FORBIDDEN CITIZENS

BY MARTIN B. GOLD

Chinese
Exclusion
and the
U.S.
Congress:
A Legislative
History

🏛 TheCapitol.Net

Alexandria, VA
2012

For more than 30 years, TheCapitol.Net and its predecessor, Congressional Quarterly Executive Conferences, have been training professionals from government, military, business, and NGOs about the dynamics and operations of the legislative and executive branches and how to work with them.

Our training and publications include congressional operations, legislative and budget process, communication and advocacy, media and public relations, testifying before Congress, research skills, legislative drafting, critical thinking and writing, and more.

Our publications and courses, written and taught by *current* Washington insiders who are all independent subject matter experts, show how Washington works.™ Our products and services can be found on our web site at *<www.TheCapitol.Net>*. TheCapitol.Net is a non-partisan firm.

Additional copies of *Forbidden Citizens* can be ordered from your favorite bookseller or online: *<www.ForbiddenCitizens.com>*.

Design and production by Zaccarine Design, Inc., Chicago, IL, *zacdesign@mac.com*. Ebook conversion by Paula Reichwald *<igossi.com>*.

The paper used in this publication exceeds the requirements of the American National Standard for Information Sciences—Permanence of Paper for Printed Library Materials, ANSI Z39.48-1992.

Forbidden Citizens: Chinese Exclusion and the U.S. Congress: A Legislative History

Library of Congress Control Number: 2011943122

Softcover	*Hardbound*	*Ebook*
ISBN 13: 978-1-58733-257-9	ISBN 13: 978-1-58733-235-7	Google Editions ISBN: 978-1-58733-258-6
		B&N nook ISBN: 978-1-58733-260-9
		Amazon Kindle ISBN: 978-1-58733-259-3

Dedicated to Senator George Frisbie Hoar,
a steadfast champion of America's
founding principles,
and to the Chinese laobaixing
in whose defense he stood.

Cover Images

The main cover image (right), is from the cover of *Puck* magazine, March 17, 1886, one month after Secretary of State Thomas F. Bayard wrote to China's Washington legation that "the violence against Chinese immigrants was precipitated by their resistance to cultural assimilation, and that racism against Chinese was typically found among other immigrants rather than the majority of the populace . . ."

The cartoonist was J.A. (James Albert) Wales.

The cartoon shows the Chinese Minister to the United States Cheng Tsao-ju handing "claims of China" to Secretary of State Thomas F. Bayard. The sign above Bayard reads, "The Chinese have no votes and no rights which this government is bound to respect, 1886."

To Secretary Bayard's right, previous Secretaries of State James G. Blaine and William M. Evarts sit below identically worded signs dated 1881 and 1877.

Cheng Tsao-ju's left hand holds another scroll that says, "The Government of China paid over to that of the United States the sum of [500,000 taels] $735,258.97 in full liquidation of all claims of American citizens in 1858." [1]

> On the night of December 14, 1856, the foreign factories at Canton were burned and foreigners were compelled to flee the city; and on the 13th of the next month [January 13, 1857] all foreigners were forced to abandon Whampoa, the port of Canton. Hostilities between China and Great Britain growing out of the controversy concerning the lorcha Arrow—a controversy which served to inflame the feelings of the Chinese against all foreign residents. "The destruction of the foreign settlements at Canton, although apparently the act of incendiaries," was "known to have been arranged by the authorities of Canton, who made no distinction between enemies and neutrals; and the subsequent proceedings of the Canton government in offering rewards for the heads of all foreigners indiscriminately." [2]

The caption below the illustration reads:

Chinese Minister: "Therefore, all things whatsover ye would that men should do to you, do ye even so to them: for this is the law and the prophets."

Secretary Bayard: "That's some nonsense of that old Confucius of yours, I suppose?"

The image is from the Library of Congress, Prints and Photographs Online Catalog, <hdl.loc.gov/loc.pnp/cph.3b49114>.

The smaller cover image (right), is from the cover of *Puck* magazine, December 19, 1900. In the spring of 1900, during the Boxer Rebellion in China, several Christian churches were burned and Chinese Christians were killed. Hundreds of soldiers from eight foreign countries were then dispatched to protect the foreign legations in Beijing. (*§ 9.12*)

The cartoonist was Frank Arthur Nankivell.

The cartoon shows a Chinese woman with two children talking to an American missionary on a street in front of a market.

The caption below the illustration reads:

The Ultimate Cause
"But why is it," asked the thoughtful Chinese, "that I may go to your heaven, while I may not go to your country?"

The American missionary shrugged his shoulders.
"There is no Labor vote in heaven!" said he.

The image is from the Library of Congress, Prints and Photographs Online Catalog, <*www.loc.gov/pictures/item/2010651356*>.

The chapter title images are the Chinese characters,

měi guó,

meaning America / American / "the beautiful country."
Pinyin: měi (third tone) and guó (second tone)

Endnotes

1. The "Claims of China" refers to the Chinese Indemnity Fund, negotiated by William B. Reed in 1858 for claims of American merchants for property destroyed in January 1857, in Whampoa (Canton).

2. (48th Congress, 2nd Session), which accompanied S. 678, December 24, 1884 (Google Books). The full text reads:

On the night of December 14, 1856, the foreign factories at Canton were burned and foreigners were compelled to flee the city; and on the 13th of the next month [January 13, 1857] all foreigners were forced to abandon Whampoa, the port of Canton. These incidents were the result of the hostilities between

China and Great Britain growing out of the controversy concerning the lorcha Arrow—a controversy which served to inflame the feelings of the Chinese against all foreign residents. "The destruction of the foreign settlements at Canton, although apparently the act of incendiaries," was "known to have been arranged by the authorities of Canton, who made no distinction between enemies and neutrals; and the subsequent proceedings of the Canton government in offering rewards for the heads of all foreigners indiscriminately," were, together with the preceding acts of injury, considered as making the "provincial government and consequently the imperial government responsible to the fullest extent." American citizens having thus been "obliged to leave Canton and Whampoa to save their lives from the indiscriminate fury of the populace, supported by the authorities," claims for their losses in consequence of the destruction of their property and the interruption of their business were preferred by the United States against China. These claims were made the subject of negotiation by Mr. William B. Reed in 1858. In the negotiation of his treaty of amity and commerce with China in that year he endeavored to secure the insertion of an article in relation to claims. The Chinese plenipotentiaries refused to admit it, and he subsequently proposed an arrangement whereby the claims might be gradually liquidated without any open acknowledgment of imperial liability. This end was to be accomplished by devoting a certain proportion of the duties collected on American goods and bottoms at three treaty ports to the payment of the American claims. To this proposal the Chinese plenipotentiaries assented, and it was agreed by means of an exchange of notes that a fund of 600,000 taels, or about $840,000, should be raised in the manner described. In this agreement, however, there were certain elements of inconvenience and uncertainty. It was provided that in the adjudication of claims, and especially of those at Canton, the Chinese Government should be represented by an officer appointed to act for it. This provision was thought to involve delay, if nothing more. Besides, no apportionment was made between the three treaty ports of the proportions of duties to be reserved in them, nor was any specification made of the time at which the agreement was to take effect, except the contingent one of the restoration of business at Canton. These features of the agreement caused Mr. Reed to desire its modification. He wished to make it more precise in its terms, as well as to give it the solemnity of a conventional form. On November 8, 1858, therefore, he signed at Shanghai a convention by which, though he accepted 500,000 taels, or $735,238.97, instead of 600,000 taels, in settlement of the claims, he obtained an exact apportionment of the fund among the ports of Canton, Shanghai, and Fuh-chau [Foochow, Fuzhou], together with a provision for the issuance of debentures by the collectors of customs on the first day of the next Chinese year.

The distribution of the fund was committed to a board of two commissioners, from whose decision and appeal was allowed to the minister of the United States in China. As commissioners the President appointed, by and with the advice and consent of the Senate, Mr. Charles W. Bradley, United States consul at Ningpo, and Mr. Oliver K. Roberts, "late vice-consul at Hongkong." According to the designation of time made by Mr. John E. Ward, then minister of the United States in China, the commissioners met at Macao November 18, 1859. They caused a notice of their meeting to be published in the China Mail, of Hongkong, and ordered all claims to be filed before December 15, 1859. They concluded their labors January 13, 1860. In most cases they came to a decision, and in every case in which they made a joint report it was approved by Mr. Ward. The total amount of the claims presented was $1,535,111.35. The claims allowed in full amounted to $75,506.83; those allowed in part amounted, so far as allowed, to $414,187.95. The whole amount allowed was, therefore, $489,187.95. The claims that were wholly disallowed amounted to $278,783.43. As the fund amounted to $735,238.97, there was a surplus left, after paying the awards, of nearly $250,000.

Some of the claims as at first presented to the board were afterward reduced "to a considerable extent by the recovery of property supposed to be lost, or by its honorable restitution by some of the principal Chinese merchants who had taken charge of it during the emergency." The board made it a rule to allow only "claims for actual losses, understanding by these words losses of actual property existing at and before the conflagration at Canton." "Besides these losses there have been," said the commissioners, "losses arising from the interruption of business by reason of the circumstance of hostilities, which may be called real losses in one sense; but these have been in every case disallowed, as well as all constructive and speculative losses of every kind. In disallowing all claims except those for destruction of actual property, we have followed the rule laid down by the Supreme Court of the United States and the usages of governments in similar cases."

The commissioners allowed interest at the rate of 12 per cent per annum on the claims from the time of their origination to December 15, 1859, in most cases a period of three years. They were induced to give this liberal rate by consideration of the fact that some time must elapse before the complete collection of the indemnity through the Chinese custom-houses could be effected; and they intended to make their awards a final settlement of the question of interest.

"The Chinese Indemnity: Convention of November 8, 1858," in "History and Digest of the International Arbitrations to Which the United States Has Been a Party," Volume 5, Appendix I, Chapter J., House of Representatives, 53rd Congress, 2nd Session, Mis. Doc. No. 212, by John Bassett Moore (GPO, 1898), pages 4627–4629 (footnotes omitted) (Google Books).

Summary Table of Contents

Introduction xix

The Principals xxiii

Chapter 1:
A Question of Naturalization 1

Chapter Two:
The Fifteen Passenger Bill of 1879 33

Chapter Three:
The Twenty-Year Exclusion Debate in the Senate 85

Chapter Four:
The Twenty-Year Exclusion
Debate in the House of Representatives 137

Chapter Five:
The Ten-Year Exclusion Legislation of 1882 193

Chapter Six:
The Amendments of 1884 219

Chapter Seven:
The Scott Act of 1888 237

Chapter Eight:
The Geary Act of 1892 281

Chapter Nine:
The 1902 Extension 319

Chapter Ten:
Permanent Law, 1904 409

Chapter Eleven:
Repeal 417

Epilogue 473

Appendices 475

Index 557

Acknowledgments 571

About the Author 572

Table of Contents

Introduction xix

The Principals xxiii

Chapter 1:
A Question of Naturalization 1

§1.0 Overview 2

    §1.10 The Senate Debate: Background 3

    §1.11 House Committee of the Whole 3

    §1.12 Senate Committee of the Whole 4

§1.20 Senate Debate, July 2, 1870:
"A requirement disgraceful to this country" 5

    §1.21 Chinese Forbidden from Holding Mining Claims 5

    §1.22 Presiding over the Senate/House 6

§1.30 Senate Debate, July 4, 1870:
"They do not value the privileges of citizenship" 13

    §1.31 Senator Sumner and Race Discrimination 29

    §1.32 The First Chinese Student to Graduate
from an American University, Yung Wing 31

    §1.33 Original Oregon Constitution Barred
Chinese Owning Real Estate and Mining Claims 32

Chapter Two:
The Fifteen Passenger Bill of 1879 33

§2.0 Overview 34

§2.10 House Debate, January 28, 1879:
"The most debased people" 35

    §2.11 Denis Kearney and the Sandlot Orators 39

    §2.12 Early China–U.S. Diplomacy 41

    §2.13 The Page Act 42

    §2.14 Absenteeism and Pairs in House and Senate Votes 48

§2.20 Senate Proceedings on the Fifteen Passenger Bill 49

    §2.21 Senate Debate, February 12, 1879:
"Consideration begins" 49

    §2.22 Senate Debate, February 13, 1879:
"An indigestible element" 49

§2.23 Senate Debate, February 14, 1879:
"Wholly unfit to become citizens" 57

§2.24 Confucian Traditions and Family Relationships 58

§2.25 Chinese Oath Swearing.. 60

§2.26 Senate Debate, February 15, 1879:
"The brightest act of my life".. 68

§2.27 James G. Blaine and the Argument for Exclusion 73

§2.28 The Nineteenth-Century Senate
versus the Modern Senate 77

§2.29 Chinese Population in the United States, 1860–1940.......... 79

§2.30 The Next Step: The House Concurs
in the Senate Amendments.. 80

§2.40 A Presidential Veto: Rutherford B. Hayes....................... 81

§2.50 The House Attempts a Veto Override 83

Chapter Three:
The Twenty-Year Exclusion Debate in the Senate 85

§3.0   Overview 86

§3.10 Proceedings in the Senate... 86

§3.11 Substitute Amendment to a Bill.................................... 87

§3.20 Senate Debate, February 28, 1882:
"A confession of American imbecility" 87

§3.21 The Politics of the 1880 Democratic Party
and Republican Party Platforms 88

§3.30 Senate Debate, March 1, 1882:
"To shame, to weakness, and to peril".................................. 95

§3.31 China–U.S. Diplomacy II... 97

§3.32 The Know-Nothing Movement..................................... 98

§3.40 Senate Debate, March 2, 1882:
"Swarm upon us like locusts" 100

§3.41 Chinese and the Transcontinental Railway.................... 102

§3.50 Senate Debate, March 3, 1882:
"Dregs of the countless hordes of China"............................. 106

§3.60 Senate Debate, March 6, 1882:
"Will not assimilate".. 110

§3.70 Senate Debate, March 7, 1882:
"An irrepressible conflict between them"............................... 116

§3.80 Senate Debate, March 8, 1882:
"A storm of condemnation".. 120

§3.90 Senate Debate, March 9, 1882:
"Fifty million sovereigns can be despotic" 127

Chapter Four:
The Twenty-Year Exclusion
Debate in the House of Representatives 137

§4.0   Overview 138

§4.10 House Debate, March 14, 1882:
"Plant a cancer in your own country".......................... 138

§4.20 House Debate, March 15, 1882:
"No more regard for his oath"................................... 140

§4.30 House Debate, March 16, 1882:
"The repulsive specter of Asiatic squalor"..................... 144

§4.40 House Debate, March 18, 1882:
"This exhaustless stream of yellow plague"..................... 150

§4.50 House Debate, March 21, 1882:
"The assimilation of oil and water" 156

§4.60 House Debate, March 22, 1882:
"Who would have them for voters?"............................. 163

§4.61 Role of the Bill Manager in the
House of Representatives............................... 165

§4.70 House Debate, March 23, 1882:
"The most hideous immoralities" 179

§4.80 A Presidential Veto: Chester Arthur:
"A breach of our national faith"............................... 184

§4.90 Senate Veto Override Debate, April 5, 1882:
"Will not disgrace our statute books" 187

§4.91 The Role of Precedent in Congress 189

Chapter Five:
The Ten-Year Exclusion Legislation of 1882 193

§5.0   Overview 194

§5.10 House Debate, April 17, 1882:
"A pack of hounds to hunt down any race" 196

§5.20 Senate Debate, April 25, 1882:
"A subject of deep respect and repentance" 199

§5.21 James A. Garfield and Race 201

§5.22 Abolition and the Timing of Chinese Immigration............ 206

§5.30 Senate Debate, April 26, 1882:
"Beyond the realm of political agitation" 207

§5.40 Senate Debate, April 27, 1882:
"They are parasites"... 210

§5.50 Senate Debate, April 28, 1882:
"A most degraded corruption" 213

§5.60 House Session of May 3, 1882:
The House Concurs in the Senate Amendments..................... 216

§5.70 Enrollment and Presidential Approval 216

Chapter Six:
The Amendments of 1884 219

§6.0 Overview 220

§6.10 House Debate, May 3, 1884 (H.R. 1798):
"This is a white man's government" 220

§6.20 Senate Debate, July 3, 1884:
"Will repent in sackcloth and ashes" 234

Chapter Seven:
The Scott Act of 1888.. 237

§7.0 Overview 238

§7.10 Senate Debate, January 12, 1888:
"Polluted with the curse of human slavery"........................... 239

§7.11 Litigation as a Means of Resistance
to the Chinese Exclusion Act..................................... 242

§7.20 Senate Debate, March 1, 1888:
"The world was created wrong" 245

§7.21 President Cleveland Responds.............................. 246

§7.30 The Senate Consents to the Bayard–Zhang Treaty................... 247

§7.31 The Senate Considers Legislation to
Implement the Bayard–Zhang Treaty (S. 3304)............... 249

§7.40 House Proceedings on the Implementation Bill (S. 3304):
"The hideous Mongolian incubus" 250

§7.41 Senate Concurs in the House Amendment,
and China's Reaction: "A response of outrage"............... 252

§7.50 The Scott Act (H.R. 11336)....................................... 253

§7.51 House Debate, September 3, 1888:
"The truth is a merchantable commodity" 253

§7.52 Senate Debate, September 3, 1888:
"Deport every single one of them"............................... 254

§7.53 Senate Debate, September 4, 1888:
"An inferior race"... 260

§7.54 Senate Debate, September 5, 1888:
"Homogeneity in races".. 262

§7.55 Senate Debate, September 6, 1888:
"A cruelty and an outrage"....................................... 264

§7.56 Senate Debate, September 7, 1888:
"Stop this ulcer"... 268

§7.57 Senate Debate, September 10, 1888:
"China is our great friend"....................................... 271

§7.58 Senate Debate, September 11, 1888:
"The evil will go on increasing" 273

§7.59 Senate Debate, September 13, 1888:
"That seething, roaring, blood-curdling curse" 274

§7.60 Senate Debate, September 14, 1888:
No quorum means stalemate.................................... 277

§7.61 Senate Debate, September 17, 1888:
Passage... 278

§7.62 House Debate, September 20, 1888:
"A demagogical way to make some capital".................. 278

§7.70 President Cleveland Signs the Scott Act,
October 1, 1888... 279

§7.80 A Political Note... 280

Chapter Eight:
The Geary Act of 1892.. 281

§8.0 Overview 282

§8.10 House Debate, April 4, 1892:
"An absolute abrogation".. 282

§8.20 Senate Debate, April 13, 1892:
"Time was of the essence"....................................... 287

§8.21 Senate Debate, April 21, 1892:
"Goes far beyond any bill"....................................... 288

§8.22 Senate Debate, April 22, 1892:
"A harsh proceeding"... 293

§8.23 Senate Debate, April 23, 1892:
"A very shrewd people"... 296

§8.24 Senate Debate, April 25, 1892:
"Intense feeling of antagonism" 301

§8.30 Bicameral Agreement: Conference Report:
"One credible white witness" 308

§8.31 Senate Debate, May 3, 1892:
"He does not stand like an ordinary person" 308

§8.32 House Debate, May 4, 1892:
"The old slavery days returned" 313

§8.40 Chinese Registration under the Geary Act 314

§8.41 Chinese Food in America 315

§8.42 Mexico, Canada, and the Chinese 317

Chapter Nine:
The 1902 Extension

The 1902 Extension 319

§9.0 Overview 320

§9.10 Senate Debate, April 4, 1902:
"One of the great policies of our country" 322

§9.11 Senate Debate, April 5, 1902:
"Amplest assurance of American friendship" 329

§9.12 Boxer Rebellion (1900) 328

§9.13 Senate Debate, April 7, 1902:
"Obnoxious social conditions" 335

§9.14 Senate Debate, April 8, 1902:
"They came like locusts" 336

§9.15 The Panic of 1873 337

§9.16 The Qing Dynasty under Siege 340

§9.17 Politics and Immigration Enforcement—
The Bureau of Immigration 347

§9.18 Senate Debate, April 9, 1902:
"Narrow, bigoted, intolerant, and indefensible" 353

§9.19 Senate Debate, April 10, 1902:
"The Chinese must be kept out" 359

§9.20 Senate Debate, April 12, 1902:
"Mere question of legislative detail" 363

§9.21 Senate Debate, April 14, 1902: Parsing words 367

§9.22 Imperialism and the Open Door Policy 370

§9.23 Senate Debate, April 15, 1902:
"Ruthlessly disregards treaty rights" 373

§9.24 Senate Debate, April 16, 1902:
"If I stand alone" 380

§9.30 House Debate, April 4, 1902:
"Largely a Pacific question" 386

§9.31 House Debate, April 5, 1902:
"To arouse this sleeping five-toed dragon" 396

§9.32 House Debate, April 7, 1902:
"Clearly unconstitutional" 401

§9.40 Resolving Differences between the Senate and
the House: The Senate Debate of April 17, 1902 407

§9.41 Resolving Differences between
the Senate and the House: Further
Proceedings on H.R. 13031, as amended 407

Chapter Ten:
Permanent Law, 1904

Permanent Law, 1904 409

§10.0   Overview 410

§10.10 Senate Debate, April 8, 1904: S. 5344:
Separating laws and treaties 410

§10.20 Senate Debate, April 22, 1904: H.R. 15054:
"There would have been great trouble" 412

§10.21 Reaction from China to the 1904 Legislation 413

§10.22 In the Year of Permanent Exclusion:
The Detention of Soong Ailing 414

Chapter Eleven:
Repeal

Repeal 417

§11.0   Overview 418

§11.10 The Last Emperor, China, Japan, and WWII 418

§11.20 The House Committee Report, October 11, 1943,
and H.R. 3070 420

§11.21 The Structure of the
National Origins Quota System 421

§11.22 The War Brides Act of 1945 422

§11.30 H.R. 3070 and House Debate, October 20, 1943:
"Important in the cause of winning the war" 424

§11.31 Madame Chiang Kaishek Speaks to the Senate
and to the House, February 18, 1943 425

§11.32 Extraterritoriality and Other Concessions 427

§11.33 The Europe-first Strategy 429

§11.34 Citizens Committee to Repeal Chinese Exclusion 452

§11.40 H.R. 3070 and House Debate, October 21, 1943:
        "Face is not just oriental" 454

§11.41 Motion to Recommit in the House 459

§11.50 H.R. 3070 to the Senate 460

§11.51 Senate Committee Consideration 461

§11.52 Senate Debate, November 26, 1943:
        "The white man feared the
        onrush of the yellow man" 462

§11.60 Bill Enrollment and Presidential Signature 472

Epilogue 473

Appendices

1. Review and Discussion Questions 477

2. Burlingame Treaty 480

3. Naturalization Act of 1870 (16 Stat. 254) 489

4. Fifteen Passenger Bill (1879) and Veto Message of
   President Rutherford Hayes of the Fifteen Passenger Bill 492

5. Angell Treaty 1880 503

6. Veto Message of President Chester A. Arthur
   of Senate Bill No. 71, April 4, 1882 506

7. The Ten-Year Exclusion Legislation of 1882, H.R. 5804 512

8. Gresham–Yang Treaty (1894) 516

9. The 1902 Extension 519

10. Permanent Law 1904 521

11. Magnuson Act (Chinese Exclusion Repeal Act of 1943) 522

12. American Immigration Laws Timeline 524

13. Bibliography 530

14. Additional Resources <TCNFCA.com> 534

Index 557

Acknowledgments 571

About the Author 572

Introduction

In 1907, immigration to the United States peaked at more than 1,285,000 (mostly European) immigrants. At twenty years old, my grandfather came to New York from Tsarist Russia the next year. Speaking no English, he went to night school for language study. He found work in the garment industry, eventually owning his own business. Escaping religious persecution in the old country, he cherished American freedom. As soon as he was eligible, he became an American citizen. For the remainder of his life, America was not merely his home but his passion.

These opportunities were open to my grandfather because he was a European. Had he been Chinese, he almost surely would have been barred from entering the United States. And if, by a quirk, he had been admitted, he could not have gotten U.S. citizenship.

Immigrants have traditionally encountered social and economic obstacles as they seek to find a place in a new society. But the United States Congress subjected the Chinese to unique legal impediments aimed squarely and solely at them. Between 1879 and 1904, a time when immigration from Europe was wide-open, Congress passed nine major Chinese exclusion bills. Two were vetoed, but seven became law. Anti-Chinese provisions were placed in other laws as well, such as those involving the annexation of Hawaii and the Philippines. When Congress finally repealed this immense body of legislation in 1943, fourteen statutes were affected.

The most notorious of these laws was popularly known as the Chinese Exclusion Act of 1882. But the act was no isolated measure passed by Congress in a weak or misguided moment. Controversial when first proposed, Chinese exclusion rapidly became consensual—and Congress continued to tighten the policy.

These laws not only involved exclusion from immigration; they also outlawed Chinese citizenship, even for those who had arrived legally before the gate was closed in 1882. Once Congress forbade naturalization, the Chinese were exposed to repeated discrimination with no political recourse. Until the 1943 repeal, no Chinese born outside of the United States could become an American citizen.

It appeared simple to single out the Chinese for this treatment. Compared to Europeans, they were different in appearance, clothing, language, diet, religion, and social structure. Insisting that the Chinese could not assimilate into American culture, lawmakers simply would not permit them to do so. While pandering for votes, especially in the Pacific region, Democrats and Republicans alike found the Chinese easy prey.

Not that the political targeting of Chinese immigrants went unchallenged in Congress. Heroes were occasionally found on Capitol Hill. Great senators such as Charles Sumner, Hannibal Hamlin, and George Hoar stood against exclusion. Representative William Rice was a leading opponent and Representatives Warren Magnuson and Walter Judd led efforts for repeal. But until 1943, opponents of exclusion were outvoted and, with each successive debate, their numbers dwindled.

Using senators' and representatives' own words, this book chronicles the sad and disturbing legislative history of the Chinese exclusion laws, with many passages transcribed from the actual debates. The appalling racism that permeated Congress becomes all too clear. Unfortunately, these vicious remarks were neither isolated nor atypical.

Members of Congress are quoted extensively. Even allowing for differences of expression over decades, the race prejudice in these debates is vivid. It is difficult to imagine that the exclusion bills could have been passed, even back then, if members of Congress had not ostracized the Chinese from the rest of American society.

The first piece of broadly anti-Chinese legislation to pass was the Fifteen Passenger Bill of 1879, described in Chapter Two, which President Rutherford B. Hayes vetoed.

However, the story really begins with the 1870 debate over naturalization rights, set out in Chapter One. But for a Senate filibuster led by Nevada's William Stewart, legislation very likely would have passed to grant legal Chinese immigrants a path to citizenship. As Stewart himself later proclaimed, had the Chinese become voters, there would have been no exclusion policy.

Chapters Three through Ten discuss exclusion debates from 1882 through 1904. Chapter Eleven is about the passage of repeal legislation in 1943.

During this period, China was in a state of continuous upheaval. The Qing Dynasty, which had ruled China from 1644, was disintegrating. When it attempted to stop the import of opium into China by the British East India Company, the Qing suffered a defeat at British hands in the First Opium War (1839–1842) and then retreated in the face of ongoing Western interference.

Domestic unrest in China during this period was also rife. The dynasty was weakened by the Taiping Rebellion (1850–1864), as well as by the Boxer Rebellion (1900).

In these years, China was poor, backward, and generally unstable. As Congress implemented Chinese-American treaties, or legislated around them, it did not pay China's wishes much heed. The dynasty was finally overthrown by the republican revolution movement late in 1911.

Established on January 1, 1912, the Republic of China, led by the Nationalist Party (Guomingdang, also Kuomintang, or KMT) attempted to modernize and unify the country. However, the republic was beset first by conflicts with local warlords and then by a Communist insurgency. While conflict between the Nationalists and Communists raged, Japan occupied Manchuria in 1931, and, in 1937, launched a general Sino-Japanese war that lasted until 1945.

The United States entered the Pacific war in 1941, following the Japanese attack on Pearl Harbor. China and America allied to oppose a common Japanese enemy. Repeal of the exclusion laws in 1943 was a war measure, undertaken by President Franklin Roosevelt and Congress to bolster America's Chinese ally.

The exclusion story is unfamiliar to most Americans, especially those not of Asian heritage. Freed from the burdens of these unjust laws, Chinese-Americans have prospered in the United States. A people Congress claimed couldn't assimilate have assimilated so well that it's hard to find the evidence of past discrimination against Chinese in America.

Chinese-Americans have been leaders in business, the professions, sports, and the performing arts. And they've worked in the top ranks of American government. In the executive branch, Elaine Chao broke ground, serving as secretary of labor (2001–2009) for President George W. Bush. Gary Locke was the first Chinese-American to be chief executive of an American state, as the twenty-first governor of Washington (1997–2005). Locke later served as secretary of commerce and then Ambassador to the People's Republic of China. Senator Hiram Fong (R-HI), a senator from 1959 to 1977, was the pioneering Chinese-American on Capitol Hill. Elected in 2009, Representative Judy Chu (D–CA) is the first Chinese-American woman to serve in either chamber of Congress.

Such success stories notwithstanding, the experience of early Chinese immigrants was uncommonly difficult because of legal discrimination against Chinese. The distress Congress caused for multiple generations of Chinese—those who were directly affected as well as their families—is still real. Shedding light on the past helps to ensure that such miscarriages do not recur.

For a more thorough discussion of the legislative procedures used in Congress, please see the *Congressional Deskbook*, also published by TheCapitol.Net.

This book's web site, *<ForbiddenCitizens.com>*, contains numerous links to additional information about the people, events, timelines, and other publications discussed herein.

The Principals

Chester Arthur

Chester Alan Arthur (R) was elected Vice President of the United States on the Republican ticket with James A. Garfield in 1880. He in turn became President on September 20, 1881, after Garfield's death by assassination and served until March 3, 1885. After vetoing legislation to exclude immigration of Chinese laborers for twenty years (§ 4.80), Arthur signed a ten-year exclusion bill on May 6, 1882 (§ 5.70), enshrining Chinese exclusion into law.

Thomas Francis Bayard, Sr.

Thomas Francis Bayard, Sr. (D-DE) was elected as a Democrat to the United States Senate in 1869 and represented Delaware until 1885. Bayard resigned from the Senate to become Secretary of State under President Grover Cleveland from 1885–1889. In that capacity, he negotiated the Bayard–Zhang Treaty (§ 7.30), which would have allowed the United States to prohibit Chinese laborer immigration. Although the Senate consented to the treaty's ratification, China did not.

James Gillespie Blaine

James Gillespie Blaine (R-ME) of Maine was elected to the United States House of Representatives in 1863 and served there until 1876. From 1869 to 1875, Blaine was Speaker. In 1876, he was appointed to a seat in the United States Senate, where he continued to serve until 1881 (*§ 2.26*). Blaine resigned from the Senate to become Secretary of State under Presidents James Garfield and Chester Arthur. Having unsuccessfully pursued the 1876 and 1880 Republican presidential nominations, Blaine was his party's candidate in 1884, but he lost the general election to Grover Cleveland. Blaine served again as Secretary of State under President Benjamin Harrison from 1889 to 1892.

Newton Booth

Newton Booth (R-CA) served as Governor of California from 1871–1875. He resigned his seat after a successful bid for the United States Senate. In the Senate, he represented California as a Republican from 1875 to 1881.

Thomas McLelland Browne

A Union general during the Civil War, Thomas McLelland Browne (R-IN) was elected to the United States House of Representatives in 1876 and served in Congress until 1891.

Matthew Hale Carpenter

Matthew Hale Carpenter (R-WI) first served in the United States Senate between 1869 and 1875. Thereafter, he engaged in private law practice until once again elected to the Senate in 1878. An outspoken opponent of Chinese exclusion, Carpenter remained a senator until his death in 1881.

Henry Laurens Dawes

Henry Laurens Dawes (R-MA) served in the United States House of Representatives from 1857 to 1875. Thereafter, he served three terms in the United States Senate (1875 to 1893). Dawes strongly opposed Chinese exclusion legislation.

George Franklin Edmunds

A Republican from Vermont, George Edmunds was appointed in 1866 to fill a vacancy in the United States Senate and won election to that seat later the same year. Between 1883 and 1885, Edmunds was the Senate's President Pro Tempore. Edmunds resigned from the Senate in 1891. He opposed efforts to exclude Chinese immigration.

William Maxwell Evarts

William Evarts (R-NY) was Attorney General of the United States during 1868–1869, under President Andrew Johnson. From 1877 to 1881, he served President Rutherford B. Hayes as Secretary of State. Evarts was a senator from 1885 to 1891.

Charles Warren Fairbanks

Charles Fairbanks (R-IN) was elected to the United States Senate from Indiana in 1896 and served until 1904, when he was elected Vice President on the Republican ticket with Theodore Roosevelt. In 1916, Fairbanks made another, this time unsuccessful, bid for candidate for Vice President on the Republican ticket with Charles Evans Hughes.

James Thompson Farley

James Farley (D-CA) was a Democratic senator from California between 1879 and 1885. It was his amendment to the 1882 Chinese exclusion act (*Chapter Four*) that barred federal or state courts from naturalizing Chinese persons.

Jacob Harold Gallinger

Jacob Gallinger (R-NH) was elected to the United States House of Representatives as a Republican in 1884. In 1890, he was elected to the United States Senate to represent New Hampshire and served until his death in 1918. Gallinger was Senate President Pro Tempore from 1911 to 1913.

Hannibal Hamlin

Hannibal Hamlin (D&R-ME) was originally elected to the United States Senate in 1848 as an anti-slavery Democrat. Hamlin split with his party after the Kansas-Nebraska Act of 1854 relaxed limitations on the spread of slavery. In 1856, Hamlin was elected Governor of Maine as a Republican, but was only briefly in that post, returning to the Senate in 1857, where he served until his inauguration as Abraham Lincoln's Vice President. After the first Lincoln administration, Hamlin returned to private life. He again served in the Senate from 1869 until 1881. As chairman of the Senate Foreign Relations Committee, he strongly opposed the Fifteen Passenger bill of 1879 (*Chapter Two*).

Rutherford B. Hayes

A Union general during the Civil War, and a former Governor of Ohio, Rutherford B. Hayes (R) began his presidency in 1877, serving until 1881. In 1879, Hayes vetoed the Fifteen Passenger Bill (*§ 2.40*), Congress' first attempt to pass Chinese exclusion legislation.

Photograph from the Library of Congress Prints & Photographs Online Catalog. loc.gov/pictures

George Frisbie Hoar

George Frisbie Hoar (R-MA) was elected as a Republican to United States House of Representatives in 1868 and served there until 1877. An ardent and courageous opponent of Chinese exclusion. Hoar was a senator from 1877 until his death in 1904.

Photograph from the Library of Congress Prints & Photographs Online Catalog. loc.gov/pictures

Charles Edward Hooker

A Democrat, Charles Hooker (D-MS) was first elected to the United States House of Representatives in 1874 and remained there until 1883. He also served during two other intervals, 1887 to 1895 and 1901 to 1903. Unlike most Southerners in Congress, Hooker opposed the exclusion laws.

John James Ingalls

A Kansas Republican, John Ingalls (R-KS) was elected to the United States Senate in 1872 and served until 1891. From 1885 to 1891, he was the Senate's President Pro Tempore. During the first exclusion debate of 1882, Ingalls tried unsuccessfully to moderate restrictions on Chinese labor immigration (*Chapter Three*).

Walter Judd

Walter Judd (R-MN) was a member of the United States House of Representatives between 1943 and 1963. Prior to his congressional service, Dr. Judd spent ten years as a medical missionary in China. After his return to the United States, he publicly advocated for repeal of the Chinese Exclusion Laws. During the 1943 House debate (*Chapter Eleven*), Judd was outspoken about the justification and urgency for repeal.

Julius Kahn

Julius Kahn (R-CA) was born in Germany and immigrated to the United States with his parents, who settled in California in 1866. Kahn was elected to the United States House of Representatives as a Republican in 1899. He lost his seat in the 1902 election, but won it back in 1904 and served until his death in 1924. He sponsored the House version of the 1902 exclusion extension bill (*Chapter Nine*).

Henry Cabot Lodge

Henry Cabot Lodge (R-MA) served as a Republican member of the United States House of Representatives from 1887 to 1893, and thereafter in the United States Senate from 1893 until his death in 1924. Lodge believed in immigration restrictions generally and was a strong advocate of Chinese exclusion. Late in his service, he chaired the Senate Foreign Relations Committee and opposed U.S. entry into the League of Nations.

Photograph from U.S. Senate Historical Office

Warren Magnuson

Warren Magnuson (D-WA) served in the United States House of Representatives from 1937 until 1944, and then in the United States Senate from 1944 until 1981. While in the House, Magnuson was the lead sponsor of successful legislation to repeal the Chinese Exclusion Laws. Near the end of his long Senate career, he became the Senate's President Pro Tempore.

Photograph from the Library of Congress Prints & Photographs Online Catalog. loc.gov/pictures

John Tyler Morgan

An Alabama Democrat, John T. Morgan signed the 1861 Alabama Ordinance of Secession and was a Confederate general during the Civil War. A strong advocate of Chinese exclusion, Morgan served in the United States Senate from 1877 to 1907.

Photograph from the U.S. Senate Historical Office

Orville H. Platt

Orville H. Platt (R-CT) served as a senator from 1879 until his death in 1905. An early opponent of Chinese exclusion, Platt later insisted on strict enforcement of Chinese immigration restrictions. In 1902, he was instrumental in derailing a harsh extension of the exclusion laws, by successfully sponsoring an amendment to make exclusion policy harmonize with China-U.S. treaties.

Photograph from the Library of Congress Prints & Photographs Online Catalog. loc.gov/pictures

William Whitney Rice

William Whitney Rice (R-MA) was elected as a Republican to the United States House of Representatives in 1876 and served there until 1887 when he lost re-election. Rice was an outspoken opponent of Chinese exclusion legislation.

Photograph from the Library of Congress Prints & Photographs Online Catalog. loc.gov/pictures

Franklin Delano Roosevelt

The thirty-second President of the United States, Franklin Delano Roosevelt (D) requested that Congress repeal the Chinese exclusion statutes, and signed the repeal measure into law in December 1943 (*§ 11.60*).

Photograph from the Library of Congress Prints & Photographs Online Catalog. loc.gov/pictures

Aaron Augustus Sargent

Aaron Sargent was a California Republican who served in the United States House of Representatives from 1861 to 1863 and again from 1869 to 1873. He was elected to the United States Senate and served there from 1873 to 1879. During his Senate tenure, he was a leading proponent of Chinese exclusion and strongly advocated passage of the 1879 Fifteen Passenger bill (*Chapter Two*).

John Sherman

John Sherman (R-OH) served in the United States House of Representatives from 1855 to 1861, in the United States Senate from 1861 to 1877, and again in the Senate from 1881 to 1897. Between 1877 and 1881, Sherman was Secretary of the Treasury under President Rutherford B. Hayes. In 1897 and 1898, he was Secretary of State under President William McKinley. While in the Senate, he chaired the Foreign Relations Committee and was a key figure in debates leading to passage of the Scott Act in 1888.

William Morris Stewart

William Morris Stewart (R-NV) was a member of the Nevada State constitutional convention in 1863 and in 1864 he was elected as a Republican to the United States Senate shortly after Nevada statehood. Stewart served until 1875. After retiring from politics for a time, he was elected to the Senate again in 1886 and served until 1905.

Photograph from the Library of Congress Prints & Photographs Online Catalog. loc.gov/pictures

Charles Sumner

Charles Sumner (R-MA) of Massachusetts was elected to the United States Senate in 1850 as a Free Soiler from Massachusetts and served as a Republican from 1857 until his death in 1874. Sumner was one of the Senate's forthright champions of slavery abolition. In 1870, he unsuccessfully sponsored an amendment to U.S. naturalization laws that would have allowed legal Chinese immigrants to become American citizens (§ 1.31).

Photograph from the Library of Congress Prints & Photographs Online Catalog. loc.gov/pictures

Henry Moore Teller

Henry Moore Teller (R/D-CO) was elected to the United States Senate in 1876. In 1882, he resigned to serve as Secretary of the Interior under President Chester Alan Arthur. In 1885, Teller was elected to the Senate again. He changed his party affiliation in 1897 to the Silver Republicans and in 1903 he switched to become a Democrat. He retired as a senator in 1909. Teller was a vigorous advocate for Chinese exclusion.

Albert Shelby Willis

Albert Shelby Willis, a Kentucky Democrat, served in the United States House of Representatives between 1877 and 1887. In 1882, he was the lead sponsor of a twenty-year Chinese exclusion bill (*Chapter Four*) that was vetoed by President Chester Arthur (*§ 4.80*).

FORBIDDEN CITIZENS

CITIZENS

Chinese Exclusion and the U.S. Congress:
A Legislative History

CHAPTER ONE

美
國
A Question of Naturalization

"Is there a Senator on this Floor who will say from anything done or said by the Chinese at this moment that there is any reason to fear peril to this Republic? Sir, the greatest peril to this Republic is from disloyalty to its great ideas."
—Senator Charles Sumner (R–MA)
41st Cong. 2nd Session Cong. Globe 5155 (1870)

"I deny, therefore, that the Declaration of Independence or the Constitution of the United States requires us to admit to naturalization Chinese, or cannibals, or Indians, or anybody, except as in our judgment their admission to political rights may comport with the best interests of the nation."
—Senator George Williams (R–OR), later Attorney General of the United States
41st Cong. 2nd Session Cong. Globe 5156 (1870)

§1.0 Overview

- Considered in the 41st Congress of the United States (1869–1871)
- Senate Party Ratio: 62 Republicans, 12 Democrats
- House Party Ratio: 169 Republicans, 67 Democrats, 10 Independents
- President: Ulysses S. Grant (R) (1869–1877)

In 1870, Congress amended America's naturalization laws, which previously allowed only white immigrants to become American citizens. During Senate debate, Senator Charles Sumner (R–MA) proposed an amendment that provided no person could be denied a path to citizenship on the basis of race. The Senate agreed to Sumner's proposal, after which Senator William Stewart (R–NV) launched a filibuster, pledging that consideration of the bill would not conclude until the Sumner amendment was removed.

At the time, the Senate lacked a cloture process to break the filibuster. When it became clear that Stewart would not back down from his threat, the Senate reconsidered its vote on the Sumner amendment and then voted the amendment down. Ultimately, the opportunity to naturalize was extended only to persons of African descent.

Decades later, Stewart would proclaim on the Senate floor that but for his efforts, Chinese immigrants could have become citizens. If Chinese had the ballot, he conceded, Congress very likely would never have passed exclusion laws.

The 41st Congress (1869–1871) championed civil rights. In April 1869, it required that Virginia, Mississippi, and Georgia ratify the Fifteenth Amendment before being readmitted into the Union following the Civil War. The Fifteenth Amendment barred the use of race as a voting qualification. In May 1870, Congress passed legislation known popularly as The Force Act (*16 Stat. 140, enacted May 31, 1870, effective 1871*). The measure was a reaction to the rise of racist organizations such as the Ku Klux Klan, and it made expressly illegal the use of violence, terror, or other tactics to impede the exercise of voting rights. Within weeks, Congress considered amendments to the country's naturalization laws, which ultimately would be changed to offer a path to citi-

§1.11 House Committee of the Whole

The House of Representatives continues to use the Committee of the Whole to expedite legislation. As the name implies, the committee is comprised of all 435 voting members of the House. However, the legislative process is eased because the quorum requirement in committee is 100, as against 218 in the House itself. Other expediting mechanisms include a five-minute rule applicable to consideration of amendments, a lower threshold for seconding demands for roll-call votes (25, versus 44 in the House), and prohibitions on motions to recommit and to reconsider. Revenue and appropriations bills must be considered in the Committee of the Whole. The procedure is optional for other measures.

When it wishes to consider legislation through this process, the House resolves itself into the Committee of the Whole. The Speaker appoints the chair. After the committee concludes its work, it "rises" and reports to the full House.

zenship for persons of African descent. In the context of the naturalization bill, lawmakers contemplated naturalizing foreign-born Chinese.

Had this been permitted, the Chinese could have become voters, like all other immigrants, and their experience in America might have been vastly altered. As it was, the attempt to allow Chinese immigrants to become citizens came to naught. Its failure left them exposed to political ostracism. Anti-Chinese legislation would come steadily between 1879 and 1904, against which the disenfranchised Chinese were largely defenseless. But the story of Chinese exclusion begins in 1870, when a Senate filibuster blocked the chance of American citizenship for the Chinese.

§1.10 The Senate Debate: Background

Before the Senate on July 4, 1870, was H.R. 2201, legislation that the House of Representatives had passed earlier to amend America's naturalization laws. Prior to this time, only whites could become naturalized citizens. As enacted, the bill would ultimately extend naturalization opportunities to "aliens of African nativity and to persons of African descent."

Once received in the Senate, the bill was referred to the Committee on the Judiciary. At the start of July 1870, the measure was pending in the Senate Committee of the Whole, a parliamentary convention that was abolished in 1930 but prior to that was an additional procedural stage to be satisfied before final dis-

§1.12 Senate Committee of the Whole

All Senate debates set out in this book, except for that of 1943, make reference to the Senate Committee of the Whole. The Senate Committee of the Whole did not operate like its House counterpart, because no special rules applied to Senate Committee of the Whole proceedings. The committee was merely one more layer of consideration. That process, which applied to every bill in the Senate, ended in 1930 for legislation and in 1986 for treaties. The sponsor of the 1930 resolution ending the practice was veteran Senator Claude Swanson (D-VA), a senator from 1910 to 1933. During Senate floor debate, he explained the redundant and cumbersome process he successfully sought to abolish:

"After a measure was considered and debated in the Committee of the Whole, and perhaps reconsidered in the Committee of the Whole, the rule provided that it should then go to the Senate, where it might be considered precisely as it had been considered in the Committee of the Whole, which meant at least two complete and thorough considerations of every bill and joint resolution introduced in the Senate. The rule could not be deviated from except by unanimous consent. Thus, a measure could be debated and argued as in the Committee of the Whole, reconsidered and again debated sometimes for two or three weeks, and then brought up in the Senate as a new proposition and the same debate had a third time, the same motions made, and then after further debate it could again be reconsidered. As a result, every question could easily have four considerations before there was a final disposition under the rules of the Senate." 72 Cong. Rec. 8975 (1930).

position in the full Senate. In the Senate, senators would sometimes attempt to redress outcomes that had occurred in the Committee of the Whole.

The Committee of the Whole initially agreed to an amendment by Senator Charles Sumner (R–MA) eliminating the word "white" in naturalization laws. A leading Abolitionist and Radical Republican, Sumner served in the Senate from 1851 until his death in 1874. Adopted on July 2, 1870, his amendment provided:

"That all acts of Congress relating to naturalization be, and the same are hereby, amended by striking out the word 'white' wherever it occurs, so that in naturalization there shall be no distinction of race or color." 41st Cong. 2nd Session Cong. Globe 5121 (1870).

The Sumner amendment generated bitter controversy. The discord arose because of the prospect that such race-neutral legislation would open the door

§1.21 Chinese Forbidden from Holding Mining Claims

In June 1859, the Gold Hill Mining District, Storey County, Nevada, adopted a regulation forbidding Chinese from holding a mining claim primarily because the Chinese in Gold Canyon (located near Alleghany, California), some fifty in number, had earned over $35,000 from gold mining. This regulation influenced mining districts in Nevada and neighboring states and eventually laid the foundation for Senator William Stewart's Mining Law of 1866 (the "Lode Law"), 14 Stat. 86, forbidding Chinese from holding an original mining claim (the Chinese could hold abandoned or second claims).

For more information about Senator Stewart, see Russell R. Elliott, *Servant of Power: A Political Biography of Senator William M. Stewart* (University of Nevada Press, 1983). For more about Chinese miners in the American West, see Sue Fawn Chung, *In Pursuit of Gold: Chinese American Miners and Merchants in the American West*. (Urbana: University of Illinois Press, 2011).

to naturalization of Chinese immigrants. Senators from Pacific Coast states were determined to derail this possibility.

§1.20 Senate Debate, July 2, 1870: "A requirement disgraceful to this country"

Under consideration in the Senate Committee of the Whole: H.R. 2201, the House-passed naturalization bill, and an amendment to it in the nature of a substitute, as proposed by the Senate Judiciary Committee.

Through an informal understanding, senators agreed to conclude proceedings on H.R. 2201 at 5:30 p.m. on Saturday, July 2, 1870. This arrangement was part of a plan to address a crush of legislation before a scheduled adjournment on July 15, 1870. Many bills were still in the queue behind the naturalization legislation.

In the Committee of the Whole, senators were considering H.R. 2201, as passed by the House, as well as a substitute amendment proposed to the House text by the Senate Judiciary Committee. The hour of 5:30 p.m. was drawing near on July 2 when Senator Charles Sumner (R-MA) proffered his amendment (striking the word "white" wherever it occurred in all acts of Congress) to the Judiciary substitute. Sumner's proposal had already been vetted by the Senate Judicia-

§1.22 Presiding over the Senate/House

The Senate's presiding officer is the Vice President of the United States. In his absence, the president pro tempore of the Senate presides. By tradition, the president pro tempore is the most senior member of the majority party. If both the vice president and the president pro tempore are unavailable to preside, Chair duty will be conferred on an acting president pro tempore, also one of the senators. In the era of the exclusion debates, it was far more common for the vice president or the president pro tempore to preside than it is now. In the modern era, junior senators of the majority party typically rotate chair duty on an hourly basis. The presiding officer recognizes senators for debate, makes procedural rulings, and is responsible for enforcing rules and decorum.

When senators are speaking on the Senate floor, they address the presiding officer as "Mr. President." In the contemporary Senate, when a female senator is presiding, she is addressed as "Madame President." The House's presiding officer performs similar functions in his chamber. The Speaker presides unless someone is designated to act in her place. When the House operates in the Committee of the Whole, a member of the House will serve as chair of the Committee of the Whole and will preside.

When representatives are speaking on the House floor, the form of address for the presiding officer depends on whether the House is sitting as the House ("Mr. Speaker" or "Madame Speaker") or as the Committee of the Whole ("Chairman" or "Chairwoman" or "Madame Chair").

ry Committee, which had favorably reported it as a stand-alone bill. But Sumner was frustrated that his bill had not progressed further. H.R. 2201 seemed attractive as a vehicle to carry his language forward.

Pacific Coast senators were alarmed that Sumner's proposal might be added to the naturalization measure. Senator George Williams (R–OR) sought to undermine Sumner's amendment with another amendment. Williams served one term in the Senate, from 1865 to 1871. Following his Senate service, he was Attorney General of the United States (1871–1875). President Ulysses Grant, in whose administration Williams served, nominated the former senator in 1873 to be Chief Justice of the United States, but the appointment stalled when the Senate Judiciary Committee did not report the nomination favorably.

Senator Williams proposed his change to the Sumner language. The Oregonian's amendment was blunt:

"But this act shall not be construed to authorize the naturalization of persons born in the Chinese empire." 41st Cong. 2nd Session Cong. Globe 5121 (1870).

Before a vote could be taken on the Williams amendment, Senator William Stewart (R–NV) rose. One of Nevada's two original U.S. senators (Nevada was the thirty-sixth state; it was admitted to the Union on October 31, 1864), Stewart served from 1864 to 1875 and again from 1887 to 1905. Representing miners and the interests of new mining capitalists, especially on the Comstock Lode in Nevada, he was to play a crucial role in denying naturalization to Chinese persons.

In debates in 1888, 1902, and 1904, Senator Stewart would boast about what he had done on July 2, 1870, to bar Chinese from the ballot box.

Senator Stewart complained that the Sumner amendment would graft onto the naturalization bill an entirely new subject, that of Chinese naturalization. Were this done, Stewart announced, he would not be bound by the informal agreement to limit debate and vote on the bill by 5:30 that evening:

"Now before the vote is taken, I wish to state that if that question, which is another question altogether, is introduced to be voted upon without giving any word of explanation, I shall not be bound by an agreement, because this is another proposition; it does not relate to the subject of the original bill. It is a separate proposition. If that is to be put on this bill, then we are not bound by any arrangement, because it is necessary that the Senate shall know what they are voting for and how they are voting, before this is voted upon. I desire to be heard and must be heard on a proposition of that character, which we on the Pacific Coast have more knowledge of than others here. I shall not be bound by any agreement if it is to be acted upon now and put on this bill. I shall desire to be heard before it is voted upon." 41st Cong. 2nd Session Cong. Globe 5122 (1870).

Stewart was threatening to filibuster. In 1870, there was no mechanism other than unanimous consent—the agreement of all senators—to impede such a strategy. Accordingly, while filibusters in the late nineteenth century were not common, they were fatal to the legislation being impeded. The cloture rule, by which a supermajority of senators could break a filibuster, was not instituted until 1917.

Senator Stewart put senators on notice he would not give way if the Sumner amendment passed. President Pro Tempore Henry Anthony (R–RI), then presiding over the Senate, observed that the agreement to commence voting on the bill by 5:30 p.m. amounted to a mere gentlemen's understanding that the chair could not enforce.

Senator Lyman Trumbull (R–IL) addressed the chamber. A three-term senator (1855–1873), Trumbull had been one of the authors of the anti-slavery Thirteenth Amendment to the Constitution. He urged that Stewart stand down from the threat to filibuster:

"I hope the Senator from Nevada will set no such example as that, by insisting that he will not be bound by an understanding. Everybody knows what this means." 41st Cong. 2nd Session Cong. Globe 5122 (1870).

Stewart would not relent. He protested that Sumner was changing the terms of the debate by pressing an amendment that was not germane to the legislation at hand:

"But this is bringing in another bill. I want to submit this proposition to the Senate: here are two distinct bills pending, involving altogether different principles; does an agreement to vote at a certain time upon one bill bind the Senate to take up another bill and put it upon that bill without a chance to say a word? I undertake to say that it is not germane, and upon that point I have a right to be heard." 41st Cong. 2nd Session Cong. Globe 5122 (1870).

Asked to explain why he thought Sumner's amendment was non-germane, Stewart replied:

"The proposition that we agreed to vote upon was simply a proposition to regulate naturalization among the persons now entitled to naturalization. The proposition introduced by the Senator from Massachusetts is to extend naturalization to a different class involving a different subject, and it is well known here that it will be discussed, and discussed thoroughly. It is a separate bill, one that has been kept separate by the Judiciary Committee, and we are not bound by the agreement when that is sought to be attached." 41st Cong. 2nd Session Cong. Globe 5122 (1870).

Senator Oliver Morton (R–IN) spoke next. A senator serving between 1867 and 1877, Morton was a staunch opponent of slavery and a member of the faction known as the Radical Republicans. Earlier in his political career, Morton was a member of the Know-Nothing Party, which was renowned for its opposition to immigration in the 1840s and 1850s.

Before his death in 1877, Morton would head a bicameral committee (the "Morton Committee," appointed in 1876) to investigate conditions in California relating to Chinese immigration. By then, Morton's anti-immigrant views had softened considerably, and he filed committee report views that were substantially sympathetic to the Chinese.

For now, though, Morton was unprepared to extend America's welcome by offering Chinese the prospect of citizenship. Such a policy departure was premature and needed more deliberation:

"This amendment involves the whole Chinese problem. Are you prepared to settle it tonight? And without discussion? The country has just awakened to the question and to the enormous magnitude of the question, involving a possible immigration of many millions, involving another civilization, involving labor problems that no intellect can solve without study and without time. Are you now prepared to settle the Chinese problem, thus in advance inviting that immigration? I am not prepared to do it." 41st Cong. 2nd Session Cong. Globe 5122 (1870).

Senator Sumner, who had been silent during the controversy, finally rose in the defense of his amendment and responded to Morton, a fellow Radical Republican:

"The Senator says it opens the great Chinese question. It simply opens the question of the Declaration of Independence and whether we will be true to it. 'All men are created equal' without distinction of color." 41st Cong. 2nd Session Cong. Globe 5122 (1870).

Discord over the amendment continued to swirl. Opponents such as Senators Eugene Casserly (D–CA), Henry Corbett (R–OR), and Willard Warner (R–AL) criticized Sumner's attempt to offer an amendment shortly before the naturalization debate was due to conclude.

Senator Williams, who had proposed the second-degree amendment expressly barring Chinese naturalization, had an idea to defuse the tension. He volunteered to withdraw his amendment, with the understanding that the Senate would then reject Sumner's proposal. But if this arrangement did not materialize, Williams would join the filibuster:

"If it is not voted down, I shall renew my amendment and intend to stand here as long as I can and fight for it. I shall not submit to have these Chinese brought here . . . ." 41st Cong. 2nd Session Cong. Globe 5123 (1870).

Sumner defended his amendment strategy. He had tried for some time to pass a separate bill for non-discriminatory naturalization, only to experience frustrating delays. Sumner's remarks, fully set forth here, demonstrate that the amendment was not aimed directly at assisting the Chinese. However, the Chinese would have benefited from what Sumner was trying to do, and opposition to his amendment arose directly from hostility to the Chinese:

"Some time during the last Congress, I had the honor of introducing a bill to strike the word 'white' from our naturalization laws. I have tried to put it on its passage. I was resisted then by the Senator from Vermont [George Edmunds], who moved its reference to the Committee on the Judiciary. There it remained until that Congress expired. During the first week of the present Congress, now more than a year ago, I introduced the same bill. It remained in the room of the Judiciary Committee from March 1869, until very recently, when it was reported favorably.

"Such, sir, have been my efforts to bring the Senate to a vote on this question. Never till this moment has it been in my power to have a vote on a question which I deem of vital importance. I have here on my table at this moment letters from different States—from California, from Florida, from Virginia—all showing a considerable number of colored persons—shall I say of African blood?—aliens under our laws, who cannot be naturalized on account of that word 'white.'

"Now, sir, there is a practical grievance which needs a remedy. This is the first time that I have been able to obtain a vote upon it, and I should be unworthy of my seat here if, because Senators rise and say they will vote it down on the ground that it is out of place, I should hesitate to persevere. The Senator from Illinois [Lyman Trumbull] properly says it is in place. Never was there a bill to which it was more germane. You are now revising the naturalization system, and I propose to strike from that system a requirement disgraceful to this country and to this age. I propose to bring our system in harmony with the Declaration of Independence and the Constitution of the United States. The word 'white' cannot be found in the two great title-deeds of this Republic. How can you place it in your statutes?" 41st Cong. 2nd Sess. Cong. Globe 5123 (1870).

A vote followed on the Sumner amendment to the Judiciary Committee's substitute to the House-passed bill. Twenty-two senators voted aye, 23 voted nay, and 27 were recorded as absent, so Sumner's effort to amend the Judiciary Committee substitute was defeated.

After brief additional debate, the Senate Judiciary Committee proposal was itself rejected by 17 ayes, 33 nays, with 22 absentees. That result left pending the House-passed bill, which remained open to amendment on the Senate floor. Senator Sumner proposed his language striking "white" from naturalization laws anew, this time as an amendment to the House bill.

Senator Stewart was first to respond. He characterized the amendment:

"That is a proposition to extend naturalization, not to those who desire to become citizens, but to those who are being imported as slaves." 41st Cong. 2nd Session Cong. Globe 5124 (1870).

Senator George Edmunds (R–VT) beseeched Stewart to forego a filibuster. Edmunds served in the Senate from 1866 to 1891 and would later be its president pro tempore.

If Stewart stood down, Edmunds promised to oppose the Sumner amendment as being outside the spirit of the gentlemen's agreement. However, were

Stewart to undermine the agreement's spirit by insisting on extended proceedings, Edmunds would support Sumner.

After additional debate, there was a vote on Sumner's amendment to the House bill. This time, it passed by 27 ayes to 22 nays, 23 senators being absent. Why Sumner failed initially and succeeded the second time can be explained by the changed votes of Senators Timothy Howe (R–WI) and Abijah Gilbert (R–FL). Without explanation, they opposed Sumner on the original roll call and supported him in amending the House bill. Sumner also won the additional votes of Senators Roscoe Conkling (R–NY), Reuben Fenton (R–NY), James Patterson (R–NH), and John Thayer (R–NE), each of whom had been absent on the first call. Senator Hiram Revels (R–MS), who supported Sumner on the initial vote, was absent on the second.

Stewart reacted negatively to Sumner's success:

"Now it is clear that I am absolved of any agreement."

"Why so?" asked Senator Trumbull.

The Nevadan Stewart responded:

"Why so? I never have made any such agreement. I never have made an agreement to extend naturalization to the Chinese on a bill to regulate naturalization. I say it is a violation of the agreement to take up another bill, a plain, palpable, clear violation of the agreement. I appeal to every fair man if I am not entitled to discuss this question upon this bill now; and before I proceed, I want a vote of the Senate whether I am to proceed to explain what the Senate is about to do. I ask leave to be heard." 41st Cong. 2nd Session Cong. Globe 5124 (1870).

Determined to speak at length, Stewart contended that he really was a friend of the Chinese who had always looked out for their best interests. He would carry this paternalistic theme throughout his remarks:

"I have done as much for them as any Senator here, or as any other individual in the United States. For twenty years, I have been their friend, and I have resisted their oppression." 41st Cong. 2nd Session Cong. Globe 5125 (1870).

Stewart was talking about his opposition to special taxes and other statutory burdens that had been imposed on Chinese miners and other early immigrants. This demonstrated he was not anti-Chinese, Stewart insisted, but naturalization presented a different question.

Williams had an amendment to propose to Sumner's and got Stewart to yield momentarily. Williams' amendment stated:

"Provided, that nothing in this act shall be construed to authorize the naturalization of persons born in the Chinese empire."

Stewart resumed the Senate floor, arguing that Chinese laborers in America were indentured coolies held to service by coercive tactics:

"They were brought here under contracts whereby they gave in security their families to be sold into slavery if they violated those contracts. They were brought here under contracts to labor a certain number of years and to be returned to those families, dead or alive. The poor coolies have kept those contracts; have behaved themselves as well as any people could; but they are still not free men." 41st Cong. 2nd Session Cong. Globe 5125 (1870).

The interests who had contracted for this labor would direct naturalized Chinese laborers on how to vote, Stewart claimed. He asked senators, "Do you want to extend naturalization to men who are liable to be dictated to by their masters who brought them here as to how they shall vote? They can not only be controlled in their labor," Stewart argued, "but in their applications to be naturalized, and they will be equally controlled in their votes. They are pagans in religion, monarchists in theory and practice, and believe in their form of government, and no other, and look with utter contempt on all modern forms as dangerous innovations." 41st Cong. 2nd Session Cong. Globe 5125 (1870).

Stewart claimed to be open to eventually naturalizing Chinese who came to America freely. Such a circumstance might occur in the future, but it did not then exist.

Stewart believed resentment of the Chinese was such that the prospect of granting them citizenship rights would provoke extreme levels of violence against them. To protect them, he reasoned, Congress must ensure they could not naturalize:

"Do you want to have the Chinese slaughtered on the Pacific Coast? Do you want to render their friends entirely helpless? Do you want their extermination? Do you want to make us utterly powerless for their good? Then pass this bill. Why, sir, how will it operate? It will be two years before any Chinaman can be naturalized under it. What will happen in the mean time? Why, sir, the conviction that the Chinaman is not fit for naturalization will seize every man who has thought on the subject at all, and the thoughtful men, those who are really desirous of protecting them, will be overpowered by the mob element that seeks to exterminate the Chinese. Our moral support will be gone; we shall be helpless; and they will be slaughtered before any one of them can be naturalized under your bill." 41st Cong. 2nd Session Cong. Globe 5125 (1870).

Minutes later, the Senate concluded the session of July 2, 1870. The time was 7:00 p.m. Proceedings had extended for an hour and a half past the understood time for the 5:30 vote, with no end to the debate apparent.

§1.30 Senate Debate, July 4, 1870:
"They do not value the privileges of citizenship"

Under consideration in the Senate Committee of the Whole:
H.R. 2201, the House-passed naturalization bill, and an
amendment to it in the nature of a substitute, as proposed
by the Senate Judiciary Committee.

The Senate returned to business on Monday, July 4, 1870, with the naturalization bill pending in the Senate Committee of the Whole. The Second Session of the 41st Congress was ten days short of closing. Confronting a clogged agenda, the Senate had chosen to work on the Fourth of July.

With Senator William Stewart (R–NV) filibustering the naturalization bill, senators who were interested in other measures were getting restless. Senator Roscoe Conkling (R–NY) spoke of turning to railroad legislation. Chairman of the Senate Finance Committee John Sherman (R–OH) urged moving to a tax measure. Pressure to get the naturalization bill out of the way was building.

Stewart held the Senate floor. As long as he did, nothing else could get done. Stewart's opponents tried to dislodge him. Senator Lyman Trumbull (R–IL) of Illinois raised a point of order that Stewart's continued obstruction violated the agreement to vote on the previous Saturday afternoon. The president pro tempore ruled against Trumbull, insisting again that the agreement amounted to an unenforceable understanding. Stewart was entitled to proceed.

Representing Nevada, Stewart was sensitive to the rising political volatility of Chinese immigration. His comments presaged years of bitter partisan warfare over the Chinese, as Republicans and Democrats struggled for primacy in the West. Himself a Republican, Stewart was determined to disprove that Sumner's amendment represented party policy. Being known as the party of emancipation did not bind Republicans to support Chinese naturalization, Stewart insisted:

"I want to be heard in the name of the Republican Party, not only of Nevada, but of the nation. It is claimed that the Republican Party have done certain things whereby they must logically do certain other things in order to be consistent. Now I propose to show that the Republican Party has never done anything to commit itself to the policy which is here proposed." 41st Cong. 2nd Session Cong. Globe 5150 (1870).

Fearing voter backlash in his region, Stewart was eager to open some distance between Sumner and other Senate Republicans:

"Our opponents said all the while that the Republican Party of the Pacific Coast desired to have these Chinese become voters, to bring them here and to trade in their votes; that we intended to naturalize them. We told people that it ought not to be a political question, that we would protect the Chinese . . . but until they renounced paganism, until they renounced imperialism, which this generation will never do, we should not propose to engraft them upon the body-politic." 41st Cong. 2nd Session Cong. Globe 5151 (1870).

Naturalizing Chinese prematurely, Stewart argued, would not only revoke the assurances made to Western voters, but also instigate overwhelming hatred against Chinese immigrants. Local authorities would not or could not shelter the Chinese from attacks, leaving the responsibility to the federal government:

"With every local office in the hands of those who hate and persecute them, with no power there to protect him, you must then protect him by the General Government . . . . How many will it take to enforce the civil rights bill then? It will take more of an army than you have now." 41st Cong. 2nd Session Cong. Globe 5151 (1870).

A decade later, in debates marked by racial denigration and stereotyping, Pacific Coast senators would lead a movement to impose widespread and onerous restrictions on immigration of Chinese laborers. However, in 1870 hostility to Chinese had not yet crystallized. Therefore, Stewart spoke not of hostility to Chinese immigration, but in opposition to coolie labor contracts. He also thought the Chinese were unfit to be American citizens:

"I want it distinctly understood now that my platform in regard to the Chinese is simply this: I would let those who choose to come here voluntarily to do so. We have a treaty to that effect. I would prohibit all coolie contracts and enforce that prohibition. I would protect them in all their civil rights by all the power of this Government. But I would not trust them with political power until they changed their devotion to pagan despotism . . . ." 41st Cong. 2nd Session Cong. Globe 5151 (1870).

Chinese could not be granted suffrage, Stewart claimed, because they did not share a common loyalty with Americans to the country's social and political institutions. How could they be expected to cherish the vote and exercise it thoughtfully?

"They do not value the privileges of citizenship. They would sell their votes for money as a matter of course. They feel no interest in it. They would sell their votes for money in order to redeem their families, to redeem the security they have given for the faithful performance of their contracts. To do that, they would sell the franchise or anything else." 41st Cong. 2nd Session Cong. Globe 5151 (1870).

Stewart wanted to be sure that no one tied Chinese suffrage to the spirit of the Fifteenth Amendment. The Fifteenth Amendment, which prohibits the use of race to deny voting rights, was ratified only five months before the naturalization debate:

"Because we did an act of justice, because we enfranchised the colored man, must we therefore necessarily abandon our institutions to the Chinese or to the people of any other country hostile to those institutions . . . . Do the Fifteenth Amendment and the Declaration of Independence mean that the Chinese have the same rights in this Government that we have?

"Because we have protected our own citizens and given them rights, because we have freed the slaves and then given them their civil and political rights, does it follow that we must extend those political rights to all people throughout the globe, whether they will accept them or not? Why, sir, it would render American citizenship a farce." 41st Cong. 2nd Session Cong. Globe 5152 (1870).

Stewart had spoken for a long while. Concluding his remarks, he said that granting Chinese the franchise would be a "crime." He would not do it himself, Stewart exclaimed, and he would work to ensure his party was not associated with it.

Sherman complained vigorously about the failure to vote on the bill the previous Saturday (July 2, 1870) and expressed strong concern about the resulting bottleneck blocking vital fiscal legislation. Stewart could untie the knot by desisting, or Sumner could end the impasse by withholding his amendment, but Sherman observed that neither senator would budge.

"I have the assurance of the Senator from Massachusetts that he will not withdraw the amendment he proposes. The Senator from Oregon also says that he will not allow a vote to be taken on that amendment without a vote on his amendment; and he is justified in making that statement. I have talked with Senators on all sides, and they say that no vote can be taken on either of these questions without a long debate, and they are prepared and ready to debate them, and propose to debate them." 41st Cong. 2nd Session Cong. Globe 5152 (1870).

Sherman was at the end of his patience. After considerable back-and-forth between senators, he secured a unanimous consent order that debate on a tax measure would commence at noon the following day, July 5, 1870. The naturalization bill would have to conclude by then or, by terms of the order, it would be supplanted on the Senate floor.

Proceedings resumed on naturalization. In an effort to collapse the time remaining until debate on the tax bill began, Senator Allen Thurman (D–OH), an opponent of Chinese suffrage, moved to adjourn the day's session. His motion failed.

Trumbull took the Senate floor, contending that it would be inconsistent with Republican Party doctrine to admit the Chinese to the country, but then leave them without political rights:

"If you allow them to come at all, I do not want them here as slaves or inferiors. I do not understand, on the principle on which the great Republican Party is based and on which it has triumphed, how we are to refuse to admit as members of the body-politic persons who we allow to come here and dwell among us." 41st Cong. 2nd Session Cong. Globe 5154 (1870). There was a hidden irony in Trumbull's position. Nearly a decade later, during debate on the Fifteen Passenger bill of 1879, Senator James G. Blaine (R–ME) would turn the argument on its head. While he agreed it was unwise to have a political underclass, Blaine would contend that because Chinese had not been given voting rights, their further immigration to America should be halted.

Senator Sumner spoke next, to refute the argument that the Chinese were an alien force, incapable of adhering to American values and becoming loyal citizens. Some Chinese might come only temporarily for jobs, Sumner said, and for them citizenship was irrelevant. Others might wish to remain permanently, and citizenship should not be denied to them. These cases were distinguishable, so Chinese immigrants should not be lumped together and stereotyped:

"We are told that they are imperialists; but before they can be citizens they must renounce imperialism. We are told that they are foreigners in heart; but before they can take part with us they must renounce their foreign character. Therefore do I say that if they come for citizenship, there is no peril; while if they come merely for labor, then all this discussion and all this anxiety is superfluous." 41st Cong. 2nd Session Cong. Globe 5155 (1870).

After a brief interlude, Senator Williams once again secured the Senate floor. Into the debate, he introduced the first serious dose of racially derogatory language. The Oregon senator challenged the notion that granting Chinese equal rights would be consistent with the principles of the Declaration:

"Does the Declaration of Independence mean that Chinese coolies, that the Bushmen of south Africa, that the Hottentots, the Digger Indians, heathen, pagan, and cannibal shall have equal political rights under this Government with citizens of the United States?" 41st Cong. 2nd Session Cong. Globe 5154 (1870).

Williams obviously did not think so, asserting that the Declaration's dominant objective was promoting public safety and happiness. Williams claimed this purpose would be best served by excluding Chinese from suffrage.

The Oregon senator asserted the legality of his amendment denying Chinese a path to citizenship. The Constitution itself recognized distinctions between native-born persons and foreigners, Williams said, citing the requirement that an individual born abroad could not become president and that naturalized persons still had waiting periods before they were eligible to serve in the House or Senate. Congress had ample power to refuse naturalization to anyone, concluded Williams.

In Senate floor debate, Sumner engaged Williams. Sumner insisted that any naturalization bill that did pass must be race-neutral to meet constitutional requirements. Rejecting that reasoning, Williams replied that Congress had absolute power in the matter and could pass whatever naturalization bill it wished.

Chinese immigrants should have no expectation of citizenship rights, Williams argued, because the Burlingame Treaty contained language that put everyone on notice. The Burlingame Treaty (*Appendix 2*), between China and the United States, was ratified in 1868. The agreement was a seminal event in Sino-American diplomacy.

Negotiated by Anson Burlingame, an American acting in the service of China, the treaty facilitated the free movement of peoples between the two nations. As Professor Harry Gelber describes it, the treaty was "in effect, China's first attempt to create ongoing modern international relationships. In 1868, Burlingame negotiated a Sino-American treaty in Washington. [Secretary of State William] Seward signed an agreement on Chinese immigration rights into the U.S. and there were promises of most favored nation treatment." Harry Gelber, *The Dragon and the Foreign Devils* (Walker & Company, 2007), p. 225.

The provision to which Williams referred, and which he claimed to author, was added as an amendment during Senate approval of the Burlingame Treaty. The language stated:

"But nothing herein contained shall be held to confer naturalization upon citizens of the United States in China, nor upon the subjects of China in the United States."

After posing the question, "Is there anybody who will say that the Chinese is a desirable population?" Williams condemned Chinese immigration, foretelling arguments that would dominate later exclusion debates.

"Mongolians, no matter how long they may stay in the United States, will never lose their identity as a peculiar and separate people. They will never amalgamate with persons of European descent; and so, as they multiply, as thousands are added to thousands, until they may be counted by millions, we shall have in the United States a separate and distinct people, an empire of China within the North American Republic." 41st Cong. 2nd Session Cong. Globe 5156 (1870).

Bringing diverse peoples together would not produce their happy coexistence but would result in the subjugation of weaker races to stronger ones, said Williams. History had already shed light on what could be expected:

"Look at the inevitable and disastrous results that have followed from the contact of the white race and the Indians upon this continent; and the red man is rapidly fading away, because notwithstanding all the schemes that may be employed to produce a contrary effect, there is an irreconcilable difference which God Almighty has made between the white man and the Indian, and the result, when they are brought together, is not an amalgamation, but the destruction of the feebler race." 41st Cong. 2nd Session Cong. Globe 5156 (1870).

If encouraged to immigrate, the immense Chinese population would present a different magnitude of racial conflict than America had suffered with native peoples or even Africans. Williams foresaw a grim situation:

"Whenever the Mongolians or Chinese become numerous and powerful in this country, we may look for tumult, convulsion, and conflict, instead of harmony, concord, and peace." 41st Cong. 2nd Session Cong. Globe 5156 (1870).

Naturalizing Africans, as the House bill proposed to do, did not bother Williams much. The affected population was small and the black population in general had already Americanized. Granting citizenship rights to Chinese was different due to greater numbers and sharper cultural distinctions. Williams inquired, "Will Congress by such a proclamation invite and encourage this influx of paganism and pollution to our shores?" 41st Cong. 2nd Session Cong. Globe 5157 (1870).

The Oregonian shuddered at the possibility of Chinese influencing the outcome of American elections. Deriding proposals to naturalize Chinese as giving "millions of benighted and groveling pagans the right to control the affairs of government," Williams rejected efforts to "put the political future of the nation into the hands of the Joss worshipers of China." Rebuking Sumner, Williams proclaimed:

"Ignorance, idolatry, immorality, vice, disease, and prostitution are the deities of the Senator's theory; and to them he is now ready to sacrifice the pride and glory of American citizenship." 41st Cong. 2nd Session Cong. Globe 5157 (1870).

Naturalization meant taking a solemn oath of allegiance, abjuring past loyalties and casting one's lot with the adopted country. Such an oath would be meaningless to the Chinese even if they were permitted to take it, Williams assured the Senate:

"Imagine such an oath administered to Chinamen, ignorant of God, Christ, the Bible, and the Christian religion; ignorant of the Constitution of the country, its language, its laws, its customs, and its habits! Would not the administration of an oath to such beings, utterly unconscious of its nature and obligations, be very much like trying to invest so many cattle with the elective franchise?" 41st Cong. 2nd Session Cong. Globe 5157 (1870).

Turning to tensions between Chinese and American laborers, Williams laid the groundwork for the 1879 and 1882 exclusion debates. Chinese labor was cheap and plentiful, he said. American workers had a right to be concerned about the degrading and impoverishing effects of competition with such a work-force. Confronted with such circumstances, Americans would take political retribution on the party that made them possible:

"Let me tell my friends not to be disappointed if this bill passes enfranchising the Chinese, if, at the next election, the black and white laborers of the country should combine to crush the party which invites competition with their labor from China; and if that combination shall be made, there will not be Representatives enough of the Republican Party in the other House of Congress, after the next election, to tell the story of its destruction." 41st Cong. 2nd Session Cong. Globe 5158 (1870).

Next to speak was Senator Carl Schurz (R–MO). Serving in the Senate for a single term, from 1869 to 1875, he was from 1877 to 1881 secretary of the interior under President Rutherford Hayes. Himself an immigrant from Germany, Schurz became one of America's leading political thinkers and writers.

Schurz began by decrying Williams' excessive rhetoric, which seemed characteristic of local citizens' meetings, but had not up to then degraded Senate debate:

"Mr. President, the so-called Chinese question is one which appears to affect the interests of a numerous class of people, and is therefore apt to produce an excitement; and I must confess that I am somewhat pained to see that this excitement has found its way to the Senate Chamber of the United States and that the remarks we have listened to are rather calculated to inflame it rather than to assuage it." 41st Cong. 2nd Session Cong. Globe 5158 (1870).

Senators from the Pacific states were seized by a "heated fancy," said Schurz, anticipating that a vast deluge of Chinese immigrants would overwhelm the region. Such fears were grossly overstated, he argued. Even with expanded rates of immigration, it would be fifty to seventy-five years before the Chinese population in America reached one million. In a country that was already 40 million strong in 1870, and whose numbers could be expected to grow rapidly, the Chinese population would remain relatively small. (In fact, the U.S. population would reach 106 million in 1920 and 140 million in 1945.)

Chinese who had come to the United States merely for temporary work were unsuitable for citizenship, Schurz agreed, and very likely would not want to be naturalized in any regard. If problems stemmed from coolie labor contracts, Schurz's remedy was not to bar suffrage but to impede such contracts. Immigration not subject to the contracts would be more like that from Europe, obviating any argument to segregate Chinese immigrants from others.

Schurz said the Williams amendment to Sumner's amendment was overbroad. It was not aimed merely at coolie labor contracts, as Williams had claimed, but targeted all Chinese. "He excludes men from the naturalization laws on the mere ground of nativity," Schurz declared.

Williams rose to defend his proposal:

"I will say that it is impossible to reach the evil which the Senator mentions without including all Chinese." 41st Cong. 2nd Session Cong. Globe 5159 (1870).

Schurz refused to accept that answer. He insisted that more precise distinctions could be drawn between Chinese who came via coolie contracts and those who arrived as free laborers:

"I am certain that something of the kind can be drafted that will meet the purpose of excluding from naturalization those birds of passage who, as a political element, would be worthless and dangerous, without, however, doing injustice to those who in good faith come to cast their lot with us." 41st Cong. 2nd Session Cong. Globe 5159 (1870).

Schurz announced he would support the Sumner amendment, with misgivings. The Chinese immigration issue deserved more nuanced reflection than was possible in an end-of-the-session crush:

"I believe the question we are now discussing is not yet fully matured, while it now serves to obstruct the passage of a useful bill." 41st Cong. 2nd Session Cong. Globe 5159 (1870).

Soon on the Senate floor was Senator Matthew Hale Carpenter (R–WI), who served from 1869 to 1875, then again from 1879 until his death in 1881. His remarks were among the most ennobling of the 1870 debate.

Carpenter dismissed Williams' prognosis of Republican doom if the Chinese were naturalized. Such predictions were overstated, and were an act of political desperation, he suggested.

Declaring his strong opposition to the Williams amendment, Carpenter characterized it as saying:

"No subject of that empire, no matter how long he has resided among us, nor how thoroughly he may have become identified in interest with us, and no matter what may be his character, intelligence, or virtue shall ever become an American citizen." 41st Cong. 2nd Session Cong. Globe 5160 (1870).

Rejecting any test for citizenship other than allegiance to the law, Carpenter argued:

"Some contend for a standard of intelligence; some would seek a standard in wealth; some in blood; some in one thing, and some in another. But we Americans have met all the discussions and arguments upon this subject with a broad American principle, which is that every man who is bound by the law ought to have a voice in making the law. This single maxim, the cornerstone of our institutions, we have laid down as our ultimate determination of the whole matter." 41st Cong. 2nd Session Cong. Globe 5160 (1870).

Comparing the arguments against the Chinese to those that had been made opposing black suffrage, Carpenter stated:

"When the war closed, emancipating four million slaves, we were confronted with the question whether they should be admitted to full rights of citizenship. It was objected that they were ignorant and degraded by their long condition of servitude. But, sir, we determined this question in a statesmanlike way. We said that every free man subject to the law ought to have a vote; that the freedman was free and subject to the law, therefore he ought to vote." 41st Cong. 2nd Session Cong. Globe 5160 (1870).

Some of the same leaders who had stood forthrightly and successfully to enfranchise freedmen were abandoning that elevated standard:

"Shall Chinamen be citizens; or permitted to emigrate to this country, shall they constitute a class inferior to citizens? And, strange to say, the very men who settled the question upon principle now hesitate to apply the principle, tested by its success in that case, to the instance before us, and now interpose the very objections to the enfranchisement of the Chinamen that Democrats urged against the enfranchisement of the freedmen." 41st Cong. 2nd Session Cong. Globe 5160 (1870).

Because Senator Williams had been a leader in ballot access for emancipated slaves, Carpenter found it ironic that the Oregonian Williams labored to block suffrage for Chinese. Such hypocrisy was hard for Carpenter to grasp:

"It is astonishing that any man whose views are so broad, and whose heart is so large, and whose faith in Americanism ought to be so exalted after witnessing the thunderings and lightnings which have attested its truth, should not hesitate to follow the great principles which guided his conduct on former occasions." 41st Cong. 2nd Session Cong. Globe 5160 (1870).

If the Senate took Williams' position, said Carpenter, it would demonstrate that the promise of self-government was a delusion. To bar citizenship for Chinese would be to abandon America's moral position. Was Congress truly prepared to say that "the Chinaman, although residing in our midst, and intelligent, industrious, and virtuous, ought not to have a voice in making the laws by which he is to be governed, by which his property is to be taxed, and by which his life is to be rendered happy or devoted to misery"? 41st Cong. 2nd Session Cong. Globe 5161 (1870).

Carpenter challenged the Senate to adhere to American ideals. Senators must not claim rights for themselves that they were unwilling to extend to the Chinese:

"Sir, this American maxim, that all freemen bound by the law, ought to have a voice in making the law is either a truth or a falsehood. If it be a truth, the Chinaman is entitled to vote; if it be a falsehood, then you must call witnesses to prove you are entitled to vote yourself." 41st Cong. 2nd Session Cong. Globe 5161 (1870).

Probing Carpenter's logic, Thurman interrupted to ask whether the Wisconsin senator should be understood to favor women's suffrage. The ballot should not be denied on the basis of gender, color, or birthplace, replied Carpenter:

"I am opposed to limiting principles geographically; I am opposed to saying that all men are created equal within certain parallels of latitude, but that God intended the people born north or south of those hues to be subjects of despotism. A man is a man, no matter where he was born, no matter what may be the color of his skin, and is entitled to be treated like a man, and to enjoy the rights, privileges, powers, and immunities of a man, under any Government which professes to be founded upon the principle that all men are created equal." 41st Cong. 2nd Session Cong. Globe 5161 (1870).

Before taking his seat, Carpenter beseeched the Republican-dominated Senate to be true to the party's ideology and history. Williams' amendment must be defeated and Sumner's must pass, regardless of controversy or risks:

"It seems to me that we must support the amendment or repudiate the principle upon which we have stood as a party; the principle upon which we have builded [sic] a nation. Often during the war the darkness was so dense that the path before us as a nation could not be seen. But with the people, when sight failed, faith inspired them, and hand in hand and shoulder to shoulder, with faces imploring uplifted to Heaven, they walked hopefully and safely through the gloom that enveloped them. So let us do here. To admit the Chinaman to full participation in the rights of citizenship may well create some apprehension; but I would sooner apply our principles to him than confess them to be erroneous, and thus destroy the only foundation upon which free government can rest." 41st Cong. 2nd Session Cong. Globe 5161 (1870).

Senator Henry Wilson (R–MA) took the floor. A senator from 1855 to 1873,

Wilson became Vice President of the United States during the second Grant administration (1873–1877), and then died in office in 1875. Although he was Sumner's Massachusetts colleague in the Senate, Wilson was not his ally.

Senator Wilson condemned coolie labor contracts and disfavored granting citizenship to Chinese laborers who came to America under such conditions. In that sense, he agreed with Stewart. On the other hand, Wilson also believed that Chinese who immigrated freely—a basic right under the Burlingame Treaty— should receive the full protection of law, including voting rights. On that score, he concurred with Sumner. But of immediate concern was that adding Chinese naturalization could jeopardize the bill's movement in the House. Alone in the Senate debate, Wilson raised the issue of potential complications in the House of Representatives. He was unwilling to put the legislation at risk, so he would vote against the amendment.

Senator Hannibal Hamlin (R–ME) rose. Lincoln's first vice president (1861– 1865), Hamlin explored an end to the stalemate. He was a Sumner amendment supporter, but could not see a way to pass the naturalization bill as amended. Stewart and his allies would not desist from the filibuster, that much was clear. It was already past 4:00 p.m. on July 4, 1870. With the consent order in place to take up tax legislation at noon the following day, the naturalization bill would die unless it was passed before time expired. To break the impasse, Hamlin thought that the Senate should reconsider the vote by which it had agreed to the Sumner amendment.

Before a formal motion to that effect could be made, Senator Henry W. Corbett (R–OR) wanted to be heard. Corbett served one term in the Senate, from 1867 to 1873.

The pending House bill was only designed to prevent corruption in elections in addition to regularizing naturalization, Corbett noted. But Sumner had added a provision to damage the body politic. Chinese were prone to debase American politics if granted suffrage:

"They come here in large numbers, including women of the most deplorable condition and the most lewd class, and they are imported in such numbers as to degrade and demoralize our people. Citizens, heretofore honest, laboring people, have been demoralized, become intemperate, become corrupt by this means. They are not only interfering with the family relations, but in every conceivable way, are introducing the most corrupt practices into our community . . . .

"If these people will sell themselves to come here and labor, they will sell themselves in flocks to vote, and the only question will be which party will pay the most for their votes." 41st Cong. 2nd Session Cong. Globe 5163 (1870).

Senator Reuben Fenton (R–NY) had served in the House as a Democrat from 1853 to 1855, split with his party, and returned to the House as a Republican representative from 1857 to 1865. Fenton was a one-term senator from 1865 to 1871.

On July 2, 1870, Fenton was one of the senators who voted with Sumner. Under Senate rules, a senator who votes with the prevailing side or who was absent may seek to reconsider. Accordingly, Fenton was eligible to seek reconsideration of the vote. Carrying the motion to reconsider required a simple majority of senators present.

Trumbull was first to his feet, urging that the vote on the Sumner amendment not be reversed. America had a policy to encourage immigration. From wherever those immigrants came, the law must be applied to them equally:

"When foreigners come here, whether from China or Japan, from England or Ireland, from Germany or Africa, no matter whence they come, if we allow them to settle among us and have a law under which they may naturalize according to the Constitution and the principles of our Government, all should be permitted to naturalize alike. Our naturalization laws, according to the Constitution of the United States, must be uniform. The authority is given by the charter of our Government to establish a 'uniform rule of naturalization,' and we can establish no other." 41st Cong. 2nd Session Cong. Globe 5164 (1870).

Senator Williams contested Trumbull's interpretation of the Constitution. A "uniform rule" meant nothing more than having identical naturalization requirements in all parts of the country, Williams argued. Drawing lines as to which persons could qualify for naturalization was wholly within Congress' discretion.

"I do not think that is a fair construction of the Constitution," replied Trumbull.

Thurman reinforced Williams. The cited provision of the Constitution meant nothing more than uniformity across states.

Trumbull answered them:

"I agree that under the Constitution you cannot pass a bankrupt[cy] act or a naturalization act that shall operate differently in different States of the Union. It has to be uniform in different States; but that is not the only uniformity; it must be uniform also in its operation upon persons; and I deny it is competent for the Congress of the United States to pass a bankrupt[cy] act that shall be applicable to particular persons only. I say it must be applicable to all classes of persons alike . . . .

"The Congress of the United States has no power to pass a bankrupt[cy] act which shall apply to a trader who is a German and not to a trader who is an Irishman or an Englishman . . . .

"And now I say that when we pass a uniform rule of naturalization, it must be applicable to foreigners from all countries." 41st Cong. 2nd Session Cong. Globe 5164 (1870).

The debate on naturalization was taking place in the immediate aftermath of constitutional amendments to end discrimination on the basis of race. Trumbull found it ironic that Congress was about to miss an opportunity to render American citizenship laws color-blind:

"It seems extraordinary to me that the Senate of the United States should be engaged in attempting to maintain this distinction on account of race or color. That is all there is of it. This whole opposition to the naturalization of the Chinese grows out of their race and color. They are Asiatics, and the color of their skin is yellow. It is not long since the color of skin being black deprived an individual of all his rights." 41st Cong. 2nd Session Cong. Globe 5164 (1870).

Senator Trumbull conceded Congress could have immigration policies that would differentiate between nations, although he personally would not support them. But Congress could not write naturalization policies that racially discriminated among persons who had been legally admitted. The Chinese then in the United States were legal immigrants:

"I do not deny the power of the Government, however unwise it might be, to build a Chinese wall around this country, and to keep foreigners out altogether; nor the power to keep those from one country out and to admit those from another; but when foreigners are admitted, settle among us, and conform to our laws, I insist that the privilege of naturalization, if it is given at all, must be by a uniform rule applicable alike to all, without regard to the particular country whence they may have come." 41st Cong. 2nd Session Cong. Globe 5164 (1870).

Concluding his statement, Trumbull was more open toward the Chinese than would be many other members in the 41st Congress or its successors over the next seventy years:

"The pending amendment provides that persons from all nations may be naturalized, except those who are born in China. Why exclude the inhabitants of China, the people from the oldest nation in the world, and who are so far advanced in arts and literature? Everybody else can be naturalized, the Hottentot and the cannibal, to use the language of the Senator from Oregon; but he proposes an amendment that shall exclude from naturalization the patient, the laborious, the industrious, the skillful, the intelligent Chinaman . . . .

"From China, there is much to learn. Their civilization is not like ours in all respects, but in some it is superior; and yet these people are to be singled out by the advocates of human rights and human liberty and equality and told they may come here and dwell among us, but not as citizens of the country . . . . Sir, I can do no such wrong." 41st Cong. 2nd Session Cong. Globe 5165–66 (1870).

By now, it was 5:15 p.m. Debate had lasted all day in the Senate Committee of the Whole, but had not been able to move forward. So that senators might have dinner, the Senate recessed until 7:00 p.m., whereupon the body would reconvene for an evening session.

Hours of fractious discussion remained. As Senate proceedings resumed, the pending question was Fenton's motion to consider the vote by which the Sumner amendment has passed on the previous weekend.

Senator Samuel Pomeroy (R–KS) rose. A senator from 1861 to 1873, Pomeroy thought reversing the vote would leave unresolved the crucial issue of racial equality:

"For us to undertake in this country to settle upon a policy that is not founded in justice, that is not in harmony with the genius and spirit of our institutions, is no settlement at all, and if we could tonight make this settlement a permanent one by taking out the word 'white' from the naturalization laws, it would be immediately acquiesced in by the American people." 41st Cong. 2nd Session Cong. Globe 5168 (1870).

While the Senate did not heed the Kansas senator, he was right. More agitation on the Chinese question would follow, as Pacific states and their representatives in Congress pressed for the kind of immigration controls that were only hinted at in 1870. Such legislation would follow. In little more than a decade, the sentiment in Congress would turn decidedly anti-Chinese.

Stewart had argued that the Chinese did not want to naturalize, because they were beyond assimilation and remained loyal to China. But Stewart had gone further, insisting that even those willing to naturalize, should nonetheless be barred. Pomeroy attacked this inconsistency:

"The Senator from Nevada [Stewart] urges a strong argument against the naturalization of Chinamen, and assigns two reasons for his position. The first is that they cannot be Americanized and do not want to be; and the second is that they do want to be! I do not know which horn of this dilemma the Senator insists on going to trial on; but if they do not want to become citizens, as he said in the first instance, then there is no danger, because no person will become a citizen involuntarily. He has got first to declare his intention and renounce his former allegiance; and then he has got to wait five years. That is some time of pupilage; that gives him some opportunity for instruction; that is some time for him to assimilate himself to the American people and the American character. If he chooses to become an American citizen after coming here, and stays five years, my opinion is that he is qualified to be and ought to be welcome to our citizenship." 41st Cong. 2nd Session Cong. Globe 5168 (1870).

Pomeroy, like Trumbull, worried about America housing a class of people without political rights. Pomeroy's remedy was not to restrict immigration but to expand suffrage:

"If you deny citizenship to a large class, you have a dangerous element; you have an element you can enslave; you have an element in the community you can proscribe. Let all be equal before the law. Let every one of them have rights that all are bound to respect, and then you will have a government as enduring as the ages that defies all attempts to destroy it." 41st Cong. 2nd Session Cong. Globe 5169 (1870).

After some thirty minutes of further debate, Sumner asked to be heard on Fenton's motion to reconsider. The New Yorker Fenton had supported the amendment on Saturday, but was now seeking a reversal of course. Sumner was indignant:

"I should like to hear from him, that we might know why the Senator, having on Saturday voted to carry out the Declaration now, on the 4th of July, declines to carry out that Declaration. On what reason? Is there any? Can any be assigned why we thus bring disgrace upon the Senate? I speak plainly, for I say such a reconsideration will be a disgrace. Such a conclusion when once adopted cannot be abandoned without the Senate suffering." 41st Cong. 2nd Session Cong. Globe 5171 (1870).

Senator Sumner countered the substantive arguments that had been raised against his amendment, particularly those from Williams. The Oregonian Williams had claimed that if the amendment became law, heathens and pagans would dominate American institutions. Sumner thought the prognosis was ridiculous; moreover, it was beside the point.

"He says it gives to millions of heathens and pagans power to control our institutions . . . . I wish the Senator were here to explain this unjustifiable exaggeration. How and when? I make no proposition that I do not find in the institutions of my country. I simply ask you to stand by the Declaration of your fathers . . . . Full well do I know that there are no millions of heathens or pagans, and no other millions on this earth that can control the institutions of this country . . . . Worse than any heathen or pagan abroad are those in our midst who are false to our institutions." 41st Cong. 2nd Session Cong. Globe 5171–72 (1870).

Stewart rose. How could Sumner feel confident that a Chinese who took a pledge of citizenship would understand the gravity of the obligation undertaken and feel bound by it?

Refusing to concede that an oath meant less to a Chinese than to other immigrants, Sumner replied:

"Precisely as an Englishman, a Scotsman, an Irishman, a Frenchman, a German, a Swede, a Dane, a Russian or an African may give a pledge; precisely as a Senator may give a pledge. I have seen the Senator go up to that table and take the oath. The Senator is able; he knows that I know that; but does the Senator suppose that he surpasses in ability many of the Chinese who might come here? Does the Senator suppose that he feels more keenly the oath that he took at that desk than a Chinese might feel it?" 41st Cong. 2nd Session Cong. Globe 5172 (1870).

Senator Williams had also said that Chinese should not be admitted to citizenship because, as well as being pagans, they were also committed imperialists, interested in spreading Chinese culture to other nations. Sumner disputed this argument, believing it showed ignorance of China's rich cultural and intellectual history.

"Then the Senator proceeded to denounce the Chinese as imperialists and pagans. Pagans perhaps, though Senators who have ever looked into those books which have done so much for the Chinese mind will hesitate before they use harsh language in speaking of their belief. Has any Senator read the system of Confucius uttered before that of the Savior, and yet containing truths marvelously in harmony with those which fell from his lips? Throughout this great, populous empire, the truths of Confucius have ever been regarded as we regard our Scriptures. And yet the Chinese are called pagans!" 41st Cong. 2nd Session Cong. Globe 5172 (1870).

As for the Chinese being imperialists, Sumner noted that America had long admitted immigrants from European imperial powers, such as Russia. If a person were born under an imperial regime, but renounced that regime to become an American, then, logically, he or she was no longer an imperialist. Country of origin mattered not at all.

Sumner referred to Pomeroy's speech of earlier that evening, considering it "exquisite, with most beautiful thought and with unanswerable argument." He fastened upon Pomeroy's point that nothing could be settled that was not settled right. Sumner proclaimed:

"This question will never be settled until it is settled according to the great principles of justice. Vainly you try, you cannot succeed . . . . I do entreat Senators not to lose this precious opportunity of completing the harmony of the statutes of this land with the Constitution of the United States and the Declaration of Independence. Only in this way can you have peace.

"Let us have peace. Sir, I tell you how you may have it. Adopt the amend-

§1.31 Senator Sumner and Race Discrimination

Twenty-six-year-old Charles Sumner arrived in Paris in 1837. There he experienced a transformative moment that would reshape his views on race discrimination:

> On Saturday, January 20, 1838, as he recorded in his journal, Sumner attended a lecture at the Sorbonne on the philosophical theory of Heraclites delivered by Adople-Marie du Caurroy, a distinguished grey-haired scholar who spoke extremely slowly. Sumner began looking about the hall.
>
> "He had a quite a large audience," Sumner wrote, "among whom I noticed two or three blacks, or rather mulattoes—two-thirds black perhaps—dressed quite *a la mode* and having the easy, jaunty air of young men of fashion, . . ." He watched closely. The black students were "well received" by the other students, he noted.
>
> "They were standing in the midst of a knot of young men, and their color seemed to be no objection to them. I was glad to see this, though with American impressions, it seemed very strange. It must be then that the distance between free blacks and whites among us is derived from education, and does not exist in the nature of things."
>
> It was for Sumner a stunning revelation. Up to this point he is not known to have shown any particular interest in the lives of black people, neither free blacks nor slaves. On his trip to Washington a few years earlier, traveling by rail through Maryland, he had seen slaves for the first time. They were working in the fields, and as he made clear in his journal, he felt only disdain for them. "They appear to be nothing more than moving masses of flesh, unendowed with anything of intelligence above the brutes." He was to think that way no longer.

David McCullough, *The Greater Journey: Americans in Paris* (Simon & Schuster, 2011), p. 131.

ment which I have proposed, strike out the word 'white' and the harmony will begin. The country will straightaway accept the result. But reject that amendment, and you open at once the floodgates of controversy." 41st Cong. 2nd Session Cong. Globe 5172 (1870).

Sumner informed senators that a vote to reconsider would not put matters to rest. If the amendment were dropped from the bill, he would continue to press the issue until he achieved satisfaction:

"But whatever may be the result, I give notice that I shall not cease my effort. I shall continue it to the end. I am a soldier for the war, and until I see this great Declaration a living letter, I shall never intermit my endeavors. I shall go forward and on every possible occasion I shall press the Senate to another vote. But I trust the Senate will not reconsider what they have done; but that they will settle this great question so that it shall never again disturb our debates." 41st Cong. 2nd Session Cong. Globe 5173 (1870).

A vote occurred on Fenton's motion to reconsider. The ayes were 27, the nays were 14, and 31 senators were absent. Senators who originally supported the Sumner amendment but voted to reconsider included Roscoe Conkling (R–NY), Hannibal Hamlin (R–ME), Alexander Ramsey (R–MN), and John Scott (R–PA). Other senators comprising the majority to reconsider came from the group of 23 absentees on the original vote. Fenton, who arranged to cut the knot, voted against his own motion.

The Sumner amendment was again before the Senate. Before it could again come to a vote, Thurman reviewed what transpired. Twenty-seven senators had supported the Sumner amendment on Saturday, July 2, 1870, but only 14 opposed reconsideration. Two of Sumner's backers had voted to reconsider and another six had abstained from voting. Thurman crowed:

"Let it be remembered that here were ten Senators who could have kept this principle in this bill, who thought it the principle of the party only last Saturday, but who are found today, two of them absent, two of them changing their votes, and six of them sitting in their seats as dumb as the sheep before the shearer." 41st Cong. 2nd Session Cong. Globe 5176 (1870).

On the reconsidered Sumner amendment, the vote was 14 in favor, 30 opposed, with 28 senators absent, and it failed.

Willard Warner (R–AL) offered an amendment to extend naturalization to Africans. His amendment, which passed with 21 yeas to 20 nays and with 31 absentees, read as follows:

"And be it further enacted, That the naturalization laws are hereby extended to aliens of African nativity and to persons of African descent."

The bill as amended was reported from the Senate Committee of the Whole to the full Senate. The presiding officer announced that the full Senate would vote en bloc on the amendments agreed to in the Committee of the Whole, unless any senator asked that a particular amendment be broken out for a separate vote. Wilson requested that African naturalization be given such separate treatment.

By voice vote the Senate agreed to the amendment proposed by the Com-

§1.32 The First Chinese Student to Graduate from an American University, Yung Wing

Yung Wing (1828–1912), the first Chinese student to graduate from an American university (Yale, 1854), was naturalized on October 30, 1852. In 1876 he married an American, Mary Kellogg, and they had two children: Morrison Brown Yung and Bartlett Golden Yung. Yung Wing is buried in Hartford, CT.

There were other instances of naturalization of Chinese, but the Naturalization Act of 1870 made it possible for citizenship to be taken away from the Chinese, usually because the person had moved to a hostile area in the West. Many judges on the East Coast and a few on the West Coast would naturalize a Chinese person, but if that person's citizenship was challenged in a court in a West Coast state, it was often taken away from him.

For more on Yung Wing, see the Yung Wing Project (<*ywproject.com*>) and Edward J.M. Rhoads, *Stepping Forth into the World: The Chinese Educational Mission to the United States, 1872–81* (Hong Kong University Press, 2011).

mittee of the Whole, then turned to the African question. It passed with 20 yeas, 17 nays, and 35 senators absent. Several senators who had opposed the Sumner amendment on the Saturday, July 2, 1870, vote crossed over to support the Warner amendment, including Warner himself. One of Sumner's backers, Senator Timothy Howe (R–WI) of Wisconsin, opposed the Warner amendment. With the single exception of Howe, none of the seventeen senators who opposed African citizenship had supported the Sumner amendment on the original roll call.

Now Sumner again offered his amendment. It was identical to the one the Senate Committee of the Whole had passed on Saturday, then reconsidered and stripped before the bill was reported to the full Senate:

"And be it further enacted, That all acts of Congress relating to naturalization be, and the same are hereby, amended by striking out the word 'white' wherever it occurs; so that in naturalization there shall be no distinction of race or color."

The amendment was rejected by 12 yeas to 26 nays, with 34 senators not voting. Sumner's supporters, as a general matter, did not defect to the other side. But apparently unwilling to confront the filibuster further, they simply abstained from the vote and were counted as absent.

§1.33 Original Oregon Constitution Barred Chinese Owning Real Estate and Mining Claims

In the Oregon Constitution adopted in 1859, the Chinese were barred from voting (Article II, Section 6) and forbidden to own real estate or mining claims (Article XV, Section 8). The Oregon legislature gradually passed numerous anti-Chinese laws, including a Chinese miner's head tax and a substantial business tax on Chinese merchants. One of the reasons for mid-nineteenth century Oregonians to question whether or not the Chinese were "free immigrants" was the fact that in 1868 the Tong Duck Chung Company of Salem/Portland, Oregon, recruited 300 to 500 Chinese from Guangdong for several years to work in Oregon.

See the original Oregon Constitution drafted in 1857 and adopted in 1859 on the Oregon Blue Book web site, <*http://bluebook.state.or.us*>. For more about Chinese in Oregon, see Marie Rose Wong, *Sweet Cakes, Long Journey: The Chinatowns of Portland, Oregon* (University of Washington Press, 2004); Chinese Consolidated Benevolent Association, *Dreams of the West: A History of the Chinese in Oregon, 1850–1950* (Ooligan Press, 2007); and Sue Fawn Chung, *In Pursuit of Gold: Chinese American Miners and Merchants in the American West* (University of Illinois Press, 2011).

Senator Lyman Trumbull (R–IL) next proposed an amendment to extend naturalization to the Chinese. His amendment read:

"That the naturalization laws are hereby extended to aliens of African nativity, and to persons of African descent, *and to persons born in the Chinese empire*" (emphasis added).

Trumbull's amendment was defeated by 9 ayes to 31 nays, with 32 senators absent. Joining Trumbull were Senators Reuben Fenton (R–NY), Joseph Fowler (R–TN), Samuel Pomeroy (R–KS), William Rice (R–MA), Thomas Robertson (R–SC), William Sprague (R–RI), and Charles Sumner (R–MA).

On final passage of the bill, there were 33 senators in the affirmative, 8 in the negative, and 31 not voting.

At 11:18 p.m. on July 4, 1870, the Senate adjourned. The opportunity for Chinese naturalization was gone, lost for a long time. It was not until 1943 that a person of Chinese descent born outside the United States was eligible to become an American citizen.

CHAPTER TWO

美
國

The Fifteen Passenger Bill of 1879

"We have this day to choose whether we will have for the Pacific Coast the civilization of Christ or the civilization of Confucius."
—Senator James G. Blaine (R–ME)
8 Cong. Rec. 1303 (1879)

§ 2.0 Overview

- Considered in the 45th Congress of the United States (1877–1879)
- Senate Party Division: 40 Republicans, 35 Democrats, 1 Independent
- House Party Division: 155 Democrats, 136 Republicans, 2 Independents
- President: Rutherford B. Hayes (R) (1877–1881)

The first major piece of anti-Chinese legislation to get through Congress was the Fifteen Passenger bill. Passed in 1879, it denied entry into the United States of any vessel carrying more than fifteen Chinese passengers.

President Rutherford B. Hayes vetoed the bill as being incompatible with Sino-American treaty obligations. Among other things, the Burlingame Treaty of 1868 provided for the free movement of peoples between China and the United States and that Chinese persons in America would be accorded the same rights enjoyed by citizens of the "most favored nation."

An attempt to override the president's veto failed. Despite never becoming law itself, the Fifteen Passenger bill laid the groundwork for exclusion laws passed by future Congresses.

U rged by members of Congress from California and neighboring states, and with numerous petitions and memorials from that region in hand, Congress finally moved to impose statutory restrictions on Chinese immigration. Passed in 1879, the Fifteen Passenger bill limited the number of Chinese persons who could arrive in the United States on any vessel to fifteen. President Rutherford B. Hayes vetoed the measure. The president's veto was sustained, temporarily halting federal efforts to limit immigration of the Chinese.

Although the bill did not become law, its importance to the history of anti-Chinese legislation was crucial. Numerous issues emerged in the Fifteen Passenger debate that would appear again during consideration and enactment of what has become popularly known as the Chinese Exclusion Act of 1882, as well as the act's successor statutes. The exclusion of many Chinese from the United States, and the political ostracism of Chinese persons already in America, had deep roots in the 1879 proceedings.

Members of Congress alleged that Chinese immigrants would undermine American workers, who could not compete for jobs with low-cost Chinese labor. The standard of living for Americans would be lowered by such competition, it was claimed, and white labor would be driven or deflected from the Pacific region.

Although immigration to America was fundamentally unrestricted in that era, and immigrants were generally welcomed, many in Congress argued that Chinese were different from Europeans, were incapable of assimilating, and should be denied the access to American citizenship and political rights to which other immigrants could aspire.

Members also asserted that Chinese already in America were but the vanguard for an immense population that would overwhelm the Pacific states. Restricting immigration was promoted as an act of national self-preservation.

Abject racial prejudice permeated the debate, with open stigmatizing of persons of Chinese descent. Members alternated between asserting white superiority and predicting American political and economic destruction from a clash of civilizations.

A few dissenters challenged such derogatory assertions and cataclysmic predictions directly, but mostly the dispute was about whether the United States could or should limit Chinese immigration in light of existing treaty obligations to China, and if restrictions would damage U.S. commercial and missionary interests in the Far East. Rhetoric defending Chinese people and their culture was not often voiced and, when expressed, was subdued.

Although the Fifteen Passenger bill carried by substantial majorities in both the House and the Senate, it was nonetheless controversial. In years thereafter, disagreement would sharply diminish, and measures based on these theories would become matters of broad consensus in Congress.

§2.10 House Debate, January 28, 1879: "The most debased people"

> *Under consideration in the House Committee of the Whole, and later in the full House, H.R. 2423 (The Fifteen Passenger Bill).*

On January 14, 1879, Representative Albert Shelby Willis (D–KY) reported from the House Committee on Education and Labor H.R. 2423, a bill to restrict immigration of Chinese to the United States. Then a freshman, Willis was to serve in the House between 1877 and 1887.

On January 28, 1879, Willis brought the bill to the House floor. The House

Committee on Education and Labor had instructed him to secure its passage without House floor amendments. Accordingly, Willis announced that he would move the previous question. As explained by Speaker Samuel Randall (D–PA):

"The effect of a demand for the previous question is to exclude all other motions except a motion to adjourn. If it be sustained, it will cut off the offering of amendments, and will allow, under the rule, one hour of debate. If not sustained, it throws the bill open to amendment and to lengthened debate." 8 Cong. Rec. 792 (1879).

Willis' maneuver to restrict amendments stirred objections across the aisle, but Republican House members had no recourse other than to attempt voting down the previous question motion. The House agreed to the motion by 116 to 33, and an hour of general debate began. Willis managed time for the majority. Representative Martin Townsend (R–NY) controlled time for the minority. The time was split along party lines, not between proponents and opponents of the bill. As became clear during the debate, the Fifteen Passenger bill had strong support among both Democrats and Republicans in the House.

Willis began the debate by asking that the House Education and Labor Committee report be read aloud. The report addressed the threshold question of whether, in light of treaty obligations to China, Congress had the power to pass a bill restricting Chinese immigration. On this point, the committee was unequivocal:

"The existing treaty with China gives its subjects an unlimited right of immigration to the United States. The second clause of Article 6 of the Constitution provides that 'this Constitution, and the laws of the United States which shall be made in pursuance thereof, and all treaties made under the authority of the United States, shall be the supreme law of the land.'

"It is contended that any law restricting Chinese immigration would contravene this provision of the Constitution and would therefore be null and void . . . .

"The clause of the Constitution above quoted does not, however, admit of the construction contended for. It elevates treaties from the status of mere compacts to the dignity of laws, but it does not clothe them with any additional authority.

"Laws made in pursuance of the Constitution are equally as binding and authoritative as treaties and, if enacted, control any contravening treaty." 8 Cong. Rec. 793 (1879).

Relying on opinions of several United States attorneys general, as well as decisions of the Supreme Court and lower federal courts, the House Education and Labor Committee concluded:

"[I]t would seem clear that Congress has the right, by appropriate legislation, to change or abrogate any existing treaty." 8 Cong. Rec. 793 (1879).

But even if Congress had the constitutional power to pass legislation contradicting treaties, was this a proper time to exercise it? The House Education and Labor Committee did not answer gently.

"The evils of Chinese immigration have been fully recognized upon the Pacific slope for many years. Welcomed at first as a unique addition to the society and a valuable ally in the development of the material resources in their new home, the Chinese by their sordid, selfish, immoral, and non-amalgamating habits, within a very short time reversed the judgment in their favor and came to be regarded as a standing menace to the social and political institutions of the country." 8 Cong. Rec. 793 (1879).

The House Education and Labor Committee report noted that immigration restrictions were beyond the power of state and local authorities to impose. Because such measures were exclusive matters of federal jurisdiction, those state and local authorities turned to Congress for relief. Their lobbying campaign had commenced even before the Burlingame Treaty of 1868, and continued well into the decade of the 1870s. Ignored at first, agitation from the Pacific states eventually got Congress' attention. As the committee recited:

"As early as the 22nd of December, 1869, at the second session of the Forty-first Congress, an effort was made, but without success, to secure restrictive legislation. In the Forty-second Congress [1871–1873], and also in the Forty-third Congress [1873–1875], numerous memorials, resolutions of public meetings, and petitions, one of which numbered over 16,000 signatures, were presented to the same effect and with the same result. At the first session of the Forty-fourth Congress [1875–1877], those renewed appeals for relief met for the first time with a favorable response. A joint resolution was introduced and passed calling upon the President of the United States [at the time, President Ulysses S. Grant] to 'open negotiations with the Chinese government for the purpose of modifying the provisions of the treaty between the two countries and restricting the same to commercial purposes.'" 8 Cong. Rec. 793 (1879).

Once Congress decided to address Chinese immigration, it did so persistently. As the House Education and Labor Committee report explained:

"Subsequently, at the same session, another joint resolution was passed, requesting the President to present to the Chinese government an additional article to the treaty of July 28, 1868, reserving mutually to the two governments the right to regulate, restrict, or prevent immigration to their respective countries." 8 Cong. Rec. 793 (1879).

The president in 1875, Ulysses S. Grant (R), eighteenth President of the United States (1869–1877), did not respond to Congress' satisfaction. Meanwhile, the House Education and Labor Committee said, "the question had assumed dangerous proportions." 8 Cong. Rec. 793 (1879). According to the committee, rising and unresolved anger and the absence of apparent relief from Washington created a combustible situation.

"The conviction that Chinese immigration was a great evil was so deep-seated and unanimous, that mob violence was openly threatened and in many instances the arm of the law seemed powerless to protect." 8 Cong. Rec. 793 (1879).

In 1876, the 44th Congress also appointed a joint committee to investigate the alleged harms flowing from Chinese immigration. Chaired by Senator Oliver Morton (R–IN), the joint committee (Morton Committee) took extensive testimony in California. The Morton Committee hearing record focused on social differences between Chinese and white Californians, and emphasized that low Chinese pay scales undercut wages for white labor. The Morton Committee recommended a renegotiation of the Burlingame Treaty.

Early in the 45th Congress (1877–1879), yet another joint resolution was passed, seeking a Burlingame Treaty revision, but President Rutherford B. Hayes (1877–1881) did not act.

The failure of these repeated congressional overtures to secure relief through the executive branch convinced the House Education and Labor Committee to pursue a statutory remedy. The committee report stated:

"So long a period of non-action proves the unwillingness or the inability of the treaty-making power to cope with the question. In either event, your committee considers that further delay would work great injustice to a large portion of our country, provided the evils whereof they complain are well-founded." 8 Cong. Rec. 793 (1879).

The House Education and Labor Committee made its case for legislation. If incompatible peoples were permitted to occupy the same country, the living standards of white labor would diminish and American cultural and political life would corrode. Congress had the power, and indeed the responsibility, to avert a cataclysm. To prevent that downward spiral, the House Education and Labor Committee would recommend legal barriers be imposed to restrict immigration and prevent race-mixing.

"There is no principle on which we are compelled to receive into our midst the natives of Asia, Africa, or any other part of the world. The character, source, and extent of immigration should be controlled with reference to our own wants

§2.11 Denis Kearney and the Sandlot Orators

Denis Kearney was an Irish immigrant who gained attention on the sandlots of San Francisco for his harsh anti-Chinese rhetoric during the Depression of the mid-1870s. He eventually brought his message to the East Coast, but with somewhat reduced impact. Anti-exclusion members accused Pacific Coast colleagues of reacting to such hysteria, while the Californians and others insisted that opposition to Chinese immigration was broadly based and not a response to demagoguery. Historian Iris Chang describes Kearney's methods and his appeal:

> Kearney, a young sailor, had invested heavily in mining stocks and lost everything in the crash. Bankrupt and embittered, he started haranguing anyone who would listen in a huge vacant lot, known to locals as "the sandlots," near San Francisco's city hall. At first his audience consisted of a few vagabonds and stragglers, but when disgruntled workers took to gathering routinely at the sandlots at night, the crowds swelled to thousands. By the glow on bonfires and torches, sandlot orators stoked the anger of the crowds by showing just how, and by whom, their lives had been stolen from them. The method was conspiracy, and the thieves were the railroads, the corporate monopolies, and the Chinese.
>
> A gifted demagogue, the thirty-one year old Kearney soon became a crowd favorite, prescribing violent solutions for those with the courage to take matters into their own hands. . . . He talked about lynching railway moguls and suggested exterminating the Chinese population by dropping balloons filled with dynamite over Chinatown. He apparently knew his psychology, ending his speeches with the rallying cry of "The Chinese must go!"

Iris Chang, *The Chinese in America* (Penguin Books, 2003), pp. 125–126.

and welfare. The difficult problems, economic and political, resulting from the presence of red and black races would be renewed in a more aggravated and dangerous form by the presence of the yellow race . . . .

"It is neither possible nor desirable for two races as distinct as the Caucasian and the Mongolian to live under the same government without assimilation. The degradation or slavery of one or the other would be the inevitable result. Homogeneity of ideas and of physical and social habits are [sic] essential to national harmony and progress." 8 Cong. Rec. 793 (1879).

From the House Education and Labor Committee's perspective, the issue of national self-preservation was squarely presented. Legislative action was urgent, if the problem of Chinese immigration was not to grow beyond Congress' capacity to address it:

"No self-governing country can afford to diminish or destroy the dignity, the welfare, the independence of its citizens. Justice to people of the Pacific slope, the dictates of common humanity and benevolence, as well as the plainest suggestions of practical statesmanship, all demand that the problem of Chinese immigration shall be solved while it is yet within legislative control." 8 Cong. Rec. 793 (1879).

From the minority, Representative Martin Townsend (R–NY) rose on the House floor to rebut. Townsend, who served in Congress between 1875 and 1879, tied the demand for legislation to passions stirred by Denis Kearney and other San Francisco sandlot orators.

Kearney's sandlot rhetoric reminded Townsend of the sort of rabble-rousing that generated discrimination against other immigrants. Now Willis and his allies on the House Committee on Education and Labor carried the cause forward in Congress:

"I say to the gentleman from Kentucky who has charge of this bill and who represents Louisville, Kentucky, that I remember the day when the cry was against the Catholic Irish, against the condemned Germans, and when the streets of his city flowed with blood and when the streets of Saint Louis, in Missouri, flowed with blood in the riots against the Irish and the Germans because they were coming here to take away the labor of the American citizen and rob his children of their bread." 8 Cong. Rec. 794 (1879).

Demands for Chinese exclusion did not arise from the true working class but rather from idle demagogues, Townsend claimed. Congress should ignore them and not heed the mob in repression of the Chinese. He drew upon a powerful historical analogy:

"I have another instance of a people whom neither oppression nor repression destroyed. The Jewish people all through the ages dressed differently from their Christian neighbors. They lived by themselves and had a different face . . . .

"These men, as I say, were persecuted; they were mobbed; they were taxed; they were oppressed; they were murdered in the streets by mobs. The mob of the Middle Ages played in advance all the fiendish tricks practiced by the hoodlums of California against the 'Heathen Chinee.'" 8 Cong. Rec. 794 (1879).

Townsend was referring to a fictional Chinese card shark depicted in a widely circulated 1870 poem called "The Heathen Chinee," by Bret Harte. The poem

§2.12 Early China–U.S. Diplomacy

The first Opium War between Great Britain and China concluded with the Treaty of Nanking in 1843. Through gunboat diplomacy, the British were able to secure significantly expanded trade, beneficial tariffs, and extraterritorial legal rights in China that the Qing Emperor had otherwise been unwilling to grant. In the aftermath of this opening, the United States pursued its own interests in China. The first Sino-American diplomatic agreement was concluded in 1844, granting Americans commercial rights within five treaty ports. Two additional treaties, in 1858, broadened commercial rights and assisted American missionaries. The Burlingame Treaty of 1868 (*§ 1.30*) further regularized relations between China and the United States, and addressed issues such as the free migration of peoples and granted most favored nation treatment to Chinese in America and Americans in China.

appeared in *Plain Language from Truthful James* (Western News, 1870), 33-35. Although Harte may not have intended the poem to cast Chinese in a negative light, it fed anti-Chinese stereotypes. The opening lines were:

> *Which I wish to remark*
> *And my language is plain*
> *That for ways that are dark*
> *And for tricks that are vain,*
> *The heathen Chinee is peculiar*
> *Which the same I would rise to explain.*

Representative Townsend turned briefly to the probable effect of exclusion legislation on American business and missionary interests in Asia. Through persistent U.S. diplomacy, hermetic China had been opened. Agreements with the Chinese had "made a step forward in the advance of civilization, Christianity, and commercial prosperity, and a step in favor of the human race." 8 Cong. Rec. 795 (1879).

Townsend claimed immigration restrictions would reverse this progress. To applause from the House gallery, he concluded:

"I am not for taking a step backward. I am for treating the human race as brothers. I will quote upon this subject the language of a man who does not live in California, the language of one whose lyre was always resonant with the best sympathies of humanity; I refer to the immortal Robert Burns:

§2.13 The Page Act

Representative Horace Page (R–CA) was the author of legislation that, as enforced, negatively affected the ability of Chinese family life to take root in the United States.

The Page Act of March 1875—passed in the midst of a depression, a rise in anti-Chinese violence, and the collapse of the myth of domesticity—sought to erase Chinese women from the social cartography of the United States. The Act prevented the "landing" of anyone for a fixed "term of service within the United States for lewd and immoral purposes." Besides Chinese felons, it banned the importation of "women for the purposes of prostitution . . . ."

Where the Page Act fell short, U.S. consuls in China stepped in, rejecting an untold number of women's applications for visas. Should a woman manage to receive a permit to sail, she often faced the ordeal of an expensive habeas corpus trial in San Francisco. Hundreds of Chinese women remained in custody, held aboard ships or in prisons, until they could explain their relationships with male emigres to hostile immigration officers or judges.

Jean Pfaelzer, *Driven Out: The Forgotten War Against Chinese Americans* (University of California Press, 2007), p 104.

'Then let us pray that come it may, as come it will for a' that
When man to man, the world o'er, shall brothers be for a' that."
8 Cong. Rec. 795 (1879).

Representative Townsend took his seat, and Representative Horace Page (R–CA) took the House floor. Page served in Congress between 1873 and 1883. His statement contrasted sharply with Townsend's and more closely resembled views of the Democratic majority, as expressed by Representative Willis and the House Education and Labor Committee.

"[F]or the past eight years or more, I have been an advocate of some restrictive legislation to prevent what I regarded as one of the greatest evils of our time, an over-influx of Chinese immigration." 8 Cong. Rec. 795 (1879).

Page observed that Asians did not immigrate to the United States on the same basis as Europeans. Instead, he charged, Chinese arrived under the pernicious influence of labor contracts arranged by the Chinese Six Companies (the Chinese Consolidated Benevolent Association), which were San Francisco-based benevolent organizations with substantial familial and commercial ties back to Guangdong Province in southern China. Guangdong was a major source of early Chinese emigration to the United States. According to Page, this exploitative system:

"... led to the formation of companies which seek to utilize the cheap labor of China for their own benefit, and under contract and by monopolistic combinations, in violation of the spirit of both the treaty and laws, have introduced multitudes of the lowest classes of these aliens in our midst ....

"The profits of labor go principally to the Chinese companies who introduce and control these aliens, with only a very limited pittance to the laborer himself." 8 Cong. Rec. 795 (1879).

American whites could not compete against workers who were paid little and did not require much to live. As Page explained:

"With demands restricted to their simplest animal needs, freed from the cost of domestic life and the burdens of government, they have been placed upon vantage-ground as competitors with American laborers and have succeeded in obtaining exclusive control of certain industries in California." 8 Cong. Rec. 796 (1879).

To support his argument that competition with Chinese labor was inherently injurious to the American workforce, Representative Page presented for the *Congressional Record* a memorial signed by some 17,000 California workers. The memorial stated that Chinese immigration had resulted in massive labor displacement and wage diminution, and that importation of Chinese was generating highly undesirable and unsustainable social conditions:

"That this immigration is in no manner homogeneous with us as a people; that the standard of labor must be debased to such a degree by their vitiating influence as to repel vast bodies of our most valuable operatives, and not only degrade the social status and moral welfare of our producing classes, but arrest the advancement of our civilization." 8 Cong. Rec. 796 (1879).

Because stigmatizing the Chinese would facilitate their exclusion, Page quoted from the writings of a prominent nineteenth-century American travel writer, Bayard Taylor, to demean Chinese people. Taylor's remarkable analysis, on which Page asked Congress to rely, was this:

"It is my deliberate opinion that the Chinese are, morally, the most debased people on the face of the earth. Forms of vice, which in other countries are barely named, are in China so common that they excite no comment among the natives. They constitute the surface level, and below them are deeps and deeps of depravity so shocking and horrible that their character cannot even be hinted.

There are some dark shadows in human nature which we naturally shrink from penetrating, and I made no attempt to collect information of this kind; but there was enough in the things which I could not avoid seeing and hearing, which are brought almost daily to the notice of every foreign resident, to inspire me with a powerful aversion to the Chinese race." 8 Cong. Rec. 796 (1879). See Bayard Taylor, *A Visit to India, China, and Japan, in the Year 1853* (G.P. Putnam, 1855).

Page told the House that he was not in principle anti-immigrant. Immigration and naturalization, he believed, were important foundations on which to build a growing county:

"We have sought population, and under the generous influence of free government, we have invited strangers to our shores by a naturalization system most liberal." 8 Cong. Rec. 796 (1879).

America was not to be open to the whole world on an equal basis, however. Page made certain to set Chinese apart from other immigrants. The country would welcome Europeans; Chinese were altogether different.

"The immigration sought has always been Caucasian, and the invitation has proceeded upon the presumption that the people who might make up the volume of foreign population should not only be of a class which the American people would deem competent for and entitled to citizenship in the Republic, but such as would from race and religious sentiment desire to become not residents only but citizens of the country." 8 Cong. Rec. 796 (1879).

Representative Page emphasized that the Chinese could not or would not assimilate into American society and should be disqualified for U.S. citizenship. Accordingly they deserved treatment that was materially different from that accorded to whites.

Europeans could expect to find in the United States a refuge from tyranny, despotism, and religious persecution, as well as a path toward American citizenship, said Page. Such immigrants were desirable, and it was in America's political ethic to welcome them. But Chinese workers were different, an alien element, incapable for deeply rooted social and cultural reasons, of ever being Americans:

"I deny that this land is an asylum for that class, who seek our shores for the mere purpose of curiosity or trade, with no appreciation of our free institutions; who refuse to adopt our customs or conform to our habits; who are not devoted to the cause of liberty or equality; who come here simply for purposes of temporary profit, or are brought here as coolies for companies formed in China under contract for servile labor; who refuse to assimilate with us, and who are unfitted by education, habits, religious superstition, and by their born prejudices to assume any of the duties that society imposes on the citizen." 8 Cong. Rec. 796–797 (1879).

Representative Page explored whether the Burlingame Treaty's obligations had to be respected or whether Congress would be better off abrogating them. The commitments in question were centered on Articles V and VI of the treaty. He felt strongly such promises should be disregarded, because they were inapplicable to the facts at hand.

Article V of the Burlingame Treaty read:

"The United States of America and the Emperor of China cordially recognize the inherent and inalienable right of man to change his home and allegiance, and also the mutual advantage of free migration and emigration of their citizens and subjects respectively from the one country or the other for the purpose of curiosity, of trade, or as permanent residents. The high contracting parties, therefore, join in reprobating any other than an entirely voluntary emigration for these purposes. They consequently agree to pass laws making it a penal offense for a citizen of the United States or Chinese subjects to take Chinese subjects either to the United States or to any other foreign country, or for a Chinese subject or citizen of the United States to take citizens of the United States to China or to any other foreign country without their free and voluntary consent, respectively." 8 Cong. Rec. 2275 (1879).

The Burlingame Treaty (*Appendix 2*) provided for the free migration and emigration of peoples, but Page contended that Chinese immigration involved contract labor and was not truly free. Accordingly, legislating to bar the influx of such labor would not contradict the treaty:

"In the fifth article, the right of free migration and emigration is recognized; but as is evident by reference to the concluding clause of this article, the word 'free' is used as the opposite of 'involuntary' and does not convey or is intended to convey the idea or the right of unrestricted introduction of the Chinese into this country, nor does it debar the United States by legislation or otherwise, from limiting or regulating the volume of people that may seek our shores." 8 Cong. Rec. 797–798 (1879).

Besides, said Page, the Chinese government itself enforced restrictions on free migration, both as to initial entry or movement within the country:

"China excludes all migration from some of its territory. It permits immigrants only to land at certain ports of the empire. An unlimited volume of emigration at the will of the parties was certainly not contemplated by China." 8 Cong. Rec. 797 (1879).

In Article VI, the Burlingame Treaty provided that America would grant Chinese subjects the same rights as citizens from the most favored nations. The text read:

"Citizens of the United States visiting or residing in China shall enjoy the same privileges, immunities, or exemptions in respect to travel or residence as there may be enjoyed by the citizens or subjects of the most favored nation; and, reciprocally, Chinese subjects visiting or residing in the United States shall enjoy the same privileges, immunities, or exemptions in respect to travel or residence as there may be enjoyed by the citizens or subjects of the most favored nation; But nothing herein contained shall be held to confer naturalization upon citizens of the United States in China, nor upon the subjects of China in the United States." 8 Cong. Rec. 2275 (1879).

Representative Page asserted that nothing in Article VI should hamper Congress from curtailing immigration. The treaty applied only to persons who had already been granted admission to the United States, not ones waiting to enter:

"By reference to the sixth article, which confers certain rights upon Chinese subjects equally with the most favored nations, it will be found that the provision does not refer to the introduction of this alien population, but only to their rights after they shall have reached our shores." 8 Cong. Rec. 797 (1879).

Having concluded that the Burlingame Treaty did not pose legal or policy barriers to exclusion legislation, Page returned to the theme of diminishing the Chinese in order to justify their political segregation:

"This people, by the deliberate judgment of the American Government, is pronounced unworthy of citizenship, and everything forecasting and characterizing their advent and presence here shows that they lack every element that enters into American home life—aliens not to be trusted with political rights, and utterly as a class devoid either of the personal or social qualities that make them a reliable and desirable element, possessing industry and economy that may make them the peers of the ants, but possessing no elements that make them valuable in building up either the social or industrial interests of the country." 8 Cong. Rec. 798 (1879).

Legislate now, Page demanded, or be prepared to perpetrate grievous injury on American labor and manufacturing interests. Without restricted immigration, limitless masses of Chinese would join their compatriots in the United States. Chinese would crowd out American workers, degrade wages, diminish living standards and inflict poverty and social decay.

"From this overflowing hive . . . they can be moved in disturbing volume to every section of the Union. They can establish factories first in the Pacific States and then farther East . . . and can proceed, for reasons heretofore given, to establish a competition against both American products and American workers, before which both will fall and disappear." 8 Cong. Rec. 798 (1879).

By the end of Page's speech, all time allocated to the Republicans in the House had expired. Willis summed up, focusing on race.

America had suffered through two difficult experiences with race-mixing, Willis said. The first was with American Indians, or in Willis' parlance, "the red race." Indian policy remained a failure:

"Millions of money and thousands of valuable lives have been sacrificed in the vain effort to make the Indian either an obedient subject or a willing citizen. He is today the same sullen, unconquered alien savage that he was in the earliest colonial history of our country." 8 Cong. Rec. 798 (1879).

The second difficult experience was with "the black race," recalled Willis, noting that bringing blacks to America produced "bitter animosities," "sectional strife," and "religious dissensions," problems that could only be solved by the "arbitrament of arms." 8 Cong Rec. 799 (1879).

Willis argued that these problems, however durable and vexatious, would not compare to what America could expect from unrestricted Chinese immigration.

"If our experience has been a failure, or at best a doubtful success, with the African and the Indian, what can we expect from the Mongolian, who has neither the docility and humility of the one, nor the consciousness of inferior civilization which distinguishes the other? The bill which is now before the House puts an end to this third experiment with an alien race." 8 Cong. Rec. 799 (1879).

If America restrained Chinese immigration, Willis said, it would follow examples that had been set in other places, as in colonial areas of the Philippines, Siam, Indo-China, Indonesia, and Australia ("Sinophobia"). The United States should learn from those experiences, he said.

Each of these other societies had found the Chinese to be detestable, Willis claimed. His stereotyping of the Chinese was brutal and condemning:

"The Chinaman, whether as a laborer, as a member of society, or of the body politic, is an undesirable element in any community. Crowded, huddled together, forty or fifty in a room not larger that would accommodate with decency and with comfort one man with a family, discarding or disregarding all the usual appliances of personal civilization as to diet and clothing, cooking, eating, and sleeping in the same apartments, they have succeeded in reducing the cost of living to its minimum and thus wherever located have forced the laboring classes to the wall.

"Nor as members of society are they less objectionable. Their personal habits consequent upon their mode of life in these squalid dens, their low grovel-

§2.14 Absenteeism and Pairs in House and Senate Votes

Roll calls in relation to the Fifteen Passenger bill demonstrate a substantial number of House members not voting, totals swelled by the extensive use of "pairs." In a "pair," a member refrains from voting as an accommodation to another member who would vote opposite but who is not present. In that way, a member's absence does not negatively affect his side of the vote. Pairing has substantially declined in modern times, as has absenteeism. In recent years, there are very few members in either the House or the Senate recorded as not-voting on roll calls.

ing ideas of virtue and religion, and their peculiar social views have been commented upon and condemned by every nation with whom they have come in contact." 8 Cong. Rec. 799 (1879).

Representative Townsend had claimed that newcomers from different lands could assimilate notwithstanding antagonistic attitudes. That might be true for Europeans but not for Chinese, Willis argued. Unlike Europeans, who were "prompt to defend the honor and to promote the interests of their adopted land," the Chinese "disdain to accept our institutions," "look with contempt upon our social customs," and "defy the authority of our laws." The experience of twenty-five years of Chinese immigration left them "unchanged and unimproved in any important particular." 8 Cong. Rec. 799 (1879).

Townsend had no basis to compare this class of persons with assimilative Europeans, said Willis. "The Chinese, unlike them, have always been and will always be an alien element in our midst" and "an indigestible element in the body-politic." 8 Cong. Rec. 799 (1879).

With the conclusion of Willis' speech, all time for Democratic debate, and all debate in the House, ended. The discussion had been dominated by reading of the report from the Committee on Education and Labor as well as speeches from Willis and Page. Townsend's defense was earnest, but his remarks were overshadowed by the vitriol from other members of the House.

The House proceeded to adopt the Committee on Education and Labor amendments, of which the most significant was increasing the number of permitted passengers from ten to fifteen.

Under the "previous question" procedure that the House imposed, no floor amendments were in order.

On January 28, 1879, after but one hour of debate, the House passed the Fifteen Passenger bill. The vote was 155 yeas to 72 nays. Of the 155 in favor, 51 were Republicans, 103 were Democrats, and one was an Independent. Of the 72 dissenters, 56 were Republicans and 16 were Democrats. Sixty-one members were recorded as not voting, including future presidents James Garfield (R–OH) and William McKinley (R–OH).

§2.20 Senate Proceedings on the Fifteen Passenger Bill

On February 7, 1879, Senator Hannibal Hamlin (R–ME), chairman of the Senate Foreign Relations Committee, reported from committee "without recommendation" H.R. 2423, the Fifteen Passenger bill that had passed the House a week earlier. As the subsequent debate would demonstrate, a majority of the committee favored the bill, but its chairman did not.

§2.21 Senate Debate, February 12, 1879: "Consideration begins"

Under consideration in the Senate Committee of the Whole:
H.R. 2423, the Fifteen Passenger Bill.

On Wednesday, February 12, 1879, Senator Aaron Sargent (R–CA) moved that the Senate proceed to the bill's consideration. After a six-year tenure in the House (1861–1863 and 1869–1873), Sargent was nearing the end of his single Senate term (1873–1879). Although any senator may move a bill's consideration, the prerogative to do so is reserved in modern Senate practice for the Senate Majority Leader. The Leader position evolved in the twentieth century. In 1879, there was no Majority Leader, so when moving the bill, Sargent was acting within the normal Senate customs of the day.

Debate began the following day.

§2.22 Senate Debate, February 13, 1879: "An indigestible element"

Under consideration in the Senate Committee of the Whole:
H.R. 2423, the Fifteen Passenger Bill.

On Thursday, February 13, 1879, Senate deliberations commenced. Unlike the single hour allocated in the House to debate, Senate consideration of the Fifteen Passenger bill would consume most of three lengthy days.

Sargent opened the debate by confronting the question of whether Congress could legislate to override treaty obligations. This topic had been addressed in the report of the House Committee on Education and Labor. Sargent drew similar conclusions to those of the House Committee, arguing that Congress was empowered to act, even if doing so caused a treaty to be abrogated.

But how should such authority be wielded? Negating a treaty should not be casually undertaken, he conceded, but urgent circumstances connected to Chinese immigration justified it.

"Now, it may be said that while this power may exist, we ought to be tender in its exercise. I admit it; it is only in the case of an emergency that we ought to exercise such a power. I will endeavor to show . . . that an emergency of this kind exists, grows greater day by day, and if there is any reserved power of the people of the United States represented in Congress to protect the people of the Pacific Coast, now is the time when that power ought to be exercised." 8 Cong. Rec. 1264 (1879).

Sargent contended that the right of self-preservation was inherent and primary, even if it caused a nation to contravene its international obligations. Stopping Chinese immigration was just such a step, he said.

Echoing comments that Representatives Page and Willis had made in the House, Senator Sargent separated the Chinese from other immigrants. While the country could welcome Europeans, it could not absorb the non-assimilative Chinese:

"They do not come as ordinary colonists; they do not come to be citizens; and the experience of over twenty-five years in California with these people shows that they are an indigestible element in our midst, a cold pebble in the public stomach which cannot be digested. They are, they remain, men of China, without any aspiration for American citizenship, without any adaptability to become citizens." 8 Cong. Rec. 1265 (1879).

Californians had been distressed by the Chinese influx, but had largely remained patient in anticipation of relief. Upon occasion, however, tolerance gave way to violence, as citizens decided "to take redress in their own hands [as] old Germanic nations did when they were threatened with an irruption of barbarians . . . ." 8 Cong. Rec. 1275 (1879).

Seething discontent was understandable, said Sargent. One need only be acquainted with despicable conditions in San Francisco's Chinatown, populated by some 40,000 Chinese immigrants:

"Left to itself, it becomes so filthy that no white man can stand the stench. White people flee from that neighborhood and property all around it depreciates. There is a strange people there. A newspaper or a book never penetrates within its precincts. They speak a foreign and impenetrable tongue." 8 Cong. Rec. 1265 (1879).

The Chinese imperiled public health and safety, Sargent exclaimed, foisting on California "two or three epidemics of smallpox," "leprosy," and "hideous immoralities," including the treatment of 6,000 women held in "the most abject bondage and brought for purposes of prostitution." 8 Cong. Rec. 1266 (1879). Chinatown was the tip of a spear aimed at America's heart, its denizens being "a slight fragment of the four hundred million people behind them." 8 Cong. Rec. 1265 (1879).

Senator Sargent addressed the effect of Chinese labor on American workers. Conditions in which the Chinese survived were deplorable, and the impact on the workforce was woeful. These conditions stemmed from the operation of coolie labor contracts, Sargent alleged. Under the contracts, Chinese workers:

". . . come and are worked so cheaply because there is a system of contract or coolie labor; they come from China consigned to one of six companies, great, powerful, wealthy corporations. They come, giving their labor in exchange for passage money for a number of years, to work wherever they are sent wherever it is profitable for their masters to put them . . . . This is not American civilization; this is filthy, squalid barbarism." 8 Cong. Rec. 1266 (1879).

American labor could not compete with Chinese workers, "who can sleep in twenty feet of cubic space, who can live on a dead rat and a few handfuls of rice, who can work for ten cents a day." Sargent forecast a social contagion. Forced into a downward wage competition, white laborers must starve, throw away hope of happy families, send their children into the street, and be stripped of hearth and home. 8 Cong. Rec. 1266 (1879).

Propelled by incessant poverty, poor agriculture, and unrest in their home country, the Chinese were driven to emigrate. Defenses must be built against them, he urged:

"They must go, they do go, and they overwhelm wherever they go. Fortunate is the people within their reach which erects barriers in time against them." 8 Cong. Rec. 1266–1267 (1879).

After Sargent concluded his argument, Senator La Fayette Grover (D–OR) took the Senate floor. Grover had been Oregon's first representative in the House after statehood for one month in 1859 (Oregon became the thirty-third state on February 14, 1859) and was later its governor (1870–1877). In the Senate, Grover served a single term (1877–1883).

Grover launched an attack on the Burlingame Treaty, in particular, its expatriation provision. As expressed in the treaty, this policy recognized "the inherent and inalienable right of a man to change his home and allegiance." Expatriation had been a core value set out in the Declaration of Independence, opposite to traditional concepts of lifetime citizenship obligations. Its expression in the Burlingame Treaty made the treaty a groundbreaking diplomatic achievement. Unless the treaty could somehow be discredited, Congress might be reluctant to abrogate it.

To erode the Burlingame Treaty's moral standing, Grover claimed that the treaty was hypocritical as applied and one-sided in China's favor. Under its terms, Chinese subjects in America could enjoy every privilege, except citizenship. They had freedom of labor, freedom to hold property, and freedom of movement. In contrast, an American in China was "limited to a few ports, and he lives and does business under every possible restriction, not amounting to exclusion altogether. The reciprocity here provided for is really Chinese privilege in America and American exclusion in China . . . . Under careful inspection, the reciprocity of this famous convention, so ostentatiously announced in every article, fades and vanishes." 8 Cong. Rec. 1268 (1879).

Senator Grover continued harshly condemning the Chinese. The immigrant he depicted was a deadly plague on society, human in form but so essentially different and non-assimilative in nature, as to overwhelm and devastate any culture he was permitted to infect.

"When he comes among us he brings all he has and all he is—his gods, his government, his language, his hieroglyphics, his unchanged customs, his clothing, his chopsticks, and, as far as possible, his food. He is a man among us but not of us. He is not bone of our bone, nor flesh of our flesh, and never can be . . . . He never adds to, but subtracts from, the resources of the country. He never builds up, but hastens a common decay every place he most inhabits." 8 Cong. Rec. 1268 (1879).

If residents of the Pacific Coast knew and had rejected the Chinese, might such immigrants be welcomed elsewhere in the country? Grover thought not, predicting severe social decay and economic degradation anywhere the Chinese settled:

"Property depreciates, mortgages carry away titles to homes for little or nothing, and the owner is homeless . . . . [G]lass is broken from tenantless houses; Christian churches are turned into heathen temples and homes for idols. The men of science are gone, the men of the professions are gone, the happy families are gone . . . . This is the deserted village, once living, now dead." 8 Cong. Rec. 1269 (1879).

At bottom, Senator Grover argued, the fundamental problem was the homogenizing of races:

"We want no more mixture of races. No strong nation was ever born of mongrel races of men." 8 Cong. Rec. 1269 (1879).

Pending legislation would forestall the assumed catastrophe. "The bill before the Senate is not all it should be, but it is a step in the right direction. Let us take that step, and Europe will rejoice with us that America in the great future is to be Caucasian and not Mongolian." 8 Cong. Rec. 129 (1879).

As Grover took his seat, the presiding officer recognized Senator Newton Booth (R–CA), Sargent's colleague from California. A former California governor (1871–1875), Booth was serving his single Senate term (1875–1881).

Booth declared the inevitability of a clash of civilizations, a looming and epic contest between incompatible peoples:

"The meeting of two civilizations antagonistic in every form and feature in a struggle for existence in the same country cannot be other than an event of momentous historical importance . . . . A people counted in the hundreds of millions, alien in race, of a civilization older than ours, so old that it regards ours with contempt, so old that it has already reached a fixed type, unchanging, unchangeable, is moving toward us. Already it has possession of half the active labor of California. It will not stop on the Pacific." 8 Cong. Rec. 1270 (1879).

If corrective legislation did not forestall the conflict, which side was destined to gain superiority? Perhaps white America would dominate, but maybe not. For whites to be confident of prevailing required an "arrogance of power," Booth observed. 8 Cong. Rec. 1270 (1879).

"When and where have races non-assimilative with diversities of character irreconcilable, been brought together under one government without the subordination of one to the other, or a conflict destructive to one and injurious to both?" 8 Cong. Rec. 1270 (1879).

Senator Booth foresaw a struggle in which the winner would be "those whose wants are reduced to a minimum." Americans had higher living standards and family responsibilities, but Chinese worked at a different level:

"The Chinaman who comes to our shore brings no family. He has no children to support, educate, and provide for . . . . He has been trained down to the lowest means of subsistence; for hundreds of generations his ancestors have been engaged in a fierce struggle for existence. By the law of heredity, their habits survive in his character; have become part of his blood and brain. His wants have been circumscribed by the narrowest circle of human possibility." 8 Cong. Rec. 1270 (1879).

The American economy of the 1870s was no longer expansive enough to provide opportunities for all:

"In a new country where labor is in the greatest demand, any form of labor is welcomed as an addition to the common stock; but as the field fills up, as labor ceases to be sought but is compelled to seek employment, the cheapest labor brings all others to its own level of wages or drives it out. It ceases to supplement; it substitutes." 8 Cong. Rec. 1270 (1879).

Under such economic conditions, Booth predicted, survival of the fittest would drive down white labor "to the Asiatic level." He continued, "Do not flatter yourselves, Mr. President and Senators, that you can preserve the externals of American society and destroy the conditions on which it rests. Do not flatter yourselves that you can preserve the independence of American citizenship and destroy the independence of American workers." 8 Cong. Rec. 1270 (1879).

The Fifteen Passenger bill represented a significant change in American immigration policy. Booth conceded that the legislation was "an innovation," but merely because the bill was unprecedented was not a reason to reject it:

"To refuse new measures in the presence of new emergencies, is as if one should refuse medicine because he had never before been sick, or to decline to insure because his house had never been burned." 8 Cong. Rec. 1270 (1879).

Senator Booth rejected the notion that Chinese and American societies could coexist. They were simply too different, or as Booth described it, "antipodal." That such diverse peoples could ever voluntarily live under the same government was "inconceivable," he declared. In place of harmony was a natural conflict and mutual contempt that could only end with the subordination of one race to the other. Destructive things would happen to America from such tension:

"The darkest passages of human history have been enacted when alien races have been brought into contact . . . . Mr. President, we do not want a conflict of races. We do not want an amalgamation of races. We do not want a subordinate race. We do not want the condition of American labor reduced to the Asiatic level. We shall eventually have one or all if Chinese immigration is free." 8 Cong. Rec. 1271 (1879).

When Booth concluded, the presiding officer recognized Senator John Tyler Morgan (D–AL), a senator between 1877 and 1907. A member of the Committee on Foreign Relations, Morgan cited congressional discontent with the failure of the Hayes administration (1877–1881) to renegotiate the Burlingame Treaty to provide for immigration controls. Diplomacy would have been a better course than abrogating a treaty through legislation, Morgan said, but Congress would act in the face of administration diffidence or stalling:

"The apparent willingness of the Government to allow this important subject to drift away from its diplomatic control into the control of the legislative department seems to imply an expectation, if not a desire, that Congress will cut the Gordian knot." 8 Cong. Rec. 1271 (1879).

Senator Morgan was not reticent about doing so. Chinese immigration had become "a danger to our country of the greatest magnitude," he said. 8 Cong. Rec. 1271 (1879).

Early Chinese immigrants, such as those who had built the transcontinental railway, had been sojourners, Morgan observed. They remained loyal to their Chinese homeland, but now the Chinese were seeking to make America home. The Burlingame Treaty was to blame for the change of attitude, declared Morgan, because it fundamentally altered the way Chinese looked at their future in America. The language of the treaty appeared to invite permanent settlement.

Senator Morgan spoke of the Burlingame Treaty as "the culmination of a national craze as to the regenerating effect that the inferior colored races would exert upon our social and political system." 8 Cong. Rec. 1271 (1879). Aware that America had broadened rights for Africans, Chinese looked at the Burlingame Treaty and expected similar benefits for themselves:

"The Chinese were not to be naturalized, and yet it was widely felt that this would only be the work of a very few years . . . . They find other inferior races admitted to the highest privileges of citizenship, which is to them an assurance that when they become sufficiently numerous, they will also become powerful and influential." 8 Cong. Rec. 1271–1272 (1879).

In China, people were condemned to live a lifetime inside the caste into which they were born. Post-Civil War America presented them with more appealing possibilities:

"They see that slaves have become masters and rulers, and they see that they may not only escape the oppressive tyranny of caste, which keeps the lower classes in worse than servitude in China, but they readily take in the situation here which opens them up to the most enticing prospects of success in becoming a ruling factor in this Government." 8 Cong. Rec. 1272 (1879).

Personal self-interest would motivate the wealthy to open America to Chinese labor, said Morgan. Among the economic elite, "there has always existed an almost irresistible desire to employ inferior races in all the necessary business of life that involves menial service . . . . Inferior races serve superior races with more docility and less friction than can be had in the service of inferior classes of the superior race." 8 Cong. Rec. 1272 (1879).

And it was not only the wealthy who would protect the interests of Chinese immigrants. Anticipating support from non-whites, Republicans had a political motivation to do so, Morgan charged.

Morgan observed America had paid an immense price for failing to deal effectively "with the inferior colored races." He meant to cauterize the wound. "I cannot hesitate to decide for myself that I should do all I can to prevent the influx of another of the inferior races into our country." 8 Cong. Rec. 1272 (1879).

The existence of treaty obligations was not reason enough to defer remedial legislation. Exclaimed Morgan, "If it is necessary to break a treaty with China to save our blood from shame and degradation, let it be broken." 8 Cong. Rec. 1272 (1879).

Senators opposed to Chinese immigration had monopolized the day's debate. Finally, there was a dissenting voice. It belonged to Senator Stanley Matthews (R–OH). Winner of an 1877 special election to fill the seat of Senator John Sherman (R–OH), who became secretary of the treasury in the Hayes administration (1877–1881), Matthews' tenure in the Senate would be short. He would resign from the Senate to become an associate justice of the United States Supreme Court in 1881.

Matthews' primary argument was that the legislation was a breach of national honor:

"If I believed that we not only had the constitutional power but the moral right to keep out from our social and political body voluntary immigrants from the Chinese Empire or elsewhere on the face of the globe . . . nevertheless my respect for the sanctity of the plighted faith of the nation in a solemn treaty with a sovereign power would compel me to seek some other method of securing these results than this arbitrary act of legislation." 8 Cong. Rec. 1274 (1879).

The Fifteen Passenger legislative remedy was extraordinary, Matthews argued, and Congress would not think to pursue it if treaty problems arose with a Western nation. "We have the constitutional power to do this thing," he acknowledged, but asked whether Chinese conduct was so egregious under the Burlingame Treaty that legislative abrogation could be justified:

"Has anything been done by the government of the Chinese Empire or by the people or inhabitants of that country in derogation of this treaty and in violation of our rights under it?" 8 Cong. Rec. 1274 (1879).

If treaty problems existed, Matthews observed, the administration could seek a renegotiation. Were that done, the Senate would consider the amendments in due course. Otherwise, said Matthews, "I am not willing, Mr. President, to bring upon this nation and country the reproach of covenant breakers." 8 Cong. Rec. 1274 (1879).

Matthews denied that a Chinese influx would degrade American society or that anything like emergency conditions existed:

"We are told that these people are aliens to us, aliens in thought, aliens in religion, aliens in language, aliens in dress, aliens in race, aliens in every circumstance of civilization, and that their presence is a fatal poison in our body-politic. Ah, Mr. President, I thought American civilization was a robuster child than that." 8 Cong. Rec. 1275 (1879).

Could restrictive legislation be squared with the American dream, and with the country's fundamental political culture? Matthews believed not. Referencing Sargent's earlier characterization of the Chinese as an "indigestible" political element, he continued:

"I thought . . . that this was a land and a country which could safely welcome to its shores the outcasts of every other clime, that its powers of digestion and assimilation were such that the very evils which afflicted mankind elsewhere would be taken up into the blood and circulation of this people and convey nutrient and health and strength to every limb and part of our economy." 8 Cong. Rec. 1275 (1879).

Senators Sargent, Grover, and Booth had forecast a clash of civilizations. Matthews saw a different kind of clash, one between the theory of exclusion legislation and America's foundational premises. He asked, "Are we compelled by voting for this bill not only to admit that our democracy is a piece of hypocrisy . . . ?" 8 Cong. Rec. 1275 (1879).

Fewer than fifteen years after the end of the Civil War, Matthews cautioned Congress not to pursue again the politics of racial division:

"We are warned by the history of the ages, and the experience of the world, and our own observation that we should be very careful how we endanger the peace and security of our age by courting the essential conflict of antagonist races." 8 Cong. Rec. 1275 (1879).

After Matthews took his seat, the Senate adjourned.

§2.23 Senate Debate, February 14, 1879: "Wholly unfit to become citizens"

Under consideration in the Senate Committee of the Whole: H.R. 2423, the Fifteen Passenger Bill.

On February 14, 1879, still meeting in the Senate as the Committee of the Whole, debate resumed on the Fifteen Passenger bill. First to speak was Senator James G. Blaine (R–ME), one of the nineteenth century's most distinguished American

§ 2.24 Confucian Traditions and Family Relationships

In view of ancient Confucian traditions of filial piety and respect for family relationships, Senator Blaine's (R–ME) assertions about Chinese families were breathtakingly misinformed. Confucius lived from 551 BC to 479 BC in an age of great turmoil in China, known as the Spring and Autumn Period (722 to 481 BC). Seeking a way to structure order out of chaos, he posited a set of mutual social responsibilities that flowed from five great relationships: ruler and subject; husband and wife; father and son; elder brother and younger brother; as well as friend and friend. The scholar-official was the leader of society and therefore education was valued. Concepts of ancestor worship and filial piety relate to Confucian philosophy, which had a central place in Chinese affairs. Remarks of Blaine and his allies about Chinese culture showed extreme ignorance of this long history. For more information on Confucianism, see, for example, Lee Dian Rainey, *Confucius and Confucianism: The Essentials* (John Wiley & Sons, 2010).

public figures. As a young man of prodigious promise, Blaine entered the House of Representatives midway through the Civil War:

"Teacher, journalist, lawyer, state legislator, political 'boss,' Blaine had already led Maine's Republican Party as state chairman, served as speaker of its state legislature, and edited two of its leading newspapers, the *Kennebec Journal* and *Portland Advertiser*, all before coming to Congress in 1863 on a pledge to support Abraham Lincoln and the war." Kenneth Ackerman, *Dark Horse: The Surprise Election and Political Murder of President James A. Garfield* (Carroll and Graf Publishers, 2003), p. 5. On his arrival in Washington, Blaine was thirty-three years old.

By 1869, then-Representative Blaine had been elected Speaker of the House. He went to the Senate in 1875, serving one term. Later, Blaine would become secretary of state under Presidents James Garfield, Chester Arthur, and Benjamin Harrison. He was also a prime contender for the Republican presidential nomination in 1876 and 1880, and was the party's unsuccessful candidate for president in 1884.

Due to the force of his personality and warm presence, Blaine was popularly known as the "Magnetic Man." Kenneth Ackerman, *Dark Horse*, p. 7. His engagement in the debate added crucial strength to the exclusionists. Blaine was a national figure and a potential president. Without him, Republican support for the bill might be only sectional, limited to Pacific Coast Senators. But Blaine broke with his fellow Republicans from the Northeast, intervening to support the Fifteen Passenger bill.

The day before, Senator Stanley Matthews (R–OH) had claimed that China was faithful to the Burlingame Treaty and had given the United States no cause to abrogate it. Blaine disagreed, contending that the Chinese government had persistently undermined the Burlingame Treaty's requirement that expatriation be wholly voluntary.

Quoting from the treaty, Blaine said: "The high contracting parties therefore join in reprobating any other than an entirely voluntary emigration for these purposes." But Blaine argued that the Chinese government had colluded with the Six Companies to facilitate commercial labor arrangements that contradicted the Burlingame Treaty's terms. "The treaty stands broken and defied by China from the hour it was made to this time." 8 Cong. Rec. 1299 (1879).

Senator Blaine observed that President Hayes had brought such violations to China's attention, without tangible results. The future secretary of state insisted that Congress had to engage in self-help. By its own terms, the Burlingame Treaty was indefinite in duration, so it lacked a natural ending point. Congress could not simply wait until the treaty expired, but would have to act.

Blaine then injected a potent new argument in the debate, that being that the United States should not allow immigration by persons who could not aspire to citizenship. Barred from naturalizing, the Chinese were a political underclass:

"We ought not admit in this country of universal suffrage the immigration of a great people, great in numbers, whom we ourselves declare are utterly unfit to become citizens." 8 Cong. Rec. 1300 (1879).

Blaine was referring to the 1870 Senate votes against the Sumner and Trumbell amendments during consideration of naturalization legislation. Blaine believed these votes settled the question of whether Chinese immigrants could aspire to American citizenship. Because they could not, the immigration laws must exclude them:

"It seems to me that if we adopt as a permanent policy the free immigration of those who by overwhelming votes in both branches of Congress we say shall ever remain political and social pariahs in a great free Government, we have introduced an element we cannot handle . . . . [However, Blaine spoke incorrectly. The House did not take a separate vote on the question of Chinese naturalization, so Blaine inferred what he assumed would have been the outcome in the House.]

§2.25 Chinese Oath Swearing

The rationale that the Chinese were not Christians and therefore could not be believed when they swore on the Bible led many courts to have them swear over a freshly killed chicken. As recently as 1903, the jurors in a Nevada murder case refused to believe the eyewitness accounts of the Chinese who swore over a killed chicken, and released the nine men who had been arrested for killing an old Chinese laundryman in Tonopah, Nevada. See Sue Fawn Chung, "The Anti-Chinese Movement in Tonopah, Nevada," in *Chinese America: History and Perspectives 2003* (January 2003), 35–45.

In Canada, this form of oath was used in the late 1800s through the early 1900s and was known as "The Chinese Oath" and the "Chicken Oath." See, for example, "The Chinese Oath," by P.S. Lampman, *The Canadian Law Review*, Volume 3 (1904), pages 24–25; and "Uncommon Oaths," by Tracy McLean, "The Stream," Courthouse Libraries | BC Blog, June 22, 2011. Also see John R. Wunder, *Inferior Courts, Superior Justice: A History of the Justices of the Peace on the Northwest Frontier, 1853–1889* (Greenwood Press, 1979).

"I am opposed to the Chinese coming here; I am opposed to making them citizens. I am opposed to making them voters . . . . I make bold to declare that you cannot maintain a non-voting class in this country." 8 Cong. Rec. 1301 (1879).

Blaine argued strenuously that the Chinese were too culturally dissimilar to whites ever to be capable of assimilating in America. One simply could not view Chinese immigration from the same favorable perspective as European immigration:

"The idea of comparing European immigration with an immigration that has no regard to family, that does not recognize the relation of husband and wife, that does not observe the tie of parent and child, that does not have in the slightest degree the ennobling and civilizing influences of the hearthstone and fireside! Why when gentlemen talk loosely about emigration from European states as contrasted with that, they are certainly forgetting history and forgetting themselves." 8 Cong. Rec. 1301 (1879).

After Blaine concluded, the presiding officer recognized Senator John H. Mitchell (R–OR). Elected in 1872, Mitchell served a full term in the Senate, and later two non-consecutive partial terms. Mitchell had been defeated for re-election in 1878, and was serving his last weeks as a senator.

Mitchell observed that opposition to Chinese immigration was non-partisan and enjoyed uncommon unanimity in the Pacific region:

"That this is so may be gleaned from the fact that of the eighteen Senators, Representatives, and Delegates from the Pacific States and Territories, where alone in the United States the shadow of this great evil has cast its blighting influence, all twelve Republicans and six Democrats are a unit upon this question . . . These Senators, Representatives, and Delegates irrespective of party, today with one voice, and that but the rightful echo of the almost universal sentiment of the people of that section, demand in the councils of the nation prompt, affirmative and efficient legislation in opposition to, in restraint of, this new, strange, imminent and deadly menace to the peace, integrity, and permanency of our institutions; legislation that will throttle in its infancy and weakness this great anaconda in whose folds the vital interests of the laboring men and women of the Pacific States and Territories . . . are being crucified." 8 Cong. Rec. 1303 (1879).

Senator Mitchell also contended that Chinese were unfit to access the American legal system because they could not give trustworthy oaths. His argument well illustrates the foundational nature of the Fifteen Passenger debate, even though the bill itself was vetoed. In subsequent years significant anti-Chinese legislation would be written on the basis that Chinese oaths were not reliable.

"They are allowed to worship their false gods," Mitchell observed. "Their worship and idolatry is not only in violation of the first command of God, but of the practice of our courts; for you could never swear a Chinaman in court, for he has nothing to swear by except that sometimes they are sworn on the bleeding form of a headless chicken or on the useless fragments of a broken saucer." 8 Cong. Rec. 1304–1305.

Senator Allen Thurman (D–OH) then took the Senate floor. A former justice on the Ohio Supreme Court (1851–1856), Thurman served a single term in the House in the early 1850s and two terms in the Senate (1869–1881). In 1888, he ran for vice president with President Grover Cleveland. Although Cleveland and Thurman secured a majority of the popular vote, they lost in the Electoral College to Benjamin Harrison and Levi Morton.

Thurman was chary about Congress legislating to abrogate treaties, but he made an exception for immigration policy, which he thought was more appropriately addressed in statutes than in international agreements:

"This country owes much of its greatness to the immigration of foreigners who have come here and taken up their homes; and I assume there is not one Senator here who would interpose any obstacle to the migration of white persons to the United States . . . . But the question of who shall come here and what provisions shall be made in respect to their coming here is more eminently a matter for legislation than for treaty . . . if you do not regulate it by law, if you surrender it wholly to the treaty-making power, you eliminate the House of Representatives, the direct representatives of the people, from any consideration whatever of the subject." 8 Cong. Rec. 1306 (1879).

If Congress were to restrict immigration, American policy would actually resemble China's own, Senator Thurman noted. Rather than having a history of free migration, for "more than ten centuries, China shut out the whole world from her borders." 8 Cong. Rec. 1306 (1879).

While China's restrictions had been relaxed, permitting trade and settlement at a few ports, severe barriers to foreigners remained. If America imposed its own limitations, said Thurman, China could not complain:

"China is the last country to insist that her people shall migrate to other countries as a matter of right," Thurman said. 8 Cong. Rec. 1306 (1879).

Enacting restrictive legislation against the Chinese was imperative, Thurman proclaimed, expressly invoking race bias:

"We have already three races besides them on this continent, the white race, the black race, and the red man. That is enough. We want no more mixture of such races in this country; but we want time to amalgamate our white people who can amalgamate until they are a homogeneous people . . . . I have always been in favor of the immigration of white people to this country . . . . I know that in the third and fourth generation, their children's children will be amalgamated with the rest of the white population of the country, and thus we have a homogeneous country. But that can never take place between the whites and the Mongolians or other colored races." 8 Cong. Rec. 1306 (1879).

After these speeches, the Senate Committee of the Whole voted on a small number of technical amendments, agreeing to some and rejecting others. The first major amendment came from Senator Aaron Sargent (R–CA), who proposed language to notify the Chinese government that treaty rights were about to be overridden. His amendment read:

"And the President of the United States shall immediately on the approval of this act give notice to the government of China of the abrogation of Articles 5 and 6 of the additional articles to the treaty of June 1858, between the United States and China, proclaimed February 5, 1870, commonly called the Burlingame treaty." 8 Cong. Rec. 1307 (1879). The amendment was agreed to by voice vote.

The next amendment came from Senator Roscoe Conkling (R–NY), a senator from 1867 to 1881. The amendment was designed to give diplomacy a last chance. It stipulated that the president must renegotiate treaty rights that permitted "the migration of subjects of the Chinese Empire and their domicile in this country." The amendment further mandated that a new or supplemental treaty should be submitted to the Senate not later than January 1, 1880. Finally, the amendment stated that if China refused to accede, the president should inform the Chinese emperor "that the United States will proceed by laws of its own to regulate or prevent the migration or importation to its shores of the subjects of China and, after January 1, 1880, to treat the obnoxious stipulations as at an end." 8 Cong. Rec. 1307 (1879).

Sargent opposed the amendment, claiming, "It is simply a promise that something shall be done hereafter, instead of taking positive action now." 8 Cong. Rec. 1307 (1879).

Senator Conkling asserted that the amendment amounted to "more than a promise." He insisted his was a disagreement over means and timing rather than over ultimate objectives:

"I feel quite sure I can speak for some members of this body beyond myself who find themselves unable to assent to such a bill at such a time, who nevertheless are as willing . . . to do that permitted by the Constitution, permitted by the comity of nations, and permitted by the civilized usages between nationalities to accomplish the whole purpose which the good of the people of the western coast demands." 8 Cong. Rec. 1308 (1879).

The Hayes administration was already in contact with China about immigration restrictions, Conkling reported, and signs were that China was willing to "do anything which may be deemed reasonable by our own Government." 8 Cong. Rec. 1308 (1879). Extraordinary tactics were not required when customary, diplomatic methods would do.

Senator Sargent retorted that not only would the treaty have to be modified but that exclusion legislation would be needed to implement the change. Adopting Conkling's amendment only postponed the day when relief would be granted. Pacific Coast senators would tolerate no delay.

Thurman took the Senate floor to assist the Westerners. He characterized the amendment as an ultimatum that would be more offensive to China than the simple passage of restriction legislation. Furthermore, said Thurman, China well understood that either party had an inherent unilateral power to override "anything in the treaty that is prejudicial to its interests." 8 Cong. Rec. 1310 (1879).

Such an argument might be legally correct, responded Senator George Frisbie Hoar (R–MA), but what of a nation's honor and solemn obligations? He asked Thurman whether he had said "that a nation which has made a treaty is at liberty to disregard it by simply proceeding to do the acts which it promised in the treaty not to do, and nothing more, whenever the refraining from those acts seems to it to be prejudicial to its interests?" 8 Cong. Rec. 1310 (1879).

Elected to the Senate in 1876, Hoar would serve until his death in 1905. His career embraced the entire period of Chinese exclusion legislation, beginning with the 1879 Fifteen Passenger bill and ending with the 1904 permanent extension of the Chinese Exclusion Act, as amended. Throughout the many debates on this issue over those years, Hoar was consistent. He stood firmly against excluding the Chinese and denying them naturalization opportunities and other civil rights. By 1902, his would be a lone voice.

Senator Thurman replied by repeating that legislation could repudiate a treaty. Such an assertion was beside the point, answered Hoar. To him, the question was "whether any nation shall make [its] promise good, so far as it be an obligation to do something in the future, depends only on . . . whether it shall find it convenient to do so." 8 Cong. Rec. 1310 (1879).

Senator Hoar condemned the argument that crisis conditions propelled Congress to legislate. No such emergency existed "as warrants this nation in resorting to the extreme and harsh measures of abrogating at once a treaty without even a notice or a request to the power with whom the treaty has been made," he said. 8 Cong. Rec. 1312 (1879).

Hoar urged three grounds to defeat the Fifteen Passenger bill: the legislation was unnecessary, it would undermine hard-won commercial concessions from China, and it contradicted basic American values:

"I am opposed to it, first, because it violates without necessity and in the absence of danger the public faith. I am opposed to it because if we had the right to accomplish the result by this method, it overthrows the guaranteed rights of so large a portion of our fellow-citizens, on which so much of their wealth and commerce depends. I am opposed to it for another reason. I am opposed to it because it violates the fundamental principle announced in the Declaration of Independence upon which the whole institutions of this country are founded, and to which by our whole history the American people are pledged.

"Wherever God has placed in a human frame a human soul, that which he so created is the equal of every other like creature on the face of the earth, equal among other things, in the right to go everywhere on this globe that he shall see fit to go, and to seek the blessings of life, liberty, and the pursuit of happiness." 8 Cong. Rec. 1312 (1879).

The white supremacy positions his colleagues had expressed dismayed Hoar. He criticized them sternly, dismissing such contentions as "the old argument of the slaveholder and the tyrant over and over again with which the ears of the American people have been deafened and which they have overthrown." 8 Cong. Rec. 1312 (1879).

Senator Sargent challenged Hoar. It was fine for the senator from Massachusetts, Hoar, to "talk in glittering generalities and sentimentality," but Hoar represented a state geographically distant from the problem. The urgency of the situation was well documented, if colleagues merely took time to acquaint themselves with the record. State legislatures had spoken to it, congressional committees had investigated it, even the 1876 platforms of both national parties had promised to address it:

"One promised respectful consideration and the other promised redress. Where was the Declaration of Independence at that time? Was that a promise made to the ear to be broken to . . . the people of California? Were those platforms put forward merely to catch votes, that the whole matter might be postponed until another presidential election should come and more platforms should be laid down?" 8 Cong. Rec. 1312 (1879).

Opposition senators misunderstood the situation, said Sargent. Self-defense was the prime issue; in view of the emergency, other principles, such as those expressed in the Declaration, must give way. Referring to Hoar, Sargent asserted:

"The Senator says that every man, no matter how humble, created by God, has a soul, and has the right to life, liberty, and the pursuit of happiness. I do not deny it. I admit that the German in Germany has those rights; that the Frenchman in France has those rights; that the Chinaman in China has those rights, and we have no right to invade their land and take away their rights or trample them down; but I do say that if it is necessary, when an element is brought into our community that destroys its morality and its integrity, that overwhelms our republican institutions; that destroys our Christian civilization; we have a right in self-defense to exclude such a crowd from access to our shores." 8 Cong. Rec. 1312 (1879).

Senators who might fear Chinese retaliation against U.S. commercial interests had no cause for concern, Sargent assured colleagues. Britain had sharply restricted Chinese immigration to Australia and Canada, and imposition of these policies had not caused trade between China and Britain to diminish.

Like Hoar, Sargent drew upon the principles of the Declaration, but he applied them differently. The right to seek life, liberty, and the pursuit of happiness belonged to whites in California, not to Chinese, Sargent said. Due to the heavy Chinese presence in their state, Californians lacked such opportunities. California was denied the benefits of white migration because, upon arrival in that state, whites were met with "a horde coming in from China with their antagonistic habits, repellant in all their qualities . . . ." 8 Cong. Rec. 1313 (1879).

Without relief, white workers would find California inhospitable, Sargent asserted. Whites would be unable to locate jobs because Chinese laborers would have crowded them out, forcing competition for scarce and unlivable wages.

Senator Sargent demanded that legislation be passed so California could better attract white settlers:

"We ask that our land may be fertilized by floods of population coming in from Europe and from other States of this Union, so that we may have a homogeneous civilization. When we plead for this, are we to be met with sneers? Are we to be told that there is no emergency? Are we to be told that we are unrepublican in the ordinary party sense; that we violate the principles of the Declaration of Independence; that we are unworthy to be believed? I say that it is unjust toward us, entirely unjust." 8 Cong. Rec. 1313–1314 (1879).

The claim that his case rested on "sentimentalities," irritated Hoar. Reclaiming the Senate floor, he pressed for adherence to fundamental tenets of American democracy. Pending legislation went far beyond the goals of restricting coolie labor contracts. His critique of the bill was scathing:

"It starts by a denial of the obligation of national faith. It starts by the abrogation at the mere will of one party of a solemn treaty. It starts by relieving the Emperor of China of obligations upon which depend the rights and the property and the business of large numbers of our own fellow citizens; and it does all these things without the slightest necessity . . . . Mr. President, the argument which I addressed to the Senate was . . . that this bill was in violation of the true principles of government." 8 Cong. Rec. 1314 (1879).

In the later nineteenth century, white immigrants flooded into America. Now, after a racially charged debate, Congress was poised to single out the Chinese for negative treatment. Hoar was deeply offended by the radical turn in national policy:

"I do not believe it is necessary for the future of this Republic to prohibit any man who seeks its shores of his own volition the right to enter in the mode and at a time he may choose, and to remain as a citizen or as a laborer or as a resident so long as he may choose." 8 Cong. Rec. 1314 (1879).

Senator James B. Beck (D–KY) confronted Hoar. Himself an immigrant from Scotland, Beck arrived in the United States at age sixteen. He was the presidential candidate of southern Democrats in the 1860 election, served four terms in the House of Representatives (1867-1875), and was three times elected to the Senate (1876, 1882, and 1888).

Beck returned to the now familiar "national self-preservation" argument, claiming that Congress had a duty to act. He offered some of the most bigoted commentary in the entire debate:

"I believe that nothing can be more detrimental to the growth and prosperity of this country in the years yet to come than to bring in vast multitudes of an inferior race of men and have them mix among our people. I have seen the Spanish cavaliers, and I have seen the Portuguese all over South America and over Central America, the descendants of Pizarro and Cortez, and the men who were the greatest of their day, who have become part of the inferior race with whom they are mixed, and they have all become a mongrel race." 8 Cong. Rec. 1314 (1879).

To achieve the benefits of racial purity one should mimic horse breeding practices, Beck said. Failure to do so would generate a national disaster:

"In all the relations of stock raising we claim to be superior to everybody else, and we do attain superiority because we maintain the purity of the blood and keep it up. There could be no greater calamity to befall a nation than to have a swarm of Chinamen come in and degrade this race of people. Such an amalgamation has degraded every race wherever it has taken place . . . ." 8 Cong. Rec. 1314 (1879).

Following Beck's diatribe, Senator Blanche Bruce (R–MS) spoke. A former slave, Bruce was the first African-American to serve a full term in the Senate (1875–1881). He did not participate in the Fifteen Passenger debate other than to offer the following brief, but poignant statement:

"Mr. President, I desire to submit a single remark. Representing as I do a people who but a few years ago were considered essentially disqualified from enjoying the privileges and immunities of American citizenship, and who have since been so successfully introduced into the body-politic, and having large confidence in the assimilative power of our institutions, I shall vote against the pending bill." 8 Cong. Rec. 1314 (1879).

Chairman of the Senate Foreign Relations Committee, Hannibal Hamlin (R–ME) sat mostly silent though two days of debate.

Hamlin began his Senate career in 1847 as a Democrat. In 1856, he opposed the Kansas-Nebraska Act, which permitted the expansion of slavery into territories previously closed to it. Because Democrats were behind this policy reversal, Hamlin left the party and became a Republican. In January 1861, Hamlin became vice president during Lincoln's first term (1861–1865). In 1869, Hamlin returned to the Senate, where he served until 1881.

Although his main speech would not occur until the following day, February 15, 1879, Senator Hamlin denounced the bill as an act of nativist bigotry:

"I am only going to enter my solemn protest against this kind of legislation that caters to your Denis Kearneys and to your unnaturalized Englishmen, and is only a counterpart of that wild craze that ran over the land known as native-Americanism . . . . Inaugurate it now and where shall it end? Shall it apply to the Lazzaroni that swarm the coasts of the Mediterranean, and shall they be excluded from our country and our Government? Shall it next enter the theological arena, and shall the Catholic be told he shall not come here to breathe the free air of this Republic? I know not where it may end." 8 Cong. Rec. 1315 (1879).

To his great dismay, Hamlin knew that the Senate would pass the bill and he had no prospect to change the outcome. As the Senate was concluding its proceedings on February 14, 1879, he offered a bitter assessment:

"I should have no hope of changing a single mind within this body. I know the power of prejudice. I know how it holds with grappled hooks of steel; and it is perhaps just as well that I utter no word, that I attempt to present no argument which satisfies me that the faith, the honor of this Government, that every Senator should hold higher and above all else, demand of us that we pause in this kind of legislation. I decline further to address this body this evening." 8 Cong. Rec. 1315 (1879).

§2.26 Senate Debate, February 15, 1879: "The brightest act of my life"

Under consideration in the Senate Committee of the Whole and later in the full Senate, H.R. 2423, the Fifteen Passenger Bill.

As the session commenced on Saturday, February 15, 1879, the Senate resumed consideration of the Fifteen Passenger bill. Senator Roscoe Conkling's (R–NY) amendment was still pending in the Committee of the Whole. Senator Hannibal Hamlin (R–ME) took the floor.

Those who opposed the legislation, Hamlin began, were not invoking mere "glittering generalities." Senator Aaron Sargent (R–CA) had offered that characterization the day before, and it rankled Hamlin, who regarded such "generalities" as America's first principles. He invoked the words of Senator Oliver Morton (R–IN), who had chaired the bicameral and bipartisan investigative committee (Morton Committee) Congress had dispatched to California to review the effects of Chinese immigration. Morton died before the committee could issue a complete report. Nonetheless, in preparing minority views, Morton had written:

"A discussion of the effect of Chinese immigration upon the country involves many considerations, and any proposition looking to its prohibition or limitation would require us to consider some of the fundamental principles of the theory and practice of our Government. It is our proudest boast that American institutions are not arbitrary in their character, and are not the simple creatures of force and circumstance, but based upon great and eternal doctrines of the equality and natural rights of man. The foundation stone in our political edifice is that all men are equal; that they are endowed by their Creator with inalienable rights; that among these are life, liberty, and the pursuit of happiness; that to obtain these, governments are instituted among men, deriving their just powers from the consent of the governed. We profess to believe that God has given to all men the same rights, without regard to race or color."

Senator Hamlin proclaimed, "It is upon this doctrine that we who oppose the passage of this bill as a restriction and a limitation stand in resisting it." 8 Cong. Rec. 1383 (1879).

Hamlin, at the time chairman of the Senate Committee on Foreign Relations, reviewed the Burlingame Treaty's achievements. It had given the United States access to China, he said, bringing down commercial barriers, opening ports, and expanding legal protections for American citizens. In exchange, America provided for the immigration of Chinese subjects. The treaty was applauded when announced, the senator reminded his colleagues:

"Who does not remember with what welcome, with what rejoicing that treaty was hailed upon the Pacific Coast?" 8 Cong. Rec. 1384 (1879).

The Fifteen Passenger bill directly contravened the Burlingame Treaty's terms and violated its promise. While doing that was within Congress' power, the course was unwise. Even if there were a basis to seek immigration restrictions, passing legislation to abrogate a treaty was a bad idea:

"I am opposed to legislating upon treaties except in extreme cases, and this is not one of them. I am opposed to legislating upon treaties until every other appropriate method has been resorted to." 8 Cong. Rec. 1384 (1879).

Senators should not be deluded into believing that they could override portions of the treaty they found burdensome while keeping the provisions they liked:

"If we abrogate that article which allows the free immigration of Chinese into this country, it is an annulment and abrogation of the treaty in all its parts if the Emperor of China shall so think fit to regard it." 8 Cong. Rec. 1384 (1879).

Hamlin refuted Senator James Blaine's (R–ME) argument that Congress was free to legislate because China had not met its treaty obligation to prevent coolie labor contracts. The record was exactly opposite, Hamlin said, and if there were fault to be found in the Burlingame Treaty's execution, it belonged to America and not to China.

"The Emperor of China has done his duty more fully than we have done ours. He has complied with every term and letter of the articles of the treaty. We have not." 8 Cong. Rec. 1385 (1879).

Senators Hamlin and Blaine clashed on the issue of naturalization. In 1870, Blaine charged, the Senate expressly rejected an amendment that would have opened a path to citizenship for Chinese, and Hamlin had voted in the majority.

His colleague had correctly stated facts, Hamlin replied, but had failed to give context. Hamlin would provide it. Prior to 1870, only whites could be naturalized. Hamlin wanted to liberalize the law, and had supported Senator Charles Sumner's (R–MA) amendment to permit naturalization without regard to race. The Senate had agreed to this, but then Pacific Coast senators threatened a filibuster unless such language was removed.

Confronted with such a threat, and dealing with a backed-up legislative schedule, senators had no choice but to reconsider the vote by which the amendment had passed, and then to scuttle the amendment itself. The Trumbull amendment that followed would have explicitly extended naturalization rights to Chinese. Given the mood of the Western senators, Senator Lyman Trumbull's (R–IL) proposal would have generated its own filibuster, so it also had to be defeated. Before final passage, the Senate agreed only to extend naturalization rights to persons of African descent.

Hamlin recalled that he had believed naturalization for Chinese was only to be temporarily deferred, not shelved forever:

"I have a clear and distinct recollection that at that time . . . I thought we might postpone for a limited period when we would bring in the Chinaman and give to him the ballot. I therefore voted as I did, first from the consideration that it was an amendment that might as well be enacted as a measure by itself or upon some other bill, not endangering the passage of that bill . . . ." 8 Cong. Rec. 1385 (1879).

Now, Hamlin had second thoughts. The failure in 1870 to extend naturalization rights to the Chinese had created a climate in which the Fifteen Passenger bill could pass. Without a path to citizenship, without voting recourse, Chinese immigrants were helpless against a political establishment that was free to stigmatize them.

"I am a little inclined to think that if all the Chinamen in our land had the ballot in their hands today, we should not have heard a word of this Chinese question here." 8 Cong. Rec. 1386 (1879).

Rather than denying Chinese citizenship, then barring them from immigrating, which was Blaine's approach, Hamlin wanted to expand access to voting rights. If the country denied a people political rights, how could they be expected to assimilate? Hamlin thought the Chinese were not really different from other immigrants and could be absorbed into America's body-politic:

"I am willing to admit them to naturalization. I think all persons who come here to make their permanent home ought to participate in our Government, ought to be citizens, and ought to have the right of franchise conferred upon them. I voted for it once; I will vote for it again; and I believe, Mr. President, that if you will treat these people upon the Pacific slope with common humanity, they will assimilate, not, perhaps, as readily as other nationalities, to our institutions, but within a reasonable time." 8 Cong. Rec. 1386 (1879).

Senator Sargent had insisted that the presence of Chinese immigrants had repelled whites from California and retarded economic growth on the Pacific slope. A fair assessment of the Chinese impact would be quite opposite, said Hamlin:

"The Chinese have built their railroads, have reclaimed their tule lands, and . . . uncounted millions of wealth have been added to that State which without the labor of the Chinese would not be in existence today." 8 Cong. Rec. 1386 (1879).

Exclusion advocates had spoken ominously about the effects that "cheap, Chinese labor" would have on living standards for white workers. To Hamlin, such an argument was a "canting cry . . . a cry addressed to the prejudices, not to the cool judgment of men." America could absorb these workers and the entire labor force would be elevated by an expanding economy. Wage disparities would be temporary and then would disappear:

"Treat the incoming immigrant as he ought to be treated, give him the protection of law, and make his home sacred to him, and my judgment is that it will require a very limited amount of time in which to solve the whole problem. A man comes from a distant country, where labor is lower than here; he does not adopt the lower scale of labor if he is skilled to occupy the higher grade; nor does it diminish the compensation of labor unless the supply is beyond the demand." 8 Cong. Rec. 1386 (1879).

Senator Hamlin declared support for the Conkling amendment because it invited negotiations rather than merely overriding a treaty. However, even if the amendment were agreed to, Hamlin remained steadfastly opposed to the Fifteen Passenger bill. He concluded:

"I shall vote against this measure, and I leave that vote the last legacy to my children that they may esteem it the brightest act of my life." 8 Cong. Rec. 1387 (1879).

As Hamlin rested his case, the presiding officer recognized Senator James B. Eustis (D–LA), then in the last year of his first Senate term (1873–1879). After a gap in service, Eustis would return for one more term between 1885 and 1891. Although he supported the bill, Eustis rejected most of the arguments used to justify it:

"I do not believe, nor would I for a moment be influenced to cast my vote for the abrogation of a treaty, where we invite another nation to send their people into our country and then turn around and tell the very people we have invited into our country under treaty stipulations that they shall not come into this country for the simple reason that they cheapen labor." 8 Cong. Rec. 1387 (1879).

Exclusion advocates had stressed cultural disparities between Chinese and Europeans, but Eustis found such differences irrelevant:

"What cause of complaint is it to say that the Chinese eat rats? Is that any reason why a treaty should be abrogated? What cause of complaint is it to say that they eat rice; or what cause of complaint would it be on our part if they did not eat anything at all, which would be cheaper?" 8 Cong. Rec. 1387 (1879).

Eustis believed that Americans had plenty of experience with Chinese immigrants before the Burlingame Treaty, and that the United States ratified the treaty with eyes open:

"There has not been a single proposition advanced which should influence any Senator to take the position that after we have made a solemn treaty with a civilized nation, we ought to abrogate that treaty on account of the habits of the people of that empire, of which we were perfectly cognizant in every particular at the very time that we made the treaty." 8 Cong. Rec. 1387 (1879).

So how could Eustis support the bill? Chinese immigration brought race-mixing to America, inevitably promoting social upheaval, he concluded. For Eustis, averting such problems was justification enough to enact the legislation:

"I shall vote for the bill, although the arguments that have been urged against its passage are overwhelming, except on a single point, and that is the race question." 8 Cong. Rec. 1387 (1879).

Senator Blaine returned to the floor to discuss the importance of the 1870 Senate vote that directly negated the possibility of Chinese naturalization. That vote was central to his thesis that the Chinese should be barred from immigrating because America should not admit persons ineligible for citizenship to reside in the country. He insisted the history not be misunderstood.

Blaine did not challenge Hamlin's account of why the Senate reconsidered the Sumner amendment. However, once the Sumner language was removed,

§2.27 James G. Blaine and the Argument for Exclusion

After his retirement, James Blaine published his memoirs, entitled *Twenty Years of Congress.* In it, he argued the case for his controversial stand in favor of Chinese exclusion:

> The argument against permitting Mongolian immigration to continue rested upon facts that were indisputable. The Chinese had been steadily arriving in California for more than a quarter of a century, and they had not in the least degree become a component part of the body politic. On the contrary, they were as far from any assimilation with the people at the end of that long period as they were on the first day they appeared on the Pacific Coast. They did not come with the intention of remaining. They sought no permanent abiding-place. They did not wish to own the soil. They built no houses. They adhered to all their peculiar customs of dress and manner and religious rite, took no cognizance of the life and growth of the United States, and felt themselves to be strangers and sojourners in a country which they wished to leave as soon as they could acquire the pitiful sum necessary for the needs of old age in their native land. They were simply a changing, ever renewing, foreign element in an American State . . . .

> To encourage or even to permit such an immigration, would be to dedicate the rich Pacific slope to them alone and to their employers— in short, to create a worse evil in the remote West than that which led to bloody war in the South . . . .

> The question stripped of all disguises and exaggerations on both sides was simply whether the labor element of the vast territory on the Pacific should be Mongolian or American. Patriotic instinct, the sense of self-preservation, the importance of having a thorough American sentiment dominant on the borders and outposts of the Republic, all demanded that the Pacific Coast should be preserved as a field for the American laborer.

James G. Blaine, *Twenty Years of Congress, Volume II* (The Henry Bill Publishing Company, 1886), pp. 654–655.

debate did not end. Trumbull had stepped forward with his amendment that expressly permitted Chinese to naturalize. The Trumbull amendment framed the issue squarely and was voted down. Hamlin had been among those voting against it. Blaine was not interested in explanations:

"Senator Trumbell [sic] moved to include 'or persons born in the Chinese Empire.' On that question, the vote was given that I spoke of yesterday. So that the question came just as palpably and as directly as it could come before the Senate, whether or not we would admit the Chinaman to citizenship in the United States. I repeat here today that the effect of that vote was adverse, and to be regarded as a settlement against Chinese immigration to this country on the simple ground that in a republic where suffrage is universal, we cannot permit a large immigration of people who are not to be advanced to the franchise." 8 Cong. Rec. 1389 (1879).

Next to speak was Senator Henry L. Dawes (R–MA). A sixteen-year veteran of the House of Representatives (1857–1875), Dawes served three terms in the Senate (1875–1893). Imbued with strong antislavery views, Dawes disdained the bill.

"Mr. President," Dawes began, "I think no one can doubt the fact that the longer this debate continues, the true philosophy of this legislation becomes more apparent . . . . The whole argument in support of this bill is that there comes in under a treaty an inferior civilization with which the civilization of Christianity is unable to contend and to which it must surrender." 8 Cong. Rec. 1389 (1879).

The Fifteen Passenger bill was not about preventing importation of coolie labor, said Dawes. Both prior statutes and the Burlingame Treaty itself guarded against that. Instead, the bill represented rank discrimination against people politically incapacitated from protecting themselves.

"It is not coolies, it is men who live on rice, it is men who work cheaply and patiently and constantly, and do not trouble themselves about political matters, who confine themselves to the industries to which they are called, who are in the way. It is because they have no other place in our history and no other function under our legislation than to attend to these duties that they are in the way and call down this hostile legislation on their heads. Had they been clothed with the function of voters . . . what a different treatment they would have received from the beginning." 8 Cong. Rec. 1389 (1879).

Senator Dawes believed Senator Blaine was engaged in political pandering to the West Coast voters who the Maine senator hoped to attract in a bid for national office. Blaine had historically stood up for the political rights of African-Americans, but took the opposite position toward the Chinese, building on their disenfranchisement to score political advantage. Dawes excoriated such hypocrisy. Blaine would have been a friend to the Chinese, rather than being their opponent, if only they could vote.

"My friend from Maine [Blaine] would have been I trust just as loud in vindication of their rights as voters as he is in his vindication of other voters suppressed in the exercise of those rights by those who claim that they are an inferior race, and who should be governed by the superior Anglo-Saxon race . . . ." 8 Cong. Rec. 1389 (1879).

The Fifteen Passenger bill and the debate around it represented a descent into racial intolerance, said Dawes, drawing upon Hoar's speech of the previous evening:

"[Senator Hoar] spoke truly last night when he said the advocates of this bill were taking up the language of the slaveholder and those who were attempting to hold the black man in subjugation as an inferior race. The debate today has demonstrated the truth of that remark." 8 Cong. Rec. 1390 (1879).

Dawes closed by noting that, in 1868, the Senate had consented to the Burlingame Treaty with great acclaim. Blaine, then Speaker of the House, had joined in the applause. What had happened within the decade to sour Congress on Chinese immigration? For instance, had the Burlingame Treaty opened the door to unexpected immigration? Not so, said Dawes, something more sinister was in play:

"What has wrought this change? The immigration of Chinese to California was as great before this treaty as since. The coolie trade in point of fact has disappeared. This opposition springs from that prejudice described by the Senator from Louisiana [Eustis] against race, a prejudice which I supposed the principles of the Declaration of Independence and of the Constitution of the United States were at war with." 8 Cong. Rec. 1390 (1879).

Given his party's roots in the antislavery Free Soil and Abolitionist movements, any Republican support for the Fifteen Passenger legislation distressed Dawes. In 1879, a majority of Republicans would oppose the bill, but there were plenty of defectors, Blaine being the most prominent. Dawes observed:

"The political organization I am proud to belong to, I supposed, was summoned into existence for the very purpose of vindicating the equality of the human race upon this continent in all political rights. If the Senator from Maine [Blaine] will permit me, I do not wonder that men are being confused by these arguments. They will find more trouble to reconcile them than the Senator from Louisiana [Eustis], for the Senator from Louisiana clearly sees the logic of this debate." 8 Cong. Rec. 1390 (1879).

Senator Dawes' sentiments still reflected mainstream Republican opinion on legislation aimed at the Chinese, but that would not be the case for much longer. In subsequent debates on Chinese exclusion, the two parties would outdo each other in an attempt to demonstrate which of them was more hostile to Chinese immigration.

It was time to begin voting on amendments. In the Senate at that time, there were seventy-five members, with one of Michigan's Senate seats vacant.

Still pending in the Senate Committee of the Whole was Conkling's proposal to seek renegotiation of the Burlingame Treaty, in lieu of abrogating the treaty by legislation. The Senate voted 31 ayes to 34 nays with 10 senators absent. 8 Cong. Rec. 1390–1391 (1879).

Senator Justin Morrill (R–VT) proposed an amendment to permit entry of persons seeking temporary residence for educational purposes. Morrill was a senator between 1867 and 1898, after serving in the House from 1855 to 1867. The most renowned achievement of his long career in Congress was his sponsorship of the Morrill Land-Grant Colleges Act of 1862.

Sargent claimed that the Morrill amendment would facilitate evasion of the Fifteen Passenger restriction, because hordes of Chinese would use the education exception to seek entry. He proposed to modify the amendment, by requiring that students carry a certificate from the Chinese government verifying that they sought admission to the United States for schooling. Morrill accepted the modification and the Senate agreed to the Morrill amendment by voice vote.

Senator George Edmunds (R–VT) was next to offer an amendment. Edmunds was troubled by the prospect that America could ignore international commitments while expecting other countries to be faithful to them. His amendment provided that if the United States abrogated the treaty, it would not consider hostile any reciprocal abrogation by China.

"I wish to declare that while we are repealing a part of the treaty, we recognize her right to repeal any part of it which she may think convenient to her interest and her own sense of propriety . . . . I wish to say to that nation, and particularly to that nation . . . that we shall not regard it as an act of hostility that will require the President of the United States to send the Army and the Navy there to reduce her to obedience to her treaty obligations." 8 Cong. Rec. 1391 (1879).

Senator Allen Thurman (D–OH) rose in opposition. Suppose China responded in a disproportional manner, such as by cutting off commercial relations? If the Senate agreed to the Edmunds amendment, the United States would have no foundation to complain about it, Thurman said. He did not want to give preemptive consent to such a response:

§2.28 The Nineteenth-Century Senate versus the Modern Senate

Although the Senate remains a body deeply wedded to its traditions, a review of the nineteenth-century debates shows major differences with the modern Senate. Among these differences are:

1. In the nineteenth century, the Senate conducted proceedings in a Committee of the Whole, but no longer does so.

2. In the nineteenth century, no one held the position of Majority Leader or Minority Leader.

3. The cloture rule did not come into being until 1917, so the nineteenth-century Senate had no way to secure a supermajority vote to overcome a filibuster.

4. There was less use in the nineteenth century of unanimous consent agreements than there is presently.

5. As against current practice, nineteenth-century proceedings do not reflect the ubiquitous use of quorum calls.

6. In contrast to the present day, the nineteenth-century Senate frequently used pairs to record positions and accommodate colleagues with opposing views.

For further reference, on Senate rules, see Martin Gold, *Senate Procedure and Practice* (Rowman & Littlefield, 2008).

"I am not willing . . . to invite her in advance to break off all commercial intercourse and go back to her policy which existed before her ports were opened at the mouth of the cannon . . . . This is an invitation for her to do that thing." 8 Cong. Rec. 1392 (1879).

Senator Samuel Maxey (D–TX) was recognized. A former Confederate general and a two-term senator (1875–1887), Maxey added another wrinkle to the race-mixing argument. Other senators had discussed problems of Chinese competing with whites in the West, but Maxey projected a time when the Chinese population would spread out from the Pacific Coast, to work as cheap labor in the South. In the 1870s, most blacks were Southerners. Untold complications could arise if hordes of Asians mixed with them:

"The supply is illimitable; and I do believe there is no portion of the Union where Chinese immigration would be so fatal to human progress and to human civilization as in the country where I live. We have there the Anglo-Saxon race and Ethiopian living side by side, speaking the same language and accustomed to each other. The negro race has been elevated by contact—association with the southern white man—from a condition of savagery in which they were when they were brought to this country, into a condition of comparative civilization and enlightenment." 8 Cong. Rec. 1393 (1879).

All this benevolent progress could be jeopardized if Asians were introduced into the South, said Texas Senator Maxey:

"Now, if you admit into that country this Chinese population, they, with their Joss gods, with their opium-smoking habits, with their superstitions, and with their gambling and filth, will break down that inferior race now in the South rather than build it up." 8 Cong. Rec. 1393 (1879).

Maxey indicated that he would rather have renegotiated the treaty than passing legislation, so he had supported Conkling's amendment. But the amendment had failed. Strongly in favor of exclusion, Maxey would now vote for the bill:

"I regard this Chinese immigration as so fearful an evil in this country, present and prospective, that if it cannot be done in a way I should like to have it done, I will take the nearest and best way to that which I believe to be right . . . ." 8 Cong. Rec. 1393 (1879).

On the Edmunds amendment, 27 senators voted yea, 39 opposed, and 9 senators were absent.

With no further amendments pending, the bill was reported from the Senate Committee of the Whole to the full Senate, which agreed by voice vote to the committee's amendments.

In the full Senate debate, Conkling renewed the amendment that had failed earlier that day in the Committee of the Whole. That vote had been close. More senators were present now, said Conkling, and the amendment might yet pass.

Senator Thurman again opposed the amendment. He characterized it as an effort to deflect the Senate from immediate action, imposing delay and uncertainty:

"After this attempt has been made to negotiate a new treaty with China, and it fails, then when we come down to the first of January, 1880, we are precisely where we are this day, not one single step taken in the direction of preventing or limiting this migration . . . . You have inaugurated some red tape, and that is the whole of it." 8 Cong. Rec. 1395 (1879).

Sargent echoed Thurman. A remedy to restrict Chinese immigration was within grasp and the opportunity to secure it should not be missed:

§2.29 Chinese Population in the United States, 1860–1940

	Foreign	Citizen	Total	Total U.S. Population
1860			34,933	31,443,321
1870			63,199	39,818,449
1880			105,465	50,189,209
1890			107,488	62,947,714
1900	80,853	9,010	89,863	76,212,168
1910	56,596	14,935	71,531	92,228,496
1920	43,107	18,532	61,639	106,021,537
1930	44,086	30,868	74,954	122,775,046
1940	37,242	40,262	77,504	132,164,569

Source: Prof. Sue Fawn Chung, University of Nevada, Las Vegas.
For further discussion of the number of Chinese who immigrated, see § 9.17, Politics and Immigration Enforcement—The Bureau of Immigration.

"The Senator from New York [Conkling], by his amendment if carried, will have this matter postponed for months, when he will come to the Senate and use every means in his power . . . to prevent any relief to the people of California. If the Senate passes the bill, it gives a mode of relief; if it passes the amendment, it simply promises relief which the Senator from New York will try his utmost to disappoint." 8 Cong. Rec. 1396 (1879).

Senator Conkling summed up the legal and psychological effect of the Fifteen Passenger bill. Enactment would turn America into a decidedly hostile place for Chinese persons:

"Here is a statute which says that no person of Chinese origin, no matter where he may be, no matter on what island of the sea or in which hemisphere he may be found, shall come by any vehicle, carrying any flag, into our waters on his way anywhere. If he is in England and wants to return to his home he shall not come within three miles, within a marine league, of our shores for any purpose. He not only shall not come to be domiciled, but he shall not come at all." 8 Cong. Rec. 1398 (1879).

Put to a full Senate vote, the Conkling amendment again failed. This time, there were 31 in the affirmative, 33 in the negative, with 11 senators absent. The Senate was committed to treaty abrogation.

Senator Morrill offered an amendment to allow entry into American waters of vessels in distress that were carrying Chinese passengers. The amendment carried by voice vote.

As final passage loomed, Edmunds dissented vehemently:

"Before this bill passes, I wish to express my utter abhorrence of the principle that the bill is founded upon, which is that, without negotiation, without notice, without any step that the fair and honest comity which should exist between nations would require to be taken, we take a step of this kind, to undertake to abrogate by legislation a provision of a treaty with a friendly power." 8 Cong. Rec. 1400 (1879).

After three days of debate, the Senate voted to pass the Fifteen Passenger bill. There were 39 yeas, 27 nays, and 9 absentees. Of the 39 in favor, 16 were Republicans, 21 were Democrats, and 2 were Independents. Of the 27 opposed, 17 were Republicans, 9 were Democrats, and 1 was an Independent. Dissenters were largely made up of "a remnant of antislavery Republicans and a bipartisan group sensitive to the international obligations of the United States." Ari Hoogenboom, *Rutherford B. Hayes, Warrior and President* (University of Kansas Press, 1995), p. 388.

§2.30 The Next Step: The House Concurs in the Senate Amendments

On February 22, 1879, Representative Albert Shelby Willis (D–KY) brought the Fifteen Passenger bill back to the House floor. He moved that the House concur in the Senate amendments. The amendments provided that the legislation would permit temporary admission to students with certificates issued by the Chinese government, and to persons rescued from shipwrecks (both originally proposed by Senator Morrill). They further required the president to notify China that the Burlingame Treaty provisions addressing the free movement of peoples were abrogated (originally proposed by Senator Sargent).

Representative Harry White (R–PA) moved to lay the bill as amended on the table, a motion that would end debate and dispose of the bill. His motion failed with 95 yeas, 140 nays, and 55 members not voting.

By voice vote, the House agreed to Willis' motion to concur in the Senate amendments. With bicameral agreement achieved, the Fifteen Passenger bill was passed. At this stage, House deliberations had lasted but a few minutes. The legislation, officially entitled "An Act to restrict the immigration of Chinese to the United States" was headed for the White House.

§2.40 A Presidential Veto: Rutherford B. Hayes

On March 1, 1879, merely three days before the 45th Congress ended, President Rutherford B. Hayes vetoed the Fifteen Passenger bill. Hayes' biographer, Ari Hoogenboom, notes:

"Since the Forty-fifth Congress was about to expire, he could have killed the bill by not signing it, but he was too forthright to use the pocket veto." Ari Hoogenboom, *Rutherford B. Hayes*, *Warrior and President* (University of Kansas Press, 1995), p. 389.

Largely drafted by Secretary of State William Evarts, President Hayes' veto message (*see Appendix 4*) emphasized the inconsistency between the bill and existing treaties, as well as the disruption the legislation would cause in Sino-American relations. The message did not complain about singling out the Chinese for unique discrimination under law.

The president reviewed the history of the bilateral relationship, including a treaty of friendship (the Treaty of Tientsin) that was ratified on August 16, 1859. In thirty articles, the 1859 treaty established "a careful and comprehensive system for the commercial relations of our people with China," the president said. 8 Cong. Rec. 2275 (1879). Included in this arrangement was a provision ensuring the United States most favored nation treatment, meaning that any rights of navigation, commerce, or intercourse China granted to any other country would also benefit Americans.

In 1868, the treaty was broadened to include the Burlingame Treaty (*Appendix 2*) immigration provisions. Under permissive U.S. immigration policies, Chinese had been coming to America for approximately two decades. The Burlingame Treaty amendments specified legal rights for those Chinese already in the country and their countrymen who arrived thereafter, as the president's veto message continued:

"The principal feature of the Burlingame treaty was its attention to and treatment of the Chinese immigration and the Chinese as forming, or as they should form, a part of our population. Up to this time, our unconvenanted hospitality to immigration, our fearless liberality of citizenship, our equal and comprehensive justice to all inhabitants, whether they abjured their foreign nationality or not, our civil freedom and religious toleration has made all comers welcome, and under these protections, the Chinese in considerable numbers had made their lodgment upon our soil." 8 Cong. Rec. 2275 (1879).

Under the Burlingame Treaty, Chinese were assured freedom of voluntary immigration. Both nations had committed to oppose servitude migration under coolie labor contracts. In addition, Chinese were to enjoy most favored nation treatment once they had entered the country, meaning, for instance, that a Chinese person in the U.S. would have the same rights, privileges, and immunities, as an Englishman, a Frenchman, or a German.

The Burlingame Treaty had opened China to America. It had done so not by force of arms but through the process of negotiations. As a consequence, economic and cultural walls were being dismantled. President Hayes thought the treaty was a remarkable diplomatic breakthrough for the United States:

"Unquestionably the adherence of the government of China to these liberal principles of freedom in emigration, with which we were so familiar and with which we were so well satisfied was a great advance toward opening that empire toward our civilization and religion, and gave promise in the future of greater and greater practical results in diffusion throughout that great population of our arts and industries, our manufactures, our material improvements, and the sentiments of government and religion which seem to us so important to the welfare of mankind." 8 Cong. Rec. 2275 (1879).

In the decade since the Burlingame Treaty was ratified in 1869, more Chinese had arrived in the United States. President Hayes was concerned that they had not readily assimilated, but instead could be considered "strangers and sojourners." 8 Cong. Rec. 2276 (1879). Mindful of rising public resentment, he did not preclude the idea of future immigration restrictions.

"I regard the very grave discontents of the people of the Pacific states with the present working of the Chinese immigration, and their still graver apprehensions therefrom in the future, as deserving the most serious attention of the people of the whole country, and a solicitous interest on the part of the Congress and the Executive." 8 Cong. Rec. 2276 (1879).

But the Burlingame Treaty did not contain a severability provision that would allow a partial renouncing of treaty obligations. Thus, Congress could not abrogate a treaty in part, while leaving the remainder of it in force. President

Hayes noted that "a denunciation of a part of a treaty, not made by the term of the treaty itself separable from the rest, is a denunciation of the whole treaty." Any denunciation would free China from all treaty obligations:

"As the other high contracting party has entered into no treaty obligations except such as include the part denounced, the denunciation of one party of the part necessarily liberates the other party from the whole treaty." 8 Cong. Rec. 2276 (1879).

Were problems generated by Chinese immigration severe enough to justify abrogation? President Hayes thought they were not. Moreover, he worried that the removal of Burlingame Treaty protections would harm America's interests in the Far East:

"Whatever urgency might in any quarter or by any interest be supposed to require an instant suppression of further immigration from China, no reasons can require the immediate withdrawal of our treaty protection from the Chinese already in this country, and no circumstances can tolerate an exposure of our citizens in China, merchants or missionaries, to the consequences of so sudden an abrogation of their treaty protections . . . . I cannot but regard the summary disturbance of our existing treaties with China as greatly more inconvenient to much wider and more permanent interests of the country." 8 Cong. Rec. 2276 (1879).

The president vetoed the bill. (*See Appendix 4 for the veto message.*)

§2.50 The House Attempts a Veto Override

The United States Constitution establishes that legislation must be presented to the president, who may either veto it and return it to Congress, allow it to become law without his signature, or pocket veto it when Congress adjourns before a veto message can be returned. Under Article I, section 7 of the U.S. Constitution, Congress may attempt to override a veto via a two-thirds vote of both the House and Senate, beginning in the chamber in which the legislation was initiated.

With the 45th Congress (March 4, 1877–March 4, 1879) in its last moments, the House took up President Hayes' veto message. If the House could muster sufficient votes to override, there would yet be time for a vote in the Senate. The vote to override received a simple majority, but not a two-thirds vote. Yeas were 110, nays were 96, and 34 members of the House did not vote. Speaker Randall declared:

"As required by the Constitution, two-thirds not having voted in the affirmative, the bill is rejected." 8 Cong. Rec. 2277 (1879).

With the failure of the House to override, further action on the legislation in the Senate was moot, and the Fifteen Passenger bill died.

After the bill's demise, interest in controlling Chinese immigration remained intense. President Hayes' decision to veto the Fifteen Passenger bill was a source of great consternation. "West of the Rocky Mountains, his veto was bitterly denounced, and he was even burned in effigy." Ari Hoogenboom, *Rutherford B. Hayes, Warrior and President* (University of Kansas Press, 1995), p. 389.

In 1880, the United States and China negotiated treaty amendments that permitted immigration restrictions to be imposed. Convening on March 4, 1881, and armed with this fresh authority, the 47th Congress (1881–1883) would address the issue.

CHAPTER THREE

The Twenty-Year Exclusion Debate in the Senate

*"If the object were to destroy our political
system, to render free government impossible,
then it would be rational and consistent
to permit the riff-raff of the nations to
be dumped into our streets and upon
our lands without restraint."*
—Senator John F. Miller (R–CA)
13 Cong. Rec. 1487 (1882)

85

§3.0 Overview

- Considered in the 47th Congress of the United States (1881–1883)
- Senate Party Division: 37 Republicans, 37 Democrats, 2 Independent (Republican majority)
- President: Chester A. Arthur (R) (1881–1885)

After failure of the Fifteen Passenger bill, the United States renegotiated its treaty obligations with China. The Angell Treaty, which amended the Burlingame Treaty, permitted the United States to restrict, but not prohibit, immigration of Chinese laborers. In 1882, Congress passed legislation to implement this agreement.

Initially, the House of Representatives passed legislation to suspend laborer immigration for twenty years. In the same bill, Congress expressly precluded the naturalization all Chinese immigrants, even those who had already been admitted to the United States. The Senate acted first on the measure, passing it after eight days of floor debate. Democrats and West Coast Republicans supported the bill. Eastern and Midwestern Republicans mostly opposed it.

§3.10 Proceedings in the Senate

In the aftermath of his veto of the Fifteen Passenger bill in 1879, President Rutherford B. Hayes the following year appointed three commissioners with authority to negotiate modifications of the Burlingame Treaty (*Appendix 2*). The principal American negotiator was James B. Angell, who had taken leave from the presidency of the University of Michigan to accept assignment as Minister to China (1880–1881). The other two commissioners were John F. Swift and William Henry Trescot. Under the amendments Angell negotiated, the United States was afforded the opportunity to restrict, but not to prohibit, Chinese immigration to America. In 1881, the Senate consented to these treaty changes. To implement the new rights, Senator John F. Miller (R–CA) introduced S. 71, which curbed Chinese immigration.

A major general in the Union Army during the Civil War, Miller was a new senator, elected in 1881. He died in office in 1886, before completion of his only term. Although a freshman, Miller would be a central figure in the passage of

§3.11 Substitute Amendment to a Bill

A substitute amendment to a bill is one that strikes the entire text of the bill and replaces it with alternative language. The term "substitute" will be important at several places in the discussion of Chinese exclusion legislation. For example, in 1882, during debate on a twenty-year exclusion bill, the Senate Committee on Foreign Relations proposed to strike the whole text of the bill that had been introduced (S. 71) and insert fresh language in its place. While jurisdictional committees often generate substitutes, individual senators may propose them. For instance, in 1902, Connecticut Senator Orville Platt (R–CT) successfully offered a substitute to replace much more complicated and onerous legislation that had been reported from committee.

the legislation, S. 71, which was formally titled "An act to execute certain treaty stipulations relating to the Chinese." (*Appendix 6*)

After introduction, S. 71 was referred to the Senate Committee on Foreign Relations. Unanimously, the committee ordered the bill reported with a substitute amendment, drafted to make the legislation hew more closely to the provisions and spirit of the Angell Treaty (*Appendix 5*). 13 Cong. Reg. 1481 (1882).

§3.20 Senate Debate, February 28, 1882: "A confession of American imbecility"

Under consideration in the Senate Committee of the Whole, S.71 with a substitute proposed by the Committee on Foreign Relations.

On February 28, 1882, Senate debate on the exclusion legislation began in earnest. Senator John Miller (R–CA) urged that Congress promptly pass legislation to implement the powers newly acquired under the Angell Treaty (*Appendix 5*).

The Fifteen Passenger bill had drawn a veto in 1879 because it contravened American treaty obligations with China. Those obligations had since been recast by the Angell Treaty negotiations, granting Congress a license to act. Miller thought it senseless to waste the moment. Deferring action would show Congress as irresolute. Besides, he asked, "Can we afford to make such a confession of American imbecility to any oriental power?" 13 Cong. Reg. 1481 (1882).

Concern about Chinese immigration had started on the Pacific Coast, but had since gained national attention and momentum. This trend could be

§ 3.21 The Politics of the 1880 Democratic Party and Republican Party Platforms

When the party platform statements were prepared, bitter memories of the 1876 election loomed, and the platforms must be understood in that context. Democrat Samuel Tilden had won the 1876 popular presidential vote by three points but lost to Republican Rutherford B. Hayes in the Electoral College by one vote, after the resolution of bitterly contested claims in three states. The final electoral count was 185 for Hayes to 184 for Tilden after a Republican-dominated congressional panel resolved in favor of Hayes electoral disputes in Florida, Louisiana, and Oregon.

When the 1880 contest began, a similarly close election was anticipated, and the parties prepared themselves to compete vigorously in the Pacific region. The 1880 party platforms reflected this politically contentious environment. Indeed, in 1880, Republican James Garfield comfortably defeated Democrat Winfield Scott Hancock in the electoral vote, 214 to 155. But in the popular presidential vote, Garfield prevailed by fewer than 10,000 votes out of almost 10 million ballots cast nationally.

observed in the strong majorities by which Congress had passed the Fifteen Passenger bill. Since then, both major political parties had addressed Chinese immigration in their 1880 platforms. Often in the 1882 debates, mention would be made of those party platforms. Members of Congress would insist that the party platforms were solemn pledges to Americans to restrict an influx of the Chinese. For example, the 1880 Democratic platform stipulated:

"No more Chinese immigration except for travel, education, and foreign commerce and therein carefully guarded."

The 1880 Republican platform, that of Senator Miller's own party, had been only slightly more nuanced:

"Since the authority to regulate immigration and intercourse between the United States and foreign nations rests with Congress, or with the United States and its treaty-making power, the Republican party, regarding the unrestricted immigration of the Chinese as an evil of great magnitude, invokes the exercise of these powers to restrain and limit the immigration by the enactment of such just, human, and reasonable provisions as will produce that result." 13 Cong. Rec. 1482 (1882).

The platform statements spotlighted the intense rivalry that was taking place between the two parties for Pacific Coast electoral votes in the narrow margin elections of the post-Reconstruction era. Republicans were dominant in the Northeast and Midwest. Democrats controlled the South. Western states were competitive and could tip electoral outcomes. Chinese ballots did not influence such results, because federal law seemed not to permit Chinese to naturalize. Democrats and Republicans could afford to pander to anti-Chinese sentiment in western states, without fear of a backlash from Chinese voters.

In addition to invoking the 1880 party platforms, Miller referred to the views of the Republican presidential nominee, Ohio's James Garfield. In that era, presidential candidates did not appear at party conventions, issuing instead letters of acceptance after being notified of their nominations. While a member of the House (1863–1881), Garfield had failed to vote on the Fifteen Passenger bill. Now with an eye toward voters in western states, Garfield addressed the immigration issue in his presidential nomination acceptance letter. His text was sensitive to an electorate that was clamoring for restrictions on the Chinese:

"The recent movement of Chinese to our Pacific Coast partakes but little of the qualities of an immigration, either in its purposes or results. It is too much like an importation to be welcomed without restriction; too much like an invasion to be looked upon without solicitude. We cannot consent to allow any form of servile labor to be introduced among us under the guise of immigration." 13 Cong. Rec. 1482 (1882).

In November 1880, Garfield was elected president, victorious over Democrat Winfield Scott Hancock. Garfield's presidency began on March 4, 1881.

Four months later, on July 2, 1881, Charles Guiteau shot President Garfield. Garfield died on September 19, 1881, his presidency barely six months old. After his death, the martyred president would continue to influence immigration policy. During the 1882 Chinese exclusion floor debates in Congress, Garfield's characterization of Chinese immigration would frequently be invoked.

Senator Miller claimed that Garfield's presidential nomination acceptance letter and the roughly parallel party platforms demonstrated political consensus on Chinese immigration:

"It would seem that the question of Chinese restriction has passed the stage of argument. To such a policy, both political parties are equally pledged, bound, and committed by the most solemn and deliberate acts and declarations . . . . The vote upon this bill will determine whether the two great political parties of this country were in earnest in making these declarations, or whether they were made merely to deceive the people and to catch votes." 13 Cong. Rec. 1482 (1882).

The widely known hostility of Californians had acted as a de facto restraint on the Chinese, holding down immigration far below what it would have been if attitudes there had been more welcoming. Even so, said Miller, almost 20,000 Chinese had arrived in San Francisco in 1881, and federal legislation was essential to choke off the influx. A negative vote on an exclusion bill would be "an invitation to the Chinese to come. It would be interpreted to mean that the Government of the United States had reversed its policy, and is now in favor of the unrestricted importation of Chinese; that it looks in favor of the Chinese invasion now in progress." 13 Cong. Rec. 1482 (1882).

Opponents of the Fifteen Passenger bill (*Chapter Two*) had claimed it was a response to mob incitement by San Francisco's sandlot orators, such as Denis Kearney (*§ 2.11*). Miller was determined to show that anti-Chinese feeling was, in fact, mainstream sentiment in California.

"It has been said that the advocates of Chinese restrictions were to be found only among the vicious, unlettered, foreign element of California society," 13 Cong. Rec. 1482 (1882), but that perspective was distorted, Miller declared. The California legislature had authorized a ballot question on Chinese immigration to be placed before voters in the 1879 general election. Miller recalled the vote:

"When the ballots were counted, there were found to be 883 votes for Chinese immigration and 154,638 against it." In Nevada, a similar referendum produced 183 votes for the Chinese and 17,259 against them, said Miller. According to Miller, the referenda "demonstrated that the people . . . who know most of the Chinese evil, and who are the most competent to judge the necessity for restriction, are practically unanimous in support of this measure." 13 Cong. Rec. 1482 (1882).

Senator Miller depicted California as a joining place for two divergent civilizations, the one proceeding westward and the other moving inexorably eastward, until "the man of the West has met the man of the Orient." Miller considered this collision not only epochal in world history, but also inherently hostile:

"The two civilizations which have here met are of diverse elements and character, both the result of evolution under different conditions, radically antagonistic, and as impossible of amalgamation as are the two great races who have produced them. The attempt to merge them must result, as both reason and experience teaches, in the displacement of one or the other. Like the mixing of oil and water, neither will absorb the other." 13 Cong. Rec. 1483 (1882).

Chinese had already lived in California for a quarter of a century, Miller observed, but he asserted they had remained immune from the influence of Western legal and religious influence on their culture:

"They have remained as fixed in their habits, methods, and modes of life as if they had all this time lived on the Mountains of the Moon. Not the slightest impression has been made upon them or on the peculiar civilization which they brought with them . . . . They have been unable or unwilling to change the habits and character which have been forced upon them and ground into them by necessity and a heredity as old as the records of man . . . . They remain Chinese always and everywhere; changeless, fixed and unalterable." 13 Cong. Rec. 1483 (1882).

Speaking in Rochester, New York, on October 25, 1858, Senator William Henry Seward (R–NY) described the divergence between free labor and slave labor as "an irrepressible conflict between opposing and enduring forces." Seward's speech was a harbinger of the civil war to come and was one of the most noteworthy and long remembered addresses from the antebellum era. Miller borrowed Seward's idea, morphing it into a prediction that there would be a clash of civilizations between Orient and Occident:

"An 'irrepressible conflict' is now upon us in full force, and those who do not see it in progress are not so wise as the men who saw the approach of that other 'irrepressible conflict' which shook the very foundations of American empire upon this continent." 13 Cong. Rec. 1483 (1882).

Miller portrayed the conflict in terms that would make Americans tremble: up against the Chinese, white society would be overwhelmed.

"We have already seen in California that the American people are far more impressible than the stoical Chinese, and the influence of Chinese methods and practices on the social economy and moral condition of our people is plainly visible." 13 Cong. Rec. 1483 (1882).

The evidence was insidious and clear, Miller said. He reported that where the two societies mingled, Americans were falling prey to Chinese practices. White farm labor mimicked the Chinese labor with whom it was forced to compete. In urban areas, idleness and crime, as well as the spread of opium, were rising in all populations. Infectious diseases were spreading across society. "These and many other evidences of the demoralizing influence of Chinese civilization are open to the dullest observation." 13 Cong. Rec. 1483 (1882).

Americans should not delude themselves into believing that the Chinese were a benign influence with whom they could happily coexist, warned Miller, because history compelled reaching a different conclusion:

"Regarded by superficial observers as the most inert and pusillanimous of all peoples, they are on the contrary the most successful conquerors the world has ever known, because they have held all they have ever conquered, and conquered every territory they have ever invaded. And not only so; whenever China has been invaded, the invaders have been absorbed and finally conquered." 13 Cong. Rec. 1483 (1882).

Senator Miller described economic conditions of the 1870s Depression, which had contributed to the rise in anti-Chinese sentiment. Over a period of three to four years, Miller said, thousands of white men and women roamed California's streets in search of jobs and, all the while, "the great steamers made their regular arrivals from China . . . ." Through the intervention of the Six Companies, the new Chinese immigrants quickly found work, and "the white people unemployed still went about the streets." 13 Cong. Rec. 1483 (1882). Labor displacement and the perpetuation of white unemployment were localized for the moment in California but would expand to a national problem as more Chinese arrived and transportation networks expanded. 13 Cong. Rec. 1484 (1882).

The social costs of using cheap labor were substantial, Miller noted, and far outstripped any economic benefits that might be derived from it:

"Temporarily, and under peculiar conditions, cheap labor might be an advantage, but when we consider our condition and are confronted by the fact that the introduction into our country of an alien race of men who perform the cheap labor operates as displacement of the natives of the soil, man for man, and substitutes a non-assimilative, heterogeneous people unfit for and incapable of free or self-government, the question assumes proportions which are not to be measured by the application of mere economic theories." 13 Cong. Rec. 1484 (1882).

One must examine the sweep of Chinese history to grasp why Chinese immigrants remained secluded from American society, said Miller. This review would show that Chinese cultural isolation was not unique to their experience in the United States:

"Alone in its busy solicitude this nation has wrought and struggled, never until lately looking up or out upon the world to note the triumphs or failures of contending nationalities . . . . They have enacted their long doleful drama of life, with its numberless tragedies, upon a stage all their own and without an audience." 13 Cong. Rec. 1484 (1882).

China was impenetrable to progressive forces, Senator Miller alleged. Literally and figuratively walled off from the world, Chinese people were socially inbred, impervious to change, and incapable of assimilation:

"Their civilization culminated before western civilization began, and has no element of progress in it. The literature, art, science, or religion of western nations has made no impression on the Chinese. They have remained the same through all the changes of the world, and they are now a people as different from other peoples in their characteristics, habits, methods, and physical appearance as if they were inhabitants of another planet." 13 Cong. Rec. 1484 (1882).

A poor country, frequently beset by natural calamities and starvation, China had produced a race of people that according to Miller could survive on a subsistence no one else could bear:

"During the thousands of years of training which this race of men has undergone, in which they have become accustomed to incessant toil and insufficient food, the individuals who were too weak to endure the strain have fallen out, and none but the 'fittest' have survived to become the progenitors of their race."

Miller described the Chinese laborers who had evolved from this struggle in terms of a master race that was not quite human:

"They are of obtuse nerve, but little affected by heat or cold, wiry, sinewy, with muscles of iron; they are automatic engines of flesh and blood; they are patient, stolid, unemotional, and persistent, with such a marvelous frame and digestive apparatus that they can dispense with the comforts of shelter and can subsist on the refuse of other men, and grow fat on less than half the food necessary to sustain life in the Anglo-Saxon." 13 Cong. Rec. 1484 (1882).

It would be impossible for white labor to compete with this workforce, Miller claimed. Wages and job conditions would be degraded to the Chinese level, and when that happened, "all that makes life worth living to those who work with their hands must be surrendered." 13 Cong. Rec. 1485 (1882). Miller predicted that the California "experiment" to permit "Chinese servile labor" to work alongside "American free labor" was an unequal contest that would generate inevitable social disaster, and no other outcome could result from such a conflict.

Senator Miller took pains to distinguish the Chinese from the multitudes of European immigrants then flooding into the United States. Europeans were like American laborers in their mental and physical characteristics, habits, aspirations, and tendencies. Such immigrants were "free and independent men" who soon became "earnest defenders of free institutions and republican government." Europeans were eager and able to assimilate:

"They unite their fortunes with ours, enjoy our prosperity, and brave our disasters. They stand shoulder to shoulder with us in the battle for the defense of the Republic and the maintenance of the national honor." 13 Cong. Rec. 1485–86 (1882).

In contrast, Miller said, "The Chinese take shelter in the hovel or mass themselves in houses like swine in the sty . . . . The Chinese come as a servile people and are held in the country in a bondage of fear by the 'Six Companies' by whose will their labor is controlled and directed." 13 Cong. Rec. 1485–86 (1882).

Californians well understood the difference between European immigrants and the Chinese. According to Miller, the former were to be welcomed; the latter, barred:

"We of the Pacific Coast have tried all varieties of men as "immigrants" and our experience suggests a warm and generous welcome to our shore of the German, the Irishman, the Scandinavian, the Italian, and all who come from beyond the Atlantic; but of the Chinese we have had enough, and we would be glad to exchange those we have for any white people under the sun." 13 Cong. Rec. 1486 (1882).

Miller thought that immigration and naturalization statutes should work in tandem. Where immigration was encouraged, naturalization laws were liberal. But imposition of "stringent and obstructive" naturalization policies demonstrated that immigration was undesirable. Racial bias in American naturalization laws made clear that only whites were wanted:

"The Chinese and other oriental colored people have never been encouraged to come by our naturalization laws. They could never upon any conditions become citizens of the United States under our laws. The policy has been a policy of discrimination as practiced by our government, and not only so, but discrimination against particular races . . . . There was and is not only this race discrimination against the Chinese in our naturalization laws, but also in the treaty with China known as the Burlingame treaty, which contains an express provision against the naturalization of Chinese in the United States." 13 Cong. Rec. 1486 (1882).

The discrimination was obvious and intentional, exclaimed Miller. Chinese were "unfit for the responsibilities, duties, and privileges of American citizenship." 13 Cong. Rec. 1486 (1882).

In unsparing terms, Senator Miller attempted to justify why it was vital to deny Chinese rights to naturalize and why they must remain politically segregated:

"The presence in this country of a great number of people of an alien race, who do not and cannot assimilate with our people, and who are so hardened and fixed in their habits and characteristics, so inflexible in all their methods of life, and who practice a civilization so antagonistic to ours that they are unfit to exercise the rights of citizenship must of necessity always be a disturbing element." 13 Cong. Rec. 1486 (1882).

Should Chinese be shown a path to citizenship, American democracy would be undermined. Chinese numbers would overwhelm the white electorate, said Miller, and their votes would be for sale on a political auction block:

"If they should be admitted to citizenship, there would be a new element introduced into the governing power of this nation, which would be the most venal, irresponsible, ignorant, and vicious of all the bad elements which have been infused into the body-politic, an element disloyal to American institutions, inimical to republican liberty, scornful of American civilization, not fit for self-government, and unfit to participate in the government of others—a people destitute of conscience or the moral sense. In every State wherein the Chinese might secure domicile, there would be a mass of voters, sufficiently numerous probably to hold the balance of power in elections, which would be for sale to the best bidder. They would esteem the suffrage only for the money they could make out of it." 13 Cong. Rec. 1486 (1882).

Senate proceedings on February 28, 1882, were about to end. Miller had spent much of the day spinning theories to support racial and political ostracism. Summing up, he framed Chinese exclusion as a life-or-death struggle for America's future:

"If the civilization of a people changes, the government must change to conform to it. In California, Chinese civilization in its pure essence appears as a rival to American civilization. It is a product of a people alien in every characteristic to our people, and it has never yet produced and can never evolve any form of government other than an imperial despotism. Free government is incompatible with it, and both cannot exist together." 13 Cong. Rec. 1487 (1882).

§3.30 Senate Debate, March 1, 1882: "To shame, to weakness, and to peril"

Under consideration in the Senate Committee of the Whole, S. 71 with a substitute proposed by the Committee on Foreign Relations.

On March 1, 1882, debate on the Miller bill (S. 71) resumed in the Senate Committee of the Whole. First recognized was Senator George F. Hoar (R–MA). As he had in the 1879 Fifteen Passenger debate (*Chapter Two*), Hoar opposed Chinese exclusion legislation, claiming it violated basic American doctrines:

"Nothing is more in conflict with the genius of American institutions than legal distinctions based on race or upon occupation. The framers of our Constitution believed in the safety and wisdom of adherence to abstract principles. They meant that their laws should make no distinction between men except as were required by personal conduct and character." 13 Cong. Rec. 1516 (1882).

Race discrimination was a shameful policy that had left deep scars on the country, said Hoar, and must be shunned. It had left "its hideous and ineradicable stains on our history in crimes committed by every generation. The Negro, the Irishman, and the Indian have in turn been its victims here, as the Jew, and the Greek, and the Hindu in Europe and Asia." 13 Cong. Rec. 1516 (1882).

Rather than absorb these lessons, advocates of the legislation had moved in the opposite direction and asked Congress to build a racially discriminatory legal structure. Hoar decried their efforts:

"It is reserved for us at the present day, for the first time, to put into the public law of the world and into the national legislation of the foremost of republican nations a distinction inflicting upon a large class of men a degradation by reason of their race and by reason of their occupation." 13 Cong. Rec. 1516 (1882).

Hoar saw no meaningful difference between the Fifteen Passenger bill and the pending measure, S. 71. The two bills "have the same origin and are parts of the same measure," he said. 13 Cong. Rec. 1516 (1882). That the Angell Treaty had been negotiated in the interim did not change or condition his assessment.

The Angell Treaty, which Hoar described as "extorted from an unwilling China," provided that the importation of Chinese laborers could be regulated, limited, or suspended, but "not absolutely prohibited" and, in any case, such "limitation or suspension shall be reasonable." 13 Cong. Rec. 1516 (1882).

Hoar criticized the legislation as exceeding what the Angell Treaty would permit. The bill, S. 71, did not structure reasonable limitations, the senator argued; instead, it erected a bar:

"Here is proposed a statute which, for twenty years, under the severest penalties, absolutely inhibits the coming of Chinese laborers to this country. The treaty pledges us not absolutely to prohibit it. The bill is intended absolutely to prohibit it." 13 Cong. Rec. 1516 (1882).

Senator Hoar did not much esteem the Angell Treaty, which the legislation purported to implement. The policies embedded in the treaty were unsound, Hoar believed, in that they institutionalized racial discrimination, promoted class bias, and undermined the expatriation principles captured in the 1868 Burlingame Treaty:

"The instrument does three things only. For the first time, as far as I know, it places in the public law of nations a denial of . . . the inalienable right of man to change his home and allegiance. It establishes a distinction between races in respect to the right to pursue their happiness in lawful ways anywhere on the face of the earth, affirming a difference degrading to the Chinese. It affirms, also, a distinction between laborers and all other persons, degrading to labor." 13 Cong. Rec. 1517 (1882).

Hoar thought the race and class distinctions set out in the Angell Treaty

§3.31 China–U.S. Diplomacy II

American diplomacy with China in the late 1800s had conflicting aims. While the United States continued to pursue the commercial and missionary objectives that led to its instigating the 1868 Burlingame Treaty (*Appendix 2*) negotiations, it now had the additional purpose of limiting labor immigration without jeopardizing those other goals. At U.S. insistence, further negotiations to this end were pursued, leading to the Angell Treaty of 1880 (*Appendix 5*). The 1880 accord amended the Burlingame Treaty to permit the U.S. to restrict the entry of Chinese laborers. In those discussions, the Chinese insisted that the restrictions be limited and that United States not be able to prohibit that immigration outright. While retaining flexibility in how Congress might implement this new authority, American negotiators reassured China that such powers would be exercised fairly, if used at all.

were disreputable. The treaty established "the principle that it is fit that there should hereafter be a distinction in the treatment of men by governments and in the recognition of their rights to the pursuit of happiness . . . based not on conduct, not on character, but upon race and occupation. You may justly deny to the Chinese what you may not justly deny to the Irishman. You may deny to the laborer what you may not deny to the scholar or to the idler." 13 Cong. Rec. 1517 (1882). These distorted policies would only be aggravated by the legislation pending to implement it, Hoar argued.

America was on the verge of setting aside its founding principles. Hoar asked the other senators:

"Are we to hold out two faces to the world, one to Europe and another to Asia? Or are we to admit that the doctrine we have proclaimed so constantly for the first century of our history is a mere empty phrase or lie?" 13 Cong. Rec. 1517 (1882).

Hoar attacked the allegation that the Chinese community in the United States was already overwhelming in size and was rapidly expanding. That allegation was a core argument for the bill, and yet census data proved trends were opposite. In a country of 50 million persons, there were but 105,000 Chinese, barely 1/500 of the population. Moreover, at a time when general immigration was vastly expanding, Chinese immigration was declining. From a peak of nearly 23,000 Chinese immigrants in 1876, each annual migration was smaller, until the number of Chinese admitted in 1880 was just 5,800. These totals demonstrat-

§3.32 The Know-Nothing Movement

Anti-Irish sentiment was not confined to hotheads and radicals, Senator George Hoar (R–MA) noted in the S. 71 debate, but was widespread in the political system. In the middle 1850s, the American Party, nicknamed the Know-Nothing Party, fielded a national ticket headed by former President Millard Fillmore (Whig) (1850-1853). The Know-Nothings were nativists who were strongly hostile to Catholic immigration. In the 1856 election, Fillmore had some success, winning 23 percent of the popular vote, although carrying only Maryland in the Electoral College. The election was the movement's political high-water mark. By the end of the decade, the American Party fractured and largely disappeared.

For more, see Tyler G. Anbinder, *Nativism and Slavery: The Northern Know Nothings and the Politics of the 1850s* (Oxford University Press, 1992).

ed, the senator said, that Chinese amounted to less than one in 100 of the total number of immigrants admitted to America in 1880. 13 Cong. Rec. 1518 (1882).

Senator Hoar mocked as hypocritical the alarms sounded by exclusionists:

"What an insult to American intelligence to ask leave of China to keep out her people, because this little handful of almond-eyed Asiatics threaten to destroy our boasted civilization. We go boasting of our democracy, and our superiority, and our strength. The flag bears the stars of hope to all nations. A hundred thousand Chinese land in California and everything is changed. God has not made of one blood all the nations any longer. The self-evident truth becomes a self-evident lie. The golden rule does not apply to the natives of the continent where it was first uttered." 13 Cong. Rec. 1518 (1882).

The true basis for exclusion was not national self-preservation but abject race prejudice, Hoar declared. Race bias ran deeply and insidiously through American history:

"The old race prejudice, ever fruitful of crime and of folly, has not been confined to monarchies or to the dark ages. Our own Republic and our own generation have yielded to this delusion and paid the terrible penalty . . . . What argument can be urged against the Chinese that has not been heard against the negro within living memory? The negroes were savages, heathens, wild beasts . . . . The great political parties vied with each other in pandering to this prejudice." 13 Cong. Rec. 1519 (1882).

Some of his Senate colleagues had denigrated the Chinese in comparison to white immigrants. It was ironic, said Hoar, that just such prejudices had been voiced in the recent past about Europeans themselves:

"It is scarcely forty years since the Irishman, who has been such a source of wealth and strength to America, began his exodus across the sea. There are men in this body, whose heads are not yet gray, who can remember how the arguments now used against the Chinese filled the American mind with alarm when used against the Irishman. He comes, said the honest bigotry of that day, only to get the means of living, and then to return; he will drive the American to starvation by the competition of his cheap labor; he lives in squalor and filth; he wants only a few potatoes for food; he is blindly attached to the Popish religion; he owes his allegiance to a foreign potentate; he is incapable of intelligent citizenship." 13 Cong. Rec. 1519 (1882).

Characterizing Chinese as culturally distinct, socially debased, and incapable of assimilation, also sounded to Senator Hoar a lot like European anti-Semitism:

"There is another most remarkable example of this prejudice of race which has happily almost died out here but which has come down from the dark ages and which survives with unabated ferocity in Eastern Europe. I mean the hatred of the Jew. The persecution of the Hebrew has never, so far as I know, taken the form of an affront to labor. In every other particular, the reproaches which for ten centuries have been leveled at him are reproduced to do service against the Chinese. The Hebrew, so it was said, was not a Christian. He did not affiliate or assimilate into the nations where he dwelt. He was an unclean thing, a dog, to whom the crime of the crucifixion of his Savior was never to be forgiven. The Chinese quarter of San Francisco had its type in every city of Europe. If the Jew ventured from his hiding place, he was stoned. His wealth made him the prey of the rapacity of the noble, and his poverty and weakness the victim of the rabble." 13 Cong. Rec. 1519 (1882).

To justify exclusion, senators had dismissed Chinese civilization as frozen in time and unequal to the West, its people wedded to their motherland and incapable of assimilating with American institutions. Hoar discredited those stereotypes. It was true that Chinese assimilation had been tortuous, but not for the reasons his colleagues proclaimed. Instead, it had been retarded because, especially in California, Chinese were subject to pervasive statutory discrimination:

"That they do not incline to become Christians or republicans may be accounted for by the treatment they have received," Hoar explained. "They are excluded by statute from the public schools. They have no honest trial by jury." What incentives would Chinese have to pledge allegiance to America, he inquired, when California's constitution contained provisions such as the following:

"No native of China, no idiot, no insane person, and no person hereafter convicted of the embezzlement or misappropriation of public money, shall ever exercise the privilege of an elector in this state.

"No corporation now existing or hereafter formed under the laws of this State shall, after the adoption of this constitution, employ directly or indirectly, in any capacity, any Chinese or Mongolian.

"No Chinese shall be employed on any State, county, municipal, or other public work, except in punishment for crime.

"The Legislature shall delegate all necessary power to the incorporated cities and towns of this State for the removal of Chinese without the limits of such cities and towns, or for their location within prescribed portions of those limits." 13 Cong. Rec. 1521 (1882).

Disputing claims that the Chinese would degrade white living standards, Senator Hoar said that, unshackled from legal barriers, they would generate an economic expansion that would raise living standards for all workers:

"Sooner or later, every new class of industrious and productive laborers elevates the class it displaces. The dread of an injury to our labor from the Chinese rests on the same fallacy that opposed the introduction of labor saving machinery, and which opposed the coming of the Irishman, and the German, and the Swede." 13 Cong. Rec. 1522 (1882).

The Senate session of March 1, 1882, was closing. Hoar had been speaking for an extended time. His remarks represented one of the most complete rebuttals that would ever be lodged against Chinese exclusion legislation. He despaired at the prospect that Congress would darken the American beacon by placing racial stigma into federal law:

"As surely as the path on which our fathers entered a hundred years ago led to safety, to strength, to glory, so surely will the path on which we now propose to enter will bring us to shame, to weakness, and to peril." 13 Cong. Rec. 1523 (1882).

§3.40 Senate Debate, March 2, 1882: "Swarm upon us like locusts"

> *Under consideration in the Senate Committee of the Whole, S. 71, with a substitute proposed by the Committee on Foreign Relations.*

On March 2, 1882, the Senate resumed consideration of S. 71. Senator La Fayette Grover (D–OR) had been a leader in the Senate for the Fifteen Passenger bill that President Hayes vetoed three years earlier. As Grover recited the history of his involvement with the issue of Chinese immigration, it became apparent that in a Congress loaded with anti-Chinese sentiment, no one had a longer or more persistent record of advocating exclusion.

"The Empire of China acts like a threatening cloud hanging over the virgin States of the Pacific." Grover began. 13 Cong. Rec. 1545 (1882). In response, Oregon had adopted "positive and leading" policies:

"In her constitution she provided that the Legislature should have the authority to prohibit the immigration of all persons not qualified to become citizens of the United States. That clause had special reference to the Chinese." 13 Cong. Rec. 1545 (1882).

Oregonians were chagrined, said Grover, that the 1868 Burlingame Treaty overrode these strategies through provisions that "opened our ports to the incursions of an unwelcome population." 13 Cong. Rec. 1545 (1882).

Grover had been governor of Oregon in 1868. After the Burlingame Treaty was ratified, he addressed the state legislature. Governor Grover boasted that his was the "first public announcement ever made to a legislative body in this country in relation to this great problem." Grover's speech in Salem to the Oregon legislature was inflammatory. In his remarks, he attacked the prospect of Chinese naturalization:

"Her people may swarm upon us like locusts. Their coming will unhinge labor, damage industry, demoralize the country, and by claiming and receiving the ballot may upturn our system of government altogether; for the most serious apprehension from the present policy of the General Government to enfranchise all inferior and servile races, and to encourage their immigration to the United States, is that the ballot system may become despicable." 13 Cong. Rec. 1545 (1882).

Affirming the governor's position, the Oregon legislature adopted an 1868 memorial to Congress, seeking the Burlingame Treaty's abrogation. According to Grover, presentation of that memorial was the first time a public body had brought the problem of Chinese immigration to Congress' attention.

A dozen years after the Oregon memorial, Congress was on the brink of passing exclusion legislation and Grover was a senator. He was determined to counter Senator George Hoar's argument that in doing so, Congress was acting contrary to the Declaration of Independence and other national principles. To ascertain the founders' meaning, Grover observed, "it is fair and necessary to consider their contemporary acts in order to construe their purposes." 13 Cong. Rec. 1546 (1882).

§ 3.41 Chinese and the Transcontinental Railway

In 1863, President Abraham Lincoln called for the construction of a transcontinental railroad. Two teams of White workers—one proceeding west from the Mississippi River and one working east from the Pacific Ocean—began work on the giant undertaking. Those proceeding west over the Great Plains made progress, but those proceeding east from the Pacific Coast hit the solid granite of California's Sierra Nevada Mountains. The white workers laid down their picks in defeat. The Chinese, from the country that had built the Great Wall, filled the gap and succeeded where the Aryan had failed. Governor Leland Stanford of California wrote President Andrew Johnson, "Without the Chinese, it would have been impossible to complete the western portion of the great National highway."

James Bradley, *The Imperial Cruise: A Secret History of Empire and War* (Little Brown and Company, 2009), pp. 279–280.

On May 10, 1869, the golden spike linking the Union Pacific and Central Pacific was pounded into the earth at Promontory Summit, Utah, and eleven thousand Chinese workers immediately lost their jobs. Though not invited to the celebrations of the Transcontinental Railroad, Chinese workers had built the railroad, hauling locomotives over the summit and sleeping by the hundreds in ice caves or tents. They worked a sunup-till-sundown day, slung from cliffs, at times throughout the night, to blast through the mountain with gunpowder and nitroglycerine . . . .

Hundreds, perhaps thousands, of Chinese died building the railroad. Recruited from teams of disillusioned miners in the West or by Charles Crocker's* brokers in China and other American labor contractors in Hong Kong, they faced relentless perils—from the Sierra winter snows to dynamite explosions to falls from ropes or wicker baskets suspended from the cliffs suspended over the American River canyon as they loaded dynamite into the rocky walls of the gorge.

Jean Pfaelzer, *Driven Out: The Forgotten War Against Chinese Americans* (Berkeley and Los Angeles: University of California Press, 2007), pp. 167–168. See also Stephen Ambrose, *Nothing Like It In the World: The Men Who Built*

§3.41 Chinese and the Transcontinental Railway (continued)

the Transcontinental Railroad 1863–1869 (Simon & Schuster, 2001), and David Haward Bain, *Empire Express: Building the First Transcontinental Railroad* (Viking, 1999).

*Charles Crocker was a senior executive with the Central Pacific Railroad. There were other American recruiters, including Albert Sisson (a younger brother of Charles) of Sisson and Wallace, later Sisson, Wallace, and Crocker, who hired railroad workers and other types of Chinese laborers for work in America.

Although the Central Pacific Railroad (CPRR) hired thousands of Chinese to cross the difficult Sierra Nevadas, once the crew reached present-day Reno, only about 5,000 Chinese remained on the payroll. The construction across Nevada was relatively easy despite the harsh weather, that is, the heat of the desert. According to James Strobridge, the Chinese were at the Golden Spike Ceremony and documents show that the gold and silver spikes had to be finally hammered down by Chinese workers since Stanford and Durant did not finish the job. There are photographs showing that the Chinese were at the ceremony—you just have to know what to look for.

See, for example, "Chinese-American Contribution to Transcontinental Railroad," on the web site of the Central Pacific Railroad Photographic History Museum: *<http://cprr.org/Museum/Chinese.html>*.

Source: Prof. Sue Fawn Chung (University of Nevada, Las Vegas).

Quite simply, the Declaration had been written for the benefit of Europeans, said Senator Grover. Examining how non-white peoples were treated at the time of the founders would conclusively establish that America's fundamental doctrines were non-universal:

"If they were intent on missionary labors in building up and sustaining a government devoted to the elevation of the colored races of mankind, why did they not seize upon the opportunity when this continent was occupied, and rightfully occupied, by the red man, to devote their great zeal and enterprise in civilizing and instructing him?" 13 Cong. Rec. 1546 (1882).

Instead, whites drove "the aborigines from the land with fire and sword," Grover proclaimed. In the "presence of the declarations of the fathers that all men are created equal," native peoples "have retired, stubbornly but certainly, before the superior race, until now the white man possesses the whole land . . . ." 13 Cong. Rec. 1546 (1882).

Treatment of Africans further reinforced this point, exclaimed Grover. The founders did not welcome them to America as equals, and actually provided in the Constitution that Congress could not interdict the slave trade before 1808, twenty years thereafter:

"They never invited the African here as a voluntary immigrant. They neither endowed him with lands nor the ballot, nor did they grant him the right of citizenship." 13 Cong. Rec. 1546 (1882).

Senator Grover said the meaning of the founding fathers was inescapable. The promise of the Declaration was extended only to whites:

"When they declared that all men were created equal, and were endowed with the inalienable right of life, liberty, and the pursuit of happiness, they undoubtedly meant all men like themselves." 13 Cong. Rec. 1546 (1882).

Grover insisted white supremacy must be preserved, and America must not pursue immigration policies that would "voluntarily create other relations with colored foreign peoples." 13 Cong. Rec. 1546 (1882). If restrictions on immigration were not imposed, America's future would darken. Grover posited what was to him a terrifying hypothetical, illustrating how America might have looked if European dominance had not been asserted and enforced:

"Had the first colonists of this country come from Asia rather than from Europe, the world would look in vain for the young colossus of nations it now witnesses . . . . In place of the temple of the true God would be the houses of heathen deities. In place of the august public assembly, convened at the behest of the people for making laws for their own government, the private consultation of emperors and autocrats would promulgate their edicts for the rule of a submissive populace. Instead of . . . our gigantic railway system traversing the entire continent, sustaining the commerce and travel of a mighty people, the world would witness a groveling throng of slowly moving human beings, plodding their footpaths with the weight of their labor's product on their backs." 13 Cong. Rec. 1547 (1882).

After Senator Grover concluded, the presiding officer directed the clerk to announce two amendments that had been filed at the desk. Both ultimately would pass. One of these was Grover's, proposing a new section to construe more broadly the expression "Chinese laborers." Worried that the bill as written might exclude only unskilled workers, Grover's amendment clarified that the term meant both skilled and unskilled laborers and Chinese employed in mining.

Senator James T. Farley (D–CA) had filed the other amendment. In 1879, Farley succeeded to Aaron Sargent's (R–CA) Senate seat, and served one term before retiring in 1885. Farley's amendment concerned naturalization and would prove to be immensely damaging to the civil rights of Chinese immigrants:

"That hereafter no state court or court of the United States shall admit Chinese to citizenship; and all laws in conflict with this act are hereby repealed."

After the Farley amendment was enacted into law, Chinese persons would be denied political recourse when the political system was used against them, as often it would be.

Members of Congress did not proceed blindly down this path. They had been warned about what might happen if the Chinese were denied political rights. In 1876, Senator Oliver Morton (R–IN) brought to California a bipartisan joint congressional committee, the Morton Committee (§ 2.10), to investigate the effects of Chinese immigration on American labor and public institutions. Morton passed away before the final Morton Committee report was issued, but had been able to file minority views. He wrote about the exposure the Chinese faced as an insular minority and their continuing peril unless given the ballot:

"The Chinese cannot be protected in the Pacific States while remaining in their alien condition. Without representation in the Legislature or Congress, without a vote in the selection of officers, and surrounded by fierce, and in many respects, unscrupulous enemies, the law will be found insufficient to screen them from persecution. Complete protection can be given them only by allowing them to become citizens and acquire the right of suffrage, when their votes would become important in elections, and their persecution, in great part, converted into kindly solicitation." 13 Cong. Rec. 1548 (1882).

Protecting the Chinese was not Farley's priority. He believed more Chinese immigration would promote greater civil unrest. Granting the franchise would encourage more people to immigrate. Blocking a path to citizenship for Chinese was one way to curtail the influx.

Senator Farley addressed Hoar, who had thus far been the sole senator to oppose the bill openly:

"Now I ask the honorable Senator from Massachusetts—I put the question broadly and squarely to him—if he would be in favor today of permitting the Chinese to exercise the elective franchise in this country." 13 Cong. Rec. 1548 (1882).

Senator Hoar was unequivocal:

"I am in favor of admitting to the privileges of American citizenship, under proper limitations in the case of foreigners who have been educated in attachments to other governments, every human being—white, black, yellow, copper-colored, or whatever color nature may have seen fit to use in painting men's skins—having first ascertained that they have abandoned all allegiance to other governments; that they are fit in character, in intelligence, in qualities that make good citizens, and are attached to our Government." 13 Cong. Rec. 1548 (1882).

Although U.S. law did not affirmatively grant Chinese a right to naturalize, Farley presented anecdotal evidence that some state courts, including those of Massachusetts, were permitting Chinese to naturalize anyway. He denounced this activity. Its effect could not simply be localized and was not a matter of curiosity or indifference to other states. If a court in Massachusetts naturalized a Chinese, that individual would have citizenship rights that courts everywhere were required to respect. Californians did not want that outcome, Farley insisted, so a uniform policy against Chinese naturalization must be declared. Such was the purpose of his amendment.

§3.50 Senate Debate, March 3, 1882: "Dregs of the countless hordes of China"

Under consideration in the Senate Committee of the Whole, S. 71, with a substitute proposed by the Committee on Foreign Relations.

As soon as debate commenced on March 3, 1882, James Farley (D–CA) took the Senate floor. He beseeched his colleagues to implement the Angell Treaty in order to halt Chinese immigration, which he said had discouraged European migration to California. Exclusion was a squarely federal responsibility, Farley noted, because California lacked the legal capacity to defend itself:

"The strong arm of the law of the State, its constitution, cannot protect us; and hence we appeal to the right that Congress has under the present treaty between the two countries." 13 Cong. Rec. 1581 (1882). Indeed, the United States Supreme Court had expressly invalidated a California statute that would have granted state officials the right to board ships in port as well as to examine and search through the immigrants aboard. *Chy Lung v. Freeman*, 92 U.S. 275 (1875). The Court held that, "[t]he laws which concern the admission of citizens and subjects of foreign nations to our shores belong to the Congress, and not to the states." 92 U.S. 275, 282.

Farley asserted that exclusion's proponents were pursuing a policy that was actually consistent with historical opposition to slave labor. Chinese in California were slaves in effect, said Farley:

"We all know that they are used as slaves by those who bring them to this country, that their labor is for the benefit of those who practically own them." 13 Cong. Rec. 1581 (1882).

Senator Farley's solution to such quasi-slavery was not to emancipate the Chinese but to exclude them. Those who clamored to stop African slavery, "ought not now to sustain Chinese labor in our country," he argued. 13 Cong. Rec. 1581 (1882).

Instead, Californians needed the federal intervention for which they had been long remonstrating. Based on experience, they knew just whom they sought to exclude:

"It is a well known fact that the Chinese are not an ignorant class of people. I do not claim that they are. They are very cunning; they are very shrewd. They are imitators, they are not inventors . . . ." 13 Cong. Rec. 1582 (1882).

Senator George Hoar (R–MA) interrupted Farley:

"Will the Senator allow me to ask him if the Chinese did not invent the printing-press, gun-powder, and the mariner's compass?" 13 Cong. Rec. 1582 (1882).

Senator John P. Jones (R–NV) intervened. A five-term senator (1873–1903), Jones proved to be quite a student of history:

"The Senator from Massachusetts has asked if Chinamen did not invent gunpowder and the printing-press. In reply to that, I can say to him that the very best authority denies to them the honor of those inventions. The Count de Gobineau, in his very able *History of the Diversity of the Races*, absolutely lays it down and, I think, conclusively proves that they had nothing to do with these inventions, but stole them from stray Aryan Caucasian people who had wandered into their midst." 13 Cong. Rec. 1582 (1882).

Hoar was astonished. He inquired, "Who were those marvelous Aryan people who wandered down into China?"

Although Jones was unable to answer Hoar, he proceeded to denigrate the Chinese further and, the Nevadan assured the Senate, "it is most distinctly shown that in the arts, the Chinese were constantly supplied with ideas by their Aryan neighbors, and they never invented anything themselves. It is a well known fact that the Chinese have been in a state of general decadence for the last five hundred years." 13 Cong. Rec. 1582 (1882).

Farley resumed the Senate floor. He admonished senators who cared about African-Americans to halt the spread of Chinese labor to the southern states. He predicted that a race war would occur if people of African descent came into contact with the Chinese:

"If you take the Chinese today and mix them with the colored people of the

South, you will find there will be a conflict between those races that will result in riot and bloodshed and the laws of the country will have to be invoked in order to protect the interests of one or both races." 13 Cong. Rec. 1582 (1882).

Senator Farley understood that some of his colleagues might oppose exclusion legislation on humanitarian grounds, but the California senator reserved such impulses for whites, whom he characterized as the victims of Chinese encroachment:

"I am inclined to be humanitarian toward my own people; I am inclined to be humanitarian toward the American people, those who were native born or Americans by adoption, in preference to a class of people who have come here and, in many cases, driven some of the white people in this country to the commission of crimes. Many white people have been driven from employment, and have found their homes in the lowest slums of the country. Why? Because they were servants, and they were driven from employment; a long pig-tailed Chinaman was admitted into the parlor to attend to the duties that an honest working girl had attended to before. These are facts that cannot be controverted." 13 Cong. Rec. 1583 (1882).

Senator Samuel B. Maxey (D–TX) backed Farley. A senator from 1875 to 1887, Maxey was certain the framers of the Constitution intended to reserve naturalization for whites only:

"The Constitution of the United States, in my judgment, never contemplated the bringing of all people of all colors, climes, races, and conditions into this country and making them citizens . . . . A careful examination of that instrument in view of the surrounding circumstances at that time, in my judgment, establishes the fact that the only people ever dreamed of to be naturalized citizens of the United States by the Framers of the Constitution or by the people of the States which ratified it were people of the Caucasian race . . . . Every word which is referred to by Jefferson and by all the other great lights in respect to inviting the oppressed of foreign nations to this country referred, and referred alone to the Caucasian race." 13 Cong. Rec. 1583 (1882).

As to the Chinese, Maxey was distinctly unwelcoming:

"I trust that the refuse and dregs of the countless hordes of China will never find a welcome here." 13 Cong. Rec. 1583 (1882).

Texas wanted to keep the Chinese out, insisted Maxey. Especially to be avoided was the potential for interaction between Chinese and Africans. According to Maxey, Chinese immigrants were unfit for citizenship, were drawn from the lowest strata of Chinese society, came with all manner of vice and degradation, and brought "a pagan religion along with them to poison the minds of the

less intelligent of our people with whom they would be brought into direct contact—the colored race . . . ." 13 Cong. Rec. 1584 (1882).

To no one's surprise, Maxey announced he would support the bill without
hesitation.

Next to speak was Senator Eli Saulsbury (D–DE), who served from 1871 to
1889. Echoing arguments made by other exclusionists, Saulsbury claimed the
Chinese were too distinctive to assimilate. If immigration were not cut off, said
Saulsbury, "not only California but the entire Pacific Coast will be largely overrun
by that heathen population." If that happened, racial tensions could boil over:

"No such people can long live in our towns and cities and villages on that
coast without being not only offensive in all their manners and degrading habits,
but their presence is calculated to engender strife and discord and lead to possible collision with the people among whom they live." 13 Cong. Rec. 1584 (1882).

Some senators justified the bill as a necessary step to protect white labor.
But Saulsbury did not find that rationale singularly persuasive. He thought a better reason to exclude was racial incompatibility:

"I would not close the gates against the immigration of the Chinese to this
country simply on the ground that they enter into competition with labor, but I
put it upon another ground, which is that it introduces a distinct race of people
with a different civilization from that to which we are accustomed, wholly incapable of assimilation with our people." 13 Cong. Rec. 1584 (1882).

Soon thereafter, Senator John J. Ingalls (R–KS) was recognized. A strong
anti-slavery advocate before the Civil War, Ingalls was a leader in the successful
movement to have Kansas admitted to the Union as a free state. He served in the
Senate between 1873 and 1891.

Ingalls told senators that the twenty-year period of Chinese exclusion was
excessive. The Angell Treaty provided that immigration could be restricted, but
not absolutely prohibited. Ingalls had an idea that he considered closer to the
spirit of the treaty: reduce the exclusion period to ten years. Ten years would
permit passions in the Pacific region to subside, allow the labor situation in those
states to stabilize, while not breaching treaty obligations to China. He proposed
a ten-year amendment to the Senate Foreign Relations Committee substitute.

Preferring no expiration date at all, Senator John Miller (R–CA) opposed the
Ingalls amendment. As introduced, the bill stated that Chinese immigration was
"declared to be unlawful, and is suspended and prohibited until otherwise provided by law." During its deliberations, the Senate Committee on Foreign Relations
had substituted a twenty-year restriction for Miller's open-ended ban. Believing
that twenty years was the best achievable outcome, Miller had acquiesced.

Senator Miller argued that a ten-year halt would appear temporary and would leave Chinese immigration unsettled, when clarity of the policy was better for everyone. While he could defend the twenty-year limit, Miller left no doubt about his personal preference:

"If there were no treaty in the way, I would make the suspension a prohibition and make it absolute and eternal." 13 Cong. Rec. 1588 (1882).

Senator Thomas Bayard (D–DE) spoke next. A senator between 1869 and 1885, Bayard resigned his seat to serve as secretary of state under President Grover Cleveland. As secretary of state (1885–1889), Bayard negotiated yet another treaty (known as Bayard–Zhang) with China to restrict immigration. In 1888, China would refuse to ratify the Bayard–Zhang treaty after the Senate added onerous amendments.

In the 1882 debate, Bayard was very attuned to the pleas from the Pacific region:

"When I hear the voice of California, and Nevada, and Oregon, and of the adjacent Territories all speaking in the same earnest tone and declaring the same truths, I must heed it," said Bayard. "They have said to us that everything which men hold dear, their traditions, their liberties, their sympathies, social habits, political rights are all in jeopardy unless a check shall be put to the incoming and terrible wave of an approaching Mongolian overflow . . . ." 13 Cong. Rec. 1588 (1882).

Senator Bayard came out strongly for exclusion. He revived the national self-preservation argument from earlier debates, insisting "a nation must be true to itself before it undertakes to expend its energies in favor of strangers and aliens." 13 Cong. Rec. 1588 (1882).

Late in the afternoon of Friday, March 3, 1882, another day of debate on Chinese exclusion legislation drew to a close.

§3.60 Senate Debate, March 6, 1882: "Will not assimilate"

Under consideration in the Senate Committee of the Whole, S. 71, with a substitute proposed by the Committee on Foreign Relations, and an amendment proposed by Senator Ingalls to the substitute.

Returning after the weekend, the Senate resumed consideration of S. 71, with the Ingalls "ten-year" amendment pending to the Committee on Foreign Relations substitute. Opening the debate was Senator James H. Slater (D–OR), who served a single term between 1879 and 1885. Slater's main concern was that the Angell Treaty was not drawn tightly enough to repel efforts to circumvent it. Permissive language in the Angell Treaty would admit educators, traders, and merchants to come without limit, he observed, even though laborers were restricted. Slater worried such provisions would offer a platform for laborers to enter under false premises.

Notwithstanding these misgivings, Slater and the Pacific Coast senators had consented to the Angell Treaty (*Appendix 5*). Believing it was the strongest bilateral agreement they were likely to get, they would rely on tough implementing legislation in order to deter evasions:

"I fear, sir, that we of the Pacific Coast will yet regret that we ever consented that this treaty might be finally consummated. But like drowning men who catch at anything which promises the possibility of escape from peril, we were unwilling to make opposition to this treaty, fearing that nothing better might be obtained in any reasonable time, and also hoping that legislation under its provisions might be so framed as to check the tide of Chinese immigration to our coast, until such time as the morbid and unnatural, though prevailing craze about the universal brotherhood of man might in some degree subside and wiser counsels prevail." 13 Cong. Rec. 1635 (1882).

Senator Slater differed with colleagues like George Hoar (R–MA) who believed Chinese had a universal right to the pursuit of happiness: "They have no right in the pursuit of their own happiness to inflict injury upon the people of other communities," 13 Cong. Rec. 1635 (1882).

Slater challenged the statistics Hoar had presented about the relatively small number of Chinese then in the United States. Tiny as their numbers might be in the country as a whole, Slater argued, on the Pacific Coast they represented a concentrated and highly combustible problem. The predicament was already acute in his region. The clash of cultures had arrived, and whites were alarmed:

"Almost from the first, their coming was objected to, and as its effects became more and more apparent, this opposition became more and more pronounced." 13 Cong. Rec. 1635 (1882). Allowed to accumulate in greater numbers and spread elsewhere, Chinese immigrants would provoke similar reaction in other regions, Slater claimed.

Slater reinforced the theme that Chinese were radically different from others in America and must be barred from the country because they would never adopt the traits of the dominant culture:

"The Chinese are aliens, born in a foreign land, speak a foreign tongue, owe allegiance to a foreign government, are idolaters in religion, have a different civilization from ours, do not and will not assimilate with our people, come only to get money, and return; and they are inimical to our laws and evade them whenever and wherever they can . . . ." 13 Cong. Rec. 1636 (1882).

Senator James Z. George (D–MS) took the Senate floor. A three-term senator (1881–1897), George had been a signer of Mississippi's Ordinance of Secession, and had been a prisoner of war during the Civil War. George succeeded Senator Blanche Bruce (R–MS), the first African-American to serve a full Senate term (1875–1881). Bruce had opposed the Fifteen Passenger bill, however, George held very different views:

"The Constitution was ordained and established by white men, as they declared in its preamble, 'to secure the blessings of liberty to themselves (ourselves) and their (our) posterity.'" Hoping that "this great pledge thus solemnly given will be as fully redeemed in favor of the white people of the South," George supported exclusion to redeem it "in favor of the white people of the Pacific States by my vote to protect them against a degrading and destructive association with the inferior race now threatening to overrun them." 13 Cong. Rec. 1638 (1882).

Senator Joseph E. Brown (D–GA) rose. Brown was the forty-second governor of Georgia (1857–1865) and served in the Senate from 1880 to 1891. He was the first southern Democrat to question seriously the arguments that had been set forth for exclusion. On final passage, he would abstain from voting.

Brown described increasingly close relations between the United States and China, including the broad expansion of American commercial interests in the aftermath of the Burlingame Treaty (*Appendix 2*). Among the leading U.S. commodities sold to China, the Georgia senator noted, was textiles. Brown feared that exclusion legislation would insult the Chinese and undermine the burgeoning trade:

"It would be foolishness on our part to seek wantonly to offend these people and destroy our commerce among them." 13 Cong. Rec. 1640 (1882).

Senator Brown argued that the bill was not a good faith implementation of the Angell Treaty and that China would be justified in regarding it as a breach. Article I of the treaty provided the United States could "regulate, limit, or suspend" immigration of Chinese laborers, but China had won American agreement that such immigration would not be barred:

"We have reserved the right to regulate, limit, or suspend the coming of Chinese laborers, but the treaty is express and positive in its provisions that we shall not absolutely prohibit it, and that our legislation on the subject shall be reasonable. Now, does any Senator here really believe, when we were negotiating this treaty with the Emperor of China, that our representatives held out to him any such idea as that our first step in limitation and suspension would be an absolute inhibition, or prohibition of the importation of a single Chinese laborer for twenty years under severe legal penalties? Do you believe, Senators, that the Chinese Government would have agreed to such a treaty if they understood that this was our interpretation of it? Would they have ratified it? I think no Senator in this Chamber can believe they would." 13 Cong. Rec. 1640 (1882).

Article II of the treaty stated that Chinese teachers, students, merchants, tourists, household servants, as well as laborers already in the United States were permitted "to go and come of their own free will and accord, and shall be accorded all the rights, privileges, immunities, and exemptions which are accorded to the citizens and subjects of the most favored nations." 13 Cong. Rec. 1640 (1882). Brown thought the committee proposal would badly undermine these guarantees.

One such provision required that non-laborers receive a certificate from the Government of China vouching for the purpose of their travel, subject to visa verification by a U.S. representative in China. The Senate Committee on Foreign Relations had added this requirement, extraordinary at the time, due to concerns that Chinese laborers might attempt to enter the country under false pretenses. Such documentation was required upon landing in the United States and could be demanded of a Chinese person at any time during his stay in America. Failure to produce papers would subject the Chinese person to a fine of up to $100 and imprisonment of up to one year, Brown noted.

A second impediment in the bill mandated that the secretary of the treasury establish a special registry for every Chinese person in the United States. The registry was to describe each person with great particularity. The bill stated:

"Entry shall be made in such books of the name of every such Chinese, and his proper signature, his place of birth (giving town or district), date of birth, last residence before coming to the United States, place of residence in the United States, if any, names and residences of his parents, if any, date and place of arrival in the United States, employment or business, height and physical marks or peculiarities by which he may be identified. Every applicant for registration shall make oath to the facts stated in his registry, which oath shall be recorded in the books of the registry. Collectors of customs and their deputies shall have power to administer and certify to all oaths under this act." 13 Cong. Rec. 1640 (1882).

Although the Angell Treaty did permit restriction of Chinese laborers, it required the United States to treat other Chinese like citizens of most-favored-nations. But the bill's onerous identification requirements applied to every Chinese and to no one else. Senator Brown mocked the incongruity:

"If he is a teacher or a merchant or a Chinaman coming here from curiosity, he has a perfect right under this treaty to go and come of his own free will and accord. But if he be one of those characters, and he has not complied with everything prescribed in reference to the passport, registration, descriptive list, and all that is set forth in this long, ponderous bill, and its numerous sections, he is to be seized and thrown into prison and fined and remain there till he pay the fine; and that is what we call extending to him the same rights, privileges, immunities and exemptions which are accorded to citizens and subjects of the most favored nation!" 13 Cong. Rec. 1641 (1882).

The legislation essentially turned the Angell Treaty on its head, Brown argued. Rather than merely restricting a labor influx, it placed unprecedented burdens on the Chinese. For them, America's welcome mat was distinctly withdrawn. Brown asked the Senate about these special disabilities:

"Do you, I ask, Senators by your law extend such denial of rights and privileges to the subjects of even the most unfavored nations? Is there any other nation on the globe whose subjects are compelled to comply with all these provisions before they can enter an American port? Is there any other nation on the globe whose subjects can be seized, tried, fined, and imprisoned for the non-compliance with provisions like those contained in this bill? If there is an instance, I am not aware of it." 13 Cong. Rec. 1641 (1882).

Senators Brown and James Farley (D–CA) then engaged in a short exchange, with Farley defending the administrative burdens placed on the Chinese. They were devised to distinguish between permitted entrants, such as teachers, and those who were barred, such as laborers. Brown dismissed Farley's explanation, contending the legislation served a more sweeping and insidious purpose:

"The object of the bill is to throw such obstacles in the way as will, without regard for the treaty, greatly limit, if it does not prevent, all Chinese from coming to this country." 13 Cong. Rec. 1641 (1882).

These special barriers contradicted U.S. treaty commitments, Brown claimed, while Europeans from most favored nations did not face such burdens or harassment:

"Have you ever heard of an instance where an Irishman or a German, before he could come to this country must get a passport at home, bring it here and have it registered, carry it with him everywhere he goes, and bring it when he returns? Have they ever been encumbered by any such provision as this? Never in any case. No; they are subjects of favored nations; they are among the most favored nations; and when the Irishman and German come here they soon have the ballot in their hands, and then they are very good people, and politicians and statesmen and everybody respect them; but the Chinaman comes in and we raise the clamor that he must not enter until he has been encumbered with all these hindrances, although we have expressly pledged our faith to China that he shall be put on the same terms and have the same exemptions, immunities, and privileges which the Irishman or the German, in the case supposed, has, or which anybody else has." 13 Cong. Rec. 1642 (1882).

Senator Brown indicated he would support the Ingalls amendment to reduce the term of restriction on laborers to ten years. Such a period, said Brown, would represent the outer limit of a good-faith implementation of the Angell Treaty. Brown of Georgia closed by addressing a more fundamental question, that being his willingness to dissent from popular opinion. In contrast to Brown, almost all other Senate Democrats favored exclusion:

"I know I do not occupy the popular side of this question . . . . The statesman who adopts the rule of pandering to popular opinion may float peacefully with the current for the time, but he will soon be called to answer at the same bar of public opinion for acts which at the time of their performance were hailed with delight. My rule is to inquire: Is it right? And if right to move forward without fear. I would rather be right than popular. I would rather have approval of my conscience than the plaudits of the multitude, or the temporary approval of those who are controlled by their passions and not by their reason and their judgment." 13 Cong. Rec. 1644 (1882).

Senator Henry Teller (R–CO) spoke next. Teller was Colorado's first senator following statehood in 1876, the thirty-eighth state admitted to the Union. Elected in 1876, he would resign his seat within a month of the exclusion debate to become secretary of the interior under President Chester A. Arthur. Teller returned to the Senate after Arthur's presidency. The Coloradan served until 1909, when he broke with the Republicans on the issue of the gold standard and became a Democrat.

Teller was an outspoken advocate of exclusion. He claimed to oppose Chinese immigration because it was undertaken for temporary financial gain. If a Chinese were ever given suffrage rights, those economic benefits would include the auction of his franchise. Other than bartering for their votes, Chinese would be disengaged from the workings of American government:

"Why, Mr. President, unless he could see some direct benefit growing out of it in a financial way, no Chinaman would ever seek to be naturalized in this country. No Chinaman desires to participate in the affairs of government of this country. He considers it beneath him; he will not repudiate his allegiance to his own country for the purpose of voting, unless he should discover that he could sell that vote, and when he discovered that, I believe the entire Chinese population of California would rush to be naturalized; not, as I say, because they want to take part in the administration of public affairs, but to make money out of it." 13 Cong. Rec. 1644 (1882).

Teller believed strongly in the doctrine of white supremacy, and the importance of enforcing it so that Caucasians would stand above other races:

"The Caucasian race has a right, considering its superiority of intellectual force and mental vigor; to look down on every other branch of the human family . . . we are the superior race today. We are superior to the Chinese, though they go back with their three or four or five thousand years of civilization." 13 Cong. Rec. 1645 (1882).

Senator Teller said he would support exclusion to defend American labor. Teller had no compunctions or second thoughts:

"I am prepared to vote for this bill, and I vote for it without excuse. I vote for it with pleasure, not speaking now of the details but of the principle, because I see no other way to protect American labor . . . . I have no apology to make when I vote for this bill." 13 Cong. Rec. 1645 (1882).

With that, the debate of March 6, 1882, ended.

§3.70 Senate Debate, March 7, 1882: "An irrepressible conflict between them"

> *Under consideration in the Senate Committee of the Whole, S. 71, with a substitute proposed by the Committee on Foreign Relations and an amendment by Senator Ingalls proposed to the substitute.*

When the Senate reconvened on March 7, 1882, Senator John Miller (R–CA) presented to the Senate a series of letters and petitions generated by fourteen mass meetings held throughout California. Sensing the chance of victory in the Senate, grassroots supporters of immigration restriction had organized to give the bill a push.

The communications from these meetings all favored exclusion legislation. An example of these was a telegram to the California senators (Miller and James Farley (D–CA)) from one A.J. McPike, chairman of the Democratic County Committee of Solano County and cosigned by S.G. Helborn, chairman of the

Republican Committee. The party leaders reported on a resolution unanimously adopted at a citizens' meeting in Vallejo, California. An excerpt from that resolution echoed the themes that had been expressed in the Senate debate of Chinese invasion and clash of civilizations, and is representative of the entire document:

"Be it therefore resolved, That as citizens of Vallejo interested in the prosperity of the State, we earnestly ask Congress for protection from this Mongolian invasion, believing as we do that, if not checked, California will before long become but little better than a Chinese province. Asiatic and American civilization cannot exist together on the same soil, there being an irrepressible conflict between them which must eventually end in the giving way of one or the other." 13 Cong. Rec. 1668 (1882).

Senator James Fair (D–NV) presented a similar communication that he had received from Nevada Governor John Kinkead. The governor said:

"Mass meetings are being held tonight in our prominent towns, and are unanimous in urging the speedy passage of Senator Miller's bill restricting Chinese immigration." 13 Cong. Rec. 1669 (1882).

In 1879, Senator Henry Dawes (R–MA), who had been an outspoken opponent of the Fifteen Passenger bill, protested the use of such propaganda and any rush to judgment. "I am aware," began the senator, "that the friends of this measure are impatient for a vote, and that in their opinion debate is exhausted."

Dawes was not ready for the Senate to vote. He condemned the bill for its harshness. Through international commitments, the United States had given its word to China, but was preparing to breach it though a legislative sleight of hand:

"We have told them, we have solemnly covenanted, that while we may put reasonable limitations and regulations upon immigration, we will not absolutely prohibit it. In this bill, we do not absolutely prohibit, for twenty years, any Chinese laborer from coming; we only declare that if he does come he shall go to the penitentiary. That is all . . . . I knew a man once who told his son, 'I do not absolutely prohibit you from going to the circus today, but I tell you that if you do, I will horsewhip you.' That is all . . . . If one of you puts his foot upon the soil of free America, though innocent of guile as a saint, with purpose as praiseworthy as ever actuated an immigrant to these shores, though you come with a sincere desire to identify yourself with our institutions and obey our laws and make a home for yourself and for your children, if you undertake to do it with the labor of your own hands, you shall find yourself in the penitentiary." 13 Cong. Rec. 1670 (1882).

Dawes viewed the campaign for Chinese exclusion as fundamentally mean-spirited. Exclusion proponents claimed the mass meetings were evidence of a public groundswell, but Dawes thought Congress should not surrender to mob impulses:

"They hold mass meetings today, their Legislatures enact a legal holiday that all of them can come together and shout 'Pass a law that will enable us to trample with the iron heel of power every man of Chinese birth who has the presumption in this land of liberty to earn his daily bread by the sweat of his brow!'" 13 Cong. Rec. 1670 (1882).

Senator Henry Teller (R–CO) defended the exclusionists:

"It is not quite fair for the Senator to attempt to make it appear that we, who believe there is an impending evil, and are anxious by the processes of law to restrict this immigration, are joining with a class of people, exceedingly few in numbers who are disposed to do personal violence to the Chinese in this country." 13 Cong. Rec. 1672 (1882).

Senator Dawes replied, "The champion of this bill from Colorado is uneasy at the position he took yesterday."

"Not a bit of it," responded Teller.

"It would do him credit if he was," the Massachusetts senator retorted, making reference to Teller's comments in the March 6, 1882, debate:

"Although the Senator yesterday was willing to admit that our civilization was superior to that of the Chinese, that the civilization of the nineteenth century was superior to that of the sixth, that the Caucasian was superior to anybody else on God's footstool, yet he turned around and said that unless we came with a statute and drove off one hundred and two thousand Chinamen from fifty million Caucasians, it was all day with the latter. He was not afraid to avow here that there was a superior and an inferior race in this country, and that the superior must have control by legislative guards and protections or they would be sure to surrender to the inferior. I should be uneasy if I were in his place at the announcement of such a proposition." 13 Cong. Rec. 1672 (1882).

The Chinese exclusion bill resembled the structure of discrimination that had in the past burdened Africans. "It is evoked," Dawes said, "from a system of legislation in disregard of human rights, to which large portions of this people once adhered, and whose consequences have been deep and lasting upon the history of the country and the character of her institutions." 13 Cong. Rec. 1672 (1882).

As an example, Dawes quoted from Oregon's constitution:

"No free Negro or mulatto, not residing in this State at the time of the adoption of this constitution, shall ever come, reside, or be within this State, or hold any real estate, or make any contract, or maintain any suit therein; and the Legislative Assembly shall provide by penal laws for the removal by public officers of all such free negroes and mulattoes, and for their effectual exclusion from the State, and for the punishment of persons who shall bring them into the State, or employ or harbor them therein." 13 Cong. Rec. 1672 (1882).

Dawes lamented that the Civil War did not seem to have resolved the race prejudice and animosity that was being revived in the exclusion debate.

Senator George F. Edmunds (R–VT) spoke next. A senator from 1866 until 1891, Edmunds indicated he would vote for the Ingalls ten-year suspension amendment. Reducing the term was more consistent with the spirit of the Angell Treaty (*Appendix 5*), he asserted.

Edmunds defended the principle of restricting immigration. Like a family, every nation enjoyed the right to determine "for its own protection and its own well-being" who shall be its members. His willingness to exclude was "based upon the belief that nations and races, as they have been constituted by the God of nature and by political divisions and arrangements, get on better as separate families with their separate independence and their separate institutions than they do amalgamated together; unless their origin, their race, their tendency, their nature is such that being put together they assimilate and become one perfect, homogeneous and prosperous mass." 13 Cong. Rec. 1673 (1882).

Unlike some of the bill's supporters, Edmunds did not believe in Caucasian racial superiority. "I do not mean to say that the Chinese race, the Chinese religion, the Chinese development is not better than the Anglo-Saxon." 13 Cong. Rec. 1673 (1882). But he could consent to a period of exclusion, because Chinese were non-assimilative. Before more Chinese were allowed to come, Congress should impose a breathing spell to see if immigrants already on the Pacific Coast could be happily absorbed. The senator doubted such assimilation would ever occur:

"Now we are not homogeneous with the Chinaman; it does not presently appear that we can be; and reducing this bill within the spirit of the treaty to ten years, it is only saying not that we deny the equality of the Chinaman, not that we deny his high civilization, if he has it, but simply that we will suspend this experiment of attempted assimilation with the elements that we already have of one hundred thousand or more in this country, until we see how it works." 13 Cong. Rec. 1673 (1882).

Edmunds affirmed his belief in the principle of expatriation, but said it was "dependent upon the willingness of the people to whom the persons expatriating themselves desired to go to receive them." 13 Cong. Rec. 1673 (1882).

For the time being, expatriation would apply to Europeans alone. Late in the afternoon, the Senate concluded its fifth day of debate on the bill and adjourned.

§3.80 Senate Debate, March 8, 1882: "A storm of condemnation"

Under consideration in the Senate Committee of the Whole, S. 71, with a substitute amendment proposed by the Committee on Foreign Relations and an Ingalls amendment proposed to the substitute.

When debate resumed on March 8, 1882, Senator Orville Platt (R–CT) was recognized. Platt was at the onset of a long career in the Senate (1879–1905), which would see him rise to a position of great influence within the Senate by the turn of the twentieth century.

While Platt would be open to appeals from the Pacific region about immigration suspension, he would not support the Miller bill:

"I cannot bring myself to vote for a bill which I believe violates the spirit of the [Angell] treaty; I cannot bring myself to vote for a bill which I believe violates principles of natural right and justice; I cannot consent, for the sake of mere expediency and good fellowship, to do this." 13 Cong. Rec. 1702 (1882).

To Platt, the intent of the legislation was clear. It masqueraded as suspension, but in fact was a ban:

"The object of this bill is to extirpate the Chinese; it is to exclude them; it is to prohibit them from coming here hereafter. I have listened to all the speeches that have been made, and I can see nothing in the utterances of the Senators who are in favor of this bill that does not tend to that end—prohibition, exclusion, extirpation." 13 Cong. Rec. 1702 (1882).

Platt contended that the exclusion bill was a breach of contract with China. "We made this contract, which we call a treaty with the Chinese Government, and we must keep it," said the senator. "We must keep it, or stand forever disgraced in the eyes of the world." 13 Cong. Rec. 1702 (1882).

Platt believed that ratification of the Angell Treaty had been secured from China as the result of "overreaching on the part of the United States and trustful confidence on the part of China." 13 Cong. Rec. 1702 (1882). If the treaty was problematic, the bill was worse. Clearly, it did not simply implement treaty rights to suspend immigration, Platt said. Exclusionists meant to bar Chinese from America forever:

"According to the law of nature, according to the law of this emigration as it is laid down here, there will be no longer any Chinese laborers within the United States. We have the right to judge the intent of a bill by what must be its inevitable results, and do you tell me that a bill, the inevitable result of which must be to destroy all Chinese occupation of the United States is simply a reasonable suspension of immigration? It seems incredible that anybody can so understand it." 13 Cong. Rec. 1702 (1882).

Senator Platt reviewed the circumstances under which the Angell Treaty (*Appendix 5*) was negotiated. Appointed by President Rutherford Hayes, Commissioners James Angell, John Swift, and William Henry Trescot had gone to China in 1880 for the purpose of negotiating the opportunity to restrict immigration of laborers. The Americans had asked for an absolute right to suspend, restrict, or prohibit such immigration, said Platt, but had encountered resistance from their Chinese counterparts:

"The Chinese commissioners said they would not accede to the prohibition, and that they wanted a detailed explanation from the United States of what they meant by limitation, specification as to the mode of limitation and as to the time of limitation, and as to the numbers which should be affected by the limitation." 13 Cong. Rec. 1703 (1882).

Platt reported that the American commissioners refused to give details, but asked the Chinese to trust that the United States would impose such restrictions fairly:

"The commissioners of the United States then said that China must leave that thing entirely to the discretion of the United States; that the United States was their friend; that the United States was just; that the United States might never have occasion to resort to any of this legislation anyway, and if it did, it would only be exercised in justice and in good faith. So our commissioners convinced China that she could safely leave this matter to the justice and good faith of the United States." 13 Cong. Rec. 1703 (1882).

The Chinese negotiators outlined what they believed would be a reasonable limitation, Platt stated, that being an influx that did not exceed the maximum number of immigrants who had come in a previous year. The Americans would not be pinned down, but said that the rights the U.S. was seeking might or might not be implemented, depending on circumstances. For instance, public unrest in one region could result in restrictions there, while labor shortages in another might be met with permissive policies. Platt cited the negotiation meeting summary, prepared by the American side, which stated:

"That two great nations discussing such a subject must always assume that they will both act in good faith and with due consideration for the interest and friendship of the other. That the United States Government might never deem it necessary to exercise this power." 13 Cong. Rec. 1703 (1882).

Trusting in the goodwill of the United States, China consented to modify the

Burlingame Treaty (*Appendix 2*), Platt noted. He inserted in the *Congressional Record* the text of a lengthy dispatch sent November 17, 1880, by the Angell commissioners to Secretary of State William Evarts. The dispatch detailed the give-and-take of the negotiations. Platt's purpose was to demonstrate that severe legislation, like the Miller bill, breached bilateral understandings. A key excerpt of the dispatch set out the following:

"We therefore communicated to the Chinese commissioners that we would consent to strike out the word 'prohibit,' provided they would accept the words 'regulate, limit, or suspend,' being satisfied that those words covered the power to devise and enforce all necessary and proper legislation . . . .

"You will observe that this language imposes no conditions upon the discretion of the United States. That the discretion should be used reasonably; that all classes of Chinese subjects not within the scope of this treaty should be protected in the enjoyment of such rights as are now conferred by existing treaties, and that the diplomatic representative of the Chinese Government should have the right from time to time to call the attention of the United States Government to any unanticipated hardship that the legislation of the United States might cause . . . .

"After a free and able expression of their own views, we are satisfied that, in yielding to the request of the United States, they have been actuated by a sincere friendship and an honorable confidence that the large powers recognized by them as belonging to the United States, and bearing directly upon the interests of their own people, will be exercised by our Government with a wise discretion, in a spirit of reciprocal and sincere friendship, and with entire justice." 13 Cong. Rec. 1704 (1882).

China was about to pay a serious price for trusting in American goodwill. Once the treaty empowered Congress, implementation became the mission of the most radically anti-Chinese members. Senators, and later representatives, from the Pacific Coast drove the debate, and reasonable restrictions gave way to something far harsher.

Senator Platt focused on the incongruities between treaty and legislation. One section of the bill especially caught his attention:

"We told them to cast themselves upon our generosity; we told them we would exercise the powers given to us wisely, justly, and in good faith. Hear our reply:

'Sec. 2 That any master of any vessel, of whatever nationality, who shall on such vessel bring within the jurisdiction of the United States any Chinese laborer from any foreign port or place shall be deemed guilty of a misdemeanor, and on conviction thereof, be punished by a fine of $500 for each and every Chinese laborer so brought, and may also be imprisoned for a term not exceeding one year.'

"Does any man suppose that we would like the Government of China to treat us in this way under a treaty such as that, wrung from us as that treaty was wrung from China upon a promise of the exercise of justice and good faith?" 13 Cong. Rec. 1704 (1882).

Platt referred to the legislation's unique and highly specific registration mandate for each Chinese immigrant. "I wonder that it does not provide for branding him," the Connecticut senator said caustically. Such registration would never be required for Europeans, Platt observed, nor would they be obliged to secure the kind of certificates from their home countries, as the bill required of the Chinese. If these directives were universally applied, "How long do you think before an act of that sort would raise a storm of condemnation throughout the civilized world? And yet we are told that we are not denying to the Chinese laborers any privilege or any exemption which is extended to the subject of the most favored nation." 13 Cong. Rec. 1705 (1882).

Senator Platt condemned the bigotry inherent in the bill:

"The true intent and meaning of it is to declare that henceforth, excepting only the Chinese now here, no man shall work in the United States except he be a white man . . . . A Chinaman is not a white man . . . he is a Mongolian; and therefore no matter how skillful he be, no matter how industrious, no matter how frugal, he shall not work in America. That is the principle of this bill for the next twenty years and for all time. I cannot accede to any such proposition.

"This is race legislation; it is avowed to be race legislation, and all the old arguments that we heard about the danger of social equality between the Negro and the white man are resuscitated and rehabilitated for the occasion." 13 Cong. Rec. 1705 (1882).

Platt implored that senators who did not care what became of the Chinese should at least concern themselves of the fate of the principles articulated in the Declaration of Independence:

"You may crystallize into this legislation the prejudice and the fear of Americans; you may crystallize into this legislation the cry 'the Chinese must go' but I ask you to pause before you put it on the ground that it is because they are not of the same race as we." 13 Cong. Rec. 1705 (1882).

A frequently expressed rationale for exclusion was that Chinese could not assimilate. The Farley (D–CA) naturalization amendment was based on the same theory. Platt considered the argument specious. He had observed the Chinese community in his home state of Connecticut. Provided they were not ostracized and repressed, Chinese were fully capable of assimilating:

"I venture to say that in that State they are as peaceable, as orderly, as industrious a class of people as we have among us . . . . I see nothing in them which leads me to believe that with fair and humane treatment, with reasonable and just and generous treatment, they may not become good citizens of the Republic . . . . But when we seek to put them down with an iron hand, when they are put in fear of their lives, how can we expect them to assimilate?" 13 Cong. Rec. 1706 (1882).

If presented with reasonable legislation to protect American labor, or to preserve American political institutions from erosion, Platt might support it. But the Miller bill was punitive and excessive:

"Harsh in its provisions, severe—I will not say barbarous—in its penalties, the bill reads more like an enactment of the seventeenth century than like a wise, humane, beneficent statute of the present age and time. It seems to speak once more the language of prejudice and fear than that of an advanced and advancing civilization." 13 Cong. Rec. 1706 (1882).

After Platt finished, the presiding officer put the question on the Ingalls ten-year suspension amendment. The count was 23 yeas to 23 nays, with 20 senators shown as not voting. On the tie vote, the Ingalls amendment failed.

Following the vote, Senator Hoar (R–MA) addressed the Senate. He renewed his claim that the Senate was preparing to shatter its pledges to China:

"It is now the purpose of a majority to proceed to prohibit, not to suspend, but to proceed to do the one thing which we promised we would not do, and which our Commissioners assured China might be left to the justice and good faith of the people of the United States." 13 Cong. Rec. 1707 (1882).

Hoar then laid bare the motives of two colleagues who stated explicitly racial reasons to support the bill. One was Senator James Z. George (D–MS), who announced he would respond to white demands from the Pacific states, in the hope that reciprocal consideration would be given to white anxieties expressed by Southerners. Hoar characterized George's statement:

"He said that this was a white man's government, framed by white men for themselves and for their white posterity, and that if the question arose of dealing with the African race, he should expect the same deference to be paid to the wishes of the white people of Mississippi that he was prepared to pay to the wishes of the white people of California." 13 Cong. Rec. 1707 (1882). As to Colorado's Henry Teller, Hoar was merciless:

"Then we are met by the Senator from Colorado [Henry Teller (R–CO)] and others who think with him, with the remark of the inferiority of this Chinese race. The Senator from Colorado seems to think that the crowning glory and dignity of every human being is to have some person or other that he can despise, and if we are not permitted to despise a Chinaman, what luxury or comfort is there left to the white man of Colorado?" 13 Cong. Rec. 1707 (1882).

Teller defended himself. He was unabashed in saying that Caucasians were simply superior to other races:

"I say the Caucasian race is superior in mental force, in intellectual vigor, and morals to any other branch of the human family." 13 Cong. Rec. 1708 (1882).

A month away from confirmation as secretary of the interior (1882–1885), Teller expanded on the racial theories he had expressed in the previous day's debate:

"I meant to say that the cultivated, intelligent Englishman and American might with propriety deny the equality intellectually and morally of the Egyptian; I meant to say that the Moor might not claim as much as we; I meant to say that there were other branches of the human family that stood lower than ours in intellectual strength, in mental vigor, and in moral worth, and a man is blind to history who does not know that is a fact." 13 Cong. Rec. 1713 (1882).

Teller insisted that one could make a claim of racial superiority and still accord inferior races legal equality and government beneficence. For instance, conditions had required extending the advantages of citizenship and government protection to Africans, who, in his judgment, were "our intellectual and mental inferiors." 13 Cong. Rec. 1713 (1882). However, the same rules should not apply to the Chinese because they were an alien, rather than a native, people:

"If we found them here when we annexed California, if we found them born upon this soil, I would extend to them every privilege that would have any tendency to make them better and increase their value as they come into the body-politic; but they are strangers in our land, they are strangers to our system of civilization, they are strangers to our Government, and they propose thus to remain."

"Mr. President, these people are not desirable in any respect, and no man can shield himself from the crime that he commits against the body of the people of the United States when he attempts to force them into our midst by the sentimental cry of the unity of the races and the brotherhood of men." 13 Cong. Rec. 1713 (1882).

Late in the afternoon, Senator Hoar again spoke. The legislation was immoral, argued the senator, because exclusion was based not on an offense against law but on an accident of birth:

"This legislation does not strike at the Chinese in person who violates the law of California or the law of the United States. This legislation says 'If your skin be yellow, if your father and mother were Mongolians, you may be as pure, as good, as law-abiding, as useful, as honorable, as honest as any man who lives, but because of that into which no moral quality possibly can enter, the color of your skin, you shall be made an exile or a criminal, or sent to the penitentiary, if you stay.'" 13 Cong. Rec. 1709 (1882).

To Hoar, only one conclusion could be drawn about the bill:

"Mr. President, if this legislation be not wrong, as Abraham Lincoln said of slavery, nothing is wrong. If it be not a violation of the moral law, then there is no moral law as it has been pronounced to us." 13 Cong. Rec. 1709 (1882).

Vermont's Senator George Edmunds had a different idea. Morality was based on community standards, those set by a body of people organized into a government. Just as the community could decide right from wrong, it could regulate who would be permitted to join society. That is what the Miller bill did, and Edmunds saw nothing immoral about it:

"I repeat what I stated yesterday, that so long as you are to have government at all, that government, like a family or a partnership, must be the judge for itself of what persons it will take into the body of the people, that at the last in our form of government constitute the government itself." 13 Cong. Rec. 1710 (1882).

Hoar evaluated the bill in relation to fundamental American principles. Chinese exclusion was a policy based on race. It contradicted deep-set values that abjured race or national origin as a basis for discrimination. For example, he noted, the Constitution required that Congress pass uniform naturalization laws, not ones "which shall distinguish between races and between nationalities." Another illustration was the Fourteenth Amendment, which provided for universal birthright citizenship. Furthermore, the Fifteen Amendment protected against abridgements of suffrage based on "race, color, or previous condition of servitude," said Hoar. 13 Cong. Rec. 1710–11 (1882).

Senate proceedings for March 8, 1882, were coming to a close. Several technical amendments were disposed of by voice vote. Then, Hoar proposed to amend the bill by adding a new section, which he hoped would respond to claims made by Senator John F. Miller (R–CA) and others that Chinese migration should be stopped because it was involuntary. The bill's proponents alleged that the Chinese Six Companies had imported workers under coercive labor contracts, and that Chinese immigrants had not come on their own volition. Hoar's amendment stated:

"Provided, That this bill shall not apply to any skilled laborer who shall establish that he comes to this country without any contract by which his labor is the property of any person other than himself."

Debate on the amendment consisted of one brief exchange between Senators Farley and Hoar. Farley spoke in opposition, arguing that the amendment invited attempts at evasion:

"I apprehend that if that amendment was adopted, they would all come here as skilled laborers and be able to prove that they had no contract with anybody, and they could prove it by their own testimony." 13 Cong. Rec. 1716 (1882).

Hoar retorted:

"This will test whether it is coolie labor that is driven at or skilled labor. I want to see which it is. This compels the laborer, puts the burden on him, to prove in defense before the court, that he is a skilled artisan and comes on his own motion." 13 Cong. Rec. 1716 (1882).

The roll call on Hoar's amendment showed 17 yeas, 27 nays, and 32 not voting, and it failed.

Hoar offered a further amendment, which provided that any person certified to be an artisan by a United States consul, and coming to the United States at his own expense and free will, would not be affected by the bill. There was no debate. The vote was 10 yeas, 24 nays, and 33 not voting, and this amendment failed.

Senator Farley's naturalization proposal was the next major amendment made pending. Before the amendment could receive a vote, the Senate adjourned for the evening.

§3.90 Senate Debate, March 9, 1882: "Fifty million sovereigns can be despotic"

Under consideration in the Senate Committee of the
Whole, S. 71, with a substitute amendment proposed
by the Senate Committee on Foreign Relations,
and a Farley amendment proposed to the substitute.

On Thursday March 9, 1882, the exclusion bill was before the Senate for a seventh day of debate. The Farley naturalization amendment to the substitute from the Senate Committee on Foreign Relations was pending. First to speak was Senator Joseph R. Hawley (R–CT).

A Union general in the Civil War, Connecticut governor (1866–1867), and a two-term member of the House Representatives (1872–1875 and 1879–1881),

Hawley served in the Senate between 1881 and 1905. He conceded that nations had a right of self-defense to control injurious immigration, especially in preparing for or conducting a war:

"Laws national or international may be set aside if we can defend ourselves, and any class of people may be excluded or any foreigners may be ordered to depart, the measure of the exercise of the power being only the degree of the necessity of self-protection." 13 Cong. Rec. 1738 (1882).

But the nation was not engaged in an armed conflict. Hawley thus claimed that a doctrine of self-protection, which might stand in wartime, was being abused to justify singling out the Chinese:

"But we are legislating for times of peace. We are legislating professedly upon the general and not the exceptional principles that are to be justified by our Constitution, by the spirit of our laws, the national spirit, character, and policy that we have freely and boastfully set forth to the whole world for a century; which are bringing to our shores this very year nearly a million of people; and which are very sensibly modifying the political aspirations and possibilities of all Europe. In this matter, we are to make a change." 13 Cong. Rec. 1738 (1882).

It was not a transformation that Hawley could embrace. The American beacon pointed only in the direction of Europe, and not of Asia. The senator considered such an abandonment of the nation's legacy to be repressive, worthy of being placed on a short list of Congress' worst moments:

"It may be that this bill will be quoted with the alien and sedition law, the repeal of the Missouri Compromise, and the fugitive-slave law, as an illustration of the truth that fifty million sovereigns can be as despotic as one sovereign." 13 Cong. Rec. 1738 (1882).

Senator Hawley challenged the premise that the Miller bill was necessary to stave off civil unrest. Such language was a dangerous basis on which to legislate. It clearly implied that Chinese should be banned not because they had taken action to threaten public safety, but because their mere presence, however peaceful, would be unwelcome and would generate violence against them.

"That if the Chinaman comes our citizens may insult him, they may raise tumults, trample upon law, that perhaps they may kill him, or perhaps they may forcibly expel him, or they may so hedge him about with fear that he would rush down in despair to the seacoast and beg to be transported home . . . . His coming here is going to make us so angry, so fierce, that we will rise up in rebellion and trample upon our own laws and wrong this man who is not charged with any dangerous purpose whatsoever." 13 Cong. Rec. 1739 (1882).

Hawley enlightened colleagues on the record of the Angell Treaty (*Appen-*

dix 5) negotiations. Pending legislation did not reflect bilateral understandings. Chinese negotiators had been very clear they would oppose prohibiting the immigration of laborers. The American commissioners, promising goodwill in treaty implementation, did not insist on it, and had settled for less restrictive language.

The bill overreached U.S. treaty rights, argued Hawley, because its effect was to prohibit immigration, even though the United States had agreed not to do that:

"These official papers of the commissioners to the Secretary of State show that nothing in the nature of prohibition was intended. But suspension for twenty years is prohibition, and it is intended as such. The bill before us is very clearly a harsh and extravagant interpretation of that treaty, just what the Chinese commissioners feared might be made, and just what our commissioners assured them our just and magnanimous nation ought to be trusted not to do." 13 Cong. Rec. 1739 (1882).

The Burlingame Treaty (*Appendix 2*) was an American initiative, Hawley said. It was undertaken to promote United States purposes in the Far East, by enhancing American commercial and missionary interests in China. "To gain these things, the civilized world bombarded China, and they granted them; and the civilized world, this part of it, appears to be sick of its bargain." 13 Cong. Rec. 1739 (1882).

Proponents of Chinese exclusion had repeatedly asserted Congress' "right" to enact restrictions on Chinese laborers. Following the Angell Treaty ratification, such a right of exclusion was said to be based on the treaty. But having a right still required care in how it was exercised. "We carelessly assert a right to do wrong things," Hawley observed. 13 Cong. Rec. 1739 (1882).

Senator Hawley urged that, if immigration and naturalization limits were imposed, they must be based other than on race or national origin. To act for racial reasons was to decimate the foundations of the American republic:

"This bill is part of a certain reactionary policy. Make your conditions what you please for immigration and for attaining citizenship, but make them such that a man can overcome them. Do not base them upon accidents of humanity. If you say that a man shall not come in or shall not become a citizen until he can read or write our language, until he can pass an examination upon the Constitution, or until he shall have accumulated a thousand dollars, or any one of many qualifications and limitations that easily suggest themselves, you still leave it open to any man in the world to overcome this and come in, but if you say that he shall not have this, that, or the other right because he is yellow, or because he is black, or because he was born in a certain place, I hold that it is a departure from the republican doctrine. I hold it to be the sound doctrine of a republican government that you have no right to base your limitations on mere accidents of humanity." 13 Cong. Rec. 1740 (1882).

Next to speak was Senator John P. Jones (R–NV), who had addressed the Senate during the opening day of the debate. He wanted to know, 'is this superior race of ours afraid of the competition with this inferior Chinese race?'" 13 Cong. Rec. 1741 (1882).

Jones assured senators that whites were up to the challenge. Whites inherently loved liberty, had fought for it for centuries, and were of the sort of stock that made good citizens, but Chinese came from different roots:

"Every fiber in their heart, every corpuscle in their blood has been molded in the spirit of despotism under which they have lived uncomplainingly." 13 Cong. Rec. 1741 (1882).

Being subjects of the emperor, in a country without democratic traditions or institutions, had left the Chinese totally unsuited for self-government, the Nevada senator insisted:

"The Chinese have lived in this condition, which conduces to crime, for unnumbered centuries. History, written and monumental, shows the Chinese Empire substantially as it exists today antedates the pyramids, antedates the law written on tablets of stone." 13 Cong. Rec. 1741 (1882).

There could be found outstanding persons of any race, but populations had to be evaluated as a whole, not by the achievements of exceptional individuals, Jones opined. How, then, to judge Chinese within the context of the modern world? Senator Jones was pitiless in his assessment:

"Oppression, barbarism, degradation. A civilization purely material, nothing spiritual about it; everything commutable in money; no injury that a man can inflict on a Chinaman that he is not willing to take a money compensation for; no sensibility to be ruffled; no honor to be outraged. I do not speak of individuals, but I speak of race." 13 Cong. Rec. 1741 (1882).

Unlike liberty-loving whites, the mercenary Chinese were incapable of creating democratic institutions or living under them. Senators like George Hoar (R–MA) and Joseph Hawley (R–CT), who had spoken confidently about prospects for Chinese assimilation, were deluding themselves, said Jones:

"Free institutions are only possible with the favored races. It is not because they are a monopoly of the favored races, but because no other race is capable of creating them . . . . [T]he favored races, as I said before, are the only ones capable of free government; and it is because we monopolize the capability that we monopolize the free institutions." 13 Cong. Rec. 1742 (1882).

Jones worried openly about the effects of further race mixing in the United States. History had demonstrated the problems with introducing into America any race besides Caucasian. Jones asked the other senators:

"Does anyone suppose for an instant that if the African were not in this country today we should be anxious to welcome him? Does any reflecting man believe he is an advantage to this country? Is it not true that if the country were occupied by smaller numbers of intelligent men of our own creative race that the country would be stronger than it is? What caused the intellectual stagnation that was observable everywhere in the South outside of politics, the bar, and the pulpit?" 13 Cong. Rec. 1744 (1882).

Senator Jones attributed such dormancy to the idea that Southern labor was performed by a "servile race," which had driven the "great creative race." 13 Cong. Rec. 1744 (1882). He analogized Chinese labor to slave labor, generating similarly degrading effects on society. As bad as those results were in the case of Africans, at least that population was able to assimilate once afforded an opportunity to do so:

"The Negro possesses in a marked degree all the humane and affectionate sympathies. He easily becomes attached to those with whom he lives and is loyal to them. He adopts our customs and is proud to imitate them . . . ." 13 Cong. Rec. 1744 (1882).

While African immigration had its problems, Jones said, an influx of Chinese would be worse. Because they would not willingly integrate into American society, and possessed cunning personalities, Chinese were a greater danger to the country than Africans:

"The skill of the Chinese enables them to invade more of the industrial pursuits than the Negro is capable of invading. Deft and subtle and able in manipulation, the Chinese can be utilized in almost any kind of factory, but his race is socially more incongruous to ours and less capable of assimilation with us than is the Negro race." 13 Cong. Rec. 1744–45 (1882).

Jones attributed the longevity of Chinese history, including the capacity of the Chinese to outlast other civilizations, to the benefits of racial homogeneity. Creating barriers that promoted racial purity, Americans could realize similar benefits for themselves, he insisted.

After additional debate, Senator John Ingalls (R–KS) attacked the Farley amendment that barred Chinese naturalization. He believed the proposal violated treaty commitments that Chinese in America would be treated equally with citizens of most favored nations:

"This amendment proposes not only to exclude from naturalization as citizens of the United States the class that is regarded by citizens of the Pacific Coast as objectionable, but declares that those Chinese who are here with the concurrence of all parties shall be excluded from the advantages which have been guaranteed to them solemnly by two treaties; that is to say, that a Chinese merchant or a Chinese trader or a Chinese scholar or a Chinese traveler, who may come here for purposes admitted by everybody to be innocent and lawful, shall be excluded from naturalization by the courts of the States and by the courts of the nation if they desire to become naturalized and are declared by the courts to be proper subjects of naturalization." 13 Cong. Rec. 1746 (1882).

Senator James Farley (D–CA) responded that Chinese coming after the Burlingame Treaty should not have had expectations of citizenship. The Burlingame Treaty contained a disclaimer, which had been insisted upon by the Senate. The disclaimer, which was unusual because treaties do not themselves grant naturalization rights, nevertheless provided:

"Nothing herein contained shall be held to confer naturalization upon citizens of the United States in China or citizens of China in the United States." 13 Cong. Rec. 1746 (1882).

Notwithstanding this policy directive, Farley noted, courts had not treated Chinese naturalization uniformly. In California, courts had interpreted existing law to bar naturalization of Chinese. But courts in some other jurisdictions, such as Massachusetts, had been willing to naturalize Chinese. If a Massachusetts court naturalized a Chinese, that person would have full citizenship rights that could be exercised in California. Farley wanted to ensure that circumstance, so unwanted by his constituents, could not materialize. He was adamant about putting the Senate on record and resolving the naturalization issue:

"If the people of the United States are in favor of admitting the Chinese to citizenship, let the Senate vote down this amendment; if they are opposed to it, let them settle that question now." 13 Cong. Rec. 1747 (1882).

Senator John Sherman (R–OH) took the floor. A former secretary of the treasury (1877–1881) and future secretary of state (1897–1898), Sherman also served three terms in the House of Representatives (1855–1861), and a total of thirty-two years in the Senate (1861–1877 and 1881–1897). During the 1880s, he was also a perennial contender for the Republican presidential nomination, which he never received. Sherman wrote and introduced the Sherman Antitrust Act in 1890.

On account of his own visits to the Pacific Coast and in light of the Senate debate, Sherman said, he was not opposed in principle to "some fair, just, prudent measure to restrain immigration from China to the United States." He also believed "every nation has an inherent right to describe who shall come and share the advantages of its institutions and its citizenship." 13 Cong. Rec. 1747 (1882).

That said, Senator Sherman was disturbed by the new direction in U.S. immigration policy. To ensure the Senate understood the enormity of the policy change at hand, Sherman framed the situation:

"It has always been the public policy of this country from the very foundation of the Government to open the doors wide to the immigration of foreigners from all the nations of the world. Never before, I suppose, in our history, has such a bill been presented to the Congress of the United States." 13 Cong. Rec. 1747 (1882).

Sherman noted that one-half of America's fifty million persons were not native-born. This demographic resulted from deliberate openess to immigration:

"It has been the public policy of this country to invite foreigners from all lands to come here. We have not only given them our public lands upon their declaring their intention to become citizens, we have made them in a very brief period citizens with the right to vote and hold office; we have protected them in their rights as against the country of their nativity; we have negotiated treaties for their protection against the rights of their parent country; we have threatened violence to protect them in their rights; and we have done the utmost that we could not only to encourage their immigration but to protect and foster the immigrants." 13 Cong. Rec. 1748 (1882).

By passing exclusion legislation, thus adopting a policy "to prevent and prohibit," Congress would reverse course. Sherman argued it was a move that should be undertaken cautiously:

"When we in Congress say that no portion of the people of Asia, no portion of more than one-half of the whole people in the civilized world shall come to this country, we take a grave and important step, and we ought to do it with care and deliberation." 13 Cong. Rec. 1748 (1882).

Such care was not being taken in the Miller bill, Sherman argued. Instead, Congress was acting in "hot haste in a new policy that is foreign to the habits of our people and of our country." 13 Cong. Rec. 1748 (1882).

The Angell Treaty allowed for immigration to be limited, but not halted. But the effect of the twenty-year ban was prohibition, the senator concluded. Exclusion's proponents were claiming to legislate against contract labor, but Sherman considered their remedy disproportionate and overbroad:

"It seems to me we have in this bill gone too far, and this bill has been framed not with the spirit of guarding the people of the Pacific Coast against a threatened inundation of a pagan horde of contract laborers but in the spirit of reversing the whole policy of this Government, of excluding all foreigners under a hue and cry against the Chinese race, however skilled, however useful, however meritorious they may be." 13 Cong. Rec. 1748 (1882).

After a short period of additional debate, a vote was taken on the Farley naturalization amendment to the Senate Foreign Relations Committee substitute. Twenty-six senators supported it, including such outspoken proponents as Senators Farley, Miller, Teller, and Jones. Twenty-two opposed it, among whom were Senators Hoar, Dawes, and Ingalls. Twenty-six senators did not vote.

Immediately thereafter, a vote occurred on Grover's (D–OR) amendment to clarify that the term "Chinese laborer" should be construed to mean both skilled and unskilled workers and Chinese employed in mining. The vote very closely paralleled the tally on the Farley amendment. Twenty-five senators voted aye, 22 voted nay, and 29 did not vote.

Senator Joseph Brown (D–GA) proposed an amendment to strike a mandate that Chinese persons admitted to the country had to carry documentation at all times and produce such "to the proper authorities of the United States whenever lawfully demanded." Brown was concerned about the unique requirements being imposed on the Chinese:

"We have agreed solemnly by the treaty that a Chinese subject shall have the same rights, privileges, immunities, and exemptions which are accorded to a British subject or a German subject, or a subject of any other nation. We require this passport and all these burdensome provisions of the subject of no other nation on earth, but propose, if the bill passes, to require these conditions hereafter of the Chinese subject." 13 Cong. Rec. 1750 (1882).

The Brown amendment was subject to a division vote, a mechanism rarely seen in the modern Senate, in which senators on each side of the question stand to be tallied. The amendment initially failed by 20 ayes to 22 nays. Brown indicated he would press for a roll call. However, Senator John Miller (R–CA) said that the amendment was harmless and that he would not contest it. Accordingly, the Brown amendment was adopted by voice vote.

For the time being, the documentation requirement was put to rest. But it would return ten years later during 1892 consideration of exclusion renewal legislation and then the result would be opposite (*Chapter Eight*).

Thus far, the Senate had been acting as in the Senate Committee of the Whole. The next step was for S. 71, as amended, to be reported to the full Senate. Thereafter, further amendments could be proposed. By voice vote, the Senate Committee of the Whole reported to the full Senate S. 71, as amended by the

Committee on Foreign Relations substitute, with the Farley (naturalization) and Grover (laborer definition) amendments included, and minus the documentation provision stricken by Brown.

In the full Senate, Senator Ingalls again offered his amendment to reduce the term of restriction from twenty years to ten. After a brief debate, the amendment came to a vote and failed. Twenty senators voted aye, 21 voted nay, and 35 did not vote. Of this tally, 18 Republicans voted in the affirmative as did 2 Independents. No Democrats were in favor. Voting in the negative were 4 Republicans and 17 Democrats.

No further floor amendments were offered. By voice vote, the Senate concurred in the action of the Committee of the Whole. The stage was set for final passage of S. 71, as amended.

Before the vote, Republican Senator George Edmunds of Vermont again spoke. Because the twenty-year exclusion term was tantamount to a prohibition, Edmunds complained that the bill violated the spirit of the Angell Treaty. Moreover, the legislation swept uniformly across the Chinese people without regard to individual differences or other ameliorating considerations:

"If he is a man who works not only with his hands as a servile laborer, but who also works like the intelligent mechanic of New England, like the Irishman or German man, who has brought his skill from another country to contribute to his own welfare and ours here, he is tabooed, with his family and his children, and is absolutely excluded for twenty years, the whole of the lifetime, for practical purposes, of any family anywhere on the face of the earth, from seeking the benefit of our free institutions and contributing his knowledge, and his skill, and his intelligence to the welfare of our own people and to the welfare of himself, when there is room on this continent yet for us all." 13 Cong. Rec. 1752 (1882).

Following eight days of Senate floor debate, the vote on final passage was 29 senators aye, 15 senators nay, and 32 senators absent. Of the votes in favor, there were 8 Republicans and 21 Democrats. Of the votes against, there were 13 Republicans, 1 Democrat, and 1 Independent.

At 5:40 p.m. on Thursday, March 9, 1882, the Senate adjourned. House debate on the bill would begin five days later. Although House proceedings are normally much more circumscribed than those of the Senate, the House consideration of Chinese exclusion legislation would be unusually lengthy.

CHAPTER FOUR

The Twenty-Year Exclusion Debate in the House of Representatives

"Instead of increasing, he lessens the resources of our country. Instead of building up, he tears down. Being in our midst, he invades and destroys our industries; he absorbs all from us he can, and in return invites us to share only his vices. Is it a people like this we should affiliate with? No! A thousand times no!"

—**Representative Romualdo Pacheco (R–CA)**
13 Cong. Rec. 2211 (1882)

§4.0 Overview

- S.71 considered in the 47th Congress of the United States (1881–1883)
- House Party Division: 151 Republicans, 128 Democrats, 14 Independents
- President: Chester A. Arthur (R) (1881–1885)

After the Senate passed the twenty-year exclusion legislation in March 1882, the House took up the measure. Unlike typical House debate, which is often far more compressed than that of the Senate, the contentious House proceedings on the twenty-year bill lasted for seven days.

The House passed the Senate bill without amendment, sending it to President Chester A. Arthur for approval. Notwithstanding enhanced U.S. rights to restrict Chinese immigration, as negotiated in the 1880 Angell Treaty, the president considered the legislation too sweeping. Believing Congress violated the treaty's spirit, Arthur vetoed the bill. His veto was sustained.

❖ ❖ ❖ ❖ ❖

§4.10 House Debate, March 14, 1882: "Plant a cancer in your own country"

Under consideration in the House Committee of the Whole, S. 71 as passed by the Senate.

On March 14, 1882, shortly after the House convened, Representative Horace Page (R–CA) moved consideration of S. 71, the twenty-year exclusion legislation that had just passed the Senate.

The House clerk read the Senate bill. By unanimous consent, the speeches that followed were limited to one hour per each House member recognized, but there was no overall ceiling on the length of debate. Page served as the House bill manager. The first member to speak was Representative William H. Calkins (R–IN), who was in the House between 1877 and 1884.

Calkins was the only House member to deliver a major speech on March 14, 1882. He had worried that congressional action could impair bilateral commercial relations, but had satisfied himself that trade retaliation was unlikely. China would be pragmatic, conducting commercial relations on the basis of economic realities rather than in response to immigration policy.

Free to legislate without such concerns, Calkins pressed to exclude a people who he said were in the United States for only pecuniary reasons, who had no inclination to adopt Christianity, nor interest in American democratic institutions. The Chinese already in America had left little legacy behind, Calkins said, other than infectious disease:

"These Chinese have brought with them to this country that loathsome disease known as leprosy . . . but it does not stop there. Ninety-nine out of every hundred of them have smallpox, and that is testified to by those who are well qualified to give information upon the subject."

Calkins also likened the work arrangements for male Chinese laborers to coolie servitude and said that the few women who had come to America were, in effect, prostitutes:

"There are perhaps two thousand women who have been brought here and are now on the Pacific slope, but not as wives. They are slaves and fill baser positions than that."

Representative Calkins summed up. Whatever qualms he had initially felt about passing a bill had been overcome. The appeals voiced from the Pacific states must get a positive response. Calkins' closing argument was notable for its crassness:

"Wherever they come they spread mildew and rot throughout the entire community. And yet, upon a mere notion of humanitarianism, you throw open the doors because you say the sentiment of this great Republic is to invite the people of other nations to these shores. By doing so you plant a cancer in your own country that will eat out its life and destroy it from among the nations of the earth . . . .

"You cannot justify your action upon the proposition that you must protect your industry and your labor, if at the same time you open wide the doors on the Pacific slope against the protest of every man and every woman and every child in that section, and allow these people to come in upon them like the locusts of Egypt.

"With these facts before us, with a bill the policy of which is simply to protect our people against that which they say is surely and certainly sapping and destroying all their industries, which is proving a sure source of pauperism and of crime, which is engrafting upon this great people the disease of leprosy, which is also disseminating among them other diseases worse than those mentioned— with all these facts staring you in the face, can you upon a simple question of sentiment say that you will extend no relief to these people? Can you reconcile that with your conscience?" 13 Cong. Rec. 1904 (1882).

After Calkins sat down, the House adjourned.

§4.20 House Debate, March 15, 1882: "No more regard for his oath"

Under consideration in the House Committee of the Whole, S. 71, as passed by the Senate.

After the House convened on Wednesday, March 15, 1882, Representative Horace Page (R–CA), who had interests in mining, was first to speak. Page served five terms in Congress, between 1873 and 1883.

The Chinese were unfit for citizenship, Page began, and the United States should bar entry of persons not permitted to naturalize. He asked his House colleagues:

"How absurd would be the idea of undertaking to naturalize a Chinaman? When the question would be put to him, 'are you attached to the laws and Constitution of the United States' what could be his answer? Why, sir, the whole proceeding would be a farce . . . ." 13 Cong. Rec. 1932 (1882).

According to Page, a large influx of Europeans was acceptable because such immigrants assimilated easily. Within a generation, descendants of European immigrants were indistinguishable from children of native-born persons. Beyond doubt, it was desirable for Europeans to go to America and valuable for the United States to attract them. But such societal benefits seemed not to apply when the immigrants were Chinese. Indeed, he said, the presence of a heavy Chinese population repelled whites from California:

"This is not a fight where the fittest survives. It is a question of whether we can maintain our nationality, whether we can maintain the peace and quiet and dignity of the State of California, provided there be nothing in that State but Chinese." 13 Cong. Rec. 1933 (1882).

Page called upon both parties to be true to what he claimed were 1880 platform commitments to control Chinese immigration. Page, a Republican, argued that these pledges were so much in agreement that the Chinese issue had been removed from the realm of partisan politics.

To establish his case, Page spoke of correspondence attributed to the late President James Garfield, a Republican. Attempting to undermine Garfield's 1880 presidential campaign, Democratic campaign workers had distributed in California what became known as the Morey letter, allegedly written on January 23, 1880, by then-Representative Garfield (R–OH) to one H.L. Morey, of the Employers' Union in Lynn, Massachusetts. The letter, which Garfield claimed was a forgery, purported to demonstrate that the future president had a lenient attitude toward Chinese immigration. The political stunt of circulating the Morey letter demonstrated how Chinese immigration had become part of the political joust between Democrats and Republicans. The text of the forged Morey letter read as follows:

"Dear Sir:

Yours in relation to the Chinese problem came duly to hand. I take it that the question of employees is only a question of private and corporate economy, and individuals or companies have the right to buy labor where they can get it cheapest.

We have a treaty with the Chinese Government which should be religiously kept until its provisions are abrogated by the action of the General Government, and I am not prepared to say that it should be abrogated until our great manufacturing and corporate interests are conserved in the matter of labor." 13 Cong. Rec. 1935 (1882).

Although not proven genuine, the Morey letter damaged Garfield's credibility in the Pacific region, because it generated suspicion among white voters that Democrats were more serious about controlling Chinese immigration than were Republicans. The Democratic presidential candidate in the 1880 election, Winfield Hancock, narrowly outpolled Garfield in California and Nevada, and almost overtook him in Oregon.

Garfield's true position was quite to the contrary, Page insisted. Republicans were ready to fight for exclusion. To demonstrate this, Page cited a passage of Garfield's letter accepting the Republican presidential nomination. In the excerpt, Garfield had contrasted the Chinese influx to the migration of Europeans to America:

"The recent movement of the Chinese to our Pacific Coast partakes but little of the qualities of such immigration, either in its purposes or its results. It is too much like an importation to be welcomed without restriction; too much like an invasion to be looked upon with solicitude." 13 Cong. Rec. 1936 (1882).

Unwilling to be outflanked on immigration by the Democrats, Page proclaimed:

"I am proud as a Republican to stand in this presence and endorse as the Republican Party of this great nation endorsed not only its platform at Chicago but the eloquent utterances of its great leader. I am here as a Republican to do my full duty in carrying out that promise to its fullest extent." 13 Cong. Rec. 1936 (1882).

By excluding the Chinese, Page insisted, if elected president Garfield would have done "no injustice to the grand claims of our country and its traditions that this was the 'land of the free, the home of the brave,' and the asylum of the down-trodden and oppressed of all nationalities." The Chinese were a people apart, because they allegedly practiced a different religion, they defied laws of morality, and their women were not virtuous. In addition, they were utterly dishonest:

"Why, sir, a Chinaman has no more regard for his oath than a savage who never saw a white man in his life. He has no regard for it absolutely. A Chinaman would not swear to the truth if it were profitable for him to swear to a lie. That is the characteristic of their race and of those of them who have come to our shores." 13 Cong. Rec. 1936 (1882).

Additional debate followed on the benefits of a twenty-year exclusion period as against a lesser ban. Representative William Whitney Rice (R–MA) took the House floor. Successor to George Hoar's (R–MA) seat in the House of Representatives, Rice served in the House between 1877 and 1887. He challenged Page's claim to represent the Republican position on Chinese immigration, laying bare a significant fissure between eastern and western Republicans on the issue. As debate and floor voting would demonstrate, the split on Chinese immigration was serious, but was confined to Republicans. Democrats were unified against the Chinese.

Rice mocked the idea that the volume of Chinese immigration confronted Congress with an emergency. He noted that the 1880 census had shown a total Chinese population of 105,000 out of 50 million Americans (two-tenths of 1 percent), that between 1870 and 1880, a total of 42,000 Chinese had come to America, and that in 1880 itself 20,000 Chinese had arrived and 10,000 had departed, leaving a net population gain of 10,000 for the year. This influx was modest, said Rice, so Congress was responding not to a real crisis but to an exaggerated distress call from the sandlots of San Francisco.

Rice insisted that Page spoke only for a faction of Republicans and not for the whole party:

"That gentleman is a good Republican. He has assumed today to speak for the Democratic side of this House. He cannot speak for the Republicans. And the reason he cannot speak for the Republican side is that, although he still represents one great wing of the party, that wing has been thrown into a panic." 13 Cong. Rec. 1939 (1882).

Rice claimed that Page distorted the Republican Party's 1880 platform's true meaning, inferring stark clarity where there was nuance. By this distortion, Page was grafting Democratic Party doctrine onto that of the Republicans:

"It is the Democratic platform that says 'no immigration'; it is the Republican platform that recognizes the right of every nation to protect itself against pauperism, disease, and crime, and it says 'restrict and regulate immigration so it shall not endanger the country or any portion of it' . . . .

"That is what the Republican platform means; not to prohibit immigration, not to suspend it but to regulate it; to restrict it, to control it, and to make it, instead of a curse, instead of a danger, a blessing and a source of prosperity." 13 Cong. Rec. 1939 (1882).

Representative Rice mused that China would retaliate by cutting the United States off from commercial relations:

"Sir, the Chinese are shrewd, they are human; they know well enough who are their friends, and they know well enough who are their enemies . . . .

"Mr. Speaker, the adoption of this bill would shut the doors of China to American influence and American trade." 13 Cong. Rec. 1939 (1882).

Rice was sure the bill violated treaty obligations with China. Passing such legislation would blacken the reputation of the United States internationally, and call into question America's trustworthiness as a treaty partner:

"Mr. Speaker, in old times the words *punica fides* were the synonym for national treachery and faithlessness. If after negotiations between China and the United States, under cover of a treaty provision modifying an old and existing treaty so that we may suspend within reasonable limits immigration of laborers from China, we declare that immigration unlawful and suspend it absolutely for twenty years, I fear we shall do much toward writing our name over that of ancient Carthage on the annals of national perfidy. I object to this bill, because I believe it is in conflict, if not with the words of the treaty, at all events with the spirit." 13 Cong. Rec. 1940 (1882).

Finally, Rice criticized the disparity between the bill and America's founding doctrine that all men are created equal:

"I do not see any reason at the end of our first hundred years to erase that legend and write over it another . . . .

"Against this bill as it now stands, against its essence and spirit, I can only utter my final protest, and say that I know it must fail because all the principles of justice and of equity, those fixed stars whose serene light falls upon Asia as well as America in all their courses, fight against it, and as surely as they were set in their places by the hand of God and made eternal they will in the end prevail." 13 Cong. Rec. 1941 (1882).

With that, House proceedings of March 15, 1882, drew to a close.

§4.30 House Debate, March 16, 1882: "The repulsive specter of Asiatic squalor"

Under consideration, S. 71, as passed by the Senate.

Representative Albert Shelby Willis (D–KY), the prime mover of the vetoed Fifteen Passenger bill of 1879, opened the March 16, 1882, debate in the House of Representatives. He suggested that sentiment in Congress had progressed steadily in the direction of exclusion. If the argument centered on the length of the restriction rather than on justification of exclusion, the critics of the policy had already conceded the argument:

"As the gentlemen who oppose this bill announce their willingness to vote for a five or ten year suspension, the principle of the present bill, its rightfulness, necessity, and propriety are admitted. At the very threshold of this discussion, therefore, there is cause for congratulation." 13 Cong. Rec. 1973 (1882).

Willis launched into a review of the history of Chinese in America. Such immigrants were welcomed in California at first, "as a unique addition to the society and a valuable ally in the development of the material resources of their new home." Indeed, Willis added, the 1862 California legislature issued a report encouraging more Chinese to come and proposed to grant citizenship rights to the Chinese already present. 13 Cong. Rec. 1973 (1882).

Then public opinion turned, and the Chinese, "by reason of their sordid, selfish, immoral, and non-amalgamating habits, came to be regarded as a standing menace to the social, industrial, and political institutions of the State." 13 Cong. Rec. 1973 (1882). Appeals to the national government in Washington, DC, followed, Willis added, culminating in a memorial to Congress by a special committee of the California legislature urging action to limit Chinese immigration. As a consequence, Congress conducted its own investigation, through the work of Senator Morton's joint committee, which held extensive hearings on the Pacific Coast. Willis quoted from the conclusion of the Morton Committee's (*§ 2.10*) majority report, which foresaw endless numbers of Chinese overwhelming local institutions:

"[T]he committee believes the influx of the Chinese is a standing menace to republican institutions upon the Pacific Coast and the existence there of Christian civilization . . . . This problem is too important to be treated with indifference. It must be solved, unless our Pacific possessions are to be ultimately given over to a race alien in all its tendencies, which will make of them practically provinces of China rather than States of the Union." 13 Cong. Rec. 1974 (1882).

Following issuance of the Morton Committee report on February 27, 1877, a series of events unfolded. These included passage and veto of the Fifteen Passenger bill (*Chapter Two*), further congressional appeals to President Rutherford B. Hayes for Burlingame Treaty renegotiation, the Angell Treaty amendments to the Burlingame Treaty, and finally the twenty-year exclusion bill already passed by the Senate (*Chapter Three*).

Willis traced his own path along this history. At first, he said, he had believed the uproar against the Chinese was the instigation of rabble-rousers, and he had been repelled:

"I thought that the cry of the Californians, 'the Chinese must go,' was an unjust, causeless, 'sandlot' cry; that it was the voice of ignorance, brutality, and fanaticism; and that the vast majority of the sober-minded and intelligent people of the Pacific slope regarded the Chinese as a frugal, peaceable, and industrious race, worthy of respect and entitled to protection." 13 Cong. Rec. 1974 (1882).

But the Kentucky Representative did not take long to reverse himself. Without really explaining his about-face, Willis noted that within a few years he had gravitated to the opposite point of view.

"I do now believe that the Chinese are a discordant and disturbing element in society; that they are an enemy to our progressive civilization, an alien, indigestible, and destroying substance in our body-politic; that the hostility which has manifested itself is the outgrowth, not of passion and prejudice, but rests upon calm, deliberate intelligence and judgment . . . ." 13 Cong. Rec. 1974 (1882).

Willis insisted that the legislation was a reasonable execution of the Angell Treaty, and that Congress should not worry about any resulting hardships. The treaty itself furnished a way to resolve grievances. It expressly provided for the Chinese minister in Washington to bring implementation problems to the attention of the American government.

Willis was adamant that pleas for relief arose from mainstream political forces, rather than from "hoodlum" or "riffraff" elements. He noted that four state legislatures had petitioned Congress for legislation to control Chinese immigration, and further cited the pro-exclusion results of the California and Nevada referenda. Willis asked the House:

"Will you heed the voices of these states, coming to you unanimously through their representatives in both Houses of Congress and through the more authoritative resolutions of their legislative assemblies, or will you reject their united testimony and suffer the dead body of an effete civilization to block the highway of their progress? Will you permit the repulsive specter of Asiatic squalor, vice, and servitude to stand at the gateways of the West to drive back the teeming millions of Caucasian immigrants who are now pressing toward its fertile plains? If you will, you do it against their best interests and in the face of their solemn protest." 13 Cong. Rec. 1975 (1882).

Representative Willis reinforced the arguments that Horace Page (R–CA) had made about the Democratic and Republican platforms. Willis contended the platforms proved that opposition to the Chinese was bipartisan, and asked whether "it can be denied that the free, unprejudiced, deliberate, and almost unanimous judgment of the United States is adverse to Chinese immigration?" 13 Cong. Rec. 1976 (1882).

Willis concluded with a broad, wholesale denunciation of Chinese people. To him, the Chinese were an alien and deeply pernicious element, unfit to be amalgamated into the American social structure:

"The Chinaman, whether as a laborer, as a member of society, or of the body-politic, is an undesirable and dangerous element in any community. Crowded, huddled together, forty or fifty in a room not larger than would accommodate with decency and comfort one man with a family, discarding or disregarding all the usual ordinary appliances of personal civilization as to diet and clothing; cooking, eating, and sleeping in the same apartment, they have succeeded in reducing the cost of living to a minimum, and thus wherever located have forced the laboring classes to the wall. As laborers, therefore, the Chinese can only exist to the exclusion or degradation of all others in the community.

"Nor as members of society are they less objectionable. Their personal habits consequent upon their mode of life in these squalid dens, their low, groveling ideas of virtue and religion, and their peculiar social views have been commented upon and condemned by every nation with whom they have come in contact . . . .

"The introduction, therefore, of a class of men like the Chinese, who are without homes or families, whose education and habits disqualify them for citizenship, whose cheap wages degrade labor, and whose want of morality and self-respect unfit them for society, is fraught with great danger to our republican institutions, and should be promptly and effectually checked." 13 Cong. Rec. 1976-77 (1882).

Representative George W. Cassidy (D–NV) was in the House from 1881 to 1885. His older brother, Christopher Columbus Cassidy (d. 1883) had been a miner in Dutch Flat, California, where the Chinese had actively been mining. (See George W. Cassidy Papers, University of Nevada Reno, Special Collections No. 98–06). Representative Cassidy was a newspaper publisher prior to serving in Congress, which contributed to his perspective. He dismissed the contention that the twenty-year exclusion period was excessive and would disturb commercial relations with China:

"We have fixed, as we think, a reasonable time during which coolies shall not come to our shores. They have had free run of this country for thirty years, coming and going at will, and now we say they must give us twenty years of quiet and rest." 13 Cong. Rec. 1978 (1882).

An additional argument opponents had made was that the bill violated fundamental equality principles expressed in the Declaration of Independence. Cassidy was not persuaded. Recalling that slavery was legal at the time of independence and had remained so for several decades thereafter, Cassidy said that the Declaration of Independence was not about equality. Thomas Jefferson's true purpose in the Declaration of Independence was to attack the British monarch's claim to stand superior to other men:

"To make himself clearly understood, he had to assail the divine-right theory in straightforward terms; he had to say that 'all men are created equal;' that no man has a right to set up as a hereditary sovereign to rule over a people . . . ." 13 Cong. Rec. 1978 (1882).

Representative Cassidy declared the Chinese as unworthy of American citizenship, even though he claimed that race was not the basis of his conclusion. As Cassidy saw it, the problem was one of Chinese culture:

"We are not legislating against the Chinaman because his skin is yellow; we have no objection to that; but we are against him because of the civilization he brings with him and which he refuses to abandon after years of residence among us . . . . Your naturalization laws as they stand today exclude the Chinaman from citizenship, and we say that if he is not desirable as a citizen, he is not desirable in any other sense or for any other purpose. They are a people without a religion, without a conscience, and without a God. There is no honesty among the men or virtue among the women." 13 Cong. Rec. 1978 (1882).

Colleagues in the House of Representatives had spoken of the economic and cultural benefits to be derived from robust trade with China. But Cassidy considered these benefits to be meaningless:

"I deny that our people have anything to learn from Asia; I deny they can be benefited or intellectually lifted up by the contact, and I also deny the advantages to the two countries are mutual and reciprocal. We may impart in some degree the examples of our civilization and energy and enterprise, but we can get nothing in return for them." 13 Cong. Rec. 1978 (1882).

Cassidy also accused the Chinese of foisting drugs and disease on America, transporting a stagnant civilization, as well as bringing about labor degradation and youth demoralization. If they were ostracized and shunned, the Chinese had brought such problems on themselves. Democrats were prepared to make good on their 1880 platform pledge, the Nevadan insisted, and the call of the House would demonstrate it.

Representative Ezra Taylor (R–OH) took the floor. Taylor succeeded James Garfield in the House of Representatives and served there from the end of 1880 until 1893. Taylor denounced the bill:

"Let me tell this House why I oppose it. It is simply because it is unnecessary, and being unnecessary, it is dangerous, unspeakably dangerous." 13 Cong. Rec. 1980 (1882).

Taylor argued that the legislation was filled with internal contradictions. He offered an example:

"Prostrated by a disease that is inbred in the Chinaman, gotten there by their close corporation at home, with their blood flowing through their veins in poisoned streams, they are still so energetic and so persistent and such eternal laborers that by the hand of labor alone they are to take possession of this country. Mr. Speaker, both of these statements cannot be true." 13 Cong. Rec. 1981 (1882). Chinese in America had been struggling against all manner of legal and social barriers erected against them, and then faced the ironic argument that they could not assimilate. Taylor's anger grew:

"They do not assimilate! Here they have been for thirty years ever since they commenced coming to this country. Have they ever been invited to assimilate? Have they been treated in California at any time as if they could assimilate? For thirty years in the lifetime of a nation they have been there and the ban has been upon them.

"Thirty years in the life of the Chinese nation, surrounded with the wall that it is proposed now to erect around the United States . . . because they have not become acquainted with our language and race, or because they have not changed from paganism to Christianity, and from heathenism to civilization, when they were laboring under all the disadvantages that have been imposed upon them by onerous restrictions and hostilities, we are told they will not assimilate." 13 Cong. Rec. 1981 (1882).

Now the barriers constructed in California were to become national barriers, cried Taylor, building upon self-fulfilling policies to isolate the Chinese and to compound the discrimination they had long experienced in America.

Representative Taylor argued that the Chinese were being victimized because they were disenfranchised. Already, California courts had refused to naturalize the Chinese. More than 100,000 such immigrants were concentrated in that state, unable to vote. Taylor spoke about the consequences of such political exclusion:

"If a hundred thousand Chinese had the ballot in California, I know some men who would not give a single vote to passing a bill of this character." 13 Cong. Rec. 1982 (1882).

Taylor denounced race prejudice as being the legislation's true foundation. He recalled the bitter history of slave auctions, which occurred in the shadow of the Capitol itself:

"Mr. Speaker, in this city men, women, and children have gone from the auction block under the Stars and Stripes of this Government; under the same cry we hear today as against the Chinese, they have been sold within the sound of my voice under the hammer. The defense was that they were an inferior race— the only defense that could ever be given. The old slogan is heard again now. I meet it as the people in my little corner of the State of Ohio met it. I meet it by saying that inequality of condition or capacity is no excuse for inequality before the law." 13 Cong. Rec. 1983 (1882). Passage of exclusion legislation would set the country on a horrible course, Taylor warned. Open immigration had built America, but if the pending bill became law, the direction of national policy would be slammed into reverse:

"They propose to build a wall across the Golden Gate; they propose to exclude the oldest of the families of the earth; and I say to this House, I say to this country, that we know not when the next wall will be erected, nor where its foundations will be laid . . . . It is the first break in the levee; when the waters stream over it the crevasse will follow as the levee gives way. This is no imaginary thought of mine. Principles will always work out, and this is the principle you are adopting in this bill." 13 Cong. Rec. 1984 (1882).

Taylor feared that once this new path was taken, America would change fundamentally for the worse. Of exclusion legislation, he said:

"It revolutionizes our traditions. I would deem it a new country we will have after this bill becomes law, as changed from the old country we have today as our country would have been if the rebellion [of the Southern States in] 1861 had succeeded." 13 Cong. Rec. 1984 (1882).

After a brief amount of additional debate, the March 16, 1882, House proceedings on the exclusion bill came to an end.

§4.40 House Debate, March 18, 1882: "This exhaustless stream of yellow plague"

Under consideration in the House Committee of the Whole, S. 71, as passed by the Senate.

The House convened a Saturday session on March 18, 1882. The entirety of that day's debate was devoted to Chinese exclusion legislation. Representative Emory Speer (D–GA), who served in the House from 1879 to 1883 and was later a U.S. district court judge (1885–1918), asserted that the proposed twenty-year restriction was a reasonable exercise of U.S. rights under the Angell Treaty. Such rights must be implemented to prevent an "Asiatic invasion" from overwhelming white populations on the Pacific Coast. The numbers of Chinese were increasing at an alarming pace:

"We see that the Chinese are coming in at a rate of 1,000 per month more than they go out. We see that last year there came into California more than 18,000 of these strange people, and that in the first three months of this year 6,000 have sailed through the Golden Gate and landed upon our shores." 13 Cong. Rec. 2028 (1882).Regardless of party affiliation, Pacific region members of Congress, senators and representatives, had been united in support of exclusion. Their demands for relief deserved to be respected, Speer said.

In general, America welcomed immigrants, Speer conceded, but Chinese must not benefit from that lenient policy. A sample of Speer's extreme racial assessments follows:

"It is extremely unjust to the generous quick-witted, gallant son of Erin to compare him to the brethren of Ah Sin with his 'smile that is childlike and bland' . . . .

"And our German population, with its quick appreciation for the character of our institutions and its devotion to those principles of independence and free government which underlie them, their industry and frugality—is there any parallel between the German and the Chinaman? Not so, Mr. Speaker . . . .

"And I say that when gentlemen advance further and as an argument why the Chinese should be admitted to this country without limitation or restriction say that the colored man belongs to an inferior race, but has become a good citizen, ergo the Chinese will also, let me tell gentlemen, whatever has been said to the contrary, that the colored man is, in every element of manhood, far superior to the Chinaman." 13 Cong. Rec. 2029 (1882).

Speer was just warming up. In tones alternately patronizing and dismissive, he detailed for the House some of the differences he observed between Africans and Chinese:

"The Negro is deeply emotional; the Chinaman is as cold as one of his ugly stone idols. The Negro is sympathetic and kind-hearted; the Chinaman callous and indifferent . . . . The Negro is intensely religious in his nature . . . the Chinaman has no love of God whatever; his religion is fear of the devil." 13 Cong. Rec. 2029 (1882).

Representative Roswell G. Flower (D–NY) served a partial term in Congress from 1881 to 1883 and returned to the House between 1889 and 1891. He was governor of New York from January 1, 1892, to January 1, 1895. Flower considered Chinese immigration in the context of its effect on labor:

"The question before the House is, in my opinion, a simple one. It can be summed up in one word: shall we protect our labor or shall we allow it to be degraded to the coolie standard? This is what we are to decide upon: whether we shall afford protection to our laborers or whether we will be content to protect capital only, and leave labor out of consideration." 13 Cong. Rec. 2030 (1882).

Chinese immigration served rich economic interests that needed to employ significant numbers of cheap hands, said Flower, who described both ends of the market for Chinese workers:

"It is bought and brought by capital to increase capital; it is a wage-saving, labor-robbing, wage-reducing machine bought and worked in the interest of capital." 13 Cong. Rec. 2030 (1882).

Flower claimed that the Chinese were mercenaries and sojourners, rather than immigrants seeking to establish roots:

"He does not want to stay; none want to have him stay; all parties are glad when he goes. He does not come like other immigrants fleeing from oppression, but voluntarily comes to be oppressed . . . . Not like the European immigrant, who brings us wealth and a love of liberty, he comes to take wealth away, and to stamp upon labor the servile characteristics of his race." 13 Cong. Rec. 2030 (1882).

Representative Peter Deuster (D–WI) took the floor. Born in Germany in 1831, Deuster immigrated to the United States in 1847. He served in Congress from 1879 to 1885. Deuster emphasized that while European immigration was mainly undertaken for political and religious reasons, Chinese came purely for economic gain:

"There are no political refugees from China, nor social or religious migrations like those of the Puritans to New England, the Huguenots to the South, like the German, Irish, or other patriots of Europe to the United States, or the persecuted, shamefully treated Israelites of Russia, seeking an asylum and new home. The Chinaman is neither socially, morally, nor politically fit to assimilate with us." 13 Cong. Rec. 2031 (1882).

Later in the debate, Representative Campbell Berry (D–CA), a member from 1879 to 1883, asserted that as a Californian he understood the true character of Chinese immigration. He, himself, had often employed Chinese, but always had negotiated their hiring through agents from the Chinese Six Companies, rather than directly with the workers:

"To be brief, I will state that the fundamental proposition in this whole question is that you cannot introduce Chinese labor without introducing Chinese conditions." 13 Cong. Rec. 2034 (1882).

Chinese laborers were not free to arrange conditions of employment, but worked under conditions akin to servitude, Berry insisted. American labor could not successfully compete with such a workforce, and tensions arising from that situation had already produced social unrest.

Both political parties were pledged to come to the relief of the Pacific Coast. Some of Berry's colleagues might find that commitment inconvenient, but they were nonetheless bound:

"Every gentleman who gave his adhesion to either of those parties is pledged to this legislation, and the treaty was negotiated for the very purpose of this legislation." 13 Cong. Rec. 2034 (1882).

Representative Berry recalled the California and Nevada referenda that had been cited in the Senate debate. The voters had been overwhelming in favor of restricting immigration, he said, so much so that "their voice comes to us as that of one man . . . . This unanimous and active opposition to the presence of the Chinese is so extraordinary that it can but arrest attention." 13 Cong. Rec. 2034 (1882).

Emotional appeals as to the "common fatherhood of God" and the "brotherhood of man" had no place in a discussion of Chinese immigration, said Berry. The moment had come to put such sentiments to rest:

"Being firm in the belief that the time is fast approaching in which that mawkish sentimentality that now pervades our people in regard to the equality of all races and all people will be laid aside, and that intelligent discrimination will be exercised in the well-defined principles of homogeneity . . . . I ask it, sir, in order that we may receive even the small relief that may be obtained under this treaty, thereby staying, so far as its provisions will allow, this exhaustless stream of yellow plague." 13 Cong. Rec. 2035 (1882).

Thus far, Democrats opposed to Chinese immigration had dominated the debate of March 18, 1882. A dissenting voice would now be heard. Representative William Robert Moore (R–TN) took the House floor. He was serving his only term in Congress.

Moore thought that imposing targeted immigration exclusions had worrisome international implications:

"The question of singling out by name a particular nation, and that nation, too, one of the oldest, largest, most docile, peaceable, and least meddlesome nations of the earth, and prohibiting by the most stringent and cruel legislation its citizens from coming like others at will into the United States, is an international question so far-reaching in its scope and consequences as to demand, it seems to me, very cautious, careful, and deliberate consideration." 13 Cong. Rec. 2035 (1882).

An exclusion policy would violate essential principles of equality that characterized the United States, and the country would long regret it, Moore opined. The precedent it set "is one that does so much violence to my own sense of justice that I cannot under any stress of evident passion consent to aid in establishing it . . . . If established, I believe it would be fraught with only mischief that would constantly return to torment us in the future." 13 Cong. Rec. 2035 (1882).

Moore was unmoved by the contention that the 1880 platforms of both major political parties were pledged to the legislation. He would not allow arguments from his fellow Republican, Horace Page, or Democrats, like Campbell Berry, to bulldoze him into such a position. The Republican Party had been founded to advocate for racial equality and he would not be driven from that path:

"As an obscure, though earnest member, therefore, of the great national Republican Party, a party that has won all its magnificent achievements upon the heaven-inspired principle of 'equal and exact justice to all men'; and as a member of a party who have for the last generation shouted ourselves hoarse for the fixing of this principle in the very framework and foundations of our grand political structure, I confess to an utter incapacity to see how we on this side of the House can reconcile a vote for this dangerous bill with any principle of Republican consistency." 13 Cong. Rec. 2035 (1882).

Representative Moore dissected points made by the bill's advocates. Fellow Republican Representative William Calkins (R–IN) had complained that the Chinese should be excluded because they carried "loathsome diseases." Moore wondered if that was not also true of Europeans.

"Is a physical disease more dangerous to the stability of our institutions when it exists among us in the person of an Asiatic rather than a European immigrant? 13 Cong. Rec. 2035 (1882).

153

Representative Speer had depicted the Chinese as a depraved civilization. Moore thought the concept was ridiculous. China had been stable and civilized longer than any nation on earth. "No other nation has shown such stability. What is the cause of it? They have evidently more to commend them than the honorable gentleman is disposed to give them credit for." 13 Cong. Rec. 2035 (1882).

Representative Albert Shelby Willis (D–KY) had introduced into the debate James Garfield's presidential nomination acceptance letter, which appeared to criticize Chinese immigration. But Garfield's letter must be considered in light of the political circumstances that prevailed when it was written, Moore stated. It was a time "when extravagant bids were being made by both great political parties for the vote of California, which was then expected to decide the Presidency." 13 Cong. Rec. 2035 (1882).

After additional debate, Representative Charles G. Williams (R–WI) stood. Williams was a five-term congressman, who served in the House from 1873 to 1883. He was greatly adverse to the Miller legislation:

"I believe the bill violates the fundamental traditions of our government; and to do this, in order to rectify a local and temporary evil, is, in my judgment, like drawing blood from the human body to quench its thirst." 13 Cong. Rec. 2038 (1882).

A person could not change his place of birth, the color of his eyes or skin, or his race, Williams observed, and yet that was the foundation on which the exclusion policy was built:

"To found a bill on any one of these should be enough to defeat it, yet this bill embraces them all." 13 Cong. Rec. 2038 (1882).

Although representing Wisconsin, Williams had been born in Rochester, New York. He recalled for the House memories from his childhood, when European immigrants traveling along the Erie Canal were subjected to bias and condemnation:

"I remember how alive prejudice was and how bitter and relentless. I remember the oaths applied to them, which cannot be repeated here, and the coarse epithets by which they were classed as 'Irish and Dutch cattle' and 'Swede and Swiss and Norwegian hogs.'

"They were humble and they were ignorant and repulsive, but they were honest, temperate, and industrious, and the greatest glory of our country is that the second generation of these same men are among its brightest jewels today." 13 Cong. Rec. 2038 (1882).

Rampant prejudices against European immigrants, often at the edge of violent expression, were tempered over time, said Williams. Prejudice had yielded to reason then. Why not now?

Representative Williams did not necessarily favor open immigration, but he could not tolerate such blatantly discriminatory legislation:

"Put into the bill any reasonable restrictions and conditions, however severe; provide for the exclusion of the vicious, the criminal, the profligate, the dissolute; go further, and provide exceptional remedies for exceptional emergencies; require that Chinamen shall learn our language, adopt our dress, attend our schools, conform to our manners and customs, become freeholders, and live in families, give bonds to remain in the country for a fixed period, or anything within the bounds of reason, and I will vote for the bill, however harsh these conditions may seem.

"But when you say the skilled and unskilled laborer, however intelligent, honest, industrious, frugal, and thrifty he may be cannot come for a period of twenty years, a period, mark you, Mr. Speaker, which measures out the life of most of the men on this floor, I cannot vote for it." 13 Cong. Rec. 2038 (1882).

Representative Charles Skinner (R–NY), a two-term member of the House (1881–1885) was next recognized. Skinner found incongruous U.S. efforts to promote strong bilateral relations while legislating discrimination against Chinese people:

"Can we consistently say to China, we will accept your representatives at the seat of government; we will place them on a social level with ourselves and all who come among us; we will encourage commercial relations with your empire; we will ask you to receive our merchants and our people who visit your country for pleasure or to grow rich in commercial transactions. But your people who are crowded in their homes and desire to come here to earn a living for the labor which they are willing to do; your people who have heard of our broad acres, and our busy industries, and desire to come here for a small share of the liberty of which we boast; your people must stay at home!" 13 Cong. Rec. 2040–41 (1882).

Once enacted, where would be principle of exclusion stop? Skinner believed that the bill was grounded on some glaring fallacies:

"It may justly be said that 'the two facts' upon which this proposed exclusion is founded are these: first, the fact that he is a Chinaman; secondly, the fact that he is a laborer. The bill is, therefore, fraught with the double inequity of being a proscription on the ground of race and a proscription on the ground of labor as an employment. In both aspects, it is entirely un-American and unjust. It is throwing a blot upon our declarations that we are a liberty-loving people.

This bill has no other basis than injustice to a race, and no measure can stand which has no better right to live." 13 Cong. Rec. 2041 (1882).

After a short amount of additional discussion, the daylong Chinese exclusion debate in the House of Representatives of Saturday, March 18, 1882, closed.

§4.50 House Debate, March 21, 1882: "The assimilation of oil and water"

Under consideration in the House Committee of the Whole,
S. 71, as passed by the Senate.

First to address the House on March 21, 1882, was Representative Addison McClure (R–OH), who served in the House of Representatives from 1881 to 1883 and again from 1895 to 1897.

McClure dismissed concerns that exclusion would jeopardize mercantile relations with China. History proved China would not condition trade on political considerations but would deal with other nations strictly on the basis of commercial advantage:

"Why, Mr. Speaker, twenty years ago England and France at the point of a bayonet exhorted a treaty from China, and yet that act of war and invasion did not compromise in the least the commercial interests of these two great and enlightened powers." 13 Cong. Rec. 2126 (1882).

McClure saw China as a civilization unchanged from ancient times and unsusceptible to modification by Western influences:

"The Chinaman of twenty centuries ago is unquestionably the Chinaman of today. The operations of time, of climate, of foreign conquest, of emigration have made no visible impression upon his rooted national characteristics. He is original, immovable, and inveterate in the preservation of his race distinctions. He never amalgamates . . . .

"He is the same unadulterated Mongolian on the banks of the Sacramento River as he is on the Huang Ho. He is the same bigoted pagan, after twenty-five years' residence under the spires of San Francisco as he is among the joss houses of Canton. He is the same unbending Asiatic, whether toiling on the Union Pacific or under the shadow of the Great Wall of China." 13 Cong. Rec. 2126 (1882).

McClure considered the Chinese a vast mass of humanity preparing to swarm the Pacific Coast. As the Chinese population grew, white workers would be subject to deadly competition:

"Wherever Mongolian labor goes in sufficient force, there white labor inevitably succumbs. No other result is possible." 13 Cong. Rec. 2126 (1882).

Congress could no longer afford to deflect public demands for action, McClure argued. Inattention was likely to provoke a violent response from aggrieved Americans, who would consider taking matters into their own hands. Such an outcome would discredit the country, and Congress had the capacity to prevent it:

"Now is the time to settle this question and to settle it peaceably and fairly. To procrastinate its solution will only aggravate the evils that surround it in the future, and possibly invite public dishonor, if not calamity. To trifle with an evil is to invigorate it." 13 Cong. Rec. 2126 (1882).

House Republicans like William Moore (R–TN) and Charles Williams (R–WI) had been among exclusion's most outspoken opponents. Others like Horace Page (R–CA) and William Calkins (R–IN) had been some of its strongest advocates, joining the vast majority of Democrats. McClure had his own interpretation of Republican doctrine, one that allowed him to vote for the bill "with a clear conscience." He believed that exclusion of the Chinese was consistent with the party's historical opposition to slavery:

"I insist that the Republican Party is now committed, and has been committed since its organization, to the principal object of this bill, the preservation of the dignity and freedom of labor . . . . As a protectionist, as a Republican, I stand by the white labor of the Pacific states against the dishonorable competition of coolie labor." 13 Cong. Rec. 2127 (1882).

Representative Thomas Bayne (R–PA) spoke next. Bayne was a seven-term member, serving from 1877 to 1891. Who was welcome in America could be understood by looking to her naturalization laws, he argued. Until 1870, those laws had only permitted white persons to naturalize, and in that year, such rights were extended only to Africans. As no other naturalization was permitted, Bayne concluded, everyone else was unwanted.

To those who argued that American civilization was robust and prosperous enough to absorb the Chinese successfully, Bayne offered a dire response:

"Disease will kill the strongest man. The social organism is no more exempt from the attacks of disease than the individual organism." 13 Cong. Rec. 2128 (1882).The disease was already rampant in California, Bayne said. The evidence was plain from assessing conditions there:

"The Chinese in San Francisco have almost wholly supplanted our own people in certain classes of skilled and unskilled work and manufactures. They have appropriated mostly the occupations which can least ensure severe competition. They drive out the poor woman as well as the strong man . . . .

"Now who will contend that such disturbances of our economic conditions are not a social malady? Who will argue that driving our own people out of their occupations and their homes is not the destruction of social functions which the law of distribution of labor had matured? Who will assert the presence of such a conflict is not a constant menace to the peace and happiness of our people?" 13 Cong. Rec. 2128 (1882).

Representative Bayne viewed the Chinese people with revulsion. Their immigration was a plague that could only bring ill tidings to America. It must be halted. The Pennsylvanian informed his colleagues:

"There are phases of the moral degradation of the Chinese which are too revolting to describe. The temptations which they place in the way of our youth, and the dreadful consequences that too often ensue, may not be spoken here. Not recognizing the marriage relation, having but little if any regard for an oath, indifferent to all things except the accumulation of money, persistent in debased habits and modes of life, their influence on our civilization would only tend to its corruption and decay." 13 Cong. Rec. 2128 (1882).

Finally, Bayne answered colleagues who suggested that if Chinese were permitted to vote, Congress would not attempt to pass an exclusion bill. "It is scarcely fair to impugn the motives of those who favor this bill, who live thousands of miles away, and whom the votes of the Chinese could in no way affect." 13 Cong. Rec. 2128 (1882).

Joseph Scranton (R–PA) represented a mining and iron-and-steel manufacturing district for five non-consecutive terms in the House of Representatives (1881–1883, 1885–1887, 1889–1891, and 1893–1897). In the 1882 debate and thereafter, labor organizations would strongly support exclusion legislation. Scranton described his constituents and their concerns:

"These miners, mine laborers, mill hands, mechanics, and all classes of daily toilers at manual labor are a thrifty, intelligent, law-abiding, patriotic people. They advocate and uphold the rights of labor and are tenacious and jealous of its power and prerogatives . . . . Their brotherhood girdles the continent and their sympathies are with their fellow-man upon the Pacific slope. They believe America is for the Caucasian race, and accepting the results of the rebellion recognize the African as a co-laborer and citizen. Not so with the Mongolian; for him they have no affiliation nor welcome." 13 Cong. Rec. 2129 (1882).

Scranton was uncomfortable with the twenty-year ban, believing it tantamount to an abrogation of the Angell Treaty. He urged reducing the restriction to ten years. A shorter term, Scranton said, would implement the treaty appropriately.

Representative Benjamin Butterworth (R–OH) followed Scranton on the

House floor. Butterworth was in the House between 1879 and 1883 and again from 1885 to 1891. He vigorously denied that the legislation was a response to race prejudice. Landslide outcomes in the California and Nevada referenda on Chinese immigration were achieved by secret ballot, so it was hard to argue that voters were swayed by public pressure to disregard their consciences. The few who opposed immigration restrictions did so for purely economic reasons, Butterworth claimed. Such voters did not act out of Christian principles or philanthropy, but were persons "who were making money out of the bone and muscle of this servile race." 13 Cong. Rec. 2130 (1882).

Some representatives had argued that Chinese did not assimilate because legal barriers prevented them from doing so. Butterworth claimed the problem was inherent, not statutory. Chinese character was hardened over forty centuries, so that they "walk in trodden paths until their very natures, their instincts, and all their feelings are as widely different from our own as it is possible to conceive of, and so widely and radically different as to render healthful assimilation out of the question." 13 Cong. Rec. 2130 (1882).

Trying to force assimilation would attempt the impossible and would portend disaster for Caucasians:

"You might as well hope to compel by law the assimilation of oil and water. We all know that as a matter of fact and of logic and philosophy that we cannot combine and unite with a lower race of people without lowering the average of our own social, physical, and moral being." 13 Cong. Rec. 2130 (1882).

Some colleagues in the House had argued that principles of Christian charity should produce a lenient and welcoming attitude toward Chinese immigration. Butterworth considered such thinking utterly unrealistic and believed the United States could not withstand the pernicious effects an influx of Chinese would produce:

"I am unwilling, in order to give play to an impracticable philanthropy, to open-wide the floodgates through which will pour a constant stream of degraded and degrading humanity, [until] at least I find our own people so purified in their morality and elevated in their virtue, and so established and fixed in their Christianity that the influence of such a flood tide of debasing leaven cannot perceptibly affect their condition . . . .

"When we shall be freed from the vices and corruption that threaten the destruction of our political system, then, and not until then, will I consent to the experiment of civilizing, humanizing, Christianizing, and enlightening the heathen of the earth by taking them into our midst. But until then I say to them 'we ask not to abide in your tents, nor you in ours.' Not with my consent shall the young Republic be made the pest-house for all the world, or a penal colony for all the nations of the earth." 13 Cong. Rec. 2133 (1882).

Representative Charles Hooker (D–MS) took the floor. Hooker, who like Anson Burlingame graduated from Harvard Law School in 1846, was elected attorney general of Mississippi in 1865 and the same year was removed with the other officers of Mississippi by the Union Army. Hooker served in the House for a total of eighteen years, spanning three non-consecutive periods (1875–1883, 1887–1895, and 1901–1903). While not opposed in principle to exclusion legislation, and inclined to support colleagues from the Pacific region, Hooker remained faithful to U.S. treaty commitments. The pending bill violated them, he believed. Hooker tried to ameliorate the conflict by backing an amendment to limit the term of exclusion to ten years. After the amendment failed, Hooker opposed final passage of the bill.

Hooker saw great promise in America's expanding relations with China and also with Japan. By this, he meant both greater trade and the extension of Christianity. He was confident in the capacity of missionaries to impart western civilization to China:

"I am not afraid, are you gentlemen, that your civilization and your power to plant the cross of Christ and the principles of liberty shall find in the oldest nation of the world a people incapable of appreciating them?" 13 Cong. Rec. 2134 (1882).

The Mississippian reviewed the history of the Burlingame Treaty (*§ 1.30*), which he considered an enormous and unique diplomatic triumph. Anson Burlingame himself had been acclaimed, and the treaty secured rights that were important to America:

"You had by that treaty opened up relations, commercial relations, with the oldest nation on the globe. You had secured to your ministers of the Gospel, bearing the banner of Christ in their hands, the right to plant it everywhere in China and you had given to the Chinaman the same rights here. The nation looked upon it as a consummation of diplomatic skill and power which had never before been manifested by any people." 13 Cong. Rec. 2134 (1882).

Exclusion legislation would build a figurative Chinese wall on the California coast and undo all these benefits, and it would take America a century backward, Mississippi Representative Hooker feared.

Unlike several of his colleagues, who had deprecated and condemned China, Hooker respected Chinese culture and history. He scoffed at the idea that the presence of Chinese in the United States would degrade American society:

"Sir, their civilization, their magnificent position in arts, in science, in politics, in everything that makes a nation great, had been attained by them hundreds of years before your nationality ever had an existence." 13 Cong. Rec. 2134 (1882).

The Burlingame Treaty had been the culmination of American diplomatic overtures to China. It was the United States that had looked west and taken the initiative, seeking to broaden relations with China, not the other way around, noted Hooker:

"Here are treaties which they never asked us to make, but which we asked them to make—begged and implored them to make. They never wanted Chinamen to come to this country. They never desired that the Chinese should emigrate. They never sought treaty relations with us, but we sought treaty relations with them. We sought them against a prejudice which at one time we thought we should never be able to overcome, because it had existed among that people for centuries, extending back across the ages to the time of Confucius; and far beyond the time of Confucius the august empire extends until its origin is lost in the twilight of fable. This people never asked you to make treaties with them. You sought them; you sent your plenipotentiaries; you asked their ports should be opened. England, aiding you, waged a war. It is a very memorable fact that almost all Chinamen come to his country from the port of Hong Kong, an English port; and you propose to establish restrictions in violation not only of the treaties you have made with the Chinese, but those you have made with England." 13 Cong. Rec. 2134–35 (1882).

In the bilateral diplomacy, China had consistently shown good faith, said Hooker. It had acceded to American requests for the Burlingame Treaty, and then it concurred in the Angell amendments, again at U.S. urging. Hooker described the forbearance China had shown to the United States:

"Do you believe, if the conditions were reversed, and our citizens were in China instead of Chinese in the United States, we could be successfully appealed to inhibit further immigration and consent to the passage of passport laws by which even those who were permitted to remain should be hampered in their every movement from one place to another? Yet, this China has done. With 100,000 of her people here, brought here by your own act, solicited to come in all your treaties, urged to emigrate, and yet been subjected to all these annoying and vexatious laws against them, China has acted more reasonable, if not as just to her own people as perhaps she should be, than could be expected of any other. She has consented to suspend that immigration which you once sought, which you regarded as the highest effort of diplomatic skill, and to modify her treaty to that end." 13 Cong. Rec. 2138 (1882).

Should the United States now reverse its policy toward China, the effect on commerce would be sharp and immediate, he predicted. That trade would be absorbed by England. However, America would suffer more than economic losses. It would no longer be a land of expansive horizons and unlimited promise:

"You will be left, when you have expelled these people and destroyed this commercial intercourse, very much as the Spaniards were left when they drove the Moors from Spain and left with their country a desert . . . ." 13 Cong. Rec. 2136 (1882).

Hooker could not understand how America could turn its back on such a large proportion of the world's people. Doing so was unreasonable and it clashed with the nation's political heritage:

"From the earliest periods of English history, the English-speaking people have asserted their right to freedom of conscience and freedom of person. Should we pause now and say that we will not extend this principle to one-third of the human race?" 13 Cong. Rec. 2136 (1882).

The last speaker of the day was Representative Aylett Buckner (D–MO), who was a member of the House from 1873 to 1885. He took special pride in announcing his support for the legislation. "I shall vote for the bill with no little pleasure," Buckner stated.

Passing the bill gave Buckner a chance to bury what he thought was an excessively sentimental commitment to the idea of racial equality:

"This bill is a reversal of the action of this Government for the last thirty years. It consigns to the grave all sublimated sentiment as to the equality of the races of men. It performs the last funeral rite over the dead body of that false and nonsensical dogma of governmental policy that 'all men are created equal.' It proclaims that this Government will not be controlled in its action on great questions of public policy by the inspiration of our emotions, or legislate under the influence of mere theoretical abstractions as to the natural rights of man." 13 Cong. Rec. 2138 (1882).

According to Buckner, the bill protected America against the pagan hordes he was convinced would invade and destroy the country:

"It seeks to preserve and protect American civilization and American Christianity against the inroads of Asiatic heathenism and Eastern semi-barbarism, and it teaches our people the great lesson that their first and very highest duty is to their own political household and to their own blood and their own race." 13 Cong. Rec. 2138 (1882).

To perform that duty meant barring Chinese immigration and denying citizenship to Chinese already in America. He said so in overtly racial language:

"We are called upon to vote for a proposition that not only excludes millions of men from citizenship and suffrage, but which I hope will be a perpetual prohibition upon their polluting our soil even with the soles of their feet . . . .

"No class of men should be permitted to locate in this country who cannot readily assimilate with our race or whose blood cannot intermingle with that of the white race without deterioration or debasement." 13 Cong. Rec. 2138 (1882).

Racial integration was a failed policy, Buckner thought. It had produced bad results for both black and white populations. Many of the same problems could be expected from blending in the Chinese. To mitigate these concerns, Buckner proposed that Africans should be segregated and the Chinese should be excluded.

"It may require scores of years of experiment before the country will be convinced that the African is an element of peril and weakness in our social and political system, which, like the Chinese, must be eliminated at any cost." 13 Cong. Rec. 2138 (1882).

Himself a Democrat, Representative Buckner took note of the split within Republican ranks, and praised those Republican colleagues who had rallied behind the bill:

"I congratulate my Republican friends who support this bill, that they have emancipated themselves for once from the influence of transcendental theorists, sublimated humanitarians, Jesuitical ecclesiastics, [and] women suffragists." 13 Cong. Rec. 2138 (1882).

On that note, the House debate of March 21, 1882, concluded.

§4.60 House Debate, March 22, 1882: "Who would have them for voters?"

Under consideration in the House Committee of the Whole,
S. 71 as passed by the Senate.

On Wednesday, March 22, 1882, the House resumed its debate on the Senate-passed bill S. 71, to exclude Chinese from the United States for twenty years. The bill's manager in the House, Representative Horace Page (R–CA), announced he would oppose all amendments. The first speaker was Representative William D. Washburn (R–MN). Washburn served in the House from 1879 to 1885 and later in the Senate from 1889 to 1895.

Washburn advocated passing exclusion legislation while the government still had the ability to control Chinese immigration. Every evil had inconspicuous beginnings, Washburn said, but then spun out of control. According to Washburn, slavery was a good example of this phenomenon:

"No one was especially alarmed when the slave traders landed their first cargoes of human beings on our shores . . . . It was regarded as somewhat immoral, it is true, but as only of a temporary character, and which could be easily checked and controlled. But as property in human beings became profitable, or was thought to be so, its power of extension and expansion became irresistible, until it was able to cast its withering blight over a large section of the country." 13 Cong. Rec. 2162 (1882).

Representative Washburn was convinced that, if left unchecked, the Chinese would not be confined to California, but would spread throughout the country. This was a curse to be nipped in the bud. "There is no time like the present to deal with an existing evil, however small proportions that evil may have attained," he said. 13 Cong. Rec. 2162 (1882).

Washburn stated that the Chinese were too different in their customs, traditions, and religious outlook ever to assimilate. The historical record was long, clear, and immutable:

"The leopard does not change his spots, neither has the Mongolian race in the long centuries changed its characteristics. It is today what it was before and since the Christian era. Instead of having been affected by the influences and teaching of the Christian religion and the high civilization that has followed it everywhere . . . nowhere in all the Mongolian world does it today find a resting place, and yet we are invited under the inspiration of a morbid sentimentalism to open wide our doors to a race of people who have not now and never have had the first sentiment or impulse in common with our own Christian civilization." 13 Cong. Rec. 2162 (1882).

Washburn claimed to be a protectionist, in the sense that he was determined to protect American workers from what he said was the degrading influence of cheap labor. As had several of his colleagues, he analogized restricting Chinese immigration to opposing slavery:

"Cheap labor has, or may seem to have, its attractions and fascinations. The people of the South once thought that the cheap labor of the slave was indispensable to their prosperity and well-being, and they held to it with a tenacity worthy of a better cause; but when we introduce, or permit to be introduced, a system of labor of a lower grade, if possible, than the slave labor of the South, we do for the whole country what slave labor did for the South, and in so doing strike a blow at the very foundations of our free Government." 13 Cong. Rec. 2163 (1882).

Giving further evidence of the split among congressional Republicans on the Chinese question, Washburn insisted that the Republican platform was not an

§4.61 Role of the Bill Manager in the House of Representatives

The bill manager in the House of Representatives is the member responsible for guiding legislation through House floor consideration. Typically, the bill manager will be the chair of the committee that reported the bill or, perhaps, a subcommittee chair. Less frequently, the bill manager may be the bill's sponsor, although that practice was more common in the nineteenth century.

Acting for the committee, it is the bill manager's job to respond to House floor amendments, indicating whether they are acceptable or will be resisted. Because of a jurisdictional committee's presumed expertise, other members give them substantial deference. Amendments the committee is willing to accept almost always prevail on the House floor. Proposals that a committee resists sometimes prevail, but most are rejected.

During 1882 House consideration of the twenty-year exclusion bill, manager Horace Page's statement that he would oppose all amendments therefore sent a signal that any amendment would have difficulty securing an affirmative vote.

exercise to pander for votes, but was a "well-considered and well-determined" statement of party policy. He concluded by emphasizing the Republicans' commitment to the "dignity of labor" through enacting restrictions on Chinese immigration. In this fashion, Washburn justified the transformation of the party of emancipation into one that supported racial discrimination:

"The Republican Party was called into existence and organized to resist the aggressions of slavery and the carrying of degraded labor into the new Territories. In all its grand history, it has never failed to respond to the appeals of the oppressed; neither has it ever failed to recognize the great truth of the dignity of labor, coupled with the universal intelligence of its people, is the bed-rock upon which all governments of the people can alone securely rest." 13 Cong. Rec. 2163 (1882).

Representative Melvin C. George (R–OR) took the floor. A two-term congressman (1881–1885), George echoed the exclusionist views of the Pacific slope. America, he said, was simply not intended to be a land open to anyone who wanted to come:

"There is no recognized principle that the ignorant, the savage, the barbarous, the brutal, the servile, the riffraff, the dangerous, or the refuse element of any foreign nation are entitled of right to enter our body-politic and become part and parcel of our governing power." 13 Cong. Rec. 2164 (1882).

Echoing Senator Blaine's argument from the Fifteen Passenger debate, (§ 2.20), Representative George said no one should be permitted to immigrate unless that person would be eligible for citizenship. What had to be asked about any people was "can we digest it and have it become part of our system and body-politic, and will it, like health [sic] blood, build up our national bone and sinew, or will it poison and canker all its surroundings?" 13 Cong. Rec. 2164 (1882). Believing that the Chinese represented a degrading presence in America, George urged that their immigration be barred:

"The capital, the energy, the vitality of our western coast has come from the East. We never got it from Asia and we never will. Asia is fossilized. It has long since attained its growth in civilization. The cheap labor imported from there are fossils, in all social and mental respects. We have nothing to hope from an infusion of their blood, or their ideas, or their institutions, nothing at all." 13 Cong. Rec. 2164 (1882).

George severely disparaged Chinese culture as backward-looking, bound by paganism, and rooted in ancestor worship. He found Chinese "the most debased people on the face of the earth." This contrasted with white workers, who he idealized as "the intelligent American laborer, married, surrounded by his wife and his children, trying to pay for his own homestead supporting his school and his church, obeying the law, and loyal to America." 13 Cong. Rec. 2164 (1882). On the other hand, Chinese were "ignorant, superstitious, childless, unmarried; (had) no home but a China hovel in narrow contracted space, and all pagans and idolaters of a different race." 13 Cong. Rec. 2165 (1882).

George refuted the claim that exclusion would not be imposed if Chinese were enfranchised. The necessity to bar them was too fundamental to be set aside for such reasons. In any event, the question of Chinese suffrage was absurd and moot:

"In this broad land, who would have them for voters? Where is there a Representative within the sound of my voice who will rise in his seat and proclaim that over 100,000 pagan idolaters, ignorant, neither able to read nor to write nor to speak our language intelligibly, who are not possessed of any of the material qualifications or sympathies of electors, who come and go in herds or under the control of some of the Six Companies that buy and sell them as they please, should have placed in their hands the elective franchise?" 13 Cong. Rec. 2165 (1882).

Representative George framed a stark choice. Either the Chinese must remain menial workers, or they must be treated like Europeans and entrusted with citizenship. "Which shall it be," he asked, "serfs or citizens?" 13 Cong. Rec. 2165 (1882).

Congress must hear the pleas from the Pacific Coast, he demanded. America faced an "irrepressible conflict" between Chinese and whites. Racial coexistence was impossible, so the conflict would continue "until one system prevails." Portions of the country would "either become Mongolian or American." Legislators would have to choose.

Representative Robert Milligan McLane (D–MD) shortly followed George. McLane served in the House from 1847 to 1851 and again from 1879 to 1883. During the administration of President Franklin Pierce (1853–1857), McLane was minister plenipotentiary to China, responsible for negotiating trading rights. The Burlingame Treaty subsequently expanded upon his efforts.

McLane detailed the reasons for America's initial outreach to China in the 1850s. Underdeveloped and relatively unpopulated, but rich in resources, California was ripe for foreign intervention. Since the Mexican War ended in 1847, the British had cast an avaricious eye on it. As an act of self-defense, America needed to fill it with workers and exploit its resources:

"That distant empire, California, a country acquired as an indemnity by our war with Mexico; not peopled, difficult to defend, fabulous, almost romantic in its history; no communication with it except by a long voyage by the Horn; impossible to defend, it excited our interest and anxiety; a great country like England, angry and jealous, watching our every step . . . menacing us in every quarter of the globe with hostility, naturally stimulated our anxiety, and excited the country to look for and encourage any population for the Pacific Coast." 13 Cong. Rec. 2167 (1882).

The government's answer to the problem was to encourage Chinese to populate California:

"Under those circumstances, for the first time in the history of our diplomacy, you will find instructions from the State Department to negotiate for Chinese immigration." 13 Cong. Rec. 2167 (1882).

American overtures were at first ill-taken in China, McLane reported. The Chinese would not receive foreigners, except in warehouse districts outside the cities:

"There was no intention to insult us seriously, but an aversion, an absolute aversion, to hold intercourse with us." 13 Cong. Rec. 2167 (1882).

The Chinese would not negotiate with the West, except under British pressure. A member of the trade mission dispatched by President Pierce, McLane said he spoke from personal experience. Chinese were neither welcoming to his mission, or even neutral, but instead were actively antagonistic:

"We had been received, but received at the hazard of our personal dignity and personal safety too. No American minister ever went into a Chinese city that he did not incur danger, even under the guard of the Chinamen and under the guard of American soldiers and sailors, side by side with Chinese officials. And yet he would be spit upon, literally spit upon by Chinese officials and the Chinese people."

"That is not much changed now," McLane concluded. 13 Cong. Rec. 2167 (1882).

This simmering hostility did not end when Anson Burlingame went to China, said McLane. The treaty Burlingame concluded in 1868 opened the door to American missionaries, who had entered parts of China previously closed to foreigners, but the Chinese would not accept Christian teachings, and the missionaries had returned disillusioned:

"The missionaries came back not only disgusted and revolted, not only humiliated and in wonder that such results could flow from these missionary efforts, but they came back baffled, intellectually speaking . . . . This was not only a pagan people, but it was a material people. It was a people without imagination, without spirituality . . . . Not only were these missionaries baffled in their hope and in their expectation that this Christianity of ours had found its way into China, but they came back loathing the people with whom they had intercourse." 13 Cong. Rec. 2169 (1882).

Representative McLane analogized restricting Chinese immigration to controlling the slave trade. Both efforts were on the same moral plane, he reasoned:

"The Negro was brought to this country, and why was he brought? He was brought to labor; he was brought to labor because his labor was cheap, and in California today we find the people subjected to exactly the same condition of affairs that this country suffered from when the mother country permitted African slavery to be introduced, and we find a question today in California equally demanding our attention." 13 Cong. Rec. 2169 (1882).

Assessing blame, McLane focused on the San Francisco-based benevolent associations known as the Chinese Six Companies. Repeatedly in the debates, the Six Companies were accused of running a squalid trade in Chinese workers. Such workers were said to have bound themselves and their families to the Six Companies in exchange for passage to America, and did not work in the U.S. except as contract laborers under the Six Companies' control. Although much American literature blames the Six Companies for being labor brokers, the actual recruiting and contracting of workers was usually done by specific Chinese labor companies or by district and fraternal organizations that sometimes fell under the umbrella of the Six Companies.

Denying such charges, the Six Companies had written to Congress. In their letter, they asserted:

"We solemnly declare that we, the Six Companies, are purely benevolent societies. We never, singly or collectively, as individuals or companies, brought one of our countrymen to this free country, under or by any contract or agreement made anywhere, as a servant or laborer. We have never before heard that our people, desiring to come here, sold their relatives to obtain the means to come. We have never yet let, hired, or contracted one of our people out to labor; neither have we ever exercised the slightest degree of control or restraint over our people after they came here, nor claimed, or demanded, or received one dollar of their earnings. We have never acted, directly or indirectly, as the agent or agents of any one of our people who advanced the means for one of our people to come here." 13 Cong. Rec. 2136 (1882).

McLane insisted the denial should be given no weight. It was a grand deception, a perjury, committed by people who had no sense of the solemnity of an oath:

"No man believes the Chinaman on oath. He [the Chinaman] despises the oath when he takes it and would not be bound by it." 13 Cong. Rec. 2169 (1882). This was the coolie trade that the United States had negotiated the right to suspend, McLane asserted. The suspension proposed in the pending bill was reasonable, and if the Chinese government thought otherwise, it had explicit treaty rights to bring the matter to the United States government for discussion. Otherwise, implementation of the Burlingame Treaty was at America's discretion.

Representative John Kasson (R–IA) served in the House between 1863 and 1867, and from 1873 to 1877, and finally from 1881 to 1884. Kasson would offer the principal amendment to the bill, proposing to reduce the term of exclusion from twenty years to ten. The honor of the country was at stake, Kasson exclaimed, because an excessive suspension would demonstrate America's treaty commitments meant little:

"I wish not to live long enough to see the time when China or any other government on the face of the globe shall revive the memory of the Carthaginians of old and instead of 'Punic faith' characterize the reckless disregard of treaties as 'American faith.'" 13 Cong. Rec. 2171 (1882).

Apart from the period of suspension, Kasson had additional objections. The bill's requirement that all Chinese obtain personal passports was unduly onerous, he felt, because China had only agreed to suspend the influx of laborers. The registration system burdened all Chinese, including the non-laborers who were supposed to receive "most favored nation" treatment. Kasson explained the discrimination:

"It requires, for example, in the certification to be made, that they have permission of the Chinese Government, and shall state their 'physical peculiarities,' who their fathers were, where they lived, etc., facts beyond anything known in the passport of any civilized country on the face of the earth. This is wrong; this is unjust; it is not within the treaty with China." 13 Cong. Rec. 2171 (1882).

To harmonize the legislation with the treaty, Kasson would propose amendments in this area as well. In addition, he would take aim at provisions that reminded him of the antebellum Fugitive Slave Laws. These provisions punished by fine and imprisonment any person who aided or abetted a Chinese laborer entering the United States, and penalized and then expelled Chinese workers found within the country.

"I should be glad if this poor miserable pursuit of one Chinaman crossing the frontier or stepping off a ship in order to see a town might be stopped; that he might not be pursued by the police, hazed into prison, and robbed of $100. My soul revolts at that sort of individual persecution of an innocent foreigner coming to this country, unable to speak our language and not knowing our institutions and laws. This is one of the most vulgar forms of barbarism." 13 Cong. Rec. 2172 (1882).

Congress had been misled about the character of the Chinese, Kasson observed. As in any society, there were hoodlum elements in China, and those persons ought not to have permission to enter the United States. But the serial condemnations of China, expressed on the House floor, had been far more sweeping and quite inaccurate:

"What is the China we know by our treaties? Is it pagan? No sir. Is it idolatrous? No sir. The China that we know as a government, embracing a religion who adherents are estimated at 100,000,000, is without an idol. It adheres to the teachings of Confucius, who before the Christian era announced doctrines which to this day have the respect of the civilized and Christian world. Every official of China is obliged to pass a civil service examination, including an examination in that moral code and system known as that of Confucius, before he can enter an office in China. Among those moral principles was that which in another and more perfect form we bind close to our hearts every Sunday. . . . Their faith is 'do unto others as they would have others do unto them.' Upon that principle, China has stood for 3000 years, as we have stood upon it for

2000 years. Let us stand upon it today in our legislation touching the rights of a friendly nation." 13 Cong. Rec. 2173 (1882).

Representative Kasson described how China had resisted, albeit ineffectively, British efforts to impose Indian opium upon it. It was a Christian society that had sought to corrupt China, not the other way around. Referring to the British-instigated Opium War (1839–1842), Kasson stated:

"Your Christian nation across the water it was that sent her naval forces to compel China to break down that barrier and admit Indian opium, that the people of that empire might continue in spite of their enlightened government to become beasts, debased at the hand of Her 'most Christian' Majesty's government." 13 Cong. Rec. 2173 (1882).

Observing China's lack of modern military preparedness, an American merchant, one Mr. Forbes (probably Robert Bennet Forbes, 1804–1889), had sent a memorial to a local official proposing China seek arms and training from the United States, Kasson said. The official had endorsed the recommendation, but the imperial government had declined it. As Kasson reported it, the response from Peking was substantially as follows:

"The imperial government, knowing of the friendship of Mr. Forbes for China, departs from its usual custom of receiving such papers in silence, and not only notifies him that it declines the proposition but gives the reasons why. The memorial proposes to educate this government in the art of war. War is barbarism and belongs to a state of barbarism. China long ago passed that stage of her existence and has no desire to return to it." 13 Cong. Rec. 2173 (1882).

Kasson pressed the House to consider what he felt was the true China, not the caricature that had been drawn. China, he said, had been "defamed" on the House floor. Congress should not legislate based on such distortions:

"Sir, I appeal to gentlemen here to make the discriminations due from fair-minded men, discriminations not founded on costumes, not founded on the way of wearing the hair, not founded on ignorance of our language, but discriminations based upon better and higher principles and facts than these paltry distinctions." 13 Cong. Rec. 2173 (1882).

Later in the day, Representative Thomas M. Browne (R–IN) took the floor. A seven-term member of the House (1877–1891), Browne believed the bill served mainly racial objectives:

"While it is said to be a measure to prevent the introduction of disease, crime, pauperism, and servile labor into the United States, the language and spirit of the bill prove that it aims only to exclude Chinese laborers, regardless of their moral, pecuniary, or physical condition." 13 Cong. Rec. 2177 (1882).

Browne called it "caste legislation" that was "supported by a spirit of intolerance and race prejudice." The debate had evoked in his mind "the crack of the master's whip." He could support narrow immigration restrictions that were not racial and were truly aimed at stopping pauperism, disease, and crime. But the bill went far beyond such limits:

"The Chinaman is not to be punished for bringing disease, vice, or pauperism; nor because he is servile, but because he brings his brain and muscle and contributes to the development of our illimitable resources his skilled and unskilled industry. It is not the pauper but the laborer; not the idle but the industrious; not the profligate but the thrifty; not the diseased but the healthy, who are feared by the promoters of this bill." 13 Cong. Rec. 2178 (1882).

Exclusion legislation written on this basis violated the Declaration's fundamental principle of expatriation, Browne contended:

"I believe a man, whether Celt or Saxon, Teuton, African, or Mongolian, has a right to withdraw from his native country and make his home in another, and that without this, his liberty is defective. This bill puts this right of expatriation, this right 'essential to perfect liberty' so far as Chinese who labor are concerned, in chains for twenty years." 13 Cong. Rec. 2178 (1882).

Such impairments to liberty were unprecedented and were being applied to one people alone, Browne declared. He inquired of the House:

"Here is the very pith of the question. Have we ever denied the right of another foreign people to come here to work and acquire property? Never. Why then deny this right to the Chinese?" 13 Cong. Rec. 2178 (1882).

Several representatives had argued that, by supporting the bill, they were protecting the dignity of American labor against the "degrading influence" of Chinese immigrant competitors. Browne also claimed to stand for the dignity of labor, but applied a more expansive meaning to it than did the exclusionists:

"I object to this bill in its present form because it attacks the freedom of labor—the liberty to work. If you would elevate labor, make it free. Servile service, such as slaves yield, is degrading, and as such I would exclude it from this country by making it free. But I insist that the right to work without trammel is a natural one, to be enjoyed alike by every race and color . . . .

"To labor, man must have a field for its employment, and to shut him out is to strike down both liberty and life. I believe a man has as much right to labor as to breathe. Moreover, I hold that man's ability to labor is his own property—that it belongs to him as much as to his hands or eyes. He may employ it in lawful pursuits upon such terms as he may choose.

"I have, Mr. Speaker, been talking of a principle—a right, if you please—that

I believe to be as sacred and as universal as the right of life itself." 13 Cong. Rec. 2178 (1882).

The principle at hand was the liberty of human labor and the bill would imperil it. Such barriers should be imposed only in the case of national emergency. "To suspend it without the gravest cause is a monstrous crime against human nature," Browne contended. Circumstances did not exist to justify the extraordinary legislation pending in the House.

Representative Browne discussed America's powers under the Angell Treaty. Because those powers were broad and unilateral, the United States was obliged to exercise them cautiously:

"It is said that this question is left wholly to the judgment of the Government of the United States. I grant it, and for this reason I insist that it is our solemn duty to so guard our legislation as to do no possible wrong. It would be little less than infamous to take advantage of a discretionary power generously accorded us by a friendly nation to interfere with or impose unusual restrictions upon the liberties of its subjects." 13 Cong. Rec. 2178 (1882).

The legislation badly implemented the Angell Treaty, Browne argued. Measured against a human lifespan, a twenty-year restriction was an extreme hardship. In the Angell Treaty negotiations, U.S. diplomats had spoken of a five-year suspension, without expressly committing to that, and even conveyed that the "United States might never exercise power of suspension at all." 13 Cong. Rec. 2179 (1882).

Through draconian legislation, Browne lamented, Congress was about to mock those assurances:

"Is the humiliating system of certificates and registrations imposed by this bill on the Chinese and not required of any other people who come among us necessary? Is it necessary to visit the degrading penalties of fines and imprisonment upon every American citizen who aids or abets a Chinese laborer to come temporarily into the United States? As was said by the distinguished gentleman from Iowa [John Kasson], it is necessary in order to protect our Pacific Coast to run down every poor Chinaman who happens to cross our frontier, or steps from a ship to see a seaboard town or city? Shall it be a crime, I ask, for a Chinaman on his way home from Cuba or Mexico to step from the ship to the wharf at San Francisco? Is a law closing every port, walling about every town, and keeping the Chinese laborer from touching our soil at every point necessary to save two States from beyond the Rocky Mountains from Chinese cheap labor?" 13 Cong. Rec. 2179 (1882).

Browne's own response to these rhetorical questions was scornful:

"Such laws have brought reproach to our own people in the past, but I have until now indulged the hope that they would disgrace us no more." 13 Cong. Rec. 2179 (1882).

Fears, such as those expressed about Chinese labor, had been voiced in the past to justify statutory discrimination against blacks, Browne said. Such measures had not been confined to slave-holding states. In Browne's own state of Indiana legislation passed that resembled what was proposed against the Chinese:

"Statesmen of the free states were devising ways for keeping Negroes from coming within our borders to cheapen and degrade white labor. So frightened were we in the North that by statutes and constitutions, we made it a crime for a colored person to come into the State. In Indiana, we declared all contracts made with colored persons so coming into the State void, and punished our citizens with fines and imprisonment if they gave these ostracized men and women employment." 13 Cong. Rec. 2179 (1882).

Several members of the House had cited the California and Nevada referenda to demonstrate broad public support for Chinese exclusion, but Browne was dismissive. Such electoral tactics were nothing new and should not be the foundation for legislating:

"The people of Indiana voted by over one hundred thousand majority for putting an article into the constitution prohibiting Negro immigration. Other states did the same thing." 13 Cong. Rec. 2179–80 (1882).

Representative Browne offered a stout defense of the Chinese people. Recounting testimony to the bicameral committee investigating the status of Chinese immigration, Browne drew conclusions that varied greatly from other colleagues:

"If it is true, it proves these abused people have by their labor added largely to the material prosperity of the States of the Pacific; that they have built railroads and ships, redeemed waste places, and planted the garden and the vineyard in the wilderness. As men, they are faithful, reliable, intelligent; as merchants, they pay promptly and are high-minded and correct. As a race, they are mentally quick, acute, and correct in their perceptions—strong and tenacious in memory. In the higher walks, they are scholars, statesmen, and diplomats—polite, adroit, and shrewd." 13 Cong. Rec. 2182 (1882).

Before ending his lengthy remarks, Browne attacked the theory that Republicans were bound by their platform to support the bill. He was a Republican, he proclaimed, and such a claim distorted the party position. He cited President Hayes' 1879 veto of the Fifteen Passenger bill, a veto that House Republicans had voted overwhelmingly to sustain:

"When in the frenzy of an excited public opinion, Congress was induced to strike down a solemn treaty made with the Chinese people, the Republican Party was true to its faith and saved the nation from dishonor by an Executive veto." 13 Cong. Rec. 2182 (1882).

Browne saw the exclusion bill as a direct contradiction of his party's founding doctrine and its emancipation record:

"It will not betray the rights of any people, nor prove untrue to its obligations to human liberty. It will not surrender its traditions or its faith to accommodate the passions or prejudices of any section. It is today, as it has ever been, the friend of the laboring classes and of the oppressed and unfortunate . . . . Whenever, sir, the Republican Party abandons the just for the expedient, or fails in its courage to denounce the popular wrong or defend the unpopular right, it will be unworthy of its past glory or the respect of a Christian people." 13 Cong. Rec. 2182 (1882).

Later in the day, Representative Charles Joyce (R–VT) addressed the House. Joyce served in Congress between 1875 and 1883. In the March 22, 1882, debate, he would conclude the case for the legislation's opponents.

Joyce cited one of the bill's great ironies: a nation built by immigrants was constructing a barrier to immigration:

"To other nations of the earth, not affected by this legislation, it must appear strange and unaccountable that a country inhabited by a people made up of immigrants from every race under Heaven should, at the very beginning of the second century of its existence, attempt to build around its territory a wall against foreigners deeper and broader and higher than that which kept China from civilization and Christianity for eighteen hundred years." 13 Cong. Rec. 2184 (1882).

Joyce charged that the bill exceeded what the Angell Treaty allowed America to do. The exclusion provisions were, in practical terms, the very prohibition the United States committed not to impose. As such, the measure was a flagrant treaty violation:

"I beg gentlemen to pause and reflect before they commit such a wrong against China and place us in such a false and cowardly position before the world."

Representative Joyce also believed denying Chinese access to the ballot was catastrophic for them:

"If the one hundred and five thousand Chinamen now in this country were armed with the freeman's great weapon of defense, the ballot, you would never have heard of this bill. The eloquent lips of gentlemen who advocate it would be silent, and we should not now be haunted with the nightmare of 'Chinese cheap labor.' It is because they cannot vote, because they are helpless to defend themselves, that these gallant gentlemen are now charging upon them with all the forces of hate, prejudice, and barbaric despotism." 13 Cong. Rec. 2184 (1882).

Pandering in the platforms to the Pacific Coast electorate greatly distressed Joyce. It reminded him of what the Whigs and Democrats had done in competing for the allegiance of Southern voters in the years before the war:

"Mr. Speaker, some gentlemen on this floor will remember when both the great political parties in this country fell upon their knees in the dust and besought the haughty slave owner in the South to save them." 13 Cong. Rec. 2184 (1882).

His party's platform did not require voting for the exclusion bill, the Vermont Republican Joyce insisted. Republicans could support alternative measures that would suspend temporarily the immigration of coolie labor, criminals, prostitutes, and diseased persons. Such legislation would be consistent with bilateral understandings, unlike the pending bill, which violated them.

Joyce disputed the idea that Chinese would not assimilate in America. Such notions were familiar and fatuous. "The same objection," he said, "was made to the Irishman in 1854–55 under the lead of the Know Nothing organization, and to the Negro, previous to 1861, by the people of the South, but these prophecies have all proved false, the fears then expressed groundless . . . ." 13 Cong. Rec. 2185 (1882).

Joyce's position that the Chinese could assimilate was contrary to popular media at the time. See, for example, Stuart Creighton Miller, *The Unwelcome Immigrant: The American Image of the Chinese, 1785–1882* (University of California Press, 1969).

Representative Joyce attacked the supporters' premises that the Chinese must be excluded because they were too different from Europeans and would never integrate into American culture and politics. Such was a self-fulfilling prophecy, he said. It was unreasonable to criticize Chinese for not assimilating, and to accuse them of being unwilling to do so, especially after so many unique legal and social barriers had been erected in their path:

"When the Englishman, the Irishman, the German, the Frenchman, or any other man comes here you extend to him the hand of welcome and give him an equal chance with the rest; but when a Chinaman appears, who has just as good a right to come here to better his condition and seek happiness as the others, you pelt him with stones and brickbats from the moment he leaves the vessel, and when at last he finds protection among his persecuted countrymen, you refuse to employ him, you will not allow him to enter your schools, you exclude him from the jury box, you do not allow him to have, exercise, or enjoy any of the rights of citizenship, and now, to complete the long list of wrongs, you declare by this bill that he shall never be naturalized." 13 Cong. Rec. 2185 (1882).

Joyce thought that colleagues who worried about the length of the proposed ban were misplacing their concern. Duration was not the issue. By restricting laborers as an entire class, rather than curing specific problems within that class, the bill was fatally overinclusive:

"I believe the total prohibition of these people from our shores for any length of time, however short, is not only unnecessary and uncalled for, but that it is a cowardly repudiation, in our dealings with a weak nation, of a just and long-established principle in our Government, as well as a bold and open violation of the letter and spirit of our solemn treaty obligations with the people of China." 13 Cong. Rec. 2185 (1882).

Joyce summarized his reasons for opposition. The bill involved clear treaty violations, hostility to the spirit of American institutions, antagonism to America's founding principles, contradiction of traditional U.S. foreign policies, repudiation of national declarations and traditional policies on immigration, undermining the historic opening to China, damage to commercial relations, and a palpable tension with the 1880 Republican platform. "I am sure this bill ought not to pass, and that every man who votes for it will in the end most deeply regret it," Joyce warned. 13 Cong. Rec. 2185 (1882).

Representative Godlove S. Orth (R–IN) spoke next. He was a six-term member of the House (1863–1871, 1875–1877, and 1879–1882). Orth considered the legislation terribly backward:

"The grave question is presented whether sufficient cause exists for our Government and people to cast aside the cherished traditions of our past history—to repeal at least by implication, the laws which by common consent have been placed upon our statute-book; to infringe upon the spirit if not the letter of treaties most solemnly ratified, and to adopt a policy in direct opposition to the genius of our institutions and the cherished principles of our fathers.

"Congress is now deliberating whether we shall forsake these principles, turn our backs upon those traditions which adorn the most brilliant pages of our history, and will take a backward step which if followed to its logical sequence will, in my judgment, place us but little in advance of the time in history known as the 'dark ages' of the world." 13 Cong. Rec. 2186 (1882).

Population trends, which had been cited with such concern by Representative Page and other Pacific Coast members of Congress, did not alarm Orth. In the 1870 census, there were fewer than 64,000 Chinese in America. Ten years later, the population was 105,000 (see § 2.29, Chinese Population in the United States, 1860–1940). Did an increase of just over 42,000 people in ten years actually portend a threat to the well-being of American institutions? Orth thought the assertion was ridiculous:

"There is one Chinaman for every five hundred Americans and I submit it is not creditable to our manhood to assert that the five hundred Americans are likely to be overcome by 'one heathen Chinee.' Then again, it is well known that they are by no means a migratory people, nor aggressive in their character." 13 Cong. Rec. 2187 (1882).

Orth pointed out additional baseless or contradictory arguments that underpinned the bill. He took aim at obvious ironies.

How could members of Congress have disdain for Chinese who did not speak English, when America admitted tens of thousands of Europeans annually who also did not speak English?

How could members of Congress comment on the Chinese manner of dress, when no one said a word about variations in the garments of European immigrants?

How could members of Congress harp on paganism, when the Constitution left religion to the conscience of every person and the United States had never imposed a religious test on immigration?

How could members of Congress complain that the Chinese took no interest in government, when American laws barred them from the franchise?

Arguments that the 1880 Republican party platform required party support for the bill were misplaced. The platform had called for legislation that was "just, humane, and reasonable." The pending legislation was anything but that, argued Representative Orth. He would not support a racially motivated bill, and he issued a challenge:

"Bring us a bill that is not founded on race or color; one that will protect our people from the influx of servile coolie labor; one that will keep us from contact with disease or crime; or from a class of immigrants who are unfit or undesirable elements of the body-politic, and no one will give it more hearty support than myself.

"But this proposed legislation is based on race or color, is in derogation of justice and right, subverts the time honored traditions of the fathers, tramples alike upon treaties and statutes, strikes at the fundamental principles of republicanism, and seeks to rob our nation of the brightest jewels in the coronet of glory." 13 Cong. Rec. 2189 (1882).

With that, the long House debate of March 22, 1882, ended.

§4.70 House Debate, March 23, 1882: "The most hideous immoralities"

Under consideration in the House Committee of the Whole, S. 71, as passed by the Senate.

Thursday, March 23, 1882, was the day the bill suspending Chinese immigration to the United States for twenty years passed. Supporters dominated the early proceedings. Representative George C. Hazelton (R–WI), a member from 1877 to 1883, spoke of the importance of immigration to America's future:

"It has come as an ally of our civilization, as a compatriot in the sacred cause of liberty, as a collaborator in our moral, intellectual, and material progress. It has come to make our battlefields illustrious and our victories secure, until, under a natural blending of the old into the new life, the national domain extends from ocean to ocean . . . ." 13 Cong. Rec. 2208 (1882).

But Hazleton made clear that he was referring to European immigration, not Chinese. Immigration should be open only to homogeneous peoples, he insisted.

Opponents had claimed the bill would contravene U.S. treaty obligations. Hazelton thought differently. He posited that America had been faithful to its commitments, while China had violated such agreements repeatedly:

"Every coolie importation from China to our shores is an open and flagrant violation of the Burlingame Treaty. Not a Chinese laborer has come through the Golden Gate to the Pacific shore of the class and character contemplated by the treaty." 13 Cong. Rec. 2208 (1882).

Hazelton wanted to send a clear message to the Chinese emperor. Congress was dissatisfied with the class of persons emigrating to the United States, and had a right to legislate a twenty-year suspension:

"We believe that their coming affects the interests and good order of our country, and especially of certain localities in the States of the Pacific. We are convinced that we cannot safely make these subjects of yours citizens of the Republic . . . ." 13 Cong. Rec. 2209 (1882).

Representative Hazelton characterized the alien and distinct nature of the Chinese community in California:

"This system of labor that now darkens the fair lands of the Pacific Coast embraces 150,000 (sic) coolies. It embraces an adult male population equal to more than one-third of the entire voting power of that State. It lives in herds and sleeps like packs of dogs in kennels. It subsists on loathsome food, and all the methods of living are revolting to human nature. It is a monstrosity whose touch blasts our civic virtues and paralyzes our system of labor. It has been there thirty years and more, and Christianity has not yet pierced the walls of its heathen superstitions or removed a pagan god from its altars." 13 Cong. Rec. 2210 (1882).

It was impossible to tolerate such a presence without risking social unrest, Hazelton suggested. The congressman did not think legislating against it would damage commercial relations with China. But even if it did, Congress had to act anyway. National self-preservation took paramount importance.

Representative Romualdo Pacheco (R–CA) spoke next. The twelfth governor of California (February 27, 1875–December 9, 1875), he served two terms in the House, between 1879 and 1883. Pacheco characterized the Chinese as unchanging and immovable, wholly incapable of assimilation. In a debate often marked by race prejudice, Pacheco's remarks were among the most bigoted delivered:

"By the laws of heredity, the habits of his ancestors live in his character and are incorporated in his blood and brain . . . . The same fierce struggle which has engaged his ancestors for centuries engages him now. He has known only the most pinching poverty and expects nothing else. His religion, if religion it may be called, is the worship of the gods which are the work of his own hands. Family ties and obligations and the sweets of home life are naught to him.

"The long course of training which has gone on for so many generations has made of the Chinaman a lithe, sinewy creature, with muscles like iron and almost devoid of nerves or sensibilities. His ancestors have also bequeathed to him the most hideous immoralities. They are as natural to him as the yellow hue of his skin, and are so shocking and horrible that their character cannot even be hinted. This is the testimony of several well-known writers, as well as the opinion of every people where this race has migrated." 13 Cong. Rec. 2211 (1882).

Discontented labor in other countries had turned to revolution when political systems had been deaf to its interests, Pacheco noted. "God forbid that we should ever see a like effect in our own land," he said. Hear the voice of his constituents, Pacheco implored. They asked not for an armed force to expel the Chinese, not even a deportation campaign. But Chinese immigration must be stopped and the wounds it opened must be healed:

"They ask merely that the evil already done them shall be restricted to its present proportions, that the mongrel race, ready to sweep down upon them in countless numbers, shall not be permitted to make of earth's garden spot a dreary wilderness, and of our white brethren homeless, famishing outcasts." 13 Cong. Rec. 2211 (1882).

Debate was drawing to a close. Representative Richard W. Townshend (D–

IL) gave the last major speech supporting the bill. His distinctly partisan remarks were a precursor of future Chinese exclusion debates. Townshend wanted to ensure that if Pacific Coast voters were giving political credit for the bill, Democrats would receive it. "Mr. Speaker, this is in fact a Democratic measure," he began. "If it becomes a law, thanks will be due to the Democrats of the Senate and the House of Representatives and a minority of Republicans in both Houses." 13 Cong. Rec. 2212 (1882).

Townshend recited a history of demands from the Pacific Coast to Congress. The first had come in 1869, merely a year after the Burlingame Treaty had been ratified. That entreaty, and ones coming in the years of Republican control that followed were rebuffed:

"In 1869, there was a Republican majority in both Houses of Congress and a Republican President presided over the destiny of this country. An appeal was made to that, the Forty-first Congress. How was it answered? The Republican Party turned their back upon the pathetic appeal of the people of California. It was renewed to the Forty-second Congress, which was likewise Republican. Numerous memorials, resolutions of public meetings, petitions, one containing over 1,000 signatures, were presented, but they were all ignored. The people of the Pacific States appealed to the Forty-third, another Republican Congress, and again relief was refused. It was not until a Democratic House assembled here for the first time since the war that the grievances of the people found a hearing." 13 Cong. Rec. 2212 (1882).

Things changed when Democrats took charge of the House in the 45th Congress (1877–1879). They passed the Fifteen Passenger bill in 1879. The vote distribution demonstrated it was Democrats who should be credited with that legislation, Townshend said. In the House, 110 Democrats supported the bill and only 9 opposed it, while 45 Republicans favored the legislation and 63 voted no. After the Senate passage, the bill had gone to President Rutherford Hayes, "a Republican President, who had it in his power by a stroke of a pen to make it the law of the land." President Hayes had vetoed the bill, so "the hopes of the people were disappointed," said Townshend.

Now, Townshend turned his vote analysis to the twenty-year exclusion bill. The Senate breakdown was instructive, he suggested:

"You will find that among all who voted against it there was but one Democratic Senator, and of those who voted for it there were but eight Senators on the Republican side; of those Republican Senators who favored the bill, there were but two of them who did not come from the Pacific slope." 13 Cong. Rec. 2212 (1882).

Representative Townshend was highly pleased about what the Senate vote illustrated:

"Mr. Speaker, the evidence discloses the fact that this is in reality a Democratic measure." 13 Cong. Rec. 2212 (1882).

The Illinois Congressman Townshend found there was a significant difference between the way Democratic and Republican party platforms of 1880 treated Chinese immigration. Both documents had been cited to justify support for exclusion, but to Townshend, the Democratic platform was explicit, while the Republican plank was "equivocating, evasive, and cringing." Democrats had said plainly that there would be "no more Chinese immigration," and congressional Democrats would obey that injunction.

Pandering to Pacific voters, Townshend accused Republicans of advocating voting rights for the Chinese. He observed that, "some seem as anxious to enfranchise the Chinese coolies as they have been to enfranchise the African."

Townshend advocated segregating Chinese from the remainder of American society, and offered a pair of remarkable analogies:

"I would deal with this evil on the same principle that the inhabitants of a city located on the lowlands of the Lower Mississippi guard against the danger of overflow when they erect a levee or barrier to keep out the submerging waters; or, as the introduction of yellow fever into the country is prevented by quarantining against it, so would I erect an impassable barrier against the inundation of servile coolies of China, and thereby guard this country from the social and political contamination of their pointing presence." 13 Cong. Rec. 2214–15 (1882).

America was approaching a fresh political divide, he said. Previously, the country had been split along North-South lines, but the new division would center on which party would be cast as a friend of labor and which would be a foe. Democrats were labor's allies, while Republicans stood for avarice and monopoly. Democrats would protect labor from Chinese competition, while Republicans wanted cheap workers to serve wealthy business interests. Concluding his remarks, Townshend issued a challenge:

"This bill draws the line of demarcation between the true friends of American labor and its oppressors. On which side of the line will representatives of the American people be found? Their answer will be given in the roll-call which will soon be made." 13 Cong. Rec. 2215 (1882).

It was by now late in the afternoon of March 23, 1882. Exclusion legislation had been pending on the floor of the House since March 14, 1882, and been debated over much of seven session days. The time for voting had been reached.

The first House vote was a roll call on the amendment by Iowa Republican John Kasson to limit the period of exclusion to ten years. The amendment failed by a count of 100 in favor, 139 against, and 61 not voting.

An amendment by Republican Representative Benjamin Butterworth of Ohio to cut the exclusion from twenty to fifteen years failed on a division vote of 87 ayes to 99 nays.

Republican Representative William Rice of Massachusetts offered two amendments, one to strike the ban on laborers and replace it with a limit on "coolies, criminals, and persons diseased with leprosy or the smallpox, from China." The second amendment would have replaced the outright ban with a 10,000-person annual ceiling on Chinese laborers. Both amendments were rejected by voice vote.

An amendment by Republican Representative William P. Hepburn of Iowa to exclude "Chinese slaves, or persons held to labor for a term of years, all Chinese criminals, paupers, and diseased persons," including deporting such individuals, was rejected by voice vote.

John Kasson of Iowa attempted one more amendment. He proposed permitting ships in distress that carried Chinese passengers, and which were bound for somewhere outside the United States, to enter American ports, provided that all Chinese passengers departed with the vessel. The bill manager, Horace Page (R–CA), had already announced his opposition to all amendments, so even this proposal went down on a voice vote.

Assessing the sentiment of the House, Kasson then withdrew from consideration an amendment to strike the Senate-passed provision barring Chinese naturalization. There was no need, he said, to trouble the House to vote on it.

By voice vote, the House turned down an amendment offered by Republican Representative Rufus Dawes of Ohio to strike the ban on "both skilled and unskilled laborers and Chinese employed in mining," and replace it with "only coolies or servile laborers, diseased or lewd persons, criminals and paupers."

Republican Representative William Cullen of Illinois proposed an amendment to limit the words "Chinese laborers" to mean someone whose transportation to the United States had been arranged by a person, company, or corporation to whom that individual had by express or implied contract agreed to be bound. The amendment was defeated by voice vote.

On behalf of Kasson, Massachusetts Republican George Robinson offered an amendment that would strike Section Seventeen of the bill. That section had defined "Chinese laborers" broadly, to include both skilled and unskilled workers and persons employed in mining. The amendment was rejected by voice vote.

The final amendment was a full substitute for the bill. Proposed by Iowa Republican Moses McCoid, the substitute was identical to the pending measure except in one material respect. It allowed for the naturalization of Chinese persons in the United States, "[p]rovided, that they have resided therein ten years, and for five years previous to their naturalization shall have adopted the manners, customs, dress, and general habits of citizens of the United States." The amendment was defeated by voice vote.

The vote on final passage of the twenty-year exclusion bill was 167 in favor, 66 opposed, and 59 not voting. Of the 167 affirmative votes, 59 were Republicans, 98 were Democrats, and 10 were Independents. Of the 66 negative votes, 62 were Republicans and 4 were Democrats. Future Speaker Joseph Cannon (1903–1911) (R–IL) and future President William McKinley (R–OH) voted for the bill. Future Speakers Thomas Reed (1889–1891 and 1895–1899) (R–ME) and David Henderson (1899–1903) (R–IA) opposed it.

Because the House had passed a Senate bill without amendment, the legislation was sent to the White House for President Chester Arthur's consideration.

§4.80 A Presidential Veto: Chester Arthur: "A breach of our national faith"

Nearly three years after President Rutherford Hayes vetoed the 1879 Fifteen Passenger bill, opponents of Chinese immigration had tried again. Their legislation had been considered on the Senate and House floors for a month. President Hayes had justified his veto in 1879 of the Fifteen Passenger bill on the basis that the bill violated existing treaty arrangements with China. The Burlingame Treaty had since been updated by the Angell Treaty, allowing for some immigration limits to be put on the Chinese. In its aftermath, the twenty-year exclusion bill had passed in 1882. Was the legislation a proper exercise of U.S treaty rights, or had Congress again overstepped? On April 4, 1882, President Chester Arthur answered with his veto message.

The president began by reciting the essence of the Burlingame Treaty:

"The treaty commonly known as the Burlingame Treaty conferred upon Chinese subjects the right of voluntary emigration to the United States for the purposes of curiosity or trade, or as permanent residents, and was in all respects reciprocal as to citizens of the United States in China. It gave to the voluntary emigrant coming to the United States the right to travel there or reside there, with all the privileges, immunities, or exemptions enjoyed by the citizens or subjects of the most favored nation." 13 Cong. Rec. 2251 (1882).

Congress found that operation of the Burlingame Treaty had not necessarily been a boon to the United States, said the president. To mitigate the effects on domestic labor from unrestricted Chinese immigration, Congress passed the Fifteen Passenger bill, but President Hayes vetoed it as inconsistent with America's Burlingame Treaty obligations.

Subsequent bilateral negotiations resulted in treaty modifications, the president observed, which left the structure of the Burlingame Treaty intact except for provisions permitting constraints on Chinese laborer immigration. The exercise of such rights was America's to implement, but it had to be consistent with the parties' intentions and understandings:

"China may therefore fully have a right to expect that in enforcing them we will take good care not to overstep the grant and take more than has been conceded to us." 13 Cong. Rec. 2251 (1882).

President Arthur would not second-guess Congress on the need to impose some restrictions on Chinese laborers, and he did not necessarily quarrel with treating Chinese immigration differently from European.

"I think it may fairly be accepted as an expression of the opinion of Congress that the coming of such laborers to the United States, or their residence here, affects our interests and endangers good order throughout the country. On this point I should feel it my duty to accept the views of Congress." 13 Cong. Rec. 2251 (1882).

But the president complained that the twenty-year restriction exceeded what the Angell Treaty negotiators on both sides had contemplated. The Chinese had proposed limitations on the right to regulate, limit, or suspend immigration. American negotiators had rejected precise limits, but had indicated that the right might never be exercised and, if it were, implementation would depend upon specific, even local, circumstances. This understanding was satisfactory to the Chinese. The president quoted the bilateral declaration that accompanied the Angell Treaty:

"The Government of China agrees that the Government of the United States may regulate, limit, or suspend such coming or residence, but may not absolutely prohibit it. The limitation or suspension shall be reasonable, and shall apply only to Chinese who go to the United States as laborers, other classes not being included in the limitations. Legislation taken in regard to Chinese laborers will be of such character only as is necessary to enforce the regulation, limitation, or suspension of immigration." 13 Cong. Rec. 2252 (1882).

President Arthur was clear that the twenty-year limitation, which was the length of an entire generation, departed excessively from the Angell Treaty understandings, so the exclusion bill did not faithfully implement the Angell Treaty. He felt compelled to veto it:

"I regard this provision of the act as a breach of our national faith; and being unable to bring myself in harmony with the views of Congress on this vital point. The honor of the country constrains me to return the act with this objection to its passage." 13 Cong. Rec. 2252 (1882).

The president also complained about the imposition of unique registration and passport requirements. These mandates were discriminatory and set a questionable precedent:

"I think it may be doubted whether provisions requiring personal registration and the taking out of passports which are not imposed upon natives can be required of Chinese. Without expressing an opinion on that point, I may invite the attention of Congress to the fact that the system of registration and passports is undemocratic and hostile to the spirit of our institutions. I doubt the wisdom of putting an entering wedge of this kind into our laws." 13 Cong. Rec. 2252 (1882).

President Arthur highlighted the contributions that Chinese immigrants had already made in America:

"No one can say that the country has not profited by their work. They were largely instrumental in constructing the railways which connect the Atlantic with the Pacific. The States of the Pacific slope are full of evidences of their industry. Enterprises profitable akin to the capitalist and to the laborer of Caucasian origin would have lain dormant but for them." 13 Cong. Rec. 2252 (1882).

If such workers were no longer needed in California, the president suggested, other regions of the country might profit from their presence.

Long-lasting exclusion policies were counterproductive to America's best interests in the Far East, he continued. The United States should avoid that backlash by being careful in how it implemented its treaty rights:

"It needs no argument to show that the policy we now propose to adopt must have a direct tendency to repel oriental nations from us and to drive their trade and commerce into more friendly hands. It may be that the great and paramount interest of protecting our labor from Asiatic competition may justify a permanent adoption of this policy. But it is wiser, in the first place, to make a shorter experiment, with a view hereafter of maintaining permanently only such features as time and experience may commend." 13 Cong. Rec. 2252 (1882).

The veto message was dated April 4, 1882. Because the bill originated in the Senate, it was returned to that body to determine whether the veto could be overridden. Senate proceedings commenced the following day.

§4.90 Senate Veto Override Debate, April 5, 1882: "Will not disgrace our statute books"

On April 5, 1882, Senator John Sherman (R–OH) moved to refer the vetoed bill as well as the veto message and accompanying documents to the Senate Committee on Foreign Relations. The motion proved controversial. The most active proponents of exclusion, such as Senators James Farley (D–CA), Samuel Maxey (D–TX), and John Tyler Morgan (D–AL), wanted an override vote without delay.

Senator Morgan made a point of order against the motion to refer the veto message to committee. He reasoned:

"The Constitution of the United States requires the Senate shall proceed now to consider the veto message and to reconsider the bill notwithstanding the objections of the President of the United States, and we have not the right to do anything else than that with the subject now before the Senate." 13 Cong. Rec. 2607 (1882).

President Pro Tempore David Davis (R–IL) did not sustain the point of order. He cited precedent for referring veto messages to committee, even though the effect of doing so may have buried legislation without the possibility of an override vote on the Senate floor.

Opening the debate on the motion to refer, Sherman said that Congress' pursuit of exclusion legislation was little better than the isolationist policies that China had itself long pursued. Such Chinese xenophobia had been sharply condemned in the West:

"Under pretense of regulating importation of Chinese laborers, Congress passed a bill which prohibits Chinese immigration for twenty years. If such a bill had been proposed in either House of Congress twenty years ago, it would have been the death warrant of the man who offered it. In order to cure an evil which we admit, we passed a Chinese bill, a bill based upon a policy peculiar to China, that of exclusion of all the world from Chinese soil. In other words, we abandoned the American principle of inviting people from all lands to come and participate with us in developing a great country, and we have adopted the old public policy of the Chinese, which is to exclude the people of all other lands from their soil." 13 Cong. Rec. 2608 (1882).

Senator Sherman expressly endorsed five complaints from the Chinese government that the vetoed bill seriously overreached American rights under the Angell Treaty. Via a memorandum from China's ambassador (then called a minister) to the United States, China had objected to the twenty-year duration, the overinclusive definition of laborer, and the passport and registration system.

China also protested that the bill failed to provide for the admission of Chinese who had to transit the United States in order to travel to China.

As to the twenty-year ban, the Chinese memorandum said:

"The time fixed in the bill, namely, twenty years, is 'unreasonable.' The language of article I that 'laborers shall not be absolutely prohibited from coming to the United States' and that the 'suspension shall be reasonable' as well as the negotiations, indicate that a brief period was intended. The total prohibition of immigration of Chinese laborers into the United States for twenty years would, in my opinion, be unreasonable, and a violation of the meaning and intent of the treaty." 13 Cong. Rec. 2609 (1882).

The Chinese ambassador further argued that the term "skilled labor" was outside the words and intent of the treaty. This addition, asserted the memorandum, would "operate with harshness upon a class of Chinese merchants entitled to admission to the United States under the treaty."

Senator Sherman was also greatly troubled by this provision:

"Here is a treaty yielded to us by China for our benefit, not for theirs . . . by which they agree that the importation of Chinese laborers shall be suspended for a time in this country. Then you make the word 'laborers' embrace a class of people that in no country in the world are classed as 'laborers.' A merchant who manufactures and sells his own wares, a mechanic, a blacksmith, the shoemaker at his last who manufacturers shoes that he sells himself . . . . You extend the meaning of the term 'laborers,' the class that the people of California complain of, so as to include all mechanics, blacksmiths, artisans, merchants, dealers, men who require capital as well as mere labor." 13 Cong. Rec. 2609 (1882).

As to the registration system, the memorandum said:

"The clauses of the bill relating to registration and passports are a vexatious discrimination against Chinese residents and immigrants, when article 2 (of the treaty) provides explicitly that they shall be entitled to all the privileges conceded to the subjects of the most favored nation." 13 Cong. Rec. 2610 (1882).

Senator Sherman concurred in this objection. At that time, passports were unprecedented in America. In their unique application to the Chinese, and in their specificity, the passports were discriminatory. Senators from California had claimed the passports would help Chinese to prove identity and affirm legal rights, but Sherman was not persuaded, and he thought the passport provision should be dropped.

The ambassador's fourth objection was that the legislation would leave the impression either that the Chinese government misunderstood the treaty it negotiated, or that Congress had willfully disregarded the Angell Treaty's mean-

§4.91 The Role of Precedent in Congress

Precedents are created when the presiding officer opines on a question of procedure, usually in response to a point of order from the floor. Rulings on points of order are subject to the possibility of an appeal to the full chamber. The rules of the Senate and the House are the foundation of procedure in those chambers, but precedents are immensely important in shaping interpretations of the rules. In some cases, rules may be silent and a precedent is all that is available to guide the presiding officer. Where precedents conflict with the text of the rules, the precedent dominates. For instance, Senate Rule 19 states that the presiding officer shall recognize the first senator who addresses him. But for more than seventy years, the Senate has followed a precedent giving preference in recognition to the Majority Leader above all other senators. Senate Rule 19 has never been amended to reflect what is now routine Senate practice.

ing. Either interpretation, said the memorandum, "will tend to prejudice the intelligent classes against the United States Government and its people, whom they now greatly admire and respect." 13 Cong. Rec. 2610 (1882).

Sherman framed this objection bluntly:

"The Chinese say, 'If you pass a bill like this, our people will feel that you cheated us in making that treaty or that you have violated your treaty with us.'" 13 Cong. Rec. 2610 (1882).

The fifth Chinese complaint was that the bill made no provision for the movement of Chinese wishing to enter the United States for purposes of transit. The memorandum stated:

"Large numbers of Chinese live in Cuba, Peru, and other countries who cannot return home without crossing the territory of the United States or touching at San Francisco. To deny this privilege, it seems to me, is in violation of international law and the comity of nations, and if the bill becomes a law it will, in this respect, result in great hardship to many thousands of innocent Chinese in foreign countries." 13 Cong. Rec. 2610 (1882).

Having endorsed the Chinese government's objections, Sherman added several thoughts of his own. While the legislation answered expressed passions, the response was disproportionate and inappropriate:

"I have no doubt that the people of California and the Pacific Coast have suffered from the evils that have grown out of Chinese immigration, but they are sensible American citizens, and they ought to feel that in passing laws for them, we ought to pass such laws as will not disgrace our statute books and set a bad example in respect to other nations. While we should do for our brethren in California all that could be expected from us to protect them from what they regard now as a great and growing evil, why should we do it in such a way as to violate the fundamental principles of the American policy which has distinguished us from the American Revolution to this hour?" 13 Cong. Rec. 2610 (1882).

The bill, S. 71, and the Angell Treaty were not consistent. For that reason, referral of the bill and related treaty documents to the Senate Committee on Foreign Relations was justified. Legislation conforming to the Angell Treaty could be crafted there.

Senator Augustus Garland (D–AR) opposed the motion to refer. Debate in the Senate had been lengthy; all arguments had been expressed. Referral to the Senate Committee on Foreign Relations would accomplish nothing, said Garland, except to sidetrack the bill. The Senate had enough information to address the veto now, he insisted.

Next to speak was Senator John Tyler Morgan (D–AL), one of exclusion's most vigorous advocates. He considered the referral to be an abdication of constitutional responsibility:

"The whole object and purpose of reference of the bill to the Committee on Foreign Relations is to relieve the President from the necessity we are under of either affirming or disaffirming his action by our vote upon a call for the yeas and nays . . . Therefore, there can be but one purpose in the motion to refer to the committee, and that is to avoid all action on the part of the Senate of the United States by which they may express their approval or their disapproval of the objections which the President has urged against the passage of such a law." 13 Cong. Rec. 2611 (1882).

Morgan stoutly criticized the Chinese government's efforts to lobby against the bill. He considered the Chinese minister's memorandum extraordinary and offensive:

"The President of the United States has invited or has allowed the Chinese Minister to come in here and to suggest objections against the legislation of Congress, and they are sent to us with a view to influence us in our course upon a great question concerning the very civilization of the people of the United States. It seems to me that it is the most extraordinary exhibition that was ever made in a legislative body or before a great people." 13 Cong. Rec. 2611 (1882).

Morgan complained that President Arthur had taken the Chinese objections more seriously than the views of the large Senate and House majorities that had passed the bill:

"It is not to be forgotten that the will of Congress upon this subject and its enlightened consideration of these questions is to have no influence in this country. It is not to be forgotten that administration after administration has thrown itself across the pathway of the people of the United States who are trying to exclude these heathens and pagans from our country and to prevent them from absorbing that which is the rightful heritage of the laboring people of our own race and kind." 13 Cong. Rec. 2612 (1882).

The Republican Party was to blame for this state of affairs, Senator Morgan said, and was guilty of using procedural devices, such as Sherman's motion to refer, in order to mask its culpability:

"The action of the Republican Party upon this subject is distinct and definite beyond all denial, and now the leader of that party in the Senate rises here and for purposes of smothering out the question, and preventing the people of the United States from having a clear view of it, undertakes to ask us to evade the Constitution of the United States by refusing to vote upon the question of reconsideration . . . ." 13 Cong. Rec. 2612 (1882).

After additional debate of this nature, the Senate rejected Sherman's motion to refer the bill and veto message to the Committee on Foreign Relations. The moment had arrived for the veto override vote. President Pro Tempore David Davis (R–IL) put the question:

"The question is, Shall the bill pass, the objections of the President of the United States to the contrary notwithstanding? The yeas and nays are to be taken on this question by the Constitution. Those who are in favor of the passage of the bill notwithstanding the objections of the President of the United States will, as your names are called answer 'yea;' those of a contrary opinion will, as your names are called, answer 'nay.'"

On the question, 29 senators voted yea, 21 voted nay, and 2 were absent. The bill had secured the support of 58 percent of the senators present and voting, but an override needed affirmation by two-thirds of senators present and voting. The twenty-year version of the Chinese exclusion legislation, known as "An act to execute certain treaty stipulations relating to the Chinese," thus failed.

When President Rutherford Hayes vetoed the Fifteen Passenger Bill in 1879, it took Congress three years to craft new legislation to exclude the Chinese. That effort had now resulted in another veto. This time, Congress would not wait long to try again. Victory for the exclusionists was at hand.

CHAPTER FIVE

美
國
The Ten-Year Exclusion Legislation of 1882

"We are driven by facts, which we cannot resist or avoid, to the conclusion that it has become a solemn necessity on our part to protect the Caucasian race on this continent against the intrusion of Oriental people."
—Senator John Tyler Morgan (D–AL)
13 Cong. Rec. 3267 (1882)

§5.0 Overview

- House Party Division: 151 Republicans, 128 Democrats, 14 Independents
- Senate Party Division: 37 Republicans, 37 Democrats, 2 Independents
- President: Chester A. Arthur (R) (1881–1885)

Following President Arthur's veto of the twenty-year exclusion bill on April 4, 1882, Congress quickly acted to pass a ten-year suspension of skilled and unskilled laborer immigration. The ten-year bill also carried the ban on naturalization of Chinese persons. Chinese who were already in the United States were entitled to government-issued certificates allowing them to return to the United States.

This time, President Arthur signed the bill. Known popularly as the Chinese Exclusion Act, the legislation became law on May 6, 1882. As a result, persons of Chinese origin born outside of the United States could not become American citizens until 1943, when the exclusion policy was repealed.

A week after the failed April 5, 1882, override vote in the Senate of President Arthur's veto of S. 71 (*§ 4.90*), an act to exclude Chinese from immigrating for twenty years, (*Chapter Four*), the House Committee on Education and Labor reported H.R. 5804, a ten-year exclusion bill. As with the vetoed bill, the House measure also barred the naturalization of Chinese persons. The committee report was three paragraphs long. It cited the state referenda that had supported immigration restrictions, the endorsement of both parties' 1880 platforms for such constraints, and Garfield's 1880 letter accepting the Republican party presidential nomination. The House committee report also stated as an "undisputed fact" that more than 100,000 Chinese laborers were in California, that they were bound under labor contracts to the Chinese Six Companies, that such immigrants undercut the local workforce, and that the Chinese had no desire to assimilate into American institutions. H. Rep. No. 1017, at p. 1 (1882).

Representative Albert Shelby Willis (D–KY), for himself and four colleagues, submitted minority views. Willis understood that the committee would seek the bill's consideration under suspension of the rules. The suspension process would provide for limited debate and no possibility of floor amendments. Shut out from amending the bill, but favoring even more rigorous exclusion, Willis

194

and his allies committed to vote for it. But they favored even more vigorous exclusion. To express their real position, they filed minority views to accompany the committee report.

A ten-year ban was simply insufficient, Willis wrote. Nothing shorter than fifteen years would respond to the pleas of Pacific Coast citizens, appeals that had been loud, widespread, and longstanding. Thus far, the hope that Congress would act had contained discontent that otherwise might have spilled over into bloodshed:

"The hope of securing that relief has hushed the voice and stayed the hand of violence. The indignant excitement born of the strange and burdensome conditions imposed by a class of immigrants self-determined upon alien, sordid, and unrepublican customs has been held in praiseworthy restraint. It has not been believed—it is not now believed—that the just, well-founded and almost unanimous demand of four sovereign States will be disregarded." 13 Cong. Rec. 2968 (1882).

Chinese were likely to interpret a ten-year suspension as merely temporary, Willis said, which would undermine the goal of repairing economies damaged by the immigration. He quoted John Franklin Swift, one of the three U.S. commissioners at the Angell Treaty negotiations in 1880 and a member of the House from California from 1877–1880, who was known to have stridently anti-Chinese attitudes. Swift had remarked:

"For my part, I would rather have no act passed at all than one suspending Chinese immigration for ten years only. It would keep us in a doubtful state of turmoil and trouble and do no good. If we are to have Chinese and nothing else it is better to know it at once so that we can either move out of the country or adapt ourselves to that form of society." 13 Cong. Rec. 2968 (1882).

Believing the principle of exclusion had been well accepted, Willis could not understand conceding to a ten-year limit. Why give up on fifteen years, he thought.

American power to control Chinese labor immigration was plenary, insisted Willis. That much could be ascertained from the report of the Angell Treaty commissioners, which stated "that the Government of the United States has the power to regulate, limit, or suspend, without conditions, Chinese labor immigration when deemed injurious to the interests of its citizens."

If it passed a ten-year bill, Congress would be making inadequate use of this power, Willis argued. The time period of exclusion should be extended and penalties for evasion should be made more severe. Nevertheless, he and the other dissenters announced support for the committee-reported bill. No harsher alternative was available to them.

§5.10 House Debate, April 17, 1882:
"A pack of hounds to hunt down any race"

*Under consideration in the House Committee
of the Whole, H.R. 5804, as reported from the
House Committee on Education and Labor.*

Representative Horace Page (R–CA) moved consideration of H.R. 5804 under suspension of the rules. In 1882, procedures governing suspension provided for thirty minutes of debate. Speaker J. Warren Keifer (R–OH) announced that Page would control the half of the time allocated to the bill's supporters and that Representative Albert Shelby Willis (D–KY) would manage the remaining time. Although Willis claimed the time in opposition, the difference between his position and Page's stance was over the duration of Chinese exclusion rather than about the soundness of the policy. The effect of dividing the time between them was that supporters of exclusion would control all time for debate. The Speaker rebuffed protests from some House members that the time allocation was unfair.

Willis commenced the debate. He would vote for the legislation, he said, although he had three objections. The bill lacked a penalty provision, he complained. While the vetoed bill, S. 71, (*see Chapter Four*) had provided for fines and imprisonment for Chinese who knowingly violated the exclusion law, the pending measure was silent. In addition, the measure lacked the registration system, which had been in the vetoed bill and to which China had objected.

"You first strike out the penalty by which Chinamen are punished for coming here unlawfully, and then you cut out the provision for registration, thus rendering it utterly impossible to distinguish or identify the lawful from unlawful residents. Could the door for Chinese immigration be more widely and safely opened?" 13 Cong. Rec. 2968 (1882).

Willis left his most significant objection for last, such being the relative brevity of the ten-year immigration suspension. Willis was convinced that a fifteen-year provision would not generate a veto:

"Is anyone here authorized to say such a bill would invoke another veto, and would not become a law? I deny it. I deny it upon the facts. I deny it unless the President is opposed to the principle of the bill. If he is not opposed to the principle, why should he not sign a fifteen-year bill?" 13 Cong. Rec. 2968 (1882).

President Chester Arthur had rejected a twenty-year ban on Chinese immigration when he vetoed S. 71. During consideration of the vetoed bill, both the

Senate and the House had defeated amendments providing for ten-year suspensions. Fifteen years would be a compromise, Willis asserted.

Under suspension of the rules, he could not offer such an amendment. Nevertheless, the sentiment of Congress was clear. And it was time to stop dithering and make a law. With misgivings that the bill was not even more stringent, Willis would vote aye.

Controversy erupted about Willis being allowed to claim the time in opposition. The following brief excerpt, which occurred just after Willis took his seat, illustrates this dispute and demonstrates the momentum under which the legislation was pushed through the House, without a meaningful opportunity for dissent:

"Mr. [William W.] Rice, of Massachusetts. I rise to a parliamentary question.

"The Speaker. The gentleman will state it.

"Mr. Rice, of Massachusetts. I desire to ask whether no time is to be given to those who are opposed to the passage of the bill.

"Mr. Pacheco. They have had their time.

"The Speaker. The Chair recognized the only gentleman who desired to be heard.

"Mr. Rice, of Massachusetts. But he is in favor of the bill.

"The Speaker. The Chair simply did what it could do under the rule. No gentleman sought recognition for that purpose except the gentleman from Kentucky [Willis], a member of the committee, who made a minority report upon the bill, and stated that he desired to oppose it.

"Mr. Rice, of Massachusetts. But by the rules of the House the time shall be evenly divided between the advocates and the opponents of the measure. [Cries of 'regular order!']

"Mr. Springer. I ask that five minutes time be allowed to the gentleman from Massachusetts [Mr. Rice] in opposition to the bill.

"The Speaker. Is there objection to the request of the gentleman from Illinois?

"Several members objected." 13 Cong. Rec. 2969 (1882).

An extended and bitter exchange followed, during which Willis stipulated that he had privately notified the Speaker of his true position and that he would have forsaken the opposition allocation if anyone had sought to claim it:

"Mr. Willis. I wish to say that in the very first sentence I uttered, I communicated my purpose to support the bill. I did so intentionally, so that if any gentleman wished to object to my holding the floor, my intention was, as the Chair knows privately, to surrender it to anyone who desired to oppose the bill.

"The Speaker. No other person claimed the right to occupy the time in opposition to the bill, and the gentleman from Kentucky did speak in opposition to the bill, but stated he preferred a different one." 13 Cong. Rec. 2970 (1882).

Representative William W. Rice (R–MA) finally was able to have this exchange with the Speaker:

"Mr. Rice, of Massachusetts. I desire in good faith to state this: when a motion to suspend the rules is seconded, the rule says fifteen minutes shall be given in opposition to the measure. When a gentleman takes fifteen minutes and makes the strongest possible speech in favor of the bill that can be made, saying that although it is objectionable to him in some respects, he shall vote for it, where is the power in this House to give the fifteen minutes to men honestly opposed to it?

"The Speaker. If the gentleman from Massachusetts were to rise and state he desired to speak in opposition to the measure, the Chair would treat him as he treats every other member, in perfect good faith; and if when he got through, other members thought he spoke in favor of it and not against it, the Chair would still have to treat it as he did." 13 Cong. Rec. 2971 (1882).

The dispute dragged on, focusing on the parliamentary situation rather than on the legislation itself.

After matters settled down, Representative John A. Kasson (R–IA) rose to endorse passage. Serving in the House from 1863 to 1867, 1873 to 1877, and 1881 to 1884, Kasson had opposed the twenty-year bill, principally for treaty reasons. He was satisfied that reducing the suspension to ten years would satisfy this concern:

"I shall support it with the hope that by ten years trial, we shall be able to ascertain whether the complete suspension of this character of immigration should be continued or not." 13 Cong. Rec. 2973 (1882).

But Kasson condemned the jockeying for political advantage, at the expense of the Chinese.

"I do not believe in the partisan spirit with which gentlemen on the other side of the House [Democrats] have pressed this question upon us. I do not believe it to be just or the duty of the Congress to make itself a pack of hounds to hunt down any race born and permitted to live on God's earth. Remember that they ask us now to assail a race of human beings in large part of high civilization and high cultivation, to separate them from all other races on the face of the earth, to exclude them from American soil, to banish those who are now here from our midst, and to introduce a spirit of persecution into the legislation of Congress, whose glory has been in the past to make America an asylum of the oppressed of all nations." 13 Cong. Rec. 2973 (1882).

All time for debate had expired. On the question of final passage, the vote on the ten-year exclusion bill was 201 in favor, 37 opposed, and 53 not voting.

The following day, April 18, 1882, H.R. 5804 was received in the Senate and referred to the Senate Committee on Foreign Relations. The Senate committee did not deliberate for long, reporting the bill with amendments on April 19, 1882.

§5.20 Senate Debate, April 25, 1882: "A subject of deep respect and repentance"

Under consideration in the Senate Committee of the Whole H.R. 5804, with amendments proposed by the Senate Committee on Foreign Relations.

On motion of Senator John Miller (R–CA), H.R. 5804 was brought to the floor for consideration in the Senate Committee of the Whole (*§1.12*). Although the House had passed the bill under suspension of the rules after only thirty minutes of debate, Senate proceedings would take five additional days.

The amendments proposed by the Senate Committee on Foreign Relations were the ones initially considered.

- The first of these delayed from sixty to ninety days the legislation's implementation date. Following ninety days after enactment, and extending for ten years thereafter, it was unlawful for a Chinese laborer to come to the United States or to remain in the country.
- The second amendment imposed criminal penalties on the master of any vessel who knowingly brought Chinese laborers from any foreign port and permitted them to be landed in the United States. Fines up to $500 were possible for each such laborer so transported, and the penalty could also include a year in prison.
- A third amendment required a separate manifest for Chinese passengers, so that such persons could be easily distinguished from other passengers.
- A fourth amendment provided for an exception for ships in distress to make port in the United States, provided that no Chinese passengers would be permitted to disembark.
- A fifth amendment "grandfathered" Chinese laborers who had been in the United States prior to November 17, 1880. The date was chosen to coincide with the ratification of the Angell Treaty. As Senator Miller explained, "The treaty provides that all laborers who were in the United States at that time should have the privilege of coming and going of their own free

will and accord. That was the reason the date was fixed on the 17th day of November, 1880 . . . ." 13 Cong. Rec. 3262 (1882).

- A sixth amendment provided that a registry book be kept by the customs collector of any port from which a "grandfathered" Chinese laborer departed the United States, such registration to be evidence of that worker's right to reenter the country. A registrant was entitled to receive from the collector a highly detailed certificate that would serve as proof of identification to the master of a vessel and to U.S. immigration authorities.
- A seventh amendment provided that no Chinese person was permitted to enter the United States from a vessel without producing the certificate, and if a person was found to be unlawfully within the United States, he was subject to immediate deportation.
- An eighth amendment proposed to exempt from application of the law all official Chinese diplomats and their household servants.

All of these amendments from the Senate Committee on Foreign Relations proved non-controversial and were approved by voice vote.

The next committee amendment would have stricken section 14 of H.R. 5804, the provision that barred any state or federal court from naturalizing Chinese persons. Senator James Farley (D–CA), who had successfully amended the twenty-year bill to include the naturalization bar, rose in opposition:

"At the time it was put into the first bill, I know that some distinguished Senators took the ground that there was no necessity for this provision because the statute already provided for it. But notwithstanding that statute, the courts have been naturalizing Chinamen; and I shall insist on the rejection of the amendment at this time." 13 Cong. Rec. 3264 (1882).

Senator Farley asked for a roll call. The vote was 26 in favor of the amendment, 32 opposed, with eighteen senators not voting. By this vote, the denial of naturalization rights remained in the bill. The policy would not be reversed for more than sixty years.

The next committee amendment was to strike the definition of "Chinese laborers." The House-passed bill language provided:

"Sec. 15. That the words 'Chinese laborers' wherever used in this act, shall be construed to mean both skilled and unskilled laborers and Chinese employed in mining."

Senator La Fayette Grover (D–OR), an outspoken advocate of exclusion, asked the Senate to oppose the amendment. He thought it created an exception that would swallow the rule:

"I hope this amendment will not be agreed to. The Chinese embassy declare

§5.21 James A. Garfield and Race

James Garfield was committed to the abolition of slavery and to granting the voting rights to freedmen. Given his attitudes, it seems unlikely that President Garfield would have approved a measure that excluded Chinese immigrants from naturalizing. Exclusion legislation doing exactly that became law during what would have been Garfield's presidency, but for his assassination:

> Throughout his life, Garfield had been an ardent abolitionist. As a young man, he had written feverishly in his diary that he felt "like throwing the whole current of my life into the work of opposing this giant evil." In the darkest days of the Civil War, he had wondered if the war itself was God's punishment for the horrors of slavery . . .

Candice Miller, *Destiny of the Republic: A Tale of Madness, Medicine, and the Murder of a President* (Doubleday, 2011), p. 26.

Elected to the House from Ohio in 1862 while serving as a major general in the Union Army, Garfield strenuously promoted racial equality once he had taken office:

> In Congress, he fought for equal rights for freed slaves. He argued for a resolution that ended the practice of requiring blacks to carry a pass in the nation's capital, and he delivered a passionate speech for black suffrage. Is freedom "the bare privilege of not being chained?" he asked. "If this is all, then freedom is a bitter mockery, a cruel delusion, and it may well be questioned whether slavery is not better. Let us not commit ourselves to the absurd and senseless dogma that the color of the skin shall be the basis of suffrage, the talisman of liberty."

Candice Miller, *Destiny of the Republic: A Tale of Madness, Medicine, and the Murder of a President* (Doubleday, 2011), p. 8.

James Garfield (R) represented Ohio in the House for nine consecutive terms, 1863 to 1881, and was elected the twentieth president of the United States in 1880. His presidency lasted just 200 days—he took office March 4, 1881, he was shot by Charles Guiteau July 2, 1881, and died on September 19, 1881, when he was succeeded in office by his vice president, Chester Arthur.

[sic] that they do not desire that artisans be excluded. This is proposed to exclude the artisans. If they are not excluded by the terms of this bill, it will be found that nearly every Chinaman desiring to come to the United States will claim to be an artisan; and they will all be admitted; and thus the purposes of the

late treaty will be avoided and the purposes of the bill will be avoided, unless this amendment is disagreed to." 13 Cong. Rec. 3264 (1882).

Notwithstanding Grover's plea, the Senate voted by 29 yeas to 28 nays, with 19 absentees to agree to the amendment. For the time being, the definition was deleted. As proceedings were still at the Senate Committee of the Whole stage, both Farley and John Tyler Morgan (D–AL) announced that they would pursue the question yet again when the bill came up in the full Senate.

Before the bill was ordered reported by the Senate Committee of the Whole, Senator George Hoar (R–MA) asked to be recognized. Throughout his long Senate career, Hoar would consistently oppose legislation that discriminated against the Chinese. He criticized the ongoing efforts of the 47th Congress (1881–1883) to enact such a bill:

"It is impossible, it is incredible that a blow at the dignity of human nature, a blow at the dignity of labor, a blow at men, not because of their individual qualities or characters, but because of the color of their skin, should not fail to be a subject of deep regret and repentance to the American people in the nineteenth century." 13 Cong. Rec. 3265 (1882).

Hoar vigorously disputed the notion, often expressed in the debate on the twenty-year bill, that the Republican party platform of 1880 and the sentiments of the party's presidential nominee, James Garfield, supported an exclusion policy. He was determined to set the record straight. The platform required just, humane, and reasonable restrictions on immigration. Hoar interpreted that to support restraining the importation of coolie contract labor, but not to restrict immigrants moving of their own free will. About President Garfield, Hoar declared:

"I believe he would have gone to the stake . . . before he would have accepted the presidency or have subscribed his name to a declaration involving such a blow to the dignity of labor and the dignity of American humanity as is involved in this bill." 13 Cong. Rec. 3265 (1882).

Senator Hoar would not acquiesce in such discriminatory legislation nor permit President Garfield's memory to be sullied:

"I denounce this legislation not only as a violation of the ancient policy of the American Republic, not only as a violation of the rights of human nature itself, but especially as a departure from the doctrine to which the great party to which I belong is committed in its latest declaration of principles, and to which our great martyred chief, whom we were so proud to acknowledge as our standard bearer affixed his declaration in almost the last public act of his distinguished life." 13 Cong. Rec. 3265 (1882).

Upon conclusion of Hoar's remarks, debate in the Senate Committee of the Whole ended, and the bill, as amended, was reported to the full Senate.

In the Senate, the amendments adopted in the Senate Committee of the Whole were agreed to en bloc, with one exception. As he had forewarned, Senator Morgan wanted the committee amendment striking the definition of "laborer" to be considered for further discussion and another vote.

With that definition amendment now before the Senate, Morgan commenced the argument. He reviewed the history of several pieces of "anti-coolie" legislation that Congress had passed since 1862. These statutes were aimed at restricting the importation of "pauper labor" from "oriental countries," said Morgan:

"What we aimed to do in these statutes was to prevent laborers from being brought into this country who, after they arrived here, were held by contract for a term of service to their foreign employers and masters." 13 Cong. Rec. 3266 (1882).

These statutes were being dodged, Morgan insisted. The Pacific region had generated vast economic possibilities for the Chinese to exploit, so they had cleverly and successfully circumvented the legislation. Violations of the law could be hard to prove because evidence was being concealed, but they were occurring:

"It became necessary that some resort should be made by them to an evasion in order to escape the penal inflictions of our statutes. And what was that resort? It was simply that the contract should be kept silent and quiet; that the men who were imported from China should come here apparently free and of their own accord, but in fact and in truth, they come as much bound by the servitude in which they had engaged in China as the coolies ever were.

"There never was a time when a coolie was absolutely sold into slavery; there never was a time when one man sold a coolie to another; but there was a time in which coolies were obtained from the vast swarms of population in the oriental countries, and they were there engaged in the stipulations of contracts which were enforced against them in this country." 13 Cong. Rec. 3266 (1882).

Senator Morgan asserted that the vast majority of Chinese had come to the United States under contracts that they could not void. They were men of the lowest class, he said, bound by economic necessity to bear hardship without hope of rising above their caste. Such men lacked the capacity for self-emancipation. If Congress, through anti-coolie legislation, had meant to keep them from immigrating, the law had simply failed.

Fresh legislation was needed to prevent the amalgamation of irreconcilable peoples, and Congress must heed history, Morgan urged. To know what was in store if Congress failed to block Chinese immigration, senators need only contemplate the consequences of race-mixing in the South:

"That calamity is not the freedom of the Negro, not the loss of $2,500,000,000 which they were worth at the time of their emancipation, but it is that our fathers, from the North and the East, had brought into our communities an abnormal and irreconcilable element of the population. There is where we suffered." 13 Cong. Rec. 3267 (1882).

The situation would be compounded and uncontrollable if the Chinese were allowed to continue migrating to America, Morgan exclaimed. Historical experience demonstrated the political impossibility of dislodging a population once it took root in the United States:

"You may think you can easily manage this question, but when you have drawn from the 450,000,000 of Chinese the lower and worst class of their people, and after you have, in the name of liberty, and manhood, and God, and religion flooded this country with that horde of pagan adventurers, you may flatter yourselves that you can manage it. Let me inform you, as I speak today with anguish and with pain, that it does not rest in the power of man to remove an evil of this character once it has been engrafted upon a free Republic . . . .

"Although every man in each branch of Congress and the Presiden t might concur that it was an absolute moral and social necessity to expel the Negro from this land, the power does not exist to do it; and after you have got the Chinese here . . . the power will be wanted to expel them. You will then have to submit to an evil that you cannot overcome, neither can you avoid it. Your hands will have been tied by a fatal indiscretion, and woe betide the people when that day comes." 13 Cong. Rec. 3267 (1882).

Congress recognized the problem and passed the Fifteen Passenger bill to address it, Morgan said. The legislation had been bipartisan, but had been vetoed by President Hayes in 1879. After treaty renegotiation, implementing legislation had likewise been vetoed by President Arthur (§ 4.80). Senator Morgan proclaimed his frustration, which he claimed was widely shared:

"Thus, for four long years we have been struggling with this question in Congress; thus for four years the people have time and again, in both Democratic and Republican platforms and through the action of men of different parties in both Houses, expressed the solemn will and pleasure of the people of the United States in respect to their protection against Chinese immigration." 13 Cong. Rec. 3268 (1882).

The will of the country was clear. How had curative legislation not yet passed? The answer, Morgan claimed, was to be found in the scheming of wealthy elitists, whose need for free labor was threatened. Similar labor relations had prevailed in the South during the antebellum period (1780–1860):

"They have risen up as one man to impose the ukase of their power to obstruct and destroy thus the solemnly expressed will of the people . . . . Go to California today and the men who want Chinese labor are the men who own large plantations and factories. What do they want? The same thing that gentlemen educated in the South wanted. Servile labor that they could control at their will and with pleasure . . . . That is the demand of the supreme classes against the substratum of society everywhere throughout this world; and we but followed in the South the same idea you follow now, when you demand in virtue of your intellectual supremacy, your capital, and your combined power that you shall be served with servile labor instead of free labor." 13 Cong. Rec. 3268 (1882).

Senator Morgan was unwilling to satisfy the wealthy interests who sought to import Chinese labor, particularly when their demands were camouflaged as arguments about racial equality:

"Are we to allow a sickly sentimentalism to induce us to violate all that belongs to our race and our Government and our country in order to let these men in here who are to become servile laborers and slaves, for they are little else, to wealthy men?" 13 Cong. Rec. 3270 (1882).

In his April 1882 veto message on the twenty-year exclusion bill, President Chester Arthur suggested that although Chinese were unwanted in one section of the country, they might provide a desirable workforce elsewhere. The president said:

"There may be, however, other sections of the country where this species of labor may be advantageously employed without interfering with the laborers of our own race. In making the proposed experiment, it may be the part of wisdom as well as of good faith to fix the length of the experimental period with reference to this fact." 13 Cong. Rec. 3269 (1882).

The suggestion outraged Morgan. It implied that the Chinese might migrate to the South, as agricultural workers. But once there, they would compete with blacks for low-wage jobs.

"The President is a pure Caucasian, more English than anything else, with the bluest of blue blood in his veins . . . . Here is a Republican, a negrophilist, a man who has pledged himself heart and soul, so far as pledges can go, to the equality of the Negro race with the white race, in every respect, who says that there may be places in this country where the Chinese can be properly employed and where the Chinaman will not come into competition with our race. If not with our race, then with what race is he to come into competition? With the

§ 5.22 Abolition and the Timing of Chinese Immigration

In many ways the Chinese began immigrating at the wrong time in history: the abolitionists and the passage of the Fourteenth Amendment had raised the color consciousness of the country, the success of large industrialists in the Gilded Age, and the Depression of 1873–1879 combined to stir workers to form labor unions that discriminated against the cheap labor (sometimes a myth and not real) of the Chinese. The nativists also cried out against those who did not look like the early immigrants to America.

Western miners were the first to react strongly against Chinese immigrants (followed by those in lumbering) because of the early financial success of Chinese miners in California, Nevada, Oregon, and Idaho in the 1850s and 1860s. See, for example, Sue Fawn Chung, *In Pursuit of Gold: Chinese American Miners and Merchants in the American West* (University of Illinois Press, 2011).

The Chinese did not benefit from the abolitionist movement or the African American victory on the Fourteenth Amendment issue, and the anti-Chinese prejudice culminated in the Ten-Year Exclusion legislation in 1882. See, for example, Najia Aarim-Heriot, *Chinese Immigrants, African Americans, and Racial Anxiety in the United States, 1848–82* (University of Illinois Press, 2003). For Chinese reactions during this period, see R. David Arkush and Leo O. Lee, eds., *Land Without Ghosts: Chinese Impressions of America from the Mid-Nineteenth Century to the Present* (University of California Press, 1989).

Source and contribution: Prof. Sue Fawn Chung, University of Nevada, Las Vegas.

Negro race. Where are the Negroes? They are in the Southern states, in our midst, in that country they love so dearly it seems impossible to divorce them from it." 13 Cong. Rec. 3269 (1882).

The Alabama senator forecast a cataclysm in his home region, which was just beginning to recover from the Civil War. Economic competition and social conflict between African labor and the Chinese would generate severe disorder:

"Picture to yourself the condition of the South, with six million of Chinese there to inhabit that country along with the six million Negroes, and the struggles of these untutored and untrained men in their controversies for the possession of the soil and the control of the country, and see how barbarism will be turned loose in that land, already sufficiently persecuted, to the destruction of the last vestige of civilization we have there. I can conceive of nothing more hideous than the strife that must arise between these people." 13 Cong. Rec. 3269 (1882).

The Chinese were not fit to live anywhere in America, Senator Morgan concluded, not in California, not in the South, nowhere at all. They were not a malleable people, and they were incapable of accepting American social and religious institutions:

"Can we think of any race of men we would not sooner invite to this country than the Chinese? I would go and open up the heart of Africa and bring those Negroes from the slavery in which they are held today by their fathers, and their kinsmen, and put them under the guidance and guardianship of the Negroes of the South with the expectation of civilizing them . . . rather than turn loose the hordes of the lower classes of Chinese on this land." 13 Cong. Rec. 3270 (1882).

With that, the Senate debate of April 24, 1882, concluded, to be resumed the following day.

§5.30 Senate Debate, April 26, 1882: "Beyond the realm of political agitation"

Under consideration, H.R. 5804, the pending question being whether to concur in the amendment made in the Senate Committee of the Whole to strike the House-passed definition of "Chinese laborers."

Senator James Slater (D–OR) opened the debate. Slater was serving in his only Senate term (1879–1885), having previously been in the House from 1871 to 1873. Slater strongly insisted on retaining the House definition of "Chinese laborers." "To strike out that clause of the bill will be in effect to destroy all its efficacy as a measure of restriction," he said. 13 Cong. Rec. 3308 (1882).

Slater reviewed the negotiation record of the Angell Treaty in order to show that it was not only manual laborers that the United States intended to restrict. In those discussions, the Chinese side had proposed that temporary restrictions on Chinese laborers apply only in California, that laborers wishing to work elsewhere be allowed to enter the United States at will, and that other Chinese, apart from "actual laborers," could enter California as well. In addition, the Chinese proposed that "artisans" be expressly included in the exempted classes.

But the United States refused to make exception for artisans because, in the words of the U.S. negotiators, "this very competition of skilled labor in the cities where the Chinese labor immigration concentrates . . . has caused the embarrassment and population discontent that we wish to avoid." 13 Cong. Rec. 3309 (1882).

As negotiated, exemptions were allowed only for diplomats, teachers, students, and tourists. If the committee amendment were agreed to, Senator Slater pointed out that restrictions would be so lax and easily evaded as to be meaningless. "We shall find that when this law goes into operation that we have a dragnet with nothing in it." 13 Cong. Rec. 3309 (1882).

President Arthur's veto of the twenty-year bill in 1882 had come as a great shock to inhabitants of the Pacific region, Slater noted. They had considered the matter to enjoy consensus "beyond the realm of political agitation." True consensus had been prematurely assumed and was apparently lacking. Unlike Democrats, Republicans had demurred from supporting the bill in the first place, and Republican senators had not voted to override the veto of a Republican president.

Senator Slater noted that even though the Burlingame Treaty met with general acclaim, substantial misgivings had been expressed on the Pacific Coast. He quoted the Oregon Democratic Party's platform of 1870, whose benchmark demands foretold later attacks in Congress against Chinese immigration:

"Urge and entreat a repeal of the recent [Burlingame] treaty concluded between the United States and China, which guarantees to the latter nation such extensive privileges and immunities without corresponding benefits to American citizens, and offers to its hordes of semi-barbarians such favorable inducements to swarm in upon us, occupying our mineral and agriculture districts; create competition with our laboring masses; establish immoral pursuits, disgusting rites, ceremonies and practices; discourage and repel the immigration of our own race; decrease the white population; retard thrift; impede the advancement of education and enlightenment; abstract from our resources and send away our valuable mineral wealth; and disorganize and apostate our community." 13 Cong. Rec. 3309 (1882).

Republicans, said Slater, had been more circumspect in opposing the Chinese, generally agreeing with Democrats to restrict naturalization rights but less willing to contain immigration:

"From the commencement of this agitation to the present hour, the Democratic Party has made and led the contest against Chinese immigration, and is today the only party substantially and honestly making resistance and warfare against this Mongolian invasion." 13 Cong. Rec. 3309 (1882).

Such political finger-pointing had arisen at other moments during the 1882 debates, especially in Representative Richard Townshend's (D–IL) comments on the twenty-year bill (*§ 4.70*). Such pandering would only worsen in later debates. By 1888, the record on the viciously anti-Chinese Scott Act (*Chapter Seven*) would be dominated by disputes regarding which party was tougher on the Chinese.

Slater said that the people of the Pacific region were no less determined to address tyranny and repression than New Englanders had been at the time of the Boston Tea Party. Governments in his area had done all they could to contain the Chinese, but the problem was beyond their capacity of self-help. Only the federal government could mitigate the damage:

"We have appealed to Congress for lo these many years. Our appeals have been scouted and derided. Measures for our relief have been twice defeated by Presidential veto. We are here again asking nothing but a small measure of justice, and we appeal to you to give us the little relief this measure will bring, in order that we may stay for the present the scourge that is now upon us . . . ." 13 Cong. Rec. 3311 (1882).

California's Senator James Farley (D–CA) took the floor to insist that Chinese employed in more skilled occupations, such as tailors, shoemakers, and cigar-makers, should nonetheless be considered laborers within a broad definition of the term. Chinese working in all these fields had supplanted whites, Farley said.

Farley's comments prompted John Ingalls (R–KS) to ask him about an apparent irony. If Chinese were so loathsome and untrustworthy, why did Californians hire them in the first place? Was it really necessary for Congress to legislate in defense of California? As a practical matter, couldn't Californians restrain immigration by not employing the Chinese?

"Mr. Ingalls. Why are these people employed? Because they do better work for less money than anyone else?

"Mr. Farley. The Senator asks me why these people are employed. I suppose it is generally understood by every person—

"Mr. Ingalls. They are employed because they do better work for less money than anyone else.

"Mr. Farley. I do not say any such thing. The Senator undertakes to put in my mouth what I never said.

"Mr. Ingalls. Why do they employ the Chinese in preference to other people?

"Mr. Farley. I can only say because they work for less money. As I apprehend, if the Senator were to select as between parties, and he wanted labor performed, if he could get a man to do certain work for fifty cents and another for a dollar, he would take the man at fifty cents.

"Mr. Ingalls. Does the Senator believe that if the people of California would abstain from hiring these Chinese they would leave?

"Mr. Farley. I believe they would . . . .

"Mr. Ingalls. You have the matter in your own hands." 13 Cong. Rec. 3311 (1882).

Senator Ingalls had posited the question of whether Chinese immigration would dry up if Californians refused to hire the immigrants. Farley did his best to evade the trap, by insisting on the need for federal intervention to structure immigration policy. The two senators simply talked past each other, resolving nothing.

After a short period of additional debate, the Senate ended that day's proceedings.

§5.40 Senate Debate, April 27, 1882: "They are parasites"

Under consideration, H.R. 5804, the pending question being whether to concur in the amendment made in the Senate Committee of the Whole to strike the House-passed definition of "Chinese laborers."

When the Senate returned to H.R. 5804 on Thursday, April 27, 1882, the pending question before the Senate Committee of the Whole remained whether to retain the House-passed definition of "Chinese laborer." Senator James Farley (D–CA) began by discussing a notorious circumstance involving Chinese shoemakers in North Adams, Massachusetts.

The incident in question had occurred in 1870. Confronting a strike by a powerful union, known as the Knights of St. Crispin, a Massachusetts shoe manufacturer, Calvin Sampson, had fired his workers and imported seventy-five Chinese from California. The Chinese made shoes in North Adams for a number of months, and the strike was broken.

The controversial tactic of using Chinese workers as strikebreakers was widely publicized. Not surprisingly, the Knights of St. Crispin fought back, organized petitions and rallies to oppose the Chinese, and were present to harass them when the new workers arrived at the train depot. See Ronald Takaki, *Iron Cages: Race and Culture in 19th-Century America* (Oxford University Press, 2000); and Anthony W. Lee, *A Shoemaker's Story: Being Chiefly about French Canadian Immigrants, Enterprising Photographers, Rascal Yankees, and Chinese Cobblers in a Nineteenth-Century Factory Town* (Princeton Univ. Press, 2008). Farley attempted to show that the Chinese workers had been received with great hostility in Massachusetts. His purpose was to establish that, even outside the Pacific region, people resented the presence of the Chinese. According to Farley, when the Chinese arrived in North Adams, they had been greeted by a sullen crowd, had been stoned, and had required police protection.

In raising the issue, Senator Farley provoked a row with both Massachusetts senators. Senator George Hoar (R–MA) answered first, claiming the Californian had distorted the North Adams situation. Any violence was scattered, and the Chinese had not been impeded from their quarters or workplace:

"Whether any boys in the crowd may have thrown stones at those Chinese, I do not know; but that any injury was inflicted upon them . . . I utterly deny. They went peaceably and quietly to their work, they remained at their work, visited freely by all classes of citizens. They came and went undisturbed, unmolested, perfectly protected by law for years in that manufacturing village . . . ." 13 Cong. Rec. 3353 (1882).

Senators Farley and Hoar engaged in an acrimonious, word-parsing debate about the disposition of the crowd, whether violence had actually occurred, and whether police protection had been required for the Chinese workers.

The senior senator from Massachusetts, Henry Dawes (R–MA), intervened. He had lived in North Adams, and the shoe manufacturer was his friend. Dawes would set the record straight. Trouble generated by strikers against strikebreakers was more modest than alleged, was temporary in nature, and was of no lasting importance. According to Dawes, the actual circumstances in North Adams were these:

"When they arrived at the depot, all manner of curiosity seized the people of the town, and they rushed to the depot in crowds. When the Crispins, who had undertaken to prescribe the terms upon which, and upon which alone, this manufacturer could hereafter manufacture shoes, were aware of what the Chinamen came for, they were angry, just as a certain class of people are intensely angry in San Francisco today, and they used violent language all around there; and one or two of them threw a stone into the crowd, but the police—the ordinary police who are about the town and about their business—interfered and there was not the slightest trouble after that. The Chinamen went in peace through the streets, a sight the people had never seen before, to their quarters, and went about their work, attracting great crowds day after day from different parts of the county to see these Chinamen work. There never was, with the exception of perhaps a stone or two that I told the Senator of, the slightest violence used toward those people. They adapted themselves with wonderful facility to the new work to which they came." 13 Cong. Rec. 3354 (1882).

Confronted by this rebuttal, Farley explained why he had raised North Adams in the debate:

"The reason I referred to at all to the North Adams matter was to show that even in Massachusetts you were not free from riot. I did in answer to the continuous charge that this kind of legislation is only desired by that class of men known as sand-lotters and common agitators in the State of California." 13 Cong. Rec. 3354 (1882).

Support for the bill was mainstream, Farley maintained, as demonstrated by the California referendum in which 154,000 out of 161,000 persons had opposed further Chinese immigration. 13 Cong. Rec. 3355 (1882).

Senator Farley wound down his remarks. People in the West were law-abiding citizens who resented condescending commentary from Easterners. Californians had a right to appeal to Congress for relief. Personally, he thought a longer exclusion period was justified, at least twenty and perhaps thirty years, but he would settle for ten, if such a bill would get the president's approval. Meanwhile, Farley concluded, the Senate should reject the committee amendment and concur in the House definition of "Chinese laborers."

The next major speaker was Senator George M. Vest (D–MO). Briefly a member of the Confederate Congress, he served four terms in the U.S. Senate (1879–1903).

Vest discussed the shared obligations between citizens and their government. Then he asked, "Do the Chinese come here to share those responsibilities?" Vest answered his own question negatively, using vivid language to argue that the Chinese were a non-assimilative population:

"They are parasites, like those insects which fasten themselves upon vegetables or upon animals and feed and feed until satiety causes them to release their hold. They come to this country not to partake in the responsibilities of citizenship; they come here with no love for our institutions; they do not hold intercourse with the people of the United States except for gain; they do not homologate in any degree with them. On the contrary, they are parasites when they come, parasites while they are here, and parasites when they go." 13 Cong. Rec. 3358 (1882).

Vest pledged to stand with citizens from the Pacific States. For the senator, such solidarity would demonstrate "that the people of California are not alone in their belief that this is under God a country of Caucasians, a country of white men, a country to be governed by white men." Senator Vest continued:

"The brains, the energy, the intellect, the sinews and nerves of the race to which we belong will never be trampled under foot by Mongolian, or African, or mixed of Indian blood. Nothing except its own blood, combining with superior force and equal brain, will ever be able for a single instant to make it lower its lofty crest." 13 Cong. Rec. 3358 (1882).

Senate debate for the day concluded shortly thereafter.

§5.50 Senate Debate, April 28, 1882: "A most degraded corruption"

Under consideration, H.R. 5804, the pending question being whether to concur in the amendment made in the Senate Committee of the Whole to strike the House-passed definition of "Chinese laborers."

At the opening of debate on April 28, 1882, Senator John Tyler Morgan (D–AL) was recognized. Morgan was the senator who had reserved the "Chinese laborer" question for consideration in the full Senate. He explained why he opposed the Senate Committee of the Whole, which had stricken a very expansive definition from the House bill.

The measure, H.R. 5804, provided for criminal penalties, he said, which made it incumbent upon Congress to provide as much certainty and precision as possible within its terms. Previously enacted laws concerning coolies had suffered from a lack of definition. The word "coolie," for instance, was a slang term that had been imported into the statute but without a clear meaning.

In any case, Morgan argued, applying the legislation to artisan workers would be consistent with bilateral understandings from the Angell Treaty negotiations. He recounted that the Chinese side had sought to exempt artisans, but the Americans insisted on retaining plenary authority to control what kind of laborers were restricted. The Chinese accepted this, once the Americans agreed that laborer immigration could only be suspended rather than prohibited altogether. Accordingly, China should not complain if implementing legislation defined "laborers" broadly.

Morgan also discussed the benefit of preserving House language banning naturalization. Even though existing statutes appeared to bar citizenship for Chinese, some vagueness and uneven treatment remained. Including an express restriction would provide needed clarity.

Senator Wilkinson Call (D–FL), who served from 1879 to 1897, was next up. Call was not persuaded by the central arguments on which exclusion was grounded. He did not believe that the bill was necessary to protect American labor from the effects of competition:

"I do not wish to be committed to the economic ideas which are urged in support of this bill, and which, in my judgment, will prove to be entire fallacies . . . I am not willing, in supporting this bill to the fullest extent to which the people of the Pacific Coast may desire it, to be committed to the proposition that the admission of any class of people into this country as laborers will of itself affect injuriously American labor, either degrade it or cheapen the price of labor. I do not believe as a principle of political economy, of industrial economy, that the proposition is a correct one." 13 Cong. Rec. 3406 (1882).

Call also disputed the idea that an influx of Chinese would undermine the foundations of Christian civilization:

"I believe as firmly as any in the superiority of the Caucasian race and that civilization which has come from it; and I believe so firmly in it that I believe all the Chinese in the world could not affect it or even corrupt it in the slightest degree . . . .

"[The bill] ought not to be placed upon the ground that here is an antagonism between the Asiatic civilization in China and the Caucasian civilization of ours which cannot be overcome and subjected to the needs of our higher and stronger race. For one, I do not give my assent to that proposition." 13 Cong. Rec. 3406 (1882).

In several respects, Call thought the legislation was poorly drafted. He criticized the bill's provision for criminal penalties applicable to persons aiding and abetting the entry into the United States of unlawful Chinese immigrants. He argued such language was vague, did not define the act to be punished, and would invite the exercise of arbitrary power.

Senator Call also found problems with the deportation provision, which read as follows:

"And any Chinese person found unlawfully within the United States shall be caused to be removed therefrom to the country from whence he came, by direction of the President of the United States."

Call objected to this language because it permitted Chinese aliens to be deprived of their liberty, solely on the basis of administrative rulings, without due process of law. No other immigrant group bore such a burden.

Having disputed the main theses for the bill, and having attacked specific portions he found troublesome, Call nonetheless would vote aye. Moreover, he would not attempt to amend the bill to fix the problems he had discovered. At bottom, if the people of the Pacific region demanded protection, the senator would provide it:

"If as a whole or with great unanimity they demand that their community not be invaded by that class of people, they have a right to do it." 13 Cong. Rec. 3408 (1882).

Before sitting down, Call clarified something else. He noted that the legislation was being promoted as "a bill to execute certain treaty stipulations with the Chinese." Considering that approach too nuanced, Call said:

"I should prefer the more manly and direct form of declaring the coming of the Chinese here to be an intolerable evil; not to endanger the good order to certain localities but to be an intolerable evil to the social system, and the political and economical system of the people of California and of the Pacific Coast, as they understand it, and directly to affirm a prohibition." 13 Cong. Rec. 3408 (1882).

The next major speaker was Senator George Pendleton (D–OH). Pendleton served one term in the Senate (1879–1885). In the 1864 election, he was the unsuccessful Democratic nominee for vice president, on a ticket headed by General George B. McClellan. As a senator, he was the prime sponsor of the Pendleton Act, which created the U.S. civil service system.

Notwithstanding concerns he had about the House bill's deportation provisions, Pendleton would vote aye. He argued that American hostility to Chinese immigration would actually improve conditions for Chinese people, because the Chinese emperor would be forced to ameliorate problems within China rather than exporting them to other countries. The senator spoke paternalistically:

"It may be, sir, that this very bill we are passing today will awaken the authorities of the Chinese Empire to such an appreciation of the fact that their hordes are down in the very depths of a most degraded corruption—will so startle them with the conviction that we, their best friends and neighbors, cannot endure the contact—that they will bring all the resources of government and institutions of education and example, to lift up their people until they shall be also fitted to join in the advancement of the races." 13 Cong. Rec. 3409 (1882).

It was time for the Senate to commence voting on a series of amendments, followed by final passage of the bill. The first vote was on the amendment adopted in the Senate Committee of the Whole to strike the House definition of "Chinese laborers." The House language read:

"Sec.15. That the words 'Chinese laborers' whenever used in this act, shall be construed to mean both skilled and unskilled laborers and Chinese employed in mining."

On the roll call, 20 senators voted to affirm the Senate Committee of the Whole, 25 voted against, and 31 did not vote. The amendment therefore failed and the House definition of "Chinese laborer" was retained. This tally represented a reversal of position. In the Committee of the Whole, 29 senators had voted to strike the provision and 28 to keep it.

Senator George Edmunds (R–VT) moved to strike Section 14, which barred state and federal courts from naturalizing Chinese persons. In the Senate Committee of the Whole an identical amendment proposed by the Committee on Foreign Relations had been defeated 26 to 32. On the Edmunds amendment, 16 senators voted aye, 25 voted no, and 35 were absent. As to the 25 senators voting to retain the ban on naturalization, 19 were Democrats and 6 were Republicans. Of the 16 senators who voted to strike the ban, all were Republicans.

Before the vote on final passage of the bill, Edmunds spoke up. He was deeply troubled by the ramifications of section 14:

"As to the fourteenth section, this is the first time in the history of this country and I think of any other, that the governing legislative power has undertaken to make an affirmative prohibition against the admission to citizenship of any race." 13 Cong. Rec. 3412 (1882).

On final passage of the bill, the vote was 32 in the affirmative to 15 in the negative, with 29 senators not voting. The vote reflected the split among Republicans. Nine Republicans joined 21 Democrats and 1 Independent to pass the legislation. All the opponents were Republicans.

H.R. 5804, as amended by the Senate, returned to the House for further disposition.

§5.60 House Session of May 3, 1882: The House Concurs in the Senate Amendments

On May 3, 1882, Representative Horace Page (R–CA) secured consent to take from the Speaker's table, H. R. 5804, as amended by the Senate, and moved that the House concur in all Senate amendments. His motion was agreed to by voice vote. Once that happened, both Houses had passed the bill in identical form, and the legislation was ready for consideration by the president.

§5.70 Enrollment and Presidential Approval

Under the signature of Speaker J. Warren Keifer, the House enrolled the bill on May 3, 1882, and the Senate, by its President Pro Tempore David Davis, followed suit on May 4, 1882. President Chester Alan Arthur approved the measure on May 6, 1882.

A bill "to execute certain treaty stipulations relating to the Chinese" was now law. It had not yet acquired the popular name "Chinese Exclusion Act." Congress would return to the subject of Chinese immigration in 1884, 1888, 1892, 1893, 1902, and 1904. These later acts would continue to address the immigration and movement of Chinese people. The issue of naturalization, settled in 1882, would not arise again in debate, but was simply an aspect of a general extension of the law in 1892, 1902, and 1904. The term "Chinese Exclusion Acts" would not appear in a bill title until 1943, when the Magnuson Act repealed all such anti-Chinese legislation.

CHAPTER SIX

美國

The Amendments of 1884

"It is a race which in all its annals and traditions has furnished to civilization nothing worthy of imitation; whose morality cannot be discussed without a blush; a people with whom no other race has ever come into contact without moral deterioration; whose literature rests upon the fame and genius of a single man; whose religion is as degrading as the fetishism of Africa."
   —**Representative Barclay Henley (D–CA)**
   15 Cong. Rec. 3752 (1884)

"They have told us that the Chinese universally are liars and thieves, that they practice infanticide, that they are guilty of acts of immorality, that they are altogether bestial. Very well; if they are, then what do people employ them for? What does this exalted nation, which is so moral, so Christian, so temperate, and so good, employ them for?"
   —**Representative Theodore Lyman (R–MA)**
   15 Cong. Rec. 3763 (1884)

§6.0 Overview

- Considered in the 48th Congress of the United States (1883–1885)
- Senate Party Division: 38 Republicans, 36 Democrats, 2 Independents
- House Party Division: 196 Democrats, 117 Republicans, 12 Independents
- President: Chester A. Arthur (R) (1881–1885)

Only two years after the 1882 Chinese Exclusion Act took effect, Congress amended the law to tighten its restrictions. With the exception of a small class of exempted persons—students, teachers, merchants, tourists, and diplomats—the exclusion policy was made to apply to all persons of Chinese origin, whether or not they immigrated from China.

Political divisions on exclusion legislation, which were evident in earlier debates, began to fade in 1884, as a consensus formed around enforcement of the law. While a small contingent of lawmakers continued to oppose exclusion legislation, members of both parties in the 1884 and future debates began to view the principles of exclusion as settled policy.

§6.10 House Debate, May 3, 1884 (H.R. 1798): "This is a white man's government"

Under consideration in the House Committee of the Whole, H.R. 1798.

On May 3, 1884, Representative John Lamb (D–IN), who was serving his sole term in Congress, moved that the House of Representatives resolve itself into the Committee of the Whole in order to consider H.R. 1798, a bill strengthening the Chinese exclusion legislation (S. 71) that passed two years earlier in 1882. The proposed legislation would extend the sweep of exclusion to all persons of Chinese origin, regardless of whether they attempted to enter from China. Few exemptions were permitted. Lamb would serve as the bill manager for the Democratic majority. He yielded to the bill's sponsor, Representative Barclay Henley (D–CA), who was a member of Congress from 1883 to 1887.

Henley indicated the California, Oregon, and Nevada delegations, as well as those from the Arizona and Washington Territories, had worked jointly to produce the legislation. It was an enforcement measure, designed to clamp down on evasions of the 1882 legislation. Implementation of the 1882 Act had proven harder than Congress contemplated, Henley observed:

"It has simply been found, through the practical operations of the prior act, that these Chinese, with the persistence and cunning that no one will deny them, have adopted methods and means to evade its provisions; and the only function of this bill is simply to strengthen and effectuate the purpose contemplated by the original act." 15 Cong. Rec. 3752 (1884).

Congress should be aware, said Henley, that curtailing Chinese migration had always been difficult, and other countries had difficulty as well. For example, the British had struggled to bar Chinese from Australia and British Columbia; the Spanish tried to keep Chinese from the Philippines. But such efforts were not always successful in deterring immigration or even preventing violence. These experiences had a common thread:

"In connection with every civilized country on earth, they have always made themselves offensive, and every country in the world where they are now to be found in any considerable numbers is making an effort for their deportation or expulsion." 15 Cong. Rec. 3753 (1884).

Henley denied that the bill was based on race prejudice. No people were "freer from the domination of any such feeling as race prejudice than the people of the State of California," he reported. 15 Cong. Rec. 3753 (1884). He then proceeded to glorify white supremacy:

"We can do nothing loftier, nothing nobler, than to declare that in no event shall the laboring masses of our country be subjected to debasing contact or degrading competition with the dark and yellow skinned races of Asia, and to the extent this is a white man's government, be it our lofty purpose to so preserve for him and his posterity forever." 15 Cong. Rec. 3753 (1884).

Next recognized was Representative Melvin George (R–OR), who served from 1881 to 1885. George reported enforcement problems with the 1882 Act. Exclusion was not working. Chinese were being discharged from ships docking in Canada, rather than from ships entering American ports. From Canada, they would travel overland, and cross the border of British Columbia and the Washington Territory.

To deter violators, punitive provisions needed to be added:

"If we have a right to say that a certain person from a foreign land shall not enter this country, we have the right, and it is absolutely necessary that we should exercise the right, of providing a punishment in case of a violation of the restriction." 15 Cong. Rec. 3753 (1884).

Representative William Rice (R–MA) sought the floor. A member from 1877 to 1887, Rice had dissented from all anti-Chinese legislation, beginning with his vote against the Fifteen Passenger bill in 1879. Denouncing the pending bill as "clap-trap and surplusage from beginning to end," Rice set out to prove it unnecessary and gratuitous. Far from being ineffective, the 1882 Act had already achieved its purpose:

"Since the passage of that act, and up to the 15th day of January of this year [1884], 17,000 Chinamen departed from these shores and only 3,415 came to this country; making during the two years this treaty has been in operation a difference of 13,600 in this country." 15 Cong. Rec. 3754 (1884).

Rice quoted from the January 13, 1884, edition of the *San Francisco Chronicle*, a newspaper he said was known for its anti-Chinese vituperation. The paper noted:

"There is of course a wide difference of monthly arrivals of 1,500 before the passage of this law and the 66 average for last year. In the ten years for which the law runs, the surreptitious arrivals would not aggregate more than 3,500." 15 Cong. Rec. 3754 (1884).

Rice believed that nearly all the Chinese who entered America had done so legally. Mostly they were returnees, using certificates that the U.S. government had issued to them pursuant to the Angell Treaty, he said. China had negotiated for the certificates to protect the interests of its subjects who had already emigrated to the United States.

But Henley alleged many of these certificates were fraudulent. California courts were impossibly clogged with entry petitions from Chinese, he said. Indeed, three hundred such cases were then pending. Rice acknowledged the backlog, but argued it was due to incessant challenges that immigration officers were raising against the certificates:

"Does the gentleman from California [Mr. Henley] want to know how these three hundred cases to which he refers came into the United States courts? It is because you do not acknowledge the validity of a single passport that has been put into the hands of the men who have the right under the treaty to come back by their government, but you arrest and try every one of them in your courts before you let them in, when they have a full right under the treaty to come in." 15 Cong. Rec. 3754 (1884).

Through all such cases, only thirty-three false passports had been discovered, said Rice.

It was not just returnees who had a right to enter the United States; the Angell Treaty had allowed for merchants to come, he observed. But public opinion in California would not allow the law to operate as parties to the treaty contemplated it would. Rice illustrated how the statute was really implemented:

"A young man from China came into California the other day from China with a passport signed by his government, seeking to exercise the right as a merchant to enter this country. His father had come to the country many years before and had established himself in a small mercantile business in one of the interior towns of the Pacific Coast. The boy of eighteen had been fitting himself to enter into partnership with his father and had come here with the passport of his government certifying that he was a merchant seeking to enter upon our shores. And he was arrested before he could set foot upon the shores of California, and was tried in the courts there; and that passport was declared to be fraudulent because he had never been a merchant and was only proposing to be one. Without being allowed to enter upon the land, without being allowed to see his father whom he had not seen for years and to join whom he had come so far, he was turned back over the weary waste of the Pacific Ocean—refused an entrance into this 'land of the free.' That is the way this act works in California. Do you want to make it any more thorough than that?" 15 Cong. Rec. 3755 (1884).

Execution of the law was overtaken by political considerations, Rice insisted. The governing principle was quite simple:

"White labor votes and yellow labor does not." 15 Cong. Rec. 3755 (1884).

Representative Rice characterized much of the bill as frivolous. For example, it tightened restrictions on ship captains, making unlawful not just an actual landing with banned human cargo but even an attempt to land. Yet another section said that Chinese laborers on a vessel "shall not be permitted to land except in case of absolute necessity." Rice taunted Henley and the other bill sponsors:

"Under the provisions of this act, no one from that forbidden country shall be permitted to land except in case of 'absolute necessity.' What is that condition? If he had the smallpox, could he be taken out of the vessel and carried to a hospital? Will you answer that? What would be a case of absolute necessity, my genial friend from California, my kind-hearted friend?" 15 Cong. Rec. 3755 (1884).

Rice criticized other provisions he believed were petty, ranging from requirements for greater specificity on the certificates of return to additional restrictions placed on merchants. Taken together, they added so little to existing law that they did not merit Congress' attention.

But the bill did contain a core provision that was new. It was aimed at impeding Chinese immigration not just from China, but also from British colonies at Hong Kong and Singapore:

"The provisions of this act shall apply to all subjects of China, and Chinese, whether subjects of China or of any other foreign power."

After the 1882 law went into effect, a Chinese person from Hong Kong had entered the U.S. through Boston, Rice reported. A local court ruled the individual admissible, holding that the 1882 Act did not apply to Chinese subjects of the British Empire. "And therefore a Chinaman got into Boston from Hong Kong, and he is at large somewhere in the country now, and for all I know he is executing a flank movement upon California," he mocked. 15 Cong. Rec. 3756 (1884).

"It is to arrest the incursion of such Chinamen that this act is prepared and presented," Rice charged. "Where are your treaty rights to do that?" He continued his inquiry:

"Think you the English Governor of Hong Kong would sit down and fill out for a Chinese sailor on an English vessel sailing thence to San Francisco that ridiculous certificate which you provide in this act he must have in order to be allowed to enter this country? Think you that if an English vessel anchored at the wharf of San Francisco with Chinese sailors on board, born in Hong Kong and without that certificate—think you that the English Government would allow these sailors to be arrested, thrown into prison, turned back if they chanced in discharging the cargo of the vessel to set foot upon your soil, because, forsooth, they had not brought this permit of the Imperial Government of England to authorize them to come in under the provisions of this Act?" 15 Cong. Rec. 3756 (1884).

Representative Rice did not harbor any hope that the bill would be defeated. Nonetheless he had taken considerable time to expose its absurdities:

"I was determined that it should not pass without spreading upon the records of this House an explanation of its provisions and its intent. I declare it to be petty in its details, presumptuous in its attempts, and impossible in its execution." 15 Cong. Rec. 3757 (1884).

After an hour, Rice yielded the floor. In opposition, Representative John Raglan Glascock (D–CA) followed him in debate, with a decidedly opposite viewpoint. Elected in 1882, Glascock was serving his only term in Congress. He regarded the policy of Chinese exclusion as settled, and he assured his colleagues that the bill broke no new ground, but merely tightened loopholes. Democrats were united in support, Glascock said proudly:

"I am glad to state that no opposition to this measure of partial relief comes from this side of the Chamber. The Democrats in Congress have uniformly responded to every cry that has come out of the West against the evil of Chinese immigration. There has been no halting, no waver with them upon this question. They have ever faced with unbroken ranks any invasion upon the rights and dignity of American labor." 15 Cong. Rec. 3757 (1884).

Glascock rejected the argument that barring Chinese from Hong Kong or Singapore would offend the British. He contended that Rice misunderstood Britain's relationship to the Chinese living in the dominions:

"They are the fruits of her aggression, the slaves of her will. They are part of her possessions, but not of her people. Her aegis is thrown before them to protect the chattel, not the man; the servant because of the service he can render, not the member of her family who has been wronged. Following out the line of cold commercial policies for the protection of her colonies, she has through those colonies adopted more stringent regulations to prevent Mongolian immigration than are contained in any bill ever submitted to an American Congress." 15 Cong. Rec. 2758 (1884).

Glascock alleged that existing legislation failed to prevent Chinese from entering the United States under a variety of subterfuges. These included use of bogus or inadequately specific return certificates, supplemented by dubious oral testimony. Requiring more detailed certificates would control fraud, as would mandating that presentation of a proper certificate should be the sole permissible basis to reenter the U.S. by sea.

A serious problem was illegal border crossings by Chinese entering the United States from British Columbia, said Glascock. He included in the *Congressional Record* a November 1883 report from a U.S. Treasury agent in Port Townsend, Washington. The agent described the method and motive behind these border crossings:

"They employ unscrupulous white men, to whom they pay large sums of money, to pilot them through, who fully understand the secret avenues of egress, both by land and by water, including the vigilance of frontier customs officers by these unprotected and exposed routes.

"Why should they not come? They are subject to no risk in making the attempt save that of being arrested and sent back; they incur no penalty or forfeiture, and the next day repeat the attempt, and so continue until they smuggle themselves, with all that the word implies, into a country they are positively forbidden to enter." 15 Cong. Rec. 3759 (1884).

Representative Glascock believed the existing law was well-purposed but ineffective:

"The expressed intention of the act of 1882 was to suspend the immigration of Chinese laborers for ten years. We have shown that the act is defective, that they still continue to come in violation of the law. It is no answer to the proof of this defect to say that the number of arrivals has greatly diminished." 15 Cong. Rec. 3759 (1884).

Critics of the pending bill were really just opposed to the underlying exclusion policy, Glascock argued. Although Glascock thought such critics were naïve about the Chinese, he personally had no such illusions:

"We are not prepared to surrender even a small portion of this great heritage of ours to an alien race, unassimilating, cunning, and treacherous; a race that looks upon our institutions and civilization with contempt, that changes not nor does it progress, that comes among us for gain and not for residence, that is debasing in all its attributes." 15 Cong. Rec. 3760 (1884).

Two years after passing the first exclusion law, Congress was again regaled with grim predictions about a clash of civilizations. The only way for whites to win a fight for race dominance was to keep the Chinese out, Glascock insisted:

"We cannot compete in the struggle of existence with such a people. Anglo-Saxon civilization, with all its pride of ancestry and achievement, cannot stand before it. It has a power of passive endurance, a grim tenacity, a cunning of hand, and a frugality that defies Caucasian energy and competition. The two civilizations cannot flourish together. One must dominate. I am no alarmist. I believe in the future of our country and the advancement of our people; but I believe that future is to be made bright, that advancement certain, only in proportion as we preserve the manhood of our people from the debasing influence of a civilization that touches but to destroy." 15 Cong. Rec. 3760 (1884).

Representative Robert Roberts Hitt (R–IL) followed Glascock. Hitt served in the House from 1882 until his death in 1906. Years before his tenure in Congress, Hitt was a close associate of Abraham Lincoln's, and had served as assistant secretary of state in 1881. The influence of Hitt's longstanding relationship with Lincoln was evident as Hitt commenced his remarks denouncing exclusion:

"It is a bill which is entitled 'to execute certain treaty stipulations.' And it departs flagrantly from the particular treaty of which it professes to be based and violates a dozen others. The bill is unfortunate. On its face, its very principle of exclusion and proscription is repugnant to an American, and it is for that reason that I have listened the more attentively to hear if those gentlemen could at this time give to us some satisfactory reason or some urgent facts to justify us in again taking so revolting a dose as this House swallowed two years ago when the restriction bill was passed." 15 Cong. Rec. 3760 (1884).

As a result of the 1882 bill, said Hitt, the flow of Chinese immigration had been checked. He placed in the *Congressional Record* statistics from the Treasury Department about the number of Chinese immigrants who had arrived in the United States between October 1, 1883, and March 31, 1884. The total was 455, of which 287 carried passports issued by China designating them as merchants.

Some in Congress had complained that the Chinese government had been too lax in granting these few merchant papers, but Hitt assured his colleagues that procedures in China had been made more stringent:

"Owing to the stoppage of the certificates by the Chinese Government, an act of good faith on their part, Chinese immigration is now substantially at an end." 15 Cong. Rec. 3761.

In addition to the curbed influx, some 20,000 Chinese had returned home since 1882. By simple attrition, Chinese laborers in California were becoming more rare. As a result, pay for Chinese workers was rising. The dreaded wage differential with white labor had pretty much been eliminated. Given these ameliorating circumstances, what was the need for fresh legislation?

"Then why ask us again to pass this measure, so obnoxious in its principle and in this amended form far harsher than ever, with new provisions of positive mischief?" 15 Cong. Rec. 3761 (1884).

Representative Hitt argued that Chinese who were exempted from exclusion, such as merchants, were entitled to the "most favored nation" rights granted to them by the 1868 Burlingame Treaty. The 1880 Angell Treaty had not replaced the Burlingame Treaty, except where contradictory to it. The inconsistency between the 1868 and 1880 treaties related to the right of the United States to restrict the influx of laborers, but the Angell Treaty had not abrogated Burlingame Treaty rights for exempted Chinese. In theory, a Chinese merchant and one from England should be treated equally. However, actual practice, as directed by Congress, led to vast disparities and overt discrimination:

"There is no citizen of Europe who is entitled to any freer ingress to the port of New York than is a Chinese merchant . . . . That is a solemn provision of that treaty and now to carry out that provision it is proposed in very mockery that these harsh, revolting, and inquisitorial provisions shall be enacted by Congress.

"What are they? It is proposed that when a Chinese merchant or traveler comes into this country, he shall be stopped and asked, 'How much money have you? What is your financial standing? Are you going through the country or will you stop here? Where did you last reside? What have you been doing?' And so on. A long inquisitional section is provided here which we have never dared to offer to other nations whose citizens have the same treaty protection for free ingress and egress to and from this country." 15 Cong. Rec. 3761 (1884).

Hitt criticized the provision barring Chinese by race, regardless of their nationality. Persons of Chinese descent who lived outside of China numbered in the many hundreds of thousands, he said. By stopping these persons from entering America, Congress was disregarding agreements with their governments:

"In utter violation of these treaties, the bill proposes to exclude Chinese persons who are subjects of any of these great powers, born under their flag, and owing them allegiance." 15 Cong. Rec. 3761 (1884).

Congress would come to regret passing such a bill, Hitt predicted. "It will lead to infinite embarrassment it is defiance of public law, (and) of the usages of international intercourse." 15 Cong. Rec. 3762 (1884).

Shortly thereafter, Representative Pleasant B. Tully (D–CA) spoke. He was a member of the House from 1883 to 1885, and had been preceded by Romualdo Pacheco (§ 4.70). Before his election, he had been a member of a California constitutional convention that urged Congress to adopt an exclusion law. Now he was serving in the House, able himself to implement that policy.

Exclusion was needed because whites and Chinese could not live or work harmoniously. "It is my own observation that whenever the Chinese have gone into any trade or avocation, the white labor is compelled to desert it," Tully said. He insisted Congress must choose "whether you would prefer to give the labor of California to white men—men of our own race and kindred—or whether you wish to give it to the Chinaman." 15 Cong. Rec. 3763 (1884).

Tully also dismissed the complaint that Chinese were denied voting rights. Based on his long familiarity with them in California, such people were unsuited for citizenship:

"In reference to the fitness of these people to become citizens of our Government, let me say that they know and care nothing for your American institutions . . . . As regards moral character, he has none so far as my observation goes. I do not speak against the whole race, but in over thirty years of experience with those people, I have never met a Chinaman who had the slightest moral sense of right." 15 Cong. Rec. 3763 (1884).

After additional debate, Representative Thomas M. Browne (R–IN) addressed the House. Browne served in the House from 1877 until 1891. "I am opposed to this bill," he announced, "because it is a revision of the act of the last Congress and violates every idea I have on the subject of human rights." 15 Cong Rec. 3764 (1884).

Browne denounced an inescapable incongruity in the exclusion debate.

Notwithstanding the criticism that the Chinese were untrustworthy and morally debased, they were employed widely in California:

"There is scarcely a respectable family on the Pacific Coast that does not employ them as cooks, waiters, and chambermaids. They are admitted into every household, they are about every table, they are in every chamber. Yet they are denounced here by gentlemen as being the most vicious and depraved in the universe." 15 Cong. Rec. 3764 (1884).

For an overview of Chinese servants and citations to numerous sources, see Terry Abraham, "Class, Gender, and Race: Chinese Servants in the North American West," a paper presented at the Joint Regional Conference Hawai'i/Pacific and Pacific Northwest Association for Asian American Studies, Honolulu, March 26, 1996 (<*www.uiweb.uidaho.edu/special-collections/papers/chservnt.htm*>).

Fear of labor competition from low-wage workers did not seem to trouble members of Congress when those workers were European immigrants, Browne observed. This, too, was an inconsistency:

"You have become frightened because in the last quarter of a century, 100,000 Chinamen have settled on the Pacific Coast. Yet when the daily papers announce that during almost every month of these years quite as large a number of low-wage people have landed at Castle Garden [a processing station for immigrants in New York operating between 1855 and 1890], it does not frighten you at all." 15 Cong. Rec. 3764 (1884).

Representative Henley interrupted to clarify. "They are not the same kind of people." The following exchange ensued:

"Mr. Browne. You make no objection to these laborers from Ireland, from Germany, from Norway, from Poland, or wherever else they may come from, notwithstanding they put themselves in competition with that of our laboring people.

"Mr. Henley. We can compete with that kind of labor.

"Mr. Browne. But gentlemen say they object because Chinese do not assimilate, because they do not come here on account of their love for liberty or in the expectation of their becoming American citizens. Yet in this very legislation you prohibit the courts of the United States from naturalizing them. You object to them because they are not naturalized; and you will not allow them to be naturalized . . . . I would like to know what a Chinaman can do that will please you.

"A Member. Stay away.

"Mr. Browne. You say you desire this legislation for the protection of American labor, yet nearly all of you who support this measure are in favor of putting the American laborer at the mercy of every laboring man and woman in the world.

"Mr. Henley. Every one that is white.

"Mr. Browne. Ah, that is the keynote of this infernal legislation. These men are not white!" 15 Cong. Rec. 3764 (1884).

Later in the day, Browne would discuss the relationship between disenfranchisement and exposure to discrimination. When a people were unable to vote, he noted, politicians could abuse them; once persons were granted the ballot, they were treated respectfully, just as attitudes toward blacks changed after they secured suffrage:

"When a particular class of people possessed no political power they had no friends. They were dangerous to our liberties . . . . As these people became voters, when it was within their power to make this party strong or the other party strong, the mere fact that they had been clothed with political power revolutionized the opinion of politicians and distinguished men." 15 Cong. Rec. 3773 (1884).

Representative Thomas Brents (R–WA) next took the House floor. From 1879 to 1885, he served as a delegate from the Washington Territory (Washington became the forty-second state in the United States on November 11, 1889). Brents considered labor protection to be a minor justification for the bill. Much more important was stability of social and political structures:

"It is a question of protection to our very institutions themselves against threatened demolition and overthrow, a question not only of dollars and cents to our people and nation, but a question of continued existence and perpetuity of virtue, morality, intelligence, civilization, and free government." 15 Cong. Rec. 3766 (1884).

Pass this bill to secure exclusion before the problem was out of hand, Brents intoned. "We have no right to make this country the dumping ground for the world's social and political offal . . . ." 15 Cong. Rec. 3766 (1884).

Representative William Eaton (D–CT) spoke next. Eaton had served in the U.S. Senate from 1875 to 1881, then in the House from 1883 to 1885. The argument that Chinese immigrants should be treated like Europeans offended Eaton. "That sort of talk is neither reason nor sense," he said. Quite simply, Europeans were welcome in America, but not the Chinese:

"We do not desire that people here. We say this country is a home for the oppressed. So it is. We say it is a home for the exile. So it is. But it is not for China to vomit 100,000,000 of its 400,000,000 population upon our shores." 15 Cong. Rec. 3767 (1884).

Representative Charles R. Skinner (R–NY) gained the House floor. He was a member of Congress from 1881 to 1885, and voted against the 1882 Act. He remained staunchly opposed to the concept of exclusion:

"The act of 1882 can never be amended to my satisfaction, except by an absolute repeal. I opposed the bill of 1882 because I believed it was un-American, because I believed it was unrepublican, because I believed it was undemocratic, because I believed it was unpatriotic. There must be an underlying principle of right to every measure of this kind to give it life or vitality, and that legislation lacked such a principle entirely. It was not founded upon mercy, justice, or patriotism. It lacked every one of those attributes. It was unworthy of a proud nation, whose great boast is its liberty and its love of freedom." 15 Cong. Rec. 3767 (1884).

Partisanship on the House floor was about to escalate. The bill manager, Representative Lamb of Indiana, followed Skinner in debate. Lamb argued that the roles of the political parties on Chinese exclusion were well-defined. Democrats were firmly on the side of white labor:

"I am proud to say that no single Democrat upon this Floor has lifted his voice today in behalf of the pauper labor of China and against the interests of the free labor of America . . . .

"When this legislation was before Congress two years ago—and I have the record here before me—sixty-six Republicans, sixty-six members of the other side of the House, who stand here pretending to protect American labor voted against that bill. When the bill to limit immigration for ten years was before the House, thirty-seven members of the House voted against that bill, and of that number thirty-four were Republicans and but three Democrats." 15 Cong. Rec. 3769 (1884).

House colleagues such as Browne and Rice argued that the pending bill was neither needed nor demanded, but Lamb thought otherwise. He called attention to the petition box of the House of Representatives. In that box were petitions from labor organizations representing a half million workers who urged that the bill be passed.

Amendments to the bill were now in order.

The first of these came from Representative Nathaniel Hammond (D–GA), a four-term member whose service began in 1879. His amendment eliminated a ninety-day grace period before implementation of the tightened restrictions. It carried by voice vote.

The proposed legislation barred not only the act of landing Chinese in America, but even making an attempt to land them. Rice offered an amendment to strike the "attempt" language. The amendment was rejected 24 to 135.

Representative Rice proposed an amendment to Section 6. The bill mandated that identification certificates be issued for Chinese persons, by whatever country in which the Chinese person happened to be a subject. Rice contended that because the legislation purported to implement a Sino-American treaty only, the requirement could not be applied to any nation other than China. He moved to strike the words "or of such other foreign government of which at the time such Chinese person shall be a subject." The amendment was defeated by 21 ayes to 134 nays.

Rice next launched a similar attack on Section 15. By treaty, China had consented to restrictions on its own laborers alone. Thinking that the United States could not bootstrap on this accord an effort to exclude Chinese from countries other than China, Rice proposed to strike the words "subjects of China or any other foreign power." On a voice vote, the amendment was rejected.

Several additional technical amendments were added. Before the amendment process concluded, Representative Albert Shelby Willis (D–KY), took the House floor. Willis had been the prime sponsor and manager of the 1882 Act in the House.

Willis extensively reviewed the history of exclusion legislation to that time. Congress had already acted on four occasions, he said. In 1878, the House passed a resolution seeking a renegotiation of the Burlingame Treaty so that limitations on immigration could be imposed. President Hayes ignored the overture. Then, in 1879, Congress passed the Fifteen Passenger bill. President Hayes vetoed it. In 1882, after the Angell mission renegotiated the Burlingame Treaty, Congress passed the twenty-year exclusion bill. President Arthur vetoed that. Finally, Congress passed the ten-year exclusion bill, which Arthur signed. In light of this record, Willis considered the policy of exclusion settled beyond further debate:

"If there is such a thing as legislative estoppel, it would certainly apply in this instance. Not once, but repeatedly within the last few years Congress has expressed itself in favor of restricting Chinese immigration." 15 Cong. Rec. 3775 (1884).

Willis was dismayed by the bill's critics, who he believed were nitpicking provisions when what they really wanted was exclusion repeal:

"And now, when we seek to make this law effective . . . we are met by arguments not affecting so much the proposed amendments, but aimed directly against the whole substantive proposition of relief . . . . Ridicule, sentimental and sensational appeal, and fierce denunciation have in turn played their part in the effort to overthrow this bill." 15 Cong. Rec. 3775 (1884).

For the Democrats, Willis claimed the exclusion issue. Opposition had come from Republicans, in both the executive and legislative branches of the federal government, and it had frustrated or delayed exclusion efforts. In the meanwhile, he said, Democrats allied with workingmen against the Chinese:

"I notice that all the speeches against this bill have been made by our Republican friends. I remember it was a Republican administration which refused the request made by a Democratic House that negotiations changing the treaty with China should be commenced with a view toward restricting Chinese immigration. I recall that two Republican Presidents have resorted to the extraordinary power of the veto to prevent the passage of bills for this purpose . . . .

"If, therefore, gentlemen insist that this measure is a Democratic measure, I shall not deny its origin and success are largely due to Democratic votes." 15 Cong. Rec. 3775-3776 (1884).

Before Willis' remarks, Rice had proposed one last amendment. It was directed at the title of the bill, which was "An act to execute certain treaty stipulations relating to Chinese." In light of the bill's provisions, particularly Section 15, Rice wanted the title changed to read "An act to violate certain treaty stipulations with China and other nations."

Now that Willis was finished, the chairman of the Committee of the Whole called the question on Rice's amendment, which was rejected by voice vote.

The Committee of the Whole rose and reported the bill favorably. In the House, the bill, as amended by the Committee of the Whole, passed with 184 yeas, 13 nays, and 125 not voting.

After that vote, the full House passed the bill, as amended, with 184 yeas, 13 nays, and 125 not voting.

Democrats favored the bill 137 to zero. Republicans supported it 44 to 13. Republican opposition to anti-Chinese legislation was rapidly collapsing.

Many representatives were recorded absent, which at the time was a means of abstaining from the vote. A breakdown of the absentees shows a disproportionately high number of Republicans, possibly demonstrating their misgivings with the bill. But their discomfort did not translate into outright opposition.

Of the 141 House Republicans, 84 were recorded absent, amounting to 60 percent of the Republican Caucus. Forty-one Democrats out of 182 were absentees, coming to 23 percent of the Democratic caucus.

Unfortunately, Representative Albert Shelby Willis was correct. A consensus had hardened in favor of Chinese exclusion; opposition seemed futile, or perhaps was too politically risky to express.

As passed by the House, H.R. 1798 went to the Senate for further disposition.

§6.20 Senate Debate, July 3, 1884: "Will repent in sackcloth and ashes"

Under consideration in the Senate Committee
of the Whole, H.R. 1798, as passed by the House.

On July 3, 1884, Senator John F. Miller (R–CA) moved that the Senate proceed to the consideration of H.R. 1798. By a vote of 40 to 7 the motion was agreed to and consideration in the Senate Committee of the Whole commenced.

First recognized was Senator Orville Platt (R–CT), who moved immediately to strike Section 15. This was the provision that would bar entry to America of persons of Chinese descent, even if they were not Chinese subjects. It was the core of the House bill and read:

"The provisions of this act shall apply to all subjects of China, and Chinese, whether subjects of China or any other foreign power."

Miller responded in opposition. Platt's amendment would interfere with an effort to resolve differences in judicial interpretations. Sitting in California as a circuit judge on the U.S. court of appeals, U.S .Supreme Court Justice Stephen Field ruled that a Chinese laborer coming from any jurisdiction was still a Chinese laborer within the meaning of the exclusion laws (*In re Ah Lung*, 18 F. 28 (C.C.D. Cal. 1883)). Other judges had ruled to the contrary. The amendment was needed to settle the conflict:

"If the law does not contain a provision of this sort, and is not so settled, Chinese laborers will come into the United States without restriction by merely taking up their residence in another country than China and then proceeding to the United States." 15 Cong. Rec. 5938 (1884).

Miller had posited a situation in which a Chinese had assumed a sham residence in order to gain access to the United States. But Platt's concern was different. It involved trying to apply Section 15 to a Chinese who was a naturalized citizen in another country:

"I doubt very much, however, whether Judge Field or any other judge has decided that this act as it now stands prevents a naturalized subject of Great Britain or other foreign power from landing in this country simply because he happened to have been born in China." 15 Cong. Rec. 5938 (1884).

Senator John Jones (R–NV) said that Platt misunderstood Field's ruling:

"The decision of Judge Field is that the act applied to the Chinese as a race, without regard to the country in which they might be domiciled or the country of which they might be subjects; that the act applied to this people as a race; and it strikes me that that answers the proposition of the Senator from Connecticut." 15 Cong. Rec. 5938 (1884).

Interjecting, Senator George Hoar (R–MA) emphasized that Field's perspective was not universally accepted. In the federal circuit court sitting in Massachusetts, other judges had determined that a law implementing a treaty with China could not be applied to subjects of nations other than China.

(On Stephen Field, see Paul Kens, *Justice Stephen Field: Shaping Liberty from the Gold Rush to the Gilded Age* (University Press of Kansas, 1997).)

The Senate was ready to decide the question. The Platt amendment was rejected on a voice vote.

Hoar concluded with a parting shot in opposition to the bill:

"I do not propose in the last day or two of the session to enter anew into a debate of this general policy. This is a bill to execute certain treaty stipulations relating to Chinese and citizens of other countries. I rest in my judgment upon sheer barbarism . . . .

"I only wish to reaffirm my disapprobation of this legislation and the principle on which it depends, and to state that in my judgment the American people will repent in sackcloth and ashes one day the policy they are inaugurating." 15 Cong. Rec. 5938 (1884).

The Senate Committee of the Whole reported the bill to the full Senate without amendment. Approximately twenty minutes of debate had transpired. By a vote of 43 yeas to 12 nays, with 21 senators absent, the bill passed.

As there were no differences between the Senate and House versions, the bill went to President Chester Arthur, who signed it into law.

The major changes from the original 1882 law involved barring immigration of Chinese persons based on their race, rather than on their citizenship; mandating greater biographical detail on certificates of return; requiring that the certificate be the sole permissible proof of a right to reenter; and imposing criminal penalties for violations of the act.

CHAPTER SEVEN

美國 The Scott Act of 1888

"*Mr. President, rather than to permit this oriental octopus to fasten its disgusting and poisonous tentacles upon us more firmly than they already are, it were better that every line of treaty stipulation with the Chinese Empire that obstructs the way should be swept from the statute book.*"
　　　　—Senator John Mitchell (R–OR)
　　　　　19 Cong. Rec. 406 (1888)

"*My mind turns on a recollection that has attended me since I was a child, of the terrible difficulties of ever eliminating from a free country like this any great, industrious, powerful race of people, either intellectually or physically, who may find a foothold in our midst. I therefore sympathize with the people of the western coast most heartily in laying the ax to the root of the tree and stop that now which hereafter it may be too late a time to stop.*"
　　　　—Senator John Tyler Morgan (D–AL)
　　　　　19 Cong. Rec. 8341 (1888)

"*We have the power by the Constitution to do things that are wrong, morally wrong, politically wrong, and in the interest of society wrong. The best evidence of that is that we frequently repeal them when we find that out. But the power and the right are two different matters.*"
　　　　—Senator William Evarts (R–NY)
　　　　　19 Cong. Rec. 8455 (1888)

§7.0 Overview

- Considered in the 50th Congress of the United States (1887–1889)
- Senate Party Division: 39 Republicans, 37 Democrats
- House Party Division: 167 Democrats, 155 Republicans, 3 Independents
- President: Grover Cleveland (D) (1885–1889 and 1893–1897)

Seeking the right to impose even more stringent restrictions on Chinese immigration, the administration of President Grover Cleveland successfully negotiated the Bayard–Zhang Treaty. Anticipating ratification, Congress passed legislation to implement the revised treaty restrictions. However, during its review of the Bayard–Zhang Treaty, the Senate added two amendments to the treaty that the Chinese government found unacceptable. Accordingly, China did not ratify the treaty.

Notwithstanding the failure of the Bayard–Zhang Treaty, Congress decided to legislate further restrictions anyway. It passed the Scott Act, which, among other things, canceled certificates granting Chinese who had left the United States a right to reenter the country.

The Supreme Court opined that the Scott Act abrogated existing treaty obligations to China but upheld the law, stating that Congress had the power to act as it did.

The 1888 debate was exceptionally partisan. Anticipating that year's elections, to win more votes both Republicans and Democrats competed for who could appear more anti-Chinese.

In Chinese culture the number eight is said to be lucky, but 1888 was to be an especially onerous year in Congress for the Chinese. In January, Senator John H. Mitchell (R–OR) brought to the Senate floor legislation to abrogate all treaties and to prohibit immigration of Chinese laborers. Debate on Mitchell's bill would generate some of the most vicious rhetoric on the Chinese question ever expressed in either chamber of Congress. The bill did not come to a vote, but the debate heralded problems the Chinese would face in the year ahead.

In March 1888, President Grover Cleveland submitted to the Senate a new treaty with China (Bayard–Zhang Treaty of 1888) that would have permitted absolute prohibition of Chinese labor immigration, rather than its mere suspension.

In May 1888, the Senate approved the Bayard–Zhang Treaty, but only after requiring amendments that would have canceled return certificates for Chinese who already held them but were then outside the United States.

Anticipating China's agreement to the Senate amendments, Congress in August 1888 passed legislation implementing the Bayard–Zhang Treaty. Chagrined at the Senate amendments, China failed to ratify it.

Responding to the lack of Chinese acquiescence, in October 1888 Congress passed the Scott Act, which imposed even more burdensome conditions on the Chinese than the Bayard–Zhang Treaty itself would have generated. The title of the legislation made clear its purpose: An act to prohibit the coming of Chinese laborers to the United States.

§7.10 Senate Debate, January 12, 1888: "Polluted with the curse of human slavery"

Under consideration, S. 559 (Mitchell).

Having enacted the ten-year exclusion legislation in 1882 (*Chapter Five*) as a result of agitation from Pacific Coast members of Congress, and having reaffirmed and refined the policy in 1884 (*Chapter Six*), Congress might have given the subject a rest. In effect for ten years, the 1882 Act was not due to expire until 1892. But Capitol Hill was not quiet. Members of Congress from the western United States demanded even further tightening. Senator John H. Mitchell (R–OR) was one of those members. Mitchell represented Oregon in the Senate on three separate occasions: from 1873 to 1879, again from 1885 to 1897, and finally from 1901 until his death in 1905.

On January 12, 1888, Mitchell called up S. 559. By day's end the bill was referred to the Senate Committee on Foreign Relations, from which it would not emerge. As such, the bill had no lasting legislative significance. But its importance comes from how the bill reflected the anger and determination of members who kept the Chinese issue alive before Congress.

Insisting that existing law had failed to stem Chinese immigration, Mitchell declared, "Our soil is once again polluted with the curse of human slavery." 19 Cong. Rec. 406 (1888). This circumstance could have been avoided if treaties and statutes had been executed in good faith, he said, but China was evasive and the U.S. government was feckless. As a consequence, "this most Herculean of all gigantic evils . . . is being imposed and impressed upon us from the shores of Asia." 19 Cong. Rec. 406 (1888).

Mitchell's comments on the effect of Chinese immigration were vivid:

"(It) embraces within it explosives more deadly than dynamite, an evil that depresses labor, corrupts morals, debases youth, makes merchandise of personal freedom and female virtue, mocks at justice, defies law, dwarfs enterprise, chains personal liberty, destroys personal freedom, menaces the public peace, invades domestic tranquility, endangers the public welfare, converts whole sections of beautiful American cities—the homes of civilized, cultivated, and refined people—into squalid, wretched, crime-smitten, and leprous-spotted habitations of the lowest and most debased classes of the pagan Mongol—in reference to all this, in reference to ridding this country of such an evil, for the purpose of saving it from deadly assault on its most vital parts, and securing it from becoming a pest-house and criminal receptacle of pagan and debauched people of a tabooed race, numbering one-half of the population of the globe, the Administration, so far as we are advised at present, has made no effort whatever." 19 Cong. Rec. 406–407 (1888).

Mitchell reported that the Chinese population was an expanding contagion in America. No longer confined to the Pacific Coast, it had crossed the Rocky Mountains and spread eastward:

"There are today in the city of New York alone 2,175 Chinese laundries, to say nothing of innumerable opium joints, gambling dens, brothels, and other sinks of vice and inequity in that modern Bedlam, carried on by Chinese." 15 Cong. Rec. 407 (1888).

How did such a transformation occur? Mitchell advised that Canada's border with America was porous, allowing Chinese to cross without much impediment, and that the problem had been exacerbated by completion of the Canadian Pacific Railway. Ease of transportation had facilitated extension of the problem east from the Pacific:

"As the means of travel between nations and across empires are improved, as the cost of travel is materially diminished, just in the same ratio is the danger which threatens this country through a superabundance of undesirable immigration increased." 19 Cong. Rec. 407 (1888).

The only barrier to an overwhelming Chinese influx via Canada was a $50 per person head tax that Canadian authorities imposed on Chinese entering that country, noted Mitchell. The head tax was an inconvenience, but not a true impediment, Mitchell said, and it was in danger of being repealed in any case.

Leaky borders created one problem; federal courts at all levels presented another.

When Chinese attempted to enter the United States, the port collector at San Francisco frequently detained them. Mitchell thought the collector's decision should be the last word, but federal courts had disagreed. They not only permitted the Chinese to access habeas corpus rights to challenge such detentions but, to the senator's further chagrin, they also permitted bail:

"It has been the practice of the federal courts in California to extend not only the right of the writ of habeas corpus but also that of bail to all Chinese persons arriving at the port of San Francisco and who may be temporarily detained on shipboard pending an investigation by the collector of the port as to their right to enter the United States, or after his decision against their right to enter, whenever complaint has been made by such Chinese persons of unlawful restraint of their liberty." 19 Cong. Rec. 414 (1888).

The 1880 Angell Treaty acknowledged the right of Chinese already in the United States to return to the country. The 1882 Act implemented this right by providing for certificates of return, and the 1884 Act amendments said the certificates would be the sole valid evidence of whether readmission to the United States could be claimed. But in habeas corpus proceedings, some courts allowed Chinese who lacked a certificate the opportunity to present testimonial evidence to justify entry.

Senator Mitchell thought these courts had overreached. He reasoned that habeas corpus rights should only attach to persons lawfully within the United States. Determining admissibility was the port collector's job. The senator was irritated by what he considered judicial encroachment:

"May it not be insisted with reason that the question as to the right of a Chinese person to enter this country, under the treaty and restriction acts, is a political and not a judicial question?" 19 Cong. Rec. 414 (1888).

One such habeas petition involved an immigrant named Chew Heong. He had lawfully entered and then departed from the United States prior to the time when the 1882 exclusion act was passed. Because he was abroad, he had never acquired a return certificate. When he attempted to reenter the U.S. without such papers, federal officers denied him admission. Chew Heong brought suit, arguing that by requiring he produce a certificate he could not possibly have obtained, Congress had unlawfully stripped him of the right of return as guaranteed by treaty.

The litigation wound up before the United States Supreme Court, which had to resolve the apparent conflict between treaty provisions and statutory language. While the treaty acknowledged the right of Chinese already in the United

§7.11 Litigation as a Means of Resistance to the Chinese Exclusion Act

When Congress passed the 1882 law, many anti-Chinese forces celebrated, believing their fight to force Chinese out of the United States had finally succeeded. Within a year, however, their hopes turned to frustration as they renamed the Chinese Exclusion Act, the "Chinese Evasion Act." Chinese in the United States did not meekly accept their exclusion from the United States. The Chinese immigrant community had a strong internal organizational network that provided an institutional basis for their resistance to the policy. The Chinese Six Companies, known to Chinese as the Zhonghua Huiguan, was composed of leaders from different huiguan or district associations to which all Chinese immigrants belonged, depending upon their birthplace. Although the Chinese consulate in San Francisco was the official representative of the Chinese government, both the Chinese Six Companies and the Chinese consulate provided crucial leadership and financial support for the fight against discriminatory treatment of Chinese immigrants.

When the Exclusion Act was passed, the Chinese organizations turned naturally to the federal courts in California to test the act's reach. Litigation had been one of the few avenues open to Chinese immigrants to resist discriminatory actions in the nineteenth century. Few Chinese managed to become American citizens because of U.S. law reserving naturalization to those who were "white" or of African descent. Lacking political power, Chinese found that the Burlingame Treaty of 1868, which guaranteed Chinese residents "the same privileges, immunities, and exemptions" extended to natives of other countries, and the Fourteenth Amendment, which prohibited states from denying any person due process or equal protection of the laws, to be potent weapons in the federal courts. Federal judges struck down many of the discriminatory state laws on the grounds that they violated the treaty rights of the Chinese or their right to equal protection under the Fourteenth Amendment. Litigation proved so fruitful that the Chinese Six Companies and Chinese consulate kept American attorneys on retainers to represent them whenever the need should arise. When exclusion went into effect, attorneys for the Chinese were kept busy as Chinese arriving at ports sought to prove their right to enter the United States.

"Chew Heong v. United States: Chinese Exclusion and the Federal Courts," by Lucy Salyer (Federal Judicial Center: Federal Judicial History Office, 2006).

States to return, implementing legislation appeared to condition this right on production of the certificate.

A decision in favor of the government would mean overriding the treaty by requiring adherence to impossible conditions. Unwilling to assume that Congress created a trap that would undermine a treaty so recently ratified, the Court ruled for the immigrant. *Chew Heong v. United States*, 112 U.S. 536 (1884).

The Court's ruling affected approximately 13,000 Chinese who left the U.S. after the treaty (November 17, 1880) but before Congress authorized the certificates (May 6, 1882). Mitchell evaluated its impact:

"The effect of this final decision of the Supreme Court . . . was to open at once a wide door to the perpetration of the most tremendous frauds upon the law, upon the part of the Chinese or those interested in their coming to the United States." 19 Cong. Rec. 414 (1888).

Such rulings, as well as ineffective border controls, confounded and enraged Senator Mitchell. Chinese exclusion had been national policy for six years, but there had been only an inconsequential reduction in Chinese immigration. Mitchell provided statistics. In 1877, 1878, and 1879, the average number of monthly Chinese arrivals at the port of San Francisco was 635. In 1880, the Angell Treaty was ratified and exclusion legislation was enacted. Nevertheless, from August 1882 to July 1887, monthly arrivals at the port averaged 621. And the numbers were increasing. The first six months of 1887 yielded the third-highest influx since Chinese immigration began at mid-century. The totals were further compounded by trans-border crossings from Canada, about which accurate statistics were not kept. As Mitchell concluded, "restriction acts do not restrict." 19 Cong. Rec. 419 (1888).

Mitchell believed the time had come to close America to Chinese altogether:

"Permit the present immigration of Chinese to go on as it has been going on ever since the passage of the restriction acts, increasing both in numbers and in baseness of character, and it will not be long until every department of labor in every city and hamlet on the Pacific Coast at least, if not elsewhere, will be monopolized and controlled by the Chinese laborer, and the wages of the white worker will be regulated, fixed, and controlled by Asiatic prices." 19 Cong. Rec. 420 (1888).

After Mitchell sat down, Nevada Senator William Stewart (R–NV) reminisced about the naturalization debate of 1870 (*§ 1.20*), during which Stewart played a crucial role by filibustering to block citizenship rights for Chinese:

"Seventeen years ago last July, the question arose in this Senate Chamber as to whether the Chinese should be naturalized. It was a fierce and protracted discussion; it continued over the 4th of July; and after the subject was fully discussed, the Senate almost unanimously decided that it would not allow them to become citizens, while in the beginning of the discussion, Senators were nearly unanimous the other way." 19 Cong. Rec. 421 (1888).

Senators Stewart and Mitchell were no longer willing to tolerate Chinese immigration in any form. They favored a policy of "absolute exclusion," recognizing no exceptions, including for people who held return certificates. Either a new treaty must be negotiated to supersede the existing one, or Congress must simply abrogate the existing treaty by legislation. That is what Mitchell's bill did, and Stewart embraced its objective:

"I say it is the duty of the Congress to pass an absolute exclusion act. I shall vote for the bill of the Senator from Oregon. We have tried various means and find that nothing else will do, and in an emergency like this, where there is so much at stake, it will not do to parley with the question. We must act at once. I shall on all proper occasions ask leave of the Senate to press this matter until we get rid of all the Chinese, and have them excluded not only from our ports, but have them prevented from invading the country through either British Columbia or Mexico. This continent must forever remain dedicated to the Anglo-Saxon race." 19 Cong. Rec. 422 (1888).

The Mitchell bill was intended as a prod. Stewart successfully moved it be referred to the Senate Committee on Foreign Relations, along with a resolution of his own, which urged the president to negotiate a new treaty with China. Under the treaty Stewart envisioned, only diplomats and merchants could enter the United States; all other Chinese would be excluded.

The Senate Committee on Foreign Relations took these measures under advisement, along with a number of related petitions and memorials and legislative initiatives. On February 29, 1888, the committee reported out an amended version of the Stewart resolution, as follows:

"Resolved by the Senate of the United States, That in view of the difficulties and embarrassments that have attended the regulation of the immigration of Chinese laborers to the United States under the limitations of our treaties with China, the President of the United States be requested to negotiate a treaty with the Emperor of China containing a provision that no Chinese laborer shall enter the United States." 19 Cong. Rec. 1580 (1888).

The committee-recommended agreement would depart significantly from the 1880 Angell Treaty, which allowed the United States to suspend Chinese labor immigration, but not to prohibit it. A treaty consistent with the resolution would mean both countries had consented to bar Chinese laborers altogether.

§7.20 Senate Debate, March 1, 1888: "The world was created wrong"

The Stewart resolution, as reported from the Senate Committee on Foreign Relations, came to the Senate floor on March 1, 1888. Committee Chairman Senator John Sherman (R–OH), in past debates an opponent of exclusion, now urged that the Senate agree to the resolution. The policy of exclusion was no longer in question. The issue had become one of enforcement:

"Whatever differences there may have been in the Senate or in the country with regard to the restriction of Chinese immigration, the time has come when I believe the general sentiment of the people is that the law on the subject should be fairly enforced; that the Chinese laborer should be excluded from enjoying the benefits of our country because he will not adapt himself to the civilization of our country." 19 Cong. Rec. 1619 (1888).

Sherman argued that existing exclusion laws were too readily evaded. Chinese presented to American authorities certificates of return guaranteed to persons grandfathered by the Angell Treaty, or sometimes proffered other evidence. Overwhelmed with habeas corpus cases, courts found it impossible to distinguish between legitimate entry claims and fraudulent ones:

"Many cases have occurred, amounting to thousands of fresh Chinese laborers, that have been recently imported into this country under pretense that they were here before 1882 and the proof furnished was absolute and clear, so clear that the courts had to decide in their favor, and yet it was equally clear that the whole statements made, the proof furnished, and the certificates furnished were all false and fraudulent." 19 Cong. Rec. 1619 (1888).

Senator Sherman added that the problem was aggravated by how easily ineligible Chinese could cross the Canadian border. Tensions in the border regions had sometimes degenerated into violence, causing the United States to pay large damages claims, he noted.

In the committee's unanimous view, the existing situation was untenable. A new treaty must be negotiated to bar Chinese laborers absolutely:

"It is utterly impossible for the courts to ascertain whether or not Chinese entitled to come back again are persons named and described in the treaty or the law. Therefore, it is that, in the opinion of the committee, and I may say in the opinion of the Department of State and of the Treasury Department as well, that the time has come when the exclusion must be absolute as to Chinese laborers coming into the United States, in order to prevent these frauds from being committed and in order to prevent our courts from being crowded with applications, many of which are admitted to be fraudulent, and our officers from being disturbed and their duties made difficult in the different departments, especially in the collector's office at San Francisco." 19 Cong. Rec. 1619–1620 (1888).

Shortly after Sherman concluded, Senator Wilkinson Call (D–FL) was recognized. Call, an adjutant general in the Confederate Army during the Civil War, served three terms in the Senate, from 1879 to 1897. Even though he had voted for limited exclusion bills, he opposed an absolute bar as overbroad and discriminatory, as well as a violation of the equal protection principles of the Fourteenth Amendment:

"This resolution practically declares the world was created wrong, that there are some four or five hundred millions of people who ought not to have been created and with whom there should be no kind of intercourse. I gravely question whether anybody can make a declaration of that kind with any propriety. Certainly you are going back on the history of this country. The Fourteenth Amendment to the Constitution . . . is an implied affirmation that every human being has the right to the equal protection of the laws and to laws which equally protect him . . . . I do not accept the theories on which this resolution is based." 19 Cong. Rec. 1621 (1888).

Immediately after Call ended his remarks, the Senate agreed by voice vote to the resolution calling for a renegotiated treaty to exclude Chinese laborers altogether.

§7.21 President Cleveland Responds

On March 8, 1888, a week after the Senate acted, it received a message from President Grover Cleveland. The president reported that much progress had been made in negotiating a new treaty with China along the lines of the Senate resolution:

"Negotiation with the Emperor of China for a treaty such as is mentioned in said resolution was commenced many months ago and has since been continued. The progress of the negotiation thus inaugurated has heretofore been freely communicated to such members of the Senate, and to the Committee on Foreign Relations as sought information concerning the same. It is, however, with much gratification that I deem myself now justified in expressing to the Senate, in response to its resolution, the hope and expectation that a treaty will soon be concluded concerning the immigration of Chinese laborers which will meet the wants of our people and the approbation of the body to which it will be submitted for confirmation." 19 Cong. Rec. 1866–1867 (1888).

§7.30 The Senate Consents to the Bayard–Zhang Treaty

Negotiations with China on a new accord concluded on March 12, 1888. Known as the Bayard–Zhang Treaty, it was submitted to the Senate on March 16, 1888. Shortly thereafter, the Senate consented to ratification, after amending the treaty to make its terms more severe.

Under the Bayard–Zhang Treaty, Chinese laborers would be absolutely barred from the United States for a period of twenty years, including Chinese who held return certificates but who were then out of the country. The provision barring entry of Chinese carrying certificates was added by Senate amendment.

Excepted from this bar was any individual who held a return certificate and who also had a lawful wife, child, or parent in the United States, or also had U.S. property or debts owed to him valued at $1,000. Written descriptions of such family, property, or claims had to be deposited in advance with the collector of customs prior to the Chinese departing.

The right of return had to be exercised within one year from the date of leaving the United States. Even if he qualified for one of the exceptions, no laborer could enter without producing the return certificate he had been issued upon departure, a requirement added by Senate amendment.

Chinese laborers who needed to traverse the United States were given transit rights, but could not remain in the country. The treaty also provided that Chinese officials, teachers, students, merchants, and tourists would not be restricted if such persons could produce a passport from their country of residence, coupled with a U.S. visa. Once admitted to the United States, all such persons, including the laborers in-transit, would continue to enjoy most-favored-nation treatment.

One of the crucial reasons the Chinese government agreed to renegotiate the treaty was concern it had for the well-being of its own subjects in an often-hostile America. Restricting further immigration of laborers was a way for the Chinese emperor to protect his people. In the United States, Chinese had suffered significant harm, both to persons and to property. Both sides recognized this sad history. Article V of the treaty addressed indemnification, and is quoted here in full:

"Whereas Chinese subjects, being in remote and unsettled regions of the United States, have been the victims of injuries in their persons and property at the hands of wicked and lawless men, which unexpected events the Chinese Government regrets, and for which it has claimed an indemnity, the legal obligation of which the Government of the United States denies; and whereas the Government of the United States humanely considering these injuries and bearing in mind the firm and ancient friendship between the United States and China, which the high contracting parties wish to cement, is desirous of alleviating the exceptional and deplorable sufferings and losses to which the aforesaid Chinese have been subjected; therefore, the United States without reference to the question of liability therefore (which legal obligation it denies), agrees to pay, on or before the first day of March 1889, the sum of $276,619.75 to the Chinese minister at this capital, who shall accept the same on behalf of his Government as full indemnity for all losses and injuries sustained by Chinese subjects as aforesaid, and shall distribute the said money among all the sufferers and their relatives." 19 Cong. Rec. 7695 (1888).

The American perspective on this indemnity was reflected in a March 16, 1888, letter dispatched to President Cleveland by the principal American negotiator, Secretary of State Thomas F. Bayard:

"This payment will, in a measure, remove the reproach to our civilization caused by the crimes referred to, as well as redress grievances so seriously complained of by the Chinese representative, and unquestionably will reflect more beneficially upon the welfare of the American residents in China." *New York Times*, March 28, 1888.

Secretary Bayard, who served three terms in the Senate (D–DE, 1869–1885), also noted that paying an indemnity would follow a precedent the Chinese government had already established concerning damages incurred by Americans living in China.

The Bayard–Zhang Treaty stated that it was to remain in force for twenty years, renewable for twenty additional years, if neither party gave formal notice of intent to terminate it.

The Senate-adopted amendments would generate severe political complications for the Chinese government. Because of the Senate amendments, China would not agree to the treaty.

Expecting the Bayard–Zhang Treaty to be ratified, and wanting to have new controls ready to operate, the Senate promptly considered implementing legislation. Because certain sections of the bill were conditional upon ratification, those sections never came into effect. Later in 1888, in response to China's failure to ratify, Congress would pass the highly restrictive Scott Act.

§7.31 The Senate Considers Legislation to Implement the Bayard–Zhang Treaty (S. 3304)

Under consideration in the Senate Committee of the Whole, S. 3304.

On July 20, 1888, Senator Joseph Norton Dolph (R–OR), a senator from 1883 to 1895, brought to the Senate floor S. 3304, a bill to prohibit the coming of Chinese laborers to the United States. The legislation, which was considered in the Senate Committee of the Whole, stipulated that it would take effect when China and the United States exchanged instruments of ratification on the Bayard–Zhang Treaty. Meanwhile, it repealed the 1882 exclusion law, effective on the date of enactment.

After some opening statements, further discussion was deferred until the session of August 7, 1888. Proceedings on that day and the following were largely characterized by political recriminations, as Democrats and Republicans took turns blaming each other for Chinese immigration. A flavor of this argument can be found in the exchange between Alabama Democratic Senator John Tyler Morgan and Nevada Republican Senator William M. Stewart, both strong advocates for exclusion. Their statements are extracted from the August 7, 1888, debate:

Senator Morgan: "The pretension will not do to set up any longer in the Senate, for the world will see through it and scout it, that the Republican Party has any responsibility for the Chinese question on the American continent, except to bring it into this country. Since it got here, they have done very little, almost nothing, with a few bright exceptions under local pressure, possibly, to get rid of it; but we have had to fight a battle of the greatest magnitude, scarcely aided by any Republicans, certainly opposed by a number of their statesmen, whose abilities have been very marked, and whose persistence has absolutely been insuperable in opposition to the restriction of Chinese immigration." 19 Cong. Rec. 7303 (1888).

Senator Stewart: "The assertion that the Republican Party is responsible for the Chinese being here and that the Democratic Party has always opposed the Chinese is not true. The attempt to make this a political issue and charge the Republicans with it is monstrous in view of the facts. The Republican Party has made every move to prevent the country being flooded with Chinese. They raised the alarm. They have gone further, day and night, in season and out of season, from the very first, to prevent the coming of Chinese. They commenced, before any Democrat thought of it, to amend the [Burlingame] treaty to prevent naturalization. When the proposition to naturalize Chinese was before the Senate, the Republicans alone made a showing against it, and it was defeated by Republican votes. When Chinese immigration became oppressive, it was the Republican Party that moved in the matter." 19 Cong. Rec. 7310 (1888).

On August 8, 1888, the Senate Committee of the Whole reported the bill, S. 3304, with no amendments. Without additional debate, the full Senate passed S. 3304 by voice vote.

§7.40 House Proceedings on the Implementation Bill (S. 3304): "The hideous Mongolian incubus"

Under consideration, S. 3304, as passed by the Senate.

The House received S. 3304 on August 9, 1888, and it was referred to the House Committee on Foreign Affairs. On Saturday, August 18, 1888, the committee reported the legislation to the House, with an amendment providing that the 1882 Act would remain in force until the new Bayard–Zhang Treaty was ratified, rather than being repealed upon enactment of the bill. The committee was concerned that, during the gap between the enactment and the exchange of treaty ratification instruments, the Senate version would inadvertently have permitted Chinese to flood American ports without restriction.

Although the House debated the bill for several hours, it did not vote on it. Proceedings resumed on Monday, August 20, 1888. Notable on that day were the comments of Representative Robert R. Hitt (R–IL), who had opposed the 1884 exclusion amendments. Now, in 1888, Hitt applauded what the Senate had done to toughen the treaty. The first Senate amendment negated the right to reenter with a certificate, unless a laborer was in an excepted class. But for the amendment, Hitt said, the treaty's purposes might have been thwarted:

"While the words of the first article seemed to prohibit absolutely the coming of Chinese laborers to this country, they did not touch the question which there was strong reason to believe the courts would soon touch . . . the question as to the right of return of those Chinese not now in the United States, and who had certificates that they had been here and might return. The courts might hold that according to the terms of the existing treaty, the certificates should be considered outstanding obligations on the part of the country. Then the whole flood of these certified Chinese would again pour in. It was well and wisely thought by the Senate that this should be prevented in advance, and the amendment to the treaty was added that none should enter even if holding return certificates." 19 Cong. Rec. 7747 (1888).

The Senate had also mandated that, as to the few Chinese who remained eligible to return, certificates be the sole acceptable evidence at the border. Absent this requirement, Hitt believed, courts could be deceived by false oral testimony:

"Under the principles recognized by our courts, a Chinaman who pretended he had lost his certificate would be allowed to prove by ordinary means or oral evidence his right to come into this country . . . . But the ordinary means of proof as existing among Christian nations are of very little value among Chinamen with whom perjury is so cheap . . . .

"It is a severe provision, but justified by the public interest and the certainty of false testimony if it is allowed. In this matter, you are dealing with a subtle race, with a body of men most cunning and evasive, who have studied all the arts possible to human ingenuity, so as to search their way through every crevice into the ports and borders of the Pacific Coast. Hence, no precaution should have been neglected by the Senate and the amendment was a wise one." 19 Cong. Rec. 7747 (1888).

Remaining discussion in the House on August 20 was consumed with the kind of political blame-casting that had marked the Senate debate. In addition, there were doses of ugly anti-Chinese rhetoric. Remarks of Representative Thomas Thompson (D–CA), then serving his sole term in Congress, are illustrative:

"It has been my province to see with my own eyes for thirty years the formation of the hideous Mongolian incubus upon that fair State, which has robbed it of much of its natural growth and prosperity. No tongue can convey or pen portray the ugliness of the monster . . . .

"With few exceptions, places from whence they have been driven by popular uprisings of the people, every town or village has its Chinese quarter, and every Chinese quarter has its gambling hells, opium joints, and other dens of infamy— a constant menace to the moral welfare of American children, both boys and girls thousands of whom, contracting for life the opium habit, become hoodlums and outcasts, and are ruined for life.

"Pitiable it is to behold these wan-faced victims of Mongolian debauchery upon our streets. The appeal to the civilization of America is to save them, and this can only be done by driving back this yellow tide from Asia that threatens to inundate and ruin our country and its people." 19 Cong. Rec. 7753 (1888).

At the conclusion of the Monday debate, the House agreed by voice vote to the amendment changing the bill's effective date, then passed the bill, also by voice.

§7.41 Senate Concurs in the House Amendment, and China's Reaction: "A response of outrage"

On August 21, 1888, after minimal debate, the Senate concurred in the House amendment. President Cleveland then approved the bill. Proceedings on S. 3304 now concluded, execution of the legislation awaited Chinese agreement to the Bayard–Zhang Treaty, as amended by the Senate. Ratification was expected imminently.

But reaction in China to the Senate's treaty amendments was outrage.

The death of the Bayard–Zhang Treaty itself did not mean the death of every provision of the implementing legislation enacted on September 13, 1888. While some of its sections were expressly conditional on the ratification of Bayard–Zhang, others survived. In particular, sections 5 through 14 of the legislation, with the exclusion of section 12, were considered by subsequent Treasury Department opinions to be valid law.

These nine sections related primarily to the conditions that Chinese laborers already in the United States would need to meet should they leave the United States and subsequently wish to return. A Chinese laborer would need to show that he had "a lawful wife, child, or parent in the United States, or property therein of the value of one thousand dollars, or debts of like amount due him and pending settlement." Marriages of less than one year would not suffice. The laborer would need to prove to a customs agent that he met these requirements in order to obtain a certificate that would function as the sole evidence of his right to return.

Perhaps most importantly, section 8 of the implementing legislation granted the Treasury Department the authority to issue regulations "to conveniently secure to such Chinese persons as are provided for in articles second and third of the said treaty . . . the rights therein mentioned, and such as shall also protect the United States against the coming and transit of persons not entitled to the benefit of the provisions of said articles." Under the auspices of this provision, Treasury officials would begin to draft extremely complicated and baroque definitions for such terms as "merchant," "teacher," and others related to the classes of Chinese immigrants permitted to enter the United States under existing treaty provisions. These definitions would later become the main focus of future Chinese exclusion debates.

§7.50 The Scott Act (H.R. 11336)

As suspicions grew in Congress that China might not ratify the Bayard–Zhang Treaty as amended, legislation (H.R. 11336) began to move that barred by law all Chinese laborers and canceled all certificates of return for Chinese persons then outside the United States. The measure would come to be known as the Scott Act. It amended the 1882 exclusion law, and the absolute bar it imposed on Chinese immigration would last until 1892, at which point, the entire exclusion policy would be up for review.

§7.51 House Debate, September 3, 1888: "The truth is a merchantable commodity"

Under consideration in the House Committee
of the Whole, H.R. 11336 (Scott Act).

The House convened at 12 noon on Monday, September 3, 1888. Up for disposition was H.R. 11336, sponsored by Representative William L. Scott (D–PA). A member of the House from 1885 to 1889, Scott spoke first. Even though his bill had not been referred to committee, he secured consent for its immediate consideration.

Because the Bayard–Zhang Treaty was not ratified, the Angell Treaty remained in force. Scott insisted that his bill to bar Chinese laborers and to cancel return certificates did not abrogate the Angell Treaty:

"This bill does not conflict in any way with any treaty stipulations now existing between the United States and China. It merely proposed under certain conditions to prohibit Chinese laborers from coming into the United States. If the treaty recently negotiated [Bayard–Zhang] has been rejected by the Chinese Government, then this bill is essential, and is the only way possible by which Chinese laborers can be kept out of the United States." 19 Cong. Rec. 8226 (1888).

According to Scott, the Angell Treaty did not actually require the United States to issue certificates of return, but Congress had provided for them anyway by law. The certificates were intended to be proof of identity, Scott said, but they had been abused and never served their original purpose:

"As the truth is a merchantable commodity from a Chinese point of view, those certificates were in many instances sold to Chinamen who had never been in this country, who took them and came to the United States in violation of the law. When a Chinaman reached the port of San Francisco, the duty of the collector of the port under the law was to determine his identity; and when the collector by positive evidence knew that the Chinaman offering the certificate was not the person to whom it had been originally issued, the collector at once required such Chinaman to leave the country. But it was just here that the United States courts came in and upon habeas corpus proceedings declared in many instances that the Chinaman offering the certificate was the original owner. By this process, Chinese laborers by the thousands have been permitted to come to the United States fraudulently, under certificates which had never been issued to them." 19 Cong. Rec. 8226 (1888).

Representative William Morrow (R–CA), in the House from 1885–1889, wanted to be sure that Scott's bill would stop the return of all Chinese laborers who had left the United States, not just ones to whom certificates had been issued. According to Morrow, some 12,000 Chinese had left the U.S. between November 17, 1880, (the date the Angell Treaty was ratified) and May 6, 1882 (the date the 1882 Act was enacted). If any person in that category was yet outside the United States, Morrow sought assurance the person could not get back in.

Scott assured him that the bill was airtight and that reentry would not be possible. Morrow was satisfied. After approximately thirty minutes of debate, H.R. 11336 passed by voice vote and was sent to the Senate.

§7.52 Senate Debate, September 3, 1888: "Deport every single one of them"

Under consideration in the Senate Committee
of the Whole, H.R. 11336, as passed by the House.

Hours after the House acted on September 3, 1888, H.R. 11336 was received in the Senate. Nevada Senator William M. Stewart (R–NV) secured consent for its immediate consideration.

Senator Henry Teller (R–CO) was recognized. In 1882, Teller's speeches in favor of exclusion had been particularly vitriolic (*§ 3.60*). Weeks after the 1882 Act passed, Teller left the Senate for service as President Chester Arthur's secretary of the interior. When the Cleveland administration took office in March 1885, Teller returned to the Senate, where he would remain until 1909.

Teller was actually pleased that the Chinese had not ratified the Bayard–Zhang Treaty. He preferred that Congress take exclusion policy into its own hands, without making such policy conditional upon the agreement of the Chinese government:

"I am in favor of legislating upon this subject without reference to treaties. I do not think that the Chinese treaty recently negotiated was a valuable treaty. It gave us the privilege of doing for twenty years that which every independent nation on the face of the earth asserts the right to do, to say who shall come here and who shall not." 19 Cong. Rec. 8216 (1888).

Teller's attitude about the Chinese remained hostile and unambiguous:

"There are now about one hundred thousand Chinese who have come into this country, and I myself will welcome any legislation that shall deport every single one of them from the United States and send them back to China, where they belong." 19 Cong. Rec. 8216 (1888).

Senator James Z. George (D–MS) spoke after Teller. The first Mississippi senator of the post-Reconstruction era, George was a strong exclusion advocate during the 1882 debates. He directly appealed to race bias:

"My objection to the immigration of Chinese into this country is not that they do not stay here, not that they do not become citizens of the United States, but it is based on an entirely different ground. They are an inferior race, unfit for citizenship in the United States and unfit to be competitors with American laborers." 19 Cong. Rec. 8216 (1888).

Shortly thereafter, Senator John Sherman (R–OH) rose. Chairman of the Senate Foreign Relations Committee, Sherman unanimously agreed with the policy of total exclusion of Chinese laborers, but wanted to institute that policy via a new treaty rather than merely passing legislation to contravene existing agreements.

Sherman spoke about the amendments that the Senate had added to the Bayard-Zhang Treaty. The Senate Foreign Relations Committee had recommended those amendments in order to close immigration loopholes, he said. In making its recommendation, the committee had not understood that the Chinese government found the amendments objectionable. Sherman now was aware of China's serious misgivings, even if its decision on ratification remained in doubt.

At various points in the debate, senators speculated on the reasons for China's delay in coming to terms. Many senators expressed that China was stalling to give its subjects time to circumvent American laws. Others thought that China worried that consenting to highly restrictive terms would set a harsh precedent for how Chinese might be treated in other places, such as in Australia.

Personally, Sherman was unable to parse Chinese motives. In any case, he was concerned primarily about procedure. Would China ratify the treaty or would Congress have to legislate in the face of Chinese recalcitrance? Sherman concluded the House would not have passed the Scott bill unless it had good cause to believe China had rejected the treaty:

"I suppose it is a matter of course that the House of Representatives has information which we have not, that the Chinese Government has refused to ratify the treaty, because I take it that the House of Representatives would never pass a bill of this kind unless they had information of that character; that they would never by unanimous consent pass a bill which practically abrogates upon the subject of Chinese immigration unless they had been advised that the Chinese Government had declined to accept the amendments of the Senate and to accept the new treaty as it now stands." 19 Cong. Rec. 8217 (1888).

If there were still a prospect that China might ratify the Bayard–Zhang Treaty, Sherman said he would object to moving the Scott bill. Believing the Bayard–Zhang Treaty was dead, he was content to legislate.

It was apparent that a consensus for exclusion had formed within Congress. In the past, there had been substantial opposition to exclusion, and Sherman had been one of the most articulate dissenters. But the policy had been established, and the issue was now one of law enforcement. On that subject, there was broad agreement:

"I am in full accord with the general sentiment of the Senate and of the House and of the people of the United States. Whatever may have been said in the past, there is no doubt a concurrent sentiment in this country that we should prohibit races so distinct, so alien, so different in habits, civilization, religion, and character from ours from coming into our country, especially when they cannot mingle in the body of our population." 19 Cong. Rec. 8217 (1888).

Senator Matthew C. Butler (D–SC), a senator from 1877 to 1895, asked Sherman whether the Scott legislation violated existing treaty obligations with China. Sherman thought it did, but saw the need to legislate anyway:

"Undoubtedly, because the existing treaty provides for the certificates; they have been issued under the existing treaty, and by virtue of those certificates, the Chinese have a right to come back here for a certain time and under certain circumstances. It is only because the provisions of the law and of the treaty have been violated by fraud and perjury that such a measure as this would be justified." 19 Cong. Rec. 8218 (1888).

Senator John H. Mitchell (R–OR) followed, admitting that the bill contravened U.S. obligations. The Angell Treaty provided that "Chinese laborers who are now in the United States shall be allowed to go and come of their own free will." The Scott legislation expressed exactly the opposite policy:

"The bill provides, it will be observed, that Chinese laborers who were in the United States at the date of the making of the treaty, the 17th of November 1880, shall not be permitted to go and come of their own free will and accord; that any class of laborers who were here on the 17th of November 1880, and who have heretofore left this country, or who may hereafter leave this country, shall not be permitted to return." 19 Cong. Rec. 8218 (1888).

Not that Mitchell disapproved of this change. The abrogation made the Scott legislation "a most excellent bill." His real problem with the bill was that it did not make exclusion of all Chinese immigrants permanent and permit deportation of Chinese already in the United States:

"While, therefore, I shall vote for this bill cheerfully, I should vote for it much more cheerfully and with much more alacrity if it went one step further and provided that no Chinese person, of whatever citizenship or from whatever port or country he may come, whether he had ever been in the United States or whether he was never here, shall from and after the date of the passage of this bill, be permitted to enter into or remain in the United States of America." 19 Cong. Rec. 8219 (1888).

Senator Butler was again recognized. Even though he would vote for the bill, he questioned why it was being pursued with such urgency. The answer was simple politics, as the 1888 election was looming and both parties were pandering for votes on the Pacific Coast:

"I think it is a game of politics, this whole business, and not a very seemly one, either, I must say. But for the fact that we are on the eve of a Presidential election and each party wants to get the vote of the Pacific slope, this Senate would not be engaged in this debate." 19 Cong. Rec. 8219 (1888).

Butler's theory was eminently plausible. The three previous presidential elections had been exceedingly close. In 1876, Hayes won by a single vote in the Electoral College while receiving a minority of the popular vote. Garfield's electoral win in 1880 was somewhat more comfortable, but he won the popular ballot by fewer than 2,000 votes nationwide. In 1884, Grover Cleveland had beaten James G. Blaine by .03 percent of the popular vote. Indeed, in the forthcoming 1888 balloting, Indiana's Benjamin Harrison would defeat Cleveland in the Electoral College while running nearly 90,000 votes behind the incumbent in the popular vote.

Butler posited that in the search for a winning electoral formula, the Democratic-controlled House had passed the Scott bill. Not to be outdone in the competition, the Republican-controlled Senate "wants to go the House one better." 19 Cong. Rec. 8222 (1888). To Butler, the timing of the Scott debate coincided with election preparation.

As if to prove Butler's point, Senator James George (D–MS) launched another round of partisan blame-casting. George wanted to demonstrate it was Republicans who welcomed the Chinese to America in the first place: "I propose to show now who opened the door and who fastened it open after it got open." 19 Cong. Rec. 8222 (1888). He cited the Burlingame Treaty as evidence of Republican leniency toward the Chinese:

"That was the door that was opened for the admission of the Chinese into this country, by a treaty right, under a treaty negotiated by Mr. Seward and by Mr. Burlingame, and ratified by a Senate of which three-fourths of the members belonged to the Republican Party. And in that treaty, sir, it is stated to be, as I have read, an inherent right on the part of the Chinese to come to this country, not only for purposes of trade and curiosity, but for permanent residence. That is the door, sir, that was opened up, which Senators on the other side of the Chamber seem now so anxious to close." 19 Cong. Rec. 8222 (1888).

George was determined to hold Republicans accountable for statements made over the years by senators such as George Hoar (R–MA), Hannibal Hamlin (R–ME), Orville Platt (R–CT), and Timothy Howe (R–WI). They had challenged exclusion as a violation of foundational American doctrines of human rights and liberties.

"A great many Chinese came in that door thus opened by the Republican Party . . . . The Republican Party had said the Chinese had an inherent and inalienable right to come—a right that inhered in them as men, a right which they could not alienate, a right which it would be an outrage of any people in the world to deprive them of. That is what is meant by an inherent and inalienable right." 19 Cong. Rec. 8222 (1888).

To back his claim of party bias, Senator George rattled off statistics. On the Fifteen Passenger bill (*Chapter Two*), Democrats voted 101 aye and 16 nay. Republicans voted 51 aye and 56 nay. "So the number of Democrats who voted for the bill double that of Republicans and the vote against the bill consisted of three times as many Republicans as Democrats." 19 Cong. Rec. 8222 (1888). In the Senate, 22 Democrats voted aye and 8 voted nay. The Republican count was 9 senators voting aye and 20 voting nay. On the House vote to override President Hayes' veto (*§ 4.90*), Democrats were 83 aye and five nay, while Republicans were 22 aye and 81 nay. "There was not a two-thirds vote for it," George noted, "and therefore this door that Republican Senators are now so anxious to close, by their own votes and the veto of their own President was kept open." 19 Cong. Rec. 8223 (1888).

George turned to the 1882 twenty-year exclusion debate. Party divisions continued to be stark. In the Senate (*Chapter Three*), 30 Democrats and only 8 Republicans had supported that bill. In the House (*Chapter Two*), 98 Democrats voted aye and only 4 voted nay, while Republicans were divided 61 ayes to 62 nays. As George put it, Republican opponents outnumbered Democratic opponents by 15 to 1.

President Chester Arthur vetoed that bill, George noted. Of the 37 senators voting to override the veto, 31 were Democrats. No Democrat voted to sustain the veto, while 28 Republicans had done so. (*§ 4.90*)

Almost immediately after the veto, the House originated the ten-year exclusion bill (*Chapter Five*). George described the voting this way:

"On April 17, 1882, the vote was taken in the House of Representatives, and 103 Democrats came up and voted to close this door which the Republican Party had opened on the Pacific Coast for the admission of the Chinese, and 91 Republicans. There were three Democrats who voted to keep the door open— just three, and there were 34 Republicans." 19 Cong. Rec. 8223 (1888).

Senator George summed up his argument. Under pressure of public opinion, Republicans had come to reverse themselves and embrace exclusion. Republicans had been the advocates of the Burlingame Treaty and the opponents of restrictions. They were the party of Presidents Hayes and Arthur. Standing tall for exclusion had been the Democrats' 1880 party platform. George would not allow latter-day Republican converts to share credit for it:

"Now we find our Republican friends, having through all this long series of years fought under this banner, not only for Chinese immigrants to take bread out of the mouth of the American laborer, but also having fought for what they called in grandiloquent language in the treaty of 1868 the inherent and inalienable right of a Chinaman to come here and to be a citizen and to vote . . . . We who have borne the heat and burden of the day, when we march forward to get toward the setting sun, covered with dust and wearied with this strife to exclude the Chinese are met by these eleventh hour men . . . ." 19 Cong. Rec. 8224 (1888).

Unwilling to permit George to marginalize the Republicans, Senator Mitchell rebutted him. It was not the Burlingame Treaty that generated Chinese immigration, argued Mitchell. Before that treaty was made, between the years 1850 and 1868, 141,800 Chinese had entered at the port of San Francisco alone. "So the basis for all the talk here today made by the Senator from Mississippi to the effect that the Republican Party opened the door to the immigration of Chinese to this country falls to the ground," Mitchell declared. 19 Cong. Rec. 8225 (1888).

Those early Chinese immigrants had been welcomed in California, not rejected. And who had welcomed them? California's second governor, Democrat John McDougal, who had delivered a message to the state legislature describing the Chinese as "the most desirable of our adopted citizens." Mitchell expanded on this theme:

"He was the first man in the United States of America who ever referred to Chinese immigrants as being the most desirable of our adopted citizens, or as being desirable at all as citizens. He was a Democrat, the head of the Democratic Party in California . . . ." 19 Cong. Rec. 8226 (1888).

Governor McDougal was not alone, Mitchell added. In the early 1850s, the Democratic-controlled California Assembly passed legislation to affirm the legality of coolie labor contracts made overseas. Every Assembly Democrat had supported the bill; every Whig had opposed it, and Whigs in the California Senate ultimately defeated it, he reported.

Senator Mitchell pointed the finger of blame back at the Democrats:

"When the Senator from Mississippi [George] therefore gets up here in his defiant way and charges the Republican Party of this country with opening the door to Chinese immigration to this country, he simply proclaims to the world his own ignorance of what he is talking about, or else he is not as careful as he should be in refraining from knowingly misrepresenting the facts. The door to Chinese immigration was opened by the Democratic Party of California in the manner I have stated . . . ." 19 Cong. Rec. 8226 (1888).

Moments later, the Senate adjourned. Neither Democrats nor Republicans wanted to be accused of welcoming the Chinese to America, and each made certain to charge the other with fault.

§ 7.53 Senate Debate, September 4, 1888: "An inferior race"

Under consideration in the Senate Committee of the Whole,
H.R. 11336 (Scott Act), as passed by the House.

The partisan recrimination continued on September 4, 1888, as the Senate resumed consideration of the Scott bill. This day, Senator Henry Teller (R–CO) would attempt to absolve the Republicans and blame the Democrats.

Teller reviewed the history of early U.S. diplomacy with China, beginning with a treaty in 1844 (Treaty of Wanghia), followed by another in 1858 (Treaty of Tientsin). These agreements gave the United States a commercial toehold in China, had been negotiated by Democratic administrations (Presidents Polk and Buchanan), and were approved by Democratic-controlled Senates. Teller noted that nothing in those treaties restricted Chinese from coming to America:

"In those treaties was there any provision that Chinamen should not come to the United States? There was not any assertion at that time of the doctrine that a man has a right to change his allegiance and his home, but the Democratic Administrations who negotiated those treaties were ready then, were ready then, as all administrations have been ready, to go to war in favor of that doctrine . . . ." 19 Cong. Rec. 8250 (1888).

The alleged evils of Chinese immigration were not apparent then to anyone outside of California, Teller observed. "On the contrary, it was supposed by nearly all classes of men that there was benefit to be derived from this immigration." 19 Cong. Rec. 8250 (1888).

Senator James George (D–MS) had insinuated that it was the Burlingame Treaty that opened America's doors to the Chinese. That impression was simply wrong, said Teller. By the time of the Burlingame Treaty's ratification in 1868, great numbers of Chinese were already in the United States:

"The Senator said that Chinese immigration arose out of the treaty of 1868. He is not familiar with the subject. He should have come to some of us who have some acquaintance with the subject for facts." 19 Cong. Rec. 8250 (1888).

Teller insisted that it was Republicans who first proposed restricting Chinese immigration to California. In his 1862 inaugural address, California Republican Governor Leland Stanford warned against Chinese immigration. Teller quoted the governor's message:

"While the settlement of our State is of the first importance, the character of those who shall become settlers is worthy of scarcely less consideration. To my mind, it is clear that the settlement among us by an inferior race is to be discouraged by every legitimate means . . . . There can be no doubt but that the presence among us of a degraded and distinct people must exercise a deleterious influence upon the superior race and to a certain extent repel desirable immigration. It will afford me great pleasure to concur with the Legislature in any constitutional action having for its object the repression of the immigration of the Asiatic races." 19 Cong. Rec. 8252 (1888).

Controlled by Democrats, the California Legislature ignored Stanford. According to Teller, this was because Democrats in California, as well as elsewhere in the sparsely populated West, were loyal to their party's longstanding predilection for cheap labor as a means of hastening economic development. Teller summarized:

"Mr. President, I might mention many other things to support my position that it was cheap labor that the Democratic Party wanted and it was cheap labor for which they went to war. It is cheap labor that they want today. Mr. President, I do not want cheap labor. I know that cheap labor may be had from Chinamen; I know it may be had from slaves, but I do not want it, and I do not intend by my vote to have it. I believe American laborers all over this country are sufficiently intelligent to see that free trade means cheap labor, that it is akin to the old system which we abolished, and I do not believe that they will kindly listen to lectures given to me from the other side of the Chamber by the Senator from Mississippi [George] or the Senator from Alabama [Morgan], or any other Senator who will stand in his place now, or who would a few years, and assert the right of one man to own and control another." 19 Cong. Rec. 8256–8257 (1888).

Senator Teller's statement concluded debate for September 4, 1888.

§7.54 Senate Debate, September 5, 1888: "Homogeneity in races"

Under consideration in the Senate Committee of the Whole,
H.R. 11336 (Scott Act), as passed by the House.

Before debate resumed on Wednesday, September 5, 1888, the Senate passed a resolution inquiring about the status of the Bayard–Zhang Treaty. The resolution read as follows:

"Resolved, That the President is requested, if not incompatible with the public interests, to inform the Senate whether the recent treaty with China and the amendments adopted by the Senate have been ratified by the Emperor of China." 19 Cong. Rec. 8365 (1888).

Then, the Senate resumed consideration of the Scott legislation for a third day. The Committee of the Whole reported the bill to the full Senate without amendment. In the Senate, no amendment was offered, so the bill was advanced to the stage of third reading. At that point, amendments were no longer in order but further debate could still occur.

Senator James George (D–MS) asked to speak. He was willing to prolong the discussion, in order not to leave Senator Henry Teller (R–CO) with the last partisan word.

Seemingly determined to prove that no one could be more against the Chinese than he, George recapitulated his own opposition to Chinese immigration, starting with his service as a freshman senator during consideration of the original 1882 exclusion legislation:

"I did not vote for that bill, I did not speak for that bill, because the presence of Chinese in this country was a special injury to the State in which I live or injury to the section from which I came. No Chinese were there, but feeling deeply from sad experience the dangers of commingling upon the same soil of diverse races, and believing as I did then and as I do now . . . that homogeneity in races was a necessary condition of government, I voted as I did.

"My own land was cursed with the want of that homogeneity, and feeling this deeply, when my brothers of the Pacific Coast came here complaining that they were being ruined by the presence of the Chinese, I went with alacrity to their help . . . .

"I never believed in the inherent and inalienable right of any foreigner to come to America and become part of our body-politic . . . . So from the very moment this Chinese question arose in the American councils for legislative action, the impulses of my heart and my head have been . . . to keep this grand country of ours for ourselves and for our posterity and for foreigners only of the white race." 19 Cong. Rec. 8297 (1888).

Senator George again took aim at the Republicans. He made special note of federal legislation enacted in 1862 to restrict trade in coolie labor contracts. Because the bill was targeted at indentured servitude, it exempted "any voluntary emigration."

George seized on the exemption to prove that Republicans had opened the door to the Chinese even sooner than had generally been supposed:

"So in the very statute . . . prohibiting the importation of Chinese into this country, there is an express provision for their coming into this country. I was a little mistaken in my speech a few days ago in supposing and stating that the treaty of 1868 opened the door. It had been opened six years before that time, by the act to which I have called attention." 19 Cong. Rec. 8298 (1888).

George proceeded to recite familiar allegations of Republican openness to Chinese immigration. These included the Burlingame Treaty; opposition to the Fifteen Passenger bill; President Hayes' veto of the Fifteen Passenger bill in 1879 and override vote; opposition to the twenty-year exclusion bill and efforts to weaken that bill; President Arthur's veto of the twenty-year exclusion bill in 1882 and the override vote; and dissension on the ten-year bill. The senator augmented this list with even more proof the Republicans were soft on the Chinese. He cited 1870 legislation passed by a Republican Congress that barred any state from imposing taxes on any particular immigrants that were not equally imposed on all immigrants. Construing the provision, George complained:

"No matter how objectionable Chinese immigration might be and no matter how desirable Irish immigration and English immigration and German immigration and Scandinavian immigration might be, they just said to the States, you shall not tax the Chinese any more that you tax the others." 19 Cong. Rec. 8298 (1888).

Debate continued through the afternoon, mostly involving sparring between George and a series of Republican interlocutors. George ended his hours-long remarks with a final broadside against the Republicans:

"But the strangest thing of all in this eventful story is that the muse of history, misled by Republican Senators, has got things mixed, and now when everybody is for Chinese restriction . . . it is made to appear that those who fought the good fight for restriction and won the victory were all the time on the other side, and that the only real friends of restriction were those who all along fought against it." 19 Cong. Rec. 8303 (1888).

President Pro Tempore John J. Ingalls (R–KS) called for a vote. The yeas were 32, the nays were zero, and 44 senators were recorded as absent. A quorum of the Senate (39) had not voted, so the bill was not passed. The Senate voted immediately to adjourn.

§ 7.55 Senate Debate, September 6, 1888: "A cruelty and an outrage"

Pending in the full Senate, H.R. 11336
(Scott Act), as passed by the House.

As the Senate turned to the Chinese issue on September 6, 1888, Senator John Sherman (R–OH) raised a question of process. Sherman thought that it was much better to secure a new treaty, rather than legislating against the old one. Passing the Scott legislation remained a distasteful last resort. The Senate remained in the dark as to what China would do, but was striving to learn. Until it was sure, Sherman believed, the Senate should not finish work on the Scott bill:

"I do not care to be embarrassed about voting on this bill, and I appeal to the Senate to let the matter stand over a day or two until we ascertain the facts. No harm can result to the people of California from a short delay . . . . I do not like to see the Congress of the United States rush pell-mell like a herd of buffaloes, at the fire of a single shot, by some rumor that may prove to be false." 19 Cong. Rec. 8329 (1888).

Senator Orville Platt (R–CT) spoke next. He had been one of the most articulate opponents of exclusion legislation in 1882. Platt began by affirming his belief in the general principle of expatriation:

"I hold that a citizen of any country on the face of this earth has a right to leave that country and to transfer his allegiance to another country with the consent of the government to which he endeavors to transfer his allegiance. That right, I think, is too sacred in American history to be denied or impeached or in any way invaded." 19 Cong. Rec. 8330 (1888).

But adhering to that principle did not require the United States to receive every willing immigrant:

"I hold that we have a right to so regulate, restrain, restrict, or prohibit immigration into this country, as that our own country and our own people shall not suffer by that immigration, and that the character of our people shall not be in any sense degraded or suffer by such immigration." 19 Cong. Rec. 8330 (1888).

As Platt saw it, the right of restriction conditioned the principle of expatriation. In 1882, he opposed exclusion because he saw insufficient basis to restrict the Chinese:

"I did not believe in the start and I do not believe now that all Chinamen are so incapable of assimilation with our citizens that they may not come here and become citizens of the United States." 19 Cong. Rec. 8331 (1888).

But Senator Platt had a change of heart. His rethinking was emblematic of how Republican opposition to exclusion had eroded. Senator Sherman had said he would support the Scott bill for law enforcement reasons. Platt went further; he had become a convert to exclusion as a policy:

"I do not take much stock in this idea that they should not be permitted to come here because they belong to a particular race; but I have come to see and believe, and in that respect my sentiments have somewhat changed, that the great bulk of the population of China, and especially that portion of it that will come here to enter into competition with our laborers, is of a character which is incapable of assimilation with us in any form, incapable of having the aspirations which an American citizen must have in order to make him a real sovereign of the Republic. I have come to believe that, and I am so thoroughly satisfied of this that I have become willing to exclude all Chinese laborers from the United States." 19 Cong. Rec. 8331 (1888).

After Platt concluded, Senator Joe Brown (D–GA) announced he would offer an amendment. A senator from 1880 to 1891, Brown proposed to exempt from exclusion Chinese laborers who were absent from the United States, who carried return certificates, and who were already in transit to return to the United States on the date of enactment. Such an individual had a right to reenter the country under existing law, and would undergo special hardship if his certificate were canceled:

"If the bill becomes a law, he would be met by an officer of the United States, who would inform him that notwithstanding he had wife and children and property in San Francisco and may have lived there for twenty years, and notwithstanding he had left home with the guarantee of both governments that he should return on his certificate, that the Congress of the United States, without giving either him or the Chinese Government any previous notice, has passed a law forbidding his return, but he must return to China. Doubtless there will be a number of such cases, and it seems to me not only a great hardship, but a cruelty and an outrage that no existing public sentiment nor any political exigency can justify." 19 Cong. Rec. 8333 (1888).

Senator Brown strongly believed that the Scott bill breached America's obligations to China and to the Chinese immigrants. The Bayard–Zhang Treaty had not yet been ratified, so the Angell Treaty remained in effect. Although Brown was personally opposed to Chinese immigration, he was troubled by overriding treaty commitments through legislative fiat. He explained to senators what the existing treaty meant, especially in light of the 1882 Act that provided return certificates be issued:

"Mr. President, the [Angell] treaty of 1880 which now exists between the two governments provides distinctly and emphatically that the Chinese laborer who was a resident of the United States at the time of the ratification of the treaty shall have the right to go and come from time to time at his own free will and accord, with all the rights of the citizens and subjects of the most favored nation. The act of Congress provides the certificates that shall be obtained when they desire to travel abroad, to enable them to return, which implies an obligation and a solemn pledge by the United States that on compliance with these terms they shall have the right to return.

"This proposed act is in the very teeth of the treaty, and is in the very teeth of the implied pledge made by this Government to each Chinaman who was a resident of the country at the time the treaty was ratified, and who has complied with the statute on that subject, that he shall have the right to return to his home in this country." 19 Cong. Rec. 8334 (1888).

Brown sent an amendment to the desk, protecting the rights of Chinese already in transit back to the United States. Brown wished he could go even further. He actually preferred to halt implementation until proper notice was given to the Chinese government and all persons overseas with certificates were afforded a reasonable opportunity to return. Unilaterally canceling the certificates, and stranding Chinese overseas who had relied on them, was an act of "palpable bad faith," Brown declared. 19 Cong. Rec. 8335 (1888).

Senator Henry M. Teller (R–CO) made a point of order that the amendment was out of order because it came too late in the Senate process. Third reading of the bill had already been ordered. Once that stage of consideration had been reached, further debate was possible, but amendments could no longer be proposed.

The presiding officer sustained Teller's point of order, so the Brown amendment fell. Brown sought unanimous consent to have the amendment considered anyway. Both Senators Teller and Mitchell objected, so the amendment died.

Soon afterward, Wilkinson Call (D–FL) took the Senate floor. He had voted for every exclusion bill ever proposed and would vote for this one. Nevertheless, he was outspoken in rejecting the rationales that were traditionally asserted to support exclusion and denial of citizenship:

"I have not deceived myself with the allegation that these people should be excluded because they do not assimilate with the people of the United States, that they do not intermix or intermarry with them, when there are twelve millions of people in this country as diverse from the white American people as any two races within the whole range of creation. Is there not as great diversity between the colored man, the African, and the white man, as there is between the Mongolian, the yellow man, and the white man? Yet the African makes a reasonably good citizen and performs a useful part in the public economy of the country . . . .

"Neither is there anything in the proposition that American labor is to be degraded, or that it is to be substituted by and with an inferior race and a different civilization. These are not the economics which are to prevail in this country or in the world's future." 19 Cong. Rec. 8336 (1888).

If the senator thought these arguments were groundless, then on what basis would he back the legislation? "My support for these measures . . . has been based upon the proposition that the people of California and Oregon, with great unanimity, were opposed to the admission and the permanent residence among them, and even to the temporary residence, of laborers of this race of people." 19 Cong. Rec. 8336 (1888).

In his earlier remarks, Senator Call offered compelling arguments why Chinese could make good citizens and strengthen America. Unfortunately, his reasons were unpersuasive to his colleagues or even to himself. If whites on the Pacific Coast wanted a particular outcome, Call would empower their wishes even if he strongly disagreed with their thinking:

"I should accord them the right to keep them out, although it be true that these foreigners, these Mongolians, may be made useful citizens. . . . I recognize the fact that they have an ancient civilization from which something is to be learned; that they have eminent examples of virtue and character in their history; that for thousands of years they have maintained government and unity of race and civilization, and that their history for the most part is unstained with the blood and human suffering which have characterized other peoples." 19 Cong. Rec. 8336–8337 (1888).

Debate continued past 5:00 p.m. When the discussion appeared exhausted, the presiding officer again put the passage of the Scott bill before the Senate. This time 37 senators voted aye, none voted against, and 39 did not vote. Once more, passage failed for the lack of a quorum. The Senate turned to other business, after agreeing by unanimous consent to vote on passage at 1:00 p.m. on the next day, September 7, 1888.

§7.56 Senate Debate, September 7, 1888: "Stop this ulcer"

Under consideration in the full Senate
H.R. 11336, as passed by the House.

The Senate convened at noon on Friday, September 7, 1888. Debate on the Scott bill entered its fifth day. House proceedings had taken fewer than thirty minutes.

The presiding officer laid before the Senate a message from President Cleveland, responding to the Senate's inquiry of September 5, 1888. The president reported that Secretary of State Thomas Bayard had asked the American Minister to China about the status of the negotiations. The minister replied on September 6, 1888, "Treaty postponed for further consideration." 19 Cong Rec. 8365 (1888). The Bayard–Zhang Treaty seemed dead in the water. The president's message added impetus to pass the Scott bill in lieu of the treaty.

Senator John Mitchell (R–OR) took the floor. He made clear that he supported the bill as useful, but that it was only a half-measure:

"The bill . . . simply relates to Chinese persons now in the United States or who have been in the United States heretofore. It provides that so far as they are concerned, if they shall go away, or if any of them have gone away heretofore, they shall not be permitted to return.

"That is this bill. That is all there is of it. It is important, radical; but radical as it is, I, inasmuch as by this step we abrogate a most material provision of our existing treaty with China, would have gone one step further and made the prohibition, the absolute exclusion, apply not only to those Chinese in the United States now, or who have been in the United States at some time heretofore, but also to the 400,000,000 Chinese who have never been to the United States." 19 Cong. Rec. 8365 (1888).

Following some additional debate, the hour of 1:00 p.m. arrived. After brief parliamentary skirmishing, a vote on the bill was taken. This time, there was a quorum. Thirty-seven senators voted aye, 3 were opposed, and 36 were counted as absent. The three senators in opposition were Joseph E. Brown (D–GA), George F. Hoar (R–MA), and James Wilson (R–IA). John Sherman (R–OH) was among the absentees.

Senator Henry Blair (R–NH), a two-term member (1879–1891), moved to reconsider the vote by which the bill was passed. Blair had voted in the affirmative to pass the bill. Because he was on the prevailing side, Senate rules entitled Blair to offer the reconsideration motion.

The motion to reconsider was debatable, and Senator Arthur Pue Gorman

(D–MD) came to the floor. Gorman served in the Senate from 1881 to 1899 and again from 1903 to 1906.

Gorman was troubled that the Scott bill had gone straight to the Senate floor and had not received consideration in the Senate Foreign Relations Committee. If the vote on passage was reconsidered, and the measure was back before the Senate, he would insist on referral of the bill and President Cleveland's message to committee.

Gorman worried about Chinese retaliation. The Scott bill was a slap in China's face. If America acted unilaterally to abrogate treaty rights and exclude Chinese, China could respond by excluding Americans and damaging U.S. business interests. A more deliberative procedure would permit the committee, "to present us with a measure that is fair and proper, that will not violate our treaty obligations, or put us in such a position that the Chinese Government will have the right, the moral right, and be justified in the eyes of the world, in excluding all our people from their shores." 19 Cong. Rec. 8370 (1888).

Senator William Stewart (R–NV) spoke next, insisting that the time for negotiation and deliberation was over. He claimed that the Chinese minister (ambassador) had signaled his government's assent to the Senate amendments, so that by delaying ratification, the Chinese were acting in bad faith:

"I say that it is the duty of the Senate to pass this bill and stop this ulcer that is destroying one of the finest cities in the Republic, besides spreading all over the country and spreading demoralization everywhere. We cannot wait, and this deliberation is an insult, after their Minister here has expressed his satisfaction with these amendments. It shows that the original treaty was a trick and intended to be evaded." 19 Cong. Rec. 8370 (1888).

Stewart explained why it was necessary to cancel return certificates, either by treaty or by statute. Fraud was rampant, he claimed:

"The [Angell] treaty of 1880 provided that legislation might be had limiting immigration. No act was passed to enforce that provision until 1882. In 1882, an act was passed. It was then said to be unfair to those who had left the country between the making of the treaty and the passage of the act—about two years. So the act provided they might come in on proof of previous residence . . . .

"Now there is a stream of previous residents—thousands of them—that have been coming in and the courts have been overloaded by cases involving their identification. All swear that they are 'previous residents' and it is impossible to detect them . . . .

"Occasionally there would be found a memorandum in Chinese in his (an immigrant's) possession, in which he had been given the directions. The memory of these people is extraordinary. They will learn a tale so well that through an interpreter you cannot investigate it.

"The courts in California have been loaded down with cases involving this question of previous residence, and they can do nothing with them. The people of the Pacific Coast have become so disgusted with the whole thing that they have asked for its stoppage. These people get all sorts of certificates and papers and bring them to this country. Our people cannot tell these Chinamen apart; hence all this trouble." 19 Cong. Rec. 8371 (1888).

Senator Wilkinson Call (D–FL) took the floor. While he favored exclusion of Chinese laborers, he disagreed with the Scott bill as a means of implementation. The bill was blatant politics, which had the potential to damage American interests in China:

"It seems to me as if this whole discussion and all these measures are intended to show which party or which individual will go farthest in appearing to persecute and oppress these Chinese people, as if that were the object rather than to devise a proper and an efficacious method of preventing their migration in any great numbers into this country, and at the same time preserving commercial relations and good feeling with the Government of China." 19 Cong. Rec. 8374 (1888).

Some of the senator's colleagues had made clear that they favored the absolute exclusion of all Chinese. Call considered that policy vastly overreaching:

"I believe the Chinese civilization has something which can be taught advantageously to all people . . . . I believe that when other peoples and nations have been committing the most horrible cruelties, religious fanaticism and political cruelties, these people, who have existed for so many years, with so many examples of the moral virtues which our religion teaches, are not . . . to be treated as pestilence and a scourge, and a necessary evil to be banished from all communication with mankind." 19 Cong. Rec. 8375 (1888).

Within moments, Senator Henry Teller (R–CO) moved to lay the motion to reconsider on the table. Teller's tabling motion was not debatable and required affirmation by a simple majority vote. If carried, it would have dispensed with the question of reconsideration and the Senate vote to pass the Scott bill would stand. What followed was a remarkable parliamentary sequence, in which abstentions prevented disposition of Teller's motion.

On the tabling motion, 23 senators voted aye, 11 voted no, and 42 were absent. Less than a majority of senators had voted and thus there was no quorum. Because there was no quorum, the motion failed.

The Constitution requires a majority of senators for a quorum, and in the absence of a quorum, the Senate cannot do business. There followed a motion to adjourn. Nineteen voted aye, 22 voted no, and 35 were absent. While the Senate refused to adjourn, the vote against the motion had produced a quorum.

With a quorum present, the Senate once more voted on Teller's motion to table reconsideration. This time, 25 senators were in the affirmative, 8 were in the negative, and 43 were recorded absent. Again, the lack of a quorum meant the tabling did not carry. Yet another motion to adjourn followed.

On the adjournment motion, the vote was 17 aye, 22 nay, and 37 absent. For a second time, the Senate refused to adjourn and the vote had produced a quorum.

This led to a third vote on Teller's tabling motion. There were 27 ayes, 7 nays, and 42 absentees. Once more, the lack of a quorum prevented agreement to the motion.

In frustration, the Senate agreed by voice vote to adjourn.

§7.57 Senate Debate, September 10, 1888: "China is our great friend"

Under consideration, the motion to reconsider (Senator Blair (R–NH)) the vote by which the Senate passed H.R. 11336 (Scott Act).

On Monday, September 10, 1888, the Senate considered the Scott bill for the sixth session day. Notwithstanding President Cleveland's message of September 7, 1888, Senator John Sherman (R–OH) reported the administration had since advised him the Chinese government was actively considering the Bayard–Zhang Treaty. The U.S. Minister to China would soon return to Washington with word on ratification. Sherman implored the Senate to withhold action on the bill:

"This treaty is still pending and not yet ratified by the contracting parties. If we pass this bill and make it a law, we nullify the treaty, a treaty that we ourselves ratified. We cannot do that consistently with national honor, unless for some flagrant act or cause; it would not be a good example to set to the nations of the world." 19 Cong. Rec. 8451 (1888).

A senator from 1885 to 1891, William M. Evarts (R–NY) had been attorney general under President Andrew Johnson (1865–1869). As secretary of state during the Hayes administration (1877–1881), he had counseled the president to veto the Fifteen Passenger bill. Evarts reinforced Sherman's misgivings about the diplomacy-wrecking step of passing preemptive legislation while the treaty was still under consideration:

"It is for the first time in the diplomatic history of this country a legislative intervention while a treaty negotiated by this Government is . . . pending for adoption by a foreign nation, and this intervention not only rebukes and repeals our action in that diplomatic conduct of affairs, but it immediately and absolutely affronts the foreign nation with the suggestion that we will no longer tolerate any such method of dealing with the matter between us." 19 Cong. Rec. 8452 (1888).

China anticipated better from the United States than it could rely on from rapacious European powers, who had coerced from them trade and territorial concessions. In light of America's good historical relations with China, Evarts observed, passing the Scott legislation would be ironic and disrespectful:

"China is our great friend, always looking to this nation to stand for justice to a non-Christian country when she could not expect it from any European power; and yet no European power, with its rude oppressions of China in the interests of its trade, has ever taken to present to that great nation and that dignified and sensitive government a proposition of this kind." 19 Cong. Rec. 8453 (1888).

Senator James Falconer Wilson (R–IA) addressed another aspect of U.S.-China relations. Serving from 1883 to 1895, Wilson had been one of the three senators to oppose the Scott bill when the Senate passed it on September 5, 1888.

The United States had long stood alone for the right of expatriation, Wilson said. No other power would concur in the principle, certainly none in Europe. Then, in the Burlingame Treaty, China assented to it. Article V of the Burlingame Treaty expressly stated:

"The United States of America and the Emperor of China cordially recognize the inalienable right of a man to change his home and allegiance . . . . "

China's validating this idea was a signal achievement of American diplomacy. Senator Wilson asked, "Could we have induced any other nation on the face of the globe, after our long search for one to agree with us, to have given that formal and emphatic recognition of our position concerning the right of expatriation?" 19 Cong. Rec. 8456 (1888).

Considering this relationship, the senator said, it was particularly inappropriate to single out China for treatment America would not mete out to any European nation.

During the September 10, 1888, debate, much had been said that was unfavorable to the Scott bill. But it is important to understand that few criticisms were aimed at reopening the Chinese exclusion policy. By 1888, support for exclusion was ingrained in Congress. Senators such as Sherman, Evarts, and

Wilson were concerned not with the policy itself, but whether Congress should proceed with preemptive legislation while treaty ratification was pending in China. Even Senator Wilkinson Call (D–FL), who spoke so affirmatively about Chinese people and their culture, was unprepared to challenge exclusion.

At 4:15, the Senate adjourned for the day, without action on the Scott bill.

§7.58 Senate Debate, September 11, 1888: "The evil will go on increasing"

Under consideration in the full Senate, the motion to table (Senator Teller (R–CO)) the motion to reconsider (Senator Blair (R–NH)) the vote by which the Senate agreed to H.R. 11336 (Scott Act).

During the afternoon of Tuesday, September 11, 1888, Senator William Stewart (R–NV) secured unanimous consent to resume debate on the legislation. More or less silent in the previous day's session, Stewart took the floor to urge the bill's passage.

Stewart noted that even the Chinese themselves claimed to be against their laborers emigrating to America. As proof, he cited the preamble to the Bayard–Zhang Treaty, which stipulated:

"Whereas the Government of China, in view of the antagonism and much-deprecated and serious disorders to which the presence of Chinese laborers has given rise in certain parts of the United States, desires to prohibit the emigration of such laborers from China to the United States." 19 Cong. Rec. 8496 (1888).

Notwithstanding this affirmation, Stewart thought the Chinese were not acting in good faith. In the four months that the treaty had been pending, 4,000 to 5,000 Chinese had entered the United States. The Chinese were stalling, in order that the implementation of the treaty would actually be delayed. "She knew very well the urgency of this case," Stewart complained:

"China knew very well that for the last four years Congress had been trying to legislate to stop this tide . . . and when this treaty was negotiated and they agreed to it, they agreed that this immigration might be stopped at once; but they have kept us for four months when there was no excuse for delay . . . ." 19 Cong. Rec. 8496 (1888).

Passing that bill now would negate any motives the Chinese had for further delay ratification, Stewart argued. He implored his colleagues not to get bogged down in procedural details:

"You all claim today that you are in favor of excluding Chinese but you want to do it in a certain way. You are all in favor of it now, but you want to do it in a certain way. If you do not pass this bill and Congress adjourns, this whole question will confront you at the next session and this evil will go on increasing and increasing . . . .

"For a man to say that he cannot vote for this bill, while he is in favor of excluding the Chinese, is to impeach his honesty or his intelligence on the subject . . . . We have a right to exclude them because China is acting in bad faith in relation to this treaty . . . . we have a right to exclude them because we have a right to protect our country from pollution." 19 Cong. Rec. 8498–8499 (1888).

In any event, Stewart's own position was not troubled by nuances, procedural or otherwise. "My record is all right. If it had not been for me, the Chinaman would be a voter before this time," Stewart boasted.

The Senate's protracted consideration of the Scott bill was becoming politically controversial. Democrats controlled the House, and the bill's sponsor in the House, Representative William Scott (D–PA), was a member of the Democratic National Committee. The House had addressed the legislation with alacrity. In the Republican-controlled Senate, the bill was now pending for the seventh day. Although the Senate had passed the bill, a motion to reconsider remained pending. Efforts to table the motion had failed several times due to the lack of a quorum. Senator Henry Teller (R–CO) accused Democrats of denying a quorum by declining to vote, so as to extend Senate proceedings and embarrass the Republicans:

"Whatever delay there has been has been occasioned by the Democrats of this body. I do not say that they have not a right, and that they ought not to so vote, but I do say that it will not do for members of the Democratic National Committee anywhere to assert that the House of Representatives put this bill through in thirty minutes and that we were a week or ten days in passing this bill through the Senate." 19 Cong. Rec. 8501 (1888).

After a brief amount of additional debate, the Senate concluded its session of September 11, 1888.

§ 7.59 Senate Debate, September 13, 1888: "That seething, roaring, blood-curdling curse"

Under consideration in the full Senate, the motion to table (Senator Teller (R–CO)) the motion to reconsider (Senator Blair (R–NH)) the vote by which the Senate agreed to H.R. 11336 (Scott Act).

The Senate did not return to the Chinese issue on September 12, 1888, but debate resumed the following day, on Thursday, September 13. Senator George M. Vest

(D–MO) took the floor. Vest was a four-term senator (1879–1903). In 1861, while a member of the Missouri legislature, Vest proposed his state's secession ordinance and later served in the Confederate Congress.

Vest strongly supported Chinese exclusion, but he had a complaint. The senator accused Republican Senators from the western States of hypocrisy, in that they asked colleagues to rid their region of Chinese immigrants, but were insensitive to Southern attitudes about Africans:

"I want know if the Republican Senators from the Pacific Slope who urge upon us to relieve them of this curse of the Chinese are willing to turn around in a single hour and vote for the most extreme measures to fix upon the white people of the South the curse of negro domination, politically, socially, and otherwise?" 19 Cong. Rec. 8565 (1888).

Vest continued to rail against a society turned upside down. He would abide the interests of the Pacific region, even if its senators had not treated the South with similar regard:

"When our friends from the Pacific Coast speak of the terrible evils of Chinese immigration, let them think of a people proud, prosperous, wealthy, who in the short period of four years saw everything they held dear stricken down, and not a foreign race, not the yellow curse from the Mongolian Empire, but their own slaves made their masters politically, and the power of those slaves pinned upon those states, by the bayonets of the National Government." 19 Cong. Rec. 8566 (1888).

White solidarity would motivate Vest to pass the Scott bill. He would do it, but it was really more than the Pacific Coast Republicans deserved:

"I want my friends from the Pacific Coast to understand that if I could be driven from my own race and people, if I could be induced to vote for a reconsideration and let them wrestle with this Chinese question by themselves, I should be made to do it by the remarkable fact that after they have got rid of the Chinese, they want to fasten African supremacy upon the white people of the South." 19 Cong. Rec. 8566 (1888).

Soon thereafter, Senator Henry Blair (R–NH) was recognized. It was he who had made the motion to reconsider the vote by which the Scott bill passed. He needed the bill reopened, in order to propose an amendment making the legislation effective on November 1, 1888, or sooner, if China rejected the Bayard–Zhang Treaty.

Blair took exception to suggestions that moving to reconsider broke faith with the exclusionists. Indeed, Blair was adamantly committed to the policy. Although as a senator from New Hampshire he had scant direct experience with the Chinese, Blair had once been in San Francisco's Chinatown. That seemed to be sufficient for him:

"From the moment I saw that seething, roaring, blood-curdling curse, Chinatown in San Francisco, I felt as though there had been planted in the vitals of American civilization the seeds of death . . . ." 19 Cong. Rec. 8567 (1888).

Lest anyone impugn his commitment to exclusion, Blair emphasized that he would go further and deport the Chinese already in the country. They had no business being in America, said Blair. Most Chinese had come in as contract laborers, in direct violation of the law. That should provide sufficient legal basis to expel them. "The evil which already exists should also be removed, and I believe that evil can be removed under existing law," he argued. 19 Cong. Rec. 8567 (1888).

Senator Blair rejected Vest's argument about Republican racial hypocrisy. It was not contradictory in the slightest for Republicans to support equal rights for Africans while demanding exclusion of the Chinese. The cases were wholly different:

"Mr. President, there is no comparison between these two races. Because we are opposed to further immigration of the Chinese, because we are in favor of elimination of the Chinese from our Northern populations for the present and for the future, it does not follow that we are involved in any inconsistency when we ask that the negro American citizen, born here and with an ancestry as old as our own on this continent, when we ask for him not social rights but that he have simply those same civil and personal rights which we demand for the white race." 19 Cong. Rec. 8568 (1888).

Later that day, Senator John Tyler Morgan (D–AL) took the floor. In negotiating the Bayard–Zhang Treaty, the Chinese government had consented to the absolute exclusion of their laborers. They had come to that position, he stated, because they feared that Chinese persons in America could not be adequately protected from harm:

"China is aware, painfully aware, as she expresses herself, that the Burlingame Treaty of 1868 and the [Angell] treaty of 1880 and all the statutes we have enacted upon that subject are really incapable of protecting the Chinese subjects in the United States from mob violence. I remember when I was in the city of Los Angeles some few years ago, it had been but a few days before that time when twenty-one Chinamen were strung up by halters and hanged, no offense having been committed except that they were Chinamen and in the way . . . . I doubt there has been a single territory in the West which has not been troubled with the presence of these mobs inflicting violence upon the Chinese." 19 Cong. Rec. 8570 (1888).

Morgan was recalling the Chinese massacre of 1871, which took place in Los Angeles, California, on October 24, 1871. All eight of the non-Chinese men convicted of manslaughter were released after serving less than a year in prison. See Scott Zesch, *The Chinatown War: Chinese Los Angeles and the Massacre of 1871* (Oxford University Press, 2012); Paul M. De Falla, "Lantern in the Western Sky," *The Historical Society of Southern California Quarterly*, 42 (March 1960), pp. 57–88 (Part I), and 42 (June 1960), pp. 161–185 (Part II); and Paul R. Spitzerri, "Shall Law Stand for Naught?: The Los Angeles Chinese Massacre of 1871 at Trial," *California Legal History*, 2008, Vol. 3, pp. 185–224. The implication of this and other trials demonstrated that the criminal courts did not protect the Chinese.

Since the Chinese could not be protected, they must be excluded, Morgan reasoned. Both the Chinese and the American governments had so concluded. "These little mobs rise, but they cannot exterminate them, and we cannot prevent it. All we can do is to keep them out of this country." 19 Cong. Rec. 8570 (1888).

After a brief period of additional debate, Senator John Sherman (R-OH secured unanimous consent that a vote on the Blair motion to reconsider occur without further debate at 2:00 p.m. the following day, Friday, September 14, 1888.

§7.60 Senate Debate, September 14, 1888: No quorum means stalemate

Under consideration in the full Senate, the motion to reconsider (Senator Blair (R–NH)) the vote by which the Senate agreed to H.R. 11336 (Scott Act).

Under the consent order, on September 14, 1888, the Senate took a roll call on the motion to reconsider the vote by which the Scott bill had passed. Eighteen senators voted aye, 17 voted nay, and 41 were absent. Once more, the vote failed due to the absence of a quorum. Senator John Sherman (R-OH) asked consent that another vote on the motion to reconsider occur at 1:00 p.m. on Monday, September 17, 1888.

The Senate had now considered the Scott bill for parts of nine session days, stretching over two weeks, without a conclusive result. A week had elapsed since the Senate voted to pass the Scott bill, and Senator Henry Blair (R-NH) submitted his motion to reconsider that vote.

§7.61 Senate Debate, September 17, 1888: Passage

Under consideration, the motion to reconsider
(Senator Blair (R–NH)) the vote by which
the Senate passed H.R. 11336 (Scott Act).

On September 17, 1888, a quorum finally materialized on the motion to reconsider. Twenty Senators voted in the affirmative, 21 voted in the negative, and 35 did not vote. Accordingly, the motion to reconsider the September 7, 1888, passage vote was defeated. Senate proceedings on the Scott bill were concluded.

§7.62 House Debate, September 20, 1888: "A demagogical way to make some capital"

The saga of the Scott bill was not quite finished. Because the legislation originated in the House, it returned there for final enrollment, the last formality before presentation to the president. However, a controversy erupted over a story in the September 19, 1888, edition of *The Washington Post* that Representative Constantine Kilgore (D–TX), chairman of the House Committee on Enrolled Bills, in collaboration with the Cleveland administration, was stalling the Scott bill's enrollment. A delay would spare the president from dealing with the Scott bill while ratification of the Bayard–Zhang Treaty was still open.

The furor resulted in Representative William Morrow (R–CA) raising a question of privilege in the House, claiming an affront to the integrity of House proceedings. Representative Benton McMillin (D–TN) made a point of order that Morrow was responding to mere newspaper speculation, delay in enrollment had thus far been slight, and no question of privilege was presented.

Representative Lewis Payson (R–IL), who served five terms between 1881 and 1891, claimed the situation was an exercise in pre-election political manipulation. Democrats, he alleged, wanted to appear aggressive and firm in pursuit of exclusion, but that was all for show. The administration, itself Democratic, preferred bilateral agreement to unilateral legislative action. Once the bill was sent to the White House, President Grover Cleveland (D) would have ten days under the Constitution to consider it. Republicans speculated that Cleveland wanted more time, until the Bayard-Zhang situation could be clarified. Better to hold the legislation in abeyance until hopes for ratification were exhausted:

"The bill is detained, without doubt, because the President of the United States wants more than the constitutional ten days. The unwarranted delay and tardiness now on the other side is a fitting sequel to the haste attending the presentation of the bill. This is a continuation of the performance begun by the gentleman from Pennsylvania [Mr. William Scott] to attempt in a demagogical way to make some capital for himself and his party. Everybody knows it. Now let the country and the House know just what it is and why it is. It is a 'performance' from first to last, and let the House and the country understand it." 19 Cong. Rec. 8789 (1888).

Speaker Pro Tempore Samuel Cox (D–NY) ruled in favor of McMillin's point of order. Cox determined that any delay in enrollment had been so minimal that a question of privilege was not presented.

§7.70 President Cleveland Signs the Scott Act, October 1, 1888

On September 21, 1888, Secretary of State Bayard received word that China refused to ratify the Bayard-Zhang treaty. That same day, President Cleveland received from the House the enrolled Scott bill. On October 1, 1888, the president approved the Scott legislation and it became law.

President Cleveland sent a message to Congress on October 1, 1888, indicating that the sticking point for the Chinese negotiating the Bayard–Zhang Treaty had been abrogation of the return certificates as well as the twenty-year duration of the treaty. The president reported the Chinese would not ratify, "unless further discussion should be had with a view to shorten the period stipulated in the treaty for the exclusion of Chinese laborers, and to change the conditions agreed on, which should entitle a Chinese laborer who might go back to China to return again to the United States." 19 Cong. Rec. 9052 (1888). These conditions were unacceptable to the United States, so the Bayard–Zhang Treaty was dead.

As had been noted several times in the debates, China was itself concerned about the mistreatment of its subjects in the United States. The president reported:

"In 1886 . . . the Chinese Government had formally proposed to our minister strict exclusion of Chinese laborers from the United States without limitation; and had otherwise and more definitely stated that no term whatever for exclusion was necessary, for the reason that China would of itself take steps to prevent its laborers from coming to the United States." 19 Cong. Rec. 9052 (1888).

China had not taken adequate steps to adhere to these promises, President Cleveland lamented. Accordingly, the United States had no choice but to act.

"An emergency has arisen, in which the Government of the United States is called upon to act in self-defense by the exercise of its legislative power. I cannot but regard the expressed demand on the part of China for a reexamination and renewed discussion of the topics so completely covered by mutual treaty stipulations, as an indefinite postponement and practical abandonment on the objects we have in view . . . ." 19 Cong. Rec. 9052 (1888).

Although he signed the Scott Act, President Cleveland did recommend passage of separate legislation to permit reentry of Chinese who were already in transit back to the United States. Senator Joseph Brown (D–GA) had raised this very idea during the Senate deliberations, but his amendment to that effect had fallen on a point of order. No such additional legislation was ever enacted, and many thousands of Chinese were stranded overseas with return certificates that Congress had rendered worthless.

The president also recommended the United States pay an indemnity to China of $276,619.75 for injury to Chinese subjects from acts of violence. The indemnity had been provided for in the Bayard–Zhang Treaty, and Cleveland remained committed to it.

§7.80 A Political Note

In all the 1888 Chinese exclusion proceedings, there was a large dose of political posturing. The debates early in the year were filled with accusations about which party was more lenient to the Chinese and which one stood tougher for exclusion. Later, politics swirled around the timing and speedy passage of the Scott bill in the House, the bill's tortuous two weeks in the Senate, and even rumors about manipulated enrollment. So what happened in the election itself, especially in the Pacific region, whose interests both parties had been so anxious to accommodate?

On November 6, 1888, barely a month after he signed the Scott Act, President Cleveland (D) lost the presidential election to Republican Benjamin Harrison of Indiana. Cleveland carried the popular vote 48.6 percent to 47.7 percent, but lost by 233 to 168 in the Electoral College. The Pacific region states of California, Oregon, and Nevada all went Republican, returning fourteen electoral votes for Harrison. In California, Harrison won the popular vote 49.6 percent to 48.6 percent. He carried Nevada 57.5 percent to 42.2 percent, and prevailed in Oregon 53.8 percent to 43.5 percent.

Cleveland's narrow margin in the overall popular vote came from his overwhelming percentages in the eleven lower South states that had originally seceded to form the Confederacy in 1860 and 1861. The New Yorker Cleveland won nearly 66 percent of the vote in Texas, and more than 70 percent in Georgia, Alabama, Mississippi, and Louisiana. Cleveland's worst performance in those states was in Florida, with 59 percent. His best state was South Carolina, with over 82 percent.

CHAPTER EIGHT

美 The Geary Act
國 of 1892

*"Through five thousand years heredity,
intensified by isolation, has produced and
reproduced their race characteristics until
they are concrete: unchangeable mentally,
physically, or morally. And wherever they
go, they disseminate vices that kill mentally
and physically . . . they are more to be feared
for their virtues than their vices."*
—Senator Charles Felton (R–CA)
23 Cong. Rec. 3478 (1892)

*"In the history of the ages of the literature
of this people, running away back from
where we can form scarcely an idea of
its antiquity, we find everywhere that this
Chinese people, this Chinese civilization,
has in the spiritual and intellectual as
well as in the material matters of human
life, contributed vastly to the benefit
and happiness of the world at large."*
—Senator Wilkinson Call (D–FL)
23 Cong. Rec. 3622 (1892)

§8.0 Overview

- Considered in the 52nd Congress of the United States (1891–1893)
- Senate Party Division: 47 Republicans, 39 Democrats, 2 Independents
- House Party Division: 238 Democrats, 86 Republicans, 8 Independents
- President: Benjamin Harrison (R) (1889–1893)

In 1892, the ten-year exclusion policy would expire unless renewed. Congress passed the Geary Act, which extended the policy for ten more years; required Chinese to carry certificates of residence that established their right to be in the United States; rendered Chinese who did not have such papers presumptively deportable; declared that paperless Chinese who attempted to prove eligibility in court would need the corroborating testimony of at least one credible white witness; and subjected Chinese who were convicted to up to a year in prison before deportation.

These unprecedented requirements applied to no one other than Chinese persons.

The 1882 exclusion law was due to expire on May 5, 1892. By that time, a consensus supporting the exclusion policy had jelled in Congress. The law had been strengthened in 1884 and in 1888. As renewal loomed, there was no serious prospect the policy would be discontinued.

§8.10 House Debate, April 4, 1892: "An absolute abrogation"

Under consideration in the House of Representatives, H.R. 6175 (Representative Thomas Geary (D–CA)).

Chinese exclusion legislation, originally enacted in 1882, was due to expire in 1892. The renewal debate, which commenced in April 1892, generated legislation far harsher than anything Congress had done in the past.

On Monday, April 4, 1892, Representative Thomas J. Geary (D–CA) moved to suspend the rules of the House of Representatives to consider H.R. 6185, a bill to absolutely prohibit the coming of Chinese persons into the United States. A member of Congress between 1881 and 1885, Geary served on the House Committee on Foreign Affairs, which affirmatively reported the bill. On the House floor, Geary was the bill manager.

Controversy immediately erupted over Section 14 of the bill, which stated:

"That all acts and parts of acts inconsistent herewith be, and the same are hereby, repealed, and the provisions of all treaties now in force between the United States and the Chinese Empire, insofar as they, or any of them conflict with the provisions of this act, be, and the same are hereby, abrogated, set aside, and repealed . . . ." 23 Cong. Rec. 2911 (1892).

Representative Charles Hooker (D–MS) complained about considering such consequential legislation, which abrogated existing treaties, under suspension procedures, which allowed for thirty minutes of overall debate:

"I am opposed to the passage of this bill in a summary way. It is a very sweeping measure. It proposes an absolute abrogation of all treaties we have on this subject, and it is a measure which the House ought to give sufficient consideration to understand and comprehend." 23 Cong. Rec. 2912 (1892).

Several members proposed extending the debate, at least for an hour or two. But doing that required unanimous consent, and objections were voiced. Thus, the House operated under its normal suspension procedures, allowing for fifteen minutes on each side.

Opening the debate, Representative Geary was very direct:

"Mr. Speaker, this bill is intended to prevent the coming of Chinese into the United States." 23 Cong. Rec. 2912 (1892).

Geary claimed that in the decade since exclusion became national policy, 60,000 Chinese had entered the United States through the port of San Francisco, while many others had come across the Canadian border. Despite Congress' best efforts, the law remained porous. Pending legislation would fix the defects, Geary argued.

Following Geary's brief remarks, Hooker spotlighted some of its extraordinary and unique features:

"The first section of the bill, it will be observed, provides for the absolute exclusion of all Chinese from immigrating into this country, for any purpose whatever, except the minister plenipotentiary from the Chinese Empire and his suite.

"The second section of the bill requires all Chinese who are here to go to an internal revenue officer and pay a certain fee for the purpose of being registered as Chinese subjects within the United States.

"Another clause of the bill proposes the most extraordinary proposition that was ever made as a law proposition, namely, that the writ of habeas corpus shall be suspended and all bail denied pending the trial of the accused.

"The concluding section of the bill proposes to abrogate every treaty that has ever been made with the Chinese Empire." 23 Cong. Rec. 2912 (1892).

Representative Hooker was appalled by the Geary legislation. In ratifying both the Burlingame Treaty and the Angell Treaty amendments to that treaty, China had consented to American overtures, even though "China did not originally want her people to come here," Hooker reported. 23 Cong. Rec. 2913 (1892).

Notwithstanding Chinese cooperation and good faith, Congress' response had been hostile. It had adopted Chinese exclusion as a policy in 1882, passed the Scott Act in 1888, and now proposed express abrogation of all treaties with China:

"China has agreed to every modification that we have ever proposed, and I do not want to see this enlightened House of Representatives putting itself on record as being willing not only to abolish all treaties with China, but also to deny to the Chinaman the benefit of the writ of *habeas corpus*." 23 Cong. Rec. 2913 (1892).

Hooker's debate time had expired. Next up was Representative Robert R. Hitt (R–IL), who objected strenuously to the provision abrogating prior treaties. "There are many considerations of interest, many great losses in business, that will follow the complete non-intercourse it will produce," exclaimed Hitt, "but they are of little importance compared to this proposed shame in falsifying our word as a nation in a legislative step so deliberately taken." 23 Cong. Rec. 2913 (1892).

Hitt noted that Chinese exclusion legislation, coupled with extreme rhetoric, was often timed to serve political ends:

"We have had many anti-Chinese bills here, each more stringent and harsher than the preceding. They come every other year with the elections, and the writer searches the dictionary for words to surpass predecessors." 23 Cong. Rec. 2913 (1892).

When the exclusion policy was aimed strictly at laborers, Hitt was open to it. But the Geary legislation went far beyond that. As to laborers, the bill was actually silent. Instead, it proposed to bar all Chinese persons. Under existing law, teachers, students, merchants, and travelers were exempt from restriction. The Geary bill would ensure such individuals were excluded as well:

"We have now a treaty which says 'shall not absolutely prohibit' and the bill selects those very words from the treaty for its title in order to make it more insulting—a bill to absolutely prohibit the coming of Chinese persons into the United States." 23 Cong. Rec. 2913 (1892).

Adding to the insult was the express abrogation language in Section 14, Hitt continued:

"[The bill] crowns all in the last section, where it deliberately, with cold perfidy that language cannot exceed, declares that all treaties and parts of treaties that are in conflict with this act are repealed, set aside, and abrogated."

Representative William Breckinridge (D–KY) interrupted Hitt. Since America would have abrogated the treaties in part, would not China have the option to declare the remaining provisions void? added Breckinridge. "Unquestionably so," Hitt responded.

"The cold, deliberate assertion in the solemn form of law that one party will, without cause, set aside an international compact which the other party has scrupulously observed, is without precedent." 23 Cong. Rec. 2914 (1892).

Representative Hitt condemned the Geary legislation as barbaric, concluding:

"This savage exclusion and extreme punishment of all strangers is a revival of the darkest features of the darkest ages in the history of man." 23 Cong. Rec. 2914 (1892).

Elaborating on his criticisms of the bill, Hitt remarked, "You can find there provisions of savagery rare in legislation—fines, imprisonments, and deportation." 23 Cong. Rec. 2914 (1892). He concluded sarcastically, "Let us keep the white history of our country unspotted, and in this vote prove ourselves faithful representatives of an enlightened, brave, Christian people . . . ." 23 Cong. Rec. 2914 (1892).

Representative Geary replied. The legislation was necessary because the Chinese government had ignored the spirit of the Angell Treaty:

"When that treaty was made [1881], China assured our people that she was more anxious to keep her laboring population at home than we were anxious to keep them out . . . but we have found from the very day that treaty was signed until the present moment that the Chinese Government, both through her officers at home and her officers in this country, has done everything in her power to violate the spirit of that treaty." 23 Cong. Rec. 2914 (1892).

Abrogating the Angell Treaty by legislation broke no ground, Geary claimed. Congress had already done so once before, when it enacted the Scott Act in 1888. "The bill passed four years ago by Congress was itself an abrogation, and declared to be so by the Supreme Court of the United States at the October term 1888, when that tribunal decided that the Scott bill in itself abrogated the Chinese treaty and that the American Congress had a right to do so." 23 Cong. Rec. 2915 (1892).

The case challenging the Scott Act was *Chae Chan Ping v. United States*, 130 U.S. 581 (1889). The Supreme Court upheld Congress' right to override a treaty by legislation. Writing for the Court, Justice Stephen Field (who had also decided the 1883 *Ah Lung* case discussed in *§ 6.20*), said:

"The power of exclusion of foreigners being an incident of sovereignty belonging to the government of the United States, as a part of those sovereign powers delegated by the Constitution, the right to its exercise at any time when, in the judgment of the government, the interests of the country require it, cannot be granted away or restrained on behalf of any one.

"The powers of government are delegated in trust to the United States, and are incapable of transfer to any other parties. They cannot be abandoned or surrendered. Nor can their exercise be hampered, when needed for the public good, by any considerations of private interest. The exercise of these public trusts is not the subject of barter or contract. Whatever license, therefore, Chinese laborers may have obtained, previous to the act of October 1, 1888, to return to the United States after their departure, is held at the will of the government, revocable at any time, at its pleasure.

"Whether a proper consideration by our government of its previous laws, or a proper respect for the nation whose subjects are affected by its action, ought to have qualified its inhibition and made it applicable only to persons departing from the country after the passage of the act, are not questions for judicial determination. If there be any just ground of complaint on the part of China, it must be made to the political department of our government, which is alone competent to act upon the subject . . . ." 23 Cong. Rec. 2915 (1892).

Congress' power to act was clear. And Representative Geary was unabashed about using that authority when useful to override a treaty:

"I am prepared to abrogate every such treaty, to violate every such law, if in doing so I may bring protection to one single laborer in my own land." 23 Cong. Rec. 2915 (1892).

Geary specifically addressed the provision denying Chinese bail in habeas corpus cases. Previously, said Geary, bail was commonly granted and had been abused:

"In one year in California over eight thousand writs of *habeas corpus* have been issued by the United States court to investigate the right of the Chinaman to come, and in each case they have been given bail for their appearance . . . and when the cases were called for a hearing, the Chinaman was gone and the bail was worthless. Since the appointment of Judge Morrow to the circuit court of the United States in San Francisco, he has declared forfeited over a quarter of a million of Chinese appeal bonds, and the United States district attorney says that he cannot collect one dollar of it." 23 Cong. Rec. 2915 (1892).

Representative John T. Cutting (R–CA) followed Geary. He insisted that Chinese would use any loophole possible to gain entry to the United States. Congress must crack down on evasions and all loopholes must be closed. Under existing law, for example, merchants were admissible. Coolies, however, posed as merchants to evade barriers erected against laborers:

"This wily race has and will resort to all manner of means in order to avail themselves of the advantages attained in this country in order to evade the law . . . . I sincerely wish the members of this House understood, as we of the Pacific Coast do from a contact with these people for over a third of a century, that no possible opportunity can be given to any of these people to enter this country of which the undesirable class will not avail themselves." 23 Cong. Rec. 2915 (1892).

Moments later, all time for debate expired. On the motion to suspend the rules, the yeas were 178 and the nays were 43. One hundred-eight members were shown as not voting. Two-thirds of the House having voted in the affirmative, the Geary bill was passed on April 4, 1892. Senate consideration would follow.

§8.20 Senate Debate, April 13, 1892: Time was of the essence

On Wednesday, April 13, 1892, Senator Joseph Dolph (R–OR) reported the Geary bill (H.R. 6185) from the Senate Committee on Foreign Relations. Dolph explained that the committee was unwilling to allow existing exclusion legislation to expire and had proposed a substitute amendment to make it more effective. Time was of the essence in passing it:

"If the 6th of May [1892] passes and no act in regard to the restriction of Chinese laborers is passed and signed by the President, our ports will be open to laborers from China and from every other part of the world, and those in British Columbia and in Canada desiring to cross the line can do so, and cannot be prevented from coming." 23 Cong. Rec. 3237 (1892).

No further action was taken on April 13, and the bill was placed on the Senate Calendar for later consideration.

§8.21 Senate Debate, April 21, 1892: "Goes far beyond any bill"

Under consideration in the Senate Committee of the Whole,
H.R. 6185 (Representative Thomas Geary (D–CA)),
as passed by the House, with an amendment proposed
by the Senate Committee on Foreign Relations.

On April 21, 1892, Senator Joseph Dolph (R-OR) moved consideration of the Geary bill, accompanied by the substitute from the Senate Committee on Foreign Relations. The substitute contained four sections. Section 1 extended for ten years the period of exclusion, thus expiring in 1902. Section 2 provided for the deportation to China of any individual of Chinese descent, unless able to prove that he was a subject or citizen of another country, in which case he would deported to that country. Section 3 created a presumption of deportation for any Chinese arrested, unless that person could affirmatively establish a lawful right to remain in the United States. Section 4 provided that a Chinese person who was convicted a second time of being unlawfully within the United States would be imprisoned at hard labor for not more than six months, and deported thereafter. The substitute did not include the controversial Geary bill language expressly abrogating prior treaties, nor the provision denying bail in habeas corpus cases.

Before Dolph could begin, Senator William Chandler (R–NH) proposed an amendment. Chandler sought to amend the text of the underlying House bill, changing its period of exclusion from ten to fifteen years. Under Senate rules, a vote on the Chandler amendment would take priority over a vote on the Foreign Relations Committee substitute. After Chandler made the amendment pending, he did not immediately speak further on it.

Opening general debate, Dolph claimed that the country would be flooded with Chinese immigrants if Congress did not pass renewal legislation before the existing law expired:

"I read in one of the New York papers yesterday morning a dispatch from Seattle which stated that there were 2000 Chinese in British Columbia along the line waiting for the opportunity to come to the United States after the 6th of May." 23 Cong. Rec. 3477 (1892).

While some of his colleagues might criticize the committee amendment as not being stringent enough, Dolph wanted to be practical. "It seems to me that the part of wisdom now is to take up some measure we can get through without unnecessary delay," he said. 23 Cong. Rec. 3477 (1892).

While open to tougher legislation, Senator Charles Felton (R–CA) concurred with Dolph. It was best to get quick action rather than delay for the perfect bill. Although some well-meaning people still opposed exclusion, Felton said he knew better:

"I represent, in part, a constituency who have suffered from the evils of Mongolian immigration for over a third of a century, and who have learned by bitter experience the great economic and moral objections to the incoming of this people." 23 Cong. Rec. 3478 (1892).

Felton thought that if barriers to Chinese immigration were lifted, Western civilization would inevitably decline. Assimilation was impossible, he said, and also inherently undesirable.

"This question is political, social, and economic. It is a question of civilization, and we of the Pacific Coast would preserve ours, the Western type, and not submit to the Eastern. To preserve ours, we must exclude the other—the Eastern. They will not mingle or fuse, and were this possible the resulting type would have the vices of both without the virtues of either." 23 Cong. Rec. 3478 (1892).

Proof of the incapacity to assimilate was to be found in the sordid record of racial violence against the Chinese, Felton observed. He cited the notorious September 2, 1885, massacre of twenty-eight Chinese miners in Rock Springs, Wyoming ("Rock Springs massacre"), as well as other incidents:

"There must be some reason for these recurrences, and if this people are permitted to further invade us, we must expect repetitions . . . . Races so dissimilar cannot assimilate and hence cannot exist together in unity, peace or prosperity—one or the other must survive and the older, the simple, will exhaust the newer and more complex." 23 Cong. Rec. 3478 (1892).

Moreover, tightening its exclusion policy would not violate any treaty obligations the United States was required to respect:

"Where conditions change and that which was intended to be mutual and equitable proves to be the reverse and either party is injured thereby, treaties naturally are and should be modified or ignored in the interests of justice and national safety." 23 Cong. Rec. 3479 (1892).

Such inequitable circumstances existed in the U.S.–China relationship, Felton insisted. There was no proportionality in it. Chinese in America outnumbered Americans in China by nearly a twenty-to-one ratio:

"They are absorbing our substance and returning no equivalent for the same. Our civilization is threatened; our industries paralyzed wherever they appear; our labor driven from employment; our women and children prevented from earning their bread; they have arrayed section against section; have and are disturbing the peace and prosperity of the land. Their presence means ruin to our laboring classes, and hence greatly complicates the labor question, fast becoming a high political one, and one that confounds the ablest thinkers— hence these very conditions have rendered the treaty nugatory." 23 Cong. Rec. 3479 (1892).

This being the case, the United States, in Felton's view, ought not hesitate to impose further restrictions on the Chinese. Existing agreements could be disregarded because China had ignored its own treaty commitments. While the movement of persons between the two countries was supposed to be free and voluntary, many Chinese still arrived under forced labor contracts. "China has committed a flagrant violation of this most important provision of the treaty." 23 Cong. Rec. 3479 (1892).

Senator Felton would propose amendments to strengthen the bill. He object- ed to the absence of a registration system, and to the fact that the committee did not restrict continued immigration of the merchant class. The failure to address these "loopholes" left open the likelihood of ongoing abuse.

Chairman John Sherman (R–OH) of the Senate Committee on Foreign Rela- tions spoke next. His committee had serious issues with the Geary bill:

"The bill as it came to us from the House of Representatives contains severe restrictions such as would read very strangely in a law of the United States. It seems to me that in severity of language and in its prohibition of the ordinary rights of humanity, it goes far beyond any bill that probably was ever introduced into the Congress of the United States." 23 Cong. Rec. 3480 (1892).

Sherman believed that legislation as stringent as the House bill was not only inhumane, but also unnecessary. He cited census figures to prove that Chinese as a percentage of persons in California were a declining population. Between 1880 and 1890, the number of whites in California had increased by 45 percent, but the Chinese population had decreased by 5 percent. And the full attrition effects of the exclusion policy had not yet been felt:

"I have no doubt in time the Chinese population in San Francisco will rap- idly decrease . . . . The natural instinct of the Chinaman is to go home to die. His dead body goes if he does not go before death. The tendency is in that direction. There are no ties of family; there is nothing to induce these people to stay here, and I have no doubt, feeling as they do that they are unwelcome guests here, that they are not in harmony with our civilization, the number of these people will gradually diminish." 23 Cong. Rec. 3481 (1892).

After offering this overarching critique, Senator Sherman began his analysis of the Geary bill. Because it excluded all Chinese except diplomatic personnel, it was a big departure from simply restricting pauper laborers. The senator complained it was overinclusive and that its penalties were severely excessive:

"The first section of this bill not only prevents anybody, except the few I will name hereafter, however educated and refined, whatever may be their interest here, their commerce, their trade relations—they are 400,000,000 people—every man of them except the few I mention is forbidden to land on our shores. If they do land, they are liable to be sent to prison for five years, as I will show hereafter, an absolutely Draconian decree, it seems to me, and a barbarous one for us. There is no occasion for it . . . ." 23 Cong. Rec. 3482 (1892).

Admitting diplomatic representatives when there was no Chinese population or property to protect seemed absurd to Sherman:

"Why should their minister come if all the Chinese are to be excluded? Why make this exception . . . . Why should they send a minister here?" 23 Cong. Rec. 3482 (1892).

Sherman thought that such a broad exclusion policy was tantamount to severing diplomatic relations between China and the United States. As a practical effect, massive disruption of commerce as well as interruption of American missionary activity would follow:

"We bombarded them in order to compel them to open their doors to the entrance of our people and our missionaries, and now we are excluding their diplomatists and consuls, for why should they come here when no Chinaman can be allowed to come here?" 23 Cong. Rec. 3482–3483 (1892).

Senator Sherman rejected House provisions that imposed criminal penalties on owners and captains of vessels who brought a Chinese person into the United States. In addition he condemned Section 14, which expressly abrogated provisions of bilateral treaties that were inconsistent with the bill:

"I do not deny that the Congress of the United States has the full power to repeal a treaty as it has a right to repeal a law, but the reasons for the repeal of a treaty must be apparent and satisfactory to the general judgment of mankind. Any nation which violates unduly and for slight cause a treaty in which it has solemnly engaged would be denounced among the civilized nations of the world." 23 Cong. Rec. 3483 (1892).

Some of the Chinese may have entered the United States unlawfully, said Sherman, but others had absolutely entered legally. The Geary bill made no meaningful distinction between Chinese who broke the law and those who were lawful immigrants. It proposed to sweep aside everyone's rights:

"This attempts to repeal by wholesale rights acquired under existing treaties by the Chinamen who are now here and are supposed to be here under existing treaties. They were either here before immigration was prohibited or are here in fraud of the law, and when they are here in fraud of the law, I do not care what measures are taken to exclude them. I know the difficulty sometimes of identifying them, but most of them are here by virtue of our treaties and in pursuance of our treaties . . . ." 23 Cong. Rec. 3484 (1892).

Senator Sherman was also worried that the bill's abrogation section set an exceedingly bad and unjustified precedent. As chairman of the Senate Committee on Foreign Relations, he knew there were conditions under which treaties could be broken, but felt China had not given the United States sufficient cause:

"The United States has never until now in its intercourse violated the terms of a treaty, so far as I know. I do not think that imputation or charge has ever been made against the American people. Our treaties are like other laws, liable to be repealed; yet we have not violated them, and here we propose by wholesale to violate them . . . .

"We have made these treaties with them; we have recognized them as among the treaty-making powers of the world. We, with the civilized nations of Europe, forced them into that position and now, sir, it would be unmanly, it would be unjust, it would be un-American for us to violate those treaties and break them without stronger cause than we have here today." 23 Cong. Rec. 3484 (1892).

Following Sherman, Senator James F. Wilson (R–IA) explained the policy of expatriation. It involved the right of a person to move from one country to the next and to change his allegiance. A founding principle of the United States, it was fundamental to the Burlingame Treaty, but exclusion legislation had contradicted it.

Wilson recounted American policy from the time of the Constitution, making clear that expatriation was not widely accepted in the eighteenth and nineteenth centuries:

"We had been insisting in the presence of all nations that the doctrine of expatriation should be recognized . . . . When we made our appeal to the crowned heads of Europe they said, 'Oh, no, once a subject, always a subject; we cannot recognize any such doctrine as that.' No country recognized it until 1868, when the Emperor of China through his embassy here, extended his hand and said, 'Yes, I will agree,' and this government grasped his hand warmly and gave him the thanks of the Republic of the United States because in the whole line of nations, he was the first to approve of our doctrine." 23 Cong. Rec. 3485 (1892).

After finally securing legitimacy for expatriation, Congress repeatedly acted against it. The very power that had agreed to the doctrine was the victim of such legislation:

"The first one of the nations consenting to our doctrine and embodying it in treaties was the first one we picked to slap in the face as the march went on." 23 Cong. Rec. 3485 (1892).

As bad as current law might be, said Wilson, nothing more directly contradicted the doctrine than the Geary bill, which absolutely barred the entry of Chinese other than diplomats.

Senator Matthew C. Butler (D–SC) amplified on what Senators Sherman and Wilson had expressed, believing passage of the Geary bill would be a national disgrace. Textiles were heavily exported to China, and South Carolina was a textile producer. Butler framed the inconsistency between the bill and American commercial interests:

"Here we are inviting the Chinese people to engage in commercial intercourse with us by every possible means known to civilized people, and yet we turn in the very teeth of it and insult them by the passage of an act like this . . . . In response to a demand from a very limited area of the country, the Pacific Coast, we are proposing now by the passage of this bill to throw insult into the face of these people and to violate every treaty stipulation which we have ever made with them." 23 Cong. Rec. 3486 (1892).

Shortly thereafter, the Senate debate of April 21, 1892, ended.

§8.22 Senate Debate, April 22, 1892: "A harsh proceeding"

Under consideration in the Senate Committee of the Whole,
H.R. 6185 (Representative Thomas Geary (D–CA)),
as passed by the House, with an amendment proposed
by the Senate Committee on Foreign Relations,
and an amendment (Chandler) to the House text.

When the Senate resumed debate on Friday, April 22, 1892, Senator William Chandler (R–NH) was recognized. Some provisions of the Geary bill were too harsh to receive Senate approval, he said. As an example, Chandler himself supported section 7 of the House bill, which provided for a maximum of five years in prison for any Chinese person found to be unlawfully in the United States, followed by deportation. But other senators thought the five-year prison term was too severe, so Chandler proposed reducing it to two years. In light of reports of illegal border crossings from Canada, he explained why imprisonment was important:

"It may be thought a harsh proceeding to imprison Chinamen coming here unlawfully and after their term of imprisonment to send them to China. The necessity, however, is a very evident one. Unless the Chinamen coming unlawfully into the country are placed in prison, the penalty of a return to China or across the border is of no value whatever . . . . Put them in prison for a limited period of time and deport them after they have served the term of imprisonment, and the penalty will be effective, and no other will be effective." 23 Cong. Rec. 3524 (1892).

The debate returned to the issue of treaty abrogation. What would be China's response? Senator Frank Hiscock (R–NY) claimed that after the United States breached the Angell Treaty with the Scott Act, China did not cancel its own treaty obligations. Perhaps it would similarly acquiesce in the abrogation provisions of the Geary legislation.

But Chandler responded that Chinese reaction had not been quite so passive. Protesting the Scott Act, China refused to accept the diplomatic credentials of former Senator Henry Blair (R–NH), who the Senate had confirmed as Minister to China. Although China's ostensible reason was the former Senator's speeches during the Scott Act debate, China said it would accept Blair if the Scott Act were repealed. Notwithstanding American remonstrance, China would not yield on this demand. Unable to be received, Blair resigned as minister.

Anger at the Scott legislation was persistent. Indeed, when China negotiated yet a further treaty with the U.S. in 1894 (the Gresham–Yang Treaty), the hated Scott Act was expressly overridden.

Chandler regarded China's rejection of Blair as the U.S. Minister to China as an insult to the United States. He thought sensitivity to Chinese concerns would ignore the affront and unduly limit U.S. policy options:

"We have permitted our accredited minister to be rejected . . . and now we are told that we ought not to amend the House bill because it abrogates a little more of the treaty than the Senate substitute does; that our friendly and amicable relations with the Emperor of China are such that we should content ourselves with violating the treaty only a little by the reenactment of the law of 1888, of which the Chinese Government demands the repeal, stating that it will make the relations of the two countries much more friendly . . . ." 23 Cong. Rec. 3530 (1892).

Preferring something less ambiguous, Chandler wanted the toughest exclusion legislation passed. The House bill was more stringent and better than the Senate substitute, needing only to be softened in certain places to win acceptance from senators. A House-Senate conference could then be had to iron out the differences.

Senator Cushman Davis (R–MN) spoke. In 1888, he had voted for the Scott Act, but was now remorseful. "For my own participation in the passage of that act of 1888," said Davis, "I have nothing but the profoundest regrets. No nation, however great, ever derived any lasting or ultimate benefit from thus proceeding against any nation, however weak or small." 23 Cong. Rec. 3531 (1892).

Davis believed U.S. relations with China had been handled quixotically and poorly:

"It is a matter of history, Mr. President, that China never sought those relations which we are abusing. She was content through unnumbered centuries, and would be content today, to remain as she was had other nations not enforced by forces, physical and moral, which were irresistible in their character, the relations of the civilized world upon her. She has a homogeneous and pacific people, strong in numbers—infinitely strong—strong in her institutions, which are almost infinitely old; but she was and is a pacific people. There is not a warlike European nation to whom, as has been remarked, we should have dared to perpetrate the injustice of the act of 1888." 23 Cong. Rec. 3531 (1892).

Pending legislation compounded the problem, said Davis. Both the House or Senate versions represented "an exhibition of our bad faith." 23 Cong. Rec. 3531 (1892). Passage would amount to breaking diplomatic relations and curtailing commercial and non-economic relations with China. Americans in China would be exposed to retribution that the Chinese government would no longer be obliged to halt:

"The Chinese are absolved from protecting anybody, great public feeling being excited there as here. Our people massacred the Chinese at Rock Springs. Can any better action be expected towards our people from those who do not possess one virtue in the world, according to my friend, the Senator from California [Mr. Felton] and yet who have preserved a state upon an immutable foundation for perhaps five thousand years?" 23 Cong. Rec. 3532 (1892).

Davis did not see a case for the stringent provisions in the House bill. There was no emergency. As Senator John Sherman (R–OH) had stated, the Chinese population in America was declining. Moreover, it was not the policy of the Chinese government to promote emigration of their subjects to the United States:

"The Chinese Government is not seeking to take possession of our institutions. It has no such desire. It does not care to see its people go abroad; it requires them to come back." 23 Cong. Rec. 3532 (1892).

At a lull in the debate, the presiding officer attempted to put the question on the Chandler amendment, which provided for a fifteen-year exclusion period. As the amendment was proposed to the underlying Geary bill text, regular Senate procedure called for the amendment's disposition before a vote on the Senate Foreign Relations Committee substitute.

Wanting to test sentiment on the substitute, Sherman sought unanimous consent to reverse the sequence. While an amendment cannot customarily be changed after it has passed, Sherman also asked consent that if the substitute were agreed to, further amendments to it would be in order. Sherman thought that if a majority of senators voted for the substitute, that would demonstrate the sentiment of the Senate, and there would be no point in wasting time on amendments, like Chandler's, that were drawn to the House text.

Senator Chandler mooted the exercise by withdrawing his amendment to the House bill. His action left the committee substitute as the sole pending amendment. Under Senate rules, the substitute was open to amendments. As the Senate adjourned on April 22, 1892, additional days of debate could be anticipated, as could numerous amendments.

§8.23 Senate Debate, April 23, 1892: "A very shrewd people"

Under consideration in the Senate Committee of the Whole,
H.R. 6185 ((Representative Thomas Geary (D–CA)),
as passed by the House, with an amendment proposed
by the Senate Committee on Foreign Relations.

The Senate convened for a Saturday session on April 23, 1892. The whole of the day's proceedings were to be devoted to the Geary bill. Senator Henry Teller (R–CO) addressed the body.

Teller recalled that a decade earlier, on humanitarian grounds, there had been serious opposition to exclusion. Over time, he observed, the argument that the Chinese simply could not assimilate had won out, and a political consensus had formed. Because he considered Chinese fundamentally and immutably different from European immigrants, Teller had been in the exclusion camp for many years:

"I remember there was very determined opposition to the bill, based on the high ground that this country is an asylum and the refuge and the home of all peoples. We who favored then the restriction of the Chinese maintained, as we maintain now, that the exclusion of the Chinese from this country is no violation of that well-established and honored rule . . . . The question of immigration of a class of people who are entirely different from ours, a class of people with whom we can have no social relations and with whom our people cannot and will not amalgamate, presents in my judgment a very different question from that which is presented even when we come to consider the undesirable immigration of persons from foreign countries who are our family. We can assimilate with the most objectionable classes that come here from Europe . . . ." 23 Cong. Rec. 3558 (1892).

Teller elaborated on why he thought the Chinese would never be interwoven in the fabric of American society. Unlike other immigrants, who approached America with a desire to build something in a new country, Chinese believed immutably in the superiority of their own culture:

"In the whole catalogue of nations, there is no nation that is so thoroughly satisfied with itself and its surroundings as the Chinese. Their civilization to them is infinitely superior to the civilization of Europe and America. They believe their scholastic attainments are infinitely greater and better than the scholastic attainments of any other people in the world, and they are as unchangeable now in this, the last of the Nineteenth Century, as they were when they were first touched and we first learned of them through Marco Polo . . . . They will, in contact with the civilization of Europe and America, remain Chinese, and so a reason exists for keeping them out of our country that exists for keeping out of the country no other class of people who desire to come here." 23 Cong. Rec. 3558 (1892).

Arguments had been made that imposing an even more restrictive exclusion regime would damage commercial relations with China. Senator Teller believed the volume and importance of Chinese trade had been exaggerated; regardless, he would subordinate economic considerations to an appropriate immigration policy:

"I would not favor harsh and unfair legislation because we do not trade with China, nor would I release and remit one iota of what is right and proper when we come to deal with those people with reference to their exclusion because of the trade with China, whether it is big or whether it is small." 23 Cong. Rec. 3559 (1892).

Senator William Stewart (R–NV) joined the debate. As always, he professed kind feelings for Chinese people, but remained a stalwart for the exclusion policy. As long as Chinese were in the United States, they would remain a "servile," "disturbing," and "immoral" element, Stewart claimed. More stringent measures were needed to keep them out:

"The Chinese are a very shrewd people, and resort to many devices which are cunning to evade our laws; and that creates the necessity for additional safeguards." 23 Cong. Rec. 3559 (1892).

In any case, Stewart said, he wanted to express his gratitude for changes in public opinion. Controversy that had existed about exclusion had faded in the face of a general consensus:

"This country has come to the conclusion that we cannot encourage these people to come among us; that their presence is destructive to our form of civilization, and that we do not want them." 23 Cong. Rec. 3559 (1882).

Later in the day, Senator Frank Hiscock (R–NY) took the floor. He focused on the consequences of making Chinese presumptively deportable unless they could affirmatively prove their right to be in the United States:

"His being here is presumed to be in violation of the law and the burden of proof is thrown upon him to establish his right to be here. When you shift the burden of proof, as it is in this bill, I believe if the people of California choose to enforce the provisions of the law, the effect will be an exodus of Chinamen from the shores of the United States." 23 Cong. Rec. 3561 (1892).

Hiscock explained how the novel and odious shift to a presumption of guilt would stack the deck against the Chinese:

"The Chinaman must, himself, affirmatively establish his right before the officers of his State; men subject to the weaknesses of human nature and doubtless not in sympathy with the immigration of Chinamen here. The officers of his state have it devolved upon them to be satisfied with the affirmative proof of the Chinese immigrant here that he does not belong to the inhibited class of laborers. The question of his employment is open, what he is doing . . . how he lives. He is to be subjected, he and his witnesses, to a searching investigation to prove he is not a Chinese workingman." 23 Cong. Rec. 3561 (1892).

Administrative officers would not have to marshal evidence of guilt, but could simply wait for Chinese to prove innocence, noted Hiscock. Proceedings would not even have to take place before a neutral magistrate. The judgment of the examining officer was deemed conclusive.

"Bear in mind that this is a summary provision. These people are not to be arrested and tried. A summary examination disposes of them." 23 Cong. Rec. 3562 (1892).

Next to speak was Senator John Tyler Morgan (D–AL), another veteran of Congress' exclusion wars. The doctrine of expatriation, embodied in the Burlingame Treaty, was superseded by the Angell Treaty, which sharply limited its application. The Angell treaty made a distinction between "the right of immigration and migration" and the "right of hospitality," remarked Morgan. China had agreed to the change. He surmised that China wanted to stop its people from emigrating in order to protect them from problems in an unwelcoming land:

"China was consenting to it because she saw, as she confessed then and more distinctly confessed in later diplomatic intercourse, that her people were entirely unacceptable in this country, and that they could not rise to any social level, even the lowest in the United States, with the white people, and that they could not even become the recognized equals of our former slaves." 23 Cong. Rec. 3562 (1892).

China's concerns had only become more acute after more incidents of violence and discrimination against its people. Morgan noted that the unratified Bayard–Zhang Treaty of 1888 contained the following provision:

"Whereas the Government of China, in view of the antagonism and much deprecated and serious disorders to which the presence of Chinese laborers has given rise in certain parts of the United States, desires to prohibit the emigration of such laborers to the United States . . . ."

Senator Cushman Davis (R–MN) asked Morgan why, in light of this consideration, China had failed to ratify the treaty. Long a member of the Senate Committee on Foreign Relations, Morgan mainly blamed the change in Chinese attitude on a Senate amendment canceling return certificates for laborers who were then outside of the United States:

"There is no doubt that the Chinese Government understood that it was a total abandonment of the former treaties and that it was a breach of faith on the part of the United States, and that it was wicked." 23 Cong. Rec. 3563 (1892).

Also problematic, said Morgan, was Congress' passage of the Scott Act while China was still considering the Bayard–Zhang Treaty. Although ratification of that treaty would have superseded the Scott Act, the Chinese were deeply offended by such preemptive legislation and shelved the treaty.

Regardless of these difficulties over immigration policy, China had maintained good diplomatic relations with the United States, Morgan said. Although a supporter of excluding laborers, Morgan saw no reason to anger China by casting the net wider, as the Geary bill proposed to do:

"Now, then, the question arises, is it proper, is it necessary, is it wise that we should start on a new scheme of legislation which destroys the right of hospitality that is provided for in the treaty of 1880, and limit that down in such a way that no man could come from China except as a foreign minister with his servants or a consul with his servants?" 23 Cong. Rec. 3564 (1892).

Senator Morgan answered his own question. "I can see no reason for giving offense to China by the further legislative modification of the rights of hospitality which were secured by the treaty with that country of 1880, when our experience has been that there has not arrived a large accession, to say the least of it, of Chinese people on the Pacific Slope or in other parts of the United States." 23 Cong. Rec. 3564 (1892).

In previous exclusion debates, Morgan had uttered fire-breathing anti-Chinese rhetoric. Believing the immigration problem was under control, and wanting to avoid damage to trade in textiles, Morgan now painted a much more benign and nonchalant picture of Chinese workers in America:

"It is costing us some money to keep them out, but that is only a part of the police expenditure of the country which we have to sustain anyhow. A few of them get through Mexico and a few get through British Columbia, but the number that come here are scarcely to be called inconvenient. They do not come in such numbers as to present any real body of competitors in the great mass of work that is to be done in this country, and when they come here, they distribute themselves among the railroads, where labor is pretty hard to secure anyway, and in the laundries, and in the kitchens, and in the gardens, and in the vineyards, and other places where careful, patient, and painstaking hand service, menial service, is required." 3 Cong. Rec. 3564 (1892).

Unwilling to inflict damage on the Sino-American relationship, Morgan would oppose anything more severe than a simple extension of existing law.

Senator Wilbur Fiske Sanders (R–MT) did not share Morgan's relatively benign attitude. Present law was not being enforced, he complained. Chinese were experienced in evading restrictions, and Canadian authorities, who profiteered from a $50 per Chinese head tax, were motivated to allow them into Canada and pay no attention when the U.S. border was crossed:

"We have five or six thousand miles of frontier. Of this, about four thousand miles is a frontier of land. On either side of us, the Chinese can come with great ease. In fact, our Northern neighbors are making their influx into their communities a matter of speculation and I know of no more happy financial situation than is occupied by the British Northwest provinces who are able . . . to collect $50 for their admission, and then to project them through the various canyons or over the prairies into the United States." 23 Cong. Rec. 3567 (1892).

Another scam was the return certificates, Sanders charged. A laborer already in the United States could leave for China and return under the guise of a merchant, still an exempted class. The reentry process was laden with fraud.

"I do not believe the law has operated to keep [out] of the United States a solitary Chinese subject or person who has desired to go to his native land and then to return here." 23 Cong. Rec. 3567 (1892).

Contrary to the purposes of American law, return certificates had spawned a big trafficking business in China, said Sanders. The certificates were sold to Chinese who wanted them to enter the United States:

"There are commercial marts there where the certificates of a right to return to the United States are for sale. Chinese persons coming over here get a certificate for leave to go back to China and return, and brokers along their riverfront buy them out, advertise them, and boldly sell them to persons who to some extent resemble the persons therein described. It is a great and remunerative industry. They are sold for a very considerable price, $200 to $300 apiece, I am advised." 23 Cong. Rec. 3568 (1892).

The deportation process was fraught with additional problems, Sanders reported. He cited the work of a joint congressional investigative committee that looked at the state of Chinese immigration and enforcement of related laws. A lot of cases remained untried on court dockets, the committee noted. Of those cases tried, 67 percent of the Chinese were ordered deported, but many of them skipped bail, so only 5 percent were actually located and expelled. Sanders believed that the need for stronger enforcement procedures was obvious:

"If 95 percent of the persons convicted escaped, we would say that the judicial tribunals had failed to fulfill their functions, and that it was time to call into exercise some other power and some other authority to the end that the august expression of a people found in their law might be enforced." 23 Cong. Rec. 3567 (1892).

Senator Sanders drew the conclusion that, "it is not desirable that these people shall be multiplied in this country, but that they shall be diminished to extinction." 23 Cong. Rec. 3569 (1892).

The Senate then agreed to adjourn for the day. The plan was to reconvene on Monday, April 25, 1892, begin proceedings on the Geary bill (H.R. 6185) at 4:00 p.m., adopt the committee substitute, and then permit amendments to H.R. 6185, as amended.

§8.24 Senate Debate, April 25, 1892: "Intense feeling of antagonism"

Under consideration in the Senate Committee of the Whole,
H.R. 6185 (Representative Thomas Geary (D–CA)),
as passed by the House, with an amendment proposed
by the Senate Committee on Foreign Relations.

Immediately after the Senate turned to consideration of H.R. 6185 (Geary bill), the presiding officer put the question on the Senate Foreign Relations Committee substitute amendment. Before a vote could occur on the substitute, Senator Watson Squire (R–WA) wanted a word.

Although he was Washington State's first senator (Washington was admitted as the forty-second state in 1889) and a former governor when Washington was a territory (1884–1887), Squire grew up on the East Coast. He told senators that upon first hearing of anti-Chinese bias, he was repelled by it and was inclined to take a more humanitarian perspective. Moving to Seattle in 1879, he became acquainted with Chinese people. His early impressions were highly favorable, but his thinking changed.

Economic conditions in the United States had worsened considerably in the mid–1870s following the Panic of 1873, leading to substantial unemployment during what is now called the Long Depression. Chinese and white workers were competing for a reduced number of jobs. Public opinion against the Chinese turned toxic:

"The work upon the railroads in that part of the country had been to a large degree suspended, and many of the laboring class were without employment. A profound feeling of dissatisfaction and unrest prevailed among the masses, and hostility against the Chinese was developed to a remarkable degree. Public meetings were held at which heated discussions prevailed. The Chinese were driven from their mines and their habitations destroyed." 23 Cong. Rec. 3608 (1892).

Once set in motion, anti-Chinese attitudes became entrenched. As governor of the then-Washington Territory, Squire worked with federal troops to protect the Chinese from harm, a difficult job, as violence periodically erupted:

"These trying events led me to understand, as I had never done before, the intense feeling of antagonism that is seated in the breasts of the great body of our laboring people in reference to the Chinese." 23 Cong. Rec. 3608 (1892).

In 1886, then-Governor Squire issued a report to the United States government. In it, he noted the problems in securing convictions of persons charged with criminal anti-Chinese activity:

"Although a large proportion of our citizens entertain feelings of loyalty and patriotism toward the Government . . . they are inclined to be lenient to those who engage in acts hostile to the Chinese, and this fact makes it extremely difficult to secure convictions of this class of offenders against the law." 23 Cong. Rec. 3608 (1892).

Then-Governor Squire went on to report that, in defiance of the exclusion policy, large numbers of Chinese were crossing the border of British Columbia, and that the restrictions were ineffective:

"It has been found with the limited customs force at it disposal, the Government is practically unable to enforce the exclusion of the Chinese under the terms of the law." 23 Cong. Rec. 3608 (1892).

Importation of Chinese labor may at one time have been beneficial for railroad construction of the Transcontinental Railroad (1863–1869) and also the Cascade Branch (1881–1888) of the Northern Pacific Railroad, but such utility had passed:

"The hiving hordes of Chinese in the towns is thought to interfere with the healthy growth and development of society, and is a constant source of uneasiness and dissatisfaction to the white laborer." 23 Cong. Rec. 3609 (1892).

As a result of his experiences as a territorial governor, Senator Squire was convinced that public welfare demanded exclusion. For the time being, he was satisfied to continue excluding laborers, while admitting merchants, visitors, scholars, and diplomats. But he worried a lot about the laborer class being admitted under false claims of identity. If this problem could not be solved by more stringent enforcement, then Squire would go along with a wholesale ban of all Chinese.

Squire had an idea about how enforcement could be improved. Since imposition of exclusion, claims by Chinese immigrants that they were actually native-born had skyrocketed. According to the San Francisco U.S. Attorney, such assertions were made in 75 percent of deportation cases, as against 5 percent before 1882. Squire was not satisfied to have the claims validated only by the testimony of Chinese witnesses:

"In accordance with the recommendation of the district attorney at San Francisco, I would legislate that at least one white witness shall be required to prove native birth." 23 Cong. Rec. 3610 (1892).

Senator John Mitchell (R–OR) followed Squire to the Senate floor. Mitchell disdained arguments that the treaty abrogation clause of the House bill demonstrated bad faith to China and should be stricken. That issue was settled in 1888 when Congress passed the Scott Act, Mitchell stressed. By canceling return certificates, the Scott Act contravened Angell Treaty rights. Many of the senators present for the immediate debate had voted in favor of that bill. The abrogation precedent had been set:

"If we are willing to go one step in the abrogation of the provisions of any one of those treaties for the purpose of protecting our own interests in this country against Chinese immigration, we should be willing to take all necessary steps to make our legislation effective. That is my position. This I think the bill of the House of Representatives does, and I think the existing legislation does not." 23 Cong. Rec. 3612 (1892).

An ardent exclusionist, Mitchell strongly endorsed the Geary bill. This was not surprising, as the House bill was nearly a verbatim replica of legislation Mitchell himself had proposed in 1886.

Senators worried excessively about the effects of treaty abrogation, Mitchell believed. China disliked the Scott Act, but did not break off diplomatic relations or curtail commercial activity. American trade was too important to the Chinese, said Mitchell, and China would be pragmatic in its own economic interest.

Mitchell considered that a greater sin than abrogating a treaty was to violate it. Citing facts drawn from judicial opinions and executive agency documents, he argued that it was China that had violated its treaty obligations by failing to have policies that effectively stopped the coolie trade, export of prostitutes, or fraudulent use of return certificates. Mitchell held the Chinese government responsible:

"It had been carried on presumably with their knowledge and consent, because it does not seem that there was any protest made or any steps taken by the Chinese Government or any representative of the Chinese Government to repress the illicit immigration or the horrors accompanying it." 23 Cong. Rec. 3615 (1892).

Senator Mitchell also condemned China for failing to ratify the Bayard–Zhang Treaty. He referenced the two Senate amendments, one canceling return certificates for most Chinese, and the second requiring presentation of the certificate for those still entitled to reenter. Mitchell contended that these amendments added clarity to the Bayard–Zhang Treaty, but did not change its substance, and that China used the amendments as an excuse to stall ratification.

Having failed in its effort to change policy through treaty amendment, Congress had acted via legislative abrogation. The Scott Act illuminated a future way forward, Mitchell thought, and Congress should not hesitate to walk that path again.

Senator Wilkinson Call (D–FL) addressed the Senate. In previous exclusion debates, Call had been willing to accede to Pacific Coast interests, but he had been uneasy with attacks on China's government or its people. Indeed, during the Scott Act debate, Call had made a point to praise the Chinese, even as he voted for the bill.

The direction of the Geary legislation had immense implications, Call believed, and Congress should be very cautious before embracing it:

"Mr. President, the importance of this bill and the policy which it establishes entitle it to a high degree of careful consideration. The bill proposes the entire exclusion of Chinese from the United States, and as a consequence, the entire exclusion of the people of the United States from China. It is a bill declaring it to be the policy of the people of the United States that there shall be absolutely no intercourse between them and the vast multitudes which comprise the population of China." 23 Cong. Rec. 3621 (1892).

Call said, in light of history and of the character of both Chinese and American civilization, such isolationism was nonsensical:

"Shall we assume that so vast a portion of the human race is incapable of civilization and progress? Shall we declare that the principles of our republican Government and our religion are a failure and can have no effect upon these people when brought into contact with them? Such a proposition finds no warrant in reason and no warrant in the history of these people." 23 Cong. Rec. 3621 (1892).

Call believed firmly in the superiority of his own religion and culture and did not fear that, in a conflict of civilizations, Christianity would lose. But the senator regarded the Chinese as a fundamentally peaceful and educated people, so he doubted a conflict would occur in the first place. To the contrary, the cultures had much to learn from each other:

"If it were for no other reason than the vast antiquity of these people, the learning and tradition that must be accumulated amongst them, this policy of non-intercourse and prohibition would be in itself subject to the severest condemnation." 23 Cong. Rec. 3622 (1892).

The hour of 4:00 p.m. had arrived. Under the April 23, 1892, unanimous consent order (§ 8.23), general debate on the bill closed. President Pro Tempore Senator Charles Manderson (R–NE) described the procedural situation:

"The pending question is on the amendment proposed by the Committee on Foreign Relations. If that amendment shall prevail by adoption, then it will be open to amendment as the text of the bill. If it should be defeated, then the bill as it came from the other House will be open to amendment." 23 Cong. Rec. 3624 (1892).

On the amendment, there were 43 yeas, 14 nays, and 31 senators were absent.

Further amendments could be proposed to the text as amended. Senator Orville Platt (R–CT) stepped forward with an amendment. Platt was an early and articulate opponent of exclusion, but by 1888 he had been won over to the policy. Platt's language extended all Chinese exclusion statutes with the exception of the Scott Act. Platt chose to carve out the Scott Act because it had been passed notwithstanding treaty obligations to the contrary:

"I cannot vote for the bill without this amendment. We are told that the passage of that act was a violation of the [Angell] treaty of 1880. It is agreed on all sides that it was a violation of that treaty. It has been remonstrated against by the Chinese Government . . . . Under those circumstances, I cannot again vote by an extension of that act to abrogate the treaty or vote for a bill which is in conflict with it." 23 Cong. Rec. 3624 (1892).

Senator Mitchell had taunted senators who had voted for the Scott Act but seemed to have qualms about abrogating again. As Platt admitted, he was one of those senators:

"I know I voted for it before. I voted for it under protest. As all Senators know, it was voted for under somewhat peculiar circumstances. It has been thrown in the face of everybody who voted for it and who is today opposed to the House bill that we violated or abrogated the treaty of 1880; that we propose to do it again by this bill; and that we should not stickle very much about going further and violating the treaty more." 23 Cong. Rec. 3624 (1892).

Agreeing to the Scott legislation was a mistake, Platt said, and it was one he would not repeat. "I do not propose hereafter to be charged with violating the treaty by voting for the bill . . . ." 23 Cong. Rec. 3624 (1892).

Predictably, Senator William Stewart (R–NV) opposed the amendment, arguing that continuing the Scott Act was essential to prevent evasions and circumventions:

"The old law led to a great deal of fraud and scandal, to *habeas corpus* proceedings, and litigation, and fraudulent certificates, and it was impractical in its operations . . . . The Chinese had learned so many ways of evading them by fraudulent contrivances that it became a public scandal . . . . The laws were exceedingly loose, without safeguards; and it would be a very dangerous step to repeal the Scott Act and revive those ancient and defective statutes." 23 Cong. Rec. 3625 (1892).

Senator John Sherman (R–OH) rose. Although he would vote against the Platt amendment because he opposed making piecemeal changes in the exclusion policy, Sherman used the moment to criticize the Scott Act as an unnecessary and harsh political exercise:

"I believe the Scott law was one of the most vicious laws that have been passed in my time in Congress. I believe now and I believed then that it was a mere political race between the two Houses, then opposed to each other in politics, in the face of a Presidential election. I say it was a mere political race to try and influence the vote in the last Presidential election." 23 Cong. Rec. 3625 (1892).

Rushing to meet political deadlines, Congress had passed legislation that put China in an untenable position and destroyed the chance to solve treaty defects by treaty amendment. "I believe the passage of that law prevented the negotiation of a treaty which would have accomplished the object," said Sherman. 23 Cong. Rec. 3625 (1892).

After a brief amount of further debate, a vote was taken on the Platt amendment. Eight senators voted in the affirmative, 45 voted in the negative, and 35 did not vote, so the amendment was defeated.

Senator William Chandler (R–NH) offered the next amendment. The Senate Foreign Relations Committee provided that a Chinese convicted a second time of unlawful presence in the United States be imprisoned at hard labor for not to exceed six months. Such punishment was too light, Chandler thought. He proposed a six-month prison term after a first conviction and a one-year term after a second. "The Senate provision is only for imprisoning a Chinaman unlawfully coming in here on a second conviction. It has already been developed in this debate that the deportation of Chinamen who come here unlawfully, without imprisoning them, does not deter them from coming." 23 Cong. Rec. 3628 (1892).

The Chandler amendment was rejected on a voice vote.

Senator Charles Felton (R–CA) recommended giving all Chinese already in the United States one year to secure a certificate of residence from the collectors of internal revenue. A Chinese person who failed to do so, or who could not produce the certificate on demand, would be presumed to have unlawfully entered the country:

"If this amendment should pass, the result would be that within the time prescribed, all Chinamen entitled to remain in this country would have a certificate or a passport practically showing that fact. If one were found without it, that one might be distinguished and suffer the penalties of the law." 23 Cong. Rec. 3628 (1892).

The Felton amendment was rejected by voice vote.

No further amendments were proposed. H.R. 6185, as amended by the Senate Foreign Relations Committee substitute, was reported from the Senate Committee of the Whole to the full Senate. By voice votes, the amendment of the Committee of the Whole was concurred in and the bill was passed. The Senate requested a conference with the House on the conflicting versions of the bill.

The House disagreed to the Senate amendment and agreed to go to conference.

§8.30 Bicameral Agreement: Conference Report: "One credible white witness"

The Senate and House submitted a conference report on the Geary bill on May 2, 1892. Overall, the House receded from its disagreement to the Senate amendment, but the conferees also added two provisions similar to those that the Senate had stricken from the Geary bill. The first of these was that no bail would be permitted in connection with Chinese habeas corpus petitions; the second was that Chinese laborers were obligated to secure a certificate of residence. If, in a deportation proceeding, the individual could not produce the certificate, oral testimony that he was a lawful resident would be permitted, but such evidence had to be supported by "at least one credible white witness."

§8.31 Senate Debate, May 3, 1892: "He does not stand like an ordinary person"

Vice President Levi P. Morton (R) laid before the Senate the conference report on H.R. 6185. Under Senate rules, the conference report could be debated but not amended.

As chairman of the Senate Foreign Relations Committee, Senator John Sherman (R–OH) was a conferee. To be presented to the Senate and the House, conference reports must be signed by a majority of conferees from each chamber. Although that had happened, Sherman himself had not signed. He took the Senate floor to explain why he had not assented to the conference agreement. He was against requiring that Chinese laborers secure certificates of residence. He also opposed placing on them the extraordinary burden of proving the lawfulness of their presence in the United States:

"Many Chinese persons must apply to our officers to get a certificate and to prove their right to obtain that certificate, and they must hold it and have it and possess it at all times as an evidence of their right to stay in this country. So we should have one hundred or two hundred thousand people, nearly all men who have to make a living by their daily labor, scattered through our country, mostly employed in the humbler occupations of life, armed with their certificates, liable to be called upon by any collector of customs or his officers, by any internal revenue collector, by any marshal, by any officer of the United States to show that certificate, and unless he can show it or prove its loss—a thing very difficult to be done, for he must make certain proof by one white witness, although very few white men can distinguish Chinamen unless they are acquainted with them—he is liable to be deported abroad to the country from which he came or to China. The burden of proof rests upon him to show he was here at the time of the passage of this law. He does not stand like an ordinary person presumed to be entitled to all rights and privileges, but he must prove himself in the affirmative." 23 Cong. Rec. 3870 (1892).

Sherman regarded the certificate system and the requirement of white witnesses to be fundamentally un-American with loathsome roots. "This inaugurates in our system of government a new departure, one I believe never before practiced, although it was suggested in conference that some such rules had been adopted in the old slavery times to secure the peaceful and quiet condition of society." 23 Cong. Rec. 3870 (1892).

According to treaty language still in force, Chinese who were lawfully in the United States were entitled to "all the rights, privileges, immunities, and exemptions which are accorded to the citizens and subjects of the most favored nation." 23 Cong. Rec. 3870 (1892). The certificate system, presumptions of guilt, and denials of bail all mocked this commitment.

Sherman was not troubled about the basic policy of excluding Chinese workers. "I believe their habits are inconsistent with our civilization," he noted, "and as soon as we can get rid of them properly, according to the treaty, I am perfectly willing to do so." 23 Cong. Rec. 3870 (1892). But it was essential that treaties be scrupulously observed. Through the Scott Act, the United States had already violated its treaty with China, however, Sherman did not consider that a license to violate it again.

Like Sherman, Senator Joseph Dolph (R–OR) had been a conferee. Unlike Sherman, Dolph supported the conference report. He regarded the certificates as a boon for Chinese because it afforded immigrants a convenient way to prove their lawful status:

"Any Chinese laborer now in the United States is liable to be arrested today on a claim that he has wrongfully come into the United States . . . and is not entitled to remain in the United States; and he is liable to be tried on that charge before a judge or before a commissioner, and anybody maliciously or otherwise may cause his arrest and the trial of that question. But if he had a certificate duly issued in legal form, he would be exempt from any interruption and annoyance of that kind. So the certificate would really be a benefit to him. It would be evidence of his right to be in the United States and to remain in the United States, which he could carry with him at all times." 23 Cong. Rec. 3872 (1892).

The conference report did not oblige Chinese other than laborers to secure certificates. Dolph pointed this out, leaving the impression that for the exempted classes, certificates were merely an option. What a Chinese merchant or scholar was to do if detained without a certificate, and under presumption of guilt, Dolph did not say.

Senator Richard Coke (D–TX) asked Dolph about the provision specifying only whites as corroborating witnesses, in case a certificate could not be produced. Did the conferees actually intend to exclude non-whites from the witness box? Dolph responded:

"I think the intention of the conference committee was to provide a witness who was not a Chinese witness. I presume that was it; the use of the word white was accidental. It was copied from the House bill but I do not think any harm can come from this provision, because all Chinese in this country are employed by white people." 23 Cong. Rec. 3872 (1892).

Dolph disputed Sherman's characterization that the bill broke new ground. The path had been laid a decade earlier when exclusion was adopted in the first place:

"My friend from Ohio [Mr. Sherman] says we are introducing something new; that we are requiring something of the Chinese we do not require of people from other countries. Well, we introduced something new when we provided that Chinese laborers should be prevented from coming to this country. There was the innovation . . . . We have discriminated against Chinese laborers. We have entered a treaty that we might exclude them from the United States. We have legislated for their exclusion from the United States." 23 Cong. Rec. 3872 (1892).

Senator John Morgan (D–AL), also a conferee, argued that the conference report significantly improved upon the original House bill. As passed by the House, the Geary legislation absolutely excluded all Chinese except for diplomatic personnel. The Senate had voted to continue admitting the exempted classes of merchants, scholars, and visitors, in addition to diplomats. The conference report adopted the Senate provision.

Morgan also addressed the provision barring access to bail in habeas corpus proceedings. It was inserted to prevent situations in which an accused person was released on bail but then failed to appear for trial. The new law would confine the Chinese person to his ship until a magistrate decided whether he was admissible. Morgan explained the conferees' reasoning:

"We took the ground, and it is ground that holds good throughout the United States and England that . . . the writ issues to the man who has custody of the party petitioning, and he remains the custodian, bringing the body of the man before the court to answer the accusation, and he remains the custodian unless the court sees proper to change it. Acting upon that now, we say this: The court shall not change the custody of the Chinaman on board his ship so as to make it necessary under our system of jurisprudence to admit the man to bail pending the investigation. We prohibit that. We leave the man exactly where he was when he arrived within the waters, we will say of San Francisco Bay, and had never put his foot upon land.

"His right has been questioned in San Francisco by the collector of customs or someone else, and the collector of customs says: 'I cannot permit you to land here; I will not permit you to land on this coast at all.'

"Thereupon, the Chinaman sues out a writ of *habeas corpus*. What does he say? Not that he is in the custody of the United States, but that he is in the custody of the captain of that ship . . . . The writ, therefore, runs to the captain of the ship. 'Bring your man here and let us see whether he is entitled to land or not under the laws of the United States.' When he comes before the magistrate, he asks for bail, and the magistrate says 'No, I shall not admit you to bail at all; I shall not change your custody; go back to your ship; you are not suffering any; you are as well off as you were on the voyage; go back and remain there until we can decide this question.'" 23 Cong. Rec. 3875 (1892).

Of course, not all Chinese attempted to enter the United States by ship. Some simply crossed the border undetected. But such persons were not home free, Morgan noted. They could be apprehended later and imprisoned subject to deportation when they failed to produce their certificates.

Saddling the Chinese with a presumption of guilt had especially bothered Sherman. Unashamed, Senator Morgan defended the provision:

"The question is raised here whether we do not put a criminal attitude upon a Chinaman the moment he undertakes to land in the United States and compel him to move out of it. Yes, we do. The treaty does that when the treaty limits his right to come here, and does not give him the full right and privilege of landing on our shores. He comes claiming a privilege, but not having it under the treaty absolutely, and he must show that he falls within the meaning of the treaty and of those laws that we have passed to carry the treaty into execution. In doing that, the onus of proof is always upon him . . . ." 23 Cong. Rec. 3875 (1892).

Morgan admitted that applying traditional presumptions of innocence in Chinese deportation cases would make the exclusion policy harder to enforce. Accordingly, the burden was arranged so that enforcement was made easier and the rights of the accused were diminished:

"It is not for the Government to show that he has come here improperly, for, if the Government had that duty imposed upon it, we should never be able to discharge it with any justice or equity." 23 Cong. Rec. 3875 (1892).

Senator Orville Platt (R–CT) addressed the chamber. During debate after adoption of the committee substitute, he had proposed an amendment that, in effect, would have caused the Scott Act to expire. He had said that he could only vote for the bill if the amendment carried. The amendment failed, and Platt had voted against final passage.

The conference report did not remedy this problem, so Platt announced his opposition. But now he had additional grounds. Platt objected to the certificate system and the presumptive deportation, which the conference committee had included under pressure from the House conferees:

"So that no Chinese laborer can obtain from the collector of internal revenue in his district a certificate of residence unless he is entitled to remain in the United States; and as laws have been in force since 1882 making it unlawful for Chinese laborers to come to the United States, it follows that no one is entitled to this certificate unless he has been in the United States prior to 1882; and the burden of proof in all these cases rests upon him. So when a Chinese laborer goes for a certificate of residence to the collector of internal revenue, he must prove to the satisfaction of internal revenue that he was in the United States prior to 1882. That will be very difficult to prove." 23 Cong. Rec. 3877 (1892).

Platt thought the problems with establishing such proof would be acute, especially if the individual had, within a decade's time, moved his location. The likely outcome would work a "very great injustice," said the senator.

Senator Wilkinson Call (D–FL) would also oppose the conference report. He focused specifically on the bail provision, which he considered unconstitutional:

"There can be no question that this new bill is in absolute violation of the rights of the Chinese who are here under the former treaty. There is no doubt that the judicial power of the United States by the Constitution is extended to every Chinaman who is here under the protection of that treaty. Now, for an act of Congress to say that Chinaman shall not have that protection according to the terms of that treaty is beyond the power of Congress, in my judgment. To say that an alien who comes here, and claims the right to come under any treaty, whether he possesses it or not, shall be denied bail when taken before a United States court for the purpose of investigating the question is unquestionably an act of barbarous legislation in respect to the people of any country whatever." 23 Cong. Rec. 3877 (1892).

On the conference report, 30 senators voted aye, 15 voted nay, and 43 did not vote. So, on May 3, 1892, the Senate concurred in the conference report.

§8.32 House Debate, May 4, 1892:
"The old slavery days returned"

With the 1882 exclusion law due to expire within the week, the House took up the conference report on Wednesday, May 4, 1892. Proceedings were quick. House conferees, led by Representative Thomas Geary (D–CA), submitted a terse statement:

"The managers of the House on the disagreeing votes of the two Houses on H.R. 6185 make the following statement to accompany the report of the conferees of the two Houses.

"The first amendment merely makes more certain the laws to be continued in force.

"The second amendment provides for the punishment of those who attempt to violate the law the first time instead of for the second offense.

"The third amendment increases the limit of punishment from six months to one year.

"The other amendments explain themselves." 23 Cong. Rec. 3922 (1892).

Geary spoke briefly. "All those drastic features that some gentlemen found so much fault with have been eliminated by the Senate. The Senate has agreed to this report, and we are anxious to get this through, because the law expires on the day after tomorrow." 23 Cong. Rec. 3922 (1892).

"The statement of the gentleman throws very little light on the bill," complained Representative Robert Hitt of Illinois (R–IL). Conferees had added new language, which Geary had not addressed. Hitt was referring to the certificate and bail provisions. He spoke with a clarity and power unsurpassed in the remainder of the 1892 debate:

"It compels every man in this country who is a Chinese laborer to go to the collector of internal revenue, prove his title to remain in the country, and apply for a certificate—a pass, a sort of ticket of leave. To obtain it he must himself prove his whole case; he is assumed not to be entitled to it; the burden of proof is all upon him. The rule of all free countries and all civil laws is reversed. He must prove residence here through a long series of years, back to the date of enactment of the whole series of stringent laws since the [Angell] treaty of 1880. He must find the witnesses in different places where he may have worked or resided, and one witness must be a white man. Even colored men are not admitted as credible witnesses. Everyone can understand how difficult, how almost impossible it is, to make out such a long and costly line of proof, especially to a laboring man. This he must prove affirmatively or he cannot get a certificate. If he is not granted a certificate, and we can readily see how officers on the Pacific

Coast would be glad to refuse it, he is arrested, imprisoned six months or less, and then expelled from the country. If he obtains it, he must carry it around with him or be liable instantly and always to arrest, imprisonment, and deportation, like a convict. It is proposed to have 100,000, or some gentlemen assert, 200,000 men in our country ticketed, tagged, almost branded—the old slavery days returned.

"Never before in a free country was there such a system of tagging a man, like a dog to be caught by the police and examined, and if his tag or collar is not all right, taken to the pound or drowned or shot. Never before was it applied by a free people to a human being, with the exception (which we can never refer to with pride) of the sad days of slavery . . . ." 23 Cong. Rec. 3923 (1892).

The bill, said Hitt, "so plainly violates our promises that none can vote for it or mention that vote without a blush." 23 Cong. Rec. 3923 (1892).

The House vote on agreeing to the conference report was 186 yeas, 27 nays, with 115 members not voting.

On May 4, 1892, with two days to spare, the Chinese exclusion laws were extended by the Geary Act, tightened by provisions that imposed unique disabilities on Chinese persons.

§8.40 Chinese Registration under the Geary Act

Significant changes generated by the Geary Act included the registration regime for Chinese laborers, putting the burden of proof on the accused, presumptive deportation, denial of bail in habeas corpus proceedings, and strengthened criminal penalties.

In 1892, the Exclusion Act expired, but if anyone had hopes it would be allowed to die a quiet death, they were disillusioned. Under the Geary Act, which replaced it, Chinese immigration was suspended for another ten years and all Chinese laborers in the United States were now required to register with the government within one year, in order to obtain certificates of lawful residence. Any Chinese caught without this residence certificate would be subject to immediate deportation, with the laws placing the burden of proof on the Chinese. The Geary Act also deprived Chinese immigrants of protection in the courts, denying them bail in habeas corpus cases.

Insulted, many Chinese residents refused to comply with the new law. A Chinese consul urged his countrymen not to register, and in cities like Los Angeles and San Francisco, the Chinese community ripped

§8.41 Chinese Food in America

Restaurants have been part of Chinese culture since at least the eleventh century.

> Restaurants have a very long history in China. At a time when fine food in western Europe was confined to a handful of great monasteries, the Song Dynasty capital, Kaifeng, supported hundreds of commercial food businesses and a rich gourmet culture . . .
>
> Some of the city's restaurants were so renowned that the emperor himself ordered out for their specialties; they could also cater the most elaborate banquets, in their own halls or at the homes of the wealthy. Kaifeng's many eateries also included teahouses where men could sip tea, gossip, and order snacks or full meals, as well as wineshops, which were more popular at night . . .
>
> China's vibrant restaurant culture continued unabated through the end of the Qing Dynasty. The English clergyman John Henry Gray [in *China: A History of the Laws, Manners, and Customs of the People* (London: Macmillan, 1878), Volume II, Chapter 19, p. 64], one of the few Europeans with a serious interest in Chinese food, summed up the typical nineteenth-century urban eatery thus:
>
> > The restaurants are generally very large establishments, consisting of a public dining-room and several private rooms. Unlike most other buildings, they consist of two or three stories. The kitchen alone occupies the ground floor; the public hall, which is the resort of persons in the humbler walks of life, is on the first floor, and the more select apartments are on the second and third floors. These are, of course, resorted to by the wealthier citizens, but they are open to persons in all classes of society, and it is not unusual to see in them persons of limited means. At the entrance-door there is a table or counter at which the proprietor sits, and where each customer on leaving pays for his repast. The public room is immediately at the head of the first staircase, and is resorted to by all who require a cheap meal. It is furnished, like a *cafe*, with tables and chairs, a private room having only one table and a few chairs in it.
> >
> > . . . All guests, rich and poor, entered the restaurant through the
> ground-floor kitchen, where they could judge for themselves the skill

§8.41 **Chinese Food in America** (continued)

of the chefs, the quality of the roasted ducks, chickens, and pigs hanging from the ceiling . . . and the facility's cleanliness. When the Chinese immigrated to the United States, they carried this style of restaurant intact to their new homeland.

Andrew Coe, *Chop Suey: A Cultural History of Chinese Food in the United States* (Oxford University Press, 2009), pp. 94–96, ISBN 0195331079.

According to Gish Jen, the "first Chinese eateries in America, known as 'chow chows,' which sprang up in California in the mid-19th century to serve Cantonese laborers. True holes in the wall, they were marked, as per a Chinese tradition, with yellow cloth triangles." "A Short History of the Chinese Restaurant," by Gish Jen, *Slate*, April 27, 2005.

With mining and railroad work no longer available [after passage of the Chinese Exclusion Act in 1882], and discrimination against Chinese at its peak, many Chinese found work as cooks. They later opened restaurants serving foods of their native land to other Chinese and those willing to try Chinese food. In the 1860s and 1870s, Chinese immigrants became involved in fishing and farming, producing foods for Asian restaurants and markets.

Among those who opened Chinese eateries, rare was a trained cook, more rare someone who knew fine Chinese food. The immigrants were poor working-class men serving foods remembered from southern China. They knew eating rice and noodles best, and being hungry. To them, meat meant pork; chicken was a luxury, beef rarely encountered, and lamb virtually unknown. In the United Sates, they found their customers liking beef, chicken, and other meats, so they prepared and served southern Chinese dishes with lots of animal protein. Chinese restaurants still emphasize more meat and serve fewer vegetables than is common in China.

"Early Chinese Food in America," by Jacqueline M. Newman, in *The Oxford Companion to American Food and Drink*, Andrew F. Smith, editor (Oxford University Press, 2007), p. 119, ISBN 0195307968.

Thanks to Prof. Sue Fawn Chung (University of Nevada, Las Vegas) and Lynne Olver at <*FoodTimeline.org*>.

§8.42 Mexico, Canada, and the Chinese

The legislative activity and news reports about Chinese in the United States surrounding the 1882 Chinese Exclusion Act and the Geary Act in 1892 influenced Mexico and Canada, which had their own anti-Chinese movements and legislative arguments.

> Faced with systematic discrimination in Canada, early Chinese immigrants had little choice but to create their own economic niche. From the turn of the twentieth century through the Second World War, a majority of Canada's Chinese immigrants were laundry workers in towns and cities from coast to coast.

Ban Seng Hoe, *Enduring Hardship: The Chinese Laundry in Canada* (Gatineau, Quebec, Canada: Canadian Museum of Civilization, 2004). Also see Lisa Rose Mar, *Brokering Belonging: Chinese in Canada's Exclusion Era, 1885–1945* (New York: Oxford University Press, 2010); Kay J. Anderson, *Vancouver's Chinatown: Racial Discourse in Canada, 1875–1980* (Montreal, Quebec, Canada: McGill-Queen's University Press, 1991).

> An estimated 60,000 Chinese entered Mexico during the late nineteenth and early twentieth centuries, constituting Mexico's second-largest foreign ethnic community at the time. . . . Chinese immigrants turned to Mexico as a new land of economic opportunity after the passage of the U.S. Chinese Exclusion Act of 1882.

Robert Chao Romero, *The Chinese in Mexico, 1882–1940* (Tucson: University of Arizona Press, 2012). Also see Grace Delgado, *Making the Chinese Mexican: Global Migration, Localism, and Exclusion in the U.S.-Mexico Borderlands* (Stanford University Press, 2012); Julia Schiavone Camacho, *Chinese Mexicans: Transpacific Migration and the Search for a Homeland, 1910–1960* (Chapel Hill: University of North Carolina Press, 2012).

up official registration notices. Three Chinese facing deportation under the Geary Act took their case to the Supreme Court. In *Fong Yue Ting v. United States*, the Court decided that just as a nation had the right to determine its own immigration policy, it also had the right to force all foreign nationals to register.

Iris Chang, *The Chinese in America* (Penguin Books, 2003) pp. 136-137.

The United States Supreme Court upheld the Geary Act against constitutional challenge in *Fong Yue Ting v. United States*, 149 U.S. 698 (1893), in which the Court stated, "The power to exclude aliens and the power to expel them . . . are in truth but parts of one and the same power." 149 U.S. at 713. It continued, "Congress, having the right, as it may see fit, to expel aliens of a particular class has undoubtedly the right to provide a system of registration and identification of the members of that class within the country . . . ." 149 U.S. at 714.

While the *Fong Yue Ting* case was being litigated, Chinese engaged in broad civil disobedience and had refused to register. See Jean Pfaelzer, *Driven Out: The Forgotten War Against Chinese-Americans* (University of California Press, 2007), pp. 298–299. Resolution of the litigation tamped down the resistance.

Meanwhile, in 1893, Congress passed the McCreary Amendment, sponsored by the chairman of the House Foreign Relations Committee, Representative James B. McCreary (D–KY). The McCreary Amendment extended by six months the deadline for Chinese to register.

CHAPTER NINE

美 國 The 1902 Extension

"*In comparatively recent years, Congress has deemed it a wise policy to discriminate and to exclude from all quarters those vicious, immoral, and undesirable elements which would not add to the well-being of our society. The restricted classes have been few, indeed. We have denied admission to idiots, insane persons, paupers, or persons liable to become a public charge, persons with a loathsome or contagious disease, persons who have been convicted of a felony, or other infamous crime or misdemeanor involving moral turpitude, polygamists, assisted immigrants, and Chinese laborers.*"

—Senator Charles Fairbanks (R–IN), later
Vice President of the United States (1905–1909)
35 Cong. Rec. 3717 (1902)

"*The Chinese have certain peculiarities that make them desirable for certain people. They are obedient. They are servile. They may be used without resentment as slaves and peons have been used. Kicks and cuffs and hard words have no particular terror to them.*"

—Senator Thomas Patterson (D–CO)
35 Cong. Rec. 3829 (1902)

§9.0 Overview

- Considered in the 57th Congress of the United States
  (1901–1903)
- Senate Party Division: 56 Republicans, 28 Democrats,
  5 Independents, 1 Vacancy
- House Party Division: 200 Republicans, 151 Democrats,
  6 Independents
- President:
  William McKinley (R) (March 4, 1901 – September 14, 1901)
  Theodore Roosevelt (R) (September 14, 1901 – March 4, 1909)

In 1894, China and the United States concluded the Gresham–Yang Treaty, in which China consented to an absolute prohibition on the immigration of Chinese laborers. With the Geary Act due to expire in 1902, Congress in that year extended the exclusion policy indefinitely. Policies set forth in the 1902 Act, which included application of Chinese exclusion to Hawaii and the Philippines, were to remain in force so long as the Gresham–Yang Treaty was active. The treaty was scheduled to expire in 1914, although either party could withdraw from it in 1904.

Extremely detailed bills were introduced in both the House and the Senate in 1902, as sponsors attempted not only to extend existing exclusion statutes but to codify a range of administrative practices and court rulings that bore upon the subject. These bills stringently interpreted the definitions of students, teachers, and merchants. Under these terms, categories that were legally exempt from exclusion would, as a practical matter, admit almost no one.

Ultimately, Senator Orville Platt (R–CT) simplified the final measure. As passed, the 1902 law essentially extended existing Chinese exclusion laws indefinitely, so long as those laws were not inconsistent with any treaty obligations.

The 1892 renewal of the Chinese exclusion laws was due to expire in 1902. Floor consideration in both chambers of Congress of extension legislation was lengthy, and occurred simultaneously in the House and Senate during April 1902.

In the intervening decade, China and the United States had ratified the

Gresham–Yang Treaty (1894) (*Appendix 8*), in which China consented to an absolute bar to Chinese immigration in exchange for the readmission to the United States of Chinese persons who had been denied return rights under the Scott Act.

In related developments, the United States annexed both Hawaii and the Philippines in 1898. Thereafter, the U.S. legislated to bar Chinese from being admitted to either territory and to stop Chinese already in those places from entering the mainland United States. (Hawaii became the fiftieth state on August 21, 1959, and the Philippines became an independent republic on July 4, 1946.)

As the time for exclusion renewal drew near, agitation from the Pacific region intensified, including from organized labor. In November 1901, San Francisco Mayor James D. Phelan called to order the Chinese Exclusion Convention. (James D. Phelan (D), was mayor of San Francisco from January 4, 1897 – January 7, 1902, and was later elected to the Senate, serving one term (1915–1921).) Composed of state and local officials, as well as labor and commercial organizations, the convention unanimously adopted a memorial for presentation to Congress, contending that the effects of exclusion had been beneficial to California. During the twenty years since exclusion, the Chinese population in California had been reduced from 75,000 to 45,600, while the numbers of whites had substantially expanded. For exclusionists, things were moving in the right direction, but the task was not complete. Renewal was essential:

"Every material interest of the State has advanced, and prosperity has been our portion. Were the restriction laws relaxed, we are convinced that our working population would be displaced, and the noble structure of our State, the creation of American ideas and industry, would be imperiled if not destroyed." S. Doc. No. 191, at p. 4 (1902).

Also see *Some Reasons for Chinese Exclusion. Meat vs. Rice. American Manhood against Asiatic Coolieism. Which Shall Survive?* Published by the American Federation of Labor, reprinted in Senate Document No. 137, 57th Congress, 1st Session (1902).

"President [Theodore] Roosevelt himself brought the matter officially to the attention of Congress in his first annual message:"

With the sole exception of the farming interest, no one matter is of such vital moment to our whole people as the welfare of the wage-workers. . . . Not only must our labor be protected by the tariff, but it should also be protected so far as it is possible from the presence in this country of any laborers brought over by contract, or of those who, coming freely, yet represent a standard of living so depressed that they can undersell our men in the labor market and drag them to a lower level. I regard it as necessary, with this end in view, to re-enact immediately the law excluding Chinese laborers, and to strengthen it wherever necessary in order to make its enforcement entirely effective.[*]

Elmer C. Sandmeyer, *The Anti-Chinese Movement in California* (Urbana: University of Illinois Press, 1991) (originally published in 1938) (* citing House Doc. No. 1, 57th Congress, 1st Session, page xviii.).

Federal legislation would have to be enacted before current law, known as the Geary Act, expired on May 6, 1902.

§9.10 Senate Debate, April 4, 1902: "One of the great policies of our country"

Under consideration in the Senate Committee of the Whole, S. 2960 (Senator John Mitchell (R–OR)).

Pending in the Senate Committee of the Whole on April 14, 1902, was S. 2960, an exceptionally lengthy and detailed bill, encompassing fifty-seven sections. It purpose was not only to extend the Chinese exclusion laws, but also to codify judicial decisions on such matters as well as administrative enforcement practices. The sponsor was Senator John H. Mitchell (R–OR), a staunch advocate of exclusion. Renewal of the basic policy to exclude Chinese laborers was not itself divisive, but specific features of the bill would prove highly controversial. As reported from the Senate Committee on Immigration, the Mitchell legislation closely resembled another measure, H.R. 13031, on which House deliberations had commenced that same day. Leading provisions of the Mitchell bill are described in these pages.

Mitchell opened the debate:

"Mr. President, I assume at the outset the time is past when argument is no longer needed in support of the policy of exclusion of Chinese laborers from this country. It has become one of the great policies of the country, as firmly supported and almost as thoroughly acquiesced in by all political parties as the Monroe Doctrine. It is a policy based on the doctrine of the general welfare; on the principle not only of the protection of the American laborer and American labor, but upon the still broader doctrine of protection against the noxious infection of those institutions of our country, which in the grand aggregate go to make up American civilization." 35 Cong. Rec. 3654 (1902).

The 1902 Mitchell legislation would extend exclusion of Chinese laborers indefinitely, rather than for a period of years. As Mitchell explained, it would also cover the movement of Chinese to and from American territories, which had been acquired since the last ten-year extension passed in 1892:

"[It] is only different from the existing law in two particulars, that it prohibits the coming of Chinese laborers to the territory of the United States and to any territory under its jurisdiction, and there is no limit as to time." 35 Cong. Rec. 3655 (1902).

The Hawaiian annexation Joint Resolution of July 7, 1898, barred Chinese from entering Hawaii or from emigrating from Hawaii to the mainland. Mitchell quoted from it:

"There shall be no further immigration of Chinese into the Hawaiian Islands, except upon such conditions as are now or may hereafter be allowed by the laws of the United States, and no Chinese by reason of anything herein contained shall be allowed to enter the United States from the Hawaiian Islands." 35 Cong. Rec. 3655 (1902).

Section 2 of the Mitchell renewal bill proposed to extend this policy to the Philippines, which had been acquired as a result of the Spanish–American War (1898). "It would be rather a strange commentary upon both the prescience and the consistency of our nation," said Mitchell, "if while strenuously to close the door against Chinese laborers from China, we at the same time left the door wide open to the hundreds of thousands—if, indeed, not millions—of Chinese laborers and laborers of Chinese descent in the Philippine Archipelago." 35 Cong. Rec. 3655 (1902).

Section 2 also made the Hawaiian and Philippine limitations applicable to Chinese born in those territories after annexation. Some senators questioned whether the policy conflicted with the birthright citizenship provision of the Fourteenth Amendment, which states that, "All persons born or naturalized in the United States and subject to the jurisdiction thereof, are citizens of the United States and of the State wherein they reside."

Convinced that constitutional protections would not extend to persons born in U.S. territories, Mitchell assured senators that the restriction-of-movement provision was sound:

"Our insular territory is not a part of the United States but, on the contrary, is territory belonging to the United States. It is believed, therefore, that the fourteenth amendment to the Constitution of the United States is not applicable to this class of persons born in this portion of our insular territory." 35 Cong. Rec. 3655 (1902).

In Section 3, the legislation broadened the definition of a Chinese laborer to apply to any Chinese person who was not part of the exempted classes of merchants, teachers, students, and diplomats. "The legislation proceeds upon the theory that only those are allowed to enter who are especially allowed," Mitchell observed. 35 Cong. Rec. 3655 (1902).

The Mitchell bill would also tighten the definitions of each excepted class, ensuring that exemptions were construed very strictly. For instance, the definition of "teacher" was extraordinarily narrow. As Mitchell described it:

"Section 6 of the bill defines the term 'teacher,' as used in this bill to mean only one who, for not less than two years next preceding his application for entry into the United States, has been continuously engaged in giving instruction in the higher branches of education, and who proves to the satisfaction of the appropriate Treasury officer that he is qualified to teach such higher branches, and has completed arrangements to teach in a recognized institution of learning in the United States, and intends to pursue no other occupation than teaching while in the United States." 35 Cong. Rec. 3656 (1902).

Mitchell claimed that this restrictive definition served to codify procedures in effect under Treasury regulations. Similar stringency applied in Section 7 to the term "students," who were limited to Chinese nationals seeking education in an institution of higher learning in courses of study for which facilities were not otherwise available in China. Under these terms, not many students would be admitted:

"It was clearly the intent of those engaged in formulating our treaties with China to provide for a limited number of Chinese youths who might come to this country to advance themselves in the higher branches of education, and not to open the doors to millions of Chinese children to come here to acquire a primary education." 35 Cong. Rec. 3657 (1902).

In the years since exclusion started in 1882, there had been great confusion over the meaning of the term "merchants." The bill was stringent. Mitchell explained that Section 8 of his bill would define "merchant" as a person "who is engaged in buying or selling at a fixed place of business, and who, during the time he claims to be a merchant, does not engage in the performance of any manual labor, except as is necessary in the conduct of his business as such merchant." 35 Cong. Rec. 3657 (1902).

If an individual claiming to be a merchant asserted return rights under the Gresham–Yang Treaty (1894), he was required to produce his certificate to a Treasury officer. If he was unable to do that, the bill provided he could establish his claim by oral testimony, but only if "two credible witnesses other than Chinese" corroborated him. 35 Cong. Rec. 3657 (1902).

Under treaty provisions reaching back to the Burlingame Treaty (1868), exempted persons were entitled to the rights of citizens of the most-favored-nation. But Mitchell was convinced the uniquely restrictive procedures and related border examinations could not be challenged as treaty violations. Such rights did not apply to Chinese seeking to enter the United States, but only to those who were already residents, he said.

Registration requirements, already established in the Geary Act, were continued in Section 12 and were extended to the territories. Mitchell noted that the Supreme Court had already upheld the constitutionality of registration. In the case of *Fong Yue Ting v. United States*, 149 U.S. 698 (1893), the Court said:

"Congress, having the right, as it may see fit, to expel aliens of a particular class or to permit them to remain, has undoubtedly the right to provide a system of registration and identification of the members of that class within the country, and to take all proper means to carry out the system which it provides." 149 U.S. at 714.

Under Section 10 of the Mitchell bill, and subject to rigorous procedures, Treasury officers were authorized to admit to the country the lawful wife and minor children of exempt-class Chinese persons actually and legally domiciled within the United States. Mitchell explained that under existing statutes, no wife or minor child had a right to enter. The law was being liberalized for humanitarian reasons, he claimed, but agents must vigilantly guard against fraud:

"At the same time, this provision is properly guarded so as to prevent the country being flooded with dissolute women, under pretense of being wives of the exempted classes, and to prevent also an influx of foreign laborers under the pretense of being children of the exempted classes." 35 Cong. Rec. 3660 (1902).

The Mitchell bill codified certain administrative policies concerning the detention of the Chinese, and extended related statutes. For instance, Section 27 required that any Chinese person seeking entrance into the United States be detained on his vessel, until a final decision had been made on his right to enter. Responsibility for detention would rest with the master, owner, agent, or consignee of the vessel, both individually and collectively. By law, such parties would bear the costs of the return passage of any individual found ineligible to enter. And, Mitchell pointed out, failure to cooperate could also be expensive in other ways:

"Every person bound under this section to detain a Chinese person who shall refuse or willfully neglect to perform such duty shall be deemed guilty of a felony and, upon conviction thereof, shall be punished by a fine of not less than $1000 nor more than $5000, or by imprisonment for a term not less than one year, or by both such fine and imprisonment." 35 Cong. Rec. 3661 (1902).

Chinese immigrants seeking admission to the United States would either do so on claim of citizenship or on the basis that they were part of an exempted class. The Mitchell bill stated that if the claim were based on citizenship, adjudication would take place before a United States district court. If an action was brought on exempted class grounds, proceedings would be solely administrative. An adverse decision by a customs officer could be appealed to the secretary of the treasury, but not to a court. And appeals were not limited to those of Chinese adversely affected; the U.S. government could also appeal, a right newly provided in the Mitchell legislation. If a Chinese immigrant lost on an initial claim, Section 48 prohibited him from pleading alternative grounds. "In other words, he must stand upon the claim he first makes. If he fails in this, it is the end of the law as to him," said the senator. 35 Cong. Rec. 3663 (1902).

Another new feature in the Mitchell bill involved banning employment of Chinese on American–flagged vessels. Mitchell explained Section 39:

"It is a provision of the bill that it shall be unlawful for any vessel holding an American register to have or employ in its crew any Chinese person not entitled to admission into the United States or into the portion of the territory of the United States to which such vessel plies, and any violation of this section shall be punishable by a fine not exceeding $2000."

Exceptions were permitted in the case of emergencies that compelled the hiring of Chinese seamen, such as in cases of distress conditions at sea. But these exceptions were to be strictly applied. Relief from fines could only come if it were "shown to the satisfaction of the appropriate Treasury officer that in such foreign jurisdiction or port, no seamen other than Chinese were obtainable, and that every such Chinese seaman was discharged from the service of such vessel upon the arrival thereof at the first port where seamen other than Chinese could be obtained." If that port were under the control of the United States, "no such Chinese seaman was permitted to depart from such vessel." Instead, the Chinese would then be transported as a passenger to a foreign port, at the vessel's expense, and be discharged there. 35 Cong. Rec. 3662 (1902).

The seaman provision would prove to be one of the bill's most controversial sections. Mitchell argued it would protect U.S. personnel and encourage the development of an American merchant marine. He defended the idea of extending the exclusion policy to the high seas:

"The deck of an American registered steamer is, in international law a part of the terra firma, so to speak, of the United States . . . ." 35 Cong. Rec. 3662 (1902).

Mitchell noted that his measure was the composite handiwork of four different interest groups: commissioners appointed from the California Chinese Exclusion Convention (1901); the entire Pacific Coast congressional membership; the American Federation of Labor; and experts from the Department of the Treasury and the Department of Justice. Before the Senate Committee on Immigration, AFL President Samuel Gompers had testified to this collaboration:

"I should say to you, gentlemen, that the California commissioners and the representatives of the American Federation of Labor have been in constant consultation . . . ." 35 Cong. Rec. 3665 (1892).

Public opinion would strongly support the resulting legislative product, Mitchell told other senators. He described how attitudes had hardened over time:

"The present policy of Chinese prohibition [has] been plainly marked by separate and distinct periods in the history of this country, wherein our country through the evolution of public sentiment, has passed from the policy of inviting Chinese immigration to this country, first to restriction, then to exclusion, and finally to absolute prohibition.

"The public sentiment which in 1868 heralded with hosannas and beckoning salutations the consummation of the Burlingame Treaty has, through enlightenment brought about by the evils following in the wake of unrestricted Chinese immigration, undergone a most decided change . . . .

"It is a grand step in the direction of freeing our people and institutions from the corrupting and corroding influences of pauper labor and those virulent and destructive vices so inseparably connected with the lower classes on Asian serfdom, and whose poisonous virus, if permitted to permeate our body politic, will inevitably lead to lamentable blight, pitiable decay, and ultimate destruction." 35 Cong. Rec. 3655 (1902).

Anticipating arguments that trade with China would suffer if the exclusion policy were extended, Mitchell was reassuring. While there had been a small drop-off in trade after exclusion was first imposed, commerce was now booming. By 1899, U.S. exports to China had exceeded their 1882 levels by approximately seven times.

Finally, the senator struck a political note. Pacific Coast voters knew that Republicans were the party in power. Failure to enact an exclusion extension would provoke dire political retribution for his party:

"One word for the Republicans of the Senate. While this is not nor should it be in any sense a party question, it should not be forgotten that the Republican Party is in control of this Government at present. It has a large majority in and controls both Houses of Congress, and we have a Republican Executive. Let me,

§9.12 Boxer Rebellion (1900)

The spasm known to history as the Boxer Rebellion began with a few peasants and youths harboring empty stomachs and dim futures and looking for someone to blame for China's troubles. The foreigners presented an easy target, whether they wore the missionary's cross or the trader's coat, or the mercenary's boots. There was much about the foreign intruders for the impoverished Chinese to dislike. They had strange customs; they stole swaths of land; they talked incessantly of their demonic religion—a "widely disseminated pamphlet," the historian Jonathan Fenby notes "said that Christians worshiped a Chief Devil who had been so wicked that he had been executed." The foreigners showed little respect for the Chinese way of life. Worst of all, their arrival signified the beginning of China's woes. With no national newspapers to inform them, and no civic organizations to represent their concerns, most of China's citizens were ignorant of the underlying causes of the nation's decline. Lacking other means of channeling their helplessness and rage, they turned against the Occidentals.

Liel Leibovitz and Matthew Miller, *Fortunate Sons* (W.W. Norton & Company, 2011) pp. 237–237.

Revolution and radical reform were for the most part responses of elites to foreign imperialism in the final years of the Nineteenth Century. A third response, more populist in its origins, was a violent anti-foreignism that culminated in the 1900 movement of the Righteous and Harmonious Fists, known to Westerners more simply as the Boxers . . . . These groups targeted foreign artifacts such as railroad and telegraph lines, and they violently attacked both foreigners and Christian converts. By the time the Boxer movement had been suppressed, some 231 foreigners and several thousand Chinese converts had been killed . . . .

In mid-summer a cobbled-together Allied Expeditionary Force took Tianjin and marched toward Beijing. The army of over 18,000 included British soldiers, Russians, French, Americans, Austrians, Italians, and—by far the largest contingent—some 8,000 Japanese. The expeditionary force took the capital with ease . . . On September 11, 1901, after prolonged deliberations, the Boxer Protocol was signed between "China" and eleven "Great Powers."

> ## §9.12 Boxer Rebellion (1900) (continued)
>
> The Boxer Protocol was a disaster not only for the Qing Empire but for its various Twentieth-century successor regimes. Particularly devastating was the combined indemnity of 450 million silver taels awarded to various foreign signatories. Since the Qing treasuries contained nothing like this amount, the sum was ordered payable over forty years at 4 percent annual interest.
>
> William T. Rowe, *China's Last Empire: The Great Qing*, (The Belknap Press of Harvard University Press, 2009), pp. 243–245.

fellow Republicans, whisper in your ears. If you fail to pass a bill on the subject of Chinese exclusion which the Senators and Representatives of the Pacific Coast States, irrespective of party, have presented to you for your consideration, and insist on forcing the passage of a statute which is inadequate and inefficient, then, at the coming elections, look out for such a vote of condemnation of the Republican Party on the Pacific Coast as you have not heard since the overthrow of the party in 1884." 35 Cong. Rec. 3668 (1902).

Mitchell had spoken for many hours. When he finished, Senate Immigration Committee Chairman Boies Penrose (R–PA), a senator from 1897 to 1921, moved a large number of technical committee amendments. Each was individually agreed to by voice vote. On April 4, 1902, the Senate worked through amendments to the first third of the bill in this fashion. Remaining amendments would be offered later in the debate.

§9.11 Senate Debate, April 5, 1902:
"Amplest assurance of American friendship"

Under consideration in the Senate Committee of the Whole,
S. 2960 (Senator John Mitchell (R–OR)).

The Senate convened on Saturday, April 5, 1902. Virtually the entire day would be consumed on the Mitchell bill (S. 2960). Senator Charles Fairbanks (R–IN) spoke first. A senator from 1897 to 1905, and then vice president under Theodore Roosevelt from 1905 to 1909, Fairbanks addressed why the bill was so lengthy and detailed:

"The pending measure is in effect a codification of existing laws and the rules and regulations which have been promulgated by the Treasury Department to carry such laws into effect. The rules and regulations have been suggested by experience in the enforcement of the exclusion laws. They have been found necessary to give the laws effect, and to prevent the success of the ingenious and systematic efforts which have been made continually to evade them." 35 Cong. Rec. 3718 (1902).

Fairbanks insisted that, notwithstanding appearances, the legislation was neither harsh, nor difficult with which to comply:

"Some of the provisions of the bill will seem to be unduly drastic, yet they are such only as experience has suggested . . . . To those who respect and obey the law, they will not seem burdensome; they will seem severe only to those who wish to nullify it and to secure the wrongful admission of the Chinese for the large profit which the nefarious traffic offers." 35 Cong. Rec. 3718 (1902).

Fairbanks explained why he thought it was essential to codify existing law enforcement policies rather than continuing to leave them to the discretion of the executive branch:

"It may seem to some that existing rules and regulations were adequate and that it was unnecessary to enact them in the form of a statute. But experience has shown that they are not regarded by some officials with that respect which they have for the written law, and that they are too and easily readily set aside by those who are appointed to administer them." 35 Cong. Rec. 3718 (1902).

The United States did not impose exclusion policies out of hostility to China, Senator Fairbanks said. Indeed, American foreign policy toward Beijing had been friendly and protective. The senator was referring to the Boxer Rebellion of 1900 (§ 9.12), in which Chinese nationalists, supported by the ruling Qing Dynasty, assaulted and laid siege to foreign legations in Beijing. The Western powers resisted the attacks, warding them off with military force and then seeking heavy indemnification and major political concessions from China. In the aftermath of the Boxer Rebellion, it was the United States who supported China to reduce the war indemnity:

"We have but to recur to the events of the past few years to find the amplest assurance of American friendship for that great and venerable Empire. When other nations sought her dismemberment and distribution of her provinces among the powers of the Earth, the United States stood first and foremost in favor of the preservation of her solidarity." 35 Cong. Rec. 3718 (1902).

Chinese exclusion was not a statement of foreign policy but an expression of domestic needs, insisted Fairbanks. While America was generally accessible to the world's peoples, it could not be open to persons unable to assimilate. "We should not admit those who will pull down and degrade our high standard." 35 Cong. Rec. 3718 (1902).

Some exclusionists said they were acting to protect labor from job competition. That rationale did not persuade Fairbanks. European immigrants were being admitted in large numbers. They would also vie for jobs and displace workers. But there was a crucial difference. Europeans could be "readily and fully incorporated into our national citizenship." To Fairbanks, the price of admission was the capacity to assimilate. Using a gastrointestinal analogy favored by exclusion advocates since 1879, he thought the Chinese failed on this key consideration:

"They do not harmonize with us. Upon their admission, they become an undigested and undigestible mass." 35 Cong. Rec. 3718 (1902).

In the end, unambiguous and fairly administered immigration policies would actually enhance Sino-American relations, Fairbanks concluded. "This is in the mutual interest of the United States and the Chinese Empire," he said, "for it will avoid inevitable friction and discontent and the disturbance of those friendly relations which have always subsisted and which now happily exist between the two great powers." 35 Cong. Rec. 3719 (1902).

Later in the day, Senator Henry Cabot Lodge (R–MA) joined the debate. Lodge was a member of the Senate Committee on Foreign Relations and an ally of President Theodore Roosevelt (R, 1901–1909). From 1887 to 1893, Lodge served in the House, and then was a senator from 1893 to 1924. Starting in 1919, Lodge would become the Senate Foreign Relations Committee's chairman, and in that capacity he was instrumental in blocking American ratification of the Treaty of Versailles (1919). On this day, April 5, 1902, Lodge worked to demonstrate that pending legislation was consistent with U.S. obligations under the Gresham–Yang Treaty.

The Gresham–Yang Treaty (*Appendix 8*) expressly required the Chinese and American governments to collaborate in prohibiting the movement of Chinese laborers to the United States, said Lodge. Consistent with its rights and obligations, the United States could impose any "proper and suitable measures to carry out the purposes of the treaty." 35 Cong. Rec. 3720 (1902).

An example of a suitable measure would be the stringent examinations required of persons who claimed entry rights as members of exempted classes:

"It is absolutely necessary, as anyone can see, to determine whether a person purporting to belong to any of the excepted classes is really of that class. That is the entire object and purpose of these clauses . . . . There is a constant and unceasing attempt to bring into this country as merchants or teachers or students or travelers, members of the prohibited class of laborers or coolies. It is to prevent that fraud that the clauses in the bill exist." 35 Cong. Rec. 3720 (1902).

If it could be shown that the Mitchell bill's provisions violated the Gresham–Yang Treaty or had the effect of barring exempted persons from entering, then Lodge would gladly amend them. But he did not think there was a problem:

"I say here on the strength of the testimony which I have heard and read that there is no difficulty in any genuine member of those classes coming in here, but when our officers are met with frauds constructed with all the ingenuity of the Oriental mind to bring coolies and laborers in here under the guise of the excepted classes, it is necessary to have stringent provisions for reaching the distinction which it is our duty to make." 35 Cong. Rec. 3720 (1902).

It was the Consolidated Chinese Six Companies that were at the center of the fraudulent activity, Lodge said. The Chinese name for the organization is the Zhonghua huiguan, which means Chinese Benevolent Association or Chinese Consolidated Benevolent Association, but Americans referred to this informal Chinese body as the Chinese Six Companies. There were more than six huiguan (benevolent associations) but the early name "Six Companies" persisted through the decades. These San Francisco-based operations had been mentioned periodically in congressional proceedings for a quarter of a century, starting with the Fifteen Passenger bill debate of 1879. A colleague asked Lodge to explain who they were and how they worked. Lodge answered:

"Chinese companies, I think of considerable antiquity, and they are nominally trading companies, I understand. They have a very powerful organization, great resources, and, if I am not misinformed, all laborers who are brought here are brought here through the Six Companies. They agree to pay a certain amount of their earnings to the company and reserve a certain amount to themselves .... They pay his expenses, as I understand it, and they bring him in here, and he pays them a certain amount of his earnings and the balance he keeps for himself or spends on himself. They make most of it. He is continually under their hands." 35 Cong. Rec. 3721 (1902).

Senator Boies Penrose (R–PA), chairman of the Senate Immigration Committee, added to the narrative. He recounted for senators testimony before his committee about the system the Six Companies allegedly used to skirt the law:

"It was distinctly testified to before the committee that the Chinese coolies paid from four to five hundred dollars for admission to this country, for their coaching papers, for various fees to corrupt the administrative officers of the Government, to the lawyers who had charge of their case at various ports of entry, and finally to the Six Companies who advanced the capital and superintended the whole business. These coaching papers are to be found in the testimony, and evidence was produced to show how they were smuggled into the detention houses, concealed in soups and pies and other forms of food, reciting at length how a Chinaman could be induced to commit perjury. There is supposed to be a profit of some $200 on every male Chinaman smuggled into the country, and two or three thousand dollars upon every female Chinese smuggled into the United States." 35 Cong. Rec. 3721 (1902).

Following Penrose to the Senate floor was Senator Jacob H. Gallinger (R–NH). Trained as a surgeon, and a representative in the House from 1885 to 1889, Gallinger served in the Senate from 1891 until his death in 1918. He worried about reports of harsh treatment of Chinese seeking entry:

"I have here a San Francisco newspaper—the *News Letter*—the entire front page of which is devoted to a discussion of the examinations that are made of these men on this side, and this newspaper from the Pacific Coast claims that the examination is exceedingly unfair and unjust to the Chinese, and that they are deported without proper authority." 35 Cong. Rec. 3723 (1902).

Defending the consuls, and the administrative practices that were being codified in the bill, Senator Fairbanks responded defiantly:

"I have more sympathy for the people of this country than I have for the Chinese seeking admission to the United States unlawfully. They know what the laws are when they go to the consuls of the United States to perpetrate fraud upon them; they have no equity which justifies us in abandoning here all effort to exclude them when they reach our shores." 35 Cong. Rec. 3723 (1902).

Next, Senator Orville Platt (R–CT) was recognized. One of the Senate's most influential members, Platt would play a crucial role in simplifying the legislation. On April 5, 1902, his main concern was that the definitions set out in the bill contradicted treaty understandings with China, at least in spirit:

"We have treaties with China, and we ought to keep those treaties not only in their letter, but in their spirit. This country cannot afford to disregard its treaties with any foreign country and least of all can it afford to disregard its treaties with a power that is not able to defend itself if those treaties are disregarded." 35 Cong. Rec. 3723 (1902).

As to the alleged consistency of the Gresham–Yang Treaty and the Mitchell bill, Platt posed a rhetorical question:

"Whether the Senators who have reported this bill believe that China thinks those definitions of teachers, scholars, and students are within the fair meaning, scope, and interpretation of that treaty?" 35 Cong. Rec. 3723 (1902).

Platt doubted seriously that was the case. "We do not consult China as to these definitions," he said "we fix them in this bill arbitrarily and, in my judgment, in a way that entitles China to seriously complain that we are not attempting in a fair spirit to observe the provisions of that treaty." 35 Cong. Rec. 3724 (1902).

To prove this, Platt focused on the extremely restrictive definition of "teacher," as previously described by Mitchell.

Mitchell had claimed he had only drawn upon existing Treasury regulations. But Platt discredited this by reading into the *Congressional Record* a Treasury ruling that was much broader and more lenient than the proposed legislation. Platt concluded that the Mitchell bill overreached:

"This proposed statute has been made very much more drastic than that Treasury ruling, which the Senator from New Hampshire [Gallinger] has read, so much so that I want to repeat here that under it, it is practically impossible that any of the exempted class known as teachers can be admitted into the United States . . . Not more than three or four Chinese teachers could possibly be admitted into the United States under this statute. Now, will Senators tell me what China understood when it said that its teachers should be admitted into the United States . . . and accorded all the privileges and immunities of the citizens or subjects of the most favored nation, and might reside here?" 35 Cong. Rec. 3724 (1902).

Senator Platt also took exception to Section 7's very restrictive definition of students, which stated:

"The term 'student' used in this act, shall be construed to mean only one who intends to pursue some of the higher branches of study, or to be fitted for some particular profession or occupation for which adequate facilities for study are not afforded in the foreign country or territory of the United States whence he comes, and for whose support while studying sufficient provision has been made, and who intends to depart from the territory of the United States immediately upon the completion of his studies."

Platt stressed the importance of bringing Chinese students to America, believing that they would take home worthy values and transformative life lessons. Such had been the experience of young Chinese who had thus far been admitted to study in the United States, Platt observed. He thought the bill was absurdly strict and offered an example:

"They have at Tientsin a university where the facilities for higher education are afforded. That will shut them out, if nothing else. It is not necessary, in my judgment, Mr. President, to so strain the provisions of this treaty and to so arbitrarily enforce them in order to prevent the coming of Chinese laborers into the United States." 35 Cong. Rec. 3725 (1902).

Defending the bill against the allegation that it introduced newly restrictive policies, Senator Lodge cited an opinion by the solicitor of the treasury. Treasury agents used the opinion, dated June 15, 1900, as guidance in enforcing immigration restrictions. The solicitor's interpretation was that the student exemption applied only to Chinese "who intend to pursue some of the higher branches of study, or who seek to be fitted for some particular profession or occupation, facilities for the study of which are not afforded in their own country." 35 Cong. Rec. 3725 (1902).

Lodge observed that, "the language of the act which the Senator [Platt] has been criticizing so severely is taken, word for word, from the interpretations of the Treasury on the existing law." 35 Cong. Rec. 3725 (1902).

But Platt thought codifying administrative rulings only made a bad immigration policy worse:

"Mr. President, I think the Senator from Massachusetts fairly shows that the proposed statute does not very much extend the rulings of the Treasury Department and Treasury officials, and that being so, I want every word I have said about this proposed statute to apply to those decisions and those rulings." 35 Cong. Rec. 3725 (1902).

Moments later, debate on the Mitchell bill ended for the day.

§9.13 Senate Debate, April 7, 1902: "Obnoxious social conditions"

> *Under consideration in the Senate Committee of the Whole,*
> *S. 2960 (Senator John Mitchell (R–OR)).*

The Senate spent only brief time on the Mitchell bill during the April 7, 1902, session. Senator Furnifold M. Simmons (D–NC) opened the day's debate. Simmons was in the second year of what would become thirty years of Senate service (1901–1931). He would vote for the exclusion bill without enthusiasm. A leader of the White Supremacy Campaigns in North Carolina from 1898 to 1900, Simmons' reluctance arose because North Carolina textile manufacturers were appealing for the bill's defeat. But important as this commerce was to his state, and as much as he hoped such trade would not be imperiled, Simmons thought it was necessary to respect the demands of the Pacific region:

"While we do not understand the prejudices of the people of the Pacific Coast toward the Chinaman, we know the fact that it exists and we believe there is foundation for it, and because we do so believe, and because the people of the Pacific Coast are chiefly concerned in this matter, we are ready to join with them . . . ." 35 Cong. Rec. 3771 (1902).

Simmons was prepared to lend his support even though he claimed Southerners had not received similar sympathy for racial policies imposed in their region:

"If the North and the West and the East are determined to saddle and fix upon us obnoxious social conditions, we will not in the spirit of retaliation seek to enforce against other sections similar and equally objectionable social conditions." 35 Cong. Rec. 3771 (1902).

After Simmons' remarks, the Senate Committee of the Whole agreed to numerous non-controversial committee amendments. Also by consent, the highly divisive seamen provision (Section 39 of the bill) was reserved for separate treatment later.

§9.14 Senate Debate, April 8, 1902: "They came like locusts"

Under consideration in the Senate Committee of the Whole, S. 2960 (Senator John Mitchell (R–OR)).

Chairman of the Senate Foreign Relations Committee, Shelby Moore Cullom (R–IL), dominated the day's debate with an extensive recapitulation of the history of Sino-American diplomacy and its correlation to domestic legislation. A senator from 1883 to 1913, Cullom believed strongly that statutes should conform to U.S. treaty obligations, and worried about obvious conflicts between the Mitchell bill and such treaties.

Senator Cullom's detailed recapitulation of the history would provide context for his pointed criticisms of the bill. The senator noted that in the 1842 Treaty of Nanking, which concluded the First Opium War, Great Britain forced China to grant numerous commercial and political concessions. Coming behind the British, the United States secured similar treatment from China, as expressed in the 1844 Treaty of Wangxia. American rights included access to five treaty ports and broad political and legal privileges.

Meanwhile, relations between Britain and China remained tense, resulting in the Second Opium War. In 1858, the Treaty of Tientsin ended that conflict. Although the United States was not a belligerent in the war, it signed the agreement, which superseded the Wangxia Treaty. Under the Tientsin Treaty, the United States gained additional rights, including those of diplomatic representation to the Qing Court in Beijing, protection for missionaries and their converts, and most-favored-nation treatment in commercial, navigational, and political

§9.15 The Panic of 1873

The Panic of 1873 began in the banking sector and quickly spread to the railroads. As economic conditions worsened around the nation, and unemployment increased, the search for scapegoats expanded. In the Pacific region, Chinese were easy targets for resentful whites. It was economic hard times that fueled the "sandlot oratory" of Denis Kearney (§ 2.11) and the violence it spawned. The Panic of 1873 was the start of a Depression in the United States that lasted from 1873–1879.

As had often been the case in past periods of unrest, the means of dealing with the Chinese who they accused of stealing their jobs was to sack and burn Chinese laundries and other businesses they operated. One of the worst examples of violence against the Chinese during the Panic of 1873 took place in Los Angeles, where 19 Chinese were hanged and shot in one brutal evening . . . .

Most Chinese who lived in San Francisco resided in the Chinatown section of that city. With San Francisco unemployment extremely high during the Panic of 1873, racial tensions in the city led to numerous riots in the Chinatown area. Responding to these rampages, the Consolidated Chinese Benevolent Association or the Chinese Six Companies, attempted to quell the violence and provide the community with a unified voice . . . . Though some peace was reestablished in Chinatown, the 1870s remained a period of great intolerance on the part of whites for the Chinese.

John Soennichsen, *The Chinese Exclusion Act of 1882* (ABC-CLIO, LLC, 2011), p. 49.

matters. Subsequent bilateral agreements between the United States and China would be framed as amendments to the 1858 Treaty of Tientsin.

Chinese immigration to the U.S. began shortly after the 1844 Wangxia Treaty was ratified, but neither that treaty nor the 1858 Treaty of Tientsin mentioned it. However, the Burlingame Treaty of 1868 focused on immigration. Anson Burlingame had resigned his post as an American diplomat in China and was entrusted by the Chinese Government to negotiate a new agreement with the United States. Led by Burlingame, a Chinese commission came to the U.S. in 1868 and was received on the floor of the House of Representatives. Cullom was at that point a representative in the House. He recalled the moment:

"We were anxious at that time to cultivate a close friendship with China, and we were perfectly willing that the Chinese should immigrate to and settle in the United States." 35 Cong. Rec. 3819 (1902).

Wanting to secure even greater rights in China, the United States had instigated the Burlingame Treaty negotiations, and was the first party to ratify, after the Senate added an amendment stating that the instrument should not be construed to extend naturalization rights to Chinese immigrants. "After much hesitation, and urging on the part of the United States under the administration of President Grant, China finally signified her adhesion . . . and the treaty was proclaimed February 5, 1870." 35 Cong. Rec. 3819 (1902).

Unlike earlier agreements, which related to U.S. rights in China, the Burlingame Treaty also spoke to the privileges of Chinese people immigrating to and residing in the United States. The Burlingame Treaty recognized the principle of expatriation and voluntary emigration. In addition, it said that visiting or residing Chinese and Americans would enjoy reciprocal rights equal to those enjoyed by the citizens or subjects of the most favored nations. Cullom stated:

"By this treaty, we invited immigration from China and guaranteed those immigrants the same protection as we guaranteed the people of other nations coming to the United States. No distinction was made between Chinese laborers and other classes of Chinese. We invited them to come, and they accepted our invitation and came in large numbers and settled principally on our Pacific Coast. That they assisted greatly in the development of the West and in the construction of railroads cannot be doubted. While they built railroads and, to a limited extent, worked in the mines, they were principally engaged in menial work which it was difficult to procure others to perform. In 1860, there were 34,933 Chinese in the United States, and in 1880 there were 105,465." 35 Cong. Rec. 3820 (1902).

Senator Cullom continued with his overview. Fear of economic competition from this immigrant influx, especially in the context of the 1870s Depression, ultimately reversed attitudes in the Pacific region. "People and officials from the Pacific Coast appealed to Congress to save them from what was termed 'the yellow invasion,'" recounted Cullom. Congress responded by passing in 1879 the Fifteen Passenger bill (*Chapter Two*), which President Hayes vetoed (*§ 2.40*), considering it contradictory to the Burlingame Treaty.

Congress sought a treaty renegotiation with China, and appropriated funds in 1880 to support a diplomatic mission for this purpose. The result was the Angell Treaty, ratified in 1881, which amended earlier agreements and which granted the United States the right to "regulate, limit, or suspend" immigration of Chinese laborers. The American delegation had sought as well the right to prohibit such immigration, but China had refused, agreeing only that the admission of laborers could be suspended:

"It was with great reluctance that China consented to this modification . . . . The Chinese commissioners asked the United States commissioners to give them some idea of the laws which would be passed to carry the powers given to the United States on the subject of Chinese immigration into execution. To this, the United States commissioners replied that they could hardly say what laws would be passed; but that both nations would act in good faith, and that the United States might never find it necessary to exercise the discretionary powers given to them under the treaty . . . . These explanations were accepted by the Chinese Government." 35 Cong. Rec. 3820 (1902).

As the Angell Treaty was intended to restrict the immigration of only Chinese laborers, other Chinese were exempted from its reach. Specifically excepted classes included merchants, students, teachers, and diplomats, as well as Chinese laborers already present in the U.S. when the Angell Treaty was ratified in 1881. Such exempted persons were to be allowed to come and go of their own free will, enjoying most-favored-nation treatment.

The twenty-year restriction that Congress attempted to enact in 1882 (*Chapters Three and Four*) ran afoul of the spirit of the Angell Treaty and provoked President Arthur's veto (*§ 4.80*). Immediately responding, Congress passed the ten-year exclusion bill, which the president signed into law on May 6, 1882 (*Chapter Five*).

"The act of 1882 was soon found to be inadequate," Senator Cullom went on. "It was found, as it is at present, that it is most difficult to obtain truthful testimony from Chinese laborers seeking to enter or to claim residence in the United States because of the utter disregard or perhaps the inability of Chinese witnesses to understand the obligations of an oath." 35 Cong. Rec. 3821 (1902).

In response, Congress passed the 1884 amendments (*Chapter Six*). In addition to applying the law to Chinese laborers from all points of emigration, the legislation also declared that presentation of a return certificate would be the sole evidence admissible to establish a right of entry. Nonetheless, there were Chinese who demanded entry rights and who had no opportunity to obtain the certificate. These would be persons who were in the U.S. prior to November 17, 1880 (the date of Angell Treaty conclusion), who left the U.S. before May 6, 1882 (the date of enactment of the exclusion law) (*Chapter Five*), and who were still out of the country on July 5, 1884 (the enactment of the law requiring presentation of the certificates) (*Chapter Six*). Persons who claimed to fit within this

§9.16 The Qing Dynasty under Siege

The history of which Senator Cullom spoke in § 9.14 coincides with a period of time when China experienced great decay, troubled by foreign incursions and domestic unrest. The Qing Court,* with which America arranged the Wangxia (1844), Tientsin (1858), Burlingame (1868), Angell (1880), Bayard–Zhang (1888), and Gresham–Yang (1894) Treaties, had disintegrating control over its empire. Each invasion by alien interests weakened the moral authority of the Throne, as the emperor appeased foreigners' endless demands, or suffered military reversals if he resisted them. Seemingly powerless to repel voracious imperialism, the Qing Dynasty (1644–1912) lost prestige inside China as well as overseas.

One reason for keeping foreigners apart from the population had always been to protect them from the perennial Chinese suspicion of outsiders, even from occasional attacks. Too often foreigners were the focus of public detestation and assumed to be responsible for oppression, humiliation, and difficulties. Economic penetration created more resentment, especially the foreign ownership of new railways, or Chinese unemployment created by foreign imports or machines. In time, resentment led to condemnation of foreign activities generally and, yet more potently, reinforced China's sense of victimhood. That also helped to stall economic modernization. Furthermore, the confused mixture of patriotism, anti-foreigner resentment, and impatience with China's impotence, began to boil over into nationalist and revolutionary movements, including a further upsurge of Han Chinese resistance to the foreign Manchus.* All that created problems for Beijing. If popular anti-foreignism was not tamped down, it could lead to even more foreign intervention. Yet seeming to take the foreigners' side would make the authorities deeply unpopular.

Harry G. Gelber, *The Dragon and the Foreign Devils* (New York: Walker & Company, 2007), p. 219.

*The Qing Dynasty was founded in 1644 by Manchurians, who invaded China proper from the northeast and overthrew the Ming Dynasty that preceded them. Most Chinese are ethnic Han, which the Manchus were not. A semi-sinicized nomadic tribe called the Manchus, who lived in northeastern China or Manchuria (as it was called) invaded China in 1644 and held power until 1911 as the rulers of the Qing Dynasty. The Manchus (not Manchurians) constitute one of the fifty-five officially recognized minorities in the People's Republic of China. The preceding Ming Dynasty (1368–1644) was under Chinese leadership. The political rally of various groups in the late 1800s to 1911 was "restore Chinese power."

time framework had generated much litigation, clogging the courts. Suspicion abounded that claimants were offering false testimony to secure admission.

In the *Chew Heong* case (*§ 7.10*), the Supreme Court in 1884 had held that claimants who could not possibly have acquired certificates should not have to produce them. Writing for the Court in *Chae Chan Ping v. United States*, 130 U.S. 581 (1889) (*§ 8.10*), Justice Stephen Field referenced legal problems that arose as courts were confronted with oral testimony from allegedly "grandfathered" Chinese laborers in lieu of documentation, Senator Cullom noted:

"Parties were able to pass successfully the required examination as to their residence before November 17, 1880, who, it was generally believed, had never visited our shores." 130 U.S. 599.

To resolve these problems via bilateral agreement, the United States negotiated the 1888 Bayard–Zhang Treaty, which would have barred entry of "grandfathered" persons, even if they possessed return certificates. China did not ratify the treaty, so Congress enacted the Scott Act of 1888 (*Chapter Seven*), imposing such restrictions by statute.

Continuing, Cullom reminded senators that the Geary Act of 1892 (*Chapter Eight*) extended the exclusion policy for ten more years. But in addition to the renewal, the Geary Act added unique and onerous legal burdens on the Chinese:

"This Act places the burden of proof on the Chinaman when arrested to prove his right to remain in the United States; or it adjudges him guilty until he proves his innocence, which is a reversal of the ordinary rule of procedure. It provides for the removal of Chinese illegally in the United States; and it also provides for the imprisonment of persons adjudged not lawfully to be entitled to remain here at hard labor, not to exceed one year, and thereafter to be removed. In other words, they are to be put in jail, kept there a year, and then sent home. It provides that no bail shall be allowed pending the disposition of the application of a Chinaman for a writ of *habeas corpus*." 35 Cong. Rec. 3821 (1902).

Congress gave the Chinese a one-year grace period to register, after which individuals caught without papers were presumptively deportable. Because court challenges to the registration requirement were not resolved until ten days after the one-year deadline, Congress passed legislation in 1893 extending the deadline for six months.

In 1894, the two countries concluded the Gresham–Yang Treaty, which absolutely forbade the immigration of Chinese laborers into the United States, excepting only registered laborers with a lawful wife or parent in the U.S., or American-based property of at least $1,000 value (much like the implementing legislation of the failed Bayard–Zhang Treaty). The Gresham–Yang Treaty was to remain in effect for ten years, to 1904. And, if neither party withdrew from it, the treaty would remain in force until 1914.

Finally, Senator Cullom described the treatment of Chinese in Hawaii and the Philippines:

"By the Acts of July 7, 1898 and April 30, 1900, the immigration of Chinese into the Hawaiian Islands is prohibited; and it is also prohibited, although not by Act of Congress, in the Philippine Islands." 35 Cong. Rec. 3821 (1902).

In the Philippines, Cullom noted, the presidential-appointed Philippine Commission imposed the bar. Headed by Governor William Howard Taft, the commission governed the Philippines in the early days of American colonial rule there (1899–1907). Taft served as the twenty-seventh president of the United States from 1909 to 1913, and was later chief justice of the Supreme Court (1921–1930).

Cullom concluded his lengthy review of the Mitchell bill with this judgment:

"It appears plain to me that the bill under consideration is a violation of our treaty with China. It is not only a violation of the spirit and general effect of the treaty, but in some instances it is a violation of the letter of the treaty." 35 Cong. Rec. 3822 (1902).

As an example, Cullom cited the bill's prohibition on the immigration of laborers. If China withdrew from the Gresham–Yang Treaty after ten years, its consent to prohibition would expire, but under the Mitchell legislation, the statutory ban would continue indefinitely:

"To determine whether this bill is a violation of our treaty with China, we must determine what is the intention of Congress in passing the bill. Is it our intention to remain in force only so long as the treaty of 1894 shall remain effective, or is it our intention to have it remain in force permanently, regardless of our treaty? If we only intend it to remain in force until the expiration of our treaty, we had better amend the bill by inserting such a provision. If it is our intention to remain in force permanently, as a reading of the first section of the bill would indicate, then we have violated the plain letter of our treaty of 1894." 35 Cong. Rec. 3822 (1902).

Collum also complained about the unusual definitions applied to the exempted classes:

"Those terms—namely, officials, teachers, students, merchants, or travelers—are not defined in the treaty and are intended to be used in their ordinary sense. This bill gives to the words 'teachers,' 'students,' and 'laborers' peculiar and unheard of definitions." 35 Cong. Rec. 3822 (1902).

Challenged by a colleague to substitute alternative definitions that might be less onerous, Cullom replied:

"I can readily understand that it is somewhat difficult perhaps to make regulations which will not seem to be a little severe, but there seems to be a studied effort on the part of the committee in charge of this bill to make a measure under which no Chinese can come into this country." 35 Cong Rec. 3822–3823 (1902).

An exchange among Senators Cullom, Mitchell, Joseph Foraker (R–OH), John Spooner (R–WI), and Thomas Patterson (D–CO) ensued. It explored what was allowable under the definition of "student." Their discussion illustrates not only the tightness of the definition, but the more fundamental point that the committee's priority was to limit, not welcome, Chinese from exempted classes:

"Mr. Cullom. If the Senator will allow me, suppose a Chinese boy wants to come here to attend the common schools, can he come in under these definitions?

"Mr. Patterson. No.

"Mr. Foraker. He could come under the treaty, but he could not come in under the definitions.

"Mr. Patterson. He has the facilities for the usual and ordinary education of Chinese in his own land. Presumably there is no—

"Mr. Spooner. Suppose he wants something better than that?

"Mr. Patterson. Then let him advance until he reaches the point where he desires to be educated in the higher branches of learning.

"Mr. Cullom. Is that the meaning of the treaty, does the Senator insist?

"Mr. Patterson. That is the meaning of the treaty and that is the meaning placed upon it by the Treasury officials.

"Mr. Mitchell. The Solicitor of the Treasury has so held.

"Mr. Patterson. That is the meaning which must be recognized, or else Chinese exclusion is a farce." 35 Cong. Rec. 3823 (1902).

Cullom consumed the next hour dissecting other parts of the Mitchell bill that he also believed contradicted treaty obligations. These included overbroad definitions of laborers (anyone failing to establish that he was not a laborer would be deemed to be one), arbitrary requirements imposed on travelers, and harsh restrictions put on return rights. Perhaps most contradictory of all was the registration requirement that was applied to all Chinese persons, whether laborers or not:

"We have certainly by these treaties guaranteed to Chinese officials, merchants, teachers, students, and travelers the treatment of the subjects of the most-favored-nation, yet section 20 of the bill provides for a system of registration and certificates of registration for those excepted classes, and provides that if they fail to obtain such certificates in any proceeding inquiring into their status, they are presumed to be laborers. There are many other stringent provisions in the bill pertaining to these exempt classes not in harmony with our guarantee to them of the treatment of the subjects of the most favored nation." 35 Cong. Rec. 3825 (1902).

Senator Cullom clarified that he supported exclusion of Chinese laborers, a policy consistent with bilateral agreements. Existing laws and enforcement tools were working. The Chinese population in America was on the decline, from approximately 105,000 in 1880 to 93,000 in 1900 (*see § 2.29, Chinese Population in the United States, 1860–1940*).

Cullom summarized his position. Legislating contrary to bilateral commitments was improper:

"My belief is that we ought not to pass any law in disregard of our treaty obligations; that we can continue the present law until the [Gresham-Yang] treaty of 1894 shall expire, if notice shall be given that this Government does not desire it to be continued for another ten years; and in the meantime a new treaty may be agreed to which will abrogate any possible treaty stipulations against the absolute exclusion of Chinese laborers and which will permit us to enact such legislation as we deem necessary for the protection of our country from the influx of these Chinese laborers into the United States." 35 Cong. Rec. 3825 (1902).

Treaty conformity was Cullom's issue, not opposition to the policy of exclusion. He stressed that if keeping out laborers was not enough to meet America's needs, he was prepared to go further and exclude all Chinese:

"I desire to say right here that if keeping out the Chinese laborers is not sufficient, let us adhere to our treaty obligations until they expire or until we regularly abrogate them, and then pass such a law as the American people deem their interest to demand, and I will vote for it if it keeps every possible Chinaman from coming to our shores." 35 Cong. Rec. 3825 (1902).

After Cullom concluded, Senator Thomas M. Patterson (D–CO) spoke. Patterson served one term in the House, between 1877 and 1879, and returned to Congress for a single Senate term from 1901 to 1907. He strongly defended adding statutory language regarding the Philippines, so that the exclusion policy administratively imposed by the Philippine Commission could be made permanent:

"The Philippines, unless they are embraced within a Federal exclusion law and unless the coming of the Chinese from the Philippine Islands to the mainland is prohibited, will simply be a stepping-stone between China and the United

States, by means of which an almost unlimited Chinese population can reach this country." 35 Cong. Rec. 3828 (1902).

Senators who favored exclusion because they "know the demoralizing influences of a Chinese group in any community," would be making a "grave mistake" in failing to codify the Philippine policy, Patterson said.

Critics of the Mitchell bill who claimed that it was over-exclusionary, he added, had only China to blame. The 1894 Gresham–Yang Treaty expressly provided for admission of merchants, students, teachers, diplomats, and travelers. Congress was merely implementing what the treaty allowed:

"When a treaty excludes all Chinese except certain excepted classes, and names those who are excepted, then, under every rule of construction, all are excluded except those expressly mentioned; and when it is complained that under this bill a banker or a physician or others cannot come in, we have a right to say it is the fault of China, for China consented to a treaty which excludes them." 35 Cong. Rec. 3828 (1902).

In essence, Patterson was saying that the United States would keep out any person that it had the right by treaty to exclude. The senator did not mention that U.S. policy could have been more lenient rather than going to the maximum of what the treaty would permit.

Americans who had particular compassion for the Chinese would do well to encourage them not to emigrate, Patterson argued. Chinese would be better off just staying at home:

"If you think of his own pleasure and happiness, there is every reason to believe they will be more enhanced at home, with his own kith and kin and those of his own caste, than here in the United States, in the midst of a hostile population, a population in which he is held as a degraded being and looked upon as an outcast and an interloper." 35 Cong. Rec. 3829 (1902).

If anyone had doubts about how hostile the U.S. population was, Senator George C. Perkins (R–CA) was determined to make the matter clear. The fourteenth governor of California (1880–1863), and a senator from 1893 to 1915, he spoke as a Californian with forty years' experience living near the Chinese:

"The better the opportunities for learning what the Chinese are and what effect their presence in large numbers would have in this country, the greater is the proportion of Americans who believe in restrictive measures and the more rigorous they believe those restrictions should be." 35 Cong. Rec. 3829 (1902).

Those who were open to Chinese immigration usually came from the East Coast, "where people have been able to see little or nothing of Chinese life, customs, and habits, and where is found a morbid sentiment based on the assertion of the Declaration of Independence that all men are equal," observed Perkins. But in the Pacific states, where the Chinese were best known, "the voice of the people is practically unanimous in favor of exclusion." 35 Cong. Rec. 3829 (1902).

Perkins was blunt about the principal reasons for this sentiment:

"They are fundamental—racial—and are bound to make themselves felt in spite of theories about moral obligations or the assumed needs of foreign trade . . . . Where two races so radically different as Chinese and Americans freely intermingle in large numbers, there must be assimilation or the subjugation of one to the other. The experience of the United States for fifty years and other countries for far longer periods, proves conclusively that the Chinese are not assimilative . . . . If they are not assimilative, they can only be a foreign body within our borders and must, in the nature of things, either suppress or be suppressed." 35 Cong. Rec. 3830 (1902).

Perkins revived the old, but obviously not extinct, argument about the clash of civilizations. "In the contest for survival between the American and the Chinese, the latter has an overpowering advantage," Perkins cried. They were a people walled off for thousands of years from the rest of humanity, compelled to live in tough circumstances, inured to hardship, bred into wanting and needing less than other people:

"They are, therefore, capable of entering into competition with any race on earth with the chances in favor of their own ultimate supremacy. The attempt to meet the Chinese on their own ground would mean decimation at once." 35 Cong. Rec. 3830 (1902).

Chinese who came to the United States were a class apart from other immigrants, Perkins insisted, not only in how they lived, but also in their aspirations and allegiances:

"The Chinese have no sympathy with and no affection for our people and our institutions. For that reason, I am opposed to their coming into this country. They come like locusts to sweep the substance from our land to carry it back to their own native heath." 35 Cong. Rec. 3832 (1902).

The picture Perkins painted of Chinese in America was profoundly depressing. In addition to coolie wage competition, he detailed problems with self-protective and aggressive labor guilds, pervasive crime, drugs, prostitution, mistreatment of women, and the spread of disease. He summarized:

"What has been said will give some idea of the character of the immigrants we desire to exclude from our shores . . . . The 25,000 Chinese in San Francisco offer an opportunity for learning how well-fitted they are to enter upon the course of life that Americans have laid out for themselves. Bringing with them slavery, concubinage, prostitution, the opium vice, the disease of leprosy, the offensive and defensive organization of clans and guilds, the lowest standard of living known, and the detestation of the people among whom they live and with whom they will not even leave their bones when dead, they form a community within a community, and there live a Chinese life." 35 Cong. Rec. 3833 (1902).

For a discussion of the Chinese practice of reburials, see Sue Fawn Chung and Priscilla Wegars, eds., *Chinese American Death Rituals: Respecting the Ancestors* (AltaMira Press, 2005).

§9.17 Politics and Immigration Enforcement— The Bureau of Immigration

Source: Prof. Sue Fawn Chung, Unpublished Research, 2012, University of Nevada, Las Vegas. For online links where available, see *<TCNFCA.com>*.

The passage of the 1875 Page Act (18 Stat. 477) (*§ 2.13*) and the 1882 Chinese Exclusion Act (29 Stat. 214) (*see Chapters Three and Four*) created an awkward situation for the federal government because the states had been in charge of regulating immigration and the federal government had no uniform policies as to how to enforce the new laws. In 1875 the Supreme Court ruled in *Chy Lung v. Freeman*, 92 U.S. 275 (1875), that immigration was a federal responsibility and the secretary of the treasury assumed the task as a part of the customs activities. In the last quarter of the nineteenth century the increasing number of new immigrants, especially those who did not fall under the category of WASP (White Anglo-Saxon Protestant), troubled many Americans, some of whom had organized themselves into associations stressing their status as "native sons and daughters." Together with newly formed labor unions of the 1870s and later, these pressure groups lobbied for more restrictive immigration.

In 1884 (23 Stat. 115), amendments were added to close loopholes in the 1882 Act and to require identification information and re-entry certificates (often with photographs) for Chinese leaving the United States (*see Chapter Six*). In 1888 (25 Stat. 476) the Scott Act (*see Chapter Seven*), as it was popularly known, added the requirement of a government-issued certificate of identification and prohibited re-entry unless one possessed this document (examples of the certificates can be found from the University of California, Berkeley collection, on the American Memory web site at the Library of Congress (*<http://memory.loc. gov>, also see links at <TCNFCA.com>*). A harsher law known as the Geary Act of 1892 (29 Stat. 25) and its amendments (*see Chapter Eight*) extended exclusion and also required registration and certificates of residence. Certificates of identity were added as documentation for American-born Chinese. According to the commissioner of immigration in 1904, the exclusion acts were enacted "in response to a purely local demand . . . that the exclusion of Chinese labor was a necessity . . . based upon considerations of self-preservation." Cong. Rec., 58 Cong., 3 Sess. (1904), Doc. 4833, "Report of Commissioner-General of Immigration" (1904), pp. 136–145 (hereafter cited Report of 1904) and Cong. Rec., 59 Cong., 1 Sess. (1906), Doc. 847 "Facts Concerning the Enforcement of the Chinese Exclusion Laws," 162 pp., online in the U.S. Congressional Serial Set, v. 4990 Session v. 50 (hereafter "Report of 1906").

In 1891, Congress established a commissioner of immigration in the Treasury Department, and its customs officials, who were appointed upon the recommendation of the governors in the ports of entry, determined immigrant eligibility to enter and remain in the U.S. Chinese laborers (the definition changed through time) were the only ethnic group excluded from immigrating to the United States. In 1895, the Bureau of Immigration was created as a separate entity for the purpose of regulating immigration and deporting illegal immigrants. New immigrants paid a head tax of fifty cents to support the new bureau, especially the branches on the West Coast that were involved in regulating Chinese immigrants.

By 1895, government agents had exposed methods of avoiding the Exclusion Acts, such as the "honorable deception" of using false documents claiming relationship to Chinese in the United States and smuggling Chinese across the Canadian and Mexican borders. See, for example, Rudolph Vecoli, ed., Research Collections in American Immigration: Records of the Immigration and Naturalization Service. Series A: Subject Correspondence Files. Part 1: Asian Immigration and Exclusion, 1906–1913, Reel 20. In addition, Bureau of Immigration agents investigated Chinese businesses throughout the United States in order to create lists of merchants, because Chinese merchants and their wives and children could travel freely in the United States and thus needed to be identified.

Labor unions made an impact upon the development of the new Bureau of Immigration and its policies from the beginning. Labor union leader Terence V. Powderly (1849–1924), son of Irish immigrant parents who joined the Knights of Labor in 1876 and moved up the administrative ranks, served as commissioner of immigration from August 1897 to 1902 and brought his anti-Chinese attitudes into the position. Delber L. McKee, "The Chinese Must Go!" pp. 37–51 and his book *Chinese Exclusion versus the Open Door Policy, 1900–1906* (Wayne State University Press, 1977), Chapter 2. Adam McKeown discusses Powderly and Sargent in his study, "Ritualization of Regulation: The Enforcement of Chinese Exclusion in the United States and China," *American Historical Review* 108:2 (April 2003), pp. 377–403.

Under Commissioner Powderly the number of Chinese admitted decreased from 3,363 in 1897 to 1,247 in 1900 (McKee, "The Chinese Must Go!" 49). Powderly reported to Congress the following Chinese arrivals and rejections at port cities: 1899—6,668 cases of which 14.2 percent (950) were rejected; 1900—6,589 of which 15.5 percent (1,065) were rejected; 1901—4,982 of which 18.4 percent (918) were rejected. McKeown compiled the data from the Annual Report of the Commissioner—General of Immigration between 1894–1924 in his article, "Ritualization," p. 390. (*For online links to Annual Reports for FY1922 and FY1924, see "Internet Resources" at <TCNFCA.com>.*)

Commissioner Powderly reinterpreted laws and legal precedents to support his anti-Chinese exclusion measures and supported the draconian, and often illegal, actions of subordinates like James R. Dunn at the powerful San Francisco office (Delber L. McKee, "Chinese Exclusion," p. 68). Powderly stepped down in 1902 but from 1907 until 1921 continued to help shape immigration policy as the Bureau of Immigration's chief information officer.

San Francisco immigration officials, California politicians, and the larger anti-Chinese public developed close and reciprocal relationships. Because the position of collector of customs was filled through a political appointment, he and the Customs Service found it politically expedient to act upon the will of the people and to comply with public demands for strict enforcement. Many of the lower-level officials in the service also owed their positions to local and state politicians. In turn, San Francisco officials were routinely called upon to give their expert testimony and support to amendments to the exclusion laws in Washington, D.C. Acting as dutiful public servants at the expense of Chinese, immigration officials in San Francisco could expect the necessary support from state congressmen and senators in their appointments and reappointments.

The effect of anti-Chinese politics on enforcement procedures was clear. Enforcement of the exclusion laws tended to follow the strictest interpretation possible. Immigration officials argued that the laws expressly allowed only five exempt classes of Chinese to immigrate— merchants, teachers, students, travelers, and diplomats. Any other Chinese would be excluded. Despite the fact that they were clearly not laborers, accountants, doctors, etc., as well as the children of exempt-class immigrants were to be excluded, for example. As the 1901 regulations for the service stated, "The true theory is not that all Chinese persons may enter who are not forbidden, but that only those who are entitled to enter are expressly allowed."

Erika Lee, *At America's Gates: Chinese Immigration During the Exclusion Era, 1882-1943* (The University of North Carolina Press, 2003), pp. 50–51.

Another labor union leader, Frank P. Sargent, succeeded Powderly as commissioner of immigration and developed even harsher regulations. Sargent was in charge of policy toward the Chinese from May 1902 until his death in 1908. He also came from a labor background with strong ties to Samuel Gompers, president of the American Federation of Labor (for Gompers' position, see Arthur Mann, "Gompers and the Irony of Racism," *Antioch Review* 13 (June 1953), p. 208), and outdid Powderly in his anti-Chinese zeal. He instituted the system of identification based on physical measurements developed by Alphonse Bertillion, thus requiring Chinese immigrants to undergo a thorough physical examination, and, in 1902 admitted only 1,523 merchants out of the 1,759 who had applied under that status (Delber L. McKee, "Chinese Exclusion," p. 68). Commissioner Sargent reported the highest percentages of rejections in the years 1903 to 1905: 1903—3,549 arrivals, 16 percent (567) rejected, 1904—4,409 arrivals, 29.4 percent (1,295) rejected, 1905—3,086 arrivals, 15.6 percent (481) rejected (McKeown, "Ritualization," p. 390). His subordinates were given great latitude in carrying out his anti-Chinese directives. Undercover agents attempted to monitor activities in Chinatowns and federal agents became more active in their efforts to keep out and deport the Chinese.

In 1903 the Bureau of Immigration was moved into the newly created Department of Commerce and Labor. The bureau was in charge of the administration of the exclusionary laws and general immigration, supervised all expenditures for the enforcement of the laws, investigated all alleged violations of the laws, including alien contract-labor laws, and submitted evidence to the United States attorney for the prosecution of the violation of any of these laws. See Darrell Hevenor Smith and H. Guy Herring, *The Bureau of Immigration: Its History, Activities, and Organization* (Johns Hopkins Press, 1924).

The Geary Act, passed in 1892 (*see Chapter Eight*), required Chinese to have in their possession documents proving their identity and legitimacy to be in the country. To demonstrate its new powers, on October 11, 1903, immigration agents raided Chinese dwellings in Boston without warrants, resulting in the arrest of approximately 250 Chinese for lack of documentation. But in the end only five of those arrested were deported. For more details, see Jung-Fang Tsai, *Hong Kong in Chinese History: Community and Social Unrest in the British Colony, 1842-1913* (New York, 1993), p. 183; K. Scott Wong, "The Eagle

Seeks a Helpless Quarry: Chinatown, the Police, and the Press, the 1903 Boston Chinatown Raid Revisited," *Amerasia Journal* 22:3 (1996), pp. 81–103; Cong. Rec., and Report of 1906, 128–129; and Erika Lee, *At America's Gates: Chinese Immigration During the Exclusion Era, 1882–1943* (University of North Carolina Press, 2007), p. 231.

Undoubtedly there was a prevailing fear that the immigration officials would conduct more of these types of raids so many Chinese began to get their papers in order, and if the originals were not found a duplicate had to be obtained. This often required assistance from lawyers. Since the first-generation Chinese were forbidden from citizenship and therefore could not be attorneys, they had to use the services of Euro-American lawyers.

In an effort to enforce the Chinese exclusion acts, the Bureau of Immigration began counting the Chinese in the United States in January 1904 and tallied the results in September 1905 in order "to identify and protect those Chinese persons who are entitled by the laws and treaty to remain within the United States" and "to detect and expel those not so entitled." (Letter from the secretary of commerce and labor to the secretary of state, dated April 6, 1905, in response to a letter of protest from the Chinese Minister Chentung Liangcheng to Acting Secretary of State Alvey A. Adee, dated March 31, 1905. National Archives and Records Administration (hereafter abbreviated NARA), Washington, DC, Immigration and Naturalization Service, Record Group (hereafter abbreviated RG) 85, Entry 132, File 13653. Professor Chung is indebted to Marian Smith of the Immigration and Naturalization Service and Robert Ellis, Jr. of the National Archives and Records Administration, both of Washington, DC, for their invaluable assistance in this study.)

In 1904 the influential Reverend NG Poon Chew (*Wu Panzhao), the founder of San Francisco's Chinese-language daily, *Chung Sai Yat Bo* (Chinese American Daily Newspaper), complained about the certificates of residence and the harassment by immigration officials, and concluded, "the U.S. Government is attempting to expel all Chinese." (Quoted in Silas K. C. Geneson, "Cry Not in Vain: The Boycott of 1905," in *Chinese America: History and Perspectives 1997* (Chinese Historical Society, 1997), ISBN 1885864051, p. 3.) The bureau noted that the 1900 Bureau of the Census counted 89,606 Chinese while the 1905 census tallied 70,690 (including 3,217 citizens, 37,735 laborers, 3,857 merchants, 281 wives of merchants, 408 children of merchants, 210 others in exempt classes, and 25,062 unknown). What was more troubling was that only 18,896 had evidence to remain, 6,239 (all outside of California) had "no evidence" but "the right to remain," and 45,555 were in the "unknown" category and potentially subject to immediate deportation. Although the report was never made public in its totality, a summary was presented to Congress in May 1906 that detailed the stricter enforcement of the exclusion laws against the Chinese and pointed out that outside of California, 16,601 had documents, but 6,239 had no documents, and 11,178 were in an "unknown" category as to their possession of documentation (Report of 1906, 77). The Chinese in China reacted to this and other discriminatory actions as well as the failure of the treaty negotiations by boycotting American goods in 1905. Pressure from the president and various American businesses dependent upon the China trade stopped the census taking.

From 1910 to 1940 a new era of restrictions began as Angel Island, located near San Francisco, California, was made the entry port for the majority of immigrants from Asia, and Chinese immigrants had an even harder time entering the country legally. The Bureau of Immigration developed into a powerful, centralized agency of career civil servants armed with regulations hostile toward the Chinese. As Erika Lee and Judy Yung have demonstrated in their book, *Angel Island*, the Chinese experienced the harshest treatment. From 1910 to 1940 over 178,000 Chinese men and women were admitted into the United States and approximately 100,000 were detained at Angel Island. Incarceration varied between a few days to a couple of years. Interrogations were demanding and any inaccurate information presented often led to deportation. When the Department of Labor was separated from Commerce in 1913, the bureau became more powerful and organized. Regulations were enforced nationwide and raids of Chinatowns and Chinese businesses were not uncommon as the bureau continually tried to deport illegal Chinese. Undercover bureau agents were directed to visit Chinese businesses, especially restaurants, to discover illegal aliens.

The main difficulty that immigration officials had with Chinese immigrants was the officials' inability to speak and comprehend Chinese, especially the various dialects that were spoken. As a result, they had to rely upon "Chinese interpreters," some of whom knew more than one dialect of Cantonese (Siyi, Sanyi, Zhongshan dialects), but many of whom did not. Usually missionaries or white American social workers recommended interpreters but eventually, according to the diary of Chinese-American activist, Walter U. Lum, of the Chinese American Citizens Alliance, the Chinese Six Companies (Zhonghua huiguan) also interpreted for the bureau. Holding such a position elevated one's political, social, and economic status in the Chinese-American community. These men, like the Caucasian officials, could be (and some were) subject to bribery and other illegal activities.

In 1933 the Bureau of Immigration was renamed the Immigration and Naturalization Service (INS), reuniting the two earlier powers, and in 1940 it was placed under the Department of Justice.

In 2003, INS was broken into three separate entities—U.S. Citizenship and Immigration Services (USCIS), U.S. Immigration and Customs Enforcement (ICE), and Customs and Border Protection (CBP)—created anew in the Department of Homeland Security.

§9.18 Senate Debate, April 9, 1902:
"Narrow, bigoted, intolerant, and indefensible"

Under consideration in the Senate Committee of the Whole,
S. 2960 (Senator John Mitchell (R–OR)).

Senator Jacob Gallinger (R–NH) opened the debate of April 9, 1902, by sharply denouncing the Mitchell bill, which he condemned as bigoted and inconsistent with U.S. obligations. He also believed it took advantage of China's travail, at a time when foreign powers were besieging it and the authority of the Qing Dynasty was disintegrating:

"Mr. President, to my mind, this bill is uncalled for, unnecessary, unwise, and un-American. It is harsh in its provisions, unjust in its definitions, and clearly violative of solemn treaty stipulations. It is the kind of legislation that prejudice engenders and unthinking agitation produces. It is a measure aimed at a weak people, and which never would be dreamed of in connection with any nation able to defend itself. It is narrow, bigoted, intolerant, and indefensible legislation." 35 Cong. Rec. 3874 (1902).

The core exclusion policy was not really at issue. "There is no serious difference of opinion as to the wisdom of excluding this class of Chinese from the United States," Gallinger assured colleagues. 35 Cong. Rec. 3874 (1902). But the bill went much further than necessary to impose tight exclusion of laborers. Section 3 provided that every person not within the expressly exempted classes was declared to be a laborer. The language read:

"Every Chinese person shall be deemed a laborer within the meaning of this act who is not an official, a teacher, a student, a merchant, or a traveler for curiosity or pleasure, as hereinafter defined."

Automatically declaring every Chinese a laborer who did not fit into narrowly defined exemption was a gross overreach:

"This is a drag-net provision which will catch every Chinaman who attempts to enter this country. The ostensible openings in this drag net are in the shape of the five exempt classes, and are more illusory than real." 35 Cong. Rec. 3874 (1902).

Gallinger reinforced the criticisms that Senator Shelby Cullom (R–IL) had leveled at the definitions (§ 9.14). They would keep out nearly all Chinese, as a practical matter, and that was an abuse of American treaty rights. For instance, the "teacher" language was so tortured that the number of persons who could qualify for admission amounted to a handful. "Let me ask," said Senator Gallinger, "did the Chinese Government have only three or four persons in mind when it inserted the word 'teacher' in the treaties?" 35 Cong. Rec. 3874 (1902).

Similarly, because there were institutions of higher education available in China, the "student" provision would restrict entrants only to a few. "It is impossible that the Chinese Government should have understood the word 'student' in the very narrow and restricted sense of post-graduate study given to it by this bill," Gallinger argued.

The Senate Committee of the Whole had defended such provisions as codifying administrative opinions and enforcement. But Gallinger pointed out that the Chinese government had repeatedly protested against such executive interpretations of treaty rights. The committee had chosen to restate the policies and ignore the protests:

"Now as long as there is a difference in interpretation of a vital point of the treaty, it hardly seems courteous to the Chinese Government to embody the disputed points in legislation in defiance of the views and opinions of the Government . . . . If we insist that our interpretation is right, and act accordingly, China has good reason to complain about our arbitrary proceedings. She may be too weak to retaliate, but she is sure to cherish ill feeling against us, which will take a long time to remove." 35 Cong. Rec. 3875 (1902).

In keeping with its Angell Treaty rights to communicate with the United States about hardships imposed by implementing legislation, the Chinese government had complained about violations of bilateral agreements. Along these lines, China expressed extreme hostility to the Mitchell bill. On March 2, 1902, the Chinese Legation submitted a lengthy letter of protest from Minister Wu Tingfang to Secretary of State John Hay (Secretary Hay had announced the Open Door Policy in regards to China in 1900). The minister's letter was referred to the Senate Committee on Immigration, which disregarded it.

On the Senate floor, Senator Gallinger read the letter aloud. The Chinese minister had written:

"The provisions of the bill as to the five exempt classes are so restrictive as to practically nullify the treaty in regard to them. The definitions as to teachers, students, and merchants are so contrary to the spirit of the treaty as to make them almost impossible of observance." 35 Cong. Rec. 3875 (1902).

The letter objected to the registration requirements. Chinese laborers had submitted to the Geary Act registration (*§ 8.40*), albeit with great protest. The Mitchell bill would cancel those registrations and mandate new ones. Such a requirement was an unnecessary hardship, said Minister Wu, and should be dropped. Even more serious was the bill's mandate for registration of exempt persons:

"The bill also contemplates the registrations of all merchants and others of the exempt class. This cannot be required under the treaty, but the bill attempts to obviate that obstacle by making the failure to register a serious prejudice of their rights." 35 Cong. Rec. 3875 (1902).

Provisions involving dragnets, the presumption of guilt, and denial of bail were also protested. Chinese Minister Wu wrote:

"I have heretofore complained to you of the great hardships to which laborers, merchants, and others have been subjected after they have been admitted to the United States and are lawfully domiciled in this country. Past experience shows that Chinese have been arrested by the wholesale, placed in jeopardy, and subjected to molestation and insult. When found innocent, no redress is obtained for such illegal arrest. Persons charged with being unlawfully in the country and taken before a court are denied the privilege of bail, but must remain in jail until their case is decided. The bill, in place of providing some relief for these hardships, rather adds restrictions thereto." 35 Cong. Rec. 3875 (1902).

The Hawaiian and Philippine provisions vexed China as well. They were simply not contemplated when the Gresham–Yang Treaty was ratified in 1894, said Minister Wu, and such language should not be enacted without Chinese consent.

These and other terms constituted an atmosphere of hostility in the United States that would repel almost all Chinese, the letter noted:

"The provisions of the bill above referred to, and others which might be cited, place so many restrictions upon Chinese persons and require them to comply with such strict provisions that no Chinese having the least respect for himself would submit to such indignities and come to this country." 35 Cong. Rec. 3875 (1902).

Minister Wu was unambiguous about the damage ensuing from the enactment of the Mitchell bill:

"It cannot fail to seriously disturb the friendly relations which have up to the present existed between the two Governments and peoples." 35 Cong. Rec. 3875 (1902).

Senator Gallinger validated Minister Wu's vehement objections. The senator thought the enmity motivating the legislation was obvious: "The animosity of those who drew up this bill against the Chinese and the extreme harshness of many of its provisions are most apparent." 35 Cong. Rec. 3880 (1902).

Mitchell and other proponents defended the stringency of the bill as necessary to prevent the unwanted entry of Chinese laborers. Gallinger would not accept this explanation:

"Shall we be justified, under the cloak of preventing frauds by a few laborers, in practically stopping all respectable classes of Chinese from coming here? Would we be justified in stopping all people from going out at night because thefts are committed under the cover of darkness? There is as much argument in this as there is for enacting some of the provisions of the bill." 35 Cong. Rec. 3880 (1902).

Statistics demonstrated that existing law was working, said Gallinger. There was no need for extreme measures. According to the 1900 United States Census, the Chinese population in the United States was some 90,000 persons, down from 107,000 a decade earlier. In California, there were 46,000 Chinese, down from nearly 73,000 in 1890. Yet advocates of exclusion continued to sound alarms, even as attrition took its toll:

"They are being blotted out rapidly, and if the decrease continues for twenty-five years, a Chinaman will be as scarce in California as an angel's visit is, and yet the Senators from the Pacific Coast lift up their hands in holy horror and declare that the best interests of this Government demand that we shall enact this harsh and unnecessary restrictive legislation." 35 Cong. Rec. 3880–3881 (1902).

Gallinger observed the hypocrisy of applying different standards to Chinese immigration than to European. For instance, a major justification for exclusion had been labor protection. Chinese workers were said to pose a threat to American labor, but far greater numbers of poor Europeans were admitted each year, and they also competed for low wage jobs:

"Mr. President, the immigration to this country from 1890 to 1900 was considerably in excess of 3,000,000 people. Last year, 487,918 came from foreign countries. They were literally of all classes and conditions . . . . While we allow nearly half a million emigrants to come into our ports in a single year, we hold up our hands in horror at the 89,000 Chinese now in this country." 35 Cong. Rec. 3885 (1902).

Gallinger concluded with a prescient admonition:

"They are a great people. The Empire is a sleeping giant, that will some time rouse from her slumbers, and it will be well for the United States to then be her friend. Let us be just in this matter. Our present laws are strict and adequate, and it seems to me that equity and wisdom both demand that Congress shall refuse to enact legislation that is clearly unnecessary, if not absolutely pernicious." 35 Cong. Rec. 3885 (1902).

Senator George Turner, elected to the Senate from Washington in 1896 on a fusion ticket of Silver Republicans and Democrats, spoke next. If Congress failed to pass the most restrictive possible legislation, it would show ignorance of "Asiatic characteristics." 35 Cong. Rec. 3885 (1902).

Chinese were radically and disturbingly distinct from other peoples, Turner said. Over many years of exclusion debates, there had been expressed much bigotry and stereotyping. Turner's speech took the language of race prejudice in Congress to new levels:

"The Chinaman is a man and brother, it is true, but with a physical and moral organization so different from ours that he might have come from another planet. His physical organization is the result of four thousand years of struggle for existence under conditions of toil and starvation without a parallel in the world's history. That struggle has made him an animal without nerves . . . .

"His affections embrace only his own immediate family. He is lacking absolutely in patriotism and in conceptions of civic duty . . . . In business matters, his chief characteristic is duplicity and deceit, and that characteristic obtains from among all classes from the highest to the lowest. He is absolutely devoid of morals, as we understand morals. He is a gambler by instinct; cheats and lies as a matter of education; injures and slays his adversary without compunction and without loss of caste among his fellows, and considers female prostitution a virtue.

"Where he congregates in numbers, he transplants China bodily, its habits and customs, its vices and crimes, its outward signs and symbols, its ineradicable racial tendencies. It is possible for him to assimilate others, but for others he is non-assimilable. He is a Chinaman first, last, and all the time." 35 Cong. Rec. 3885 (1902).

At some point in the past, Turner had visited Chinatown in San Francisco. It made a negative impression on him:

"There were gathered there within limits not to exceed a quarter mile square, in business buildings given over to Chinese inhabitants, probably 30,000 Chinamen and a few Chinese women. They burrowed in the ground like rats. They roosted in the air like crows. They were packed in every available space like sardines . . . . I should say that there were 500 Chinamen in this one building.

The stench was something not to be forgotten . . . . The general impression left on one's mind is that of a seething, reeking, heaving mass of vermin, intermixed and intertwined, each striving with all its might to satisfy some animal need or craving, and having nothing in common with anything human except an ugly, debased, and stunted human form." 35 Cong. Rec. 3886 (1902).

Senator Turner's negative impressions were reinforced by contemporary drawings in popular magazines, such as the *The WASP* and *Harper's Weekly*.

Weaken the system of exclusion, Turner warned, and "we will have these seething, swarming sink holes of inequity in every city in the Union within twenty years . . . ." 35 Cong. Rec. 3886–3887 (1902).

Turner ended with an appeal to Southern senators, who he considered well experienced in dealing with racial issues:

"We appeal with especial confidence to our friends from the South, who have in their body politic a growing cancer second only in virulence to that which would be fastened on the Pacific Coast by a further propulsion to their shores of the pagan hordes of China. The Caucasian and the Mongolian are as far apart as the Caucasian and the Ethiopian.

"We have had the race problem with us from the beginning as a result of the presence of the Ethiopian . . . . How it will end no man can foresee, but one thing is certain, since the black man is nonassimilable and cannot reach up to the standard of the Caucasian, nor pull the latter down to the level of the Ethiopian, he will remain a disturbing factor in our nationality so long as he remains one of its constituent elements." 35 Cong. Rec. 3892 (1902).

This condition of irreconcilable racial animosity must not be replicated, Turner insisted. He fashioned a plea to the Senate:

"In the name of American progress and American civilization, let us avoid adding another such plague spot to the body politic." 35 Cong. Rec. 3892 (1902).

Senator William P. Dillingham (R–VT), who served in the Senate from 1900 to 1923, made the last major speech of the day. Although he was uncomfortable with the bill in certain specifics, neither he nor anyone else attacked the basic exclusion policy:

"If there is any member of the Senate who opposes this measure or any other upon the ground that he objects to the policy of Chinese exclusion, I do not know who he is." 35 Cong. Rec. 3894 (1902).

But Dillingham believed both that the Mitchell bill was unduly harsh and that existing exclusion laws were effective. He proffered some statistics in addition to ones that had been given earlier, showing a decade-long 40 percent reduction in the Chinese population in California:

- Since the 1894 treaty superseded the Scott Act, the right of Chinese laborers to return certificates had been restored. In the ensuing years, 12,638 Chinese left the U.S., but only two-thirds, 8,712, actually returned.
- Since 1894, the number of Chinese who passed through the United States in transit to other countries averaged only 1,495 annually.
- In the same period, notwithstanding the fact that authorities had "raked and scraped this nation of ours in each of those years to find and deport Chinese illegally here," the average number of annual deportations was just over 200. 35 Cong. Rec. 3895 (1902).

"The fear which has been expressed of a large influx into this country of Chinese of the prohibited class is greater than the facts warrant," Dillingham concluded. 35 Cong. Rec. 3895 (1902).

The Senate soon adjourned for the day.

§9.19 Senate Debate, April 10, 1902: "The Chinese must be kept out"

Under consideration in the Senate Committee of the Whole, S. 2960 (Senator John Mitchell (R–OR)).

The United States had annexed the Philippines as a U.S. territory as a result of the 1898 Treaty of Paris between the United States and Spain. As consideration of the Mitchell legislation resumed on April 10, 1902, the matter in controversy was Section 2, which restricted even those Chinese born in the Philippines after annexation. The Mitchell bill read:

"That from and after the passage of this act, the entry into the American-mainland territory of the United States of Chinese laborers coming from any of the insular territory of the United States shall be absolutely prohibited; and this prohibition shall apply to all Chinese laborers, as well as those who were in such insular territory when the same was acquired by the United States as to those who have come there since, and it shall also apply to those who have been born there since and to those who may be born there hereafter."

Senator William Dillingham (R–VT), who had closed the previous day's Senate debate, opened this one by arguing that the provision was unconstitutional because it conflicted with the birthright citizenship language of the Fourteenth Amendment, which states:

"All persons born or naturalized in the United States, and subject to the jurisdiction thereof, are citizens of the United States and of the State wherein they reside."

In *United States v. Wong Kim Ark*, 169 U.S. 649 (1898), the Supreme Court held that a laborer of Chinese descent, born in the United States, was an American citizen. But was the Philippines part of the United States? Dillingham thought so. If he was right, then persons born there after annexation would have birthright citizenship, and the Mitchell bill would violate their constitutional rights.

Dillingham cited a line of Supreme Court cases that defined the United States to include places that were not themselves states. One such case was *Loughborough v. Blake*, 18 U.S. 317, 5 Wheat. 317 (1820), which affirmed Congress' power to tax in the District of Columbia. The Court said:

"The provision that direct taxes shall be apportioned among the several states according to their respective numbers, to be ascertained by a census, was not intended to restrict the power of imposing direct taxes to states only." 5 Wheat. at 317.

Dillingham also referred to the terms of the 1898 Treaty of Paris. Inasmuch as the Philippines had previously been under Spanish dominion, the 1898 treaty gave Spanish natives of the Philippines a one-year grace period after ratification to declare their continued allegiance to Spain. It then provided:

"In default of which declaration, they shall be held to have renounced it and to have adopted the nationality of the territory in which they reside." 35 Cong. Rec. 3933 (1902).

Also pertinent, said Dillingham, was the case of *Fourteen Diamond Rings v. United States*, 183 U.S. 176 (1901), in which the government failed in an attempt to impose a duty on products imported from the Philippines. No import duty was owed, held the Court, because the Philippines was American territory:

"By the third article of the treaty, Spain ceded to the United States 'the archipelago known as the Philippine Islands,' and the United States agreed to pay Spain the sum of $20,000,000 within three months. The treaty was ratified; Congress appropriated the money; the ratification was proclaimed. The treaty making power, the executive power, the legislative power, concurred in the completion of the transaction.

"The Philippines thereby ceased, in the language of the treaty, 'to be Spanish.' Ceasing to be Spanish, they ceased to be foreign country. They came under the complete and absolute sovereignty and dominion of the United States, and so became territory of the United States over which civil government could be established. The result was the same although there was no stipulation that the native inhabitants should be incorporated into the body politic, and none securing to them the right to choose their nationality. Their allegiance became due to the United States, and they became entitled to its protection." 183 U.S. at 179.

After consenting to the 1898 Treaty of Paris, Dillingham noted, the Senate separately passed a joint resolution disclaiming intent to incorporate the Philippines into the United States. The Senate vote was 26 yeas to 22 nays; the House never acted upon it. The joint resolution stated in part:

"That by the ratification of the treaty of peace with Spain, it is not intended to incorporate the inhabitants of the Philippine Islands into citizenship of the United States, nor is it intended to permanently annex said islands as an integral part of the territory of the United States . . . ." 35 Cong. Rec. 3934 (1902).

But in the *Fourteen Diamond Rings* case, the Supreme Court considered whether the Senate's declaration limited the rights of Filipinos. The Court refused to give any legal effect to what the Senate had done:

"We need not consider the force and effect of a resolution of this sort, if adopted by Congress, not like that of April 20, 1898, in respect of Cuba, preliminary to the declaration of war, but after title had passed by ratified cession. It is enough that this was a joint resolution, that it was adopted by the Senate by a vote of 26 to 22, not two-thirds of a quorum, and that it is absolutely without legal significance on the question before us. The meaning of the treaty cannot be controlled by subsequent explanations of some of those who may have voted to ratify it. What view the House might have taken as to the intention of the Senate in ratifying the treaty we are not informed, nor is it material, and if any implication from the action referred to could properly be indulged, it would seem to be that two-thirds of a quorum of the Senate did not consent to the ratification on the grounds indicated." 183 U.S. at 180.

Senator Dillingham concluded that the requirements of allegiance, and the dominion of the United States over its territories, met the requirements of citizenship for Filipinos. He was sure that persons owing allegiance to the United States were entitled to its protection:

"What kind of protection does that imply, Mr. President? Does it not imply that the protection that is guaranteed by the Constitution and the laws, that they shall be protected in their liberty, in all of their personal rights, in the right of travel and of entry into this country? And yet, if this bill becomes a law, I do not see how one of that class coming to the port of San Francisco can, under the measure, be admitted." 35 Cong. Rec. 3934 (1902).

Later in the day, Senator William Stewart (R–NV) took the floor. Stewart had been Nevada's first senator, serving from 1864 to 1875, and then returning to the Senate in 1887, where he would serve until 1905. He received substantial support from the mining industry. See Russell R. Elliott, *Servant of Power: A Political Biography of Senator William M. Stewart* (University of Nevada

Press, 1983); and Ruth Hermann, *The Gold and Silver Colossus: William Morris Stewart and His Southern Bride* (Dave's Printing, 1975).

In the 1902 debate, Stewart reminisced at length and without regret about his role in the 1870 naturalization debate, in which he successfully filibustered citizenship rights for Chinese immigrants (*§ 1.20*). He drew the obvious conclusion that but for him the history of Chinese in America would have been different:

"If we had failed in that contest, of course there would have been a great many Chinese citizens, and there would have been no exclusion bills pending now. That would have ended the matter; but knowing the Chinese as I did, and knowing very well that they would have been brought here by the millions under the control of these Chinese merchants, I resisted it." 35 Cong. Rec. 3942 (1902).

Stewart was gratified that "it has now become the settled judgment of the American people that the Chinese must be kept out . . . . The sentiment of the whole country demands it, the safety of labor demands it, and Congress will comply with those demands. The situation is not now as it was in 1870, when the struggle lasted over the Fourth of July to prevent the extension of the right of naturalization to the millions [sic] of Asiatic coolies who were being imported into this country. The sentiment is universal, or nearly so, that Chinese laborers not be permitted to come here." 35 Cong. Rec. 3942 (1902).

Senator George Hoar (R–MA), a dedicated opponent of Chinese exclusion, addressed the Senate soon after. Unlike many senators who had spoken during the course of the debate, Hoar objected not just to overreaching implementation, but also to the basic policy itself. As the April 10, 1902, debate was winding down, Hoar concluded:

"This great Republic puts itself on record that men differ essentially in the matter of human rights because of race and not because of the quality of the individual, and that a laborer is degraded being in comparison with a scholar or the gentleman or the idler. Now that is a stab at the essential principle on which the Republic rests, and I for one will not mark the close of my life, as my eyes are about to close, by joining in such an act in consequence of any alleged or fancied necessity . . . . I will not bow to the knee of Baal in dealing with the Philippine Islands or with the Chinese. I will not vote that labor shall not stand on equality with other conditions of men . . . . I will not worship this god you have set up. My opposition to this policy has nothing to do with the details of the measure." 35 Cong. Rec. 3943 (1902).

Before adjournment, Senator Stephen Russell Mallory (D–FL) proposed an amendment to strike the following language from the Philippine emigration restriction:

"And it shall apply to those who have been born there since and to those who may be born there hereafter."

Mallory explained that the purpose of this amendment was "simply to leave open the question of the right of people born in the Philippine Islands since the acquisition of that territory to come to this country." 35 Cong. Rec. 3944 (1902).

On behalf of the Senate Committee on Immigration, Chairman Boies Penrose (R–PA) agreed to accept the amendment.

By unanimous consent, the Senate agreed to begin voting on amendments to the Mitchell bill, and thereafter on the bill itself, commencing at 3:00 p.m. on Tuesday, April 15, 1902.

Senator Orville Platt (R–CT) gave notice that he would propose a complete substitute for the bill. It would simplify the legislation considerably just by extending existing laws in parallel with the Gresham–Yang Treaty. Chinese exclusion would last so long as the treaty remained in force.

"The idea of my amendment is to continue existing laws just as they are until the expiration of the treaty, whether it shall expire on the 7th day of December [1904] by having been denounced or whether it shall continue longer by not having been denounced." 35 Cong. Rec. 3945 (1902).

Then, the Senate adjourned.

§9.20 Senate Debate, April 12, 1902: "Mere question of legislative detail"

Under consideration in the Senate Committee of the Whole,
S. 2960 (Senator John Mitchell (R–OR)).

As debate opened on April 12, 1902, Senator Henry Cabot Lodge (R–MA) hoped to arrest any momentum that might build in the direction of Senator Orville Platt's (R–CT) announced amendment. In principle, he said, both the Senate and Platt shared the objective of excluding the Chinese:

"What we have before us, therefore, to determine is neither a principle nor a policy, but a pure question of legislative detail." 35 Cong. Rec. 4033 (1902).

Lodge claimed codification would bring needed clarity to the law:

"We are now living under three statutes, innumerable Treasury regulations, decisions of the law officers of the departments, and of the courts of the United States . . . . I think it would be far better for the Chinese, as well as for the United States, that we should act under an intelligent, well-considered statute than under a loose body of regulations and overlapping and sometimes contradictory acts." 35 Cong. Rec. 4033 (1902).

Lodge turned to the Philippine question, which had gained the Senate's attention earlier in the 1902 debate. On April 10, 1902, the Senate had accepted an amendment to remove language prejudicing the rights of Chinese descendants born in the Islands after annexation (*§ 9.14*). But that amendment did not touch upon the emigration rights of Chinese in the Philippines who were already there when the 1898 Treaty of Paris was ratified.

Congress possessed the power to "exclude the inhabitants or a portion of the inhabitants of an organized territory from entering other portions of the United States," Lodge said. 35 Cong. Rec. 4034 (1902). There was recent precedent. In the Hawaiian annexation resolution ("Joint Resolution To provide for annexing the Hawaiian Islands to the United States," also called "Newland's Resolution," 55th Congress, 2nd Session, 1898) and related organic legislation, Congress barred Chinese laborers in Hawaii from migrating to the mainland. Best to extend that policy now to the Philippines, Lodge contended, rather than leave the matter unclear:

"When the Senate and the Congress of the United States have prohibited the passage of Chinese laborers from an organized territory, inhabited by citizens of the United States, into the mainland of the country, it is idle, I think, to argue that we have not the power to prevent the immigration of Chinese from the Philippines into Hawaii, or into the United States, or into Puerto Rico. My own belief is that it would be better to shut them out." 35 Cong. Rec. 4034 (1902).

Lodge did not believe the Platt substitute served this purpose. By just extending existing laws, the substitute left the rights of Chinese and the Philippines unresolved:

"In the substitute bill, it is left open to bring Chinamen from the Philippines into Hawaii and from the Philippines into the United States for the simple reason that the existing laws did not contemplate, as they could not have contemplated a the time of their enactment, the exclusion of Chinese in one part of the territory under the jurisdiction of the United States from entering the mainland territory of the United States . . . .

"We have shut out the Hawaiian Chinese. I think we have the undoubted right and, in my opinion, it is proper also to shut out the Philippine Chinese. I do not think the proposed substitute meets that point." 35 Cong. Rec. 4034 (1902).

The detailed provisions affecting the exempted classes had also provoked serious controversy during the debate. But Lodge believed such specificity was essential:

"If you simply say, in the language of the treaty, that Chinese merchants, students, and teachers can come into the country, you will have a million laborers here in five years. You have got to apply some test; you must do it. If you do not, the country will be flooded with them." 35 Cong. Rec. 4038 (1902).

Senator Lodge thought it would be better for the Chinese if these tests were regularized in law, in order to lessen the chances for arbitrary administrative decisions.

Pressing forward with the exclusion policy was not intended to show disrespect for China and its culture, Lodge claimed:

"One great misconception that I have seen running through these debates is that we treat the Chinese and talk about them as of they were a lot of simple, guileless savages . . . . The truth is widely different from this conception.

"The Chinese, Mr. President, live under one of the oldest civilizations in the world . . . . They have a civilization that has been great in art, great in poetry, great in literature. Our ancestors were running wild in the forests of Europe when they were a highly civilized people." 35 Cong. Rec. 4039 (1902).

While some senators had been overtly bigoted and denigrating toward the Chinese, Lodge cast the problem differently. China was a society apart, he said, and its people did not want to adapt to American culture:

"They do not come here with admiration for our civilization. They come here with contempt for it. They are children of a civilization older, and they think, mightier than ours. They differ from us in many of their ways and habits. It does not follow that they are worse for that, but when they come to this country, they do not come to seek our civilization or adopt our habits. They come to a country whose civilization they despise. They are a highly educated and very astute people. The great difficulty, in my judgment, is that they are products of a civilization which has been not only high and intelligent but which has shown itself immutable and immovable." 35 Cong. Rec. 4039 (1902).

Tightly applied rules were the only way to have a successful exclusion policy, Lodge argued. Anything more permissive would not keep them out. The Chinese were adept in devising ways to evade the law:

"The Chinese know the law and the way to get into this country better than any Senator in this Chamber . . . . There is not a Chinaman who comes to these shores who is not instructed on every single point as to how to get in . . . . They regard us as the Greeks regarded the rest of the world. Everybody outside of the Greek language was a barbarian, and the Chinaman regards everybody outside the sacred boundaries of his Empire as a barbarian also. They come to us in that attitude, and they come with keen intellects and sharp intelligence, knowing exactly what they mean to do. Such a people trying to evade our laws and get into our country require thorough restrictions and careful tests if we are to keep them out." 35 Cong. Rec. 4039 (1902).

The House measure, which the Senate would have to address in conference, was even harsher than the Mitchell bill, said Lodge. To have hope of reaching a reasonable bicameral compromise, Senate conferees had to be armed with the most detailed possible legislation. Working with the committee bill, rather than the Platt substitute, would advantage the Senate in this regard.

Lodge's colleague, Senator Jacob Gallinger (R–NH), had pointed out the hypocrisy of restricting Chinese laborers to protect American workers while concurrently leaving America wide open to the entry of working-class Europeans. Lodge agreed immigration policy was inconsistent. Accordingly, he had pressed several times for overall immigration restrictions, but had fallen short:

"I think nothing is more important than additional restriction of the immigration coming from eastern Europe now pouring in and taking the place of the races that have made up and built the United States." 35 Cong. Rec. 4040 (1902).

But the failure to secure broader restrictions would not deter Lodge from legislating where he could. "It is no argument to say that because we fail in one place that we should not succeed in another." 35 Cong. Rec. 4040 (1902).

Lodge had dominated that day's Senate debate almost exclusively. It was time for him to wrap up his case, which he did forcefully. Senators should not be deceived into thinking that the bill was merely responsive to radical elements or sandlot orators:

"Upon any great popular movement or upon a popular desire the agitator and the demagogue are sure to fasten . . . . But, Mr. President, if Senators think that the feeling or the movement behind this legislation are only the work of the professional agitator or the sandlot orator, they make, in my judgment, a very great mistake. I think this is a question of dealing with a people who are utterly alien to us, who can never become part of our civilization, who present economic conditions which we cannot meet, and in the presence of whose labor our labor would perish." 35 Cong. Rec. 4040 (1902).

Oil and water could not mix:

"The Chinese are of the great Mongol family. We are of the Aryan race . . . with a different language, a different past, a different hope, and a different future. Theirs is the Mongol race; and when Chinese labor is brought into competition with our labor, our labor cannot meet it on the standard and in the environment that the Chinaman creates and lives. That is why, as I believe, the great mass of the American people, with a strong race instinct, believes they should be shut out. I think that deep popular instinct is sound and wise." 35 Cong. Rec. 4040 (1902).

§9.21 Senate Debate, April 14, 1902: Parsing words

Under consideration in the Senate Committee of the Whole,
S. 2960 (Senator John Mitchell (R–OR)).

Senators representing Southern textile interests, such as Matthew C. Butler (D–SC) (*§ 8.21*) had periodically voiced concern about the effect of exclusion laws on commercial relations with China. While foreign trade issues were mostly absent from the 1902 debate, Senator John L. McLaurin (D–SC) brought them to the Senate's attention early on Monday, April 14, 1902. The Mitchell bill was unnecessarily imperiling trade with China, the senator said.

Commercial interests would have to give way, of course, if impairing commerce were the only way to impose effective immigration policies:

"If this Chinese trade could not be secured by us except at the price of coolie immigration, I would be the last man to raise my voice in behalf of it. The South has had quite enough of the 'race issue,' as it is, and heaven forbid that another race issue should be precipitated upon the South, or the North either, by any further irruption of a Mongolian nature!" 35 Cong. Rec. 4092 (1902).

McLaurin insisted, however, that good immigration policy and sound commercial relationships were not mutually exclusive. During the exclusion period, bilateral trade had expanded. It had been interrupted somewhat during the 1900 Boxer Rebellion, but had already recovered to pre-Boxer levels. An important part of that trade was in Southern textiles. If exclusion laws were working, and McLaurin was sure they were, why irritate China by violating treaty commitments?

"No doubt exclusion would be effective by the proposed law, but exclusion is also satisfactorily effected by the present law. Why, then, should we change, unless we can derive some benefit from the proposed new law that we fail to derive from the existing law?

"The United States would derive no benefit from the proposed change, Mr. President, but on the contrary, a positive and serious injury. The pending bill is calculated, by its restrictive action and inimical spirit, to kill our trade with China." 35 Cong. Rec. 4092 (1902).

While exclusion policy was intended to protect Pacific Coast workers, McLaurin noted, the need for economic fairness did not just apply to a single region. Instead, the country must legislate to "secure fair play for all its sections and all its citizens alike—for rich and for poor, for the laborers on the Pacific Coast and also for the laborers on the Atlantic coast, for the miners of California and also for the mill workers of South Carolina. Aye, fair play, too, for the Governments and respectable citizens of all foreign nations as well, including China." 35 Cong. Rec. 4092 (1902).

By narrowly defining the exempted classes, the Mitchell bill would take exclusion policy to a new and counterproductive level:

"You have only to accept the logical results of the policy toward China and the Chinese which is embodied in the provisions of the bill before you to bring about a condition of commercial warfare between this country and its chief customer in the Orient . . . ." 35 Cong. Rec. 4093 (1902).

Should aggressive American legislation alienate the Chinese market, McLaurin predicted, Europeans would be glad to fill the trade vacuum. And if China retaliated for the humiliation by rescinding American rights to most-favored-nation status, the United States would have no basis to complain:

"I do not see that we should have any cause for protest if China were to place the same embargo on our merchants, students, and travelers visiting the Empire that we are now asked by the advocates of the pending bill to make perpetual in regard to hers." 35 Cong. Rec. 4094 (1902).

When McLaurin concluded, Senator Joseph Foraker (R–OH) addressed the body. A senator from 1897 to 1909, Foraker had no quarrel with excluding laborers, but objected to legislation he believed was tantamount to barring all Chinese:

"The provisions of the bill of course are such, and intended to be such, as to keep out Chinese laborers. In my opinion, the provisions of this bill as to the so-called exempted classes, those who are not laborers, are designed in practical effect to keep out everybody else who is a Chinaman, but not a laborer. In other words, Mr. President, it is not stating it any too strongly to say that the difference would not be material in practical results if we were to strike out all after the enacting clause and make this bill read as follows: 'that from and after the passage of this act no Chinaman shall be allowed to come into the United States.' That is what the effect of it is." 35 Cong. Rec. 4095 (1902).

That an exclusion policy aimed at restricting laborers was now prejudicing the interests of exempted persons was beyond dispute, said Foraker. Treaty rights were under assault. In 1858, at American instigation, China and the United States ratified the Treaty of Tianjin (Tientsin), which provided in part:

"It shall be lawful for the officers or citizens of the United States to employ scholars and people of any part of China, without distinction of persons, to teach any of the languages of the Empire and to assist in literary labors. And the persons employed shall not for that cause be subject to any injury on the part of either the Government or of individuals . . . ." 35 Cong. Rec. 4095–4096 (1902).

The section quoted was still in force. As a result, said Foraker, "Any citizen of the United States has the right by that treaty, any person in China has a right, if a person in the United States sees fit to exercise his right, to accept employment as a scholar or as a literary man in the United States and to come to the United States for that purpose." 35 Cong. Rec. 4096 (1902).

Foraker observed that only a few scholars would qualify for admission under the Mitchell bill's definition. Without amending the Treaty of Tianjin , the bill would effectively abrogate it:

"We have no right to render nugatory, null, and void a provision of that kind; and an attempt to do it is a violation of the honor of this country—something you cannot afford to do, no matter at whose behest we are asked to do it." 35 Cong. Rec. 4096 (1902).

Advocates of codification had argued that they were only putting Treasury regulations into statute. This assurance did not comfort Foraker, who believed the regulations were faulty in the first place. Codifying them would make a bad problem worse, he thought, and would provoke China to retaliate:

"If China were to treat us reciprocally—and by what authority do Senators say she would not treat us reciprocally if we enact legislation such as this—she would by an edict, which could be issued in an hour's time by the Emperor, debar from China every missionary who is there, shut up every educational institution we have there, shut out every civil engineer we have there engaged in carrying on American work, in which American capital has been invested. We are building railroads there. We are spending millions of dollars in China. They could drive every American out, if they would only act reciprocally. That is all they would have to do. Who has the right to say they would not do it? Why should they not mete out to us our measure to them?" 35 Cong. Rec. 4097 (1902).

Foraker also raised a question of statutory interpretation. While everyone agreed that laborers should be excluded, was the list of exempted classes intended to be exclusive or merely illustrative concerning which Chinese would be admitted? Earlier in the debate, Senator John Mitchell (R–OR) had argued for exclusivity, using a canon of statutory construction: *expressio unius est exclusio alterius* (the express mention of one thing excludes all others). And Section 3 of the bill stated that "every Chinese person shall be deemed to be a laborer" who did not fall within the expressly exempted classes.

Senator Foraker sharply disagreed with this narrow interpretation. Exclusion policy was aimed solely at laborers, and the exemptions most recently affirmed in the Gresham–Yang Treaty (1894) were merely examples of who was not restricted. Foraker drew this conclusion from reading the negotiation

§9.22 Imperialism and the Open Door Policy

Theodore Roosevelt deemed the Chinese a "race-foe" and called upon the United States to maintain "race-selfishness" to exclude "the dangerous alien who would be ruinous to the white race." When he became president,* Roosevelt inherited two competing U.S. approaches to China. In America, voters demanded Chinese exclusion. In China, U.S. businessmen demanded "The Open Door."

The United States had come late to the slicing of the Chinese melon. It wasn't until 1898 that the nation had acquired the Pacific links—Hawaii, Guam, and Manila—required to tap China's riches. President McKinley's challenge at the time had been how to insert U.S. business interests into the powers' ongoing scramble for the Middle Kingdom. For his China policy, be chose the kindly slogan "The Open Door." The Open Door called on the Western powers to benevolently avoid partitioning China to the point that it could not function as a national entity, allowing all to compete within another's allotted sections . . . .

In fact, McKinley's policy had no practical effect on commercial competition in China. It did, however, humiliate the Chinese. Outraged at the attitude of these distant powers who felt they had rights to dismember their country, Chinese patriots arose to oppose the Foreign Devils in their midst. Because these athletic young men often practiced martial arts, foreigners called them Boxers. In June of 1900, the Boxers entered Beijing and laid siege to the embassies of the Foreign Devils, who held out for fifty-five days until twenty thousand troops from the Eight-Nation Alliance came to their rescue.

James Bradley, *The Imperial Cruise: A Secret History of Empire and War* (Little Brown and Company, 2009), pp. 285–286.

* Theodore Roosevelt became the twenty-sixth president of the United States on September 14, 1901, upon the death by assassination of President William McKinley.

records of both the 1880 Angell Treaty and the 1894 Gresham–Yang Treaty. In the Chinese text of both documents, Foraker told senators, the words "et cetera" followed the exempted class list:

"Those classes were enumerated by way of illustration not as an intended enumeration of all the educated classes who might come in, and that is the way to read it . . . . It was the intention of the parties to bar out laborers and let everyone else come in, and they enumerated a number of classes only to indicate what classes might come." 35 Cong. Rec. 4098 (1902).

Mitchell challenged Foraker. Did not the construction of *expressio unius* apply? Otherwise, why have a list at all?

Foraker responded:

"*Expressio unius est exclusio alterius* would apply if there were nothing else here but a simple statement that certain enumerated classes should have a right to come, but you must read the whole instrument together, and that rule does not apply and cannot apply here, because, in the first place, it says all other laborers shall be kept out and no other classes shall be kept out. Only laborers are to be excluded. Then it proceeds, 'Chinese subjects, whether proceeding to the United States as teachers, students, etc.' That is for illustration, in my contention, and the Chinese text of this treaty sustains that contention." 35 Cong. Rec. 4099 (1902).

Senator Orville Platt (R–CT) entered the discussion, citing the negotiation record to demonstrate that while the Americans had originally proposed a construction consistent with Mitchell's position, it was not part of the final accord. The U.S. proposal said:

"And the words 'Chinese laborers' are herein used to signify all immigration other than that for teaching, trade, travel, study, and curiosity hereinbefore referred to." 35 Cong. Rec. 4099 (1902).

The Chinese negotiators resisted this overture. "That was objected to by the Chinese commissioners and was abandoned by our commissioners," Platt noted. 35 Cong. Rec. 4099 (1902).

Foraker added that overly restrictive policies on exempt persons had originated from an 1898 Treasury Opinion, which he believed violated the 1894 Gresham–Yang Treaty. If he could have found the votes in the Senate, Foraker would have preferred to strike down the Treasury opinion. Such an outcome did not seem possible. Adopting the Platt substitute amendment meant existing law would be extended, which would leave the 1898 Treasury opinion standing. While that result was not ideal, Foraker considered it better than incorporating the Treasury opinion into statute law through the Mitchell bill's codification. If Congress codified, then it owned the policy:

"The continuance of the existing law is far less objectionable than to enact into law a statute that embodies in the way of codification and compilation all these unwarranted and obnoxious rulings of the Treasury Department. So long as it is only the Treasury Department proceeding under general authority of statute and enacting this, that, and the other provision, prohibitory for all that it is, we have no responsibility except only in the sense that we do not act to right a wrong, but when we deliberately take up those regulations and make them the law of the land, we endorse and approve, and put into operation all that Treasury, without any authority, has done." 35 Cong. Rec. 4104 (1902).

Senator Foraker asserted objections to the peculiarity and narrowness of the exemption definitions. In the Gresham–Yang Treaty, China had consented to a prohibition on Chinese labor immigration. Longstanding rights of other Chinese were not to be disturbed. Being a transparent effort to bar them in the guise of labor restrictions, the Mitchell bill must be opposed:

"I do not care how emphatically you exclude the laborer; I do not care how drastic, so long as they not be unreasonable, the provisions of your bill may be to enforce the exclusion of the classes to be excluded, but I do protest against imposing conditions upon classes that have a right to come under pretense that it is necessary to annoy them and debar them to keep out the laborer." 35 Cong. Rec. 4106 (1902).

Foraker also worried about the Mitchell bill undermining President William McKinley's Open Door policy in China. Transmitted to the major powers via two notes (1899 and 1900) issued by Secretary of State John Hay, the Open Door policy sought to ensure that America would have equivalent rights in China to each of the countries strengthening a foothold there (France, Germany, Great Britain, Italy, Japan, and Russia). It was of high importance to U.S. merchants that they have an opportunity to trade as equals in the Chinese market, the senator noted.

But while the McKinley administration insisted on this access, Congress was crafting legislation almost certain to alienate China and drive commerce elsewhere. Foraker found the disconnect highly ironic:

"While we are keeping the laborer out, while we have induced the Government of China to agree with us that he shall be kept out, we are not going to offend and insult the people of China and thus close in our face the door that President McKinley and Secretary Hay, with their wise diplomacy, opened wide for the American merchant and manufacturer and wage worker. What does the wage worker want? He wants a market for this country in which we can sell the products he manufactures." 35 Cong. Rec. 4107 (1902).

Foraker had been speaking for approximately two hours. When he concluded, the Senate agreed to several non-controversial amendments. By previous agreement, action on amendments that required roll-calls would be deferred until the following day, April 15, 1902.

§9.23 Senate Debate, April 15, 1902: "Ruthlessly disregards treaty rights"

Under consideration in the Senate Committee of the Whole, S. 2960 (Senator John Mitchell (R–OR)).

Shortly after the Senate convened on Tuesday, April 15, 1902, Senator Henry Heitfeld (Populist-ID) took the floor.

No promise of commerce with China should be allowed to mask the evils of Chinese immigration, Heitfeld asserted:

"I do not undervalue the advantage of the oriental trade, but I would rather have us do without a dollar of the China trade forever than to open our doors to her coolie population . . . . If no Chinaman had ever set foot on our soil, we would be tenfold better off. Wherever the Chinese laborers go in any considerable number, there the white workingman does not care to remain . . . .

"The only possible way of solving this vexed question is by effectually barring the doors to every Chinaman who labors for a living. It gives me a great deal of satisfaction to learn from the last census reports that although our Chinese population is not decreasing as rapidly as I would like, it is at least gradually relieving many sections of our coast of its obnoxious presence." 35 Cong. Rec. 4148 (1902).

Heitfeld was sure that worry over trade relations was overblown. "Sentiment must not be allowed to warp our judgment," said Heitfeld. Nor would it warp China's. "No exclusion laws that may be passed by the lawmaking power of this country will keep her from buying from us if we can sell cheaper than other countries," he assured his colleagues. 35 Cong. Rec. 4148 (1902).

Japan was Heitfeld's example. In 1895, Japan had initiated a war against China. But notwithstanding Japanese aggression, trade between the two countries had more than doubled from the pre-war period. Commerce was commerce, Heitfeld concluded.

Southerners were not mollified by such arguments. They continued to express concerns about textiles. So it was with Senator Jeter Pritchard (R–NC), a senator from 1895 to 1903: "It is the sheerest folly to assert that the Chinese Government will submit to any further measures than are embodied in the present Geary law, especially when the pending bill so ruthlessly disregards and openly violates existing treaty rights," observed Pritchard. "That she will as a self-respecting nation adopt some means of retaliation goes without saying." 35 Cong. Rec. 4154 (1902).

Pritchard was loathe to jeopardize commerce in order to tighten Chinese exclusion. He preferred to move in the opposite direction. To expand trade, Pritchard was for building a trans-oceanic canal and subsidizing ship construction:

"The people of the South are in favor of both of these propositions, upon the ground that their adoption will facilitate the extension of our trade into foreign countries." 35 Cong. Rec. 4154 (1902).

China policy must move in tandem with such measures, not work against them, said Pritchard. Otherwise, the unintended victims would be the economy in the American South:

"I cannot support the bill which has been reported by the committee, for its adoption would prove disastrous to the cotton manufacturers of the South, and would result in curtailing the amount of goods manufactured and lessen the demand for labor, which would necessarily result in lower wages of operatives employed in the cotton mills of the Southern States." 35 Cong. Rec. 4154 (1902).

At this point in the debate, Senator Charles Fairbanks (R–IN) offered a pair of amendments. Trying to salvage the bill from the threat posed by the Platt substitute to extend existing law, Fairbanks proposed deleting the highly controversial definitions of "students" and "teachers."

Although he expressed some misgivings about accepting the amendments, Senator Boies Penrose (R–PA), chairman of the Senate Committee on Immigration, felt constrained to do so. He understood the jeopardy that the Platt amendment posed for the bill, so he would try to cauterize the wound. The consequence would be to leave such definitions where they currently rested—in the hands of the Treasury regulations. Said Penrose:

"If the amendment be adopted, the result will be that the Treasury regulations will be amply sufficient, and that these two amendments will remove many objections which have been made to the bill." 35 Cong. Rec. 4157 (1902).

With voting soon to commence on more controversial amendments, Penrose wanted to be sure that senators knew of the breadth of public support for the bill. In particular, he highlighted endorsements from organized labor. Chinese exclusion had begun decades earlier as a labor protection movement on the Pacific Coast, and labor unions remained a key force in promoting the policy:

"The bill which is now under consideration is as urgently demanded by the laboring people of the State of Pennsylvania as it is by the people of the Pacific Coast. All our great industrial centers, all our miners unions and other labor organizations throughout the anthracite and bituminous regions of Pennsylvania urgently demand and insist upon the enactment of effective legislation to exclude Chinese laborers from our territory." 35 Cong. Rec. 4157 (1902).

The American Federation of Labor (AFL) was formed in Pittsburgh in 1891, noted Penrose. Its founding documents insisted upon Chinese exclusion. Penrose quoted from them:

"Whereas the experiences of the last thirty years in California and on the Pacific Coast have proved conclusively that the presence of Chinese and their competition with free white labor is one of the greatest evils with which any country can be afflicted: Therefore, be it Resolved, that we use our best efforts to get rid of this monstrous evil which threatens, unless checked, to extend to other parts of the Union, by the dissemination of information reflecting its true character and by urging upon our representatives in the United States Congress the absolute necessity of passing laws entirely prohibiting the immigration of Chinese into the United States." 35 Cong. Rec. 4157 (1902).

Penrose observed that enforcement without codification would depend upon reference to portions of nine different laws, as well as numerous judicial and administrative opinions. "It is not an exaggeration to say that there is hardly a vital departure to be found in this bill in any of its many sections. The bill is in the interest of uniformity in enactment and in practice." 35 Cong. Rec. 1458 (1902).

A coherent policy was especially urgent in light of fresh American interests in Hawaii and the Philippines. Leaving those new territories open to Chinese immigration, or allowing them to be a pathway to the mainland, would negate any good that could come from merely extending the 1892 Geary Act.

Senator Penrose conceded that his committee had proposed unusual and harsh legislation:

"It is admitted and must be understood that this legislation is extraordinary in its character. The reason is that we are confronted with the menace that has threatened the white peoples of Europe for thousands of years. First, it was military and warlike competition with the Mongolians; now it is industrial competition with them. It is legislation directed against a particular people. The provisions of the law are stringent and unusual. The principle of exclusion herein embodied is the product of national development, and has become a vital principle of national policy, essential for the protection of American citizenship and for the preservation of American civilization." 35 Cong. Rec. 4158 (1902).

Penrose explained why Americans were originally open to Chinese and then decided to exclude them. Although America and China had trade relations starting in 1783, called "Old China Trade," official government Sino-American contacts originated in 1844 after the first Opium War, said Penrose. "American diplomacy was then engaged in enabling American citizens to secure admission into

China and to break up that exclusion and isolation in which the great oriental empire had been involved for ages." 35 Cong. Rec. 4158 (1902).

Penrose continued. The 1858 Treaty of Tianjin secured further American advances into China, he said, and Chinese began immigrating in greater numbers. The country had need of them then:

"In order to unify the nation and bring the Pacific States into easy communication with the rest of the Union, the construction of a railroad across the continent and over the mountains became a necessity. Labor was scarce on the Pacific Coast. The construction of a railroad was delayed and resort was had to China for workmen. They came in large numbers, and by their aid the great transcontinental work was being carried to successful completion." 35 Cong. Rec. 4158 (1902).

The Burlingame Treaty of 1868 cemented bilateral relations. The treaty was hailed as a triumph of American diplomacy, Penrose observed, because it marked another step forward for the nation's China policy. At the time, the Chinese were welcome:

"Our people beheld the immigration of thousands of Chinese to the Pacific Coast without any great apprehension, and were disposed to entertain a good opinion of their assiduity, patience, and fidelity." 35 Cong. Rec. 4158 (1902).

Thus, the United States had taken steps to secure commercial and missionary rights in China. And at first, Chinese immigration to the United States was useful. Later, public perceptions formed that the immigration was a threat and needed to be curbed. This attitude came to dominate American diplomacy in China in the years that followed:

"Our early treaties were controlled by conditions utterly different from those existing at the present day. Then it was the effort of the people and the merchants of the United States, as well as the nations of Europe, to break into the exclusion which the Chinese Empire had maintained with rigid consistency in all the recorded time of existence. It was to open to our merchants and to our traders those rich oriental markets which have always dazzled the minds of men. It was only as our own Pacific Coast developed that the menace of Chinese coolie labor grew darker and darker upon us." 35 Cong. Rec. 4158 (1902).

Restrictions on immigration were not an American innovation, Penrose claimed. China itself imposed such controls on aliens, based on theories not particularly different from those on which U.S. exclusion laws were based:

"From the outset, the position of the foreigner in China has been one of violation and exclusion. His rights have been limited under the treaties to specific objects within the narrow limits of the treaty ports and extended only at the will of the Chinese Government to residence and travel in the interior . . . .

"Innumerable incidents might be mentioned where citizens of the United States, peacefully dwelling or traveling in China, have been the victims of mob violence and of hostile aggression on the part of the local authorities.

"The restrictions upon foreigners in China are especially narrow as to vocation, residence, and travel. In fact, Chinese legislation is based on the great primitive fact that natural barriers exist which seem to forbid the assimilation of the foreign element with the great Chinese race . . . ." 35 Cong. Rec. 4159 (1902).

Penrose's point was that exclusion policies worked in both directions. And he had no problem living with either set of restrictions. Just as Americans could not assimilate in China, Chinese could not assimilate in the United States. "It is the inherent prerogative of sovereignty to take cognizance of such incompatibilties," said Penrose. "Chinese exclusion can be justified on these grounds and this sovereign right is freely exercised by the United States . . . ." 35 Cong. Rec. 4159–60 (1902).

Exceeding normal legislative bounds, said Penrose, was justifiable because America was facing uncommon circumstances:

"Legislation of the character of the Chinese exclusion bill is necessarily exceptional and extraordinary. It can hardly be said that ordinary rules of consistency and propriety apply. We are face to face with a fact originating in prehistoric times—the immiscibility of the white European races and the Mongolian races." 35 Cong. Rec. 4159–60 (1902).

Senator George Turner (D–WA) launched upon a bitter speech. A senator from 1897 to 1903, Turner was an unsuccessful Republican Senate candidate in 1888 and 1892 after which he switched parties and was elected in 1896 on a "fusion ticket" made up of Silver Republicans, Democrats, and Populists. He denounced Senate Republicans, who he claimed were committed to weakening the exclusion policy. He had hoped, he said, that the Mitchell legislation could move forward without partisanship, but certain Republicans were too wedded to big commercial interests, and had decided to undermine the bill through the Platt amendment:

"The Republican finds its chief end and aim and object in life in the conservation of wealth, instead of in the protection of the common people of the land . . . . I believe that those who vote in favor of the Platt substitute will do so because way down in their hearts, they are opposed to restricting the immigration of Chinese to our country, and they are opposed to it because the manufacturing corporations, the transcontinental railroads, and the steamship companies want unrestricted Chinese immigration into this country." 35 Cong. Rec. 4167 (1902).

Turner scolded supporters of the Platt substitute:

"Do you want a lame, a halting, an inefficient administration of the laws relating to the exclusion of Chinese from our shores? Do you want as many holes to be punched into those laws as possible? Do you want to leave as many loopholes as possible to enable Chinese to come here? If you do, then you want to vote for the Platt substitute for the pending bill, because that is what it will do." 35 Cong. Rec. 4167 (1902).

Turner submitted for the *Congressional Record* telegrams he had received from eleven different labor organizations in the State of Washington, each urging passage of the Mitchell bill.

Senator John Spooner (R–WI) interrupted Turner. Spooner, who served in the Senate from 1885 to 1891 and again from 1897 to 1907, reproached Turner:

"I am, I confess, quite amazed that he should find it in harmony with his inclination or belief to impute to every member of this body on this side of the Chamber who does not happen to agree with him unworthy motives or a surrender to influences which ought not to affect any Senator on either side of the Chamber." 35 Cong. Rec. 4168 (1902).

Senator Turner disclaimed intent to impute bad motives to any particular senator. The problem, he said, was with "the peculiar tenets and policies of the Republican Party which had become ingrained in the consciousness of the members of that party." 35 Cong. Rec. 4168 (1902).

Spooner would not back down. "The Senator thinks apparently that the moment he left the party all the virtue, all the patriotism, all its traditional regard for the interests of labor and for humanity departed with him. The Senator is mistaken," Spooner exclaimed.

For almost twenty years, both the Democratic and Republican parties had been aligned on the exclusion of Chinese laborers, noted Spooner. Distinctions existed not on the basic policy, but on issues like the treatment of exempted classes and the execution of treaty obligations. Those differences were not minor, as the vote on the Platt substitute was soon to reveal. Nevertheless, Spooner felt obliged to demonstrate that he and his fellow Republicans were fully committed to labor's anti-Chinese agenda:

"So today, Mr. President, there is no man, so far as I know, who is in favor of throwing open the gates to the immigration of Chinese labor. We are afraid of them; that is the truth about it. They cannot become citizens of the United States. They create Chinese societies in our midst which are as isolated as if they were in China. They are acute, patient, thrifty, imitative, able, and with a standard of living which would enable them, if they could come here at will, to drive American labor to the poorhouse, if America would permit it, which American labor would not . . . .

"I do not yield—and I think I speak in that respect for every Senator on this side of the Chamber—to the Senator from Washington in the slightest degree in strength of purpose and desire to exclude Chinese labor from the United States." 35 Cong. Rec. 4169 (1902).

Spooner was uncomfortable with aspects of the Platt substitute, such as its failure to mention the Philippines, but he trained most of his criticism on the Mitchell bill. If that legislation passed, the United States would override the Gresham–Yang Treaty. And abrogation would result from an Act of Congress, not just some regulation. Statutes stood on equal legal status to a treaty, and could supplant it, while interpretative regulations were inferior to both treaties and laws:

"Anyone whose right under a treaty is invaded by Treasury regulations incompatible with the national obligation has his day in court; and if the Treasury regulation made by the Commissioner of Immigration is not in harmony with the treaty—if it deprives someone of a right in fact conferred on him by the treaty—the courts will say that . . . . But if the Congress, whose duty it is not to construe laws but whose duty it is to make laws, enacts into a statute regulations incompatible with a treaty, *pro tanto* it abrogates the treaty. That is the difference, and it is a wide difference." 35 Cong. Rec. 4171 (1902).

Sparring continued between advocates of the Platt substitute and defenders of the Mitchell bill. The main points of contention were whether the Mitchell bill violated treaty obligations and whether the Platt substitute was sufficiently comprehensive. Responding to criticisms from Spooner and others that the Platt substitute had omitted reference to the Philippines, Senator Orville Platt (R–CT) modified his amendment to bar movement of Chinese from the Philippines to the U.S. mainland.

Before adjournment, Senator Henry Cabot Lodge (R–MA) moved an amendment to strike from the Mitchell bill a provision barring employment of Chinese on American merchant vessels.

No votes were taken. Shortly after 6:00 p.m., on April 15, 1902, the Senate adjourned.

§9.24 Senate Debate, April 16, 1902: "If I stand alone"

Under consideration in the Senate Committee of the Whole, S. 2960 (Senator John Mitchell (R–OR)), and an amendment concerning merchant seamen (Senator Henry Cabot Lodge (R–MA)).

The Senate entered upon its eleventh day of debate on the Chinese exclusion bill on April 16, 1902. President Pro Tempore William P. Frye (R–ME) caused to be read a communication he had received from the American Federation of Labor (AFL). Signed by AFL President Samuel Gompers, and the remaining members of the AFL Executive Council, the message insisted that statutory exclusion policy be extended to the Philippines; said that any legislation that did not strictly define the exempted classes would be a "mockery and of no value"; demanded retention of the provision excluding Chinese from American merchant vessels, in order to protect seamen from Chinese "contamination"; opposed the Platt substitute; and exhorted the Senate to pass the Mitchell bill. It concluded:

"We therefore urge all true friends of the policy of the exclusion of Chinese laborers from the United States to vote for the bill and to defeat any amendment offered thereto to weaken it in any of its essential or effective features." 35 Cong. Rec. 4208 (1902).

Senator George Turner (D–WA) opened the debate by renewing his attack on the Republican Party. He spoke with the special passion of the converted. Turner had himself been a Republican during Lincoln's time and for many years following. Then, the party stood for human rights, but its precepts had changed, causing him to abandon it, Turner claimed:

"It would be a brave man who would assert and undertake to establish that the Republican Party of today has anything in common with the Republican Party of Abraham Lincoln's day . . . . It stands today not for a pure and simple administration of this government in the interest of the common people of the land, but it stands for the material interests of the nation, for the corporations, for the trusts, and for the enormous aggregation of capital which come to the halls of Congress and demand exceptional legislation in their favor." 35 Cong. Rec. 4210 (1902).

Tying this critique to Chinese exclusion, Turner argued that moneyed interests had lobbied Republicans to weaken the bill:

"The transcontinental railroads have had their agents here, inveighing against this measure. The great shipping companies on the Atlantic and Pacific

Coasts have had their agents here inveighing against this measure. The business interests, the commercial interests, the trade interests, affect to have been frightened by this measure. They have all exerted their influence to bring about the operation of this ingrained tendency of the Republican Party to oppose everything which wealth wants defeated and to deny to the people everything which they want enacted." 35 Cong. Rec. 4211 (1902).

Turner dismissed arguments made against the Treasury Department procedures. Such complaints sounded as if the United States had no right to execute the treaty, except in a manner agreed to by China. But if the United States had to wait for China to acquiesce to U.S. regulations, he said, implementation would be impossible:

"This fails to take account of the duplicity of the Chinese character, which everybody who has been in that country and who has written upon the subject tells us extends from the highest to the lowest. Even the Emperor of China is not exempt from this trait of duplicity." 35 Cong. Rec. 4211 (1902).

Turner also insisted the Chinese were dishonest: "It is known that not only deception but corruption prevails from the highest to the lowest in the governmental service of China." 35 Cong. Rec. 4212 (1902).

Voting on amendments was about to begin. Before that happened, Senator Charles Fairbanks (R–IN) once again took the floor. He advocated for a realigned immigration policy:

"I shall be glad to see the Chinese labor population diminish and their places taken by Germans, by Dutch, by English, by Scandinavians, by other nationalities from whose blood we have sprung and have become the most puissant people on the face of the globe." 35 Cong, Rec. 4218 (1902).

The American exclusion policy did not demonstrate hostility to China, Fairbanks contended. Exclusion was a matter of domestic concern. Had not the United States just proven its friendship, by protecting China against excessive indemnity demands following the Boxer Rebellion?

"When the great nations of the earth sat about the international council chamber and many of them looked with covetous eyes upon the harbors, upon the cities, and provinces of China, the United States said, 'the integrity of the Chinese Empire shall not be destroyed'; and when other governments undertook to exact indemnities which would have bankrupted the Empire, the United States spoke for moderation, and for equity, and saved to China many millions of dollars." 35 Cong. Rec. 4218 (1902).

Fairbanks closed with an argument to support the bill and deflect the substitute. Codification was merely a change in form, not in substance, he said.

The president pro tempore announced that the bill was open to amendment. First up was Senator Henry Cabot Lodge's amendment to strike the bar to Chinese employment on American-flag vessels.

Speaking for the amendment was one of exclusion's most venerable advocates, Senator William Stewart (R–NV). "I suppose it would be impossible for an American ship to cross the Pacific Ocean and return if it could employ only American citizens," Stewart argued. 35 Cong. Rec. 4218 (1902).

The true effect of the Senate Immigration Committee-reported language would be counter-productive. The provision would cause ship owners to circumvent it by flagging their vessels elsewhere. The alleged beneficiary of the provision—American laborers—would be ill-served by it:

"Now to say that this is in the interest of labor, it seems to me, is a burlesque. If we make it impossible to carry the American flag on our ships, we will injure shipbuilding here, and we will put out of employment in that business a thousand men . . . ." 35 Cong. Rec. 4218 (1902).

Some advocates for labor seemed to believe it was locked into a zero-sum contest with management. Stewart was not one of them. "It is an absurdity," he declared, "to assume that anything which benefits commerce, which benefits industry, which makes wealth, is prejudicial to labor. All wealth is produced by labor, and if you destroy the means of producing wealth, you destroy labor . . . . The laboring people of this country are not such imbeciles as to think that this particular provision would be in their interest." 35 Cong. Rec. 4218–19 (1902).

Leaders of organized labor, such as the Executive Council of the AFL, had singled out the seamen's provision for support. Going against them could incur political wrath, but Stewart was not worried about it. His credentials in support of Chinese exclusion were impeccable. He spotlighted his filibuster, some thirty years ago (§ 1.20), of the Sumner amendment that would have allowed Chinese legally in America to naturalize:

"There appears to be a desire to pander to some false sentiment. I am under no necessity to do it on this subject. But for me, as the *Record* will show, the Chinaman could have become a citizen." 35 Cong. Rec. 4219 (1902).

Senator Thomas M. Patterson (D–CO) closed for the opponents. Ships flying the American flag were American territory, he reasoned. American workers at sea deserved as much protection from Chinese labor competition as workers on land.

The Lodge amendment to strip the bar on Chinese workers at sea carried. Forty-seven senators voted aye, 29 voted nay, and 10 were listed absent.

Senator Edward Carmack (D–TN), a senator from 1901 to 1907, proposed an amendment to allow Chinese persons who were American citizens to travel between the territories and the U.S. mainland. Senator George Hoar (R–MA) endorsed the amendment:

"The term 'Chinese' is defined in Section 52 of the bill, and it includes 'all male and female persons who are Chinese either by birth or descent, as well as those of mixed blood as those of the full blood.' So the term 'Chinese,' without any limitation or qualification, includes an American citizen . . . . That being true, we should either make the exception which the Senator from Tennessee proposes, or we have got to rely on the fact that it would be unconstitutional to pass the bill without the exception." 35 Cong. Rec. 4223 (1902).

Carmack concurred with Hoar. "We have no right to bar any person who is a citizen of the United States," Carmack stated, "but the language of the section as it stands now may be construed as an attempt to do that very thing." 35 Cong. Rec. 423 (1902).

Even Senator John Mitchell (R–OR) agreed to cure the defect. The language of the amendment should have been in the bill in the first place, he said.

The amendment carried by voice vote.

Senator William Dillingham (R–VT) proposed an amendment that would have expanded the list of exempted classes to include "five good-faith representatives of each regularly established Chinese wholesale commercial house." Senator Boies Penrose (R–PA) opposed this, claiming the additional exemption would be abused:

"It would let down the bars in a class of cases where most of the frauds are permitted, namely, the admission to the country of laborers in the guise of merchants." 35 Cong. Rec. 4240 (1902).

The Dillingham amendment was rejected on a vote of 13 ayes, 57 nays, with 18 senators not voting.

Senator Orville Platt (R–CT) formally offered his substitute. It continued in operation "all laws prohibiting and regulating the coming of Chinese persons and persons of Chinese descent into the United States, and the residence of such persons therein . . . ." for so long as the Gresham–Yang Treaty of 1894 remained in force. That treaty could be renounced in 1904, but otherwise would continue until 1914. As the termination date of the treaty was undetermined, the duration of the Platt extension was indefinite.

Amendments were in order both to the substitute and to the underlying Mitchell bill. A series of minor amendments to the bill was agreed to by voice vote. One proposed amendment to the bill was especially curious. Offered by Senator Matthew S. Quay (R–PA), it would have exempted Chinese Christians from the exclusion policy. A senator from 1887 to 1899 and again from 1901 to 1904, Quay explained:

"I regard, although I do not profess to be an apostle, the Christian religion the basic stone, the living root of all Western civilization and government and society." 35 Cong. Rec. 4241 (1902). Chinese who conformed to it would have proven capable of assimilating, Quay reasoned, so he would admit them on presentation of "proper ecclesiastical certificates." 35 Cong. Rec. 4241 (1902).

The amendment drew immediate opposition. Platt stated, "I do not know that we can admit a Christian laborer any more properly than we can a Chinese laborer who is not a Christian." 35 Cong. Rec. 4241 (1902). Senator Joseph Rawlins (D–UT), a senator from 1897 to 1903, raised constitutional objections:

"The First Amendment of the Constitution of the United States forbids Congress to make any law respecting an establishment of religion or prohibiting the free exercise thereof . . . . Congress has no function and has no right to discriminate in favor of a Christian or against a Christian, in favor of a Mohammedan or against a Mohammedan, in favor of the followers of Confucius or against those of other religious denominations. It is a queer idea, it seems to me to inject into this bill a sort of inquisition to ascertain what may or may not be the religious faith of a person knocking at the doors of the Republic . . . ." 35 Cong. Rec. 4242 (1902).

Senator John C. Spooner (R–WI) quipped that if the amendment passed, Senator Quay would instantly become the most successful Chinese missionary in the world.

The amendment was rejected by voice vote.

Quay sent up another amendment, to admit Chinese who had acted in defense of the foreign legations or Beijing's Beitang Cathedral (also known as Xishiku Cathedral) during the Boxer disturbances. Without assistance from those Chinese, reported Quay, the defense would have failed. Under his proposal, some 600 to 800 Chinese would be eligible for admission.

On a roll call, the amendment was voted down. Seven senators voted in the affirmative, 68 were in the negative, and 13 did not vote.

Platt spoke on behalf of the substitute, and he affirmed yet again his commitment to the exclusion policy: "Suggestions from any quarter that Senators on this side desire to break down that policy . . . are entirely gratuitous and without foundation." 35 Cong. Rec. 4245 (1902).

But while there was a consensus on the ends, there was serious division over the means. Platt insisted the bill too much contradicted the Gresham–Yang Treaty:

"I believe it violates the letter, but unquestionably it violates the spirit of that treaty, and if we would keep faith with China, and if we would preserve the open door and not close it, we should not offend China in this matter." 35 Cong. Rec. 4245 (1902).

For example, Platt cited the bill's provision that anyone not an official, teacher, student, or merchant, would automatically be deemed a laborer. As Senator Joseph Foraker (R–OH) noted earlier in the debate (*§ 9.14*), this very concept had been advanced by the American Gresham–Yang Treaty negotiators (commissioners), and the Chinese side had expressly rejected it. Accordingly, the provision had been left out of the treaty. "To go now and put it into this bill would be a direct insult to China," said Platt. 35 Cong. Rec. 4245 (1902).

Platt summarized his argument against the bill:

"This legislation is unnecessary to continue the exclusion of Chinese laborers; it is offensive to the Government of China, with which we wish to remain on good terms; and then it is bad legislation in that no bill ought to include all Treasury regulations and decisions in it." 35 Cong. Rec. 4245 (1902).

Senator John Mitchell (R–OR) proposed an amendment to the substitute requiring that all Chinese laborers in the Philippines secure a certificate of residence within eight months, without which they would be presumptively deportable. Under laws related to Hawaiian annexation, such a requirement had already been imposed on Chinese laborers in the Hawaiian Islands. Chinese who were American citizens due to birthright citizenship were made exempt from this requirement.

Mitchell defended the amendment as being in the best interest of Chinese laborers in the Philippines. Without possessing the certificates, they would have no line of defense against presumptive deportation:

"I simply want to state to the Senate, Mr. President, and to those Senators who are friends of the Chinese, if there are any such here, who think the legislation produced by the Committee on Immigration is too drastic, that this amendment is as much in the interest of the Chinese in our insular territory as it is in the interest of the Government." 35 Cong. Rec. 4250 (1902).

Despite Platt's resistance, the Mitchell amendment was agreed to by 41 yeas to 40 nays, with 7 senators not voting.

The Platt substitute passed by 48 yeas to 33 nays, with 7 senators absent. Outspoken proponents of exclusion, such as Senators Mitchell, Penrose, Fairbanks, Teller, and Turner had all opposed it.

The Senate Committee of the Whole reported the bill, as amended by the Platt substitute, to the full Senate.

It was only left to the Senate to pass the bill. Before that happened, Senator George Hoar (R–MA) spoke. Hoar had been a Senator since 1877, all through the exclusion era, and he had been an unceasing opponent of the policy. Hoar, who would die in office in 1905, made one last statement denouncing it:

"I cannot agree with the principle upon which this legislation or any legislation we have had in the country since 1870 rests. I feel bound to enter a protest. I believe that everything in the way of Chinese exclusion can be accomplished by reasonable, practical, and wise measures that will not involve the principle of striking at labor because it is labor, and will not involve the principle of striking at any class of human beings merely because of race, without regard to the personal and individual worth of the man struck at. I hold that every human soul has its rights, dependent upon its individual personal worth and not dependent upon color or race, and that all races, all colors, all nationalities contain persons entitled to be recognized everywhere they go on the face of the earth as the equals of every other man.

"As this bill violates that principle, in my judgment, I am bound to record my protest if I stand alone." 35 Cong. Rec. 4252 (1902).

Stand alone, Hoar did. The vote on final passage was 76 to 1.

§ 9.30 House Debate, April 4, 1902: "Largely a Pacific question"

Under consideration in the House Committee of the Whole,
H.R. 13031 (Representative Julius Kahn (R–CA)),
with amendments proposed by the House Committee
on Foreign Affairs.

Himself an immigrant from Germany, in 1902 Representative Julius Kahn (R–CA) was at the beginning of a long career representing San Francisco in the U.S. House of Representatives, serving from 1899 to 1903 and again from 1905 to 1924. Kahn was the principal sponsor of H.R. 13031, the House version of Senator Mitchell's Chinese exclusion bill. On April 4, 1902, Representative Robert Hitt (R–IL), chairman of the House Committee on Foreign Affairs, presented the bill before the House Committee of the Whole.

A companion measure to the Senate Mitchell bill, the Kahn legislation in the House was also a joint product of members from the Pacific region. Hitt's committee reported the measure with few modifications.

Hitt characterized the bill as balanced:

"We have endeavored to make the provisions effective and prevent fraud, but to avoid harassing or tormenting merchants, officials, and teachers whom we desire to come and for whose presence we are all of us very anxious. We have a large and growing commerce with China." 35 Cong. Rec. 3678 (1902).

Hitt deferred to Representative James B. Perkins (R–NY) for a more detailed explanation of the House Committee on Foreign Affairs reasoning. A congressman from 1901 to 1910, Perkins defined the legislation's purpose:

"What is the object of this bill, Mr. Chairman? It is, as stated in its heading, to exclude Chinese coolies from the United States. And every member of that committee is glad, and certainly I as much as any member am glad, to do anything that will exclude Chinese laborers, Chinese coolies, from the United States." 35 Cong. Rec. 3680 (1902).

Perkins discussed an important committee recommendation to strengthen exclusion policy. Any ship entering American ports would suffer heavy economic penalties if it transported Chinese not within the exempted classes eligible for admission:

"When a ship comes alongside any wharf or dock of the United States on which there are Chinese coolies who are not to be landed, the steamer must give bond in the penal sum of $2000 for every Chinaman on board, to see to it that the Chinamen whom they have on board do not get on land—the ship that brings them carries them away." 35 Cong. Rec. 3680 (1902).

Since the last time the exclusion laws had been extended, the Philippines had come under American jurisdiction. What to do about the substantial Chinese population there? Perkins talked about three questions the House Committee on Foreign Affairs had addressed:

Should Chinese living there be permitted to enter the United States? Given the presence of at least 250,000 Chinese in the Philippines, the House Committee on Foreign Affairs unanimously decided that none should be permitted to immigrate to the U.S. mainland.

Should the exclusion laws operate within the Philippines? The House Committee on Foreign Affairs determined that the Filipinos themselves wanted to be free of competition with Chinese labor. Although there was division in the committee on this question, Perkins noted a consensus "that Chinese laborers be excluded from the colonial possessions of the United States on the same terms and in the same manner as they are excluded from the mainland of the United States." 35 Cong. Rec. 3679 (1902).

How, if at all, should Chinese in the Philippines be registered? Registration of mainland-based Chinese had been required since the Geary Act had passed a decade earlier in 1892. As introduced, the Kahn bill would have required a substantial force of Treasury Department agents to conduct the registration. The Kahn bill deferred to the Philippine Commission, headed by William Howard Taft, the question of how best to conduct this registration.

The House Committee on Foreign Affairs also differed with Kahn on applying Chinese exclusion to American-flagged merchant vessels, which Kahn had included in the bill to be introduced. The committee thought the provision impractical, for the same reasons that Senator Lodge had attacked such language in the Mitchell bill in the Senate. As reported to the House, the Kahn bill did not contain the seaman provision.

Representative James Beauchamp "Champ" Clark (D–MO) followed Perkins to the floor. Clark served in the House from 1893 to 1895 and again from 1897 to 1921. Between 1911 and 1919, Clark was Speaker of the House. He spoke of the difficulties legislators faced crafting a balanced policy:

"The task which Congress seems to have set for itself of excluding as many Chinese as possible without giving such offense as will destroy our trade with the Chinese Empire is one of the most vexatious problems that the legislative mind has ever considered." 35 Cong. Rec. 3681 (1902).

The problem was made worse when the Supreme Court decided in *United States v. Wong Kim Ark*, 169 U.S. 649 (1898), that a Chinese person born in the United States was entitled to American citizenship as a birthright. Would the Court hold that persons in the Philippines, now annexed, were citizens of the United States? Clark, who was opposed to Philippine annexation in the first place, thought that imperialistic U.S. policies in the Far East had unnecessarily complicated Congress' work on Chinese exclusion.

Clark addressed other parts of the bill. He noted a difference of opinion over the provision barring Chinese labor on U.S. merchant vessels. Republicans opted to strike it; but Clark and his fellow Democrats preferred to retain it. He would offer an amendment to restore it.

Clark quoted from the House Committee on Foreign Affairs report's minority views. "The question of Chinese exclusion is largely a racial question and largely a labor question." 35 Cong. Rec. 3681 (1902). The future Speaker expanded upon the racial theme:

"Individually, I go further and say that the Chinese question is the race question of the Pacific Coast. There is no use dodging it. The Chinese problem is to the Pacific Coast what the negro problem is to the southern States, except that the race question of the South is entirely a domestic question, while the race question on the Pacific is complicated with international questions. I believe, moreover, that the white people of the South are the most capable of dealing with their race question just as the white people of the Pacific Coast are most competent to deal with their Chinese race question.

"Upon these race questions, I unhesitatingly take my position with the white people of the South and the white people of the Pacific Coast." 35 Cong. Rec. 3681 (1902).

Proudly, Representative Clark declared that the Democratic minority would offer a substitute that would be tougher than the majority bill. In addition to the seaman provision, Democrats wanted to add texture to the definition of Chinese person. The majority provision stated:

"That the term 'Chinese' and the term 'Chinese person' as used in this act are meant to include all male and female persons who are Chinese either by birth or descent."

This definition was not good enough for the minority, which proposed to add to the end of it the words "as well as those of mixed blood as those of the full blood." Clark explained what they had in mind:

"If you cut that section off at the word 'descent,' there is not a Chinese in Hawaii or in the Philippines who will not be able to prove that he has a strain of some other sort of blood in him. Every one of them will turn out to be a mulatto." 35 Cong. Rec. 3683 (1902).

If of mixed-race, then the person must be classified as a Chinese, Clark said. That is how such matters were resolved in the South:

"By common consent down South, anybody who has one drop of negro blood in him is classed as a negro. If that applies to the negroes, it certainly ought to apply to the Chinese." 35 Cong. Rec. 3683 (1902).

Democrats proposed stricter definitions for the exempted classes, the issue that was to feature so prominently in the Senate debate. This was required due to the "utter duplicity of the Chinese character," Clark asserted. 35 Cong. Rec. 3683 (1902).

Clark highlighted bill language that barred entry of Chinese born in the territories after annexation by the United States. The Senate had stricken such a provision from the Mitchell bill on constitutional grounds, even before adoption of the Platt substitute.

But it was just that constitutionality that Clark wanted to test. He believed that if the provision became law, a suit would challenge it. That was fine by Clark, because he wanted to give the Supreme Court an opportunity to reverse *Wong Kim Ark*:

"I do not believe that the decision of the United States Supreme Court in Wong Kim Ark against the United States, declaring that the Chinese born in this country of Chinese parents are American citizens, is a sound and just decision. I want to see them compelled to decide that case over again, and the only way you can compel them to decide that question again is to put that language in this bill." 35 Cong. Rec. 3684 (1902).

Clark described the holding with which he disagreed:

"It decides that Chinese born in the United States of Chinese parents subject to our jurisdiction—and that means everybody except diplomats—are American citizens, clothed with all the immunities, privileges, and duties of American citizens." 35 Cong. Rec. 3684 (1902).

The ruling rested on an interpretation of the Fourteenth Amendment. Clark scoffed, "I do not believe a syllable of it." The Thirteenth, Fourteenth, and Fifteenth Amendments were passed "for the sole benefit of the negroes," he said. 35 Cong. Rec. 3684 (1902). Clark added:

"I do not believe that the Congress that passed the Fourteenth Amendment was thinking any more about making citizens out of the Chinese than they were about making a citizen of the man in the moon." 35 Cong. Rec. 3684 (1902).

Why was it necessary to have a detailed bill rather than simple legislation that merely extended existing law? Clark argued the case. A core statute, on which later legislation was built, was the Scott Act of 1888. While the Scott Act's cancellation of return certificates had been overridden by the Gresham-Yang Treaty (1894), other provisions of the act were still under legal challenge. What if the Court struck down the act? "You will go through the performance of continuing the laws that are in existence, and the Supreme Court will declare them all bad, and in three weeks they will import 100,000 Chinese coolies, and there you are." 35 Cong. Rec. 3685 (1902).

The consequence of opening the floodgates would be catastrophic, Clark predicted. "If they ever get here in large numbers, they will drive the American laborers out, or the American laborers will kill them, mob them—one or the other." 35 Cong. Rec. 3685 (1902).

The core question for Clark, like many other exclusion advocates before him, was the capacity of Chinese immigrants to assimilate. "I am totally opposed to anybody coming here that you cannot make an American citizen out of, and the Chinese will not assimilate with white people." 35 Cong. Rec. 3685 (1902).

Clark spoke approvingly of a 1901 anti-miscegenation law passed by the California legislature, barring intermarriage between Chinese and whites (California Civil Code section 60, California Statutes 1901, p. 335, declared unconstitutional in *Perez v. Sharp*, 32 Cal.2d 711, 198 P.2nd 17 (1948)). Evidence showed that "the cross between the Chinese and the white race or the Chinese and the negro, is inferior to either the white man, the Chinaman, or the negro," he assured the House. 35 Cong. Rec. 3685 (1902). See also Najia Aarim-Heriot, *Chinese Immigrants, African Americans, and Racial Anxiety in the United States, 1848–82* (University of Illinois Press, 2003).

Nevada passed the first anti-miscegenation law in 1861 prohibiting the marriage between whites and Mongolians (Chinese/Asians). See Deenesh Sohoni, "Unsuitable Suitors: Anti-Miscegenation Laws, Naturalization Laws, and the Construction of Asian Identities," *Law and Society Review* 41:3 (September 2007), pp. 587–618.

Chinese exclusion policy also involved the law of self-preservation, according to Representative Clark. "It is largely a racial question, and it raises the paramount issue, 'Shall the white man continue to dominate the Western Hemisphere, or shall he be placed in the process of ultimate extinction and be supplanted by the yellow man?'" 35 Cong. Rec. 3685 (1902).

Clark would do whatever was necessary to preserve Caucasian dominance, and if that meant passing extraordinary legislation, so be it:

"I know that the provisions of this bill seem cruel. I understand perfectly well that they seem to run counter to everything we have ever advocated or offered to the world; but, in my judgment, they are absolutely necessary to secure the desired end." 35 Cong. Rec. 3685 (1902).

Representative Robert Adams (R–PA) followed Clark. A member of the House from 1893 to 1906, Adams' principal focus was expanded trade in the Far East. While he supported exclusion of laborers, he was against "over-strict regulations" that impeded exchanges between the educated classes of both countries:

"China was civilized for centuries while we were wandering Huns and Goths in the forests of Europe and wild men on the heather of Scotland and Ireland. I believe China can teach us much out of her past history and much of her great sciences that were known to her before we were ever heard of. I want intercourse between the two countries. I want that development between the Orient and the rapidly growing West which will tend to the advancement of the world . . . ." 35 Cong. Rec. 3688 (1902).

The committee-amended bill would promote those ends while still maintaining a labor exclusion policy, Adams suggested.

Representative Julius Kahn (R-CA) spoke next, walking through a history of the restrictions in Chinese immigration. He particularly criticized the alleged abuse of return rights for Chinese guaranteed to Chinese who had been living in the United States before the 1882 exclusion was imposed:

"This provision gave rise to no end of fraud. By a decision of our courts, it was held that parol evidence was sufficient to establish the prior residence of a Chinese laborer in this country.

"With a supreme contempt for our judicial system, and with a duplicity that is almost unparalleled among the nations of the earth, hordes of Chinese laborers did not hesitate to swear themselves into the country as former residents, and the acts of Congress which the people of the Pacific Coast had hailed with joy and expectancy, were soon found to have turned out Dead Sea fruit." 35 Cong. Rec. 3688 (1902).

Failure to control the tide led to progressively stricter tactics, said Kahn. These included negotiation in 1888 of the proposed Bayard–Zhang Treaty, which would have permitted the United States to prohibit, rather than merely to suspend, the entry of laborers. But China never ratified the treaty. Filling the vacuum, Congress enacted the Scott Act (*Chapter Seven*) on October 1, 1888, which cancelled all return certificates, and which became law over China's vigorous protest.

In 1892, Congress passed the Geary Act (*Chapter Eight*), which not only extended for ten years the original 1882 exclusion policy but also imposed unique registration requirements on Chinese laborers. The Chinese had refused to comply, but instead litigated the constitutionality of the registration. After the Supreme Court upheld the Geary Act in *Fong Yue Ting v. United States*, 149 U.S. 698 (1893), Congress extended the registration window for six months. That supplementary legislation, which passed in 1893, also contained further safeguards against registration fraud.

In 1894, China and the United States ratified the Gresham–Yang Treaty, which repealed the Scott Act, reactivated return rights, and prohibited the immigration of Chinese laborers into the United States. It also provided for continued rights of entry for the exempt classes.

Nevertheless, Kahn believed Chinese immigration problems continued to fester:

"In recent years, the frauds that have been attempted and have been committed in the matter of bringing Chinese laborers into this country have been practiced principally under the exemptions of these privileged classes." 35 Cong. Rec. 3689 (1902). Ninety percent of these frauds, Kahn posited, were perpetrated by laborers posing as merchants.

If the laws were harsh, Kahn observed, then the Chinese had only themselves to blame:

"It has been maintained that the attitude of our Government is exceedingly severe in the matter of Chinese exclusion; that our laws have been becoming more and more stringent and drastic; but I submit if the Chinese people themselves would deal honestly with us, and if they resorted less to trickery and duplicity to circumvent our laws, then there would be no need of closing up all possible loopholes in the law with the seemingly severely restrictive measures that the Chinese themselves make necessary." 35 Cong. Rec. 3689 (1902).

Kahn detailed various methods by which he said fraud was committed. These included the use of "coaching papers," with questions and answers supplied to "enable the prospective Chinese immigrant to evade the questioning and cross-examination of the inspectors at our various points of entry." 35 Cong. Rec. 3689 (1902).

Chinese who were refused entry attempted to bribe their way in, Kahn claimed. If such methods failed, they turned litigious. "When the corrupt offers are spurned, the wily Chinese begins to prefer charges against the inspector and does everything in his power to make his position a burden and a discomfort." 35 Cong. Rec. 3690 (1902). Every inspector in San Francisco was subjected to such harassment, Kahn reported.

Representative Kahn dismissed arguments that passing the legislation would damage commerce with China. Such claims had been made every time an exclusion bill went through Congress, but retaliation did not materialize. Highs and lows of U.S.-China trade pretty much mirrored the experience of the British and French, even though those countries had never enacted exclusion laws. "It is universally conceded that commerce is not influenced by sentiment," said Kahn, "and that commercial peoples purchase where they can buy to the best advantage." 35 Cong. Rec. 3691 (1902).

Kahn ended his lengthy speech by condemning Chinese society. He quoted Bayard Taylor, the travel writer whose depiction of the Chinese in *A Visit to India, China and Japan in the year 1853* had been cited in the first exclusion debate, in 1879 (*§ 2.10*). Taylor had since died, but his denigrating comments lived on. The passage Kahn cited began this way:

"'It is my deliberate opinion that the Chinese are morally the most debased people on the face of the earth. Forms of vice which in other countries are barely named are in China so common they excite no comment among the natives. They constitute the surface level, and below them there are depths of depravity so shocking and horrible that their character cannot even be hinted.'" 35 Cong. Rec. 3693 (1902).

Kahn embraced Taylor's bigoted views as his own. "For nearly fifty years the Chinese have lived in this country," Kahn said. "Their daily intercourse with the Caucasian has not materially changed their customs or habits. Mr. Taylor's description of conditions in China is undoubtedly equally applicable to any Chinese community in our country." 35 Cong. Rec. 3693 (1902).

Next to address the House was Representative Henry Naphen (D–MA), a member of the House from 1899 to 1903.

"We are charged with disloyalty to our grand traditions, and our high ideals of hospitality by legislating against the Chinese." 35 Cong. Rec. 3695 (1902). But all Congress had done was to act in self-preservation against aliens unable to assimilate, he said. In all the debates on exclusion, no one had better captured the essence of the policy than did the two-term Massachusetts Democrat:

"With one exception, the tests imposed or suggested against those seeking the hospitality of our shores have been standards of character, education, and property, not racial. We have drawn the race line only against one nationality. In other cases, we admit the people and exclude the individual. In the Chinese case, we admit the individuals and exclude the people." 35 Cong. Rec. 3695 (1902).

Naphen asked rhetorically:

"Are these bland Orientals, stealing in and out, tireless as automata, seemingly impervious to impressions, the material for American citizenship?" 35 Cong. Rec. 3696 (1902).

In this own mind, the question answered itself. A Chinese could no more fit into American citizenship than an American could become Chinese. "Can it be wondered, then, that this race should act as an irritant upon the populations amidst which it intrudes, and be made the object of special legislation?" 35 Cong. Rec. 2696 (1902).

Mindful of periodic anti-Chinese riots and related violence, Naphen was ready to blame the Chinese for being the cause of the unrest that surrounded them. "The presence of Chinese has given rise to serious disorder on many occasions," he noted. "It is part of justice, I admit, to punish the perpetrators of such wrongs, but it is part of prudence to remove the inciting cause." 35 Cong. Rec. 3696 (1902).

But pro-exclusion as Naphen might be, he did have his limits. He could not concur in the challenge that Clark and the House minority posed to Chinese birthright citizenship:

"Much as I am in favor of an exclusion act, I desire to place on record my opposition to section 2 in its present form, which provides that the prohibition of Chinese immigration shall apply to those born in our insular possessions since their acquisition, and those who may be born there hereafter. We have no right to prevent the free transit of any person born in the insular possessions whose parents have a permanent residence and domicile therein, be they Mestizos or Chinese." 35 Cong. Rec. 3698 (1902).

Some members of Congress argued that the Treaty of Paris, ending the Spanish–American War in 1898, granted Congress plenary powers to determine the rights of Filipinos, but Naphen believed the Constitution limited that authority. A crucial distinction had to be made between persons who were already alive at the time of annexation and ones who were born in the Philippines thereafter:

"It may be urged that under the treaty Congress has a right to determine the civil rights and political status of the native inhabitants of the territory ceded. That referred to the native inhabitants then there, and not to those who have been born there since or may be born there hereafter. The Constitution takes care of their status . . . .

"We hold our insular possessions under authority from the Constitution, and must be governed by its terms. You cannot violate or set aside a single sentence or clause under any circumstances. If we admit that Congress can do this, then the whole instrument falls to the ground and there would be no Constitution and no Congress." 35 Cong. Rec. 3698–99 (1902).

"We cannot by legislative action discriminate against persons born in our insular territories, after ratification of the treaty, so as to exclude them from their natural, civil, or political rights," Naphen concluded. 35 Cong. Rec. 3699 (1902).

The day's last speaker was Representative Henry W. Palmer (R–PA). He served from 1901 to 1907 and then from 1909 to 1911. Palmer's remarks were notable for their concluding lines. While the American dream was to be open to some persons, he said, it must be off-limits to others:

"To those who fly from the persecution of tyrants, if they are industrious, law-abiding, and God-fearing, and if they seek homes and citizenship in this fair land of opportunity and freedom; if they come to cast their lot with us, renouncing all allegiance to foreign princes and potentates, to help in building up the great Republic, the gates should not be closed. For the anarchist, who would destroy all government; for the criminal, fleeing from punishment for crimes committed, and for the Chinese, whose coming in large numbers would tend to lower the standard of citizenship, lessen intelligence and impair virtue, and therefore weaken the support upon which the perpetuity of the Republic depends, we have no room." 35 Cong. Rec. 3700 (1902).

§9.31 House Debate, April 5, 1902: "To arouse this sleeping five-toed dragon"

Under consideration in the House Committee of the Whole, H.R. 13031 (Representative Julius Kahn (R–CA)), with amendments proposed by the House Committee on Foreign Affairs.

Debate opened with remarks from Representative Frederick H. Gillett (R–MA), a member of the House from 1893 to 1925. During his tenure, he succeeded Representative James "Champ" Clark (D–MO) as Speaker, serving as Speaker from 1919 to 1925. Thereafter, Gillett was in the Senate from 1925 to 1931.

There was no dissension on the need to exclude Chinese laborers, Gillett said, but discord existed on how best to do it. Overreacting to political pressures from the Pacific region had proven to produce bad legislation:

"I think the chapter of Chinese exclusion laws passed under the compulsion of Pacific politics is one which is not creditable to the American nation. The purpose to be accomplished, which was to exclude laborers, I believe, was wise and necessary, but the methods pursued were injudicious and improper." 35 Cong. Rec. 3730 (1902).

Gillett leveled particular criticism at the 1888 Scott Act, which intentionally abrogated U.S. commitments to China flowing from the Angell Treaty. "I do not think that when treaties become unendurable they must forever be observed," he said, "but I think the manly and honorable way is to abrogate them with due notice and not insultingly disregard them." Gillett added, "I think China has ever since had a just grievance against the United States." 35 Cong. Rec. 3731 (1902).

How presently to implement Gresham–Yang Treaty rights to prohibit laborers without being too restrictive on the exempted classes? Gillett found both the Kahn bill and the prospective minority substitute amendment excessive:

"While we wish to keep out all laborers, it is not only a wise policy for us to allow Chinese merchants free access to this country, but the right is specifically guaranteed by treaty, so I think it would be unwise and illegal for us to interfere with it, and I think that the provisions for admitting the exempt classes are too severe in both bills and ought to be moderated." 35 Cong. Rec. 3731 (1902).

Gillett was optimistic that, as China opened to the West and began to modernize, commerce with America would expand, provided that the U.S. did not chill it with gratuitously harsh legislation:

"We are all looking forward to the East as a profitable market. We hope in the coming years to find there a large outlet for our surplus products, and also a field for our inventions, and that we may take part in the development there of materials of the new civilization." 35 Cong. Rec. 3731 (1902).

Excessive restrictions on exempted classes would damage those prospects, Gillett believed. The Kahn provisions were likely to be treaty violations, would damage bilateral relations, and direct trade to other nations. A simple extension of existing laws would be sufficient to maintain exclusion policy and avoid such counterproductive controversies.

Representative Theobald Otjen (R–WI) followed Gillett to the House floor. A member of the House from 1895 to 1907, Otjen agreed with Gillett on the need to foster strong commercial relations and to be scrupulous in observing treaty obligations. But Otjen parted ways with Gillett on the need for strict scrutiny of the exempted classes. According to Otjen, very restrictive provisions were the only way to prevent fraud:

"No one advocates the placing of annoying or harsh conditions upon the exempted classes seeking admission to our shores, but such provisions and safeguards must be placed around their admission as experience has shown to be necessary to prevent Chinese laborers from gaining admission under the pretense of belonging to the exempted classes." 35 Cong. Rec. 3731 (1902).

No other people on Earth were subjected to the discrimination that Congress foisted on the Chinese, Otjen said approvingly. He explained the basis for it:

"The character of this legislation is unusual; it is not directed at any other nation in the world excepting China . . . . To permit the coming here of an alien race, and to place them side by side with our own people, a race whose social plane is so radically different, whose standard of living is so much lower than our own, a race which can never be assimilated, cannot but bring deplorable and disastrous results." 35 Cong. Rec. 3732 (1902).

Continuing efforts by the Chinese to immigrate, as well as any attempts at assimilation and race-mixing, would damage everyone, Otjen stated. All would be better served if government policy kept the races apart:

"The two races cannot live side by side; one or the other must go under. Can anyone fail to see that there would spring up strife and hatred between the two races, resulting in disorders, riots, and bloodshed? This being so, are we not justified in preventing such a state of affairs, not only for the best interests of our people, but also for the best interests of the Chinese people?" 35 Cong. Rec. 3732 (1902).

Labor leaders had urged strong exclusion legislation and must be heard,

Otjen declared. Anti-exclusionists had condemned them as agitators and demagogues; in fact, such movements must be seen as "public benefactors." Unions were not motivated by "enmity toward the Chinese race," but by self-preservation. It was not just union leaders who were behind exclusion, but also the rank and file:

"Thousands of petitions have been received by this House from labor organizations located in all parts of the country praying for passage of this bill, and that Congress express in unmistakable terms its determination to protect them from this threatened and most serious menace to their welfare." 35 Cong. Rec. 3732 (1902).

Next to speak was Representative Charles E. Hooker (D–MS). He served in the House three times (1875–1883, 1887–1895, and 1901–1903). Especially in the context of the overall debate, Hooker's statement was noteworthy for its strongly anti-discriminatory tone:

"It is true that they are copper-complexioned and almond-eyed," Hooker began, "but the gentlemen who want to exclude all classes in contravention of the [Gresham-Yang] treaty certainly do not intend to get up an indictment of the Almighty because He created from the same origin people of different colors." 35 Cong. Rec. 3735 (1902).

Hooker mocked the prejudice that Representatives Clark and Naphen had displayed in their rhetoric:

"My honorable friend from Missouri [Clark], to whose oratory I always listen with great pleasure, and by whom I am always instructed, seems to think that because there is a Caucasian race to which he belongs, that therefore there are no other races. I am sure my honorable and amiable and Christian friend from Missouri [Clark] and the gentleman from Massachusetts [Naphen], who comes from the same State that Burlingame did, would not want to write an indictment against the Almighty because He made people of different color." 35 Cong. Rec. 3735 (1902).

It all sounded to Hooker like the attacks that nativists had made decades before against Irish immigrants. Hooker cautioned the House:

"We must not set ourselves up as judges against all the balance of the world because we happen to be Caucasian and white." 35 Cong. Rec. 3736 (1902).

"We all admit," Hooker continued, "that under the Christian religion, we are all descended from one ancestor—all the nations of the earth—and that we ought to be governed by the great cardinal principles of right and justice between governments as we are governed in our conduct in the observance of the laws toward our neighbor." 35 Cong. Rec. 3736 (1902).

Hooker had accepted the need to exclude Chinese laborers, a policy he acknowledged was urged by labor interests. But he was firm that the exempted classes be able to enter the U.S. without burdensome limitations, such as hyper-strict definitions that imposed de facto exclusion:

"It behooves us to treat these people with justice and deal with them fairly, because the God of nature, the God of power, has . . . given them the color they have. We ought not to undertake to violate the treaty because of that." 35 Cong. Rec. 3736 (1902).

After Hooker sat down, Representative Abraham Brick (R–IN) offered remarks that went in the opposite direction. A member of the House from 1899 to 1909, Brick sounded the alarm:

"So important is this bill that if its general object should fail I believe it would be the most paralyzing blow ever aimed at American labor or leveled at American civilization." 35 Cong. Rec. 3738 (1902).

The matter was all the more urgent because of complications arising from Hawaiian annexation and the Spanish–American War, Brick said. An era of imperialism had dawned, bringing new populations under American gover- nance. "Today we have new and untried problems to solve," he observed. "They are the problems of American supremacy and of the markets of the world. They are the problems of our ever-marching, ever-conquering civilization . . . . We will govern all these new and strange peoples with all the kindness and liberty that play around our institutions; but I insist that always and forever it shall be done in just regard for our people here at home." 35 Cong. Rec. 3738 (1902).

The concept of "just regard" must include vigorously enforced Chinese exclusion policies, including restrictions on movements of Chinese to, from, and within the insular territories, Brick insisted. The Kahn bill met this objective:

"It says, in emphatic terms, that not a single Chinese laborer shall set his foot upon American soil. It promises the men of America that they are not only protected in their employment here, but also against cheap labor and its every result, directly or indirectly, from our island territory." 35 Cong. Rec. 3838 (1902).

In comments reminiscent of the early exclusion debates, Brick insisted that exclusion was essential to resolve the future of American civilization:

"Shall the Anglo-Saxons and kindred races possess the country or shall the Mongolian control it? That proposition will be absolutely settled in the passage of this bill." 35 Cong. Rec. 3738 (1902).

Without tight exclusion, Brick predicted catastrophe. Chinese would arrive unabated, bringing with them "social vices and national habits that would surely contaminate the clear stream of Christian civilization and American institutions." 35 Cong. Rec. 3738 (1902).

Representative Brick expanded on his fear-mongering diatribe. "Dangerous as are their peculiar vices, their virtues are still more perilous," he continued. "Intelligent in their own way . . . crafty, patient, diplomatic, they are painfully industrious, brutally frugal, and fanatically fatalistic; a people to be feared; as changeless and unrelenting as eternity; the immutable progeny of ages gone and civilizations passed away . . . .

"Shall we now pursue a policy—a Fabian, cowardly, procrastinating policy —that shall usher in the countless hosts of an alien people to degenerate our race and despoil our labor—a people who have no regard for family, whose language holds no name of 'home,' in whose breast there comes no redeeming rapture even in the consecrated presence of a noble woman, and whose heart yields no responsive, civilizing throb even in the sanctified light of the fires of the hearthstone or the eye of wife and child?" 35 Cong. Rec. 3738–39 (1902).

After such overwrought oratory, Brick answered his own question. "Every instinct of God-given self-defense, that law higher than all human statutes, revolts against it." 35 Cong. Rec. 3739 (1902). Supporting a law that denied the possibility of citizenship to Chinese, Brick offered an ironic argument:

"Then let this bill pass. Let us so act that we may go home in the consciousness of a duty well performed, and be able to say with a prouder boast than did that old Roman, 'I thank God that I, too, am an American citizen.'" 35 Cong. Rec. 3739 (1902).

Representative Henry Green (D–PA), a member from 1899 to 1903, closed the day's proceedings with a warning. There was a price to be paid for stirring up China by engaging that country with treaties and trade. China left to slumber in its isolation was better than a China awakened:

"I believe it will be the worst of policies for us to stir up the Chinese country and its people and even urge them to adopt our ideas of civilization and progress. She is a sleeping giant who, when once aroused, may do us great harm. It may seem very smart for some of our American exploiters to laugh and sneer whenever the yellow peril is mentioned; but gentlemen, the yellow peril will be a practical peril when its breaks its bonds of conservatism . . . .

"They are physically and mentally strong and have the important elements which go into making of good soldiers and sailors. They will soon be able to handle the weapons of war with the soldiers of the military powers of the world. The step is not a great one and the time will soon come, aye, sooner than most men expect it. Nor is her commercial growth and development far away. We who live day-to-day may see the time when she, with her great natural resources and cheap labor, will be an active and irresistible competitor in the markets of the world.

"Let us keep an eye on China and not allow our greed for gain to arouse this sleeping five-toed dragon." 35 Cong. Rec. 3750 (1902).

§9.32 House Debate, April 7, 1902: "Clearly unconstitutional"

Under consideration in the House Committee of the Whole, H.R. 13031 (Representative Julius Kahn (R–CA)), with amendments proposed by the House Committee on Foreign Affairs.

The House was not in session on Sunday, April 6, 1902, but resumed consideration of the Kahn bill on the following day.

Representative Rudolph Kleberg (D–TX), who served between 1896 and 1903, initiated the debate by complaining about Section 2 of the bill, which undermined birthright citizenship. "I think the clause is clearly unconstitutional," he observed. "I believe that our insular possessions are clearly part of the United States." 35 Cong. Rec. 3870 (1902). He threatened to oppose the bill if the section were not deleted.

Representative Henry Naphen (D–MA) was certain that Congress had not meant to except the Chinese when the Fourteenth Amendment was adopted:

"It had been urged that the Fourteenth Amendment was not intended to confer rights of citizenship upon the children of Chinese parents. An examination of the debate in the Senate and House when the Fourteenth Amendment was under consideration proves that it was understood that children born of Chinese parents in the United States would come under the terms of the Amendment." 35 Cong. Rec. 3780 (1902).

The insular possessions were part of the United States, asserted Naphen. In *De Lima v. Bidwell*, 182 U.S. 1 (1901), the Supreme Court had said so. Persons born in those territories had the natural rights of citizens:

"The Constitution takes care of their rights. Though we may suspend their political rights and define what their civil status may be, we cannot take away their natural right to go to any part of the Republic." 35 Cong. Rec. 3870 (1902).

Inasmuch as it was unconstitutional to deprive those people of those rights, Naphen proposed an amendment to strike the section. But if the amendment failed, he planned to vote for the bill anyway.

Representative Champ Clark (D–MO) assumed the House floor. In addition to the litigation it would spawn, Clark added a second reason for challenging birthright citizenship. Many Democrats were uncomfortable with the Republican President William McKinley's imperialistic foreign policy, now continued by the slain president's Republican successor, Theodore Roosevelt. Clark thought the birthright citizenship issue was a way to disgorge the Philippines:

"If the United States Supreme Court ever decides that the residents of the Philippine Islands are American citizens, and that we have no right to keep out of the country Filipino Chinese, then the American people will rise in their might and drive Congress in to getting rid of the Philippines, and that is just exactly what I want to see done—precisely." 35 Cong. Rec. 3788 (1902).

The Naphen amendment was defeated on a voice vote.

The clerk continued to read the Kahn bill section-by-section, each section being open to amendment in turn. In due course, there was additional debate about the highly specialized definitions for the exempted classes. Clark defended the detailed restrictions:

"The whole intent of this law is to shut out Chinese laborers. If there were some way of branding the Chinaman right across his forehead that he is a laborer, there would be no trouble about it. You cannot do that . . . . The men who drew this bill, and the proponents of this bill, are simply trying to keep Chinese coolies out of here, and the reason they have not succeeded in doing so is, as I have explained in my main speech, on account of the duplicity of the Chinese character." 35 Cong. Rec. 3791 (1902).

Representative William H. Douglas (R–NY), who was in the House from 1901 to 1905, offered an amendment to expand the definition of "merchant" to allow Chinese purchasing agents to enter the United States. "My objection to this section of the bill as it now stands," Douglas reasoned, "is that it permits a Chinaman to come to this country and establish a place for the sale of Chinese goods, but does not permit a Chinese corporation of firm or individual to come or send an agent here for the purpose of buying our goods." 35 Cong. Rec. 3791 (1902).

Douglas thought American policy was backwards. "I should prefer to exclude the seller rather than the purchaser," he added. 35 Cong. Rec. 3792 (1902).

Douglas tried to reassure his colleagues who might worry about his amendment that he was as pro-exclusion as the rest of them:

"This bill does not present a dividing line politically. Members of all parties favor it. China, with her 400,000,000 inhabitants is as thickly populated as an ant hill. Throw down the bars and the lower classes of her people will swarm in upon us, lowering the present high grade of American citizenship, lowering the character and dignity of American labor, and lowering the compensation of labor . . . . They do not assimilate with our people, they are not interested in our institutions, and do not breathe their spirit." 35 Cong. Rec. 3792 (1902).

The Douglas amendment was defeated by 15 yeas to 67 nays.

Representative William Sulzer (D–NY) rose. He was a representative from 1895 to 1912. The proposed bill much expanded upon existing law, Sulzer noted, and he was glad of it. The only governor of the State of New York ever to be impeached (in 1913), Sulzer on this afternoon further inflamed an already over-heated debate:

"If the immigration bars are ever let down in this matter, the Chinese will come into this country in droves, overrun the land, menace our domestic institutions, threaten our tranquility, imperil the Republic, and destroy American labor.

"This bill is for self-preservation. It is largely a racial question of supremacy and essentially for the protection of labor. We offer no apologies to the Chinese for this legislation, but we declare it the first duty of Congress to legislate for the rights of the American workmen . . . .

"In this matter, we should not quibble. We should not split hairs to favor the Chinaman." 35 Cong. Rec. 3794 (1902).

Over the next hour, a number of technical amendments were agreed to by voice vote. Disposition of only a few controversial amendments remained. Representative Charles E. Hooker (D–MS) offered one, proposing to relax certain conditions the bill would impose on the rights of Chinese travelers to enter the United States. Such rights had been expressly guaranteed in the Gresham–Yang Treaty, and Hooker thought the pending measure created undue interference. The amendment was defeated by voice vote.

Representative George Perkins (R–CA) proposed an amendment to augment the proposed statutory restrictions on Chinese in the Philippines with a grant of discretionary regulatory authority to the Philippines Commission. Such authority would give the commission flexibility to ameliorate unnecessarily harsh consequences from the War Department's implementation of the statute:

"We are endeavoring absolutely to preclude these people from coming into those islands as much as we are from coming into this country. I am thoroughly in accord with every provision of this act which is not illiberal and illogical; but when it comes down to a simple question of pure persecution, and unnecessary persecution at that, I believe we are putting on the statute books a law which, if extended to the islands that have recently come into our possession . . . will be doing something that is not worthy of this country, and that will react on us to such an extent that we will be heartily ashamed of ourselves . . . ." 35 Cong. Rec. 3801 (1902).

Representative Julius Kahn (R–CA) opposed the amendment, which was defeated on a voice vote.

Then Kahn offered Clark's seaman amendment, making unlawful the employment of any Chinese sailor on American-flagged vessels. Perkins made a point of order that the amendment was non-germane, because it regulated employment but was being added to legislation controlling immigration:

"It says it shall be unlawful—that is unlawful anywhere—for any vessel with an American register to have or employ in its care any Chinese person not entitled to admission to the United States." 35 Cong. Rec. 3803 (1902).

The chairman of the Committee of the Whole was prepared to rule on the point of order, on the basis of House Rule XVI, which required that all amendments be germane:

"No motion or proposition on a subject different from that under consideration shall be admitted under cover of an amendment."

In his ruling, the chairman stated:

"The Chair will say that if this amendment had been proposed to prohibit the presence as employees of Chinese persons on American ships touching American ports, where there would be an opportunity to escape from the ship from time to time, the Chair would have ruled that germane to the general purpose of the bill, which is to prohibit the entering of Chinese persons into American territory; but . . . (as) this bill is not engaged in the regulating of the employment of labor, but in excluding of persons of Chinese blood and descent from our territories, the Chair sustains the point of order." 35 Cong. Rec. 3803 (1902).

The ruling gave Kahn a way out of his procedural dilemma. Upon hearing it, the Californian responded immediately with an amendment that provided:

"And it shall be unlawful for any vessel holding an American register, *on a voyage terminating at an American port*, to have or employ in its crew any Chinese not entitled to admission into the United States or any portion of the territory of the United States to which such vessel plies, and any violation of this provision shall be punishable by a fine not exceeding $2,000." 35 Cong. Rec. 3803 (1902) (emphasis added).

Representative Perkins thought Kahn's new language was a mere circumvention of the rules and he had offered merely a cute evasion. "Mr. Chairman," said Perkins, "I submit it does not change it at all. It still regulates the employment of Chinese." 35 Cong. Rec. 3804 (1902).

The chairman entertained a bit of debate, then ruled once more:

"This bill is to prohibit the entrance of Chinese laborers into the United

States. Seamen are laborers within the distinctions made in this bill, and the amendment now before the committee proposes to prohibit the coming of such laborers into an American port. It is based upon the theory that great safeguards are needed to carry out the purpose of the law. The bill is full of provisions which are intended to guard against evasions of the law. For instance, upon page 10 of the bill it is provided that even the Chinese who are entitled under this bill to enter our ports can only come in at certain points of entry. In other words, the regulation of American ships or foreign ships bearing Chinese to our shores is prescribed by this bill. The Chair thinks, therefore, that with the modifications which have been made in the amendment, it is clearly in order and overrules the point of order." 35 Cong. Rec. 3804 (1902).

With the amendment now in order, further debate occurred, largely centered on whether the employment restrictions would protect American labor or destroy American shipping. By a vote of 100 ayes to 74 nays, the Clark seaman amendment carried.

Representative Clark had one more amendment to offer. Section 48 of the bill stated, "That the term 'Chinese' as used in this act, includes all persons who are Chinese by birth or descent." After the word "descent," Clark proposed to add: "And as well those of mixed blood and those of the full blood, as well as males as females; and wherever herein personal pronouns are used the masculine includes the feminine." 35 Cong. Rec. 3807 (1902).

Clark explained his thinking:

"I confess very frankly that at one time I thought the language used by the majority of the committee was sufficient; but when you take into consideration the fact that if you leave this phrase out about the mixed blood, every Chinese who wants to get into the United States will claim that he has another strain of blood in him, and you will never be able to find out the truth. I am in favor of fixing it so there can be no doubt about it, and that is what this amendment will do exactly." 35 Cong. Rec. 3807 (1902).

On a vote of 74 yeas and 70 nays, the amendment carried.

Two closing statements remained, one from each side of the aisle on this largely bipartisan bill. The first came from Representative Frank Wheeler Mondell (R–WY), who would serve in Congress for twenty-seven years, including four years as the House Majority Leader (1919–1923). He strongly supported the bill:

"The Chinaman in America is forever and always an alien. For the most part he does not attempt to be or appear to be anything else, and when he does, the veneer of Americanism is so thin as to disclose the Tartar at the slightest touch.

It is safe to say that no Chinaman ever landed on our shores who fulfilled the conditions . . . requisite in a useful immigrant.

"Not only does the Chinaman land on our shores without the slightest thought or expectation of adopting our views or of conforming to our methods, but he comes with habits fixed and inflexible, with racial characteristics and racial vices which render him unfit for American citizenship even if he desired it . . . .

"I am thankful, Mr. Chairman, that our portals are to be still more safely guarded against the coming of the yellow peril. I have no fear that continued escalation will affect in any way our trade with China; but if it should, it would be infinitely better that we never sold China a dollar's worth of our merchandise or produce than we should degrade our people by compelling them to compete with coolie labor or endanger our institutions by an influx of hordes of the heathen Chinee." 35 Cong. Rec, 3807–08 (1902).

Clark took the floor to summarize. Democrats had enjoyed great success in toughening the legislation:

"The situation about the bill is this: The Majority reported the bill; the Democratic minority reported a substitute, making the provisions more drastic. Every single solitary amendment that has been offered or adopted here today was contained in that Democratic substitute. Having got into the bill by way of amendment what we started to get into it, we shall not press the substitute, because we have already accomplished our object of making the bill stronger and more effective." 35 Cong. Rec. 3808 (1902).

Then the Committee of the Whole rose and reported the bill to the full House as amended.

No separate vote being demanded in the House on any of the amendments, they were agreed to en bloc. The Kahn bill, as amended, was read for the third time and passed by voice vote.

Having completed its work on August 7, 1902, the House would await the conclusion of Senate action, still more than a week off, with a conference to convene afterwards to settle differences between the chambers.

§9.40 Resolving Differences between the Senate and the House: The Senate Debate of April 17, 1902

On April 17, 1902, Senator Orville Platt (R–CT) called from the Senate calendar H.R. 13031, the House-passed exclusion bill. He successfully proposed an amendment to strike the text of the House bill and to substitute in its place the text of the Senate-passed bill. The Senate Committee of the Whole reported H.R. 13031, as amended by the substitute, to the full Senate, which passed the bill as amended. A conference with the House was sought.

§9.41 Resolving Differences between the Senate and the House: Further Proceedings on H.R. 13031, as amended

In general, House conferees were willing to accept the Senate's approach to exclusion extension but, as Senator Platt informed other senators, there was one point of outstanding disagreement. The House did not want to tie the extension of exclusion to the expiration of the Gresham–Yang Treaty:

"The House committee [sic] asks that the Senate conferees shall agree to eliminate from the amendment passed by the Senate as a substitute for the House bill that portion of the amendment which provides that the present laws shall be extended and continued while the treaty remains in force, and also the section which provides that if the treaty shall be terminated according to the provisions of the treaty, such laws so extended shall be continued in force until another treaty shall have been negotiated and appropriate laws to carry it into effect shall have been passed.

"The House committee asks us to eliminate that provision and to extend and continue the present laws, reenacting them indefinitely without limit as to time." 35 Cong. Rec. 4709 (1902).

The Senate conferees did not accede to the House request. To resolve the matter, Platt secured the Senate's agreement to a further conference with the House. Although the difference between the chambers was focused on this one issue, technically the entire conference remained open. Nothing was settled until everything was settled.

While the conference continued, Senator George Turner (D–WA) presented to the Senate a petition from the Chinese Exclusion Commission of the State of California. Placed in the *Congressional Record* on August 28, 1902, it urged conferees to reject the Senate substitute and support the House-passed bill.

Later on that same day, the conferees reached accord. The conference report largely bore the structure of the Senate proposal. The Senate no longer insisted on marrying the exclusion policy to the Gresham–Yang Treaty expiration dates (either 1904 or 1914). Instead, the legislation would continue in force indefinitely, so long as not inconsistent with treaty obligations, until otherwise provided by law.

The conferees agreed to bar immigration of Chinese laborers to U.S. insular possessions and to forbid the passage of such persons from the possessions to the mainland. They did not include the provision challenging birthright citizenship.

Certificates of residence would be required in the Philippines, but the system of implementing them was left to the Philippine Commission.

The language barring employment of Chinese seamen on American-flagged vessels was dropped.

By voice votes on April 28, 1902, both the Senate and the House agreed to the conference report. After President Theodore Roosevelt signed it on April 29, 1902, the 1902 extension legislation became law.

CHAPTER TEN

美
國

Permanent Law, 1904

"They came as peons, held by the great companies in chains of serfdom. They came with their filth and opium, and their pagan rites and superstitions, with their utter lack of morals, with their imitative skill and patient industry. They came in ignorance of the worth of their toil and incapable of individual contact. They came ready to live on their frugal meals of rice and the flesh of rats and mice and cats. They lived as ants live. They burrowed in droves, sleeping in the fumes of opium."

—Senator Thomas Patterson (D–CO)
38 Cong. Rec. 4473 (1904)

"China today is weak and helpless, but China some day will be strong and aggressive; and I hope that the relations of this country with that Empire may be such that when that day comes we shall have the good will and sympathy and not the hatred of that great people."

—Senator Jacob Gallinger (R–NH)
38 Cong. Rec. 5419 (1904)

§10.0 Overview

- Considered in the 58th Congress of the United States (1903–1905)
- Senate Party Division: 56 Republicans, 28 Democrats, 5 Independents, 1 Vacancy
- House Party Division: 209 Republicans, 176 Democrats, 1 Independent
- President: Theodore Roosevelt (R) (September 14, 1901 – March 4, 1909)

In 1904, China withdrew from the Gresham–Yang Treaty. Wanting to assert control over U.S. immigration policy, and no longer tethered to any bilateral agreements with China, Congress simply reenacted the 1902 extension permanently and unconditionally.

§10.10 Senate Debate, April 8, 1904: S. 5344: Separating laws and treaties

Under consideration, S. 5344
(Senator Thomas Patterson (D–CO)).

In January 1904, the Chinese government notified the U.S. Department of State that the Gresham–Yang Treaty would not be extended. As a result, the treaty would expire on December 7, 1904.

On April 8, 1904, Senator Thomas Patterson (D–CO) brought before the Senate S. 5344, legislation extending the Chinese exclusion laws permanently. The senator was greatly concerned about the effect of China's treaty renunciation, believing it would bring the terms of the 1880 Angell Treaty back into force. Under the Angell Treaty, the United States could restrict or suspend the immigration of Chinese laborers, but not absolutely prohibit it (*§ 3.10*). Such prohibition was in fact permitted for a minimum of ten years by the Gresham–Yang Treaty. But because as of December 1904, China would no longer be bound to that prohibition, a statute conditioned upon harmony with treaty obligations could be subject to legal challenge.

Patterson was not willing to revert to the more permissive policies of earlier years, and did not think the public would want to do so either: "The time of the debates is not so remote from the present generation that their recurrence is needed to prick the American instinct of self-preservation from the yellow peril into activity." 38 Cong. Rec. 4473 (1904).

Remedial legislation was needed, Patterson insisted. Without it "every barrier against Chinese immigration that has been built will be removed on the 7th of December next, and the ports of the country will be thrown open to the unrestricted coming of the Chinese hordes . . . ." 38 Cong. Rec. 4473 (1904).

Patterson said the problem arose from the conference report on the 1902 law (*see discussion in § 9.41*), which attempted to ensure harmony between U.S. legislation and Sino-American treaties. The conference report stated:

"All laws not in force prohibiting and regulating the coming of Chinese persons and persons of Chinese descent into the United States and the residence of such persons therein . . . are hereby reenacted, extended, and continued so far as the same are not inconsistent with treaty obligations." 38 Cong. Rec. 4475 (1904).

The Gresham–Yang Treaty superseded rather than extinguished the Angell Treaty of 1880 and the Burlingame Treaty of 1868. Once the Gresham–Yang Treaty was no longer in force, the earlier treaties would spring back to life, Patterson said. The senator did not believe the 1902 immigration prohibitions could be sustained after the Gresham–Yang Treaty ceased to operate in December 1904. Litigation would strike them down:

"The Supreme Court would clearly hold that the purpose of Congress in the enactment of this law was to keep its statutory provisions in harmony with treaty obligations. Whenever the law was contested if it were contested before December 7, the question would be whether it was in conflict with the obligations of that treaty because it was in existence. If the question arose after the abrogation of the treaty of 1894, then the question before the Supreme Court would necessarily be 'what treaty obligations are in existence?' The treaty of 1894 is at an end. The treaty of 1880 or the treaty of 1868, either one or the other or both, so far as they are not in conflict are revived. And looking at existing treaty obligations, the court would be bound to declare that the law was invalid." 38 Cong. Rec. 4476 (1904).

Senator Patterson proposed to divorce exclusion policy from treaties, by amending the 1902 law to strike the words "so far as the same are not inconsistent with treaty obligations."

The Second Special Session of the 58th Congress (December 7, 1903–April 28, 1904) was due to conclude by the end of April, 1904. Patterson opined that, in the few remaining weeks, there might not be time to accomplish his purposes by passing a stand-alone measure. The most expeditious path would be to include these provisions in an appropriations bill, which Congress was due to pass before adjournment:

"This may be accomplished by a separate act, or, if there is not time for that—and there is no disposition upon any part of anybody to prolong the present session—a proper amendment can be added to the sundry civil appropriation bill when the clause that provides funds for carrying into effect the exclusion laws is reached. It is a matter of a few words and twenty minutes of time . . . ." 38 Cong. Rec. 4478 (1904).

The Senate would defer further action until the House sent over an appropriations bill containing exclusion provisions.

§10.20 Senate Debate, April 22, 1904: H.R. 15054: "There would have been great trouble"

Under consideration in the Senate Committee of the Whole, H.R. 15054, a supplemental appropriations bill for the Fiscal Year ending June 30, 1904.

In H.R. 15054, the House of Representatives used a supplemental appropriations bill for the Fiscal Year ending June 30, 1904, as a vehicle for language that separated the Chinese exclusion laws from U.S. treaty commitments and included aggressive provisions to tighten the laws, not just to extend them. In the House bill:

- Section 5 reenacted the 1902 law (*Chapter Nine*), dropping the requirement that such be consistent with treaties.
- Section 6 stated that entry of persons of Chinese descent would be limited to only those "who are citizens of the United States by reason of birth and those who are specifically granted by law such privilege, and no other." 38 Cong. Rec. 5310 (1904).
- Section 7 defined the terms "Chinese person" or "person of Chinese descent" to be an individual of the "Mongolian race" whose ancestors were, prior to the year 1800, subjects of the emperor of China; further, that the statement of an immigration inspector that an individual was a Chinese person would be presumptively valid.
- Section 8 stated that the term "laborers" meant any Chinese person not expressly authorized by law to enter or to remain in the United States.
- Section 9 allowed immigration officers to decide claims of citizenship, subject only to an appeal to the secretary of the treasury. No appeal to the courts was permissible.

§10.21 Reaction from China to the 1904 Legislation

On the other side of the Pacific, Chinese were stunned by the news from Washington. On May 10, 1904, the Headquarters of the Shanghai Commerce Association called the Board of Trustees to a meeting, and a decision was made to urge all merchants home and abroad not to deal in goods from the United States. The action, which won wide support, lasted for a whole year. It was the first national boycott in Chinese history.

I-yao Shen, *A Century of Chinese Exclusion Abroad* (Beijing: Foreign Languages Press, 2006), pp. 47–48.

The following year, however, President Theodore Roosevelt tried to ease up.

President Roosevelt has sent a letter to Secretary Metcalf of the Department of Commerce and Labor directing him to see that the immigration officers exercise discretion in the enforcement of the Chinese exclusion law, to the end that the relations of this Government with China may continue to be cordial.

"President Aids Chinese: Issues Order for Discretion in Enforcing Exclusion Laws." *The New York Times*, June 15, 1905.

The threats of Chinese at Shanghai and other ports to boycott American goods in retaliation for operation of the exclusion act in the United States appears to have had the desired effect. President Roosevelt has directed the "exercise of discretion in the enforcement of the exclusion law, to the end that the relations of this government with China may continue cordial." That is to say, in order to please eastern manufacturers who are courting Chinese trade the Pacific coast ports shall leave their gates slightly ajar for the Chinaman's convenience.

Los Angeles Herald, June 16, 1905, p. 6.

- Section 10 was a technical section that made no changes to substantive law.
- Section 11 authorized different rights of appeal from decisions by immigration officers that did not involve citizenship claims. These rights strongly advantaged the government over the immigrant. An individual

§10.22 In the Year of Permanent Exclusion: The Detention of Soong Ailing

Soong Ailing was the eldest of three girls in the Soong family of Shanghai. All three came to great prominence in twentieth-century China. Soong Ailing married H.H. Kung, a descendent of Confucius, a major financier, and a minister in Chiang Kaishek's Nationalist Government. The middle sister, Soong Chingling, married the founder of the Republic of China, Sun Yat-sen, and in her later years was a revered figure in the People's Republic of China. The youngest sister, Soong Meiling married Chiang Kaishek and was China's First Lady.

Their father was Charlie (C.J.) Soong, who was trained in missionary work at Vanderbilt University. All three girls were reared as Christians and were sent to the United States for education. For more about C.J. Soong, see "The Soong's Saga," Vanderbilt University, Divinity Library (2009).

In 1904, in the company of missionaries, Ailing journeyed to America. It was the year that the Chinese exclusion policy became permanent. Ailing traveled on a Portuguese passport that her father had obtained for her in Macao, in cabin class on a vessel called the *Korea*. As the ship docked in San Francisco, Ailing was rudely welcomed. Meiling's biographer, Hannah Pakula, recounts what happened upon Ailing's arrival in the United States:

> When they docked and began unloading, Ailing, who was surprised to see "white men doing coolies' work," presented her passport for inspection in the lounge.
>
> "Trying to get by on one of these things, are you?" the immigration officer said. "That's been tried by a lot of other Chinese, little sister. It won't work. You just stay here until we're ready to take you to the detention home."
>
> "You cannot put me in a detention home," Ailing snapped back. "I am a cabin-class passenger, not from the steerage."
>
> "You certainly won't put her in a detention home," added Anna Lanius.* "I'm staying right here to see that you don't." One of the immigration officers agreed, referring to the detention home in question—a cell block on the waterfront—as "not fit for a self-respecting animal." Ailing, he said, should remain on the *Korea* until a ship could be found to take her back to China . . . . Ailing remained in custody for another two weeks, transferred from

§10.22 In the Year of Permanent Exclusion: The Detention of Soong Ailing (continued)

one ship to another, until Reid** finally reached Washington and arranged for her to enter the United States.

Hannah Pakula, *The Last Empress: Madame Chiang Kaishek and the Birth of Modern China* (Simon & Schuster, 2009), p. 22.

Many Chinese were detained upon arrival, especially at the Angel Island Immigration Station in San Francisco Bay, for periods far exceeding that which Soong Ailing experienced.

*Among the missionaries was Anna Lanius.

** Dr. Reid was a missionary based in San Francisco.

could appeal an adverse decision to the U.S. district court, and could seek review of an adverse district court ruling by applying for writ of certiorari to the Supreme Court. But such writs are rarely granted. Conversely, the federal government was given a right to appeal adverse decisions directly to the court of appeals and thereafter to the Supreme Court.

- Section 12 transferred certain authority from the Department of the Treasury to the (then-named) Department of Commerce and Labor.
- Section 13 allowed for the commissioner-general of immigration, subject to the approval of the (then-named) secretary of commerce and labor, to grant exceptions from expulsion for persons who had entered the U.S. prior to December 8, 1894, and to except from exclusion persons who had rendered "meritorious service" to the United States government.

According to Senator Orville Platt (R–CT), the vaguely expressed concept of "meritorious service" meant rewarding informers:

"It shows that the desire to keep out Chinese laborers is not so real a desire after all; because if one Chinese laborer turns informer and testifies against one who is trying to get in, the informer may be permitted to remain in the United States. It is said that they have given evidence in smuggling cases; but the real point of it is to offer an inducement to a Chinaman who might be expelled from this country to get a right to remain here by testifying against another Chinaman who wants to get in. I do not think we ought to do that." 38 Cong. Rec. 5418 (1904).

Senator Shelby Cullom (R–IL) proposed an amendment to the supplemental appropriations bill that would strike all House-passed exclusion provisions, except Section 5, which simply reenacted the 1902 legislation without the words "insofar as the same are not inconsistent with treaty obligations."

Senator Weldon B. Heyburn (R–ID), who served from 1903 to 1912, offered an amendment to the House language that Cullom proposed to strike. Heyburn's amendment would have permitted excluded Chinese to be admitted as workers in the Panama Canal Zone (under construction 1903–1914); provided, however, that such entry was for canal work only and that it did not constitute a waiver from exclusion or deportation from the United States.

Thereafter, the Senate began voting. Under its rules of procedure, the Senate would vote first on the Heyburn amendment. It was defeated on a voice vote. A vote followed on Cullom's amendment to strike all exclusion provisions but Section 5. It was agreed to, also by voice vote.

As amended, H.R. 15054 passed. The House later accepted the Senate's amendments. Unleashed from any treaty obligations, the policy of Chinese exclusion was thus made permanent.

Before Senate action was taken on the amendments, Senator William Stewart (R–NV) reprised his role in stopping Senator Charles Sumner's (R–MA) naturalization amendment thirty-four years earlier (*§ 1.20*). In the twilight of his long Senate career, Stewart wore this history proudly. On Saturday, July 2, 1870, the Senate had agreed to Sumner's effort to strike "white" from the naturalization laws. Stewart reviewed what transpired next:

"The then Senator from Oregon, Mr. Williams, and myself started in to protest. We kept up the debate on Saturday. Monday was the 4th, and the bill went over to Monday, when, by explaining the effect of naturalizing the Chinese, we gained converts—not a majority, but a very respectable minority. Finally, a compromise was effected extending the naturalization laws to the whites and persons of African descent, thus leaving out the Asiatics." 38 Cong. Rec. 5418 (1904).

Stewart's trophy was Chinese exclusion.

"At that time there were probably 125,000 Chinese in the United States. If they had been allowed to be naturalized and become voters, there probably never would have been any exclusion, but there would have been great trouble." 38 Cong. Rec. 5418 (1904).

CHAPTER ELEVEN

美
國

Repeal

"Nations, like individuals, make mistakes. We must be big enough to acknowledge our mistakes of the past and to correct them."
  —President Franklin Delano Roosevelt
  October 11, 1943
  89 Cong. Rec. 8576 (1943)

"Is that where Americans want to leave the matter? Do we still want officially to stigmatize as congenitally inferior because their skins happen to be yellow instead of white, black, or red, the Chinese people?"
  —Representative Walter Judd (R–MN)
  89 Cong. Rec. 8588 (1943)

§11.0 Overview

- Considered in the 78th Congress of the United States (1941–1943)
- Senate Party Division: 58 Democrats, 37 Republicans, 1 Independent
- House Party Division: 222 Democrats, 209 Republicans, 4 Independents
- President: Franklin D. Roosevelt (1933–1945)

During the Second World War, President Franklin D. Roosevelt asked Congress to end the Chinese exclusion laws. The existence of such discriminatory, racial laws had been fodder for Japanese wartime propaganda within China. Both the Roosevelt and Chiang Kaishek governments were concerned about the corrosive effect of such propaganda on Chinese morale.

Anxious to reinforce America's alliance with China against a common Japanese enemy, the president sought repeal of Chinese exclusion laws. Although there was some dissent in both the House and the Senate, and labor and veterans organizations expressed misgivings, repeal was broadly supported by Democrats and Republicans in both chambers and passed by voice votes.

§11.10 The Last Emperor, China, Japan, and WWII

By 1943, the Chinese exclusion policy had been in effect for over sixty years. Nearly four decades had passed since Congress had made the restrictions on immigration and the denial of naturalization rights permanent (*Chapter Ten*). More than seventy years had elapsed since Senator Charles Sumner's failed amendment, which would have granted the Chinese the chance for American citizenship (*Chapter One*).

In the meantime, open immigration had been replaced by a less permissive country quota system, which Chinese could not access because they were subject to the exclusion laws.

Since the last of the exclusion acts had passed in 1904, China had undergone massive changes. The Qing Dynasty, which had reigned from 1644, fell in 1911.

After a period of internal upheaval and conflicts with local warlords, the writ of the Republic of China ran across most of the country. Founded on January 1, 1912, by Sun Yat-sen (1866–1925), the republic was in 1943 under the leadership of Generalissimo Chiang Kaishek and the Guomindang Party (Chinese Nationalist Party, also Kuomintang of China, or KMT).

Since 1927, Chiang had been engaged in a civil war with the Chinese Communists. In 1943, the Communists were essentially confined to a stronghold in north central China, observing with Chiang a rough version of a ceasefire, so that both sides could pursue a united front in the war against Japan.

The Japanese war started in 1931, when Japan occupied Manchuria, installing the abdicated Qing Emperor, Puyi, on the throne as a figurehead. The occupation expanded into a general Sino-Japanese war, following a violent incident on July 7, 1937, at the Marco Polo Bridge near Beijing.

Japan had swept through eastern China, occupying Beijing and Shanghai, before routing Chiang from his capital at Nanjing in late 1937. While Japan established a puppet regime in Nanjing under Wang Jing-wei, Chiang relocated 800 miles to the west, across the Yangtze River gorges, setting up his government in Chongqing.

For more than four years, China stood essentially alone against Japan. The Pearl Harbor attack of December 7, 1941, thrust China and the United States into an anti-Japanese alliance. Long pilloried in Congress for backwardness, China became a symbol of heroism and resistance.

On February 18, 1943, Madame Chiang (Soong Meiling, *see § 10.22*) journeyed to Capitol Hill to address separate meetings of the House and the Senate. Educated in the United States between 1907 and 1917, Madame Chiang was an immensely effective emissary to Congress from a war-torn ally. Her galvanizing presence, the fact of the alliance itself, the exigencies of America's war effort in the Far East, the work of grassroots American leaders, and a call from President Franklin Roosevelt, led that year to the repeal of Chinese exclusion legislation.

Soong Meiling's friendship with Henry R. Luce, a prominent American publisher who was born in China in 1898, contributed greatly to her popularity and acceptance by American politicians. There are several books on the connection, for example, Robert E. Herzstein, *Henry R. Luce, Time, and the American Crusade in Asia* (Cambridge University Press, 2005).

§11.20 The House Committee Report, October 11, 1943, and H.R. 3070

On October 11, 1943, the House Committee on Immigration and Naturalization favorably reported H.R. 3070, legislation introduced by Representative Warren Magnuson (D–WA), repealing the Chinese exclusion laws. The Committee Report (Repealing the Chinese Exclusion Laws: Report, H. Rep. 78–732) succinctly described the bill's purpose:

"The legislation proposed in this bill is for the purpose of repealing the Chinese exclusion laws, to place Chinese persons on a small quota basis, and to make persons of the Chinese race eligible to become naturalized citizens." H.R. Rep. No. 78–732, at 1.

Under the Immigration Act of 1924 (P.L. 68–139, 43 Stat. 153, enacted May 26, 1924), China was granted an annual quota of one hundred persons eligible for admission to the United States. But as the report noted, the quota of one hundred had to be filled by persons born in China who were not themselves racially Chinese, because "existing provisions of law prohibit, generally speaking, the coming to the United States of Chinese, they being persons of a race ineligible for citizenship." H.R. Rep. No. 78–732, at 2.

H.R. 3070 would reform this regrettable policy, by placing Chinese under a unique quota of 105 persons worldwide. An individual of Chinese descent coming from any country other than China would be charged against the Chinese quota, rather than his own country's quota. So that the entire 105 would not be absorbed by persons from outside China, the legislation provided that 75 percent of the quota be allocated to persons born and resident in China.

The bill, H.R. 3070, also removed the bar to citizenship for Chinese. A preliminary step in this direction had been taken on March 27, 1942, in the Second War Powers Act. 56 Stat. 176 (1942), in which persons serving in the U.S. military were made eligible for naturalization. The barrier to Chinese citizenship having been partially breached by the Second War Powers Act, the House Committee on Immigration and Naturalization proposed to finish the job and remove statutory impediments to the Chinese.

For Chinese persons to take advantage of these new rights, they had to have been lawful permanent residents of the United States. Due to the exclusion laws, only a relative handful of Chinese were in that status. Many of the foreign-born Chinese then in America had been temporarily admitted as students, or perhaps as professors or government ministers, but they were not permanent residents. As a result, the initial impact of the legislation was symbolic. Fears expressed by

§11.21 The Structure of the National Origins Quota System

The new national origins quota system was among a series of measures that marked a new era in American immigration history. The system used the number of previous immigrants and their descendents to formulate a quota of how many from a country could enter annually. The Quota Act of 1921 provided that the total number of immigrants to the United States should be 357,803 for each year and the quota for each nation was set at three percent of the number of people descended from each nationality recorded in the 1910 census. Three years later, this act was replaced by the Quota Act of 1924, which reduced the number of immigrants to 164,677 and the quota was changed to two percent of the population from each nationality according to the 1890 census.

I-yao Shen, *A Century of Chinese Exclusion Abroad* (Beijing: Foreign Languages Press, 2006), p. 49.

some in Congress about an immigration influx of Chinese hordes, or a massive padding of the voter rolls, were groundless. As the House Committee on Immigration and Naturalization noted, under the new law not many Chinese would be admitted or could secure American citizenship:

"The number of Chinese who will actually be made eligible for citizenship under this section is negligible. There are approximately 45,000 alien Chinese persons in the United States (continental, territorial, and insular). However, a large number of these Chinese have never been admitted to the United States for lawful permanent residence, which is a condition precedent to naturalization and, therefore, many of this number would not be eligible for naturalization, not because of racial disability, but because they cannot meet statutory requirements of law. The number of Chinese who will be made eligible in the future, in addition to those already here, will of necessity be very small because the quota for China is limited to 105 per annum as provided in section 2 of the bill." H.R. Rep. No. 78–732, at 3.

The House Committee on Immigration and Naturalization recognized that the exclusion laws had been a "source of misunderstanding" in Sino-American relations and had "aroused widespread resentment" in China. The committee cited purely economic motives as being the reason these laws were enacted

§11.22 The War Brides Act of 1945

Barriers to immigration for the Chinese were lowered after the war concluded, again in connection with military service, under the War Brides Act of 1945. (H.R. 4857; P.L. 79-271; 59 Stat 659. 79th Congress, December 28, 1945).

> After World War II, the U.S. Government decided to overhaul [its] immigration to reward Chinese American veterans for their service. The 1945 War Brides Act permitted them to marry in China and bring their wives to the United States. Given the low number of Chinese women at home (the male-female ratio was three to one), many servicemen decided to wed foreign-born Chinese women. Before the act expired on December 30, 1949, almost six thousand Chinese American soldiers went to China and returned with brides. For many, there was no time for elaborate rituals or lengthy, romantic courtships. They faced not only the deadline of the Act's expiration date but also the time constraints of their own furloughs . . . . As a result of such hasty marriages, after the war about 80 percent of all new Chinese arrivals were female.

Iris Chang, *The Chinese in America* (Penguin Books, 2003) p. 234.

in the first place. Changes had occurred in the years since the first of the laws was enacted in 1882, the committee said, and these changes had caused a reassessment of China and the discriminatory laws Congress had passed against the Chinese:

"We have had time and abundant occasion to reflect on the extraordinary qualities of the Chinese people. Above all, the tenacity and courage of the Chinese in their terrible ordeal of the last seven years has impelled a respect that we are proud to acknowledge . . . .

"It is fitting, therefore, that the incongruity of discriminatory legislation, inconsistent with the dignity of both our peoples, should be eliminated." H.R. Rep. No. 78–732, at 4.

For himself and three other committee members, Representative John B. Bennett (R–MI) filed minority views. Bennett was in his first term in the House. Defeated for re-election in 1944, he won in 1946 and served until 1964. In the minority views, Bennett and others opposed the bill because they felt that longstanding immigration policy should not be changed during wartime. Immigration, they stated, could be anticipated to be a significant matter for postwar debate. Bennett and his allies proposed to defer the question for comprehensive discussion once the war was over.

Their second objection dealt with the piecemeal unraveling of what was known as the Asiatic Barred Zone. The zone had been created in the Immigration Act of 1917. Extending policies originally developed in Chinese exclusion legislation, the 1917 Act put the United States off-limits to peoples from much of the east and south Asia region. Repealing the Chinese Exclusion Acts would have the effect of putting Chinese in a preferred position as against other Asians, who would remain barred. Such inequities would inevitably drive demand from non-Chinese peoples for increased immigration, the congressmen feared.

The minority views also complained that the legislation was largely an empty gesture. Paradoxically, because of the unique nature of the Chinese quota arrangement, the bill perpetuated discrimination against Chinese:

"This bill simply extends the Chinese a few 'crumbs' and does not put them on an equality basis with other nations because, for example, in the case of other nationalities or races, they may be admitted from other countries as non-quota aliens when born in non-quota countries [such countries included most of the Western Hemisphere except a few West Indian Islands], or when coming here as the members of a family of a citizen parent. While under this bill, any Chinese, no matter in what country he was born, is charged to the Chinese quota." H.R. Rep. No. 78–732, part 2, at 2.

Emphasizing that they bore no racial prejudice against Chinese people, the minority members urged that all possible aid be given to China in the war against Japan. But the proposed legislation would do nothing important for the war effort, they alleged, and was counterproductive as a matter of domestic policy:

"This type of legislation is of no material benefit to China. It amounts to nothing more than a feeble gesture to do a futile thing at the expense of a sound and long-established rule of immigration." H.R. Rep. No. 78–732, part 2, at 2.

On October 7, 1943, Representative Samuel Dickstein (D–NY), chairman of the Committee on Immigration and Naturalization, filed H.R. 3070 and the accompanying Committee Report with the clerk of the House, who in turn referred it to the House Committee of the Whole.

§11.30 H.R. 3070 and House Debate, October 20, 1943: "Important in the cause of winning the war"

Under consideration: H. Res. 314, providing a procedure
for consideration of H.R. 3070, the bill repealing the Chinese
exclusion laws. Later under consideration, H.R. 3070 itself.

On October 20, 1943, Chairman Adolph J. Sabath (D–IL) of the House Rules Committee brought to the floor of the House H. Res. 314, a procedural resolution to govern consideration of H.R. 3070. Sabath was a member of the House from 1907 until 1949. The procedural resolution, also known as a "rule," provided that the bill would be considered for up to four hours of debate and that it would be open to amendments.

Sabath told the House that existing law permitted the Japanese to significantly damage American interests in China: "Their propaganda stresses that we are not, in fact, a friend of China because we discriminate against her nationals." 89 Cong. Rec. 8573 (1943).

Reflecting the importance of Madame Chiang (*§ 11.10*), Sabath commented on her 1943 visit to the House to call for aid to China and draw attention to the war in her country:

"I do not see how anyone who was present and heard the urgent plea of that great woman, Madame Chiang Kaishek, in this House, can possibly oppose this meritorious, just legislation." 89 Cong. Rec. 8573 (1943).

Sabath noted that the original exclusion legislation had been a response to labor competition, parroting the rationale that it had been enacted purely for economic protection. But in light of the damage these laws would impose on America's military objectives, there was no longer sufficient justification to continue them:

"I feel it is our duty to remove, and justice demands that we should as speedily as possible remove, from Japanese propagandists the opportunity to create resentment by China, and therefore discord to our Allied Nations' effort." 89 Cong. Rec. 8573 (1943).

Representative Samuel Dickstein (D–NY), the chairman of the House Immigration and Naturalization Committee, interrupted Sabath to emphasize this point. The committee had received testimony, Dickstein said, of the breadth and effect of such exploitation by the Japanese:

"The evidence before our committee definitely establishes the fact that there is short-wave propaganda by Japan almost daily and weekly, advising the Chinese that we are just using them as a means to our own end, and that we do

§11.31 Madame Chiang Kaishek Speaks to the Senate and to the House, February 18, 1943

The House was packed, with many wives sitting on the steps, as Meiling made a dramatic entrance, with her four-inch heels failing to prevent her diminutive frame from being dwarfed by the cluster of tall men protectively surrounding her as she walked down the center aisle. Congressmen held their small daughters on their knees . . . .

Diminutive and erect, clenching a white silk handkerchief in her right hand and tracing the lines of her speech with red-lacquered fingernails, Meiling spoke slowly, in soft, clear tones imbued with "tremendous vitality." Her English was flawlessly American, a pleasing mix of "Georgia softness and Massachusetts cultivation," resonant yet gentle, neither Southern drawl nor Yankee twang. She had an extraordinary mastery of drama and timing, beginning a sentence in a low tone, then working up to an emotional crescendo, only to drop her voice at exactly the right moment before raising it again to drive home her point.

Laura Tyson Li, *Madame Chiang Kai-shek: China's Eternal First Lady* (Atlantic Monthly Press, 2006), pp. 200-201.

According to the official record of [Meiling's] visit,* "a veritable storm of cheering and handclapping" followed the end of her address, which was carried live on radio. "Goddam it," said one congressman, "I never saw anything like it. Mme. Chiang had me on the verge of bursting into tears." It was a brilliant presentation, carefully thought out, engagingly presented. If the Chinese are known for face, the substitution of the correct appearance for the reality, the effects of Madame Chiang's two appearances before the Congress have probably seldom been equaled.

Hannah Pakula, *The Last Empress: Madame Chiang Kai-shek and the Birth of Modern China* (Simon & Schuster, 2009), p. 421.

* Referring to her speech before the House of Representatives. An audio recording of the speech is available online (link at <*TCNFCA.com*>).

not intend to use them in the proper way; that they belong to Japan and that they should form oriental unity with Japan to fight the United States." 89 Cong. Rec. 8573 (1943).

The hearing record to which Dickstein referred contained powerfully worded samples of Japanese propaganda transcripts. The samples were compelling because they contained more than a kernel of truth. Reference was made to the "Chungking authorities," which referred to Chiang Kaishek's government. (Chungking is written as "Chongqing" in the Mandarin pinyin transliteration, and will be found that way on modern maps of China.) An excerpt from one of the propaganda samples that Dickstein read on the House floor said:

"In all the colonies of the dominions of the British Empire, and most conspicuously of all, in the United States, which makes the greatest pretense of professing justice and equality, the Chinese along with other Asiatics are treated as pariahs, unworthy of enjoying the simple rights or courtesies accorded to other people as a matter of fact. The Chungking authorities must certainly know that Chinese are rigidly prohibited from emigrating to the United States and that this ban on Chinese immigration was established in the latter portion of the last century after a campaign of venomous vilification of the character of the Chinese people.

"The Chungking authorities must know that the few Chinese who are temporarily permitted to enter the United States such as international merchants, professional men, and tourists, are forced to undergo the most humiliating and discourteous treatment and detention at the various immigration stations. They are practically treated like a class apart from the rest of humanity. The Chungking authorities must also know that in most of the cities in America, unfriendly social pressure forces the few Chinese who have managed to establish their residence there, to live in segregated Chinatowns, located in the most disreputable district. Chungking authorities must also know that, throughout the greatest part of the Western States of America, the Chinese are rigidly prohibited through crafty legal racial restrictions from residing anywhere except in the most undesirable neighborhoods.

"The Chungking authorities must also know that Chinese are rigidly excluded from attaining American citizenship by naturalization, a right which is accorded to the lowest immigrant from Europe. The Chungking authorities must also know that the social customs in America force the Chinese to remain in the most menial of occupations, despised and mistreated, and at best patronizingly tolerated with a contemptuous humor." 89 Cong. Rec. 8573 (1943).

The many Congresses that enacted the exclusion laws and barred Chinese

§11.32 Extraterritoriality and Other Concessions

Starting with the Opium Wars of the 1840s, first Britain, then France and the United States, and finally Japan and Germany all brought pressure to bear on China from along its eastern seaboard. In part because they were wary of one another and feared triggering a territorial scramble, the powers for the most part did not seize land or establish direct colonial rule. But they did demand and, thanks to their superior coercive power, were able to extract extraordinary concessions. Through a series of "unequal treaties," foreigners claimed "rights, privileges, dignities, and prerogatives which . . . backed by force, developed . . . into a special corpus of international law controlling practically every aspect of Chinese life." In addition to the so-called treaty ports, where they controlled trade and were beyond the reach of local law, foreign powers used gunboats to protect businessman and missionaries upriver, and, in general, to extend their influence deep into the interior.

Aaron L. Friedberg, *A Contest for Supremacy: China, America, and the Struggle for Mastery in Asia* (W.W. Norton & Company, 2011), pp. 15-16.

from citizenship had developed a lengthy debate record that denigrated China's people and civilization. Often, viciously bigoted rhetoric marked those debates. Now, in wartime, it was the Japanese who were stereotyped, and the Chinese were somehow cleansed of stigma. Sabath continued:

"The Chinese people cannot be charged with being derelict or disloyal. They cannot be charged with not being law abiding. It cannot be charged that they are repugnant and dishonest, because everyone who has come into contact with the Chinese people recognizes that they are so much different from the Japanese that there is no comparison." 89 Cong. Rec. 8573 (1943).

Next to speak was Representative Hamilton Fish III (R–NY), a member from 1920 to 1945. A scion of American politics, Fish was a grandson of a secretary of state and father of a thirteen-term member of the House, Hamilton Fish IV (R–NY, 1969–1995). Normally an opponent of President Franklin Roosevelt, Fish III supported the repeal legislation. In addition, he advocated legislation calling for an end to American extraterritorial rights in China.

Like the exclusion laws, extraterritorial privileges were a bone in the Chinese throat. These extraterritorial rights had been granted by China in the nineteenth century, under foreign coercion. They gave Western nations legal status in China that was supreme over local law.

Extraterritoriality was a vestige of colonialism, and Fish could see no justification for it. Strengthening bilateral relations required abjuring extraterritorial rights along with repealing exclusion. The United States, along with the United Kingdom, renounced extraterritorial privileges very early in 1943, the same year that the exclusion laws ended.

Representative Everett M. Dirksen (R–IL) asked to speak next. A member of the House from 1933 to 1949, Dirksen served in the Senate from 1951 until his death in 1969, including tenure as Senate Minority Leader from 1959 to 1969.

Although he would support repeal, Representative Dirksen did not believe that the laws were a mistake when first enacted:

"I do not agree with the President that mistake was made on Chinese exclusion 60 years ago. The essential point is that the condition was different from what it is today. Chinese exclusion back in 1879, which was the date of the first act that was enacted, was aimed as much against the abuses of our own people as much as it was against the Chinese." 89 Cong. Rec. 8575 (1943).

Dirksen took special note of the political situation that had driven exclusion in the prior century. He quoted from the 1884 Democratic and Republican platforms, to demonstrate how continuing and tightened enforcement of the exclusion laws had become an article of faith for both parties:

"In the Democratic national platform of 1884 it is stated, 'American civilization demands that against the immigration or importation of Mongolians to these shores, our gates are closed.' In that same year, the Republican platform denounced the importation of contract labor and stated further, 'We pledge ourselves to sustain the present law restricting Chinese immigration and to provide such further legislation as is necessary to carry out its purpose.' " 89 Cong. Rec. 8575 (1943).

Now that the issue of contract labor had disappeared, there was no longer a purpose served by anti-Chinese immigration restrictions, said Dirksen.

"I believe it is high time to put that great republic in the Orient on the same basis with some of the other countries and give them the benefit of the quota statute." 89 Cong. Rec. 8575 (1943).

Representative Noah M. Mason (R–IL) followed Dirksen. Elected to the House in 1937, he served until 1963. Mason reviewed the 1924 quota law, explaining how it operated. The system was confusing, Mason said, and he wanted his colleagues to understand why China would be subject to a quota of 105 persons permitted to immigrate annually.

§11.33 The Europe-first Strategy

Following the Pearl Harbor attack on December 7, 1941, President Franklin Roosevelt and Britain's Prime Minister Winston Churchill conducted a series of meetings in Washington, DC, known as the Arcadia Conference. Held between December 22, 1941, and January 14, 1942, the conference reaffirmed the policy of giving top priority to the war in Europe, over the fighting in Asia and the Pacific.

There was a vocal school in the United States that thought America's central focus should be Japan, not Germany. That Japan would consume Roosevelt worried Churchill as he wandered the White House. As Roosevelt and his generals saw it, however, Hitler represented the most significant long-term threat. "The principle of Germany first was based strictly on military reasoning," [White House aide Robert] Sherwood wrote. "It was assumed—and, it would seem from the results, correctly—that Germany had far greater potential than Japan in productive power and scientific genius, and, if time to develop this during years of stalemate in Europe, would prove all the more difficult if not impossible to defeat." It would be Hitler first, Tojo after.

Jon Meacham, *Franklin and Winston* (Random House, 2003), p. 140.

For Churchill, the moment of truth had come. He was edgy, desperate to know how Pearl Harbor had affected the President's thinking. Would Roosevelt stick to the old "Europe-first" strategy? Or would he yield to the public clamor that he strike out against Imperial Japan? FDR obviously appreciated the Prime Minister's concerns and immediately assured him that there would be no change in strategy from "Europe-first." Churchill was greatly relieved. His worst fears had been laid to rest.

David Bercuson and Holger Herwig, *One Christmas in Washington* (The Overlook Press, 2005), pp. 126–127.

Due to the effects of the exclusion acts, in 1920 there were 74,000 Chinese in the United States within a total U.S. population of nearly 106,000,000. This compared to pre-exclusion 1880 census figures of 105,000 Chinese among a U.S. population of 50,000,000. (*See § 2.29.*) Therefore, during the exclusion years, the American population more than doubled, while Chinese in the United States fell by 25 percent. As a consequence of this attrition, the statutory quota worked out to only 105, just over the minimum national quota of 100. The most generous quota of more than 60,000 per year belonged to Great Britain:

"The erroneous understanding by most people is that a quota is arrived at on the basis of the number of people in that country, not here. Of course, on the basis of four hundred or five hundred million people in China, that is a different story; but our quota law is based on this formula and it cannot be changed unless we change the quota law." 89 Cong. Rec. 8575 (1943).

Mason inserted in the *Congressional Record* nine editorials supporting exclusion repeal. The most compelling came from the October 11, 1943, edition of the *Washington Post*, because it addressed not only pragmatic and strategic issues but moral concerns as well:

"It would repeal the ugly and antiquated Chinese Exclusion Act—which serves no purpose save as propaganda fuel for our Japanese enemies who persistently hold it up before the Chinese people as evidence of America's racial prejudice . . . .

"The House cannot fail to pass this bill without dealing a serious blow to one of our allies—and thus to ourselves and the whole United Nations cause. If the bill is enacted speedily and overwhelmingly, as it should be, it will do much to cement the good relations between China and the United States and to spur the war effort in the Far East. These are considerations which, of themselves, should insure its prompt passage. Beyond them is the important fact that the bill would at last expunge from our national record a piece of wanton discrimination which has always been a source of shame." 89 Cong. Rec. A4415 (1943).

After a brief interlude of additional debate, Representative Martin J. Kennedy (D–NY) took the floor. A member of the House from 1930 to 1945, Kennedy had little patience with quibbling over quotas and formulas. He insisted that the House look at the bigger picture, that being ending discriminatory treatment against the Chinese.

Barely a month into the 78th Congress (1943–1945), Kennedy introduced H.R. 1882, which called for the outright repeal of the exclusion laws. He had timed his legislation to secure a symbolic bill number. Kennedy's bill was the first of its kind to be proposed in the 78th Congress.

Kennedy submitted for the *Congressional Record* a letter he had sent on February 17, 1943, to Madame Chiang, two days before her appearance in the House of Representatives (§ *11.31*). The letter discussed the importance of Chinese-American friendship and steps that could be taken to deepen bilateral ties. One such tactic was repeal of the exclusion laws. With the correspondence, he included a copy of his bill. Kennedy wrote:

"During the difficult period of the settlement of our West, the importation of 'cheap Chinese labor' brought with it a wave of alarmed misunderstanding and a prejudice on the part of some of our people. There was no justification for this fear. Even under the 1930 census, there were only 46,129 Chinese people in our country. We have more than that number of European refugees in a few months." 89 Cong. Rec. 8577 (1943).

In a week's time, Madame Chiang responded warmly to Kennedy's letter, congratulating him for his "farsightedness."

Kennedy also had placed in the *Congressional Record* President Franklin D. Roosevelt's October 11, 1943, message endorsing exclusion repeal. The president began:

"There is now pending before this Congress legislation to permit the immigration of Chinese people into this country and to allow Chinese residents here to become American citizens. I regard it as important in the cause of winning the war and of establishing a secure peace." 89 Cong. Rec. 8577 (1943).

President Roosevelt noted that China understood that the United States was pursuing a Europe-first strategy in the war, but that substantial aid would be flowing as soon as capacity and logistics would permit. This flow would help China in a material sense, but it was not enough:

"China's resistance does not depend alone on guns and planes and on attacks on land, on the sea, and from the air. It is based as much on the spirit of her people and her faith in her allies. We owe it to the Chinese to strengthen that faith. One step in this direction is to wipe from the statute books those anachronisms in our law which forbid the immigration of Chinese people into this country and which bar Chinese residents from American citizenship." 89 Cong. Rec. 8577 (1943). The exclusion policy had been a mistake that should be corrected, said Roosevelt.

Roosevelt addressed two issues arising out of the new 105-person quota that would be assigned to China. First, he said that the number was small enough so that no reasonable fear should exist that Chinese immigration would generate unemployment or hamper job opportunities for other workers; second, although the quota would, in principle, advantage China over other countries within the Asiatic Barred Zone (established with the Immigration Act of 1917), such preference was appropriate for a steadfast ally:

"While it would give the Chinese a preferred status over certain other oriental people, their great contribution to the cause of decency and freedom entitled them to such preference." 89 Cong. Rec. 8577 (1943).

Exclusion repeal was long overdue, said the president.

Not everyone favored repeal, Representative John Marshall Robsion (R–KY) countered. A member of the House from 1919 to 1930, Robsion resigned in 1930 to take an appointment to the Senate. In the 1930 election, he lost his Senate seat. He returned to the House in 1935 and served there until his death in 1948.

Robsion tracked the criticism expressed in the committee report's minority views. Granting China a quota was bound to generate increased demands from other equally friendly Asian peoples, so that the pending measure would not only affect China but might weaken the entire Asiatic Barred Zone policy.

Such immigration law changes were untimely during wartime, Robsion argued. They should wait until servicemen returned home and the effect of enhanced immigration on job opportunities could better be assessed. He saw repeal as a convenient means to promote immigration reform:

"This question was not brought up in China. It is being developed here in our own country, and some of the sponsors have been trying for years to break down our immigration laws, and they are using the war as a vehicle in this instance to help accomplish their purpose." 89 Cong. Rec. 8577 (1943).

If labor protectionism had been the leading motivation for enactment of the exclusion laws, as the House Immigration and Naturalization Committee and others had already expressed, the issue was not yet buried. Robsion noted that the American Legion had passed a resolution opposing repeal. The Legion insisted upon maintaining immigration restrictions, without regard to the origin of the limitation, in order to protect returning service personnel from job competition. Repeal of Chinese exclusion was problematic in and of itself and would foster demands for even more relaxation and reforms, they feared. Robsion quoted from testimony the American Legion gave during hearings on the bill:

"Certainly our most immediate and more important job after the cessation of hostilities will be to find jobs for the millions of men and women who are or will serve in our armed forces, and no one can predict what economic conditions will prevail in this country at that time.

"We appreciate and commend the Chinese people for the wonderful service they have performed holding the Japanese at bay . . . . The naturalization and immigration question as it affects the Chinese can wait until the war is over when basic and sound consideration can be given it without the influence of war hysteria . . . .

"The sum total of this proposed legislation if enacted by Congress would go far toward the breaking down of the safeguards provided by our immigration and naturalization laws . . . .

"We feel that the naturalization and immigration rights granted the Chinese at this particular time will be used as an opening wedge toward following through with similar rights for other groups." 89 Cong. Rec. 8577–78 (1943).

Robsion noted that the Veterans of Foreign Wars and various labor organizations, including the American Federation of Labor, had expressed similar opposition. He concluded by asking:

"Will we have jobs and opportunities for our 12,000,000 defenders when they come home after the war? Will we again have millions walking the streets and highways, looking for jobs and opportunities to make a living and not being able to find them?" 89 Cong. Rec. 8578 (1943).

Labor protection after World War I had been the main reason for enacting immigration restrictions in 1921 and tightening them in the Immigration Act of 1924, said Robsion. Of course, the quotas had been controversial and countries that were subject to the restrictions had long tried to dispense with them. Exclusion repeal legislation would intensify their lobbying:

"The bill before us is an entering wedge to aid in further efforts to break down our immigration laws and take away their protection for our own citizens." 89 Cong. Rec. 8578 (1943).

Next to speak was Representative John W. McCormack (D–MA). Serving in the House from 1928 to 1971, McCormack was Speaker of the House from 1962 until he left Congress. At the time of the exclusion repeal fight, McCormack was House Majority Leader.

In hearing testimony, the American Legion argued that people in China, busy fighting the war, were unlikely to care much about exclusion repeal. McCormack disputed this, believing that repeal would have a major impact on Chinese public opinion. Although characterizing the original exclusion legislation as a tool for labor protection, McCormack considered it dishonorable. Repeal would heal old wounds.

"It removes the insult of an ignoble act committed some years ago of excluding by name from admission into the United States anybody from China.

"How would we like it if any other country in the world, by express act of its legislative body or those in control of its government were to say that no American should be admitted into that country as an immigrant? Without regard to whether or not we wanted to go or whether we thought any other American should enter that country as an alien, you and I as Americans would feel insulted if we were picked out from the nations of the world as the one nation excluded expressly from admission as immigrants into any other country." 89 Cong. Rec. 8579 (1943).

To be sure, the Chinese felt the insult, and that is why Japanese propaganda had been so effective. Keeping such laws on the statute books were worth twenty divisions to the Japanese, the Majority Leader contended.

Individuals and organizations that worried about the effect of repeal on American jobs had no cause for concern, he said. Only a few Chinese could enter under the quota:

"The smallest country in the world, under the immigration laws, is entitled to have admitted into the United States 105 immigrants each year, and that is all we are giving to a nation of over 400,000,000 persons." 89 Cong. Rec. 8579 (1943).

McCormack saw repeal as generating substantial benefits to the United States, such as erasing the stain of racial prejudice and burnishing the country's international standing. Passing the bill would allow America to be true to itself, strengthen its wartime posture, and enhance its place in the peacetime world:

"It is a step toward salutary internationalism based upon justice and understanding. It is a denial of the false doctrine of racism and a reiteration of the principles of equality of opportunity for life, liberty, and happiness for all mankind . . . .

"And when the noise of cannon and shell has ceased, the post-war quiet must fall upon an America surrounded by friends—international friends looking to America in trust and confidence and faith that her spoken ideals were the real ideals for which the war was fought." 89 Cong. Rec. 8579 (1943).

The wartime strategy of the United States was to position China as one of the leading world powers. To this end, President Roosevelt and Prime Minister Winston Churchill held a summit meeting with Chiang Kaishek in Cairo in November 1943, and China was made a permanent member of the United Nations Security Council when that body was created in 1945. A friendly relationship with China was a cornerstone of American foreign policy.

McCormack argued that repeal was crucial in binding China and America closer together. He considered that the Chiang government was actually a form of American constitutional democracy transplanted in Asia:

"China is more to America than an ally. She is our friend, united in her sentiment of friendship for the people of the United States. Our Constitution has been her governmental inspiration . . . .

"The American Constitution means to China equality of race, religion, class, and liberty under the law for all. The principles of the Government of China of today flow from their [sic] understanding of the principles of American Government . . . .

"It is time for us to realize that if nations cannot be gracious to each other, cannot respect each other's race, all talk of democracy is in vain." 89 Cong. Rec. 8580 (1943).

As he ended his remarks, McCormack returned to Japanese exploitation of racial resentment, which he suggested would have devastating immediate and long-term effects if Congress did not act to neutralize it:

"The average American may not care what the average oriental may think of him. But beware the attitude of the peacock in our international relationships. The future world must respect the opinions of the half billion citizens of the Orient . . . .

"Let us not underestimate the Nipponese in their propagandizing of the natives in captive countries. Japan is stressing in the Philippines, as in all Asiatic countries, the word which has meant little to orientals under white rule 'freedom.' Japan places emphasis on our nationalistic tendencies and accuses us of imperialistic design. We are charged with having for 19 months forgotten the Filipinos because they are colored peoples and America is rushing all her troops to the aid of other white men in Europe . . . .

"Race hatred is the master weapon of the Nippon as well as the Nazi. It is our greatest threat to world peace.

"The enactment of the proposed legislation is legally obligatory, morally necessary, and economically indispensable for our own best interests. It is not only an act of faith, but of interest, sentiment, and justice on our part. By its passage, we are showing ourselves big enough nationally to admit and correct a mistake. We remove the sting of Japanese propaganda. We eradicate the stigma of the enduring insult America gives to the people of China." 89 Cong. Rec. 8580 (1943).

Following McCormack's statement, the House agreed by voice vote to House Resolution 314, the rule establishing the procedure for consideration of H.R 3070, the Chinese exclusion repeal bill.

Representative Ed Lee Gossett (D–TX), who served in the House from 1939 to 1951, moved that the House resolve itself into the Committee of the Whole to address H.R. 3070. Taking this procedural step was customary in the House because a quorum of only one hundred was needed to operate in the Committee of the Whole, as opposed to 218 in the House itself.

Gossett reviewed the Chinese exclusion acts in the context of laws that later barred other Asian peoples from immigration:

"While orientals generally have been excluded from admission to this country, it is interesting to note that the Chinese are the only nationals repeatedly specified by race in our statutes." 89 Cong. Rec. 8581 (1943).

The original genesis of the laws was fear of a massive labor incursion, Gossett said, making it appear that the concerns so starkly expressed by Pacific Coast representatives and senators were actually more broadly felt:

"At the time the original Chinese exclusion acts were passed our immigration laws were very lax, we had no quota system, and the Chinese were immigrating to our west coast in hordes. There was great fear throughout the country, especially in the West, that cheap Chinese labor was going to vitally affect the American standard of living." 89 Cong. Rec. 8581 (1943).

Changes in immigration policy, particularly imposition of the quota system, had removed the basis for these fears, Gossett argued. Quotas had made immigration more manageable, and diminished the possibility that domestic labor might be swamped. As to the Chinese, imposing a 105-person quota eliminated the prospect of a major influx.

Immigration policy was actually a secondary issue in the repeal effort, Gossett insisted. Repeal would be better considered in light of its effect upon the war:

"The bill now under consideration is not an immigration bill. This bill is a war measure and a peace measure." 89 Cong. Rec. 8581 (1943).

Gossett noted that Japanese pan-Asian propaganda had two thrusts: the first was agitation over extraterritoriality; the second was the Chinese exclusion laws. "There is no propaganda quite as effective as true propaganda," he said. 89 Cong. Rec. 8581 (1943). These Japanese arguments and generous peace terms represented an effort to weaken Chinese resolve or, worse yet, convert China from a friend to an enemy.

To enhance Chiang's position and bolster Chinese commitment to the war, the U.S. had surrendered extraterritorial rights. Now, it was time to finish the job by repealing exclusion, Gossett argued.

Representative Fred Busbey (R–IL) interrupted Gossett with a question. Busbey served from 1943 to 1945, 1947 to 1949, and 1951 to 1955. He had heard that the 105-person quota would not truly limit the Chinese because individuals of Chinese origin could enter under the British quota, which exceeded 60,000. Hong Kong, after all, was a British Crown colony; Britain, deeply enmeshed in a war, was unlikely to exhaust its substantial quota.

Gossett responded that China had a special quota under the bill, in that the number of 105 applied to Chinese persons worldwide, regardless of citizenship:

"I am glad to have that question asked. Under that section, no more than 105 Chinese can come in from England, France, Germany, Italy, or from the ends of the earth. Section 2 is based on race. Only 105 persons of the Chinese race can come into this country. Seventy-five percent of this quota of 105 is given to China proper, to persons born in and resident in China. In that particular, this quota provision differs from existing quotas granted to other nations now permitted immigration. In other words, an English Chinaman, a Chinaman who is a citizen of England, would have to come into the country under this quota of 105." 89 Cong. Rec. 8582 (1943).

Representative John Hinshaw (R–CA), who served from 1939 to 1956, spoke to the question of how many Chinese might actually be affected by ending the ban on naturalization. Census data from 1940 showed that there were approximately 77,000 Chinese in the United States, of whom 40,000 were foreign-born and 37,000 were native-born. These data demonstrated the effects of several generations of exclusion, Hinshaw noted:

"In the period from 1890 to the present time, the number of Chinese of foreign extraction has dropped from over 100,000 to 40,000. They are dying off. They are the old people of the Chinese race in this country." 89 Cong. Rec. 8583 (1943).

Shortly thereafter, Representative John Bennett (R–MI) was recognized. He had been the principal author of the minority views filed with the report of the House Committee on Immigration and Naturalization.

As he expressed in the minority views, Bennett was opposed to making changes in American immigration laws during wartime. Immigration had been and was likely to remain a complex question. Since it could be projected to be a leading post-war issue, Bennett thought the entire matter should be reserved for comprehensive consideration later.

Bennett disputed the arguments that passage of the bill would cement bilateral relations and deprive Japan of a propaganda tool. These theories were the rationale for repeal, but neither objective would be served. In his view, the new quota system merely perpetuated discrimination:

"In the first place, this bill does not give the Chinese equality of immigration with any European nation . . . for it very definitely discriminates against the Chinese in the following manner: Europeans may enter this country as non-quota immigrants if they were born in another country. For example, an Englishman born in South America comes to the United States as a non-quota immigrant, whereas a Chinese born in South America would be charged to the Chinese quota. Thus, you compel Chinese to come here by race and permit Europeans to come on the basis of nativity." 89 Cong. Rec. 8594 (1943).

The pending measure was inherently hypocritical, suggested Bennett:

"It was brought about by a studied and intentional limitation in this particular bill which says in one breath to China, we are treating you on the basis of equality with Europeans, but in the next breath, it positively limits the number of Chinese by restricting their entry to race regardless of the country of birth." 89 Cong. Rec. 8584 (1943).

The Chinese were not likely to be fooled by meaningless overtures, Bennett predicted. Better to tell them that, regardless of outstanding inequities, immigration policy should not be addressed piecemeal. Immediate action was not needed; the Chinese would be satisfied by a commitment to consider the problem when the war was over, he argued.

Representative Bennett believed the bill would exacerbate, rather than solve, the Japanese propaganda issue. The unique Chinese quota created a problem, rather than presenting a solution:

"The Japanese have been telling the Chinese that we are prejudiced against them because we do not treat them on an equality basis with the white race so far as immigration is concerned. This bill will do nothing to correct that criticism by the Japanese because, while we pretend to give the Chinese equality in this legislation, we do not do so . . . ." 89 Cong. Rec. 8584 (1943).

Living with the pressures of war, China would not benefit from empty gestures, Bennett said. The best immediate thing the United States could do to make up for old sins and to strengthen relations with China was to help it secure victory over Japan:

"Irrespective of what our past record toward China may have been, we are now making atonement in a very positive and material way. We have American boys by the tens of thousands scattered all over the Pacific islands and Far East areas, with only one objective in mind—to crush the military might of Japan, and the day Japan is crushed, China will be free." 89 Cong. Rec. 8585 (1943).

In addition, America would take the lead in helping China with post-war reconstruction. China would have to be rebuilt and its people would have to be fed. Such concrete efforts would be sufficient to convince China of America's regard, argued Bennett, without having to rewrite United States immigration policy.

Next up was Representative Warren Magnuson (D–WA). A congressman from 1936 to 1944, Magnuson also served in the Senate from 1944 to 1980.

Magnuson was the principal sponsor of H.R. 3070, the Chinese exclusion repeal bill. When enacted, the legislation was also known as the Magnuson Act.

The presence of the exclusion statutes had been a source of misunderstanding between the United States and China over many decades. Even if the motive for those laws was to protect against contract labor, Magnuson asserted, the legislation had been "a source of humiliation to a great nation and a great people." 89 Cong. Rec. 8585 (1943).

The laws were no longer needed, because the quota system eliminated the possibility of an influx of cheap labor. Under the quota, only a handful of Chinese could enter per year. The number was small enough to dispel any fears of labor competition, he said.

Bennett interrupted to affirm that his disagreement was not with the quota number, but with the fact that basic immigration law was being repealed during wartime on a piecemeal basis. Not so, Magnuson responded. Basic immigration law, including the quota system, remained intact. The Chinese were simply being placed within that system instead of remaining outside it.

Insisting that Magnuson admit that, due to the special quota, the Chinese were being treated differently from Europeans, Bennett asked, "Why should we try to fool them by the sop this bill pretends to give them?" 89 Cong. Rec. 8586 (1943). Representative Noah Mason (R–IL) interjected that China had not been misled and was totally in accord with the legislation: "I just wish to state in answer to the gentleman from Michigan [Mr. Bennett] that the bill is exactly as the Chinese Nation asked and wanted, and are perfectly satisfied with." 89 Cong. Rec. 8586 (1943).

Mason's suggestion that the bill had been drawn to the specifications of the Chinese engendered some controversy. Representative Fred E. Busbey (R–IL) wanted to know more, because he had read the hearing record thoroughly and had found no evidence of a witness or written submission from the Chinese government.

Mason replied that Chinese leaders had told him personally that the legislation was exactly as they desired. Magnuson added that the Chinese had not formally appeared before the committee or lobbied through official channels, but that communications had been undertaken privately:

"Why should they not talk about it? It is a thing of utmost importance to them; but they are not going to come to us with their hat in their hand and their hands out, asking for equality; they should expect us to give them equality of their own volition and our own initiative, and we should." 89 Cong. Rec. 8587 (1943).

After a brief interlude, Representative Walter Judd (R–MN) addressed the House. Judd was then in his first of the ten terms he would serve in Congress (1943–1963), but he was already highly respected as a China expert. An orator of spellbinding capability, Judd would deliver the keynote address at the 1960 Republican National Convention. Staunchly anti-Communist, he would later become a leader in the "China Lobby," promoting continued support for Chiang Kaishek after the 1949 establishment of the People's Republic of China. For the time being, Judd would be a key ally for President Franklin D. Roosevelt's China policies.

A physician, Judd had been a medical missionary in China from 1925 to 1931 and again from 1938 to 1941. In hearings before the House Immigration and Naturalization Committee, Dr. Judd gave eloquent testimony in support of repeal.

Representative Judd commenced his statement on the House floor by providing an overview of the situation Congress was about to correct. How had Chinese come to America in the first place?

"When gold was discovered in California in 1848, and white men flocked to the West to get rich quick and become gentlemen of leisure, it soon became clear that someone would have to do some hard work building railroads and bringing the soil under cultivation. Agents of the railroads and shipping companies recruited laborers in China and brought them here in large numbers, until by 1876 there were about 110,000 on the Pacific Coast." 89 Cong. Rec. 8588 (1943).

With such a large workforce present in the region, Judd said, social and economic dislocation followed:

"The American population was still small and there were fears of being overwhelmed by Chinese laborers. We had not yet evolved the quota system for controlling and regulating immigration." 89 Cong. Rec. 8588 (1943).

When quotas finally arrived, Chinese were not eligible for them due to exclusion laws already in force. Instead, they were subject to "outmoded laws which single out the Chinese for special humiliating discriminations," Judd observed. 89 Cong. Rec. 8588 (1943).

Arguing that such legalized ostracism should not continue, Judd asked:

"Is that where Americans want to leave the matter? Do we still want officially to stigmatize as congenitally inferior because their skins happen to be yellow instead of white, black, or red, the Chinese people who recognized the nature of this world struggle and held the line [against Japan] single-handed for 4½ years before we woke up?" 89 Cong. Rec. 8588 (1943).

Judd implored Congress to take three steps: repeal the exclusion laws, put Chinese on the same footing as other immigrants for naturalization, and make China eligible for a quota.

Establishing a special quota would alleviate concerns that repealing exclusion would result in a large Chinese migration, said Judd. Left unattended, such fears could generate real political obstacles. Judd observed that major veterans and labor organizations had already opposed the bill because of its possible impact on post-war jobs.

Representative George Dondero (R–MI), a member of the House from 1933 to 1957, sought further amplification about the quota. This was his exchange with Judd:

"Mr. Dondero. The claim has been made here this afternoon that if a member of the Chinese race came here from South America, he would be charged against the quota for China itself.

"Mr. Judd. No; he would not be charged to the quota of China proper, because you will notice that this bill does not give a quota to China, the quota is of Chinese persons or persons of Chinese descent . . . .

"Mr. Dondero. If that is so, and a person who came here from South America who is of Chinese descent, would he not be charged against the quota of the Chinese Government proper?

"Mr. Judd. The quota would not be limited to the Chinese Government proper. If the gentleman will look on page 3 of the bill, line 17, he will see that it states 'all Chinese persons entering the United States annually as immigrants.' The Chinese would be a Chinese person even though he was born in Mexico or Brazil and is a citizen of Mexico or Brazil . . . .

"Mr. Dondero. But he would not be chargeable against China proper?

"Mr. Judd. He would be charged against this quota of 105 a year. The quota includes 'Chinese persons and persons of Chinese descent' even though they are not citizens of China proper." 89 Cong. Rec. 8589 (1943).

Moments later, in response to an inquiry, Judd also clarified that of the 105 Chinese persons worldwide, seventy-five slots were reserved to persons from China proper.

Representative Bertrand "Bud" Gearhart (R–CA), who served from 1935 to 1949, asked Judd how such an inconsequential quota could generate friendly relations with China. Judd responded that quota numbers themselves were incidental, so long as exclusion was repealed. Racial discrimination deeply offended Chinese pride, and the stigma had to be removed:

"The fact that it figures out to be 105 is relatively unimportant. The important fact is that by our present laws they are excluded because of their color. It is not red, white, or black. This bill would remove that stigma of biological inferiority. If the same formula used for other peoples figured out to admit only two Chinese a year, it would still do the job. It would start treating them as equals racially instead of inferiors. It would be justice. That is what they want, just as we would want it if we were in their place . . . .

"People live by roses as well as by bread. No one is suggesting that roses will do what bread can do. But surely no one believes that bread will do what roses can do. We who are the descendants of 1776 ought to know of people who fought in the snow with bare, bleeding feet for such things as equality. That is the principle involved here. It is more important than guns or even food. The actual numbers to be admitted do not count. The chief thing is the principle of being treated as equals." 8 Cong. Rec. 8589 (1943).

Judd observed that most Americans failed to grasp Asian psychology. Americans tended to rely too heavily on statistics, and insisted upon seeing the world only from a U.S. perspective. Such ignorance had led to costly policy errors in the Far East. As a private citizen, Judd had appeared before the House Committee on Foreign Affairs in 1939 to warn about this myopia. He did so in the hope of illuminating how Japanese militarists intended to use the power available to them. "Coequal in value with any set of facts is a knowledge of the psychology of the people who are going to use those facts," Dr. Judd had told the committee. 89 Cong. Rec. 8590 (1943).

Americans had not come to terms with Japanese psychology in time, Judd lamented. Would they repeat the same mistake with China?

"We were too late and too little with Japan. Are we going to be too late and too little with China too? Are we going to insist stubbornly, against the testimony of every single witness who has lived in China and knows the Chinese well, that just because we cannot imagine granting an insignificant quota would mean much to us, therefore, it cannot really mean much to them? Must a lot of American boys die needlessly before we realize that there are still some peoples in the world who care more about the things of the spirit than about things that can be counted, measured, and weighed?

"Tanks and planes and food are important; but equally important is the heart of the man who uses them." 89 Cong. Rec 8590 (1943).

Representative Judd was not suggesting that, if the bill failed, China would necessarily withdraw from the war and reach a separate peace with Japan. But he was confident that repeal would strengthen China's fighting spirit. It greatly mattered how China could expect to be treated in the post-war family of nations, he said. If it could forecast the prospect of equality, then the war was particularly worth fighting. If, instead, China faced a perpetuation of racial discrimination and colonialism, then a separate peace would be more attractive:

"If we were Chinese, and had been fighting for over six years, much of it on the verge of starvation, without drugs or anesthetics, without weapons or industrial plants to make them, and with increasing inflation and growing discontent, and therefore divisions among the people, would we not begin to ask, 'Why are we going through all this? If by enduring and struggling till victory is ultimately won we are still going to be just sort of a sub-colony, treated as inferiors by 'master' races, the white men, then why do we not make peace now and get the best terms we can from Japan?' " 89 Cong. Rec. 8590 (1943).

Shortly after the Pearl Harbor attack on December 7, 1941, President Roosevelt and Prime Minister Winston Churchill met in Washington, drawing plans to give primacy to the battle for Europe over the fighting in Asia (*§ 11.33*). For that plan to succeed, China had to remain engaged. As Judd observed, the viability of American war prospects in Asia greatly depended on Chinese resistance to Japanese aggression:

"The hard experience of a year and a half of war against Japan indicates all too clearly that we cannot win alone in the Pacific, or at least not without almost prohibitive costs. We can succeed only if our allies, and particularly if China, can hold against Japan until we can defeat Germany and get our full strength into the Pacific." 89 Cong. Rec. 8590 (1943).

Judd noted that a key Tokyo war aim was to win terms from China that would secure Japan's rights to a dominant presence in continental Asia. "With China as her base on the continent, Japan would be impregnable, or so nearly so that it would require 4 or 5 or even 10 years to defeat her." 89 Cong. Rec. 8590 (1943). To gain that overpowering position, Japan was working to undermine Chinese faith in the Western allies:

"The Chinese have endured over 6 years of bombings and invasion, famine, disease, uncontrolled inflation, enforced migration of over 50,000,000 people, and a year and a half of almost complete blockade. All of these physical disasters have not caused them to waver. Only one thing could cause them to waver, a loss of expectation that they will eventually get full independence and equal treatment by the other nations of the world, a loss of confidence in the real and ultimate motives of us, their allies." 89 Cong. Rec. 8591 (1943).

China would have good cause to doubt those allies, Judd stated. These reasons included the failure of Western nations to engage Japan until their own interests were directly threatened, slowness in delivery of war materiel, Churchill's stated intention to re-establish colonial empires after the war, and apparent American acquiescence to Britain's imperialistic policies in Asia:

"Surely it is understandable why many tired, starving, and sick Chinese might begin to wonder whether help to them is being deliberately delayed until after Hitler's defeat, so that the white man can then come in to make the kill and thus be left sitting on top in Asia, the old status quo restored." 89 Cong. Rec. 8592 (1943).

The United States could put such concerns to rest by passing the exclusion repeal bill, Judd assured the House. Doing so would assuage the Chinese, and was manifestly in America's self-interest:

"We are sacrificing American lives insofar as we fail to mobilize fully the will and the confidence of so indispensable an ally. I do not want on my hands the blood of a single additional American soldier who had to die in China because we failed here to show our purpose to treat the Chinese as equals . . . ." 89 Cong. Rec. 8592 (1943).

China would be crucial to America's objectives not only in battle, but also in the post-war world. The days of American isolationism were over. "We have learned the hard way that we cannot get security by ignoring the rest of the world, because the rest of the world simply will not ignore us." 89 Cong. Rec. 8592 (1943).

Major international challenges would emerge after the war, Representative Judd foresaw. For the United States to police the world alone would be impractical, outlandishly expensive, and would lack support from the American people, he said. America would need to foster alliances. As did Roosevelt, Judd thought strengthening the bond with China was essential:

"In short, America after this war is going to need friends and need them badly. Therefore, we dare not trifle with the friendship of that nation which will inevitably be the strongest in Asia. The burning question is not whether we will help China, but whether she will help us, now in the war, and afterward in the peace." 89 Cong. Rec. 8593 (1943).

Judd pointed out a great anomaly in America's immigration law as then written. Adolf Hitler was eligible for citizenship, while Madame Chiang Kaishek was not. Echoing the sentiments long ago expressed by exclusion opponents Senators Hannibal Hamlin, Charles Sumner, and George Hoar, Representative Judd denounced the existing law as immoral and anti-American:

"In addition to the disservice which our exclusion of the Chinese does to our own military, economic, and political interests, it violates the finest traditions and the moral sense of the American people . . . .

"Do we really believe in 1943, as our forefathers did in 1776, that all men are created equal in worth and in the right to be treated justly on the basis of what they are as individual human beings, not on the basis of the race to which they happen to belong? Do we really believe that there are certain inalienable rights, such as life, liberty, and the pursuit of happiness? If so, then let us make it unmistakably clear by our words and our deeds, and quickly." 89 Cong. Rec. 8593 (1943).

Supporting Judd's view was the Federal Council of Churches of Christ in America. Eight hundred leading seminarians and divinity scholars signed a petition to Congress, dated October 19, 1943. Judd inserted it in the *Congressional Record*:

"Whereas our immigration and naturalization laws affecting orientals are based on discrimination on account of race; and

"Whereas such racial discrimination does violence to the Christian view of one humanity under God, is contrary to the democratic principles upon which this country was founded, and to proved [sic] scientific fact;

"We, the undersigned, express the hope that the Congress, taking into account these principles, will take immediate steps to modify these laws with respect to China so that natives of that country, otherwise admissible, may enter this country under the existing quota system and become citizens on the same terms as immigrants from nonoriental countries." 89 Cong. Rec. A 4417 (1943).

Although only a freshman, and serving in the minority, Representative Judd had spoken longer than any other representative, including Majority Leader John McCormack and the repeal bill's sponsor, Representative Warren Magnuson. Concluding with a warning, Judd said:

"Those who think we can continue to leave it as a statute which is an insult to our friends and not eventually suffer for it are, I believe, grievously mistaken." 89 Cong. Rec. 8593 (1943).

Decades earlier in Chinese exclusion debates, particularly ennobling speeches would seem to be followed by especially depressing ones. So it was in 1943. After Judd relinquished the House floor, Representative William P. Elmer (R–MO) followed him. Elmer served a single term, from 1943 to 1945.

The Missouri congressman began by denying the Chinese had suffered special discrimination that needed to be rectified:

"No injustice is done to China, greater or above that to other Asiatics, and any country has a right to protect itself; that is what these laws did." 89 Cong. Rec. 8593 (1943).

Elmer observed that American attitudes toward China were chameleon-like and tended to oscillate between extremes. He cited the example of the 1900 Boxer Rebellion, the turn-of-the-century uprising in China against foreign influences (§ 9.12). The Boxers attacked and surrounded foreign legations in Beijing. After nearly two months foreign forces, called the International Allied Forces, lifted the siege. (Originally consisting of seventy-five Russians, seventy-five British, seventy-five French, fifty Americans, forty Italians and twenty-five Japanese, by the time the Boxers were suppressed, the Japanese had contributed 50 percent of the fighting forces.) The violence, which caused huge indemnities to be imposed on China, also stirred anti-Chinese sentiment abroad. Elmer noted:

"A few years ago, the Boxer Rebellion was on and for years afterwards our pet name for them was 'Chinese devils.' They were fighting then for their country, just as they are now. They were trying to defeat a partition of China. The exclusion acts were heartily approved then. We just did not like the Chinese. But now we want to show our sympathy so we repeal the exclusion laws because some Americans want to ease their consciences over more recent treatments and others want to arouse our sympathy to a high pitch for other motives, ulterior to our safety and wellbeing." 89 Cong. Rec. 8593 (1943).

Representative Elmer thought this fluctuation made no sense. "When did the Chinese devils become Chinese saints?" 89 Cong. Rec. 8593 (1943). He thought the Chinese had not changed much from the old exclusion days:

"They did not fit into our system of things. To us they are aliens in China; they are aliens in this country. They did not assimilate." 89 Cong. Rec. 8593 (1943).

Elmer claimed that he had worked to familiarize himself with Chinese history, reading more than 1,000 pages of recent texts. Nowhere in such texts were the American exclusion acts mentioned as a consequential issue, he said. Colleagues in Congress who argued the subject was important to the Chinese were distorting things out of proportion:

"The Chinese felt it was an American question to be discussed and settled by us. Why, then, this agitation? Why this self-incrimination over a policy of 60 years ago? Why this sudden face about? You will have to dig deeper than the Exclusion Act to find it." 89 Cong. Rec. 8593 (1943).

When German armies invaded the Soviet Union, Ukrainian people at first cheered them as liberators from Stalinist domination. Lest Congress believe that the Chinese had inherently friendly attitudes toward the West, Elmer told a similar story about what happened when the Japanese freed Hong Kong from British control:

"The Chinese applauded when the English colonials were taken from the Hill in Hong Kong and jailed. They could not restrain their happy feeling. This was on the basis of 'Asia for the Asiatics,' and the foreign domination by occidental nations was so bad that any change was welcome." 89 Cong. Rec. 8594 (1943).

American views toward China were fundamentally schizophrenic, Elmer suggested. Two days before the Japanese attacked Pearl Harbor, the United States permitted Japanese ships to leave U.S. ports with significant amounts of war materiel destined for military use against China. Protests from the Chinese government were rebuffed in Washington, and the activity was defended as merely commercial transactions. "Perhaps we were aiding our exclusion laws by making sure a lot of Chinese would not apply for entry and citizenship," Elmer said wryly. 89 Cong. Rec. 8594 (1943).

The Japanese attack on Hawaii on December 7, 1941, changed American attitudes towards China. "All at once we discovered the saintly qualities of the Chinese people. If it had not been for December 7, I do not know if we would ever have found out how good they were." 89 Cong. Rec. 8594 (1943).

Representative Elmer suggested exclusion repeal was little more than a hypocritical effort to salve American consciences. Calling repeal a "cheap gesture," he ridiculed the argument that it was important to stiffen Chinese war morale, or that China was an essential partner to help America win in the Pacific. "If we have to rely on China to win the war, we have already lost it. We are the one to help China," he commented. 89 Cong. Rec. 8594 (1943).

Exclusion repeal could not be seen in legislative isolation. It meant opening up America's immigration laws. Demands for additional changes and a relaxation of the quotas would surely follow. Such demands must be resisted, as must exclusion repeal, Elmer demanded:

"You enact this law and you have taken off the stakes and riders of the immigration fence. It will be easy to push down the rest of it. Raise it higher, strengthen it more, close the gaps. Make it like the Missouri lawful fence: horse high, bull-strong, and pig-tight." 89 Cong. Rec. 8595 (1943).

Following Elmer to the podium was Representative James A. Wright (D–PA), a member of the House from 1941 to 1945. Wright wanted to make clear how Chinese would regard repeal. Some of his House colleagues, like Judd, theorized that repeal would matter a lot to the Chinese; others, like Bennett, thought it would matter little. Who was correct? Wright thought it best to have the Chinese speak for themselves. He inserted in the *Congressional Record* editorials from major Chinese newspapers and government spokespersons. Typical of these was commentary from *The China Times*, a major Chongqing daily:

"We hope that the new law not only will be passed by the United States Congress, but will be passed by an overwhelming vote, so as to manifest the American people's sense of justice and to produce favorable effects on the future relations between the two nations." 89 Cong. Rec. 8595 (1943).

Similarly, the Chinese Foreign Ministry issued a statement saying:

"Although it is a domestic issue, the repeal of the act, as recommended by President Roosevelt, will be exceedingly welcomed here and will be considered as further cementing the traditional friendship between the United States and China." 89 Cong. Rec. 8595 (1943).

After additional member statements, Representative Carl Curtis (R–NE) entered the debate. Elected to the House in 1939, Curtis served there until he won a Senate seat in 1954. Curtis was a senator from 1955 to 1979. As a member of the House Committee on Immigration and Naturalization, he generally supported strict immigration controls, and was willing to reduce existing immigration quotas. However, Curtis would support exclusion repeal. He saw it as a distinct issue from immigration:

"I would vote today to cut down all quotas for the post-war period, but this Chinese problem must not be confused with that problem. The Chinese recognize our right to limit immigration to prevent unemployment or for any other like reason. They grant to the United States the right to shut off all immigration, if we so desire, but they do object to a policy that permits the immigration into this country of hundreds of thousands and not one Chinese." 89 Cong. Rec. 8597 (1943).

Repealing exclusion was key to depriving the Japanese of an argument that might resonate in war-weary China, said Curtis. If that argument actually took hold, and the Chinese reversed allegiances, there would be monumental security problems for the United States:

"I think it is of utmost importance that we retain the friendship of the Chinese. Suppose the Chinese do capitulate and join Japan, then all Asia is apt to go with her. Then you will have a race struggle in which we are hopelessly outnumbered that will last, not for one year, not for five years, but throughout the generations to come. It will mean much not only in our day, but to our children and grandchildren to have a strong, powerful China that is a friend to the United States and with whom we can have a working cooperation." 89 Cong. Rec. 8597 (1943).

Representative Cameron Morrison (D–NC) followed Curtis. A former governor of North Carolina, Morrison was in the Senate from 1930 to 1932, and served one term in the House, from 1943 to 1945. Morrison commented that congressional attitudes toward the Chinese people had changed dramatically since the era in which the exclusion laws were passed:

"There is no doubt that the law was enacted with a conception of the Chinese character which does not now abide in the hearts and brains of the American people. We have more respect for the Chinese today than we had when that law was enacted. I am not going to strike back and reflect upon our great fathers who enacted those ancient laws, but today General Chiang Kaishek and his lady are crowned with glory and honor in the heart of every true patriot in the United States. Why should we keep upon the books an insulting and irritating discrimination whose repeal will do us no harm, when General Chiang Kaishek and his lady and the great Republic of China, and our own great Government . . . tell us that it ought to be repealed?" 89 Cong. Rec. 8598 (1943).

Unlike Morrison, Representative Thomas A. Jenkins (R–OH) opposed the bill because it included a new quota for Chinese. A congressman from 1925 to 1959, Jenkins, like many other Magnuson Act opponents, emphasized that he favored maximum assistance to China in the war, but insisted on separating the military issue from changes to immigration policy. Jenkins did not want to add a new quota for China. Doing so was purely symbolic, he felt, and immigration policy was not an appropriate place for symbolism:

"We are now asked to deviate from that policy and to grant a favor to very deserving people simply as a gesture. There are no gestures in immigration law. The immigration law is stern and it should be recognized as such . . . . We still want to do the best we can by the whole world but we must also remember that we owe an obligation to our own people. That is the reason why the American Federation of Labor and all the patriotic societies of the land are opposed to this legislation." 89 Cong. Rec. 8599 (1943).

Jenkins did not agree that the original exclusion acts were a mistake. "I do not think it was an injustice, because everything we did was under and in line with a treaty to which they agreed," he observed. 89 Cong. Rec. 8599 (1943). Given the subsequent development of the quota system, however, he felt the exclusion laws no longer served a useful purpose and should be repealed. "In fact, I think we should do so now, and I am enthusiastically in favor of passing a law to that effect." 89 Cong. Rec. 8599 (1943).

But repealing exclusion was different from granting the Chinese a quota and according them naturalization rights. Existing law granted the right to become a naturalized citizen to "white persons, persons of African nativity or descent, and descendants of races indigenous to the Western Hemisphere." The pending measure proposed to add the words "And Chinese persons or persons of Chinese descent."

Jenkins suggested that the gesture amounted to little more than bait-and-switch tactics, granting express naturalization rights and then providing such a restrictive quota that few Chinese could ever take advantage of them. The gesture would be empty, if not counterproductive:

"I do not rate the Chinese as being so ignorant and so easy as not to notice how they are being discriminated against . . . . To make him eligible and then say that he is not eligible, and we will tolerate only seventy-five of them per year is not putting them on a par with other peoples and other countries." 89 Cong. Rec. 8599 (1943).

Enacted in 1924, the operative quota system was skewed in favor of immigrants from Europe, particularly Northern Europe, and especially Great Britain. Jenkins defended the bias:

"It was only natural and fair . . . that the nations of northern Europe should have larger quotas than the countries who had not contributed to the founding and building of our country. Who built up this country? It was the English, the Scotch, the Welsh, the Irish, the Scandinavians, the Germans, the French, and the Spanish, and the Dutch, and the Italians, and other nations of that kind. The Japs or the Chinese were not here in any numbers when the country was built up. They did not contribute to the building of the country as other nations. Consequently, when Congress passed the quota laws, they provided that the principle quotas should go to those countries whose people predominated in the country. But to be fair and courteous, the Congress provided that every country should have a minimum quota of 100." 89 Cong. Rec. 8599 (1943).

Chinese, of course, suffered badly under this system. Due to attrition attributable to the exclusion policy, the number of Chinese present when quotas were developed was lower than it otherwise would have been. Since the quota was sized to a population whose growth was restricted by statute, quota restrictions perpetuated the effects imposed by the exclusion laws.

After additional debate, Representative John Main Coffee (D–WA) addressed the House. Coffee, who served in Congress from 1937 to 1947, was the only member in House debate to characterize exclusion repeal as an apology for prior misdeeds:

"I think this bill is an apology for certain mistakes we have made in the past. Let us recollect that we have been culpable of many blunders in the treatment of our neighbors across the Pacific." 89 Cong. Rec. 8601 (1943).

The bill would demonstrate that the Americans regarded the Chinese as equals, said Coffee. No step could be more potent to contradict Japanese claims that the Americans and British believed in white superiority and that Asians must band together to defeat white nations. If the United States did not promptly repeal exclusion, the corrosive effect of the Japanese argument would increasingly be felt. The message was already working, Coffee argued. It was rooted in the stunning Japanese naval victory over Russia in the Straits of Tsushima during the Russo–Japanese War of 1905:

"From 1905, when the treaty of Portsmouth was signed in the United States with the help of Theodore Roosevelt, the Japanese have preached to the orientals, 'Now, you see that a colored race can win over a white race because we, a colored race, won victory over a white race, Russia.' From 1905 to 1943, this propaganda has been assiduously sown throughout the Orient, namely, 'If you join with us and rally together as one co-prosperity sphere and entity, we can combine together and defeat the white race.'

"That pronunciamento has been more productive of results than anything else. It left its mark in Burma; it had its effect in Malay; it helped weaken resistance to invasion in the Dutch East Indies; it is making inroads in the Philippine Islands. This bill will do more to counteract that propaganda than any other bill we can enact. I hope we will pass this legislation." 89 Cong. Rec. 8602 (1943).

Following a brief interlude of additional debate, Representative Samuel Dickstein (R–NY), chairman of the House Committee on Immigration and Naturalization, again took the floor. He assured colleagues that no major news publication opposed the bill. As to other domestic opinion, Dickstein added:

"Every religious organization in this country, representing almost every denomination, has been urging the passage of this bill; 40 or 50 witnesses, from groups which represented approximately 80,000,000 people, have gone on record appealing to this committee and the Congress to pass this bill at the earliest possible moment for the good of the country. The wide range of people interested in repeal is astonishing. Missionaries acquainted with the reaction of the Chinese people to exclusion; most of the chambers of commerce on the west coast interested in post-war trade; labor organizations eager to see an old wrong, for which they were partly responsible, corrected; social and welfare organizations anxious to show their sympathy and understanding of the problems facing our ally; (and) military experts thinking of the best strategy to defeat our enemies . . . ." 89 Cong. Rec. 8603 (1943).

Also important would be the reaction within China itself. To illustrate that, Dickstein quoted from the hearing record. In testimony, the Most Reverend Bishop Paul Yu Pin, the Catholic bishop of China, spoke of the psychological importance of the legislation and the negative consequences that would flow from not passing it:

"Should thousands of tanks and airplanes from America to China not be forthcoming immediately, the Chinese people and soldiers perhaps will understand that Allied strategy of global warfare dictates otherwise for the time. But should your honorable committee look unfavorably upon these bills before you today, then I assure you my country and my people will not be able to under-

§11.34 Citizens Committee to Repeal Chinese Exclusion

Many Americans were involved in the repeal movement, including Chinese-Americans, especially members of the Chinese American Citizens Alliance.

The committee was organized by James Walsh, a prominent New York publisher and the husband of writer Pearl S. Buck. Although the committee was relatively small—with never more than about 240 persons—it was highly influential in organizing support for repeal of the federal law. Meeting first on May 25, 1943, the committee functioned as a pressure group that induced larger forces to lobby Congress for repeal. Although lobbying against the law on moral grounds was decades old, the committee sought to take advantage of the new military situation in the Pacific by making the U.S. alliance with China a central feature.

The committee's members were mostly East Coast elites and their allies in other parts of the country who could use their social and professional positions to generate action against the Exclusion Act. Urged by the committee, business groups, for example, lobbied Congress to change the law, arguing that total exclusion and mistreatment of Chinese by customs officials were bad for business. When pressed, members such as Buck emphasized that repeal was necessary as a measure to win the war.

From "Citizens Committee to Repeal Chinese Exclusion," in the *Encyclopedia of Immigration*, by Charles F. Bahmueller, September 22, 2011.

See also: Xiaohua Ma, "A Democracy at War: The American Campaign to Repeal Chinese Exclusion in 1943," *Japanese Journal of America Studies* 9 (1998): pp. 121–142; Frederick Riggs, *Pressures on Congress: A Study of the Repeal of Chinese Exclusion* (Columbia University Press, 1950); and L. Ling-chi Wang, "Politics of the Repeal of the Chinese Exclusion Laws," *Remembering 1882: Fighting for Civil Rights in the Shadow of the Chinese Exclusion Act* (Chinese Historical Society of America, 2007).

stand. It would be a great blow to our morale in China, irreparable harm to the Allied cause." 89 Cong. Rec. 8602 (1943).

Shortly thereafter, Representative Mike Mansfield (D–MT) joined the debate. Mansfield served in the House from 1943 to 1953. In 1952, he was elected to his first of four Senate terms. Before his retirement in 1977, Mansfield had served sixteen years as the Senate Majority Leader. Immediately after Mansfield's retirement from the Senate, President Jimmy Carter appointed him as Ambassador to Japan. In 1981, President Ronald Reagan renewed Mansfield's appointment as Ambassador to Japan.

Mansfield had been a professor of Far Eastern history at the University of Montana. After explicitly endorsing Judd's remarks from earlier that day, Representative Mansfield focused on America's checkered past in China. He placed special emphasis on imperialism and extraterritoriality:

"Do we by any chance have the idea that we have treated China fairly, that our policy has been for the best? Do we favor the right of extraterritoriality? Do we realize it was formally incorporated in a treaty—the Treaty of Wangxia—first by America? Do we derive any satisfaction out of the Opium War—the so-called First Anglo–Chinese War—which preceded that treaty? Do we uphold the idea of treaty ports? Do we uphold the idea of foreign concessions and compounds? Do we uphold the idea of having American consular courts in China, and a district court at Shanghai dispensing justice to Americans on Chinese soil? No. We have a good many things to answer for, and this is one way we can make good on some of the things we owe to our Chinese friends." 89 Cong. Rec. 8605 (1943).

Mansfield also spoke of excessive American reparations demands arising out of the Boxer Rebellion:

"We stole everything we possibly could of real value and transported a great deal of it back to this country. Some of it is still in the Capital City of the United States today, where it does not belong." 89 Cong. Rec. 8604 (1943).

When exclusion was enacted and reaffirmed, congressional debates were littered with frequent references degrading China's culture and promoting the alleged superiority of European peoples. Such venal commentary reflected profound ignorance in Congress, and Mansfield worked to set matters straight:

"When we think of our superiority, we ought to keep in mind the fact that Chinese culture is approximately 4000 years old . . . . China was a great and powerful nation long before there was such a thing as a Greece or a Rome. Those are the places which we consider as the foundation of our civilization, but, believe me, they cannot compare with China in antiquity." 89 Cong. Rec. 8605 (1943).

Most Americans came from European origin, and America was naturally Eurocentric in outlook. But Mansfield believed that enhanced awareness of Asia was essential to the United States, both during the war and thereafter:

"We must awaken from our lethargy about the Orient and put the manifest sympathy of the American people to a practical use. We must realize just how much we need China; not how much China needs us. We must never forget that we will have full need of all our energies, abilities, and real friends in our barbaric struggle with Japan. We must never forget that our future lies, in large part, in the Pacific." 89 Cong. Rec. 8605 (1943).

Following a brief additional debate, the House concluded its October 20, 1943 proceedings on H.R. 3070. The following day, debate would resume.

§11.40 H.R. 3070 and House Debate, October 21, 1943: "Face is not just oriental"

Under consideration in the House Committee of the Whole, H.R. 3070; later reported to the full House.

On Thursday, October 21, 1943, the House again resolved itself into the Committee of the Whole to consider H.R. 3070. Representative John Bennett (R–MI) moved an amendment to strike section 2 of the bill, which granted an immigration quota to Chinese persons. The amendment was one of two he intended to propose, the other being to eliminate section 3, which expressly permitted Chinese persons who were lawful resident aliens a right to naturalize while other Asians remained barred. He explained the effects of the amendments:

"If this amendment is adopted, and the amendment which I subsequently intend to offer to strike out section 3, it will leave the bill with section 1 only. Section 1 repeals the Chinese exclusion laws, which have had the effect of stigmatizing the Chinese as against all other Asiatics and, in my judgment, have been unfair to them, but it will not disturb any part of our basic immigration structure. It will give the Chinese the same immigration status as other Asiatics. It will not give them any preference, but it will end the present discrimination. We ought to stop there." 89 Cong. Rec. 8622 (1943).

Bennett again observed that the bill did not put Chinese on an equal footing with other immigrants. This was due to the unique Chinese quota, which was based on race, rather than nationality. But while the Chinese were in that sense disadvantaged, he observed, they were paradoxically given preference over other Asians, because they got a quota, while the others remained in the Asiatic Barred Zone. The bill would not only fail to counter Japanese propaganda, but would be counterproductive, because the "Chinese preference" would generate resentments in Asia that Japan could exploit:

"We are taking our immigration structure apart under the guise of war legislation to do a thing which will be appreciated by no nation and resented by many. It will not mislead anyone, even the Chinese whom it is intended to mislead, and go down in history as one more master stroke of meaningless diplomacy at the expense of a very important part of our immigration system." 89 Cong. Rec. 8622 (1943).

Representative Warren Magnuson (D–WA) opposed the amendment. He noted that it was consistent with what Bennett had expressed in the House Committee on Immigration and Naturalization report of minority views. Japanese propagandists were explicitly feasting on Bennett's positions, quoting him in broadcasts spread across China:

"May I say to the gentleman, and for the information of the House, bearing out what many Members said here yesterday regarding Japanese propaganda, that last night at 11 o'clock the radio of Tokyo in a broadcast beamed all over the Orient quoted the minority report on this bill." 89 Cong. Rec. 8623 (1943).

Magnuson denied that the Chinese were being given a special preference. By being granted an accessible quota, they were being put on the same footing as other nations. Moreover, it was not fair to deny a quota to the Chinese merely because other Asians were not granted one. Those peoples, such as Filipinos and Indians, were not then part of independent countries, so they could not qualify for a quota in the first place. "I have no doubt that they will be put on an equality basis or a quota basis when their independence is given to them," Magnuson said. 89 Cong. Rec. 8623 (1943).

Representative Thomas Jenkins (R–OH) supported the amendment. Repealing exclusion would erase a stigma, but granting a quota was an unnecessary step toward dismantling America's immigration system. "Why do you not repeal those provisions against which they complain and stop at that," he queried. 89 Cong. Rec. 8623 (1943).

Jenkins explained to the House how existing immigration law worked. For a person to be admitted to the United States in 1943, there was a two-prong test, he said. One prong was racial. The prospective immigrant had to be white, or be of African descent, or be descendents of persons indigenous to the Western Hemisphere. The other prong dealt with nationality. The prospective immigrant had to be from either a country for which quotas were expressly granted or a country exempt from quota altogether. If both prongs of the test were not satisfied, the person was inadmissible. Jenkins offered an example, in which an individual could satisfy one test (nationality) and not the other (racial):

"Let us suppose that a man living in England, born there of Chinese parents who were living there, and who were born there, wanted to come to the United States for citizenship. He would not be admitted. Why? Because he was not a white man, according to our immigration laws. He is an Englishman, but he still cannot be admitted. Under our law, Great Britain, of which England is a part, has an enormous quota of 65,000. Englishmen, or citizens of British provinces, are eligible to this quota if they do not come within the excludible class. A Chinese Englishman is not now eligible." 89 Cong. Rec. 8623–8624 (1943).

Representative James A. Wright (D–PA) addressed a weakness in the argument that Bennett and Jenkins presented: they would repeal exclusion but not authorize a quota. That would mean Chinese were not specifically excluded, but were nonetheless stopped because they were subject to the Asiatic Barred Zone. Wright denounced the Bennett amendment:

"If I understand this amendment, we will say in effect to the Chinese, 'We will not exclude you because you are Chinese, but we will exclude you because you are orientals.' What weasel words, what an insult to a people! I would far rather vote against this entire act, I would far rather have Congress go on record as saying to the Chinese people, 'We do not consider you equals at all' than to be guilty of this double-dealing. The gentleman would remove the discrimination against them, because of the fact that they are Chinese nationals, and still retain it because they are orientals." 89 Cong. Rec. 8625 (1943).

After a brief interlude, it was Representative Compton I. White's (D–ID) turn. An Idaho Democrat, White was in the House from 1937 to 1947 and again from 1949 to 1951. He vigorously opposed exclusion repeal. His speech was a throwback to the language of the formative exclusion debates, and his were the most racially derogatory remarks expressed in the 1943 proceedings.

White was born in Iowa, but at twelve years of age moved to Idaho, where his father was a railroad station agent. There he encountered Chinese, which enabled White to say that he had lived among them and understood them.

"I think there were 200 Chinese coolies employed in the immediate environs of the little town where I landed. It was simply a station along the railroad line. I saw the Chinese. I know something of the Chinese mentality. I wonder how much these people here who want to open the gates to Chinese immigration know of the perils that Chinese immigration raised in California in the early days, and all the troubles that the people had to maintain themselves against being displaced wholly and bodily by the Chinese coolies, exploited by a few whites . . . . In dealing with this bill, you are opening the doors, if you please, to coolie labor." 89 Cong. Rec. 8625–8626 (1943).

According to White, exclusion legislation had saved California from being overrun by Chinese immigrants. Whether rational or not, the fear of an overwhelming influx of Chinese had galvanized support on the West Coast for the original bills and later amendments. White used the same logic to validate those old messages:

"There were enough Chinese on the Pacific Coast to have colonized that country and taken it over from the white people completely. San Francisco today would be a Chinese city if you had not enforced this law that we are now trying to repeal." 89 Cong. Rec. 8626 (1943).

White denigrated the Chinese and their influence on the rest of society:

"I know the habits of the Chinese. They are inveterate opium smokers most of the day. They brought that hideous opium habit to this country. These Chinese coolies provide a means of spreading it out among our boys and girls. If you stop to think about what you are doing here in dealing with this Chinese question, you will not repeal this law." 89 Cong. Rec. 8626 (1943).

Reviving arguments about incapacity to assimilate, White contended that a new influx of Chinese would not integrate well in America. Permitting them to immigrate was likely to provoke severe racial tensions:

"I do not think we can take the Chinese with their habits and mentalities in this year and time into our great American melting pot and in 10 years or a hundred years bring them up to our standards of civilization. It is impossible. We may be placed in the same position as the sentimentalists were in the South after the Civil War who wanted to do something grand for civilization. You have got a long, tough job to bring them up, and you still have race riots and other racial problems confronting you." 89 Cong. Rec. 8626 (1943).

White posed a rhetorical question to his colleagues:

"How many of you know anything of the devious ways of the 'wily Chinese'?"

In concluding his remarks, White turned oddly benevolent and paternalistic:

"I have no animosity against the Chinese. We children loved the Chinese cooks and laundrymen who lavished Chinese 'goodies' on us on Chinese New Year's—and even remembered our own Christmas. Let us help the Chinese—but help them in their own country." 89 Cong. Rec. 8627 (1943).

A former teacher at the College of Yale in Changsha, China, Representative John Martin Vorys (R–OH) served in Congress from 1939 to 1959. He contradicted White's stridently anti-Chinese comments made earlier that afternoon. Moreover, Vorys was determined that Congress put the "gesture" of exclusion repeal into proper perspective:

"I cannot sit here in silence and hear things said about the Chinese through ignorance that simply are not true. The Chinese were a civilized people when your ancestors and mine were wearing skins for clothes and fighting with clubs . . . .

"We have all heard about 'face,' how important 'face' is in China—'face,' pride, dignity. Although the Chinese have their own standard of 'face,' we have the same thing in our country. If the situation were reversed, and we were doing more for a certain nation than any other nation, and they treated us with contempt, we would 'lose face.' 'Face' is not just oriental. It is universal.

"You say this is only a gesture. Gestures are important. Shaking your fist is a gesture, but an important one. Shaking hands is a gesture, but an important one. This is an important gesture to a people to whom we owe much and for whom we are in a position to do so little at a crucial time . . . ." 89 Cong. Rec. 828–8629 (1943).

Several of Vorys' colleagues had expressed reservations about the Chinese quota, believing it would set a precedent for demands for enhanced quotas for other countries or for a dismantling of immigration law generally. This argument did not persuade Vorys, who made plain that war exigencies trumped such concerns:

"If the precedent we are creating here is that we will remove discriminations against any nation on this planet that is fighting our battles for us at a time when we cannot do much about it, who are a race of great people, a civilized people, a fine people, all right, let us create that precedent; it is an excellent precedent to create. It will not only help the Chinese, but will help us." 89 Cong. Rec. 8629 (1943).

Representative Thomas F. Ford (D–CA) also rebutted the exclusionists. A congressman from 1933 to 1945, Ford insisted that public opinion on the West Coast strongly favored repeal. His stance represented an extraordinary reversal of position in his region. It was agitation from western representatives and senators that fostered exclusion legislation in the first instance (*Chapters One through Three*). Believing that exclusion had social costs that were not limited to the Chinese themselves, Ford added:

"I have always felt that Chinese exclusion was a mistake. It has deprived us of a type of citizenship that would have been a real contribution to our body politic. I sincerely hope that the Congress will promptly rectify this erroneous discrimination against a great people who, if permitted to enter on equal terms with other nations in our American body politic, will make a distinct and tremendously valuable contribution to freedom as conceived by democracy." 89 Cong. Rec. 8628 (1943).

Following additional speeches, Representative Walter Judd (R–MN) again took the House floor. He disputed the idea that the smallness of the quota would render the legislation meaningless to the Chinese. Judd emphasized that the point was equality of treatment, not quota numbers. To underline this, Judd quoted Bishop Paul Yu Pin, whose testimony before the House Immigration

§11.41 Motion to Recommit in the House

Customarily, under House procedure, before a final vote is taken on a measure, the minority party offers a motion to recommit the bill to the committee from which it came, which can have the effect of killing the legislation. Alternatively, the recommittal motion may be accompanied with instructions. Customarily, the instructions require that the bill be reported back "forthwith" with a particular amendment. Were such a recommittal motion to carry, the measure would immediately be back before the House with the minority-crafted amendment pending.

For more, see § 6.140 House Floor: Motion to Recommit and Final Passage, *Congressional Deskbook* (TheCapitol.Net, 2012).

and Naturalization Committee had been referred to earlier in the debate. The passages Judd cited appeared in an interview the bishop gave to *Commonweal* magazine. Bishop Yu Pin's comments demonstrated that moral symbolism was crucially important. Failure to pass the bill would neuter America's moral position; worse yet, it would seriously escalate racial tension:

"We do not wish to have you open your country to a flood of Chinese immigrants. That is your own problem, for you to solve precisely as you wish. It is an internal problem. But we do object to being branded not only as inferior to you but as inferior to all the other nations and races in the world . . . .

"Certainly China will keep in the fight until Japan is defeated. In this defeat you, of course, will play a great part. But if your attitude of superiority continues, if the Far East becomes convinced that the United States has forfeited her moral right to leadership, and is fixed in her determination to look down upon the colored races, I can foresee only a prospect which makes me tremble at its horrors.

"In that case, the next war would almost inevitably be a war between the races . . . ." 89 Cong. Rec. 8633 (1943).

Judd insisted that the possibility of major racial tensions was significant. Japanese propaganda in the Far East was using racially discriminatory American statutes to fan resentment. Race riots in the United States during the summer of 1943 were a harbinger of the problems Americans could anticipate if the Japanese were permitted to succeed. Judd urged rejection of the Bennett amendment.

The Bennett amendment to strike the quota was rejected: 21 representatives supported Bennett and 128 opposed him.

Representative A. Leonard Allen (D–LA) proposed the next amendment. It provided that no immigrant could be admitted to the United States until the number of unemployed persons was fewer than 1 million persons. Allen said he was offering the amendment on behalf of the American Legion. In their convention held during September 1943, the Legion had adopted a resolution that read:

"*Be it resolved by the American Legion in convention assembled in Omaha, Nebraska, September 21-23, 1943,* That all immigration be barred from the United States from the date of the end of hostilities of the present war until unemployment has dropped to less than 1,000,000." 89 Cong. Rec. 8633 (1943).

The Veterans of Foreign Wars were also anti-immigration, Allen assured the House. The VFW resolution, which also passed their convention in September 1943, provided:

"*Resolved by the Forty-fourth National Encampment of the Veterans of Foreign Wars of the United States,* To hereby go on record in opposition to any let-down in United States immigration or exclusion laws, under any guise whatsoever." 89 Cong. Rec. 8634 (1943).

Adopting his amendment would result in a ban on all immigration, noted Allen. It was offered to head off a post-war rush of immigrants, as had occurred after the First World War. It was not aimed expressly at the Chinese, Allen assured the House.

Allen's immigration ban amendment raised a subject that went beyond the scope of the underlying repeal bill. On a point of order, the amendment was ruled non-germane and thus out of order.

No further floor amendments were offered. The House Committee of the Whole reported the bill, as amended, to the full House. Before the vote on final passage, the minority was afforded a customary opportunity to move to recommit the bill. Representative Bennett offered the motion. He asked that the bill be recommitted to the House Committee on Immigration and Naturalization with instructions that it report the bill with an amendment striking section 2, which provided for the quota. The motion to recommit was rejected on a voice vote.

Final passage of H.R. 3070 in the House also occurred by voice vote, and the bill was passed. The measure would now be considered in the Senate.

§11.50 H.R. 3070 to the Senate

On Monday, October 25, 1943, the Senate received H.R. 3070, which was referred to the Senate Committee on Immigration.

The response of Chinese in America to the reversal of policy, both at the local and national levels, was joyous. Nowhere was this reaction more vivid than in San Francisco, where decades earlier sandlot orators had stoked the fires of exclusion. As noted in the *New York Times* of October 31, 1943:

"San Francisco itself was the leading center of severe discriminatory measures against the Chinese in the early Eighteen Eighties. So when the San Francisco Board of Supervisors took the lead, after three weeks of consideration, in unanimously voting to ask Congress to put Chinese immigration on a quota basis, that was regarded jubilantly among the Chinese themselves as a great victory for justice."

§11.51 Senate Committee Consideration

On November 16, 1943, Senator Charles O. Andrews (D–FL) submitted to the Senate the report of the Senate Committee on Immigration on H.R. 3070. The report recited that the committee had appointed a five-member subcommittee, which met on four occasions. Andrews chaired the subcommittee; other members were Senators George Radcliffe (D–MD), Burnet Maybank (D–SC), Rufus Holman (R–OR), and C. Douglass Buck (R–DE). The Senate subcommittee reviewed the House hearing record and took its own witness testimony.

The Senate Committee on Immigration proposed no amendments to H.R. 3070. In its "General Statement Relating to All Sections," the report observed:

"From a reading of the bill and a study of this report, it will be seen that it is proposed to remove discriminations against the Chinese, which have been a source of misunderstanding in the relations between our two people for over 60 years and have aroused widespread resentment among the Chinese people." S. Rep. No. 535, at p. 3 (1943).

Ignoring the virulently racial rhetoric that accompanied the exclusion debates, the committee whitewashed the motive for the old laws as purely economic.

"The original act of exclusion was not born of ill will toward the Chinese people. The motivation was exclusively economic." S. Rep. No. 535, at p. 3 (1943).

Somehow, the passage of years and the war in China illuminated for the senators characteristics of the Chinese people that Congress had ill-understood when passing the exclusion laws:

"We have had time and abundant occasion to reflect on the extraordinary qualities of the Chinese people. Above all, the tenacity and courage of the Chinese in their terrible ordeal of the last 7 years has impelled a respect we are proud to acknowledge." S. Rep. No. 535, at p. 4 (1943).

The Senate Committee on Immigration recommended the bill be passed without amendment. Repeal, it said, would square with the "realization of the

American people that freedom depends upon the respect for the integrity of others and that their own freedom and security demand that they accord to others the respect that they ask for themselves." S. Rep. No. 535, at p. 4 (1943).

§11.52 Senate Debate, November 26, 1943:
"The white man feared the onrush of the yellow man"

Under consideration: H.R. 3070, as passed by the House.

On November 26, 1943, the Friday after Thanksgiving, Senate Majority Leader Alben Barkley (D–KY) secured unanimous consent to turn to the consideration of H.R. 3070.

A senator from 1936 to 1946, Charles O. Andrews (D–FL) opened the debate. In September 1943, he had introduced S. 1404, which also proposed to repeal exclusion. Given its view that the House bill was acceptable, the Senate Committee on Immigration chose to order it reported, rather than to proceed with the Andrews legislation. By acting on the House bill, the Senate would expedite congressional treatment of exclusion repeal and speed the measure to President Roosevelt.

Andrews described the unique, discriminatory characteristics of the exclusion acts and their impact within the Chinese population:

"The Chinese are the only persons who were singled out by nationality or origin for discrimination in our immigration laws. It naturally has been a source of embarrassment to the Chinese, because they feel the inference is that the United States has set them apart as an inferior people." 89 Cong. Rec. 9989 (1943).

Senator Rufus C. Holman (R–OR) asked Andrews to yield. A senator from 1939 to 1945, Holman took exception to the use of the word "inferior":

"I wish to call attention to the use of the word 'inferior' in the Senator's statement. I protest against the use of the word 'inferior' in this discussion." 89 Cong. Rec. 9989 (1943).

Holman conceded that the Chinese were not a lesser people, but he contended that they were unable to assimilate in American society. Such was reason enough to maintain an exclusion policy:

"I do not contend that the Chinese are an inferior race, but they, in large numbers, are incompatible in that their civilization and racial characteristics are entirely divergent from our own. I base my thoughts on the subject not on the ground of inferiority of any race or group but on the ground of incompatibility when in large unassimilable groups they settle permanently among us." 89 Cong. Rec. 9989 (1943).

Senator Andrews did not respond, and resumed his prepared remarks about legal barriers to Asian immigration. He noted that other Asian peoples, notably Japanese and Koreans, had been restricted from the United States since early in the twentieth century. Originally, the bar was imposed via executive orders in 1907 and 1913. The original statute establishing the Asiatic Barred Zone was enacted in the Immigration Act of 1917. The Immigration Act of 1924 established a quota system for certain parts of the world, but expressly prohibited persons from the Asiatic Barred Zone from naturalizing. Andrews explained:

"When Congress passed the [Immigration Act of 1924], which became effective on July 1, 1924, it put in a provision in that act—section 13(c), to be specific —which provided with very limited exceptions such as ministers and professors, that no person racially ineligible to naturalization could be admitted to the United States. As a matter of fact, the Chinese exclusion laws could very well have been repealed at that time, because this broad provision of the 1924 Act, in a comparatively few words, accomplished the major objectives of the various Chinese exclusion laws." 89 Cong. Rec. 9989 (1943).

Although the exclusion acts had been rendered outmoded by the 1924 statute, they had remained in force until their effectiveness as a tool of war propaganda caused Congress to repeal them explicitly.

Section 2 of the repeal bill granted the Chinese a quota. This was the provision that had stirred controversy in the House and that had been the subject of Bennett's failed amendment. Senator Andrews told his colleagues about the distinctive nature of the Chinese quota:

"All that section 2 does is to grant an annual quota of 105 to cover all Chinese persons, no matter where they are born. This differs from the present quota laws, in which nativity is almost the sole determining factor as to the quota to which a person may be charged. The Chinese quota is based entirely on the Chinese people as such. In fact, it states that 'all Chinese persons entering the United States annually as immigrants shall be allocated to the quota for Chinese.' Under this language, a Chinese coming to the United States as an immigrant to reside permanently shall be charged to the one quota of 105 set aside for persons of the Chinese race, regardless of where they are born." 89 Cong. Rec. 9889–9990 (1943).

Later in his remarks, Andrews explained what would happen to Chinese of mixed blood. If an individual was at least one-half Chinese, and also half of a race eligible for citizenship, then that person could be admitted up to the limits of the Chinese quota. For instance, a person half-Chinese and half-white, or half-black would be admitted. But other combinations could not immigrate:

"If he is as much as one-half of a blood still ineligible for citizenship, such as

Jap, Hindu and so forth, he will be classed as a person racially ineligible to citizenship and neither admissible to the United States nor admissible to naturalization." 89 Cong. Rec. 9991 (1943).

Andrews inserted in the *Congressional Record* an October 13, 1943, letter from Attorney General Francis Biddle to Senator Richard Russell, chairman of the Senate Committee on Immigration. With regard to immigration controls, Biddle claimed that the 1924 quota restrictions had rendered the exclusion laws obsolete. As to citizenship rights, Attorney General Biddle estimated that 45,000 Chinese, then resident in the United States, would be able to qualify.

Senator Elbert Thomas (D–UT) followed Andrews to the Senate floor. Prior to his time in the Senate, he had been a leader in the national immigration debate. As an academic, serving with a group called the National Committee for Constructive Immigration Legislation, he had helped to formulate proposals that were the foundation for the 1924 quota law. By 1933, Thomas had been elected to the Senate, where he served until 1951.

As a young man, Thomas had been a Mormon missionary in Japan. He learned to speak Japanese and, as a professor at the University of Utah, taught Japanese culture.

Statutes based on the concept of racial superiority, said Senator Thomas, were morally wrong. Striking them down was the right thing to do. But Thomas distinguished between racial "superiority," which he felt was unsupportable, and racial "incompatibility," which he thought was self-evident:

"There are no superior and inferior races, Mr. President. There are races with different habits of life, with different outlooks on life, with racial differences which make them incompatible, as the Senator from Oregon [Holman] has stated, and there will probably always be an incompatibility between the white and the yellow races so long as they live apart from each other and follow the habits of their ancestors." 89 Cong. Rec. 9993 (1943).

Thomas preferred to acknowledge racial differences rather than to obscure them with noble arguments about racial equality. To illustrate this, the senator drew upon an historical analogy.

At the Paris Peace Conference in 1919 following World War I, the Japanese government asked President Woodrow Wilson to support inclusion of a "racial equality" declaration in the League of Nations Covenant. Wilson refused, causing great consternation among the Japanese. Nonetheless, Thomas believed Wilson had acted wisely because, like President Wilson, the senator also did not believe in racial equality:

"Our President—and I am proud that he was able to face the question on the basis of right and justice and with an understanding of history—stated to the Japanese that there was no such thing as racial equality. And since there is no such thing as racial equality, a declaration to that effect in any kind of document, no matter how universally that doctrine may be preached, will not bring about racial equality. It does not exist.

"Then President Wilson, with his genius in dealing with the subject, instead of saying 'These yellow people are inferior to our people,' stated the facts. He said we could not compete with the yellow man, because of his racial characteristics and racial habits. The yellow man works longer. He sleeps less. He lives on a lower standard. He wants less leisure. He marries earlier. He has more children. All that may be a sign of strength rather than a sign of weakness." 89 Cong. Rec. 9993 (1943).

Senator Thomas contended it was primarily apprehension, mixed with a dose of racism, that drove enactment of the exclusion laws:

"The white man feared the onrush of the yellow man, and it was that fear which brought the Exclusion Act. The action was not based on a superiority–inferiority comparison." 89 Cong. Rec. 9993 (1943).

Thomas was not troubled by arguments about the peculiar nature of a Chinese quota. Granting a quota of whatever kind would at least bring China into the family of other quota nations. If the quota reflected bias rather than even-handedness, that was not problematic. The immigration system was not intended to be egalitarian:

"We do discriminate in our immigration legislation, but we do so in a fair way. We lay down first of all the principle that a certain racial and ethnical compatibility exists in the American Nation, and we want to keep it that way. Therefore, one nationality does not have an equal chance with another nationality in coming into the United States. Immigration is highly graded.

"One might think that because of the fact that there are more than 400,000,000 Chinese, more Chinese should be allowed to come into our country than nationals of other countries, but less are allowed to come in, because immigration rests upon the basis of the stock of the American people . . . . We do discriminate between various peoples under our immigration legislation, and that would continue, but we discriminate on the basis of our own ideas of what we want our national stock to be." 89 Cong. Rec. 9994 (1943).

Thomas expounded upon the impact of psychological warfare throughout history. In many instances, the effect of such tactics had been profound. Repealing exclusion presented an opportunity to secure a psychological advantage against the Japanese that should not be missed:

"As I have pointed out, the measure we are considering today, and what we say and do about it, are part of the psychological warfare we are waging against Germany and Japan. Its passage will signify that we mean what we say when we talk about justice and the sovereignty of free nations." 89 Cong. Rec. 9998 (1943).

After Thomas sat down, Senator Holman received unanimous consent to insert in the *Congressional Record* a lengthy statement prepared by Senator Hiram Johnson (R–CA). The document had originally been submitted to the Senate Committee on Immigration and was entitled "The Story of Legislation on Oriental Labor." The ranking minority member of the Committee on Immigration, Johnson was long a fixture in both California and national politics. He served in the Senate from 1917 to his death in 1945. From 1911 to 1917, Johnson had been California's governor and, in 1912, was Theodore Roosevelt's running mate on the Progressive Party (Bull Moose) ticket. When exclusion repeal was debated in the Senate, Johnson was ill, so Holman placed the statement in the *Record* on Johnson's behalf.

Notwithstanding the fact that Johnson had decided to oppose the bill, his paper disavowed any race prejudice toward the Chinese:

"My opposition to the pending bill does not indicate a lack of appreciation for the courageous fight of the Chinese people to preserve their independence. Nor is it inspired by any prejudice toward the Chinese at home or abroad . . . . At the outset, I want to make it emphatically clear that my position, and that of those who appear here on my behalf, does not imply in any degree inferiority of the Chinese race in those matters to which they give their attention." 89 Cong. Rec. 9999 (1943).

Johnson recounted that the original opposition to Chinese labor had sprung from the white miners in California. Their objections spread to other parts of the white population, especially the working class. In response, the California state legislature took steps to bar Chinese immigration, passing a state exclusion law in 1858. "If Californians had been able to legislate on the subject, it would have been settled," he said. Because any such state statute was unconstitutional, California led demands for federal legislation. "It is well known that California has borne the brunt of the long struggle for effective Asiatic exclusion," noted Johnson. 89 Cong. Rec. 9999 (1943).

The "long struggle" to which Johnson referred took many forms. As Johnson described it:

"For three decades, the white residents of California and adjacent states tried out every conceivable method to discourage Chinese immigration. There was an unending series of discriminatory state laws and city ordinances. There were anti-Chinese demonstrations, riots, and persecutions without number." 89 Cong. Rec. 9999 (1943).

The cause of this unrest was self-preservation, Johnson reported. In retrospect, critics might think that sentiment was overblown, but Johnson insisted otherwise:

"There are those who now maintain that Chinese immigrants were never a menace to our country, but the record speaks for itself. Without restriction, the teeming population of China could have literally overwhelmed our western shores in an incredibly short period. The opposition to Chinese immigration was not a racial but wholly an economic issue." 89 Cong. Rec. 9999 (1943).

Stymied by federal courts, Californians had no place to turn but to Congress, where most members were inexperienced in dealing with Chinese immigration. Johnson described the dilemma:

"Thus the final action on this question, which was of the most vital importance in the social and economic development of California, was left to the representatives of States where no such problems had ever been met, and where there was more or less complete ignorance of their significance." 89 Cong. Rec. 10000 (1943).

Senator Johnson noted that the motivating influence for exclusion had been labor organizations, which heavily petitioned Congress at the time of exclusion and, even in 1943, opposed repeal. Organized labor was relentless in its efforts:

"During the eighties, the efforts to solve the Chinese problem were transferred from the State to the National legislative bodies, but the workingmen's organizations of the Pacific Coast were still in back of the whole movement. They never relaxed their strenuous efforts to enlist the active support of their fellow trade-unionists in the East, or ceased to make known their grim determination to prevent the continued influx of organized labor, even if by a last resort to violence. They ignored all party lines and voted steadily and consistently with a view to the promotion of this one issue." 89 Cong. Rec. 10000 (1943).

Johnson narrated the long history of Chinese exclusion efforts within Congress, beginning with the Fifteen Passenger bill of 1879 (*Chapter Two*) and ending with the 1904 statute that made exclusion permanent (*Chapter Ten*). Immigration pressures from Japan began to rise just as Chinese exclusion was cemented into law, the senator noted:

"Japanese immigration became an issue during the early years of the present century. The anti-Japanese agitation was mild and innocuous in comparison with the virulent anti-Chinese movement that had raged in the coast states for several decades." 89 Cong. Rec. 9999 (1943).

Seeing Japan as an ally for American foreign policy in the Far East, President Theodore Roosevelt (1901–1909) opposed legislation to exclude Japanese, said Johnson. Instead, the president entered into an informal 1907 Gentlemen's Agreement with Tokyo by which the Japanese government would refrain from issuing passports to Japanese laborers. While the Gentlemen's Agreement of 1907 preempted restrictive legislation, it was not altogether effective, said Johnson. Exclusion statutes had worked better:

"Investigations made by the California State Board of Control showed that the Japanese population of California increased during the decade 1910–1920 by more than 25,000 from immigration only. During the same period, the net increase of the Chinese population, including births, was only 789. In other words, the Chinese Exclusion Act actually excluded. The Japanese Gentlemen's Agreement did not." 89 Cong. Rec. 9999 (1943).

According to Johnson, the remedy was to preempt all this with the 1924 Immigration Act. In addition to establishing the quota system for certain countries and making others quota-free, the 1924 Act barred from immigration any person who was not eligible to naturalize:

"Exclusion of all aliens ineligible to citizenship offered a logical, simple, practical, and effective solution of the entire Asiatic immigration problem. It followed federal law which since 1790 made all the yellow and brown races ineligible to citizenship because of unassimilability and the menace they would offer if established here." 89 Cong. Rec. 9999 (1943).

Reaffirming the logic first expressed by Senator James G. Blaine (R–ME) in the 1879 Fifteen Passenger debate (*Chapter Two*) and that of other members as time went along, Johnson remarked, "Certainly, if immigration is to be restricted, we should commence with that element which is barred from citizenship." 89 Cong. Rec. 9999 (1943).

The Japanese government vigorously objected to the exclusionary effect of the 1924 immigration statute, but Senator Johnson thought the protests were excessive. Japanese were not specifically targeted and had themselves restricted immigration to Japan from China and Korea:

"The measure is not discriminatory against Japan, for it applies to half the population of the globe, and the Japanese constitute not more than 7 or 8 percent of those affected. It should be remembered, too, that Japan in protection of her own people, wisely excludes Chinese and Koreans, thus discriminating against people of her own color." 89 Cong. Rec. 9999 (1943).

For Johnson, existing U.S. law had the virtue of fairness. All Asians were barred from naturalization, so all were stopped from immigrating. As passed by the House in H.R. 3070, repeal legislation would replace the blanket exclusion of Asians with a structure that would prefer Chinese above other Asians:

"Having placed all Asiatic peoples on an equal basis with respect to immigration and naturalization, Congress is now about to pass a bill discriminating in favor of one Asiatic nation against all other peoples of the Orient, who were excluded because of ineligibility to citizenship . . . .

"Is not this proposed legislation a deliberate slap in the face for all Asiatic peoples, except only for the Chinese? Is it not a complete reversal of America's carefully considered, nondiscriminatory immigration policy toward all nations and races of Asia?" 89 Cong. Rec. 9999 (1943).

While Johnson did not object to erasing the stigma of exclusion, he believed the Chinese quota would generate fresh problems: "Enactment of this bill will place upon our statute books an immigration policy frankly and clearly discriminatory against a far greater number of Asiatics than Chinese." 89 Cong, Rec. 9999–10000 (1943).

Next recognized was Senator Robert Rice Reynolds (D–NC), who served from 1933 to 1945. Reynolds opposed repeal on the grounds that enhanced immigration, however modest, would complicate the post-war employment prospects for returning servicemen. The American Federation of Labor had made precisely the same point, an argument to which Reynolds would return before concluding his remarks. Reynolds couched his position as supporting the troops:

"I want any jobs available after the war to go to our soldiers; I am going to fight for those soldiers; and when I vote against repeal of the Chinese exclusion acts, I believe conscientiously in my heart and soul that I am voting for every American man and woman in uniform . . . ." 89 Cong. Rec. 10012 (1943).

Reynolds then opened a broad attack on immigration generally:

"If we were to follow the advice of some radical internationalists we would permit anyone from any country in the world to come to the United States of America and take over the United States of America." 89 Cong. Rec. 10012 (1943).

"I have nothing against the Chinese," Reynolds proclaimed, but he refused to relax immigration law, even to let 105 Chinese enter the country. Such immigrants should not lay claim to a single job, he said.

Reynolds took President Franklin D. Roosevelt to task for characterizing Chinese exclusion as a mistake. "This seems an extraordinary pronouncement for the President to make," he objected. Drawing upon the fear of yellow hordes overwhelming the United States with immigration, Reynolds argued that the exclusion acts had preempted severe race trouble in America and, through their extension into the Asiatic Barred Zone, had prevented the formation of a Japanese "fifth column":

"Had Congress not enacted the Chinese Exclusion Acts when it did, our country would now have on its hands a race problem. In fact, if Congress had not finally developed the principle of Chinese exclusion into total Asiatic exclusion, our existing Japanese problem would have been so magnified as to constitute a grave military menace." 89 Cong. Rec. 10013 (1943).

Defending the policy of excluding Chinese by race, Reynolds argued that it had prevented circumventions. He opined that, otherwise, Chinese subjects of the British Crown could have accessed substantial numbers of unused quota spots available to Britain; alternatively, they could have traveled to Latin America and entered the U.S. from Western Hemisphere countries, none of which had a quota.

Reynolds believed the public would be intolerant of such evasions. Accordingly, the Chinese were given a special quota that prevented them from entering the United States using anyone else's quota. However, solving one problem meant creating another. Echoing Senators Thomas and Johnson, Reynolds complained that the special quota advantaged Chinese over other Asians.

Such a pro-Chinese preference would not last, Reynolds said. Forecasting the effects of exclusion repeal, he anticipated pressure to relax immigration quotas for Asians generally, such as those from British India. Between 10,000 and 50,000 Asian immigrants could be expected to seek admittance every year if this first step were taken, Reynolds predicted.

Senator Reynolds inserted in the *Congressional Record* an October 4, 1943, report of the Executive Council of the American Federation of Labor. The report makes clear the instrumental role unions had in promoting passage of exclusion legislation:

"One of the first acts of the first convention of the American Federation of Labor in 1881 was to declare: 'Thirty years' experience of the Pacific Coast with the Chinese had proved their competition with white labor was the greatest evil with which a country could be afflicted; that publicity as to its true character be disseminated throughout the country, and Congress be urged to enact an exclusion act.'

"The question of Chinese exclusion was one of the most important questions pending before the American Federation of Labor conventions, beginning with its first one, and including the present law enacted in 1924, which prohibits the entry into this country of persons ineligible to citizenship . . . .

"From its inception, the American Federation of Labor has vigorously maintained that orientals should be barred from entering this country and that they should not be permitted to become citizens . . . .

"The fact that China is our ally in the present world war should not influence us to permit repeal of the oriental exclusion law any more than the fact that Russia is an ally should influence us to embrace communism." 89 Cong. Rec. 10014 (1943).

Reynolds also submitted a letter from James L. Wilmeth, National Secretary of the National Council, Junior Order United American Mechanics. The letter recited the ritual union complaints about relaxing immigration quotas and exclusion bars, but also directly advocated exclusion based on race:

"The yellow race is not assimilable with the white or Caucasian race. The introduction of a large number of Asiatic orientals at this time would complicate the race situation in the United States. We have all the race troubles at the present time that we can handle." 89 Cong. Rec. 10015 (1943).

Wilmeth's letter also raised a unique issue. No one else in the 1943 debate had spoken about Chinese Communism, a subject that would roil the Congress only a half-decade later when Mao Zedong would overthrow the Chiang Kaishek government in 1949. In Wilmeth's letter, the subject was casually, but expressly, mentioned:

"Communism has been introduced into China during the last decade or two. If we are to believe the reports we read, there are large numbers of Chinese people who have espoused and are devoted to the doctrines and principles of communism. The introduction of even a small number of Chinese who are indoctrinated with communism will further complicate our political and economic condition." 89 Cong. Rec. 10015 (1943).

Concluding his remarks, Senator Reynolds offered two amendments. The first, like Representative Allen's amendment, barred immigration unless the number of unemployed persons in the United States was under 1 million. The second barred the issuance of any visas to any immigrant for a period of one year following conclusion of the war. The amendments were defeated by voice votes.

No other amendments were proposed. After a single day of debate, H.R. 3070 passed in the Senate on a voice vote without amendment on November 26, 1943.

§11.60 Bill Enrollment and Presidential Signature

On December 8, 1943, the second anniversary of America's Declaration of War against Japan, Speaker of the House Sam Rayburn (D–TX) and Vice President Henry Wallace signed the enrolled copy of H.R. 3070 and transmitted it to the White House.

Returning to Washington after the Tehran Conference (November 28 to December 1, 1943) with Premier Joseph Stalin and Prime Minister Winston Churchill, President Franklin Roosevelt signed the bill. On Friday, December 17, 1943, more than sixty years after they were first imposed, the Chinese exclusion acts were repealed.

美 Epilogue
國

On May 26, 2011, in a hearing room at the Rayburn House Office Building, Representative Judy Chu (D–CA), along with two of her principal cosponsors, Representatives Judy Biggert (R–IL) and Mike Coffman (R–CO), held a press conference to announce introduction of House Resolution 282, which expressed the House's regret for passing legislation targeted at Chinese immigrants. Representative Dana Rohrabacher (R–CA) joined as an original cosponsor.

That same day, Senator Scott Brown (R–MA) introduced Senate Resolution 201, expressing regret on behalf of the Senate. Senators Dianne Feinstein (D–CA), Orrin Hatch (R–UT), Patty Murray (D–WA), Daniel Akaka (D–HI), Marco Rubio (R–FL), and Ben Cardin (D–MD) were his original cosponsors. Shortly thereafter, Senators Tom Carper (D–DE), Chris Coons (D–DE), Mark Kirk (R–IL), and John Hoeven (R–ND) added their cosponsorship.

As the Senate was concluding its proceedings of October 6, 2011, Senate Majority Leader Harry Reid (D–NV) secured unanimous consent to discharge the Senate Judiciary Committee from further consideration of Senate Resolution 201 and to bring it to the Senate floor. By unanimous consent that evening, the Senate agreed to the resolution.

Senator Brown upheld the traditions of his predecessors, Senators George Hoar (R–MA, Senate 1877–1904) and Henry Dawes (R–MA, Senate 1875–1893), who opposed exclusion from the first moment. He also stood in the shoes of another Massachusetts senator, Charles Sumner, who worked tirelessly to erase the stain of racial prejudice and discrimination in America.

Brown's prime co-sponsor, Dianne Feinstein, understood all too well the effects of a policy that germinated in her state. Long a champion of civil rights and a friend of the Chinese–American community, she worked with Brown to shine the light of truth on a sad historical record and to make things right.

On June 8, 2012, after discussions with House Judiciary Committee Chairman Lamar Smith (R-TX), Representative Chu introduced an updated text, House Resolution 683. Cosponsored by Chairman Smith, the new resolution was referred to the House Judiciary Committee.

House Resolution 683 was discharged from committee on June 18, 2012. Later that day, under suspension of the rules, it passed the House. House Majority Leader Eric Cantor (R-VA) stated to the press, "Throughout our history, America has been a country of promise and opportunity. While we have done much to fulfill that promise, we've also made serious missteps and we didn't always get it right. More than a century ago, Congress enacted legislation that discriminated against people of Chinese origin and went against the very principles of liberty and opportunity for all that our country has always held dear. Today, as a sign of friendship to the many Chinese-Americans who are an essential part of the fabric of our nation, the House formally acknowledged these wrongs. I thank Representative Chu for submitting this resolution and I am proud that the House had the opportunity to consider it today."

It is very rare for a sitting Congress to reflect on U.S. history and to pass resolutions evaluating the deeds of its predecessors. But the Chinese exclusion laws so strongly clashed with America's values and national purpose that Congress was motivated to act.

Leaving the Capitol Building after passage of the Chu resolution, I stopped at the statue of Hannibal Hamlin in Statuary Hall, steps away from the House Floor. It was Hamlin who proclaimed that his vote against the 1879 Fifteen Passenger Bill would be a legacy to his children, that they might deem it the brightest act of his life. The resolutions of the House and Senate of the 112th Congress redeemed his foresight. "Thank you, Senator," I said aloud.

BACK OF THE BOOK

Appendix 1. Review and Discussion Questions

Appendix 2. Burlingame Treaty (1868)

Appendix 3. Naturalization Act of 1870 (16 Stat. 254)

Appendix 4. Fifteen Passenger Bill (1879) and Veto Message of President Rutherford Hayes of the Fifteen Passenger Bill, March 1, 1879, 1879 Congressional Record—House 2275–2277

Appendix 5. Angell Treaty 1880 (ratified 1881)

Appendix 6. Veto Message of President Chester A. Arthur of Senate Bill No. 71, April 4, 1882

Appendix 7. The Ten-Year Exclusion Legislation of 1882, H.R. 5804 "An act to execute certain treaty stipulations relating to Chinese." (Sess. I, Chap. 126; 22 Stat. 58. 47th Congress; Approved May 6, 1882.)

Appendix 8. Gresham–Yang Treaty (1894)

Appendix 9. The 1902 Extension. "An act to prohibit the coming into and to regulate the residence within the United States, its Territories, and all territory under its jurisdiction, and the District of Columbia, of Chinese and persons of Chinese descent." (Sess. I Chap. 641; 32 Stat. 176. 57th Congress; April 29, 1902.)

Appendix 10. Permanent Law 1904 (Sess. 2 Chap. 1630, Section 5, 58 Stat. 428, April 27, 1904.)

Appendix 11. Magnuson Act (Chinese Exclusion Repeal Act of 1943), H.R. 3070, "An act to repeal the Chinese Exclusion Acts, to establish quotas, and for other purposes." (Chap. 344, Public Law 78–199, 57 Stat. 600, December 17, 1943.)

Appendix 12. American Immigration Laws Timeline

Appendix 13. Bibliography

Appendix 14. Additional Resources <TCNFCA.com>

Index

Acknowledgments

About the Author

APPENDIX 1

Review and Discussion Questions

Chapter 1

- Why did Senator William Stewart filibuster the naturalization bill?

- If a majority of senators supported the Sumner amendment, why couldn't they overcome the filibuster?

- If naturalization rights had been extended in 1870 to Chinese immigrants, would the history of Chinese exclusion efforts likely have been different?

- The 1870 debate involved a major issue that recurs in future debates—the choice between expanding suffrage and restricting immigration. What were the primary arguments in the debate for either choice? Why are the positions of senators on either side so hard to reconcile?

Chapter 2

- What happened in the decade after the Burlingame Treaty to change attitudes in Congress toward Chinese immigration?

- How did the Fifteen Passenger Bill breach American treaty obligations to China?

- Is it proper for Congress to legislate in a way that violates U.S. treaty obligations?

Chapter 3

- How did the veto of the Fifteen Passenger bill propel forward efforts to pass the twenty-year 1882 exclusion bill?

- How did the Angell Treaty change U.S. obligations to Chinese immigrants?

- How did the history of previous racial and ethnic conflicts in the United States affect the debate?

Chapter 4

- Why did Congress welcome immigrants from Europe while rejecting immigrants from China?

- Several representatives who previously supported the emancipation and enfranchisement of African-American slaves also supported unequal treatment of Chinese immigrants. How did these representatives explain their seemingly contradictory positions?

- Why did President Chester Arthur believe that the twenty-year exclusion bill exceeded U.S. rights under the Angell Treaty?

Chapter 5

- Why did Congress deny the right of naturalization to Chinese who had already legally immigrated to the United States?

- What effect did exclusion from naturalization have on the ability of Chinese to seek redress through the U.S. political system?

- What procedural issues affected the passage of the ten-year bill in the House of Representatives?

- If President Arthur vetoed the twenty-year exclusion bill because it contradicted U.S. treaty obligations, why did he sign the ten-year bill?

Chapter 6

- Why did Congress again address the subject of Chinese exclusion so soon after passing the 1882 Act?

- Why did Congress expand exclusion to cover all persons of Chinese origin rather than just individuals immigrating from China? Why did some representatives and senators think that this expansion would have a large impact on U.S. foreign policy?

- In the 1884 debate, certain representatives and senators credited the Chinese exclusion policies to their own political parties. Why do you think the debate was more expressly partisan than earlier debates?

Chapter 7

- Why did Congress insist on the renegotiation of treaty arrangements with China?

- How did Senate amendments to the Bayard–Zhang treaty render it unacceptable to China?

- Why did Congress consider passage of the Scott Act an urgent matter?

- How did the Scott Act conflict with existing Sino-American agreements?

Chapter 8

- Why did Congress insist that Chinese workers carry documentation?

- How could a Chinese person without documentation prove his right to remain in the United States?

- In deportation proceedings, why did Congress make the Chinese guilty unless proven innocent?
- Some representatives and senators found the Geary Act's enforcement provisions, including the habeas corpus provision, too stringent. How did proponents of the Geary Act justify the act's enforcement tools? Are their justifications persuasive?

Chapter 9

- Why did the House pass complex legislation rather than just extending existing law?
- Why did Representative Clark support the provision that barred Chinese persons born in U.S. territories from immigrating to the United States?
- Why did the Senate pass a simpler bill to extend the exclusion laws?
- What was the relationship between the 1902 extension and the Gresham–Yang treaty?

Chapter 10

- What was the impact on Chinese immigration of China's ending the Gresham–Yang treaty?
- Why did Congress believe it was necessary to separate Chinese exclusion laws from Sino-American treaties?
- By what legislative path did Congress make exclusion policy permanent?

Chapter 11

- What was the relationship between the Chinese exclusion laws and America's war strategy?
- Why was a special immigration quota created for Chinese people?
- In the 1943 debate, several senators and representatives discussed what they believed to be the reasons that the Chinese exclusion laws were originally enacted. Now that you have reviewed the major debates, do you agree with these characterizations?

APPENDIX 2

Burlingame Treaty
(Burlingame-Seward Treaty of 1868)

TREATY CONCERNING TRADE, CONSULS, RELIGIOUS TOLERATION AND EMIGRATION, BEING ADDITIONAL ARTICLES TO THE TREATY OF JUNE 18, 1858.

Concluded July 28, 1868; Ratifications exchanged at Peking, November 23, 1869; Proclaimed February 5, 1870.

Whereas since the conclusion of the treaty between the United States of America and the Ta Tsing Empire (China) of the 18th of June, 1858, circumstances have arisen showing the necessity of additional articles thereto, the President of the United States and the august sovereign of the Ta Tsing Empire have named for their plenipotentiaries, to wit: the President of the United States of America, William H. Seward, Secretary of State, and his Majesty the Emperor of China, Anson Burlingame, accredited as his Envoy Extraordinary and Minister Plenipotentiary, and Chih-Kang and Sun Chia-Ku, of the second Chinese rank, associated high envoys and ministers of his said Majesty, and the said plenipotentiaries, after having exchanged their full powers, found to be in due and proper form, have agreed upon the following articles:

ARTICLE I

His Majesty the Emperor of China, being of the opinion that, in making concessions to the citizens or subjects of foreign Powers of the privilege of residing on certain tracts of land, or resorting to certain waters of that empire for purposes of trade, he has by no means relinquished his right of eminent domain or dominion over the said land and water, hereby agrees that no such concession or grant shall be construed to give to any Power or party which may be at war with or hostile to the United States the right to attack the citizens of the United States or their property within the said lands or waters; and the United States from resisting an attack by any hostile Power or party upon their citizens or their property, It is further agreed that if any right or interest in any tract of land in China has been or shall hereafter be granted by the Government of China to the United States or their citizens for purposes of trade or commerce, that grant shall in no event be construed to divest the Chinese authorities of their right of jurisdiction over persons and property within said tract of land, except so far as that right may have been expressly relinquished by treaty.

ARTICLE II

The United States of America and his Majesty the Emperor of China, believing that the safety and prosperity of commerce will thereby best be promoted, agree that any privilege or immunity in respect to trade or navigation within the Chinese dominions which may not have been stipulated for by treaty, shall be subject to the discretion of the Chinese Government and may be regulated by it accordingly, but not in a manner or spirit incompatible with the treaty stipulations of the parties.

ARTICLE III

The Emperor of China shall have the right to appoint consuls at ports of the United States, who shall enjoy the same privileges and immunities as those enjoyed by public law and treaty in the United States by the consuls of Great Britain and Russia, or either of them.

ARTICLE IV

The twenty-ninth article of the treaty of the 18th of June, 1858, having stipulated for the exemption of Christian citizens of the United States and Chinese converts from persecution in China on account of their faith, it is further agreed that citizens of the United States in China of every religious persuasion and Chinese subjects in the United States shall enjoy entire liberty of conscience and shall be exempt from all disability or persecution on account of their religious faith or worship in either country. Cemeteries for sepulture of the dead of whatever nativity or nationality shall be held in respect and free from disturbance or profanation.

ARTICLE V

The United States of America and the Emperor of China cordially recognize the inherent and inalienable right of man to change his home and allegiance, and also the mutual advantage of the free migration and emigration of their citizens and subjects respectively from the one country to the other, for purposes of curiosity, of trade, or as permanent residents. The high contracting parties, therefore, join in reprobating any other than an entirely voluntary emigration for these purposes. They consequently agree to pass laws making it a penal offence for a citizen of the United States or Chinese subjects to take Chinese subjects either to the United States or to any other foreign country, or for a Chinese subject or citizen of the United States to take citizens of the United States to China or to any other foreign country, without their free and voluntary consent respectively.

ARTICLE VI

Citizens of the Untied States visiting or residing in China shall enjoy the same privileges, immunities or exemptions in respect to travel or residence as may there be enjoyed by the citizens or subjects of the most favored nation, and, reciprocally, Chinese subjects visiting or residing in the United States shall enjoy the same privileges, immunities and exemptions in respect to travel or residence as may there be enjoyed by the citizens or subjects of the most favored nation. But nothing herein contained shall be held to confer naturalization upon citizens of the United States in China, nor upon the subjects of China in the United States.

ARTICLE VII

Citizens of the United States shall enjoy all the privileges of the public educational institutions under the control of the government of China, and reciprocally, Chinese subjects shall enjoy all the privileges of the public educational institutions under the control of the government of the United States, which are enjoyed in the respective countries by the citizens or subjects of the most favored nation. The citizens of the United States may freely establish and maintain schools within the Empire of China at those places where foreigners are by treaty permitted to reside, and, reciprocally, Chinese subjects may enjoy the same privileges and immunities in the United States.

ARTICLE VIII

The United States, always disclaiming and discouraging all practices of unnecessary dictation and intervention by one nation in the affairs or domestic administration of another, do hereby freely disclaim and disavow any intention or right to intervene in the domestic administration of China in regard to the construction of railroads, telegraphs or other material internal improvements. On the other hand, his Majesty, the Emperor of China, reserves to himself the right to decide the time and manner and circumstances of introducing such improvements within his dominions. With this mutual understanding it is agreed by the contracting parties that if at any time hereafter his imperial Majesty shall determine to construct or cause to be constructed works of the character mentioned within the empire, and shall make application to the United States or any other Western Power for facilities to carry out that policy, the United States will, in that case, designate and authorize suitable engineers to be employed by the Chinese Government, and will recommend to other nations an equal compliance with such application, the Chinese Government in that case protecting such engineers in their persons and property, and paying them a reasonable compensation for their service.

In faith whereof the respective Plenipotentiaries have signed this treaty and thereto affixed the seals of their arms.

Done at Washington the twenty-eighth day of July, in the year of our Lord one thousand eight hundred and sixty-eight.

[SEAL]   WILLIAM H. SEWARD
         ANSON BURLINGAME
[SEAL]   CHIH-KANG
         SUN CHIA-KU

Signed in the English and Chinese languages, at Washington July 28, 1868. Ratifications exchanged at Peking, November 23, 1869.

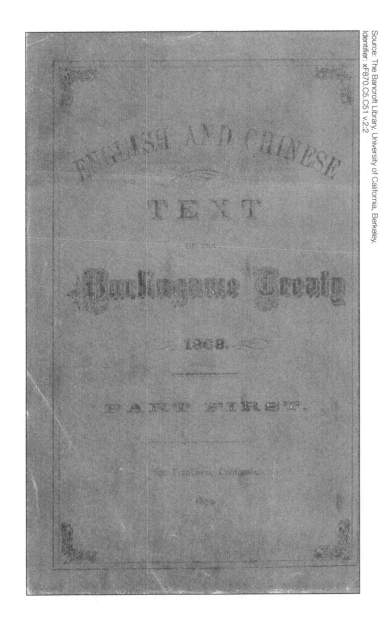

第一款　大清與　　大合衆兩國並其民人各皆照前和平友

好毋得或異更不得互相欺凌偶因小故而啓爭端若他國

有何不公輕視之事一經照知必湏相助從中善為調處以

示友誼關切　第三款

　　　　　　一俟　大清

　　大合衆國　大伯理璽天德既得選舉國會紳耆

帝　　大皇帝批准原册　　　　　　　　大合

大臣議允各將條約之批准互易後必湏敬禮收藏

衆國當著首相恭藏　大清

於華咸頓都城　　大清國當著内閣學士恭藏　大合

衆國　　大伯理璽天德批准原册於北京都城則兩國之

　友誼歷久弗替矣

紙筆人厘利士謹録

第三款　一條約各欵必使兩國軍民人等盡得聞知俾可遵守

大合衆國於批准互易後立即宣布照例刊傳　大清國於

批准五易後六即通諭都城並著各省督撫一體頒行　第四欵

一因欲堅立友誼嗣後　大清内閣大學士大將之大臣任聽以平行

之禮信義之道與　大合衆國駐劄中華之大臣往來並得與兩廣閩

浙兩江督撫一體公文往來至京會商　京師内閣文件或交公文如有

督撫照例代送或交提塘驛站賫遞均無不可其照會公文加

印封者必湏謹愼費遞遇有劄照等件　内閣暨各督撫當卽量

迅速照覆　第五欵

一嗣後無論何時倘有中華

別國或立約或為別故允准與衆國　大皇帝情願與

再行計議特許應准　大合衆國　欽差一律照辦無沾掛碍

公家事件　大合衆國

第六欵　一　大合衆國大臣遇　事不論何時應准到北京暫住與

内閣大學士或與派出平行大憲酌議關涉彼此利益事件惟每年

不得逾一次到京後卽速定議不得耽往來應由海口或由陸

路不得駕馭兵船進天津海口先行知照地方官派員船迩接若保小

事不得因有此條輕請到京至上京必湏先行照會禮部俾得

循辦一切事歟往返邊送彼此以礼相待富京之日按品撙備

公館所有費用自備貨斧其跟從　大合衆國

欽差人等不得逾二十人之數僱客華人供役在外到處不

得帶貨貿易

紙筆人厘利士謹録

第七款
一、嗣後中國督撫與合衆國大臣會晤或在公署
或在行轅均須彼此酌定合宜之處毋得藉端推辭常事以
文移往來不可煩瑣會面
第八款
一、大合衆國如有官船在通商海口遊奕巡查
該地方大員當與船中統領以平行礼儀相待以示兩國和好
之誼如有採買食物淡水或須修理等事中國官員自
當襄助購辦遇有　大合衆國船隻或因毀壞刧或雖未
毀壞而尚被刻被擄及在大洋等處如有事故
船追捕盜賊交地方官訊究應辦　大合衆國官、

紙筆人厘利士謹錄

第九款
一、大合衆國領事及管理貿易等官在中華議
之所開各港居住保護貿易者當與道臺知府平行
過有與中華地方官交涉事件或公文往來或會晤面
商務須兩得其平即所用一切字樣体制尚應平
行如地方官及領事等官有侮慢欺觌之事准其彼此
將委曲情由申訴　本國各大憲秉公查辦候領事等官
六不得率意任情致與中華官民動多抵牾嗣後遇事官
派到港口大合衆國大臣即行照知該省督撫當以優禮
欵接致可行其職守之事

本館紙筆人厘利士謹錄

第十款
一、大合衆國民人在中華安分貿易辦事者當
與中國人一体和好友愛地方官必時加保護俾身家二
安不使受欺侮撓等事倘其屋宇産業有被内地
不法匪徒逞兇恐嚇焚毀侵害一經領事官報明地方官
立當派撥兵役彈壓驅逐並將匪徒查拏按律重辦倘華
民與　大合衆國人有爭鬥詞訟等案華民歸中國官
按律治罪　大合衆國人無論岸上海面與中國華民歐
每傷損毀壞物件戕傷害命一切非礼不合情事應歸領事等官
按　本國例懲辦至捉拏犯人以偹貿訊或由本地方官或由
大合衆國官均無不可

本館紙筆人厘利士謹錄

第十一款
一、嗣後中國大臣與合大衆國大臣公文往來應
照平行之礼用照會字樣領事等官與中國地方官公文
往來六用照會字樣申報大憲用申陳字樣若平民稟
報官憲仍用稟呈字樣均不得欺觌不恭有傷友誼至
兩國均不得互相徵索礼物
第十二款
一、大合衆國民人在通商各港口貿易或久居或
暫住均准其相賃民房或租地自行建樓並設立醫舘礼拜
堂及墳塋之處聽大合衆國人與内民公平議定租息内
民不得抬價捐勒如無礙民居不關方内照例用税契須各出
地方官不得阻止大合衆國人勿許強租硬占務須各出
情愿以昭公允倘坟垦墓或被中國民人毀掘中國地方官

嚴拏照例治罪其大合眾國人治船寄居處兩商民水手人
等只許在近地行走不准遽赴內地鄉村市鎮私行貿易以期
永久彼此相安

第十三款 一 大合眾國船隻在中國洋面遭風觸礁擱淺遇
盜致有損壞等害者誠處地方官一經查知即應設法拯
救保護並加撫卹俾得駛至最近港口修理准其採買糧
食汲取淡水俾商船有在中國兩轄內洋被盜搶刼者地方
文武員弁一經聞報即當嚴拏賊盜照例治罪起獲原贓無
倫多少或交本人或交領事官俱可但不得宵關失草至中
國地廣人稠萬一正盜不能緝獲或起贓不全不得令中國賠
還貨欵但若地方官通盜沿染一經證明行文大憲奏明嚴行

治罪將該員家產查抄抵償

第十四款 一 大合眾國民人嗣後均照舊章赴廣東之廣州潮州
福建之廈門福州臺灣浙江之寧波江蘇之上海盖嗣後與合眾
國或他國定立條約准開各港口市鎮在彼居住貿易任其船
隻裝載貨物於以上所立各港互相往來俾該船隻不得駛
赴沿海口岸及未開各港私行違法貿易如有犯此禁令者
應將船隻貨物充公歸中國入官其有走私漏稅或攜帶
各項違禁貨物至中國者聽中國地方官自行辦理治罪
大合眾國民人不得稍有袒護若有別國船隻宵大
合眾國旗號作不法貿易者大合眾國自應設法以嚴為
禁止

第十五款 一 大合眾國民人在各港貿易者除中國例禁下
准攜帶進口出口之貨外其餘各項貨物俱准任意販運往來
買賣完納稅餉惟照前粘附在望廈兩立條約之例冊除是別國
必須照例與中華至好之國一律辦理
按條約有何更改即應即應一體同因大合眾國人兩納之稅
第十六款 一 大合眾國船隻進通商各港口時必將船牌
等件呈交領事官轉報海關即按牌上兩載噸數輸納
船鈔每噸以方停四十官尺為准又往一百五十噸以上者
每噸納銀四錢不及一百五十噸者每噸納銀一錢凡船
隻曾在本港納鈔因貨未全消復載往別口出售或因
無回貨滇空船或未滿載之船駛赴別港覽載者領

事官報明海關將鈔已完納之處在紅牌上註明並行交別
口海關查照俟讀船進別口時止納貨稅不輸船鈔以免重
微設立浮樁亮船建造塔表亮樓由通商各海口地方官會
同領事酌量辦理

第十七款 一 大合眾國船隻進口即准其僱用引水帶進俟
正項稅欵全完仍令帶出並准僱覓廠役買辦工匠水手延
請通事司書及必須之人並僱用內地艇隻其工價若干由談
商民等自行定議或由領事等官酌辦

第十八款 一 大合眾國船隻一經進口即由海關酌派妥役
隨船管押或搭坐商船或自僱艇隻均聽其便倘大合眾國
民人有在船上不安本分離船逃走至內地避匿者一經領

7

事官知照中國地方官即派役訪查拏送領事官治罪
若有中國犯法民人逃至大合衆國人寓館及商船潛匿
者中國地方查出即行文領事等官挐拏送回均不得稍有
庇匿至大合衆國商民水手人等均歸領事等官隨時稽查
約束倘兩國人有倚強滋事輕用火器傷人致釀殺重案
兩國官員均應執法嚴辦不得稍有偏徇致令衆心不服
第十九款 一 大合衆國商船進口或船主或貨主或代辦
商人限二日之內將船牌貨單等件呈遞本國領事等官
收存領事及將船名人數及所載噸數貨色詳細開明
照會海關方准領取牌照開艙起貨倘有未領照之先
擅行起貨者罰洋銀五百大員並將擅行卸運之貨一

概歸中國入官或有商船進口止起一分貨物者按其
所起一分貨物輸納稅餉未起之貨均准其載往別口售沽
倘有進口並未開艙即欲他往者限二日之內即行出口
不得停留六未征收稅餉均俟到別港發售再行
照例輸納倘進口貨船已逾二日之限即須輸納船
鈔遇有領事等官不在港內應准大合衆國船主
商人祇友國領事代為料理否則逕赴海關呈明
法妥辦
第二十款 一 大合衆國商船出貨進口出口將起貨
下貨日期呈報領事官由領事等官轉報海關屆期交
派官役與該船主貨主或代辦商人等須秉公將貨物

聽明以便按例徵稅若內有估價空稅之貨或因議價
高下不等多寡不齊致有辯論不能了結者限該貨高
於即日內稟報領事官俾得通知海關會商酌奪若稟
報稽遲即不為准理
第二十一款 一 大合衆國民人運貨進口既經納清稅餉
倘有欲將已卸之貨運往別口售賣者稟明領事等管
轉報海關檢查貨稅底部相符即將某貨若干担已完稅
原貨並無拆動抽換情弊委員驗明寔係原已
若干之處填入牌照發該商收執一面行文別口海關查照
俟船進口准開艙出售免其重納稅餉若
有影射夾帶情事經海關查出罰貨入官如大合衆國

8

船隻運載往外洋載米進各港口者並未起卸六准其復還
出口
第二十二款 一 大合衆國船隻進口後方納船鈔進口貨
物於起貨時完稅出口貨物於下貨時完稅俟稅鈔全
完由海關發給紅牌然後領事官方給還船牌等件所
有稅銀中國官役銀號代納或以紋銀或以洋銀按時價
折交均無不可倘有未經完稅領事官先行繳還船牌者
所欠稅鈔當為領事官是問
第二十三款 一 大合衆國船停泊口內如有貨物須要
剝過別船者應先呈明領事官轉報海關委員查明確當
方准剝運倘不稟明候驗批准竟行剝運者即將所剝之

貨歸中國入官

第二十四款　一　中國人有該欠大合眾國人債項者准其

按例控追一經領事官照知地方官立即設法查究嚴追

給領倘大合眾國人有該欠華民者亦准由領事官知

會計取或直向領事官控追俱可但兩國官員均不能

保償

第二十五款　一　大合眾國官民延請中國各方士民人

等教習各方語音並幫辦文墨事件不論所請係何

等之人中國地方官民等均不得稍有阻撓陷害等情

並准其採買中國各項書籍

顧利士謹錄

唐人花旗和約全部

Bancroft Library

APPENDIX 3

Naturalization Act of 1870 (16 Stat. 254)

254   FORTY–FIRST CONGRESS. Sess. II. Ch. 252, 253, 254. 1870.

tion until after the fifty-four millions granted in the first section shall have been taken up.

After six months from, &c. any bank in a State having excess of circulation may remove to State having less, &c. Proviso.

SEC. 7. *And be it further enacted,* That after the expiration of six months from the passage of this act any banking association located in any State having more than its proportion of circulation may be removed to any State having less than its proportion of circulation, under such rules and regulations as the comptroller of the currency, with the approval of the Secretary of the Treasury, may require: *Provided,* That the amount of the issue of said banks shall not be deducted from the amount of new issue provided for in this act.

APPROVED, July 12, 1870.

July 13, 1870.

CHAP. CCLIII. — *An Act to extend the Time for presenting Claims for additional Bounties.*

Time for presenting claims for certain additional bounties extended. 1866, ch. 296, §§ 12, 13. Vol. xiv. p. 322 Claims not then presented to be void. Repeal of 1866, ch. 133, § 4. Vol. xv. p. 334.

Be it enacted by the Senate and House of Representatives of the United States of America in Congress assembled, That the time for presenting claims for additional bounties granted to soldiers by the twelfth and thirteenth sections of the act of July twenty-eighth, eighteen hundred and sixty-six, is hereby extended until the expiration of six months after the passage of this act, after which time all claims for such bounties not presented in due form shall be void; and the fourth section of the act approved March third, eighteen hundred and sixty-nine, entitled "An act in relation to additional bounties and for other purposes," is hereby repealed.

APPROVED, July 13, 1870.

July 14, 1870.

CHAP. CCLIV. — *An Act to amend the Naturalization Laws and to punish Crimes against the same, and for other Purposes.*

Knowingly taking, &c. a false oath, required in the naturalization of aliens, to be deemed perjury, and how punished.

Be it enacted by the Senate and House of Representatives of the United States of America in Congress assembled, That in all cases where any oath, affirmation, or affidavit shall be made or taken under or by virtue of any act or law relating to the naturalization of aliens, or in any proceedings under such acts or laws, and any person or persons taking or making such oath, affirmation, or affidavit, shall knowingly swear or affirm falsely, the same shall be deemed and taken to be perjury, and the person or persons guilty thereof shall upon conviction thereof be sentenced to imprisonment for a term not exceeding five years and not less than one year, and to a fine not exceeding one thousand dollars.

The doing of certain acts in connection with the naturalization of aliens declared felony, and penalty therefor.

SEC. 2. *And be it further enacted,* That if any person applying to be admitted a citizen, or appearing as a witness for any such person, shall knowingly personate any other person than himself, or falsely appear in the name of a deceased person, or in an assumed or fictitious name, or if any person shall falsely make, forge, or counterfeit any oath, affirmation, notice, affidavit, certificate, order, record, signature, or other instrument, paper, or proceeding required or authorized by any law or act relating to or providing for the naturalization of aliens; or shall utter, sell, dispose of, or use as true or genuine, or for any unlawful purpose, any false, forged, ante-dated, or counterfeit oath, affirmation, notice, certificate, order, record, signature, instrument, papor, or proceeding as aforesaid; or sell or dispose of to any person other than the person for whom it was originally issued, any certificate of citizenship, or certificate showing any person to be admitted a citizen; or if any person shall in any manner use for the purpose of registering as a voter, or as evidence of a right to vote, or otherwise, unlawfully, any order, certificate of citizenship, or certificate, judgment, or exemplification, showing such person to be admitted to be a citizen, whether heretofore or hereafter issued or made, knowing that such order or certificate, judgment, or exemplification has been unlawfully issued or made; or if any person

APPENDIX 3

Naturalization Act of 1870 (16 Stat. 254)

FORTY-FIRST CONGRESS, Sess. II. Ch. 254. 1870.   255

shall unlawfully use, or attempt to use, any such order or certificate, issued to or in the name of any other person, or in a fictitious name, or the name of a deceased person; or use, or attempt to use, or aid, or assist, or participate in the use of any certificate of citizenship, knowing the same to be forged, or counterfeit, or ante-dated, or knowing the same to have been procured by fraud, or otherwise unlawfully obtained; or if any person, and without lawful excuse, shall knowingly have or be possessed of any false, forged, ante-dated, or counterfeit certificate of citizenship, purporting to have been issued under the provisions of any law of the United States relating to naturalization, knowing such certificate to be false, forged, ante-dated, or counterfeit, with intent unlawfully to use the same; or if any person shall obtain, accept, or receive any certificate of citizenship known to such person to have been procured by fraud or by the use of any false name, or by means of any false statement made with intent to procure, or to aid in procuring, the issue of such certificate, or known to such person to be fraudulently altered or ante-dated; or if any person who has been or may be admitted to be a citizen shall, on oath or affirmation, or by affidavit, knowingly deny that he has been so admitted, with intent to evade or avoid any duty or liability imposed or required by law, every person so offending shall be deemed and adjudged guilty of felony, and, on conviction thereof, shall be sentenced to be imprisoned and kept at hard labor for a period not less than one year nor more than five years, or be fined in a sum not less than three hundred dollars nor more than one thousand dollars, or both such punishments may be imposed, in the discretion of the court. And every person who shall knowingly and intentionally aid or abet any person in the commission of any such felony, or attempt to do any act hereby made felony, or counsel, advise, or procure, or attempt to procure, the commission thereof, shall be liable to indictment and punishment in the same manner and to the same extent as the principal party guilty of such felony, and such person may be tried and convicted thereof without the previous conviction of such principal. *(The doing of certain acts in connection with the naturalization of aliens declared felony, and penalty therefor. Penalty for knowingly and intentionally aiding, &c. the doing of such acts. Trial, &c.)*

SEC. 3. *And be it further enacted,* That any person who shall knowingly use any certificate of naturalization heretofore granted by any court, or which shall hereafter be granted, which has been, or shall be, procured through fraud or by false evidence, or has been or shall be issued by the clerk, or any other officer of the court without any appearance and hearing of the applicant in court and without lawful authority; and any person who shall falsely represent himself to be a citizen of the United States, without having been duly admitted to citizenship, for any fraudulent purpose whatever, shall be deemed guilty of a misdemeanor, and upon conviction thereof, in due course of law, shall be sentenced to pay a fine of not exceeding one thousand dollars, or be imprisoned not exceeding two years, either or both, in the discretion of the court taking cognizance of the same. *(Penalty for knowingly using any fraudulent &c. certificate of naturalization; for fraudulently falsely representing one's self to be a citizen.)*

SEC. 4. *And be it further enacted,* That the provisions of this act shall apply to all proceedings had or taken, or attempted to be had or taken, before any court in which any proceeding for naturalization shall be commenced, had, or taken, or attempted to be commenced; and the courts of the United States shall have jurisdiction of all offenses under the provisions of this act, in or before whatsoever court or tribunal the same shall have been committed. *(This act to apply to all proceedings for naturalization, before any court. Courts of the United States to have jurisdiction of offences under this act.)*

SEC. 5. *And be it further enacted,* That in any city having upwards of twenty thousand inhabitants, it shall be the duty of the judge of the circuit court of the United States for the circuit wherein said city shall be, upon the application of two citizens, to appoint in writing for each election district or voting precinct in said city, and to change or renew said appointment as occasion may require, from time to time, two citizens resident of the district or precinct, one from each political party, who, when so *(In cities of more than 20,000 inhabitants, judge of circuit court, upon application, to appoint two citizens in each election district)*

APPENDIX 3

Naturalization Act of 1870 (16 Stat. 254)

256   FORTY-FIRST CONGRESS. Sess. II. Ch. 254, 255. 1870.

to supervise registration, voting, &c. in certain elections. [Repealed, 1871, ch. 99, § 18. Post. p. 440.]

designated, shall be, and are hereby, authorized to attend at all times and places fixed for the registration of voters, who, being registered, would be entitled to vote for representative in Congress, and at all times and places for holding elections of representatives in Congress, and for counting the votes cast at said elections, and to challenge any name proposed to be registered, and any vote offered, and to be present and witness throughout the counting of all votes, and to remain where the ballot-boxes are kept

Authority of such persons.

at all times after the polls are open until the votes are finally counted; and said persons and either of them shall have the right to affix their signature or his signature to said register for purposes of identification, and to attach thereto, or to the certificate of the number of votes cast, *and* [any] statement touching the truth or fairness thereof which they or he may ask

Penalty for obstructing them.

to attach; and any one who shall prevent any person so designated from doing any of the acts authorized as aforesaid, or who shall hinder or molest any such person in doing any of the said acts, or shall aid or abet in preventing, hindering, or molesting any such person in respect of any such acts, shall be guilty of a misdemeanor, and on conviction shall be punished by imprisonment not less than one year.

In cities of over 20,000 inhabitants the marshal may appoint special deputies at congressional elections, &c. Post, p. 440.

SEC. 6. *And be it further enacted,* That in any city having upwards of twenty thousand inhabitants, it shall be lawful for the marshal of the United States for the district wherein said city shall be, to appoint as many special deputies as may be necessary to preserve order at any election at which representatives in Congress are to be chosen; and said deputies are hereby authorized to preserve order at such elections, and to arrest for any offence or breach of the peace committed in their view.

Aliens of African nativity and descent may become citizens.

SEC. 7. *And be it further enacted,* That the naturalization laws are hereby extended to aliens of African nativity and to persons of African descent.

APPROVED, July 14, 1870.

July 14, 1870.   CHAP. CCLV. — *An Act to reduce internal Taxes, and for other Purposes.*

Be it enacted by the Senate and House of Representatives of the United States of America in Congress assembled, That on and after the first day

Special internal revenue taxes upon occupations repealed after May 1, 1871. 1864, ch. 173, § 79. Vol. xiii. p. 251. 1866, ch. 184, § 0. 1867, ch. 169, § 2. Vol. xiv. pp. 115, 471. Except upon brewers, distillers, &c. and dealers in liquors and tobacco. 1868, ch. 186. Vol. xv. p. 125. 1869, ch. 18. Ante, p. 41.

of May, eighteen hundred and seventy-one, the special taxes imposed by the seventy-ninth section of the act entitled "An act to provide internal revenue to support the government, to pay interest on the public debt, and for other purposes," approved June thirty, eighteen hundred and sixty-four, as amended by section nine of the internal revenue act approved July thirteen, eighteen hundred and sixty-six, and as amended by section two of the internal revenue act approved March two, eighteen hundred and sixty-seven, be, and the same are hereby, repealed; but this act shall not be held to repeal or in any way affect the special tax on brewers imposed by said section, or the special taxes imposed by the act approved July twenty, eighteen hundred and sixty-eight, entitled "An act imposing taxes on distilled spirits and tobacco, and for other purposes," or the acts amendatory thereof.

Taxes on sales, except, &c. to cease October 1, 1870.

SEC. 2. *And be it further enacted,* That on and after the first day of October, eighteen hundred and seventy, the several taxes on sales imposed by the internal revenue laws now in force, saving and excepting such taxes on sales as are by existing law paid by stamps, and the taxes on sales of leaf tobacco, manufactured tobacco, snuff, cigars, foreign and domestic distilled spirits, and wines, imposed by said act, approved July twenty, eighteen hundred and sixty-eight, and acts amendatory thereof, be, and the same are hereby, repealed.

Taxes in schedule A on boats, &c. legacies, &c. passports and gross

SEC. 3. *And be it further enacted,* That on and after the first day of October, eighteen hundred and seventy, the taxes imposed by the internal revenue laws, now in force, herein specified, be, and the same are hereby, repealed, namely: on articles in schedule A; the special tax on boats,

APPENDIX 4

Fifteen Passenger Bill (1879) and Veto Message of President Rutherford Hayes of the Fifteen Passenger Bill, March 1, 1879, 1879 Congressional Record– House 2275–2277

Transcribed by Yi Ping Caitlin Roberts

VETO OF THE CHINESE IMMIGRATION BILL.

The SPEAKER laid before the House the following message from the President of the United States:

To the House of Representatives:

After a very careful consideration of House bill No. 2423, entitled "An act to re-strict the immigration of Chinese to the United States," I herewith return it to the House of Representatives, in which it originated, with my objections to its passage.

The bill, as it was sent to the Senate from the House of Representatives, was con-fined in its provisions to the object named in its title, which is that of "An act to restrict the immigration of Chinese to the United States." The only means adopted to secure the proposed object was the limitation on the number of Chinese passengers which might be brought to this country by any one vessel to fifteen, and as this number was not fixed in any proportion to the size or tonnage of the vessel or by any consideration of the safety or accommodation of these passengers, the simple purpose and effect of the enactment were to repress this immigration to an extent falling but little short of its absolute exclusion.

The bill, as amended in the Senate and now presented to me, includes an independent and additional provision which aims at, and in terms requires, the abrogation by this Government of articles 5 and 6 of the treaty with China, commonly called the Burlingame treaty, through the action of the Executive enjoined by this provision of the act.

The Burlingame treaty, of which the ratifications were exchanged at Peking, November 23, 1869, recites as the occasion and motive of its negotiation by the two governments that "since the conclusion of the treaty between the United States of America and the Ta Tsing Empire (China) of the 18th of June, 1858, circumstances have arisen showing the necessity of additional articles thereto," and proceeds to an agreement as to said additional articles. These negotiations, therefore, ending by the signature of the additional articles July 28, 1868, had for their object the completion of our treaty rights and obligations toward the government of China by the incorporation of these new articles as, thenceforth, parts of the principal treaty to which they are made supplemental. Upon the settled rules of interpretation applicable to such supplemental negotiations the text of the principal treaty and of these "additional articles thereto" constitute one treaty, from the conclusion of the new negotiations, in all parts of equal and concurrent force and obligation between the two governments, and to all intents and purposes as if embraced in one instrument.

The principal treaty, of which the ratifications were exchanged August 16, 1859, recites that "the United States of America and the Ta Tsing Empire desiring to maintain firm, lasting, and sincere friendship, have resolved to renew, in a manner, clear and positive, by means of a treaty or general convention of peace, amity, and commerce, the rules of which shall in future be mutually observed in the intercourse of their respective countries," and proceeds, in its thirty articles, to lay out a careful and comprehensive system for the commercial relations of our people with China. The main substance of all the provisions of this treaty is to define and secure the rights of our people in respect of access to, residence and protection in, and trade with China. The actual provisions in our favor, in these respects, were framed to be, and have been found to be, adequate and appropriate to the interests of our commerce, and by the concluding article we receive the important guarantee, "that should at any time the Ta Tsing Empire grant to any nation, or the merchants or citizens of any nation, any right, privilege, or favor connected either with navigation, commerce, political or other intercourse which is not conferred by this treaty, such right, privilege, and favor shall at once freely inure to the benefit of the United States, its public officers, merchants, and citizens." Against this body of stipulations in our favor, and this permanent engagement of equality in respect of all future concessions to foreign nations, the general promise of permanent peace and good offices on our part seems to be the only equivalent. For this the first article undertakes as follows: "There shall be, as there have always been, peace and friendship between the United States of America and the Ta Tsing Empire, and between their people respectively. They shall not insult or oppress each other for any trifling cause, so as to produce an estrangement between them; and if any other nation should act unjustly or oppressively, the United States will exert their good offices, on being informed of the case, to bring about an amicable arrangement of the question, thus showing their friendly feelings."

At the date of the negotiation of this treaty our Pacific possessions had attracted a considerable Chinese emigration, and the advantages and the inconveniences felt or feared therefrom had become more or less manifest, but they dictated no stipulations on the subject to be incorporated in the treaty. The year 1868 was marked by the striking event of a spontaneous embassy from the Chinese Empire, headed by an American citizen, Anson Burlingame, who had relinquished his diplomatic representation of his own country in China to assume that of the Chinese Empire to the United States and the European nations. By this time the facts of the Chinese immigration and its nature and influences, present and prospective, had become more noticeable and were more observed by the population immediately affected and by this Government. The principal feature of the Burlingame treaty was its attention to and its treatment of the Chinese immigration and the Chinese as forming, or as they should form, a part of our population. Up to this time our uncovenanted hospitality to immigration, our fearless liberality of citizenship, our equal and comprehensive justice to all inhabitants, whether they abjured their foreign nationality or not, our civil freedom and our religions toleration had made all comers welcome, and under these protections the Chinese in considerable numbers had made their lodgment upon our soil.

The Burlingame treaty undertakes to deal with this situation, and its fifth and sixth articles embrace its most important provisions in this regard and the main stipulations in which the Chinese government has secured an obligatory protection of its subjects within our territory. They read as follows:

"ARTICLE V.

"The United States of America and the Emperor of China cordially recognize the inherent and inalienable right of man to change his home and allegiance, and also the mutual advantage of the free migration and emigration of their citizens and subjects respectively from the one country to the other for the purpose of curiosity, of trade, or as permanent residents. The high contracting parties, therefore, join in reprobating any other than an entirely voluntary emigration for these purposes. They consequently agree to pass laws making it a penal offense for a citizen of the United States or Chinese subjects to take Chinese subjects either to the United States or to any other foreign country, or for a Chinese subject or citizen of the United States to take citizens of the United States to China or to any other foreign country without their free and voluntary consent, respectively.

"ARTICLE VI.

"Citizens of the United States visiting or residing in China shall enjoy the same privileges, immunities, or exemptions in respect to travel or residence as may there be enjoyed by the citizens or subjects of the most favored nation; and reciprocally, Chinese subjects visiting or residing in the United States shall enjoy the same privileges, immunities, and exemptions in respect to travel or residence as may there be enjoyed by the citizens or subjects of the most favored nation. But nothing herein contained shall be held to confer naturalization upon citizens of the United States in China, nor upon the subjects of China in the United States."

An examination of these two articles in the light of the experience then influential in suggesting their "necessity" will show that the fifth article was framed in hostility to what seemed the principal mischief to be guarded against, to wit, the introduction of Chinese laborers by methods which should have the character of a forced and servile importation, and not of a voluntary emigration of freemen seeking our shores upon motives and in a manner consonant with the system of our institutions and approved by the experience of the nation. Unquestionably the adhesion of the government of China to these liberal principles of freedom in emigration, with which we were so familiar and with which we were so well satisfied, was a great advance toward opening that empire to our civilization and religion, and gave promise in the future of greater and greater practical results in the diffusion throughout that great population of our arts and industries, our manufactures, our material improvements, and the sentiments of government and religion which seem to us so important to the welfare of mankind. The first clause of this article secures this acceptance by China of the American doctrines of free migration to and fro among the peoples and races of the earth.

The second clause, however, in its reprobation of "any other than entirely voluntary emigration" by both the high contracting parties, and in the reciprocal obligations whereby we secured the solemn and unqualified engagement on the part of the government of China "to pass laws making it a penal offense for a citizen of the United States or Chinese subjects to take Chinese subjects either to the United States or to any other foreign country without their free and voluntary consent" constitutes the great force and value of this article. Its importance both in principle and in its practical service toward our protection against servile importation in the guise of immigration cannot be overestimated. It commits the Chinese government to active and efficient measures to suppress this iniquitous system where those measures are most necessary and can be most effectual. It gives to this Government the footing of a treaty right to such measures and the means and opportunity of insisting upon their adoption and of complaint and resentment at their neglect. The fifth article, therefore, if it fall short of what the pressure of the later experience of our Pacific States may urge upon the attention of this Government as essential to the public welfare seems to be in the right direction and to contain important advantages which once relinquished cannot be easily recovered.

The second topic which interested the two governments under the actual condition of things which prompted the Burlingame treaty was adequate protection under the solemn and definite guarantees of a treaty of the Chinese already in this country and those who should seek our shores. This was the object and forms the subject of the sixth article, by whose reciprocal engagement the citizens and subjects of the two governments, respectively, visiting or residing in the country of the other are secured the same privileges, immunities, or exemptions there enjoyed by the citizens or subjects of the most favored nations. The treaty of 1858, to which these articles are made supplemental, provides for a great amount of privilege and protection, both of person and property, to American citizens in China, but it is upon this sixth article that the main body of the treaty rights and securities of the Chinese already in this country depends. Its abrogation, were the rest of the treaty left in force, would leave them to such treatment as we should voluntarily accord them by our laws and customs. Any treaty obligation would be wanting to restrain our liberty of action toward them, or to measure or sustain the right of the Chinese government to complaint or redress in their behalf.

The lapse of ten years since the negotiation of the Burlingame treaty has exhibited to the notice of the Chinese government, as well as to our own people, the working of this experiment of immigration in great numbers of Chinese laborers to this country, and their maintenance here of all the traits of race, religion, manners and customs, habitations, mode of life, and segregation here, and the keeping up of the ties of their original home, which stamp them as strangers and sojourners, and not as incorporated elements of our national life and growth. This experience may naturally suggest the reconsideration of the subject, as dealt with by the Burlingame treaty, and may properly become the occasion of more direct and circumspect recognition, in renewed negotiations, of the difficulties surrounding this political and social problem. It may well be that, to the apprehension of the Chinese government no less than our own the simple provisions of the Burlingame treaty may need to be replaced by more careful methods, securing the Chinese and our-selves against a larger and more rapid infusion of this foreign race than our system of industry and society can take up and assimilate with ease and safety. This ancient government, ruling a polite and sensitive people, distinguished by a high sense of national pride, may properly desire an adjustment of their relations with us, which would in all things confirm, and in no degree endanger, the permanent peace and amity and the growing commerce and prosperity, which it has been the object and the effect of our existing treaties to cherish and perpetuate.

I regard the very grave discontents of the people of the Pacific States with the present working of the Chinese immigration, and their still graver apprehensions therefrom in the future, as deserving the most serious attention of the people of the whole country and a solicitous interest on the part of Congress and the Executive. If this were not my own judgment, the passage of this bill by both Houses of Congress would impress upon me the seriousness of the situation, when a majority of the representatives of the people of the whole country had thought fit to justify so serious a measure of relief.

The authority of Congress to terminate a treaty with a foreign power by expressing the will of the nation no longer to adhere to it, is as free from controversy under our Constitution as is the further proposition that the power of making new treaties or modifying existing treaties is not lodged by the Constitution in Congress, but in the President, by and with the advice and consent of the Senate, as shown by the concurrence of two-thirds of that body. A denunciation of a treaty by any Government is, confessedly, justifiable only upon some reason both of the highest justice and of the highest necessity. The action of Congress in the matter of the French treaties, in 1798, if it be regarded as an abrogation by this nation of a subsisting treaty, strongly illustrates the character and degree of justification which was then thought suitable to such a proceeding. The preamble of the act recites that "the treaties concluded between the United States and France have been repeatedly violated on the part of the French government, and the just claims of the United States for reparation of the injuries so committed have been refused, and their attempts to negotiate an amicable adjustment of all complaints between the two nations have been repelled with indignity;" and that "under authority of the French government there is yet pursued against the United States a system of predatory violence, infracting the said treaties, and hostile to the rights of a free and independent nation."

The enactment, as a logical consequence of these recited facts, declares "that the United State are of right freed and exonerated from the stipulations of the treaties and of the consular convention heretofore concluded between the United States and France, and that the same shall not henceforth be regarded as legally obligatory on the Government or citizens of the United States."

The history of the Government shows no other instance of an abrogation of a treaty by Congress.

Instances have sometimes occurred where the ordinary legislation of Congress has, by its conflict with some treaty obligation of the Government toward a foreign power, taken effect as an infraction of the treaty, and been judicially declared to be operative to that result. But neither such legislation nor such judicial sanction of the same has been regarded as an abrogation, even for the moment, of the treaty. On the contrary, the treaty in such case still subsists between the Governments, and the casual infraction is repaired by appropriate satisfaction in maintenance of the treaty.

The bill before me does not enjoin upon the President the abrogation of the entire Burlingame treaty, much less of the principal treaty of which it is made the supplement. As the power of modifying an existing treaty, whether by adding or striking out provisions, is a part of the treaty-making power under the Constitution, its exercise is not competent for Congress, nor would the assent of China to this partial abrogation of the treaty make the action of Congress, in thus procuring an amendment of a treaty, a competent exercise of authority under the Constitution. The importance, however, of this special consideration seems superseded by the principle that a denunciation of a part of a treaty, not made by the terms of the treaty itself separable from the rest, is a denunciation of the whole treaty. As the other high contracting party has entered into no treaty obligations except such as include the part denounced, the denunciation by one party of the part necessarily liberates the other party from the whole treaty.

I am convinced that, whatever urgency might in any quarter or by any interest be supposed to require an instant suppression of further immigration from China, no reasons can require the immediate withdrawal of our treaty protection of the Chinese already in this country, and no circumstances can tolerate an exposure of our citizens in China, merchants or missionaries, to the consequences of so sudden an abrogation of their treaty protections. Fortunately, however, the actual recession in the flow of the emigration from China to the Pacific coast, shown by trustworthy statistics, relieves us from any apprehension that the treatment of the subject in the proper course of diplomatic negotiations will introduce any new features of discontent or disturbance among the communities directly affected. Were such delay fraught with more inconveniences than have ever been suggested by the interests most earnest in promoting this legislation, I cannot but regard the summary disturbance of our existing treaties with China as greatly more inconvenient to much wider and more permanent interests of the country.

I have no occasion to insist upon the more general considerations of interest and duty which sacredly guard the faith of the nation in whatever form of obligation it may have been given. These sentiments animate the deliberations of Congress and pervade the minds of our whole people. Our history gives little occasion for any reproach in this regard, and in asking the renewed attention of Congress to this bill I am persuaded that their action will maintain the public duty and the public honor.

R. B. HAYES.
EXECUTIVE MANSION, March 1, 1879.

An act to restrict the immigration of Chinese to the United States.

Be it enacted by the Senate and House of Representatives of the United States of America in Congress assembled, That no master of any vessel owned in whole or in part by a citizen of the United States or by a citizen of any foreign country, shall take on board such vessel, at any port or place within the Chinese Empire, or at any other foreign port or place whatever, any number exceeding fifteen Chinese passengers, whether male or female, with the intent to bring such passengers to the United States, and leave such port or place and bring such passengers to any number exceeding fifteen on one voyage within the jurisdiction of the United States: *Provided,* That this section shall not apply to any master of a vessel seeking a harbor in stress of weather.

SEC. 2. That whenever the master or other person in charge of any such vessel takes on board the same, at any foreign port or place, any greater number of Chinese passengers than is prescribed in the first section of this act, with intent to bring such passengers to the United States, and leave such port or place and brings such passengers to any number exceeding fifteen on one voyage within the jurisdiction of the United States, he shall be deemed guilty of a misdemeanor, and shall, for each passenger so taken on board and brought within the jurisdiction of the United States exceeding the number of fifteen, be fined one hundred dollars, and may also be imprisoned for not exceeding six months.

SEC. 3. That the master of any vessel arriving in the United States, or any of the Territories thereof, from any foreign place whatever, at the same time that he delivers a manifest of the cargo, and if there be no cargo, then at the time of making report or entry of the vessel pursuant to law, shall, in addition to the other matters required to be reported by law, deliver and report to the collector of the district in which such vessel shall arrive a separate list of all Chinese passengers taken on board the vessel at any foreign port or place, and of all such passengers on board the vessel at that time; such list shall be sworn to by the master in the same manner as directed by law in relation to the manifest of the cargo; and the refusal or neglect of the master to comply with the provisions of this sec-tion shall receive the same penalties, disabilities, and forfeitures as are provided for a refusal or neglect to report and deliver a manifest of the cargo.

SEC. 4. That the amount of the several penalties imposed by the foregoing pro-visions shall be in liens on the vessels violating those provisions; and such vessels shall be libeled therefor in any circuit or district court of the United States where such vessel shall arrive.

SEC. 5. That nothing herein contained shall be held to repeal or modify any law forbidding the importation of coolies, or of females for immoral purposes, into the United States: *Provided*, That no consul or consular agent of the United States residing at any port from which any vessel taking Chinese passengers may take her departure shall grant the certificate provided for in section twenty-one hundred and sixty-two of the Revised Statutes for more than fifteen Chinese passengers on any one vessel.

SEC. 6. That this act shall not apply to persons officially connected with the Chi-nese government, or any embassy thereof, or to persons rescued from shipwreck during the voyage of and by the vessel bringing the same within the jurisdiction of the United States, or to persons who may only seek a temporary residence for educational purposes, and who shall have a certificate from the Chinese government for that purpose.

SEC. 7. That this act shall take effect from and after the first day of July, eighteen hundred and seventy-nine. And the President of the United States shall immediately on the approval of this act give notice to the government of China of the abrogation of articles five and six of the additional articles to the treaty of June eighteenth, eighteen hundred and fifty-eight, between the United States and China, proclaimed February fifth, eighteen hundred and seventy, commonly called the Burlingame treaty.

SAM. J. RANDALL,
Speaker of the House of Representatives.
W. A. WHEELER,
Vice-President of the United States and President of the Senate.

APPENDIX 4

Fifteen Passenger Bill (1879) and Veto Message of President Rutherford Hayes of the Fifteen Passenger Bill, March 1, 1879, 1879 Congressional Record–House 2275–2277

The result of the vote was then announced as above stated.

Mr. CONGER. I move to reconsider the vote just taken; and also to lay that motion upon the table.

Mr. SPRINGER. If the gentleman makes that motion I shall call for the yeas and nays on it.

Mr. CONGER. I withdraw the motion.

BUSINESS ON THE SPEAKER'S TABLE.

Mr. HARRIS, of Virginia. I now move to suspend the rules in order to proceed to business on the Speaker's table, under Rule 54.

Mr. EWING. I desire to inquire of the Chair how the gentleman from Virginia [Mr. HARRIS] gets the floor to move a suspension of the rules?

The SPEAKER. He gets the floor by the recognition of the Chair. [Laughter.]

Mr. EWING. I am first on the list.

The SPEAKER. The gentleman from Ohio [Mr. EWING] is first on the list of individual members. But the gentleman will notice that to-day the Chair has recognized only such members as were authorized by their committees to submit motions to suspend the rules.

Mr. EWING. The object of my inquiry was to ascertain whether the gentleman from Virginia [Mr. HARRIS] was authorized by any committee to make that motion.

Mr. HARRIS, of Virginia. The gentleman has no right to catechise the Speaker as to what authority he has to recognize any member he chooses.

Mr. EWING. I am not catechising the Speaker.

The SPEAKER. The Chair recognizes the gentleman from Virginia [Mr. HARRIS] because he submits a motion to suspend the rules in order to proceed to the consideration of business on the Speaker's table, where there rests a large number of bills of a public character.

Mr. EWING. The Chair announced that he would recognize——

[Cries of "Regular order!]

The SPEAKER. The Chair would prefer that the gentleman be allowed to make his statement.

Mr. EWING. The Chair announced that he would recognize gentlemen in the order in which they are on the book, unless a committee should instruct some gentleman to move a suspension of the rules.

The SPEAKER. The Chair has always reserved the right to recognize any motion to proceed to the consideration of public business.

Mr. EWING. The Chair did not make that reservation when he made the statement the other day.

The SPEAKER. The Chair has never made any other statement since he has been in the chair.

Mr. EWING. The Chair did not make that statement the other day.

The SPEAKER. The question is on the motion of the gentleman from Virginia, [Mr. HARRIS,] to suspend the rules for the purpose of proceeding to the consideration of business on the Speaker's table.

Mr. TOWNSHEND, of Illinois. Is it in order now to move that the House take a recess until to-morrow morning at ten o'clock?

The SPEAKER. Not pending a motion to suspend the rules.

Mr. TOWNSHEND, of Illinois. But before the motion is put to the House?

The SPEAKER. The Chair thinks not.

The question was taken upon the motion to suspend the rules; and upon a division there were—ayes 151, noes 20.

Mr. EDEN. Before the result of the vote is announced I desire to make a parliamentary inquiry.

The SPEAKER. The gentleman will state it.

Mr. EDEN. I desire to inquire if we proceed to business on the Speaker's table at this time under a suspension of the rules, will we proceed to that business with all the rights that are given us under the rules?

The SPEAKER. The motion is to proceed to the business under Rule 54, and all other rules applicable are reserved. It is a mere motion to suspend the rules in order to get to the Speaker's table; and every bill is subject to the other rules of the House.

Mr. COX, of New York. All points of order being reserved?

The SPEAKER. They are. Two-thirds having voted in favor thereof, the rules are suspended and the House will now proceed to the consideration of business upon the Speaker's table.

VETO OF THE CHINESE IMMIGRATION BILL.

The SPEAKER laid before the House the following message from the President of the United States:

To the House of Representatives:

After a very careful consideration of House bill No. 2423, entitled "An act to restrict the immigration of Chinese to the United States," I herewith return it to the House of Representatives, in which it originated, with my objections to its passage.

The bill, as it was sent to the Senate from the House of Representatives, was confined in its provisions to the object named in its title, which is that of "An act to restrict the immigration of Chinese to the United States." The only means adopted to secure the proposed object was the limitation on the number of Chinese passengers which might be brought to this country by any one vessel to fifteen, and as this number was not fixed in any proportion to the size or tonnage of the vessel or by any consideration of the safety or accommodation of these passengers, the simple purpose and effect of the enactment were to repress this immigration to an extent falling but little short of its absolute exclusion.

The bill, as amended in the Senate and now presented to me, includes an independent and additional provision which aims at, and in terms requires, the abrogation by this Government of articles 5 and 6 of the treaty with China, commonly called the Burlingame treaty, through the action of the Executive enjoined by this provision of the act.

The Burlingame treaty, of which the ratifications were exchanged at Peking, November 23, 1869, recites as the occasion and motive of its negotiation by the two governments that "since the conclusion of the treaty between the United States of America and the Ta Tsing Empire (China) of the 18th of June, 1858, circumstances have arisen showing the necessity of additional articles thereto," and proceeds to an agreement as to said additional articles. These negotiations, therefore, ending by the signature of the additional articles July 28, 1868, had for their object the completion of our treaty rights and obligations toward the government of China by the incorporation of these new articles as, thenceforth, parts of the principal treaty to which they are made supplemental. Upon the settled rules of interpretation applicable to such supplemental negotiations the text of the principal treaty and of these "additional articles thereto" constitute one treaty, from the conclusion of the new negotiations, in all parts of equal and concurrent force and obligation between the two governments, and to all intents and purposes as if embraced in one instrument.

The principal treaty, of which the ratifications were exchanged August 16, 1859, recites that "the United States of America and the Ta Tsing Empire desiring to maintain firm, lasting, and sincere friendship, have resolved to renew, in a manner, clear and positive, by means of a treaty or general convention of peace, amity, and commerce, the rules of which shall in future be mutually observed in the intercourse of their respective countries," and proceeds, in its thirty articles, to lay out a careful and comprehensive system for the commercial relations of our people with China. The main substance of all the provisions of this treaty is to define and secure the rights of our people in respect of access to, residence and protection in, and trade with China. The actual provisions in our favor, in these respects, were framed to be, and have been found to be, adequate and appropriate to the interests of our commerce, and by the concluding article we receive the important guarantee, "that should at any time the Ta Tsing Empire grant to any nation, or the merchants or citizens of any nation, any right, privilege, or favor connected either with navigation, commerce, political or other intercourse which is not conferred by this treaty, such right, privilege, and favor shall at once freely inure to the benefit of the United States, its public officers, merchants, and citizens." Against this body of stipulations in our favor, and this permanent engagement of equality in respect of all future concessions to foreign nations, the general promise of permanent peace and good offices on our part seems to be the only equivalent. For this the first article undertakes as follows: "There shall be, as there have always been, peace and friendship between the United States of America and the Ta Tsing Empire, and between their people respectively. They shall not insult or oppress each other for any trifling cause, so as to produce an estrangement between them; and if any other nation should act unjustly or oppressively, the United States will exert their good offices, on being informed of the case, to bring about an amicable arrangement of the question, thus showing their friendly feelings."

At the date of the negotiation of this treaty our Pacific possessions had attracted a considerable Chinese emigration, and the advantages and the inconveniences felt or feared therefrom had become more or less manifest, but they dictated no stipulations on the subject to be incorporated in the treaty. The year 1868 was marked by the striking event of a spontaneous embassy from the Chinese Empire, headed by an American citizen, Anson Burlingame, who had relinquished his diplomatic representation of his own country in China to assume that of the Chinese Empire to the United States and the European nations. By this time the facts of the Chinese immigration and its nature and influences, present and prospective, had become more noticeable and were more observed by the population immediately affected and by this Government. The principal feature of the Burlingame treaty was its attention to and its treatment of the Chinese immigration and the Chinese as forming, or as they should form, a part of our population. Up to this time our uncovenanted hospitality to immigration, our fearless liberality of citizenship, our equal and comprehensive justice to all inhabitants, whether they abjured their foreign nationality or not, our civil freedom and our religious toleration had made all comers welcome, and under these protections the Chinese in considerable numbers had made their lodgment upon our soil.

The Burlingame treaty undertakes to deal with this situation, and its fifth and sixth articles embrace its most important provisions in this regard and the main stipulations in which the Chinese government has secured an obligatory protection of its subjects within our territory. They read as follows:

"ARTICLE V.

"The United States of America and the Emperor of China cordially recognize the inherent and inalienable right of man to change his home and allegiance, and also the mutual advantage of the free migration and emigration of their citizens and subjects respectively from the one country to the other for the purpose of curiosity, of trade, or as permanent residents. The high contracting parties, therefore, join in reprobating any other than an entirely voluntary emigration for these purposes. They consequently agree to pass laws making it a penal offense for a citizen of the United States or Chinese subjects to take Chinese subjects either to the United States or to any other foreign country, or for a Chinese subject or citizen of the United States to take citizens of the United States to China or to any other foreign country without their free and voluntary consent, respectively.

"ARTICLE VI.

"Citizens of the United States visiting or residing in China shall enjoy the same privileges, immunities, or exemptions in respect to travel or residence as may there be enjoyed by the citizens or subjects of the most favored nation; and, reciprocally, Chinese subjects visiting or residing in the United States shall enjoy the same privileges, immunities, and exemptions in respect to travel or residence as may there be enjoyed by the citizens or subjects of the most favored nation. But nothing herein contained shall be held to confer naturalization upon citizens of the United States in China, nor upon the subjects of China in the United States."

An examination of these two articles in the light of the experience then influential in suggesting their "necessity" will show that the fifth article was framed in hostility to what seemed the principal mischief to be guarded against, to wit, the introduction of Chinese laborers by methods which should have the character of a forced and servile importation, and not of a voluntary emigration of freemen seeking our shores upon motives and in a manner consonant with the system of our institutions and approved by the experience of the nation. Unquestionably the adhesion of the government of China to these liberal principles of freedom in emigration, with which we were so familiar and with which we were so well satisfied, was a great advance toward opening that empire to our civilization and religion, and gave promise in the future of greater and greater practical results in the diffusion throughout that great population of our arts and industries, our manufactures, our material improvements, and the sentiments of government and religion which seem to us so important to the welfare of mankind. The first clause of this article secures this acceptance by China of the American doctrines of free migration to and fro among the peoples and races of the earth.

The second clause, however, in its reprobation of "any other than entirely voluntary emigration" by both the high contracting parties, and in the reciprocal obligations whereby we secured the solemn and unqualified engagement on the part of the government of China "to pass laws making it a penal offense for a citizen of the United States or Chinese subjects to take Chinese subjects either to the United States or to any other foreign country without their free and voluntary consent" constitutes the great force and value of this article. Its importance both in principle and in its practical service toward our protection against servile importation in the guise of immigration cannot be overestimated. It commits the Chinese government to active and efficient measures to suppress this iniquitous system

APPENDIX 4

Fifteen Passenger Bill (1879) and Veto Message of President Rutherford Hayes of the Fifteen Passenger Bill, March 1, 1879, 1879 Congressional Record–House 2275–2277

2276 CONGRESSIONAL RECORD—HOUSE. MARCH 1,

where those measures are most necessary and can be most effectual. It gives to this Government the footing of a treaty right to such measures and the means and opportunity of insisting upon their adoption and of complaint and resentment at their neglect. The fifth article, therefore, if it fall short of what the pressure of the later experience of our Pacific States may urge upon the attention of this Government as essential to the public welfare seems to be in the right direction and to contain important advantages which once relinquished cannot be easily recovered.

The second topic which interested the two governments under the actual condition of things which prompted the Burlingame treaty was adequate protection under the solemn and definite guarantees of a treaty of the Chinese already in this country and those who should seek our shores. This was the object and forms the subject of the sixth article, by whose reciprocal engagement the citizens and subjects of the two governments, respectively, visiting or residing in the country of the other are secured the same privileges, immunities, or exemptions there enjoyed by the citizens or subjects of the most favored nations. The treaty of 1858, to which these articles are made supplemental, provides for a great amount of privilege and protection, both of person and property, to American citizens in China, but it is upon this sixth article that the main body of the treaty rights and securities of the Chinese already in this country depends. Its abrogation, were the rest of the treaty left in force, would leave them to such treatment as we should voluntarily accord them by our laws and customs. Any treaty obligation would be wanting to restrain our liberty of action toward them, or to measure or sustain the right of the Chinese government to complaint or redress in their behalf.

The lapse of ten years since the negotiation of the Burlingame treaty has exhibited to the notice of the Chinese government, as well as to our own people, the working of this experiment of immigration in great numbers of Chinese laborers to this country, and their maintenance here of all the traits of race, religion, manners and customs, habitations, mode of life, and segregation here, and the keeping up of the ties of their original home, which stamp them as strangers and sojourners, and not as incorporated elements of our national life and growth. This experience may naturally suggest the reconsideration of the subject, as dealt with by the Burlingame treaty, and may properly become the occasion of more direct and circumspect recognition, in renewed negotiations, of the difficulties surrounding this political and social problem. It may well be that, to the apprehension of the Chinese government no less than our own the simple provisions of the Burlingame treaty may need to be replaced by more careful methods, securing the Chinese and ourselves against a larger and more rapid infusion of this foreign race than our system of industry and society can take up and assimilate with ease and safety. This ancient government, ruling a polite and sensitive people, distinguished by a high sense of national pride, may properly desire an adjustment of their relations with us, which would in all things confirm, and in no degree endanger, the permanent peace and amity and the growing commerce and prosperity, which it has been the object and the effect of our existing treaties to cherish and perpetuate.

I regard the very grave discontents of the people of the Pacific States with the present working of the Chinese immigration, and their still graver apprehensions therefrom in the future, as deserving the most serious attention of the people of the whole country and a solicitous interest on the part of Congress and the Executive. If this were not my own judgment, the passage of this bill by both Houses of Congress would impress upon me the seriousness of the situation, when a majority of the representatives of the people of the whole country had thought fit to justify so serious a measure of relief.

The authority of Congress to terminate a treaty with a foreign power by expressing the will of the nation no longer to adhere to it, is as free from controversy under our Constitution as is the further proposition that the power of making new treaties or modifying existing treaties is not lodged by the Constitution in Congress, but in the President, by and with the advice and consent of the Senate, as shown by the concurrence of two-thirds of that body. A denunciation of a treaty by any Government is, confessedly, justifiable only upon some reason both of the highest justice and of the highest necessity. The action of Congress in the matter of the French treaties, in 1798, if it be regarded as an abrogation by this nation of a subsisting treaty, strongly illustrates the character and degree of justification which was then thought suitable to such a proceeding. The preamble of the act recites that "the treaties concluded between the United States and France have been repeatedly violated on the part of the French government, and the just claims of the United States for reparation of the injuries so committed have been refused, and their attempts to negotiate an amicable adjustment of all complaints between the two nations have been repelled with indignity;" and that "under authority of the French government there is yet pursued against the United States a system of predatory violence, infracting the said treaties, and hostile to the rights of a free and independent nation."

The enactment, as a logical consequence of these recited facts, declares "that the United States are of right freed and exonerated from the stipulations of the treaties and of the consular convention heretofore concluded between the United States and France, and that the same shall not henceforth be regarded as legally obligatory on the Government or citizens of the United States."

The history of the Government shows no other instance of an abrogation of a treaty by Congress.

Instances have sometimes occurred where the ordinary legislation of Congress has, by its conflict with some treaty obligation of the Government toward a foreign power, taken effect as an infraction of the treaty, and been judicially declared to be operative to that result. But neither such legislation nor such judicial sanction of the same has been regarded as an abrogation, even for the moment, of the treaty. On the contrary, the treaty in such case still subsists between the Governments, and the casual infraction is repaired by appropriate satisfaction in maintenance of the treaty.

The bill before me does not enjoin upon the President the abrogation of the entire Burlingame treaty, much less of the principal treaty of which it is made the supplement. As the power of modifying an existing treaty, whether by adding or striking out provisions, is a part of the treaty-making power under the Constitution, its exercise is not competent for Congress, nor would the assent of China to this partial abrogation of the treaty make the action of Congress, in thus procuring an amendment of a treaty, a competent exercise of authority under the Constitution. The importance, however, of this special consideration seems superseded by the principle that a denunciation of a part of a treaty, not made by the terms of the treaty itself separable from the rest, is a denunciation of the whole treaty. As the other high contracting party has entered into no treaty obligations except such as include the part denounced, the denunciation by one party of the part necessarily liberates the other party from the whole treaty.

I am convinced that, whatever urgency might in any quarter or by any interest be supposed to require an instant suppression of further immigration from China, no reasons can require the immediate withdrawal of our treaty protection of the Chinese already in this country, and no circumstances can tolerate an exposure of our citizens in China, merchants or missionaries, to the consequences of so sudden an abrogation of their treaty protections. Fortunately, however, the actual recession in the flow of the emigration from China to the Pacific coast, shown by trustworthy statistics, relieves us from any apprehension that the treatment of the subject in the proper course of diplomatic negotiations will introduce any new features of discontent or disturbance among the communities directly affected. Were such delay fraught with more inconveniences than have ever been suggested by the interests most earnest in promoting this legislation, I cannot but regard the summary disturbance of our existing treaties with China as greatly more inconvenient to much wider and more permanent interests of the country.

I have no occasion to insist upon the more general considerations of interest and duty which sacredly guard the faith of the nation in whatever form of obligation it may have been given. These sentiments animate the deliberations of Congress and pervade the minds of our whole people. Our history gives little occasion for any reproach in this regard, and in asking the renewed attention of Congress to this bill I am persuaded that their action will maintain the public duty and the public honor.

R. B. HAYES.

EXECUTIVE MANSION, *March* 1, 1879.

An act to restrict the immigration of Chinese to the United States.

Be it enacted by the Senate and House of Representatives of the United States of America in Congress assembled, That no master of any vessel owned in whole or in part by a citizen of the United States or by a citizen of any foreign country, shall take on board such vessel, at any port or place within the Chinese Empire, or at any other foreign port or place whatever, any number exceeding fifteen Chinese passengers, whether male or female, with the intent to bring such passengers to the United States, and leave such port or place and bring such passengers to any number exceeding fifteen on one voyage within the jurisdiction of the United States: *Provided*, That this section shall not apply to any master of a vessel seeking a harbor in stress of weather.

SEC. 2. That whenever the master or other person in charge of any such vessel takes on board the same, at any foreign port or place, any greater number of Chinese passengers than is prescribed in the first section of this act, with intent to bring such passengers to the United States, and leave such port or place and brings such passengers to any number exceeding fifteen on one voyage within the jurisdiction of the United States, he shall be deemed guilty of a misdemeanor, and shall, for each passenger so taken on board and brought within the jurisdiction of the United States exceeding the number of fifteen, be fined one hundred dollars, and may also be imprisoned for not exceeding six months.

SEC. 3. That the master of any vessel arriving in the United States, or any of the Territories thereof, from any foreign place whatever, at the same time that he delivers a manifest of the cargo, and if there be no cargo, then at the time of making report or entry of the vessel pursuant to law, shall, in addition to the other matters required to be reported by law, deliver and report to the collector of the district in which such vessel shall arrive a separate list of all Chinese passengers taken on board the vessel at any foreign port or place, and of all such passengers on board the vessel at that time; such list shall be sworn to by the master in the same manner as directed by law in relation to the manifest of the cargo; and the refusal or neglect of the master to comply with the provisions of this section shall receive the same penalties, disabilities, and forfeitures as are provided for a refusal or neglect to report and deliver a manifest of the cargo.

SEC. 4. That the amount of the several penalties imposed by the foregoing provisions shall be in liens on the vessels violating those provisions; and such vessels shall be libeled therefor in any circuit or district court of the United States where such vessel shall arrive.

SEC. 5. That nothing herein contained shall be held to repeal or modify any law forbidding the importation of coolies, or of females for immoral purposes, into the United States: *Provided*, That no consul or consular agent of the United States residing at any port from which any vessel taking Chinese passengers may take her departure shall grant the certificate provided for in section twenty-one hundred and sixty-two of the Revised Statutes for more than fifteen Chinese passengers on any one vessel.

SEC. 6. That this act shall not apply to persons officially connected with the Chinese government, or any embassy thereof, or to persons rescued from shipwreck during the voyage of and by the vessel bringing the same within the jurisdiction of the United States, or to persons who may only seek a temporary residence for educational purposes, and who shall have a certificate from the Chinese government for that purpose.

SEC. 7. That this act shall take effect from and after the first day of July, eighteen hundred and seventy-nine. And the President of the United States shall immediately on the approval of this act give notice to the government of China of the abrogation of articles five and six of the additional articles to the treaty of June eighteenth, eighteen hundred and fifty-eight, between the United States and China, proclaimed February fifth, eighteen hundred and seventy, commonly called the Burlingame treaty.

SAM. J. RANDALL,
Speaker of the House of Representatives.
W. A. WHEELER,
Vice-President of the United States and President of the Senate.

The SPEAKER. The question is, Will the House on reconsideration pass this bill, notwithstanding the objections of the President?

Mr. WILLIS, of Kentucky. I move the previous question.

Mr. BUTLER. I ask leave to have printed in the RECORD some remarks on this message.

The SPEAKER. The Chair hears no objection.

Mr. MCKENZIE. I hope that general consent will be given.

Mr. WILLIS, of Kentucky. I ask that general consent be given to print remarks on this subject.

The SPEAKER. The gentleman from Kentucky asks that such members as may desire it shall have leave to print in the RECORD remarks on the subject of this veto message. The Chair hears no objection.

The previous question was seconded and the main question ordered.

Mr. TOWNSEND, of New York. I call for the yeas and nays.

The SPEAKER. The Constitution requires that this question be taken by yeas and nays.

The question was taken; and there were—yeas 110, nays 96, not voting 84; as follows:

YEAS—110.

Atkins,	Cook,	Finley, Ebenezer B.	Herbert,
Banning,	Covert,	Finley, Jesse J.	House,
Bayne,	Cox, Samuel S.	Forney,	Hubbell,
Beebe,	Cravens,	Fort,	Jones, Frank
Bell,	Crittenden,	Foster,	Jones, James T.
Blackburn,	Culberson,	Garth,	Jorgensen,
Boone,	Davis, Horace	Gause,	Kenna,
Brentano,	Davis, Joseph J.	Giddings,	Kimmel,
Bridges,	Deering,	Glover,	Knott,
Butler,	Dibrell,	Goode,	Ligon,
Cabell,	Dickey,	Gunter,	Luttrell,
Caldwell, John W.	Durham,	Hale,	Maish,
Carlisle,	Eden,	Hamilton,	Majors,
Chalmers,	Eickhoff,	Harmer,	Manning,
Clarke of Kentucky,	Elam,	Hartzell,	Marsh,
Clark of Missouri,	Errett,	Hayes,	Martin,
Cobb,	Evans, I. Newton	Hazelton,	Mayham,
Cole,	Evins, John H.	Henkle,	McKenzie,
Collins,	Ewing,	Henry,	McMahon,

APPENDIX 4

Fifteen Passenger Bill (1879) and Veto Message of President Rutherford Hayes of the Fifteen Passenger Bill, March 1, 1879, 1879 Congressional Record–House 2275–2277

| 1879. | CONGRESSIONAL RECORD—HOUSE. | 2277 |

Mills,	Reilly,	Slemons,	Whitthorne,
Money,	Rice, Americus V.	Southard,	Wigginton,
Muldrow,	Robertson,	Sparks,	Williams, Jere N.
Muller,	Ross,	Steele,	Williams, Richard
Neal,	Sayler,	Steuger,	Willis, Albert S.
Page,	Scales,	Townshend, R. W.	Wright,
Patterson, T. M.	Shallenberger,	Turner,	Yeates.
Rea,	Shelley,	Turney,	
Reagan,	Singleton,	Walker,	

NAYS—96.

Aldrich,	Danford,	Killinger,	Sampson,
Bacon,	Denison,	Landers,	Serfon,
Bagley,	Dunnell,	Lapham,	Sinnickson,
Baker, William H.	Dwight,	Lathrop,	Smalls,
Ballou,	Eames,	Lindsey,	Smith, A. Herr
Banks,	Evans, James L.	McCook,	Starin,
Blair,	Frye,	Mitchell,	Stewart,
Bliss,	Gardner,	Monroe,	Stone, John W.
Boyd,	Garfield,	Morse,	Stone, Joseph C.
Brewer,	Hardenbergh,	Norcross,	Strait,
Briggs,	Harris, Benj. W.	Oliver,	Thompson,
Browne,	Harris, Henry R.	Overton,	Townsend, Amos
Bundy,	Harris, John T.	Patterson, G. W.	Townsend, M. I.
Burchard,	Henderson,	Peddie,	Waddell,
Burdick,	Hewitt, Abram S.	Phelps,	Wait,
Camp,	Hunter,	Phillips,	Ward,
Candler,	Humphrey,	Price,	Warner,
Cannon,	Humperford,	Pridemore,	Watson,
Caswell,	Ittner,	Pugh,	White, Harry
Clark, Rush	James,	Rainey,	White, Michael D.
Conger,	Jones, John S.	Randolph,	Williams, Andrew
Crapo,	Keifer,	Rice, William W.	Williams, C. G.
Cummings,	Kelley,	Robinson, G. D.	Williams, James
Cutler,	Ketcham,	Robinson, M. S.	Willis, Benj. A.

NOT VOTING—34.

Acklen,	Clymer,	Hunton,	Roberts,
Aiken,	Cox, Jacob D.	Joyce,	Ryan,
Bailey,	Davidson,	Keightley,	Sapp,
Baker, John H.	Dean,	Knapp,	Smith, William E.
Beale,	Ellis,	Lockwood,	Springer,
Benedict,	Ellsworth,	Loring,	Stephens,
Bicknell,	Felton,	Lynde,	Swann,
Bland,	Fleming,	Mackey,	Thornburgh,
Blount,	Franklin,	McGowan,	Throckmorton,
Bouck,	Freeman,	McKinley,	Tipton,
Bragg,	Fuller,	Metcalfe,	Tucker,
Bright,	Gibson,	Morgan,	Vance,
Brogden,	Hanna,	Morrison,	Van Vorhes,
Brokner,	Harrison,	O'Neill,	Voeder,
Cain,	Hart,	Pollard,	Walsh,
Caldwell, W. P.	Haskell,	Potter,	Willits,
Calkins,	Hatcher,	Pound,	Wilson,
Campbell,	Hendoc,	Powers,	Wood,
Chittenden,	Hewitt, G. W.	Reed,	Wren,
Claflin,	Hiscock,	Riddle,	Young, Casey
Clark, Alvah A.	Hooker,	Robbins,	Young, John S.

During the roll-call the following announcements were made:

Mr. CALDWELL, of Tennessee. I am paired with Mr. McGOWAN. If he were present, he would vote "no" and I would vote "ay."

Mr. ROBBINS. I am paired with Mr. HANNA.

Mr. ROBERTS. I am paired with Mr. WALSH.

Mr. ATKINS. I wish to announce that Mr. BLOUNT, Mr. CLYMER, and Mr. BAKER, of Indiana, are absent on conference committees.

Mr. WILSON. I am paired with Mr. WHEN.

Mr. DAVIDSON. I am paired with Mr. KEIGHTLEY. If he were present, I would vote "ay" and I presume he would vote "no."

Mr. CALKINS. I am paired with Mr. HOOKER. If he were present, I would vote "ay."

Mr. CLAFLIN. I am paired with Mr. LORING.

Mr. O'NEILL. I am paired with Mr. ELLIS. If he were present, I would vote "no" and he would vote "ay." I wish also to announce that my colleague, Mr. FREEMAN, is paired with Mr. RIDDLE.

Mr. BUCKNER. I am paired with Mr. CHITTENDEN.

Mr. TOWNSEND, of Ohio. Mr. McKINLEY is paired with Mr. MORSE on questions generally, but on this question both would vote "no."

Mr. MORSE. I vote "no."

Mr. HASKELL. I am paired with Mr. RYAN. If he were here, I would vote "ay."

Mr. TIPTON. I am paired with my colleague, Mr. KNAPP. If he were present, I would vote "ay."

Mr. HANNA. I am paired with Mr. ROBBINS.

Mr. METCALFE. I am paired with Mr. BLAND.

Mr. BEEBE. My colleague, Mr. LOCKWOOD, is paired with Mr. ELLSWORTH.

Mr. SPRINGER moved by unanimous consent that the reading of the names be dispensed with.

Objection was made.

The vote was then announced as above recorded.

The SPEAKER. As required by the Constitution, two-thirds not having voted in the affirmative, the bill is rejected.

POTTAWATOMIE INDIANS.

The SPEAKER laid before the House a letter from the Secretary of the Interior, relative to certain stocks belonging to the Pottawatomie Indians; which was referred to the Committee on Indian affairs, and ordered to be printed.

KISKIMINETAS AND CONEMAUGH RIVERS.

The SPEAKER also laid before the House a letter from the Secretary of War, transmitting the report of Major William E. Merrill, Corps of Engineers, of the results of the examination of the Kiski-

minetas and Conemaugh Rivers, Pennsylvania; which was referred to the Committee on Commerce, and ordered to be printed.

CANEY FORK RIVER, ETC.

The SPEAKER also laid before the House a letter from the Secretary of War, transmitting the report of Captain W. R. King, Corps of Engineers, of the results of investigation of Caney Fork River and Obies River, Tennessee, and of the survey of the Cumberland River, Kentucky; which was referred to the Committee on Commerce, and ordered to be printed.

FEES OF DISTRICT ATTORNEYS.

The next business was the bill (H. R. No. 3124) to amend section 824 of the Revised Statutes of the United States, returned from the Senate with amendments; which were read, as follows:

Add at the end of the bill:

"Provided, however, That informations shall not be filed in such cases except when the accused has been committed in default of bail, or is under a recognizance for his appearance to answer for crimes charged in the information."

Amend the title so as to read:

"An act to amend section 824 of the Revised Statutes of the United States relative to fees of district attorneys."

Mr. HERBERT. Mr. Speaker, that bill places indictments and informations upon the same footing. Its effect is to give to district attorneys the same fees for convictions under information as for convictions under indictment. It is an encouragement to the district attorneys to dispense as far as possible with grand juries, to do away with the protection which grand juries afford to the citizens, and pay them for resorting to information. In these days when affidavits can be hired to be made for a penny apiece, by the bushel, it seems to me that we ought not to pass such a bill, and I therefore move to lay the bill and amendments on the table.

The motion was agreed to.

Mr. HERBERT moved to reconsider the vote just taken; and also moved that the motion to reconsider be laid on the table.

The latter motion was agreed to.

SUPERVISORY JURISDICTION OF CIRCUIT COURTS.

The next business on the Speaker's table was the bill (H. R. No. 5065) to give circuit courts supervisory jurisdiction in certain criminal cases, with amendments by the Senate.

The amendments of the Senate were read.

Mr. HANNA. This is a bill which it seems to me every lawyer that practices in circuit courts should take an interest in and favor its passage.

Mr. HARRIS, of Virginia. I move to concur in the Senate amendments.

The motion was agreed to.

Mr. HARRIS, of Virginia, moved to reconsider the vote by which the amendments of the Senate were concurred in; and also moved that the motion to reconsider be laid on the table.

The latter motion was agreed to.

ORDER OF BUSINESS.

Mr. WHITE, of Pennsylvania, (at eleven o'clock and fifty-five minutes p. m.) I move that the House do now adjourn. It is now almost Sunday morning.

The SPEAKER. The Chair would advise the gentleman from Pennsylvania that it is desirable that the House, before adjourning or taking a recess, should receive from the Senate the sundry civil bill.

Mr. WHITE. I withdraw the motion.

ACKNOWLEDGMENT OF DEEDS, ETC.

The next business on the Speaker's table was the bill (H. R. No. 1651) to validate and confirm certain acknowledgments of deeds and other instruments of writing under seal, made in a foreign country, for lands lying in the District of Columbia, and the records thereof, with amendments by the Senate.

The amendments of the Senate were read.

Mr. FRYE. This bill was unanimously reported by the Judiciary Committee of the House, unanimously passed the House, went to the Senate, and has been amended by the Senate in certain particulars. I have examined the amendments, all that I have under my charge when it passed the House, and I find they are only put in for the protection of innocent parties. The bill simply provides to make valid certain acknowledgments of deeds made in foreign countries. The amendments are all right. I move that they be concurred in.

The amendments of the Senate were concurred in.

Mr. FRYE moved to reconsider the vote by which the amendments of the Senate were concurred in; and also moved that the motion to reconsider be laid on the table.

The latter motion was agreed to.

ENROLLED BILLS SIGNED.

Mr. SAMPSON, from the Committee on Enrolled Bills, reported that the committee had examined and found truly enrolled bills of the following titles; when the Speaker signed the same:

An act (S. No. 362) granting a pension to A. G. Ege;
An act (S. No. 399) granting a pension to Abigail S. Tilton;
An act (S. No. 663) granting a pension to William H. H. Buck;
An act (S. No. 687) granting a pension to William H. Bagley;
An act (S. No. 801) to amend section 2403 of the Revised Statutes of the United States, in relation to deposits for surveys;

APPENDIX 5

Angell Treaty 1880
(ratified 1881)

TREATY REGULATING CHINESE IMMIGRATION
INTO THE UNITED STATES.

Concluded November 17, 1880; Ratifications exchanged
at Peking July 19, 1881; Proclaimed October 5, 1881.

Whereas, in the eighth year of Hsien Feng, anno Domini 1858, a treaty of peace and friendship was concluded between the United States of America and China., and to which were added, in the seventh year of Tung Chih, Anno Domini 1868, certain supplementary articles to the advantage of both parties, which supplementary articles were to be perpetually observed and obeyed:– and

Whereas the Government of the United States, because of the constantly increasing immigration of Chinese laborers to the territory of the United States, and the embarrassments consequent upon such immigration, now desires to negotiate a modification of the existing Treaties which shall not be in direct contravention of their spirit:–

Now, therefore, the President of the United States of America has appointed James B. Angell, of Michigan, John F. Swift, of California, and William Henry Trescot, of South Carolina as his Commissioners Plenipotentiary; and His Imperial Majesty, the Emperor of China, has appointed Pao Chiin, a member of His Imperial Majesty's Privy Council, and Superintendent of the Board of Civil Office; and Li Hungtsao, a member of His Imperial Majesty's Privy Council, as his Commissioners Plenipotentiary; and the said Commissioners Plenipotentiary, having conjointly examined their full powers, and having discussed the points of possible modification in existing Treaties, have agreed upon the following articles in modification.

ARTICLE I.
Whenever in the opinion of the Government of the United States, the coming of Chinese laborers to the United States, or their residence therein, affects or threatens to affect the interests of that country, or to endanger the good

order of the said country or of any locality within the territory thereof, the Government of China agrees that the Government of the United States may regulate, limit, or suspend such coming or residence, but may not absolutely prohibit it. The limitation or suspension shall be reasonable and shall apply only to Chinese who may go to the United States as laborers, other classes not being included in the limitations. Legislation taken in regard to Chinese laborers will be of such a character only as is necessary to enforce the regulation, limitation or suspension of immigration, and immigrants shall not be subject to personal maltreatment or abuse.

ARTICLE II.

Chinese subjects, whether proceeding to the United States as teachers, students, merchants or from curiosity, together with their body and household servants, and Chinese laborers who are now in the United States shall be allowed to go and come of their own free will and accord, and shall be accorded all the rights, privileges, immunities and exemptions which are accorded to the citizens and subjects of the most favored nation.

ARTICLE III.

If Chinese laborers, or Chinese of any other class, now either permanently or temporarily residing in the territory of the United Treatment of the States, meet with ill treatment at the hands of any other persons, the Government of the United States will exert all its power to devise measures for their protection and to secure to them the same rights, privileges, immunities and exemptions as may be enjoyed by the citizens or subjects of the most favored nation, and to which they are entitled by treaty.

ARTICLE IV.

The high contracting Powers having agreed upon the foregoing articles, whenever the Government of the United States shall adopt legislative measures in accordance therewith, such measures will be communicated to the Government of China. If the measures as enacted are found to work hardship upon the subjects of China, the Chinese Minister at Washington may bring the matter to the notice of the Secretary of State of the United States, who will consider the subject with him; and the Chinese Foreign Office may also bring the matter to the notice of the United States Minister at Peking and consider the subject with him, to the end that mutual and unqualified benefit may result.

In faith whereof the respective Plenipotentiaries have signed and sealed the foregoing at Peking in English and Chinese being three originals of each text of even tenor and date, the ratifications of which shall be exchanged at Peking within one year from date of its execution.

Done at Peking, this seventeenth day of November, in the year of our Lord, 1880. Kuanghsii, sixth year, tenth moon, fifteenth day.

[SEAL.] JAMES B. ANGELL.
[SEAL.] JOHN F. SWIFT.
[SEAL.] WM. HENRY TRESCOT.
[SEAL.] PAO CHON.
[SEAL.] LI HUNGTSAO.

And whereas the said Treaty has been duly ratified on both parts and the respective ratification were exchanged at Peking on the 19th day of July 1881:

Now, therefore, be it known that I, Chester A. Arthur, President of the United States of America, have caused the said Treaty to be made public to the end that the same and every article and clause thereof may be observed and fulfilled with good faith by the United States and the citizens thereof.

In witness whereof, I have hereunto set my hand and caused the seal of the United States to be affixed.

Done in Washington this fifth day of October in the year of our Lord one thousand eight hundred and eighty-one, and of the Independence of the United States the one hundred and sixth.

[SEAL.] CHESTER A. ARTHUR, By the President:
        JAMES G. BLAINE, Secretary of State.

APPENDIX 6

Veto Message of President Chester A. Arthur of Senate Bill No. 71, April 4, 1882

April 4, 1882

To the Senate of the United States:

After careful consideration of Senate bill No. 71, entitled "An act to execute certain treaty stipulations relating to Chinese," I herewith return it to the Senate, in which it originated, with my objections to its passage.

A nation is justified in repudiating its treaty obligations only when they are in conflict with great paramount interests. Even then all possible reasonable means for modifying or changing those obligations by mutual agreement should be exhausted before resorting to the supreme fight of refusal to comply with them.

These rules have governed the United States in their past intercourse with other powers as one of the family of nations. I am persuaded that if Congress can feel that this act violates the faith of the nation as pledged to China it will concur with me in rejecting this particular mode of regulating Chinese immigration, and will endeavor to find another which shall meet the expectations of the people of the United States without coming in conflict with the rights of China.

The present treaty relations between that power and the United States spring from an antagonism which arose between our paramount domestic interests and our previous relations.

The treaty commonly known as the Burlingame treaty conferred upon Chinese subjects the right of voluntary emigration to the United States for the purposes of curiosity or trade or as permanent residents, and was in all respects reciprocal as to citizens of the United States in China. It gave to the voluntary emigrant coming to the United States the right to travel there or to reside there, with all the privileges, immunities, or exemptions enjoyed by the citizens or subjects of the most favored nation.

Under the operation of this treaty it was found that the institutions of the United States and the character of its people and their means of obtaining a livelihood might be seriously affected by the unrestricted introduction of Chinese labor. Congress attempted to alleviate this condition by legislation, but the act which it passed proved to be in violation of our treaty obligations, and, being returned by the President with his objections, failed to become a law.

Diplomatic relief was then sought. A new treaty was concluded with China. Without abrogating the Burlingame treaty, it was agreed to modify it so far that the Government of the United States might regulate, limit, or suspend the coming of Chinese laborers to the United States or their residence therein, but that it should not absolutely prohibit them, and that the limitation or suspension should be reasonable and should apply only to Chinese who might go to the United States as laborers, other classes not being included in the limitations. This treaty is unilateral, not reciprocal. It is a concession from China to the United States in limitation of the rights which she was enjoying under the Burlingame treaty. It leaves us by our own act to determine when and how we will enforce those limitations. China may therefore fairly have a right to expect that in enforcing them we will take good care not to overstep the grant and take more than has been conceded to us.

It is but a year since this new treaty, under the operation of the Constitution, became part of the supreme law of the land, and the present act is the first attempt to exercise the more enlarged powers which it relinquishes to the United States.

In its first article the United States is empowered to decide whether the coming of Chinese laborers to the United States or their residence therein affects or threatens to affect our interests Or to endanger good order, either within the whole country or in any part of it. The act recites that "in the opinion of the Government of the United States the coming of Chinese laborers to this country endangers the good order of certain localities thereof." But the act itself is much broader than the recital. It acts upon residence as well as immigration, and its provisions are effective throughout the United States. I think it may fairly be accepted as an expression of the opinion of Congress that the coming of such laborers to the United States or their residence here affects our interests and endangers good order throughout the country. On this point I should feel it my duty to accept the views of Congress.

The first article further confers the power upon this Government to regulate, limit, or suspend, but not actually to prohibit, the coming of such laborers to or their residence in the United States. The negotiators of the treaty have recorded with unusual fullness their understanding of the sense and meaning with which these words were used.

As to the class of persons to be affected by the treaty, the Americans inserted in their draft a provision that the words "Chinese laborers" signify all immigration other than that for "teaching, trade, travel, study, and curiosity." The Chinese objected to this that it operated to include artisans in the class of laborers whose immigration might be forbidden. The Americans replied that they "could" not consent that artisans shall be excluded from the class of Chinese laborers, for it is this very competition of skilled labor in the cities where the Chinese labor immigration concentrates which has caused the embarrassment and popular discontent. In the subsequent negotiations this definition dropped out, and does not appear in the treaty. Article II of the treaty confers the rights, privileges, immunities, and exemptions which are accorded to citizens and subjects of the most favored nation upon Chinese subjects proceeding to the United States as teachers, students, merchants, or from curiosity. The American commissioners report that the Chinese Government claimed that in this article they did by exclusion provide that nobody should be entitled to claim the benefit of the general provisions of the Burlingame treaty but those who might go to the United States in those capacities or for those purposes. I accept this as the definition of the word "laborers" as used in the treaty.

As to the power of legislating respecting this class of persons, the new treaty provides that we "may not absolutely prohibit" their coming or their residence. The Chinese commissioners gave notice in the outset that they would never agree to a prohibition of voluntary emigration. Notwithstanding this the United States commissioners submitted a draft, in which it was provided that the United States might "regulate, limit, suspend, or prohibit" it. The Chinese refused to accept this. The Americans replied that they were "willing to consult the wishes of the Chinese Government in preserving the principle of free intercourse between the people of the two countries, as established by existing treaties, provided that the right of the United States Government to use its discretion in guarding against any possible evils of immigration of Chinese laborers is distinctly recognized. Therefore if such concession removes all difficulty on the part of the Chinese commissioners (but only in that case) the United States commissioners will agree to remove the word 'prohibit' from their article and to use the words 'regulate, limit, or suspend.'" The Chinese reply to this can only be inferred from the fact that in the place of an agreement, as proposed by our commissioners, that we might prohibit the coming or residence of Chinese laborers, there was inserted in the treaty an agreement that we might not do it.

The remaining words, "regulate, limit, and suspend," first appear in the American draft. When it was submitted to the Chinese, they said: "We infer that of the phrases regulate, limit, suspend, or prohibit, the first is a general expression referring to the others. We are entirely ready to negotiate with your excellencies to the end that a limitation either in point of time or of numbers may be fixed upon the emigration of Chinese laborers to the United States." At a subsequent interview they said that "by limitation in number they meant, for example, that the United States, having, as they supposed, a record of the number of immigrants in each year, as well as the total number of Chinese now there, that no more should be allowed to go in any one year in future than either the greatest number which had gone in any year in the past, or that the total number should never be allowed to exceed the number now there. As to limitation of time they meant, for example, that Chinese should be allowed to go in alternate years, or every third year, or, for example, that they should not be allowed to go for two, three, or five years." At a subsequent conference the Americans said: "The Chinese commissioners have in their project explicitly recognized the right of the United States to use some discretion, and have proposed a limitation as to time and number. This is the right to regulate, limit, or suspend."

In one of the conferences the Chinese asked the Americans whether they could give them any idea of the laws which would be passed to carry the powers into execution. The Americans answered that this could hardly be done; "that the United States Government might never deem it necessary to exercise this power. It would depend upon circumstances. If Chinese immigration concentrated in cities where it threatened public order, or if it confined itself to localities where it was an injury to the interests of the American people, the Government of the United States would undoubtedly take steps to prevent such accumulations of Chinese. If, on the contrary, there was no large immigration, or if there were sections of the country where such immigration was clearly beneficial, then the legislation of the United States under this power would be adapted to such circumstances. For example, there might be a demand for Chinese labor in the South and a surplus of such labor in California, and Congress might legislate in accordance with these facts. In general the legislation would be in view of and depend upon the circumstances of the situation at the moment such legislation became necessary. The Chinese commissioners said this explanation was satisfactory; that they had not intended to ask for a draft of any special act, but for some general idea how the power would be exercised. What had just been said gave them the explanation which they wanted.

With this entire accord as to the meaning of the words they were about to employ and the object of the legislation which might be had in consequence, the parties signed the treaty, in Article I of which "the Government of China agrees that the Government of the United States may regulate, limit, or suspend such coming or residence, but may not absolutely prohibit it. The limitation or suspension shall be reasonable, and shall apply only to Chinese who may go to the United States as laborers, other classes not being included in the limitations. Legislation taken in regard to Chinese laborers will be of such a character only as is necessary to enforce the regulation, limitation, or suspension of immigration."

The first section of the act provides that "from and after the expiration of sixty days next after the passage of this act, and until the expiration of twenty years next after the passage of this act, the coming of Chinese laborers be, and the same is hereby, suspended; and during such suspension it shall not be lawful for any Chinese laborer to come, or, having so come after the expiration of said sixty days, to remain within the United States."

The examination which I have made of the treaty and of the declarations which its negotiators have left on record of the meaning of its language leaves no doubt in my mind that neither contracting party in concluding the treaty of 1880 contemplated the passage of an act prohibiting immigration for twenty years, which is nearly a generation, or thought that such a period would be a reasonable suspension or limitation, or intended to change the provisions of the Burlingame treaty to that extent. I regard this provision of the act as a breach of our national faith, and being unable to bring myself in harmony with the views of Congress on this vital point the honor of the country constrains me to return the act with this objection to its passage.

Deeply convinced of the necessity of some legislation on this subject, and concurring fully with Congress in many of the objects which are sought to be accomplished, I avail myself of the opportunity to point out some other features of the present act which. in my opinion, can be modified to advantage.

The classes of Chinese who still enjoy the protection of the Burlingame treaty are entitled to the privileges, immunities, and exemptions accorded to citizens and subjects of the most favored nation. We have treaties with many powers which permit their citizens and subjects to reside within the United States and carry on business under the same laws and regulations which are enforced against citizens of the United States. I think it may be doubted whether provisions requiring personal registration and the taking out of passports which are not imposed upon natives can be required of Chinese. Without expressing an opinion on that point, I may invite the attention of Congress to the fact that the system of personal registration and passports is undemocratic and hostile to the spirit of our institutions. I doubt the wisdom of putting an entering wedge of this kind into our laws. A nation like the United States, jealous of the liberties of its citizens, may well hesitate before it incorporates into its polity a system which is fast disappearing in Europe before the progress of liberal institutions. A wide experience has shown how futile such precautions are, and how easily passports may be borrowed, exchanged, or even forged by persons interested to do so.

If it is nevertheless thought that a passport is the most convenient way for identifying the Chinese entitled to the protection of the Burlingame treaty, it may still be doubted whether they ought to be required to register. It is certainly our duty under the Burlingame treaty to make their stay in the United States, in the operation of general laws upon them, as nearly like that of our own citizens as we can consistently with our right to shut out the laborers. No good purpose is served in requiring them to register.

My attention has been called by the Chinese minister to the fact that the bill as it stands makes no provision for the transit across the United States of Chinese subjects now residing in foreign countries. I think that this point may well claim the attention of Congress in legislating on this subject.

I have said that good faith requires us to suspend the immigration of Chinese laborers for a less period than twenty years; I now add that good policy points in the same direction.

Our intercourse with China is of recent date. Our first treaty with that power is not yet forty years old. It is only since we acquired California and established a great seat of commerce on the Pacific that we may be said to have broken down the barriers which fenced in that ancient Monarchy. The Burlingame treaty naturally followed. Under the spirit which inspired it many thousand Chinese laborers came to the United States. No one can say that the country has not profited by their work. They were largely instrumental in constructing the railways which connect the Atlantic with the Pacific. The States of the Pacific Slope are full of evidences of their industry. Enterprises profitable alike to the capitalist and to the laborer of Caucasian origin would have lain dormant but for them. A time has now come when it is supposed that they are not needed, and when it is thought by Congress and by those most acquainted with the subject that it is best to try to get along without them. There may, however, be other sections of the country where this species of labor may be advantageously employed without interfering with the laborers of our own race. In making the proposed experiment it may be the part of wisdom as well as of good faith to fix the length of the experimental period with reference to this fact.

Experience has shown that the trade of the East is the key to national wealth and influence. The opening of China to the commerce of the whole world has benefited no section of it more than the States of our own Pacific Slope. The State of California, and its great maritime port especially, have reaped enormous advantages from this source. Blessed with an exceptional climate, enjoying an unrivaled harbor, with the riches of a great agricultural and mining State in its rear and the wealth of the whole Union pouring into it over its lines of railway, San Francisco has before it an incalculable future if our friendly and amicable relations with Asia remain undisturbed. It needs no argument to show that the policy which we now propose to adopt must have a direct tendency to repel Oriental nations from us and to drive their trade and commerce into more friendly lands. It may be that the great and paramount interest of protecting our labor from Asiatic competition may justify us in a permanent adoption of this policy. But it is wiser, in the first place, to make a shorter experiment, with a view hereafter of maintaining permanently only such features as time and experience may commend.

I transmit herewith copies of the papers relating to the recent treaty with China, which accompanied the confidential message of President Hayes to the Senate of the 10th January, 1881, and also a copy of a memorandum respecting the act herewith returned, which was handed to the Secretary of State by the Chinese minister in Washington.

CHESTER A. ARTHUR

The veto message was read, and, after debate, was ordered to be printed and to lie on the table. It was taken up the next day, and, after debate, the question was taken on its passage, the objections of the President to the contrary notwithstanding, which was decided in the negative by a vote of 29 yeas against 21 nays, 26 Senators not voting. So the bill was not passed, two-thirds of the Senators present not voting in the affirmative.

APPENDIX 7

The Ten-Year Exclusion Legislation of 1882, H.R. 5804
"An act to execute certain treaty stipulations relating to Chinese."
(Sess. I, Chap. 126; 22 Stat. 58. 47th Congress; Approved May 6, 1882.)

---

58   FORTY-SEVENTH CONGRESS. Sess. I. Ch. 117-120, 126. 1882.

award in acknowledgment of the services of masters and crews of foreign vessels in rescuing American citizens from shipwreck.

Appointments made by reason of fitness, and not for political reasons. SECTION TEN.—That the appointment of district superintendents, inspectors, and keepers and crews of life-saving stations shall be made solely with reference to their fitness, and without reference to their political or party affiliations.

SECTION ELEVEN.—That this act shall take effect from and after its passage.

Approved, May 4, 1882.

May 4, 1882.   CHAP. 118.—An act to amend the laws with reference to elections in West Virginia.

Be it enacted by the Senate and House of Representatives of the United States of America in Congress assembled, That on the second Tuesday of October, eighteen hundred and eighty-two, there shall be elected in each Congressional District in the State of West Virginia, one representative to represent said State of West Virginia in the Forty-eighth Congress.

West Virginia. Election of Representatives for the Forty-eighth Congress.

SEC. 2.—That said election shall be conducted according to the laws now in force, except so far as the same relate to and fix the time of such election.

Approved, May 4, 1882.

May 4, 1882.   CHAP. 119.—An act making an immediate appropriation for the removal of obstructions at Hell Gate, New York.

Be it enacted by the Senate and House of Representatives of the United States of America in Congress assembled, That the sum of fifty thousand dollars be and is hereby appropriated, to be paid out of any money in the Treasury not otherwise appropriated, for the removal of obstructions in East River, Hell Gate, New York, the same to be expended under the direction of the Secretary of War, and to be immediately available.

Removal of obstructions from Hell Gate, N. Y. Appropriation.

Approved, May 4, 1882.

May 4, 1882.   CHAP. 120.—An act to repeal the discriminating duties on goods produced east of the Cape of Good Hope.

Be it enacted by the Senate and House of Representatives of the United States of America in Congress assembled, That section two thousand five hundred and one of the Revised Statutes of the United States which reads as follows:

Repeal of discriminating duties on goods produced east of the Cape of Good Hope when imported from places west of the Cape of Good Hope, from and after January 1, 1883. R. S., 2501, 459, repealed.

"There shall be levied, collected and paid on all goods, wares, and merchandise of the growth or produce of the countries east of the Cape of Good Hope (except wool, raw cotton and raw silk, as reeled from the cocoon, or not further advanced than tram, thrown, or organzine,) when imported from places west of the Cape of Good Hope, a duty of ten per centum ad valorem in addition to the duties imposed on any such article when imported directly from the place or places of their growth or production", be and the same is hereby repealed from and after the first day of January, eighteen hundred and eighty-three.

Approved, May 4, 1882.

May 6, 1882.   CHAP. 126.—An act to execute certain treaty stipulations relating to Chinese.

Preamble. Whereas, in the opinion of the Government of the United States the coming of Chinese laborers to this country endangers the good order of certain localities within the territory thereof: Therefore,

APPENDIX 7

The Ten-Year Exclusion Legislation of 1882, H.R. 5804
"An act to execute certain treaty stipulations relating to Chinese."
(Sess. I, Chap. 126; 22 Stat. 58. 47th Congress; Approved May 6, 1882.)

FORTY-SEVENTH CONGRESS. SESS. I. CH. 126. 1882.   **59**

Be it enacted by the Senate and House of Representatives of the United States of America in Congress assembled, That from and after the expiration of ninety days next after the passage of this act, and until the expiration of ten years next after the passage of this act, the coming of Chinese laborers to the United States be, and the same is hereby, suspended; and during such suspension it shall not be lawful for any Chinese laborer to come, or, having so come after the expiration of said ninety days, to remain within the United States. — *Immigration of Chinese laborers to the United States suspended for ten years.*

SEC. 2. That the master of any vessel who shall knowingly bring within the United States on such vessel, and land or permit to be landed, any Chinese laborer, from any foreign port or place, shall be deemed guilty of a misdemeanor, and on conviction thereof shall be punished by a fine of not more than five hundred dollars for each and every such Chinese laborer so brought, and may be also imprisoned for a term not exceeding one year. — *Penalties for violation of act.*

SEC. 3. That the two foregoing sections shall not apply to Chinese laborers who were in the United States on the seventeenth day of November, eighteen hundred and eighty, or who shall have come into the same before the expiration of ninety days next after the passage of this act, and who shall produce to such master before going on board such vessel, and shall produce to the collector of the port in the United States at which such vessel shall arrive, the evidence hereinafter in this act required of his being one of the laborers in this section mentioned; nor shall the two foregoing sections apply to the case of any master whose vessel, being bound to a port not within the United States,.shall come within the jurisdiction of the United States by reason of being in distress or in stress of weather, or touching at any port of the United States on its voyage to any foreign port or place: *Provided,* That all Chinese laborers brought /on such vessel shall depart with the vessel on leaving port. — *Exemptions.* — *Masters of vessels with immigrants, when exempt.* — *Proviso.*

SEC. 4. That for the purpose of properly identifying Chinese laborers who were in the United States on the seventeenth day of November, eighteen hundred and eighty, or who shall have come into the same before the expiration of ninety days next after the passage of this ac., and in order to furnish them with the proper evidence of their right to go from and come to the United States of their free will and accord, as provided by the treaty between the United States and China dated November seventeenth, eighteen hundred and eighty, the collector of customs of the district from which any such Chinese laborer shall depart from the United States shall, in person or by deputy, go on board each vessel having on board any such Chinese laborer and cleared or about to sail from his district for a foreign port, and on such vessel make a list of all such Chinese laborers, which shall be entered in registry-books to be kept for that purpo e, in which shall be stated the name, age, occupation, last place of residence, physical marks or peculiarities, and all facts necessary for the identification of each of such Chinese laborers, which books shall be safely kept in the custom-house; and every such Chinese laborer so departing from the United States shall be entitled to, and shall receive, free of any charge or cost upon application therefor, from the collector or his deputy, at the time such list is taken, a certificate, signed by the collector or his deputy and attested by his seal of office, in such form as the Secretary of the Treasury shall prescribe, which certificate shall contain a statement of the name, age, occupation, last place of residence, personal description, and facts of identification of the Chinese laborer to whom the certificate is issued, corresponding with the said list and registry in all particulars. In case any Chinese laborer after having received such certificate shall leave such vessel before her departure he shall deliver his certificate to the master of the vessel, and if such Chinese laborer shall fail to return to such vessel before her departure from port the certificate shall be delivered by the master to the collector of customs for cancellation. The certificate herein provided for shall entitle the Chinese laborer to whom the same — *Privileges to Chinese laborers in United States November 17, 1880, under treaty November 17, 1880.* — *List to be made and kept in custom-house.* — *When leaving to receive certificate entitling person described to a return to the United States.* — *Certificate filed and canceled, when.*

APPENDIX 7

The Ten-Year Exclusion Legislation of 1882, H.R. 5804
"An act to execute certain treaty stipulations relating to Chinese."
(Sess. I, Chap. 126; 22 Stat. 58. 47th Congress; Approved May 6, 1882.)

60   FORTY-SEVENTH CONGRESS. Sess. I. Ch. 126. 1882

is issued to return to and re-enter the United States upon producing and delivering the same to the collector of customs of the district at which such Chinese laborer shall seek to re-enter; and upon delivery of such certificate by such Chinese laborer to the collector of customs at the time of re-entry in the United States, said collector shall cause the same to be filed in the custom-house and duly canceled.

Certificate to issue on departure from United States, by land, free of cost. SEC. 5. That any Chinese laborer mentioned in section four of this act being in the United States, and desiring to depart from the United States by land, shall have the right to demand and receive, free of charge or cost, a certificate of identification similar to that provided for in section four of this act to be issued to such Chinese laborers as may desire to leave the United States by water; and it is hereby made the duty of the collector of customs of the district next adjoining the foreign country to which said Chinese laborer desires to go to issue such certificate, free of charge or cost, upon application by such Chinese laborer, and to enter the same upon registry-books to be kept by him for the purpose, as provided for in section four of this act.

Chinese other than laborers to be identified by certificate from Chinese Government. SEC. 6. That in order to the faithful execution of articles one and two of the treaty in this act before mentioned, every Chinese person other than a laborer who may be entitled by said treaty and this act to come within the United States, and who shall be about to come to the United States, shall be identified as so entitled by the Chinese Government in each case, such identity to be evidenced by a certificate issued under the authority of said government, which certificate shall be in the English language or (if not in the English language) accompanied by a translation into English, stating such right to come, and which certificate shall state the name, title, or official rank, if any, the age, height, and all physical peculiarities, former and present occupation or profession, and place of residence in China of the person to whom the certificate is issued and that such person is entitled conformably to the treaty in this act mentioned to come within the United States. Such certificate shall be prima-facie evidence of the fact set forth therein, and shall be produced to the collector of customs, or his deputy, of the port in the district in the United States at which the person named therein shall arrive.

Fraudulent certificates. SEC. 7. That any person who shall knowingly and falsely alter or substitute any name for the name written in such certificate or forge any such certificate, or knowingly utter any forged or fraudulent certificate, or falsely personate any person named in any such certificate, shall be **Penalties.** deemed guilty of a misdemeanor; and upon conviction thereof shall be fined in a sum not exceeding one thousand dollars, and imprisoned in a penitentiary for a term of not more than five years.

Lists of Chinese passengers on vessels arriving at ports of United States to be kept and delivered by masters of such vessels to collector of customs. SEC. 8. That the master of any vessel arriving in the United States from any foreign port or place shall, at the same time he delivers a manifest of the cargo, and if there be no cargo, then at the time of making a report of the entry of the vessel pursuant to law, in addition to the other matter required to be reported, and before landing, or permitting to land, any Chinese passengers, deliver and report to the collector of customs of the district in which such vessels shall have arrived a separate list of all Chinese passengers taken on board his vessel at any foreign port or place, and all such passengers on board the vessel at that time. Such list shall show the names of such passengers (and if accredited officers of the Chinese Government traveling on the business of that government, or their servants, with a note of such facts), and the names and other particulars, as shown by their respective certificates; and such list shall be sworn to by the master in the manner required by law in relation to the manifest of the cargo. Any willful refusal or neglect of any such master to comply with the provisions of this section shall incur the same penalties and forfeiture as are provided for a refusal or neglect to report and deliver a manifest of the cargo.

Collector of customs to examine SEC. 9. That before any Chinese passengers are landed from any such vessel, the collector, or his deputy, shall proceed to examine such pas-

APPENDIX 7

The Ten-Year Exclusion Legislation of 1882, H.R. 5804
"An act to execute certain treaty stipulations relating to Chinese."
(Sess. I, Chap. 126; 22 Stat. 58. 47th Congress; Approved May 6, 1882.)

FORTY-SEVENTH CONGRESS. SESS. I. CH. 126, 127. 1882.   **61**

sengers, comparing the certificates with the list and with the passengers; and no passenger shall be allowed to land in the United States from such vessel in violation of law. *(marginal note: and compare certificates and lists.)*

SEC. 10. That every vessel whose master shall knowingly violate any of the provisions of this act shall be deemed forfeited to the United States, and shall be liable to seizure and condemnation in any district of the United States into which such vessel may enter or in which she may be found. *(marginal note: Forfeiture of vessels for violation of provisions of act.)*

SEC. 11. That any person who shall knowingly bring into or cause to be brought into the United States by land, or who shall knowingly aid or abet the same, or aid or abet the landing in the United States from any vessel of any Chinese person not lawfully entitled to enter the United States, shall be deemed guilty of a misdemeanor, and shall, on conviction thereof, be fined in a sum not exceeding one thousand dollars, and imprisoned for a term not exceeding one year. *(marginal notes: Misdemeanor. Penalty.)*

SEC. 12. That no Chinese person shall be permitted to enter the United States by land without producing to the proper officer of customs the certificate in this act required of Chinese persons seeking to land from a vessel. And any Chinese person found unlawfully within the United States shall be caused to be removed therefrom to the country from whence he came, by direction of the President of the United States, and at the cost of the United States, after being brought before some justice, judge, or commissioner of a court of the United States and found to be one not lawfully entitled to be or remain in the United States. *(marginal note: Chinese not entitled to residence in United States to be removed by direction of the President.)*

SEC. 13. That this act shall not apply to diplomatic and other officers of the Chinese Government traveling upon the business of that government, whose credentials shall be taken as equivalent to the certificate in this act mentioned, and shall exempt them and their body and household servants from the provisions of this act as to other Chinese persons. *(marginal note: Officers of Chinese Government exempt.)*

SEC. 14. That hereafter no State court or court of the United States shall admit Chinese to citizenship; and all laws in conflict with this act are hereby repealed. *(marginal note: Admission of Chinese to citizenship prohibited.)*

SEC. 15. That the words "Chinese laborers", wherever used in this act, shall be construed to mean both skilled and unskilled laborers and Chinese employed in mining.

Approved, May 6, 1882.

CHAP. 127.—An act for the erection of a public building at Denver, Colorado. *(marginal note: May 8, 1882.)*

Be it enacted by the Senate and House of Representatives of the United States of America in Congress assembled, That the Secretary of the Treasury be, and he is hereby, authorized and directed to procure a proper site and cause to be erected thereon a suitable building, with fire-proof vaults, in the city of Denver, Colorado, for the accommodation of the United States district and circuit courts, post office, land-office, and other government offices in said city, at a cost not exceeding three hundred thousand dollars, including cost of site, which site shall be such as will afford an open space between the building hereby authorized and any other building of not less than forty feet; and the sum of one hundred thousand dollars is hereby appropriated, out of any moneys in the Treasury not otherwise appropriated, for the purpose herein mentioned: *Provided,* That no money shall be used or applied for the purpose mentioned until a valid title to the land for the site of such building shall be vested in the United States; and no expenditure of money shall be made on the building proposed to be erected on said site until the State of Colorado shall duly release and relinquish to the United States the right to tax or in any way assess said site or the property of the United States that may be thereon, and shall cede jurisdiction over the same during the time that the United States shall remain the owner thereof. *(marginal notes: Denver, Colo. Public building. Site. Cost. Appropriation. Proviso. Title.)*

Approved, May 8, 1882.

APPENDIX 8

Gresham–Yang Treaty (1894)

IMMIGRATION PROHIBITION TREATY BETWEEN THE UNITED STATES OF AMERICA AND CHINA, 1894.

RATIFICATIONS EXCHANGED AT WASHINGTON, 7TH DECEMBER, 1894.

Whereas, on the 17th of November, A.D. 1880, and of Kwanhsiu, the sixth year, the tenth month, and the 15th day, a treaty was concluded between the United States and China for the purpose of regulating, limiting, or suspending the coming of Chinese labourers to and their residence in the United States, and, whereas, the Government of China, in view of the antagonism and much depreciated and serious disorders to which the presence of Chinese labourers has given rise in certain parts of the United States, desires to prohibit the emigration of such labourers from China to the United States; and, whereas, the two Governments desire to co-operate in prohibiting such emigration and to strengthen in many other ways the bonds of relationship between the two countries; and, whereas, the two Governments are desirous of adopting reciprocal measures for the better protection of the citizens or subjects of each within the jurisdiction of the other; now, therefore, the President of the United States has appointed Walter Q. Gresham, Secretary of State, as his Plenipotentiary, and his Imperial Majesty, the Emperor of China, has appointed Yang Yui, Officer of the Second Rank, Sub-director of the Court of Sacrificial Worship and Envoy Extraordinary and Minister Plenipotentiary, and the said Plenipotentiaries having exhibited their respective full powers, found to be in due form and good faith, have agreed upon the following articles:-

ART. I.—The high contracting parties agree that for a period of ten years, beginning with the date of the ratifications of this Convention, the coming, except under the conditions hereinafter specified, of Chinese labourers to the United States shall be absolutely prohibited.

ART. II.—The preceding article shall not apply ,to the return to the United States of any registered Chinese labourer who has a lawful wife, child, or parent in the United States or property therein of the value of $1,000, or debts of like amount due to him and pending settlement. Nevertheless, every such Chinese labourer shall, before leaving the United States, deposit, as a condition of his return, with the collector of customs of the district from which he departs, a full description in writing of his family or property or debts as aforesaid, and shall be furnished by the said collector with such certificate of his right to return under this treaty as the laws of the United States may now or hereafter prescribe, and not inconsistent with the provisions of the treaty; and, should the written description aforesaid be proved to be false, the rights of return thereunder, or of continued residence after return, shall in each case be forfeited. And such right of return to the United States shall be exercised within one year from the date of leaving the United States; but such right of return to the United States may be extended for an additional period, not to exceed one year, in cases where, by reason of sickness or other course of disability beyond his control, such Chinese labourer shall be rendered unable sooner to return, which facts shall be fully reported to the Chinese Consul at the port of departure, and by him certified to the satisfaction of the collector of the port at which such Chinese subject shall land in the United States. And no such Chinese labourer shall be permitted to enter the United States by land or sea without producing to the proper officer of the Customs the return certificate herein required.

ART. III.—The provisions of the convention shall not affect the right at present enjoyed of Chinese subjects, being officials, teachers, students, merchants, or travellers for curiosity or pleasure, but not labourers, of coming to the United States and residing therein. To entitle such Chinese subjects as are above described to admission into the United States they may produce a certificate either from their Government or from the Government of the country where they last resided, *viséd* by the diplomatic or consular representative of the United States in the country or port whence they depart. It is also agreed that Chinese labourers shall continue to enjoy the privilege of transit across the territory of the United States in the course of their journey to or from other countries, subject to such regulations by the Government of the United States as may be necessary to prevent the said privilege of transit from being abused.

ART. IV.—In pursuance of Article 3 of the Immigration Treaty between the. United States and China, signed at Peking on the 17th day of November, 1880, it is hereby understood and agreed, that Chinese labourers or Chinese of any other class, either permanently or temporarily residing in the United States, shall have for the protection of their persons and property all rights that are given by the laws of the United States to citizens of the more favoured nations, excepting the right to become naturalized citizens. And the Government of the United States reaffirms its obligations, as stated in the said Article 3, to exert all its power to secure protection to the person and property of all Chinese subjects in the United States.

ART. V.—The Government of the United States having, by an Act of Congress, approved May 5th, 1892, as amended and approved November 3rd, 1898, required all Chinese labourers lawfully within the United States, before the passage of the first-named Act, to be :registered, as in the said Acts provided, with a view of affording them better protection, the Chinese Government will not object to the enforcement of the said Acts, and reciprocally the Government of the United States recognises the right of the Government of China to enact and enforce similar laws and regulations, for the registration, free of charge, of all labourers, skilled or unskilled (not merchants, as defined by the said Acts of Congress), citizens of the United States in China whether residing within or without the treaty ports. And the Government of the United States agrees that within twelve months from the date of exchange of the ratifications of this convention, and annually thereafter, it will furnish to the Government of China registers or reports showing the full name, age, occupation, and number or place of residence of all other citizens of the United States, including missionaries residing both within and without the treaty ports of China, not including, however, diplomatic and other officers of the United States residing or travelling in China upon official business, together with their body and household servants.

ART. VI.—This convention shall remain in force for a period of ten years, beginning with the date of the exchange of ratifications, and, if six months before the expiration of the said period of ten years neither Government shall have formally given notice of its final termination to the other, it shall remain in full force for another like period of ten years.

In faith whereof, we, the respective plenipotentiaries, have signed this Convention and have hereunto affixed our seals.

Done, in duplicate, at Washington, the 17th day of March, A.D. 1894.

> WALTER Q. GRESHAM,
> Secretary of State.
>
> YANG YUI,
> Chinese Minister to the United States.

Source: "Treaties Between the Empire of China and Foreign Powers, Together with Regulations for the Conduct of Foreign Trade, Conventions, Agreements, Regulations, Etc. Etc. Etc.," Fourth Edition, William Frederick Mayers, Editor First Edition (North China Herald Office, 1902).

APPENDIX 9

The 1902 Extension. "An act to prohibit the coming into and to regulate the residence within the United States, its Territories, and all territory under its jurisdiction, and the District of Columbia, of Chinese and persons of Chinese descent." (Sess. I Chap. 641; 32 Stat. 176. 57th Congress; April 29, 1902.)

176   FIFTY-SEVENTH CONGRESS. SESS. I. CHS. 640, 641. 1902.

April 29, 1902.
[Public, No. 89.]

CHAP. 640.—An Act To refund the amount of duties paid in Porto Rico upon articles imported from the several States from April eleventh, eighteen hundred and ninety-nine, to May first, nineteen hundred, to confer jurisdiction on the Court of Claims to render judgment thereon, and making an appropriation therefor.

Porto Rico.
Duties to be refunded.
Jurisdiction conferred on Court of Claims.

Be it enacted by the Senate and House of Representatives of the United States of America in Congress assembled, That jurisdiction be, and is hereby, conferred upon the Court of Claims of the United States of all claims against the United States arising out of the payment of customs duties to the military authorities in the island of Porto Rico upon articles imported from the several States, which articles were entered at the several ports of entry in Porto Rico from and including April eleventh, eighteen hundred and ninety-nine, to May first, nineteen hundred, and the Court of Claims is empowered and directed to ascertain the amounts of such duties paid during said period and to enter judgment against the United States for the several amounts so paid, with interest thereon at the rate of six per centum per annum from the several dates of payment of such duties to the dates of such judgments, respectively, in all actions for the recovery of such duties now pending in the Court of Claims and in all actions for the recovery of such duties which may be brought in said court within six months from the date of the passage of this Act.

Payment of judgments.

SEC. 2. That the Secretary of the Treasury, upon the certification of such judgments, or any of them, from which the United States does not take an appeal, is authorized to pay the same.

Approved, April 29, 1902.

April 29, 1902.
[Public, No. 90.]

CHAP. 641.—An Act To prohibit the coming into and to regulate the residence within the United States, its Territories, and all territory under its jurisdiction, and the District of Columbia, of Chinese and persons of Chinese descent.

Chinese exclusion.
Immigration prohibited.
Prohibition extended to island territories.
Vol. 25, p. 476.

Be it enacted by the Senate and House of Representatives of the United States of America in Congress assembled, That all laws now in force prohibiting and regulating the coming of Chinese persons, and persons of Chinese descent, into the United States, and the residence of such persons therein, including sections five, six, seven, eight, nine, ten, eleven, thirteen, and fourteen of the Act entitled "An Act to prohibit the coming of Chinese laborers into the United States" approved September thirteenth, eighteen hundred and eighty-eight, be, and the same are hereby, re-enacted, extended, and continued so far as the same are not inconsistent with treaty obligations, until otherwise provided by law, and said laws shall also apply to the island territory

Immigration from island territories to mainland prohibited.

under the jurisdiction of the United States, and prohibit the immigration of Chinese laborers, not citizens of the United States, from such island territory to the mainland territory of the United States, whether in such island territory at the time of cession or not, and from one portion of the island territory of the United States to another portion

Proviso.
Transit permitted.

of said island territory: *Provided, however,* That said laws shall not apply to the transit of Chinese laborers from one island to another island of the same group; and any islands within the jurisdiction of any State or the District of Alaska shall be considered a part of the mainland under this section.

Secretary of Treasury to prescribe regulations, etc.
Vol. 28, p. 1210.

SEC. 2. That the Secretary of the Treasury is hereby authorized and empowered to make and prescribe, and from time to time to change, such rules and regulations not inconsistent with the laws of the land as he may deem necessary and proper to execute the provisions of this Act and of the Acts hereby extended and continued and of the treaty of December eighth, eighteen hundred and ninety-four, between the United States and China, and with the approval of the President to

APPENDIX 9

The 1902 Extension. "An act to prohibit the coming into and to regulate the residence within the United States, its Territories, and all territory under its jurisdiction, and the District of Columbia, of Chinese and persons of Chinese descent." (Sess. I Chap. 641; 32 Stat. 176. 57th Congress; April 29, 1902.)

FIFTY-SEVENTH CONGRESS. Sess. I. Chs. 641, 642. 1902.   177

appoint such agents as he may deem necessary for the efficient execution of said treaty and said Acts.

Sec. 3. That nothing in the provisions of this Act or any other Act shall be construed to prevent, hinder, or restrict any foreign exhibitor, representative, or citizen of any foreign nation, or the holder, who is a citizen of any foreign nation, of any concession or privilege from any fair or exposition authorized by Act of Congress from bringing into the United States, under contract, such mechanics, artisans, agents, or other employees, natives of their respective foreign countries, as they or any of them may deem necessary for the purpose of making preparation for installing or conducting their exhibits or of preparing for installing or conducting any business authorized or permitted under or by virtue of or pertaining to any concession or privilege which may have been or may be granted by any said fair or exposition in connection with such exposition, under such rules and regulations as the Secretary of the Treasury may prescribe, both as to the admission and return of such person or persons. *(margin: Alien contract labor. Permission to foreign exhibitors at expositions authorized by Congress.)* *(margin: Regulations.)*

Sec. 4. That it shall be the duty of every Chinese laborer, other than a citizen, rightfully in, and entitled to remain in any of the insular territory of the United States (Hawaii excepted) at the time of the passage of this Act, to obtain within one year thereafter a certificate of residence in the insular territory wherein he resides, which certificate shall entitle him to residence therein, and upon failure to obtain such certificate as herein provided he shall be deported from such insular territory; and the Philippine Commission is authorized and required to make all regulations and provisions necessary for the enforcement of this section in the Philippine Islands, including the form and substance of the certificate of residence so that the same shall clearly and sufficiently identify the holder thereof and enable officials to prevent fraud in the transfer of the same: *Provided, however,* That if said Philippine Commission shall find that it is impossible to complete the registration herein provided for within one year from the passage of this Act, said Commission is hereby authorized and empowered to extend the time for such registration for a further period not exceeding one year. *(margin: Certificates of residence of Chinese in insular territory.)* *(margin: Philippine Commission to prescribe regulations, etc.)* *(margin: Proviso. Registration time may be extended.)*

Approved, April 29, 1902.

CHAP. 642.—An Act For the relief of certain indigent Choctaw and Chickasaw Indians in the Indian Territory, and for other purposes. *(margin: April 29, 1902. [Public, No. 91.])*

Be it enacted by the Senate and House of Representatives of the United States of America in Congress assembled, That the Secretary of the Treasury be, and he is hereby, authorized, upon the request of the Secretary of the Interior, to deposit in the United States subtreasury at Saint Louis, Missouri, to the credit of the treasurer of the Choctaw Nation, the sum of twenty thousand dollars of the fund now in the United States Treasury to the credit of the Choctaw and Chickasaw nations, derived from the sale of town lots under an Act approved June 28, 1898, being "An Act for the protection of the people of the Indian Territory, and for other purposes," the said sum to be used for certain destitute Choctaw Indians in the manner hereinafter provided, and charged against the proportionate share of said fund due to each Choctaw Indian receiving relief under the provisions hereof. *(margin: Choctaw and Chickasaw Indians. Fund for relief of indigent Choctaws.)* *(margin: Vol. 30, p. 509.)*

Sec. 2. That Gilbert W. Dukes, principal chief of the Choctaw Nation, George W. Scott, treasurer of the Choctaw Nation, and Green McCurtain, ex-principal chief of the Choctaw Nation, are hereby constituted a commission, with authority to investigate and determine what Choctaw citizens are destitute and in absolute need of help; and *(margin: Commission to supply food, etc., to destitute Choctaws.)* *(margin: Restrictions.)*

VOL XXXII, PT 1——12

APPENDIX 10

Permanent Law 1904

(Sess. 2 Chap. 1630, Section 5, 58 Stat. 428, April 27, 1904.)

428　　　　FIFTY-EIGHTH CONGRESS. Sess. II. Ch. 1630. 1904.

pany, of Pittsburg, Pennsylvania, William L. Jones, receiver, five thousand dollars, reported in Senate Executive Document Numbered Five, Fifty-third Congress, third session.

Mi-souri.
Claim to be reopened.
The accounting officers of the Treasury are hereby authorized and directed to reopen and adjust the claim of the State of Missouri, under the Act to reimburse the State of Missouri for moneys expended for the United States in enrolling and equipping and provisioning militia **Vol. 14, p. 38.** forces to aid in suppressing the rebellion, approved April seventeenth, eighteen hundred and sixty-six, on the basis of like claims of Indiana, Michigan, New York, Maine, and Pennsylvania.

Texas.
Payment for expenses, Greer County.
To pay to the State of Texas as reimbursement to said State for expenses incurred in maintaining a civil government, and so forth, in what was then known as Greer County, Texas, now known as Greer County, Oklahoma, as shown by reports of the Secretary of the Interior contained in House Document Numbered Five hundred and seventy-one, Fifty-seventh Congress, first session, and House Document Numbered Five hundred and seventy-one, Part Two, Fifty-seventh Congress, first session, fifty thousand eight hundred and seventy-four dollars and fifty-three cents, and the acceptance of payment hereunder shall be in full for all claims, of the character herein provided for, by the State of Texas.

New Jersey and Wisconsin.
Adjusting claims of.
Vol. 32, p. 1078.
That the accounting officers of the Treasury be, and they are hereby, authorized and directed to reopen and adjust the claims of New Jersey and Wisconsin, for which appropriation was made by Act of Congress approved March third, nineteen hundred and three, on the basis of like claims of Indiana, Michigan, Kentucky, Maine, and Pennsylvania, with the same force and effect as though appropriation therefor had not been made or accepted by the said States.

James D. Longstreet.
Payment to widow.
For the relief of Helen D. Longstreet, widow of General James Longstreet, the sum of one thousand two hundred and fifty dollars.

Chinese exclusion.
Vol. 32, p. 176, amended.
SEC. 5. That section one of the Act of Congress approved April twenty-ninth, nineteen hundred and two, entitled "An Act to prohibit the coming into and to regulate the residence within the United States, its Territories, and all territory under its jurisdiction, and the District of Columbia, of Chinese and persons of Chinese descent," is hereby amended so as to read as follows:

Laws reenacted without limitation.
"All laws in force on the twenty-ninth day of April, nineteen hundred and two, regulating, suspending, or prohibiting the coming of Chinese persons or persons of Chinese descent into the United **Vol. 25, p. 477.** States, and the residence of such persons therein, including sections five, six, seven, eight, nine, ten, eleven, thirteen, and fourteen of the Act entitled 'An Act to prohibit the coming of Chinese laborers into the United States,' approved September thirteenth, eighteen hundred and eighty-eight, be, and the same are hereby, reenacted, extended, and continued, without modification, limitation, or condition; and said laws shall also apply to the island territory under the jurisdiction of the United States, and prohibit the immigration of Chinese laborers, not citizens of the United States, from such island territory to the mainland territory of the United States, whether in such island territory at the time of cession or not, and from one portion of the island territory of the United States to another portion of said island terri- **Proviso.** tory: *Provided, however,* That said laws shall not apply to the transit **Transit permitted in insular possessions.** of Chinese laborers from one island to another island of the same group; and any islands within the jurisdiction of any State or the District of Alaska shall be considered a part of the mainland under this section."

Approved, April 27, 1904.

APPENDIX 11

Magnuson Act (Chinese Exclusion Repeal Act of 1943), H.R. 3070, "An act to repeal the Chinese Exclusion Acts, to establish quotas, and for other purposes." (Chap. 344, Public Law 78–199, 57 Stat. 600, December 17, 1943.)

600   PUBLIC LAWS—CHS. 343, 344—DEC. 17, 1943   [57 STAT.

*Death of benefici-
ary before payment.*

following: "*And provided further,* That in the event of the death of any beneficiary before payment to and collection by such beneficiary of the amount authorized herein, such gratuity shall be paid to the next living beneficiary in the order of succession above stated: *And*

*Determination of
payee if dependent
relative not desig-
nated.*

provided further, That if there be no widow, child, or previously designated dependent relative, the Secretary of War shall cause the amount herein provided to be paid to any grandchild, parent, brother or sister, or grandparent shown to have been dependent upon such officer or enlisted man prior to his death, and the determination of such fact by the Secretary of War shall be final and conclusive upon the accounting officers of the Government: *And provided further,* That the last foregoing proviso shall be effective as of August 27, 1940."

Prior payments.

SEC. 2. Nothing herein shall be construed to invalidate or in any manner affect any payments made prior to the date of the approval of this Act, but no gratuity payment shall hereafter be made to the representative of the estate of a beneficiary who died prior to such approval.

Approved December 17, 1943.

[CHAPTER 344]

December 17, 1943
[H. R. 3070]
[Public Law 199]

AN ACT

To repeal the Chinese Exclusion Acts, to establish quotas, and for other purposes.

*Chinese Exclusion
Acts, repeal.*

Be it enacted by the Senate and House of Representatives of the United States of America in Congress assembled, That the following Acts or parts of Acts relating to the exclusion or deportation of persons of the Chinese race are hereby repealed: May 6, 1882 (22 Stat. L. 58); July 5, 1884 (23 Stat. L. 115); September 13, 1888 (25 Stat. L. 476); October 1, 1888 (25 Stat. L. 504); May 5, 1892 (27 Stat. L.

8 U. S. C. § 263 *et
seq.*
8 U. S. C. § 293.

25); November 3, 1893 (28 Stat. L. 7); that portion of section 1 of the Act of July 7, 1898 (30 Stat. L. 750, 751), which reads as follows: "There shall be no further immigration of Chinese into the Hawaiian Islands except upon such conditions as are now or may hereafter be allowed by the laws of the United States; and no Chinese, by reason of anything herein contained, shall be allowed to enter the United States from the Hawaiian Islands."; section 101 of the Act of April

8 U. S. C. § 294.
8 U. S. C. § 262.

30, 1900 (31 Stat. L. 141, 161); those portions of section 1 of the Act of June 6, 1900 (31 Stat. L. 588, 611), which read as follows: "And nothing in section four of the Act of August fifth, eighteen hundred and eighty-two (Twenty-second Statutes at Large, page two hundred and twenty-five), shall be construed to prevent the Secretary of the Treasury from hereafter detailing one officer employed in the enforcement of the Chinese Exclusion Acts for duty at the Treasury Department at Washington. * * * and hereafter the Commissioner-General of Immigration, in addition to his other duties, shall have charge of the administration of the Chinese exclusion law * * *, under the supervision and direction of the Secretary of the Treasury."; March 3, 1901 (31 Stat. L. 1093); April 29, 1902 (32 Stat. L.

8 U. S. C. § 263 *et
seq.*
28 U. S. C. § 49.
8 U. S. C. § 271.

176); April 27, 1904 (33 Stat. L. 428); section 25 of the Act of March 3, 1911 (36 Stat. L. 1087, 1094); that portion of the Act of August 24, 1912 (37 Stat. L. 417, 476), which reads as follows: "*Provided,* That all charges for maintenance or return of Chinese persons applying for admission to the United States shall hereafter be paid or reimbursed to the United States by the person, company, partnership, or corporation, bringing such Chinese to a port of the United States as applicants for admission."; that portion of the Act

8 U. S. C. § 299.

of June 23, 1913 (38 Stat. L. 4, 65), which reads as follows: "*Provided,* That from and after July first, nineteen hundred and thirteen, all Chinese persons ordered deported under judicial writs shall be

APPENDIX 11

Magnuson Act (Chinese Exclusion Repeal Act of 1943), H.R. 3070, "An act to repeal the Chinese Exclusion Acts, to establish quotas, and for other purposes." (Chap. 344, Public Law 78–199, 57 Stat. 600, December 17, 1943.)

57 STAT.]   78TH CONG., 1ST SESS.—CHS. 344–346—DEC. 17, 1943   601

delivered by the marshal of the district or his deputy into the custody of any officer designated for that purpose by the Secretary of Commerce and Labor, for conveyance to the frontier or seaboard for deportation in the same manner as aliens deported under the immigration laws."

SEC. 2. With the exception of those coming under subsections (b), (d), (e), and (f) of section 4, Immigration Act of 1924 (43 Stat. 155; 44 Stat. 812; 45 Stat. 1009; 46 Stat. 854; 47 Stat. 656; 8 U. S. C. 204), all Chinese persons entering the United States annually as immigrants shall be allocated to the quota for the Chinese computed under the provisions of section 11 of the said Act. A preference up to 75 per centum of the quota shall be given to Chinese born and resident in China. *[Immigration quota; preference.]*

SEC. 3. Section 303 of the Nationality Act of 1940, as amended (54 Stat. 1140; 8 U. S. C. 703), is hereby amended by striking out the word "and" before the word "descendants", changing the colon after the word "Hemisphere" to a comma, and adding the following: "and Chinese persons or persons of Chinese descent :". *[Eligibility for naturalization.]*

Approved December 17, 1943.

[43 Stat. 159. 8 U. S. C. § 211.]

[CHAPTER 345]

AN ACT

To suspend temporarily the application of sections 3114 and 3115 of the Revised Statutes, as amended.

[December 17, 1943 [H. R. 3309] [Public Law 200]]

Be it enacted by the Senate and House of Representatives of the United States of America in Congress assembled, That the application of the provisions of sections 3114 and 3115 of the Revised Statutes, as amended (U. S. C., 1940 edition, title 19, secs. 257 and 258), is hereby suspended. *[Duty on equipments, etc., for vessels. Suspension of R. S. §§ 3114, 3115.]*

SEC. 2. This Act shall remain in force until two years after the date of the enactment of this Act, or until the day following the date of the cessation of hostilities in the present war (as defined in section 780 (e) of the Internal Revenue Code), whichever shall first occur, and shall apply to all duties which have accrued on repairs made, or equipment purchased, on or after December 8, 1941: *Provided,* That no claim for a refund of duty pursuant to this Act shall be allowed unless a written application for such refund is filed by the party in interest within six months from the date of the enactment of this Act with the collector of customs at the port where entry was made or the Bureau of Customs: *Provided further,* That nothing in this Act shall be construed to require any Federal department or agency to obtain a refund of duty pursuant to this Act. *[Effective period. 56 Stat. 937. 26 U. S. C., Supp. II, § 780 (e). Refund of duty.]*

Approved December 17, 1943.

[CHAPTER 346]

AN ACT

Extending the time within which applications under section 722 of the Internal Revenue Code must be made.

[December 17, 1943 [H. R. 3363] [Public Law 201]]

Be it enacted by the Senate and House of Representatives of the United States of America in Congress assembled, That (a) section 722 (d) of the Internal Revenue Code (prescribing the time for filing applications for general relief under the excess-profits tax) is amended to read as follows: *[Internal Revenue Code, amendments. 56 Stat. 916. 26 U. S. C., Supp. II, § 722 (d). Ante, p. 56.]*

"(d) APPLICATION FOR RELIEF UNDER THIS SECTION.—The taxpayer shall compute its tax, file its return, and pay the tax shown on its *[Relief under excess-profits tax.]*

APPENDIX 12
American Immigration Laws Timeline

1788 The **U.S. Constitution** restricts the presidency to native born citizens and grants Congress the authority to establish rules governing naturalization. (**Article 2, Section 1.**)

1790 Congress passes the **Naturalization Act**, limiting the opportunity for naturalization to white persons who have had two years of U.S. residency. 1st Congress, Sess. II, Chap. 3; Stat. 103. March 26, 1790.

1798 **Alien and Sedition Acts**, four bills passed in 1798. An attempt to control French radicals after the revolution, stipulates fourteen years of residency before citizenship; regulation repealed 1801.

1808 U.S. forbids the importation of slaves (**Act Prohibiting Importation of Slaves** (aka 1808 Transatlantic Slave Trade Act) signed into law March 2, 1807, went into effect January 1, 1808).

1819 **On March 2, 1819, the U.S. Congress passed an Act Regulating Passenger Ships and Vessels** (15th Congress, Sess. II, Chap. 46, 3 Stat. 489. 1819), which required masters and captains of vessels arriving at U.S. ports to submit a list of passengers to the collector of the district beginning January 1, 1820.

1857 *Dred Scott v. Sandford*, 60 U.S. 393 (1857), declared free Africans non-citizens.

1862 Anti-coolie law, "**An Act to prohibit the 'Coolie Trade' by American Citizens in American Vessels**" 37th Congress, Sess. II, Chap. 27; 12 Stat. 340. February 19, 1862.

1864 1864 Immigration Act, "**An Act to encourage Immigration**" allowed recruiting of foreign labor. 38th Congress, Sess. I, Chap. 246; 13 Stat. 385. July 4, 1864.

1865 Slavery and involuntary servitude abolished by the **Thirteenth Amendment**.

1868 The **Fourteenth Amendment** is ratified. Among other things, it establishes citizenship rights for all persons born or naturalized in the United States.

1868 The **Burlingame Treaty** between the United States and China is ratified. The treaty permits free and voluntary immigration from China and grants Chinese immigrants treatment equivalent to that accorded to the citizens or subjects of most-favored nations. *(Appendix 2)*

1870 Congress passes amendments to the naturalization laws in **Naturalization Act of 1870. 41st Congress, Sess. II, Chap. 254; July 14, 1870.** Persons of African descent who do not otherwise enjoy birthright citizenship can be naturalized. In the Senate, an amendment by Senator Charles Sumner (R-MA) to permit naturalization of persons without regard to race is defeated. An amendment by Senator Lyman Trumbull (R-IL) to extend naturalization rights to persons of Chinese descent is also defeated. (*Ch. 1 and Appendix 3*)

1875 The **Page Act** passes, barring the importation of women for purposes of prostitution. The Page Act also bars the transportation of "any subject of China, Japan, or any Oriental country, without their free and voluntary consent." 43rd Congress, Sess. II, Chap. 141; 18 Stat. 477. March 3, 1875. (*§ 2.13*)

1875 In ***Henderson v. Mayor of City of New York*, 92 U.S. 259 (1875)**, the U.S. Supreme Court declares state laws on immigration unconstitutional.

1875 In ***Chy Lung v. Freeman*, 92 U.S. 275 (1875)**, the U.S. Supreme Court declares that control over immigration is a federal responsibility and that state efforts to burden immigration are unconstitutional.

1879 The **Fifteen Passenger bill** passes, but is vetoed by President Rutherford B. Hayes as incompatible with U.S. treaty obligations. (*Ch. 2 and Appendix 4*)

1881 The Angell Treaty is ratified, permitting the United States to restrict or suspend, but not to prohibit, immigration of Chinese laborers. (*Appendix 5*)

1882 Congress passes legislation to halt the immigration of Chinese laborers for twenty years and to bar Chinese persons from naturalizing. President Chester A. Arthur vetoes the bill, regarding the twenty-year ban as incompatible with U.S. treaty obligations. (*Chs. 3 and 4, and Appendix 6*)

1882 Congress passes legislation to halt the immigration of Chinese laborers for ten years and to bar Chinese persons from naturalizing. "**To execute certain treaty stipulations relating to Chinese**." 47th Congress, Sess. I, Chap. 126; 22 Stat. 58. On May 6, 1882, President Chester A. Arthur signs it into law. The measure becomes popularly known as the **Chinese Exclusion Act**. Chinese already in the United States are afforded certificates of return, which allow them to reenter the country notwithstanding the bar. (*Ch. 5 and Appendix 7*)

1884 In ***Chew Heong v. United States*, 112 U.S. 536 (1884)**, the U.S. Supreme Court upholds the right of a Chinese immigrant who did not possess a return certificate to enter the United States because he could establish his previous residence in the country and had been abroad when the Chinese Exclusion Act's return certificates were authorized and issued.

1885 The Chinese Exclusion Act is amended by the **Alien Contract Labor Law** to apply to all laborers of Chinese descent seeking to enter the United States from anyplace in the world, not just from China. "An act to prohibit the importation and migration of foreigners and aliens under contract or agreement to perform labor in the United States, its Territories, and the District of Columbia." **48th Congress, Sess. II, Chap. 164; 23 Stat. 332. February 26, 1885.** (*Ch. 6*)

1888 The United States and China negotiate the **Bayard-Zhang Treaty**, which allows the U.S. to prohibit immigration of Chinese laborers. The Chinese Government ultimately refuses to ratify the treaty. (*Ch. 7*)

1888 Anticipating the ratification of the **Bayard-Zhang Treaty of 1888**, Congress passes implementing legislation. Some provisions of the legislation—addressing the conditions that Chinese laborers already in the United States would need to meet should they leave and wish to reenter, as well as authorizing the Treasury Department to craft definitions regarding the classes of Chinese persons entitled to immigrate to the United States—survive, even though the treaty was not ratified. (*Ch. 7*)

1888 After China does not ratify the Bayard-Zhang Treaty, Congress passes the Scott Act, which cancels the certificates of return that had been issued under the 1882 exclusion law. Thousands of Chinese who had anticipated the right to reenter the United States are stranded overseas. (*Ch. 7*)

1889 In **Chae Chan Ping v. United States, 130 U.S. 581 (1889)**, the U.S. Supreme Court, while recognizing that the Scott Act contravenes the Burlingame and Angell Treaties, upholds the Scott Act as a constitutional exercise of Congress' power to regulate immigration.

1892 **Ellis Island Immigration Station** opens in January 1892

1892 In the **Geary Act**, Congress extends the exclusion policy for ten years, requires Chinese to carry papers proving their right to be in the United States, makes Chinese caught without such papers presumptively deportable, places the burden of proof on the Chinese immigrant in deportation proceedings, and allows oral testimony on behalf of the immigrant only if corroborated by a white witness. "**An act to prohibit the coming of Chinese persons into the United States.**" **52nd Congress, Sess. I, Chap. 60; 27 Stat. 25. May 5, 1892.** (*Ch. 8*)

1893 In *Fong Yue Ting v. United States*, 149 U.S. 698 (1893), the U.S. Supreme Court upholds the registration requirements set forth in the Geary Act. Congress passes legislation extending the registration deadline by six months, to accommodate the registration of Chinese who had declined to comply while the Geary Act's validity was being challenged.

1894 China and the United States ratify the **Gresham-Yang Treaty (1894)**, allowing the U.S. the right to prohibit immigration of Chinese laborers. The Scott Act is abrogated and the use of certificates of return is again permitted. (*Appendix 8*)

1898 In *United States v. Wong Kim Ark*, **169 U.S. 649 (1898)**, the U.S. Supreme Court upholds the application of birthright citizenship under the Fourteenth Amendment to a Chinese person born in the United States.

1898 Exclusion policy is extended to cover the newly annexed territory of Hawaii.

1902 Congress continues the exclusion policy indefinitely in the 1902 extension, to operate in a manner consistent with U.S.-China treaty obligations. The exclusion policy is extended to cover insular possessions of the United States, including the Philippines. "An Act To prohibit the coming into and to regulate the residence within the United States, its Territories, and all territory under 1ts jurisdiction, and the District of Columbia, of Chinese and persons of Chinese descent." **57th Congress, Sess. I, Chap. 641; 32 Stat. 176. April 29, 1902**. (*Ch. 9 and Appendix 9*)

1903 Secretary of Commerce and Labor assumes control over immigration until 1940; anarchists excluded. (*§ 9.17*)

1904 China renounces the Gresham-Yang Treaty. (*Ch. 10*)

1904 Congress permanently extends the exclusion laws. **58th Congress, Sess. II, Chap. 1630, Sec. 5**; 58 Stat. 428, April 27, 1904. (*Ch. 10 and Appendix 10*)

1907 Under a policy known as the **Gentlemen's Agreement of 1907**, the United States and Japan informally agree to restrict Japanese immigration to the United States.

1907 "**An Act to regulate the immigration of aliens into the United States, 1907**," aka Alien Immigration Act, Chap. 1134, 3; 34 Stat. 898. February 20, 1907—Head tax on immigrants raised; No persons with physical or mental defects, tuberculosis, children not accompanied by a parent.

1910 **Angel Island Immigration Station** opens in January 1910.

1917 The **Immigration Act of 1917** provides broad immigration restrictions, especially with respect to "undesirables" of other countries (for example, individuals with contagious diseases, prostitutes, and criminals). The geographically defined "**Asiatic Barred Zone**" is established, preventing immigration from much of east Asia. **64th Congress, Sess. II, Chap. 29; H.R. 10384; Pub.L. 301; 39 Stat. 874. February 5th, 1917.**

1921 Emergency Quota Law, "An Act To limit the immigration of aliens into the United States." Quotas established. **67th Congress, Sess. I; H.R. 4075; Pub.L. 67-5; 42 Stat. 5. May 19, 1921.**

1924 The temporary quota system established by the **Emergency Quota Act of 1921** is extended and modified by the **Immigration Act of 1924 (Johnson-Reed Act).** Both laws use a national origins-based quota system. The 1924 Act excludes from entry any alien who by virtue of race or nationality is ineligible for citizenship. "An act to limit the immigration of aliens into the United States, and for other purposes" aka National Origins Law (Johnson-Reed Act). **68th Congress, Sess. I, Chap. 190; H.R. 7995; Pub.L. 68-139; 43 Stat. 153. 68th Congress; May 26, 1924.**

1928 Congress makes annual immigration quotas permanent effective July 1, 1929.

1939 Refugee bill (**Wagner-Rogers Child Refugee Bill**) defeated that would allow admittance of 20,000 children from Nazi Germany. (**"Wagner-Rogers Refugee Bill Backed at Hearing; 1,400 Adoption Offers Reported."** *Jewish Telegraphic Agency* **21 Apr 1939.**)

1940 Attorney General given control of immigration. (*§ 9.17*)

1940 "In 1940 and 1941, President Franklin D. Roosevelt formalized U.S. aid to China. The U.S. Government extended credits to the Chinese Government for the purchase of war supplies, as it slowly began to tighten restrictions on Japan. The United States was the main supplier of the oil, steel, iron, and other commodities needed by the Japanese military as it became bogged down by Chinese resistance but, in January, 1940, Japan abrogated the existing treaty of commerce with the United States. Although this did not lead to an immediate embargo, it meant that the Roosevelt Administration could now restrict the flow of military supplies into Japan and use this as leverage to force Japan to halt its aggression in China.

"After January 1940, the United States combined a strategy of increasing aid to China through larger credits and the Lend-Lease program with a gradual move towards an embargo on the trade of all militarily useful items with Japan. The Japanese Government made several decisions during these two years that exacerbated the situation. Unable or unwilling to control the military, Japan's political leaders sought greater security by establishing the 'Greater East Asia Co-Prosperity Sphere' in August, 1940. In so doing they announced Japan's intention to drive the Western imperialist nations from Asia." (**State Dept.**) (*§ 11.10*)

1942 Bracero program begun.

1943 The **Magnuson Act (Chinese Exclusion Repeal Act of 1943)** repeals the Chinese exclusion laws and establishes a unique immigration quota for Chinese persons worldwide. **78th Congress, Sess. I, Chap. 344; H.R. 3070; Pub.L. 78-199; 57 Stat. 600. December 17, 1943.** *(Ch. 11 and Appendix 11)*

1945 Congress passes the **War Brides Act (1945)**, which puts Chinese wives of American citizens on a non-quota basis. "An act to expedite the admission to the United States of alien spouses and alien minor children of citizen members of the United States armed forces." **79th Congress, Sess. I, Chap. 591; H.R. 4857; Pub.L. 79-271; 59 Stat 659. December 28, 1945.** *(§ 11.22)*

1946 Chinese War Brides Act, "An act to place Chinese wives of American citizens on a nonquota basis." **79th Congress, Sess. II; H.R. 4844; Pub.L. 79-713; 60 Stat. 975. August 9, 1946**.

1948 Displaced Persons Act, "An act to authorize for a limited period of time the admission into the United States of certain European displaced persons for permanent residence, and for other purposes." **80th Congress, Sess. II, Chap. 647; S. 2242; Pub.L. 80-774; 62 Stat. 1009. June 25, 1948.**

1950 Internal Security Act of 1950, aka Subversive Activities Control Act (**McCarran Internal Security Act**). 81st Congress, Sess. II, Chap. 1024; 64 Stat. 993.

1952 The Immigration and Nationality Act (**McCarran-Walter Act**). **82nd Congress, Sess. H.R. 5678; Pub.L. 414; 66 Stat. 163. June 27, 1952**.

1965 **Immigration and Nationality Act,** aka **Hart-Cellar Act**, ends the system of immigration quotas based on national origins. **89th Congress, H.R. 2580; Pub.L. 89-236; 79 Stat. 911. October 3, 1965.** (12-page PDF)

1986 **Immigration Reform and Control Act**.

Sources: The Flow of History (*<flowofhistory.org>*); Prof. Sarah Starkweather's site "U.S. Immigration Legislation Online"; American Immigration Laws Timeline from the National Archives.

APPENDIX 13

Bibliography

Online links can be found at <TCNFCA.com>.

- Aarim-Heriot, Najia. *Chinese Immigrants, African Americans, and Racial Anxiety in the United States, 1848–82.* Urbana: University of Illinois Press, 2006.

- Ackerman, Kenneth. *Dark Horse: The Surprise Election and Political Murder of President James A. Garfield.* Viral History Press, 2011.

- Ambrose, Stephen. *Nothing Like It in the World: The Men Who Built the Transcontinental Railroad, 1863–1869.* New York: Simon & Schuster, 2000.

- Anbinder, Tyler G. *Nativism and Slavery: The Northern Know Nothings and the Politics of the 1850s.* New York: Oxford University Press, 1992.

- Anderson, Kay. *Vancouver's Chinatown: Racial Discourse in Canada, 1875–1980.* Montreal Buffalo: McGill-Queen's University Press, 1991.

- Arkush, R. David (ed.). *Land Without Ghosts: Chinese Impressions of America from the Mid-nineteenth Century to the Present.* London: University of California Press, 1989.

- Bain, David. *Empire Express: Building the First Transcontinental Railroad.* New York: Penguin Books, 2000.

- Bercuson, David. *One Christmas in Washington: Roosevelt and Churchill Forge the Grand Alliance.* Woodstock, NY: Overlook Press, 2006.

- Blaine, James Gillespie. *Twenty Years of Congress, Vol. 1— From Lincoln to Garfield, with a Review of the Events Which Led to the Political Revolution of 1860.* Fili-Quarian Classics, 2010.

- Blaine, James Gillespie. *Twenty Years of Congress, Volume 2— From Lincoln to Garfield, with a Review of the Events Which Led to the Political Revolution of 1860.* Fili-Quarian Classics, 2010.

- Bradley, James. *The Imperial Cruise: A Secret History of Empire and War.* New York: Little, Brown and Co, 2009.

- Camacho, Schiavone. *Chinese Mexicans: Transpacific Migration and the Search for a Homeland, 1910–1960.* Chapel Hill: University of North Carolina Press, 2012.

- Cassel, Par Kristoffer. *Grounds of Judgment: Extraterritoriality and Imperial Power in Nineteenth-Century China and Japan.* New York: Oxford University Press, 2012.

- Chang, Iris. *The Chinese in America: A Narrative History*. New York: Penguin, 2004.

- Chinese Consolidated Benevolent Association. *Dreams of the West: A History of the Chinese in Oregon, 1850–1950*. Portland, OR: Ooligan Press Chinese Consolidated Benevolent Association, 2007.

- Chung, Sue Fawn, and Wegars, Priscilla (eds.). *Chinese American Death Rituals: Respecting the Ancestors*. Lanham, MD: AltaMira Press, 2005.

- Chung, Sue Fawn. *In Pursuit of Gold: Chinese American Miners and Merchants in the American West*. Urbana: University of Illinois Press, 2011.

- Coe, Andrew. *Chop Suey: A Cultural History of Chinese Food in the United States*. New York: Oxford University Press, 2009.

- Delgado, Grace. *Making the Chinese Mexican: Global Migration, Localism, and Exclusion in the U.S.-Mexico Borderlands*. Stanford, CA: Stanford University Press, 2012.

- Elliott, Russell. *Servant of Power: A Political Biography of Senator William M. Stewart*. Reno: University of Nevada Press, 1983.

- Friedberg, Aaron. *A Contest for Supremacy: China, America, and the Struggle for Mastery in Asia*. New York: W. W. Norton & Co, 2011.

- Gold, Martin B. *Senate Procedure and Practice*. Rowman & Littlefield, 2008.

- Gray, John Henry. *China: A History of the Laws, Manners and Customs of the People*. Dover Publications Reprint, 2003.

- Hermann, Ruth. *The Gold and Silver Colossus: William Morris Stewart and His Southern Bride*. Nevada Publications, 1975.

- Herzstein, Robert. *Henry R. Luce, Time, and the American Crusade in Asia*. Cambridge New York: Cambridge University Press, 2005.

- Hoe, Ban Seng. *Enduring Hardship: The Chinese Laundry in Canada*. Gatineau, Quebec, Canada: Canadian Museum of Civilization, 2004.

- Hoogenboom, Ari. *Rutherford B. Hayes: Warrior and President*. Lawrence, KS: University Press of Kansas, 1995.

- Kens, Paul. *Justice Stephen Field: Shaping Liberty from the Gold Rush to the Gilded Age*. Lawrence, KS: University Press of Kansas, 1997.

- Lee, Anthony. *A Shoe-maker's Story: Being Chiefly About French Canadian Immigrants, Enterprising Photographers, Rascal Yankees, and Chinese Cobblers in a Nineteenth-century Factory Town*. Princeton, NJ: Princeton University Press, 2008.

- Lee, Erika, and Yung, Judy. *Angel Island: Immigrant Gateway to America*. Oxford New York: Oxford University Press, 2010.

- Lee, Erika. *At America's Gates: Chinese Immigration During the Exclusion Era, 1882–1943*. Chapel Hill: University of North Carolina Press, 2003.

- Leibovitz, Liel, and Miller, Matthew. *Fortunate Sons: The 120 Chinese Boys who Came to America, Went to School, and Revolutionized an Ancient Civilization*. New York: W.W. Norton, 2011.

- Li, Laura Tyson. *Madame Chiang Kai-Shek: China's Eternal First Lady*. New York: Grove Press, 2006.

- Li, Tien-Liu. *Congressional Policy of Chinese Immigration: or, Legislation Relating to Chinese Immigration to the United States*. Nashville, TN: Publishing House of the Methodist Episcopal Church, 1916.

- Mar, Lisa. *Brokering Belonging: Chinese in Canada's Exclusion Era, 1885–1945*. New York: Oxford University Press, 2010.

- McCullough, David. *The Greater Journey: Americans in Paris*. New York: Simon & Schuster, 2011.

- McKee, Delber. *Chinese Exclusion Versus the Open Door Policy, 1900–1906: Clashes over China Policy in the Roosevelt Era*. Detroit, MI: Wayne State University Press, 1977.

- Meacham, Jon. *Franklin and Winston: An Intimate Portrait of an Epic Friendship*. New York: Random House Trade Paperbacks, 2004.

- Millard, Candice. *The Destiny of the Republic: A Tale of Madness, Medicine and the Murder of a President*. New York: Doubleday, 2011.

- Miller, Stuart. *The Unwelcome Immigrant: The American Image of the Chinese, 1785–1882*. Berkeley: University of California Press, 1974.

- Pakula, Hannah. *The Last Empress: Madame Chiang Kai-Shek and the Birth of Modern China*. New York: Simon & Schuster Paperbacks, 2010.

- Pfaelzer, Jean. *Driven Out: The Forgotten War Against Chinese Americans*. Berkeley: University of California Press, 2008.

- Rainey, Lee. *Confucius & Confucianism: The Essentials*. Oxford Malden, MA: Wiley-Blackwell, 2010.

- Rhoads, Edward. *Stepping Forth into the World: The Chinese Educational Mission to the United States, 1872–81*. Hong Kong: Hong Kong University Press, 2011.

- Romero, Robert Chao. *Chinese in Mexico, 1882–1940*. Tucson: University of Arizona Press, 2012.

- Rowe, William. *China's Last Empire: The Great Qing*. Cambridge, MA: Belknap Press of Harvard University Press, 2009.

- Salyer, Lucy. *Laws Harsh as Tigers: Chinese Immigrants and the Shaping of Modern Immigration Law*. Chapel Hill: University of North Carolina Press, 1995.

- Sandmeyer, Elmer. *The Anti-Chinese Movement in California*. Urbana: University of Illinois Press, 1991.

- Schneider, Judy, and Koempel, Michael. *Congressional Deskbook: The Practical and Comprehensive Guide to Congress, 6e*. Alexandria, VA: TheCapitol.Net, 2012.

- Shen, I-yao. *A Century of Chinese Exclusion Abroad*. Beijing: Foreign Languages Press, 2006.

- Smith, Andrew F. (ed.). *The Oxford Companion to American Food and Drink*. Oxford New York: Oxford University Press, 2007.

- Smith, Darrell, and Herring, H. Guy. *The Bureau of Immigration, Its History, Activities, and Organization*. New York: AMS Press, 1974.

- Soennichsen, John. *The Chinese Exclusion Act of 1882*. Santa Barbara, CA: Greenwood, 2011.

- Takaki, Ronald. *Iron Cages: Race and Culture in 19th-century America*. New York: Oxford University Press, 2000.

- Taylor, Bayard. *A Visit to India, China and Japan in the Year 1853*. British Library, Historical Print Editions, 2011.

- Tsai, Jung-Fang. *Hong Kong in Chinese History*. New York: Columbia University Press, 1995.

- Wong, Marie Rose. *Sweet Cakes, Long Journey: The Chinatowns of Portland, Oregon*. Seattle: University of Washington Press, 2004.

- Wunder, John R. *Inferior Courts, Superior Justice: A History of the Justices of the Peace on the Northwest Frontier, 1853–1889*. Greenwood Press, 1979.

- Zesch, Scott. *The Chinatown War: Chinese Los Angeles and the Massacre of 1871*. London New York: Oxford University Press, 2012.

APPENDIX 14
Additional Resources

Links to these and other resources can be found online at <TCNFCA.com>.

People

Andrews, Charles O. (D-FL)

Angell, James Burrill

Arthur, Chester A. (R-NY)

Bayard, Thomas F. (D-DE)

Bayne, Thomas M. (R-PA)

Beck, James Burnie (D-KY)

Bennett, John B. (R-MI)

Berry, Campbell P. (D-CA)

Blaine, James G. (R-ME)

Blair, Henry W. (R-NH)

Booth, Newton (R-CA)

Brick, Abraham L. (R-IN)

Brown, Joseph E. (D-GA)

Browne, Thomas M. (R-IN)

Bruce, Blanche (R-MS)

Buckner, Aylett Hawes (D-MO)

Burlingame, Anson (R-MA)

Butler, Matthew C. (D-SC)

Butler, Smedley

Butterworth, Benjamin (R-OH)

Calkins, William H. (R-IN)

Call, Wilkinson (D-FL)

Carpenter, Matthew Hale (R-WI)

Cassidy, George W. (D-NV)

Chandler, William E. (R-NH)

Chiang Kai-shek

Chew, NG Poon (Wu Panzhao)

Clark, Champ (James Beauchamp) (D-MO)

Coffee, John Main (D-WA)

Conkling, Roscoe (R-NY)

Corbett, Henry W. (R-OR)

Cullom, Shelby Moore (R-IL)

Curtis, Carl T. (R-NE)

Davis, Cushman K. (R-MN)

Dawes, Henry L. (R-MA)

Dickstein, Samuel (D-NY)

Dillingham, William P. (R-VT)

Dirksen, Everett M. (R-IL)

Dolph, Joseph N. (R-OR)

Dondero, George A. (R-MI)

Edmunds, George Franklin (R-VT)

Elmer, William P. (R-MO)

Evarts, William M. (R-NY)

Eustis, James B. (D-LA)

Fairbanks, Charles W. (R-IN)

Farley, James T. (D-CA)

Felton, Charles N. (R-CA)

Fenton, Reuben E. (D&R-NY)

Fish, Hamilton III (R-NY)

Flower, Roswell P. (D-NY)

Foraker, Joseph B. (R-OH)

Ford, Thomas F. (D-CA)

Gallinger, Jacob H. (R-NH)

Garfield, James A. (R)

Geary, Thomas J. (D-CA)

George, James Zachariah (D-MS)

George, Melvin C. (R-OR)

Gilett, Frederick H. (R-MA)

Glascock, John Raglan (D-CA)

Gompers, Samuel

Gorman, Arthur Pue (D-MD)

Gossett, Ed Lee (D-TX)

Grover, La Fayette (D-OR)

Hamlin, Hannibal (D&R-ME)

Hawley, Joseph R. (R-CT)

Hay, John M.

Hayes, Rutherford B. (R-OH)

Hazleton, George C. (R-WI)

Heitfeld, Henry (P-ID)

Henley, Barclay R. (D-CA)

Heyburn, Weldon B. (R-ID)

Hiscock, Frank (R-NY)

Hitt, Robert Roberts (R-IL)

Hoar, George Frisbie (R-MA)

Hooker, Charles E. (D-MS)

Howe, Timothy Otis (R-WI)

Ingalls, John James (R-KS)

Jenkins, Thomas A. (R-OH)

Johnson, Hiram W. (R-CA)

Jones, John Percival (R-NV)

Joyce, Charles H. (R-VT)

Judd, Walter H. (R-MN)

Kahn, Julius (R-CA)

Kasson, John A. (R-IA)

Kennedy, Martin J. (D-NY)

Kleberg, Rudolph (D-TX)

Lamb, John E. (D-IN)

lao baixing (laobaixing)

Lodge, Henry Cabot (R-MA)

Luce, Henry R.

Magnuson, Warren G. (D-WA)

Mansfield, Mike (D-MT)

Mason, Noah M. (R-IL)

Matthews, Stanley (R-OH)

Maxey, Samuel B. (D-TX)

McCormack, John W. (D-MA)

McCreary, James B. (D-KY)

McDougall, John (D-CA)

McLane, Robert Milligan (D-MD)

McLaurin, John L. (D-SC)

McClure, Addison S. (R-OH)

Miller, John Franklin (R-CA)

Mitchell, John Hipple (R-OR)

Mondell, Frank W. (R-WY)

Moore, William Robert (R-TN)

Morgan, John Tyler (D-AL)

Morrill, Justin Smith (R-VT)

Morton, Oliver H. (R-IN)

Naphen, Henry F. (D-MA)

Orth, Godlove Stein (R-IN)

Otjen, Theobald (R-WI)

Pacheco, Romualdo (R-CA)

Page, Horace F. (R-CA)

Palmer, Henry W. (R-PA)

Patterson, Thomas M. (D-CO)

Penrose, Boies (R-PA)

Perkins, George C. (R-CA)

Perkins, James B. (R-NY)

Platt, Orville H. (R-CT)

Pomeroy, Samuel (R-KS)

Powderly, Terence V.

Quay, Matthew S. (R-PA)

Reynolds, Robert Rice (D-NC)

Rice, William Whitney (R-MA)

Robsion, John M. (R-KY)

Sanders, Wilbur Fiske (R-MT)

Sabath, Adolph J. (D-IL)

Sargent, Aaron (R-CA)

Schurz, Carl (R-MO)

Scott, William L. (D-PA)

Seward, George F.

Seward, William H. (R-NY)

Sherman, John (R-OH)

Simmons, Furnifold McLendel (D-NC)

Skinner, Charles R. (R-NY)

Slater, James H. (D-OR)

Soong Ai-ling (Madame Chiang Kai-shek)

Soong, Charles Jones

Speer, Emory (D-GA)

Spooner, John C. (R-WI)

Squire, Watson C. (R-WA)

Stewart, William Morris (R-NV)

Swift, John Franklin (R-CA)

Sulzer, William (D-NY)

Sumner, Charles (R-MA)

Sun Yat-sen

Taft, William Howard (R)

Taylor, Bayard

Taylor, Ezra B. (R-OH)

Teller, Henry M. (R-CO)

Thomas, Elbert (D-UT)

Thurman, Allen G. (D-OH)

Townsend, Martin I. (R-NY)

Townshend, Richard W. (D-IL)

Trumbull, Lyman (D&R-IL)

Tully, Pleasant Britton (D-CA)

Turner, George (R&D-WA)

Vest, George G. (D-MO)

Vorys, John Martin (R-OH)

Washburn, William D. (R-MN)

White, Compton I. (D-ID)

Williams, Charles G. (R-WI)

Williams, George Henry (R-OR)

Willis, Albert Shelby (D-KY)

Wilson, Henry (R-MA)

Wilson, James Falconer (R-IA)

Wright, James A. (D-PA)

Yu Pin, Paul

Links online at <TCNFCA.com>.

Internet Resources

- 1882 Project: American Civil Rights and the Chinese Exclusion Laws
- "Allies, Enemies and Aliens: Migration and U.S.-Chinese Relations, 1940–1965," by Meredith Leigh Oyen, PhD Dissertation, Georgetown University, December 14, 2007—Google Books
- "An Alleged Wife: One Immigrant in the Chinese Exclusion Era," by Robert Barde, *Prologue Magazine*, Spring 2004, Vol. 36, No.1—National Archives
- Angel Island: Immigrant Journeys of Chinese-Americans—"An oral history of Chinese Immigrant Detainees" by Lydia Lum
- Angel Island Immigration Station Foundation
- Angell Treaty of 1880 (22 Stat. 826)—from the Federal Judicial Center
- Angell Treaty of 1881—from the Yung Wing Project, Transcribed by Cassandra Bates (4-page PDF)
- "Annual report of the Commissioner General of Immigration, to the Secretary of Commerce and Labor, for the Fiscal Year Ended June 30, 1906," Washington, Government Printing Office, 1906—Google Books
- "Annual report of the Commissioner General of Immigration, to the Secretary of Commerce and Labor, for the Fiscal Year Ended June 30, 1911," Washington, Government Printing Office, 1912—Archive.org (for more Annual Reports, see Archive.org)
- "Annual report of the Commissioner-General of Immigration, to the Secretary of Commerce and Labor, for the Fiscal Year Ended June 30, 1922," Washington, Government Printing Office, 1922—Archive.org (for more Annual Reports, see Archive.org)
- "Annual report of the Commissioner-General of Immigration, to the Secretary of Commerce and Labor, for the Fiscal Year Ended June 30, 1924," Washington, Government Printing Office, 1924—Archive.org (for more Annual Reports, see Archive.org)
- Anti-Chinese Legislation and Court Cases—from the Museum of Chinese in America
- Arcadia Conference (WWII)—Wikipedia
- "A Short History of the Chinese Restaurant," by Gish Jen, *Slate*, April 27, 2005
- "Asian Immigrants In American Law: A Look At The Past And The Challenge Which Remains," by Chin Kim and Bok Lim C. Kim, 26.2 *American University Law Review*, page 373, 1977 (35-page PDF)
- "Asian Pacific Americans in the United States Congress," by Lorraine H. Tong, CRS Report 97-398, May 19, 2011 (27-page PDF)
- Asiatic Barred Zone (Immigration Act of 1917)—Wikipedia
- "A visit to India, China, and Japan, in the year 1853," by Bayard Taylor (G.P. Putnam, 1855)—Internet Archive (also available on Amazon)
- Bayard-Zhang Treaty of 1888 (unratified)—from Encyclopedia of Immigration (§ 7.30)
- Bertillon system, developed by Alphonse Bertillon—Wikipedia
- Bing Cherry—Wikipedia. See also Ah Bing

- Boxer Indemnity Scholarship Program—Wikipedia
- Boxer Protocol (1901)—Wikipedia
- Boxer Rebellion (1900)—Wikipedia
- Bureau of Immigration—Wikipedia
- Burlingame Treaty of 1868 (English and Chinese Text)—
  from the University of California
- Canada
  - Anti-Chinese sentiment in Canada—Wikipedia
  - Chinatowns in Latin America—Wikipedia
  - Mar, Lisa. *Brokering Belonging: Chinese in Canada's Exclusion Era, 1885–1945.* New York: Oxford University Press, 2010
  - Hoe, Ban Seng. *Enduring Hardship: The Chinese Laundry in Canada.* Gatineau, Quebec, Canada: Canadian Museum of Civilization, 2004
  - Anderson, Kay. *Vancouver's Chinatown: Racial Discourse in Canada, 1875–1980.* Montreal Buffalo: McGill-Queen's University Press, 1991.
- Canons of Statutory Construction—Wikipedia
- Cartoons
  - "Blaine Language" and "Just So" From *Harper's Weekly*, Vol. 23 (March 15, 1879)—Berkeley Digital Library, University of California (also at HarpWeek) (see § 9.17)
  - "The Chinese Question," From *Harper's Weekly*, Vol. 15 (February 18, 1871)— Library of Congress (more images from the Library of Congress) (see § 9.17)
  - Used on the cover of *Forbidden Citizens*
- Certificate of Residence (Wong Fay)—Library of Congress (more)
- *Chae Chan Ping v. United States*, 130 U.S. 581 (1889)—FindLaw | Encyclopedia of Immigration (cited in § 8.10)
- *Chew Heong v. United States*, 112 U.S. 536 (1884)—Legal Information Institute (§ 7.10)
- "*Chew Heong v. United States*: Chinese Exclusion and the Federal Courts," by Lucy Salyer, Federal Judicial Center, Federal Judicial History Office, 2006 (82-page PDF) (§ 7.11)
- *China: A History of the Laws, Manners, and Customs of the People,* by John Henry Gray (1878)—Volume 1 | Volume 2—Google Books
- "China as 'Victim'? The Opium War That Wasn't," by Harry G. Gelber, Center for European Studies at Harvard University, Working Paper Series #136 (2006) (10-page PDF)—Harvard Center for European Studies
- "China's Age of Invention," with Robin Yates, "Secrets of Lost Empires," NOVA, February 29, 2000.
- Chinese American Citizens Alliance
- Chinese-American Contribution to Transcontinental Railroad— from Central Pacific Railroad Photographic History Museum
- Chinese American Museum—Los Angeles

Links online at <TCNFCA.com>.

- Chinese Cemetery of Los Angeles
- Chinese Character A Day—from Adeline Yen Mah
- Chinese Culture Center of San Francisco
- Chinese Educational Mission—Wikipedia | CEM Connections | China Daily (April 22, 2004)
- Chinese Exclusion Act (1882)—ourdocuments.gov | Harvard University Library Open Collections Program | Wikipedia | Newspaper articles about Chinese Exclusion from the Library of Congress, Chronicling America collection
- Chinese Exclusion Commission of California
  - "Chinese Exclusion Convention Opens Fight in Defense of American Labor," *The San Francisco Call*, November 22, 1901—Library of Congress (1-page PDF)
  - "Course of Exclusion Legislation in Present Congress," *The American Federationist*, Volume 9, January 1902—Google Books
  - Letter from Edward James Livernash to Theodore Roosevelt, April 16, 1902—Theodore Roosevelt Center
  - "Employment of Chinese on Vessels Flying the American Flag, Etc.," March 15, 1902, 57th Congress, 1st Session, S. Doc. No. 254—Google Books
  - "Employment of Chinese on Vessels Flying the American Flag, Etc.," April 3, 1902, 57th Congress, 1st Session, S. Doc. No. 281—Google Books
  - "Exclusion of Chinese Laborers," April 14, 1902, 57th Congress, 1st Session, S. Doc. No. 304—Google Books
  - More newspaper articles about the Commission from the Library of Congress, Chronicling America collection
- "Chinese Exclusion, Photography, and the Development of U.S. Immigration Policy," by Anna Pegler-Gordon, *American Quarterly*, Vol. 58, Number 1, March 2006. (Also found in *The Best American History Essays 2008* (Palgrave Macmillan 2008).)
- Chinese Historical Society of America
- Chinese Indemnity Fund
  - "Report in the Senate Committee on Foreign Relations, June 24, 1870" (Google Books)
  - Letter from Anson Burlingame to Secretary of State Seward, August 12, 1865 (Google Books)
  - Senate Report No. 934, December 24, 1884, 48th Congress, 2nd Session. A Report to Accompany S. 678, "A bill in relation to the Chinese indemnity fund." (Google Books)
- Chinese in Oregon—from Center for Columbia River History
- "Chinese Immigration," by Prof. E. W. Gilliam, 143 *The North American Review* 26, July 1886—Google Books
- "Chinese Immigration," by Mary Roberts Coolidge (Henry Holt, 1909)—Google Books
- Chinese Immigration and the Chinese in the United States—National Archives (U.S.)
- "Chinese Opposition to Legal Discrimination in Arizona Territory," by Andrea Pugsley, Journal of Arizona History, Volume 44, Summer 2003
- Chinese Residents in Tombstone (AZ)—Sam Shueh and Eric Chen

Links online at <TCNFCA.com>.

- Chinese restaurants—Food Timeline (Lynne Olver)
- Chinese Servants in the North American West—Terry Abraham
- Chinese Six Companies (aka Chinese Consolidated Benevolent Association aka Zhonghua Huiguan)—Wikipedia I FoundSF
  - History of the Chinese Consolidated Benevolent Association
- *Chy Lung v. Freeman*, 92 U.S. 275 (1875)—FindLaw
- Citizens Committee to Repeal Chinese Exclusion—Encyclopedia of Immigration
- "Class, Gender, and Race: Chinese Servants in the North American West"— A paper by Terry Abraham, presented at the Joint Regional Conference Hawai'i/ Pacific and Pacific Northwest Association for Asian American Studies, Honolulu, March 26, 1996 (cited in § 6.10)
- CRS Reports
  - "Immigration and Naturalization Fundamentals," CRS Report RS20916
  - "Immigration Policies and Issues on Health-Related Grounds for Exclusion," CRS Report R40570
- *De Lima v. Bidwell*, 182 U.S. 1 (1901) (Puerto Rico not a foreign country after annexation)—FindLaw I Wikipedia (cited in § 9.30)
- Denver, Colorado—"Remembering when Denver had a Chinatown," by Christian Toto, The Denver Post, May 7, 2011 I Remembering the Destruction of Denver's Chinatown and Avoiding the Mistakes of the Past I Hop Alley / Chinese Riot of 1880
- Diplomat Rescuers and the Story of Feng Shan Ho—from the Center for Holocaust & Genocide Studies at the University of Minnesota
- "Early Chinese Food in America," by Jacqueline M. Newman, in *The Oxford Companion to American Food and Drink*, Andrew F. Smith editor (Oxford University Press 2007), page 119, ISBN 0195307968—Google Books
- Encyclopedia of Immigration
- Europe First Strategy (WWII)—Wikipedia
- "Exclusion of Chinese"—U.S.C.: heading of Chapter 7 of Title 8 of the United States Code
- Extraterritoriality—Wikipedia I British-Chinese Treaty for the Relinquishment of Extra-Territorial Rights in China I ChinaPage I Treaty Ports
- "Eye on the East: Labor Calls for Ban on Chinese Immigration"—"This memorial from a 1901 Chinese exclusion convention in San Francisco devoted to strategies for preventing Chinese immigration, called on Congress to use its legislative powers to limit the arrival of Asian aliens to America. It was reprinted in a 1902 AFL pamphlet."—History Matters, George Mason University
- Flavor & Fortune: Dedicated to the Art and Science of Chinese Cuisine— from The Institute for the Advancement of the Science & Art of Chinese Cuisine
- *Fong Yue Ting v. United States*, 149 U.S. 698 (1893) (upheld the Geary Act)— FindLaw
- Force Act of 1870—Wikipedia
- *Fourteen Diamond Rings v. United States*, 183 U.S. 176 (1901) (No duty owed on Philippine imports because the Philippines was American territory)—FindLaw

Links online at <TCNFCA.com>.

- "From the Party of Lincoln to the Party of "Chinese-must-go": Position Taking and Policy Change in the post-Reconstruction Congress," by Jungkun Seo, paper prepared for presentation at the 2007 meeting of the Midwest Political Science Association, Chicago, IL, April 12–15, 2007 (Also by Jungkun Seo, see "Wedge-issue Dynamics and Party Position Shifts: Chinese Exclusion Debates in the post-Reconstruction U.S. Congress,1879–82," *Party Politics*, November 2011, 17(6): 823-847 (25-page PDF)
- Geary Act (1892)—Wikipedia I Text from Hastings College of Law
- Gentlemen's Agreement of 1907—Wikipedia
- Gresham-Yang Treaty (1894) (Immigration Prohibition Treaty Between the United States of America and China, December 7, 1894)—Google Books
- History of U.S.-China Relations: Timeline of Important Events 1784–1979—from Kris McClellan
- H.RES. 282, 112th Congress, "Expressing the regret of the House of Representatives for the passage of discriminatory laws against the Chinese in the United States, including the Chinese Exclusion Act."—Thomas
- "Humors of a Congressional Investigating Committee: A Review of the Report of the Joint Special [Morton] Committee to Investigate Chinese Immigration. Washington, 1877." By Samuel E. W. Becker, Secretary to the Bishop of Wilmington, De., late Professor in The University of Virginia ("Experience has, in our country, abundantly demonstrated that both political parties have been, are, and will in all human probability always be ready to pander to the last extent to the prejudices of the ignorant, who are in all countries a vast majority, and, in this of ours, have and make use of their votes. Both Democrats and Republicans inserted an anti-Chinese plank in the platform of the last Presidential campaign [1876]. It is, therefore, not to be wondered at that the members of this [Morton Committee]--men who make a profession of politics--should have come to the work as partisans, and with mentally forgone conclusions.")—from the Library at Michigan State University (36-page PDF)
- Hyphen—Asian America Unabridged
- Immigration Act of 1917 (Asiatic Barred Zone Act), H.R. 10384; Pub.L. 301; 39 Stat. 874. 64th Congress; February 5th, 1917—Wikipedia
- Immigration Restriction Act of 1921 (Emergency Immigration Act of 1921; Emergency Quota Act), H.R. 4075; Pub.L. 67-5; 42 Stat. 5. 67th Congress; May 19, 1921—Wikipedia
- Immigration Act of 1924 (Johnson-Reed Act)—Wikipedia I National Archives I State Dept.
- National Origins Formula—Wikipedia
- Immigration and Nationality Act of 1952 (McCarran-Walter Act)—Wikipedia
- Immigration and Nationality Act of 1965 (Hart-Celler Act), H.R. 2580; Pub.L. 89-236; 79 Stat. 911. 89th Congress; October 3, 1965—Wikipedia I Harvard Crimson I Asian Nation
- "Immigration to the United States," by Raymond L. Cohn—EH.net
- Knights of St. Crispin, Order of—Wikipedia

Links online at <TCNFCA.com>.

- Know Nothing Party—Wikipedia
- Long Depression (1873–1896)—Wikipedia
- *Loughborough v. Blake*, 18 U.S. 317, 5 Wheat. 317 (1820) (affirmed Congress' power to tax in DC)—FindLaw
- Lue Gim Gong—Wikipedia| Sampson's Chinese, by Paul W. Marino (2-page PDF) | Forbidden Friendship: Finding the Facts Behind the Historical Fiction, Lori Austin, 4th Grade Teacher, Gabriel Abbott Memorial School, Florida, MA | West Volusia (FL) Historical Society | Lue Gim Gong Valencia orange—University of California, Riverside | Adopted Son—Paul Marino | 'Lue Gim Gong (OPS)'—USDA Agriculture Research Service, Germplasm Resources Information Network
- Madame Chiang Kai-Shek Addresses Congress, February 18, 1943 (audio recording)—History.com
- Magnuson Act (Chinese Exclusion Repeal Act of 1943)—Wikipedia
- Mark Twain's Observations about Chinese Immigrants in California— Library of Congress
- Mexico
  - Chinese immigration to Mexico—Wikipedia
  - Chinatowns in Latin America—Wikipedia
  - Romero, Robert Chao. *Chinese in Mexico, 1882-1940*. Tucson: University of Arizona Press, 2012
  - Delgado, Grace. *Making the Chinese Mexican: Global migration, localism, and exclusion in the U.S.-Mexico borderlands*. Stanford, CA: Stanford University Press, 2012
  - Camacho, Schiavone. *Chinese Mexicans: Transpacific migration and the search for a homeland, 1910–1960*. Chapel Hill: University of North Carolina Press, 2012.
- "Mongolian Immigration," by George F. Seward, 134 *The North American Review* 563, June 1882—Google Books
- Monroe Doctrine—Wikipedia
- Morey letter—Wikipedia
- Morton Committee (Committee on Chinese Immigration) (1876) (from "Chinese Immigration," by Mary Roberts Coolidge (Henry Holt, 1909))—Google Books (see "Humors of a Congressional Investigating Committee" above.)
- Museum of Chinese in America (MOCA)
- Naturalization Act of 1870 (16 Stat. 254)—Wikipedia
- "Newlands Resolution"—Joint Resolution To provide for annexing the Hawaiian Islands to the United States, 55th Congress, 2nd Session (1898)—OurDocuments. gov (see also 20 U.S.C. § 7512) ((cited in § 9.20)
- Old China Trade (1783–1844)—Wikipedia
- Open Door Policy (Sec. of State John Hay)—Wikipedia | State Dept.
- Opium Wars—Wikipedia
  - First Opium War (1839–1842)—Wikipedia
  - Second Opium War (1856–1860)—Wikipedia

- Oregon Constitution, Original 1857 Version—from Oregon Blue Book: Article II, Section 6 (suffrage); Article XV, Section 8 (real estate and mining claims)
- Panic of 1873—Wikipedia
- *Perez v. Sharp*, 32 Cal.2d 711, 198 P.2nd 17 (1948) (California's bans on interracial marriage violate the Fourteenth Amendment of the U.S. Constitution)—Wikipedia
- "Plain Language from Truthful James," by Francis Bret Harte—Bartleby.com
- "Problems of Immigration," by Frank P. Sargent, in The Making of America, Volume 2 (John D. Morris & Company, 1905), page 437—Google Books
- "President Aids Chinese: Issues Order for Discretion in Enforcing Exclusion Laws." *The New York Times*, June 15, 1905 (1-page PDF)
- *punica fides*—"The Romans had a saying, '*Punica fides*' (the reliability of a Carthaginian) which for them represented the highest degree of treachery: the word of a Carthaginian (like Hannibal) was not to be trusted, nor could a Carthaginian be relied on to maintain his political relationships." (Carthage) (§ 4.20)
- Qing Dynasty (1644–1912)—Wikipedia
- Race Riots, 1943—Wikipedia
- Radical Republicans—Wikipedia
- Reed, William Bradford (1806–1876)—State Dept. | Wikipedia | "President Buchanan's Minster to China 1857–1858," by Foster M. Farley, in Pennsylvania History, Volume 37, Number 3 (July 1970), 269–280 (12-page PDF)
- Remembering 1882—8 Videos of expert panel, from the Chinese Historical Society of America
- Report of the Joint Special Committee to Investigate Chinese Immigration, February 27, 1877 (Morton Committee report)—Google Books. See also Humors of a Congressional Investigating Committee: A Review of the Report of the Joint Special Committee to Investigate Chinese Immigration (1877), by Samuel E. Becker (36-page PDF)
- "Rise & Fall of the Canton Trade System—III, Canton and Hong Kong," by Peter C. Perdue, 2009 (46-page PDF)
- Rock Springs massacre" (Rock Springs, WY, September 2, 1885)—Wikipedia
- Salem's (Oregon) Chinese Americans—from Salem (Oregon) Public Library, Salem Online History
- Scott Act (1888)—from HarpWeek
- Scott Act (1888)—Wikipedia
- Scott Act of 1888—from Hastings College of Law
- "Some Reasons for Chinese Exclusion. Meat vs. Rice. American Manhood against Asiatic Coolieism. Which Shall Survive?" Published by the American Federation of Labor, reprinted in Senate Document No. 137, 57th Congress, 1st Session (1902)—Google Books
- Sinophobia—Wikipedia
- S.RES. 201, 112th Congress, "Expressing the regret of the Senate for the passage of discriminatory laws against the Chinese in America, including the Chinese Exclusion Act."—Thomas

Links online at <TCNFCA.com>.

- Taiping Rebellion (1850–1864)—Wikipedia
- Terms and Sessions of Congress—TermsOfCongress.com
- *Territory of New Mexico v. Yee Shun*, (3 N.M. 100) (1884)—
  Encyclopedia of the Great Plains
- The Chinese American Experience: 1857–1892—from HarpWeek
- The Chinese Exclusion Act—from Maryland State Archives
- The Chinese Experience in 19th Century America—
  University of Illinois at Urbana-Champaign
- "The Chinese in America," by Bryan J. Clinche, 9 *American Catholic Quarterly
  Review* 57, January 1884—Google Books
- The Chinese in California, 1850–1925 (Teacher's version)—Library of Congress
  (links to numerous resources). Also see Chinese in California, 1850–1925
  from the Bancroft Library at the University of California, Berkeley.
- The Chinese in San Francisco—Virtual Museum of the City of San Francisco
- "The Chinese Must Go," by John F. McClymer, Assumption College
- "The Chinese Must Stay," by Yan Phou Lee, North American Review, 148
  (April 1889) pages 476–483, Federal Judicial Center. Also available as an
  8-page PDF transcribed by Cassandra Bates in 2006.
- "The Chinese Question," *Fibre and Fabric Magazine*, June 17, 1905, page 441
  (columns 2 and 3)—Google Books
- "The Coolie Question in 1856–1862: A Brief Vindication," by Gideon Nye, Jr.
  (Hongkong, 1869), Harvard University Library
- "The Debate on the Chinese Exclusionary Act and Its Repeal," by Jay B.
  Martens, AP History Teacher, Williamsville (IL) High School (11-page PDF)
- "'The Eagle Seeks a Helpless Quarry'—Chinatown, the Police, and the Press:
  the 1903 Boston Chinatown Raid Revisited," by K. Scott Wong, in "A Reader:
  Asian American Studies" (Rutgers, 2000)—Google Books
- The History of Jim Crow—Arizona | California | Colorado | Idaho |
  Massachusetts | Montana | Nevada | New Mexico | New York | Oregon |
  Texas | Utah | Virginia | Washington | Wyoming
- "The international relations of the Chinese empire," by Hosea B. Morse,
  Volumes 1–3 (Longmans, Green and Co., 1910)—Google Books
- "The Other Side of the Chinese Question," *The Nation*, April 1, 1886,
  pages 272–273—Google Books
- "The Sandlot and Kearneyism," by Jerome A. Hart—
  Virtual Museum of the City of San Francisco
- The Soong's Saga. "In 2009 the [Vanderbilt University] Divinity Library mounted
  an exhibit featuring Charles Soong, one of Vanderbilt's alums from 1882–1885.
  Soong's children and their spouses played significant roles in the history of
  twentieth-century China. His eldest daughter, Ai-ling, married H.H. Kung, minister
  of finance under the Nationalist government. His second daughter, Ching-ling,
  married Sun Yat-sen, the first leader of republican China. His third daughter,
  Mei-ling, married the Nationalist leader Chiang Kai-shek. T.V. Soong, Charles

Links online at <TCNFCA.com>.

Soong's oldest son, was centrally involved in establishing modern China's financial system."—Vanderbilt University (§ 10.22)

- "The Supreme Court and the Rights of Aliens," by Leonard Dinnerstein, Fall 1985 (10-page PDF)
- "To the Person Sitting in Darkness," by Mark Twain—Wikipedia | Text on Google Books | Twain-Ament Indemnities Controversy
- Treaties between the Empire of China and foreign powers—Google Books
- Transcontinental Railroad (1863–1869)—Wikipedia
- Treaty of Nanking (1842)—Wikipedia
- Treaty of Paris (1898)—Wikipedia
- Treaty of Tientsin (1858)—Wikipedia | text on Wikipedia | State Dept.
- Treaty of Versailles (1919)—text on Wikipedia
- Treaty of Wangxia (Wanghia) (1844)—Wikipedia | State Dept.
- Tucson's (AZ) Chinese Heritage—The Promise of Gold Mountain—Univ. of AZ
- Uncommon Oaths—Tracy McLean, "The Stream," Courthouse Libraries | BC blog, June 22, 2011
- *United States v. Bhagat Singh Thind*, 261 U.S. 204 (1923) (A Punjabi Sikh, settled in Oregon, could not be a naturalized citizen of the United States, because he was not a "white person")—FindLaw | Wikipedia
- *United States v. Wong Kim Ark*, 169 U.S. 649 (1898) (A person of Chinese descent, born in the United States to Chinese parents, is an American citizen by birthright)—Findlaw | Wikipedia
- Veto Message of President Rutherford Hayes of the Fifteen Passenger bill, March 1, 1879 (House bill No. 2423, "An Act to restrict the immigration of Chinese to the United States")—Google Books
- Veto Message of President Chester A. Arthur of Senate bill No. 71, April 4, 1882 (Senate bill No. 71, "An act to execute certain treaty stipulations relating to Chinese")—Google Books
- War Brides Act (1945) H.R. 4857; Pub.L. 79-271; 59 Stat 659. 79th Congress, December 28, 1945—Wikipedia
- "yellow peril"—Wikipedia
- "Yellow peril, yellow press: 100 years ago today, city saw roundup of Chinese," by Chris Berdik, *The Boston Globe*, October 12, 2003
- *Yick Wo v. Hopkins*, 118 U.S. 356 (1886) (even if a law is race neutral on its face, if it is applied in a prejudicial manner, it violates the equal protection clause (Section 1.) in the 14th Amendment)—FindLaw | Wikipedia | State Dept.
- Yung Wing Project—site includes transcript of: "My Life in China and America," by Yung Wing,
- Introduction of Resolution in the House of Representatives Expressing Regret for Chinese Exclusion Act, May 26, 2011 (video)

Links online at <TCNFCA.com>.

Books

See also Appendix 13, Bibliography.

- Ahmad, Diana. *The Opium Debate and Chinese Exclusion Laws in the Nineteenth-century American West.* Reno: University of Nevada Press, 2007. 0874178444

- Ancheta, Angelo. *Race, Rights, and the Asian American Experience.* New Brunswick, NJ: Rutgers University Press, 2006. 0813539021

- Anderson, Eugene. *The Food of China.* New Haven: Yale University Press, 1988. 0300047398

- Aronson, Virginia. *Gift of the Unicorn: The Story of Lue Gim Gong, Florida's Citrus Wizard.* Sarasota, FL: Pineapple Press, 2002. 1561642649

- Barth, Gunter. *Bitter Strength: A History of the Chinese in the United States 1850–1870.* Harvard University, 1964. B003KDF72A

- Baughman, James L. *Henry R. Luce and the Rise of the American News Media.* Baltimore: The Johns Hopkins University Press, 2001. 0801867169

- Bieler, Stacey. *Patriots or Traitors?: A History of American-educated Chinese Students.* Armonk, NY: M.E. Sharpe, 2004. 0765611864

- Blum, Edward. *Reforging the White Republic: Race, Religion, and American Nationalism, 1865–1898.* Baton Rouge: Louisiana State University Press, 2005. 0807132489

- Brady, Marilyn. *The Asian Texans.* College Station: Texas A & M University Press, 2004. 1585443123

- Brockey, Liam. *Journey to the East: The Jesuit Mission to China, 1579–1724.* Cambridge, MA: Belknap Press of Harvard University Press, 2007. 0674030362

- Brook, Timothy. *The Troubled Empire: China in the Yuan and Ming Dynasties.* Cambridge, MA: Belknap Press of Harvard University Press, 2010. 0674046021

- Brooks, Charlotte. *Alien Neighbors, Foreign Friends: Asian Americans, Housing, and the Transformation of Urban California.* Chicago: University of Chicago Press, 2009. 0226075974

- Brundage, David. *The Making of Western Labor Radicalism: Denver's Organized Workers, 1878–1905.* Urbana: University of Illinois Press, 1994. 0252020758

- Buck, Pearl. *The Good Earth.* New York: Pocket Books, 2005. 1416500189

- Bush, Sara. *Arizona's Gold Mountain: Oral Histories of Chinese Americans in Phoenix.* 2000. B0006RNBGM

- Butler, Smedley. *General Smedley Darlington Butler: The Letters of a Leatherneck, 1898–1931.* New York: Praeger, 1992. 0275941418

- Carpenter, Francis. *The Old China Trade: Americans in Canton, 1784–1843.* New York: Coward, McCann & Geoghegan, 1976. 0698203585

- Chan, Sucheng. *Asian Americans: An Interpretive History.* Boston: Twayne, 1991. 0805784373

Links online at <TCNFCA.com>.

- Chan, Sucheng, and Hsu, Madeline Y. *Chinese Americans and the Politics of Race and Culture*. Philadelphia: Temple University Press, 2008. 1592137539

- Chan, Sucheng. *Entry Denied: Exclusion and the Chinese Community in America, 1882–1943*. Philadelphia: Temple University Press, 1991. 0877227985

- Chan, Sucheng. *This Bittersweet Soil: The Chinese in California Agriculture, 1860–1910*. Berkeley: University of California Press, 1986. 0520067371

- Chang, Derek. *Citizens of a Christian Nation: Evangelical Missions and the Problem of Race in the Nineteenth Century*. Philadelphia: University of Pennsylvania Press, 2010. 0812242181

- Chang, Iris. *Thread of the Silkworm*. New York: Basic Books, 1995. 0465006787

- Chang, K. C. *Food in Chinese Culture*. London: Yale University Press, 1977. 0300019386

- Chang, Pang-Mei. *Bound Feet & Western Dress*. New York: Anchor Books, 1997. 0385479646

- Chen, Yong. *Chinese San Francisco, 1850–1943: A TransPacific Community*. Stanford, CA, Cambridge: Stanford University Press Cambridge University Press, 2002. 0804745501

- Cheung, Sidney, and Wu, David Y. H. (eds.). *The Globalization of Chinese Food*. New York: RoutledgeCurzon, 2004. 0415338301

- Chin, Tung. *Paper Son: One Man's Story*. Philadelphia: Temple University Press, 2000. 1566398010

- Chinese Historical Society of America. *Chinese America: History and Perspectives, 1997*. ISBN *1885864051*

- Cho, Jenny. *Chinatown in Los Angeles*. San Francisco, CA: Arcadia Pub, 2009. 0738569569

- Choy, Philip P., Lorraine Dong, and Marlon K. Hom. *Coming Man: 19th Century American Perceptions of the Chinese*. Seattle: University of Washington Press, 1994. 0295974532

- Chung, Sue Fawn. *The Chinese in Nevada*. Charleston, SC: Arcadia Pub, 2011. 0738574945

- Clayborn, Hannah. *Historic Photos of the Chinese in California*. Nashville, TN: Turner Pub. Co, 2009. 1596525193

- Clunas, Craig. *Empire of Great Brightness: Visual and Material Cultures of Ming China, 1368–1644*. Honolulu: University of Hawaii Press, 2007. 0824831497

- Collis, Maurice. *Foreign Mud: Being an Account of the Opium Imbroglio at Canton in the 1830's and the Anglo-Chinese War that Followed*. New York: New Directions, 2002. 0811215067

- Corbett, Christopher. *The Poker Bride: The First Chinese in the Wild West*. Grove Press, 2011. 0802145272

- Daniels, Roger. *Asian America: Chinese and Japanese in the United States Since 1850*. Seattle: University of Washington Press, 1992. 0295970189

Links online at <TCNFCA.com>.

- Daniels, Roger. *Guarding the Golden Door: American Immigration Policy and Immigrants Since 1882*. New York: Hill and Wang, 2005. 0809053446

- De Leon, Arnoldo. *Racial Frontiers: Africans, Chinese, and Mexicans in Western America, 1848–1890*. Albuquerque: University of New Mexico Press, 2002. 0826322727

- de Tocqueville, Alexis. *Democracy in America*. Library of America, 2004. 1931082545

- Dirlik, Arif (ed.). *Chinese on the American Frontier*. Rowman & Littlefield Publishers, 2003. 0847685330

- Dong, Jielin and Hu, Sen (eds.). *The Rocky Road to Liberty: A Documented History of Chinese Immigration and Exclusion*. Saratoga, CA: Javvin Press, 2010. 1602670285

- Dyer, Thomas G. *Theodore Roosevelt and the Idea of Race*. Baton Rouge, LA: Louisiana State University Press, 1992 0807118087

- Dyke, Paul. *The Canton Trade: Life and Enterprise on the China Coast, 1700–1845*. Hong Kong: Hong Kong University Press, 2007. 9622098282

- Eber, Irene (translator). *Voices from Shanghai: Jewish Exiles in Wartime China*. Chicago: University of Chicago Press, 2008. 0226181669

- Elliott, Mark. *Emperor Qianlong: Son of Heaven, Man of the World*. New York: Pearson Longman, 2009. 0321084446

- Elsensohn, M. Alfreda. *Idaho Chinese Lore*. The Caxton Printers, 1993. B0006C99E0

- Fairbank, John King. *The Chinese World Order: Traditional China's Foreign Relations*. Cambridge MA: Harvard University Press, 1968. 0674126017

- Fairbank, John King. *The Great Chinese Revolution, 1800–1985*. New York: Perennial Library, 1987. 006039076X

- Fairbank, John King. *The United States and China*. Cambridge, MA: Harvard University Press, 1983. 067492438X

- Falbaum, Berl (ed.). *Shanghai Remembered: Stories of Jews who Escaped to Shanghai from Nazi Europe*. Royal Oak, MI: Momentum Books, 2005. 1879094738

- Fay, Peter Ward. *Opium War, 1840–1842: Barbarians in the Celestial Empire in the Early Part of the Nineteenth Century and the War by Which They Forced Her Gates*. Chapel Hill, NC: The University of North Carolina Press, 1974. 0807847143

- Fong, Timothy. *The First Suburban Chinatown: The Remaking of Monterey Park, California*. Philadelphia: Temple University Press, 1994. 1566392624

- Friday, Chris. *Organizing Asian-American Labor: The Pacific Coast Canned-Salmon Industry, 1870–1942*. Philadelphia: Temple University Press, 1995. 1566393981

- Gates, E. Nathaniel. *Race and U.S. Foreign Policy from 1900 through World War II*. New York: Garland Pub, 1998. 0815329571

- Genthe, Arnold. *Genthe's Photographs of San Francisco's Old Chinatown*. New York: Dover Publications, 1984. 0486245926

Links online at <TCNFCA.com>.

- Gong-Guy, Lillian. *Chinese in San Jose and the Santa Clara Valley*. Charleston, SC: Arcadia Pub, 2007. 0738547778

- Graham, Gerald. *The China Station: War and Diplomacy 1830–1860*. Oxford Eng. New York: Clarendon Press Oxford University Press, 1978. 0198224729

- Greenberg, Michael. *British Trade and the Opening of China 1800–42*. Cambridge: Cambridge University Press, 2008. 0521079160

- Greenwood, Roberta. *Down by the Station: Los Angeles Chinatown, 1880–1933*. Los Angeles: Institute of Archaeology, University of California, Los Angeles, 1996. 0917956877

- Gross, Ariela. *What Blood Won't Tell: A History of Race on Trial in America*. Cambridge, MA, London: Harvard University Press, 2010. 0674047982

- Gungwu, Wang. *Chinese Overseas: From Earthbound China to the Quest for Autonomy*. Cambridge, MA: Harvard University Press, 2000. 067400986X

- Gyory, Andrew. *Closing the Gate: Race, Politics, and the Chinese Exclusion Act*. Chapel Hill: University of North Carolina Press, 1998. 0807847399

- Hahn, Emily. *China to Me: A Partial Autobiography*. E-reads, 1999. 0759240604

- Hahn, Emily. *The Soong Sisters*. New York: E-reads, 2003. 0759253412

- Hee-Chorley, Lorraine. *Chinese in Mendocino County*. Charleston, SC: Arcadia, 2009. 073855913X

- Heppner, Ernest. *Shanghai Refuge: A Memoir of the World War II Jewish Ghetto*. Lincoln, NE: University of Nebraska Press, 1993. 0803272812

- Higham, John. *Strangers in the Land: Patterns of American Nativism, 1860–1925*. New Brunswick, NJ: Rutgers University Press, 2002. 0813531233

- Hing, Bill. *Making and Remaking Asian America through Immigration Policy, 1850–1990*. Stanford, CA: Stanford University Press, 1993. 0804723605

- Ho, Chuimei (ed.). *Chinese in Chicago, 1870–1945*. Charleston, SC: Arcadia, 2005. 0738534447

- Holmes, David. *Chinese Milwaukee*. Charleston, SC: Arcadia Pub, 2008. 0738552240

- Hom, Marlon K. *Songs of Gold Mountain: Cantonese Rhymes from San Francisco Chinatown*. Berkeley: University of California Press, 1987. 0520081048

- Hoobler, Dorothy. *The Chinese American Family Album*. New York: Oxford University Press, 1994. 0195124219

- Huang, Yunte. *Charlie Chan: The Untold Story of the Honorable Detective and his Rendezvous with American History*. New York: W. W. Norton, 2010. 0393340392

- Ingold, Jeanette. *Paper Daughter*. Boston: Houghton Mifflin Harcourt, 2010. 015205507X

- Jacobson, Matthew. *Barbarian Virtues: The United States Encounters Foreign Peoples at Home and Abroad, 1876–1917*. New York: Hill and Wang, 2001. 0809016281

- Jeung, Russell. *Faithful Generations: Race and New Asian American Churches*. New Brunswick, NJ: Rutgers University Press, 2005. 0813535034

- Johnston, Reginald. *Twilight in the Forbidden City*. Soul Care Publishing, 2008. 0968045952

- Joppke, Christian. *Selecting by Origin: Ethnic Migration in the Liberal State*. Cambridge, MA: Harvard University Press, 2005. 0674015592

- Jorae, Wendy. *The Children of Chinatown: Growing up Chinese American in San Francisco, 1850–1920*. Chapel Hill: University of North Carolina Press, 2009. 0807859737

- Jung, John. *Chinese Laundries: Tickets to Survival on Gold Mountain*. S.l: Yin & Yang Press, 2007. 1466302054

- Jung, John. *Chopsticks in the Land of Cotton: Lives of Mississippi Delta Chinese Grocers*. California: Ying & Yang Press, 2008. 0615185711

- Jung, John. *Southern Fried Rice: Life in A Chinese Laundry in the Deep South*. Lulu.com, 2006. 1411640349

- Jung, John. *Sweet and Sour: Life in Chinese Family Restaurants*. Cypress, CA: Yin and Yang Press, 2010. 061534545X

- Jung, Moon-Ho. *Coolies and Cane: Race, Labor, and Sugar in the Age of Emancipation*. Baltimore, MD: Johns Hopkins University Press, 2006. 0801890829

- Keay, John. *China: A History*. New York: Basic Books, 2009. 0465015808

- Keeton, George Williams. *The Development of Extraterritoriality in China*. New York: Howard Fertig 1969. B0006BTV8U, 9780865270428

- Keevak, Michael. *Becoming Yellow: A Short History of Racial Thinking*. Princeton, NJ: Princeton University Press, 2011. 0691140316

- Kim, Hyung-Chan. *Asian Americans and Congress: A Documentary History*. Westport, CT: Greenwood Press, 1996. 0313285950

- Kindleberger, Charles. *Manias, Panics, and Crashes: A History of Financial Crises*. Hoboken, NJ: John Wiley & Sons, 2005. 0471467146

- Kwong, Peter. *Chinese America: The Untold Story of America's Oldest New Community*. New York: New Press Distributed by W.W. Norton, 2005. 1565849620

- Kwong, Peter. *Forbidden Workers*. New York: New Press, 1997. 156584517X

- Kwong, Peter. *The New Chinatown*. New York: Hill and Wang, 1996. 0809015854

- Lai, Him Mark. *Island: Poetry and History of Chinese Immigrants on Angel Island 1910–1940*. Seattle: University of Washington Press, 1991. 0295971096

- Lau, Estelle. *Paper Families: Identity, Immigration Administration, and Chinese Exclusion*. Durham, NC: Duke University Press, 2006. 0822337479

- Laven, Mary. *Mission to China: Matteo Ricci and the Jesuit Encounter with the East*. London: Faber, 2011. 0571225179

- Lee, Anthony. *Picturing Chinatown: Art and Orientalism in San Francisco*. Berkeley: University of California Press, 2001. 0520225929

- Lee, Gus. *Chasing Hepburn: A Memoir of Shanghai, Hollywood, and a Chinese Family's Fight for Freedom*. New York: Three Rivers Press, 2003. 140005155X

Links online at <TCNFCA.com>.

- Lee, Jennifer 8. *The Fortune Cookie Chronicles: Adventures in the World of Chinese Food*. New York: Twelve, 2008. 0446580074

- Lee, Joann Faung Jean. *Asian Americans: Oral Histories of First to Fourth Generation Americans from China, the Philippines, Japan, India, the Pacific Islands, Vietnam, and Cambodia*. New York: New Press Distributed by W.W. Norton, 1992. 1565840232

- Lee, Josephine and Lim, Imogene L. *Re/collecting Early Asian America: Essays in Cultural History*. Philadelphia: Temple University Press, 2002. 1566399645

- Lee, Robert G. *Orientals: Asian Americans in Popular Culture*. Philadelphia: Temple University Press, 1999. 1566397537

- Lescohier, Don D. *The Knights of St. Crispin, 1867–1874*. BiblioLife, 2009. 1115862871

- Ling, Huping. *Chinese Chicago: Race, Transnational Migration, and Community since 1870*. Stanford, CA: Stanford University Press, 2012. 0804775591

- Ling, Huping. *Chinese in St. Louis, 1857–2007*. Charleston, SC: Arcadia Pub, 2007. 0738551457

- Ling, Huping. *Surviving on the Gold Mountain: A History of Chinese American Women and their Lives*. Albany, NY: State University of New York Press, 1998. 0791438643

- Liu, Haiming. *The Transnational History of a Chinese Family: Immigrant Letters, Family Business, and Reverse Migration*. New Brunswick, NJ: Rutgers University Press, 2005. 0813535972

- Loewen, James. *The Mississippi Chinese: Between Black and White*. Long Grove, IL: Waveland Press, 1988. 0881333123

- Louie, Vivian. *Compelled to Excel: Immigration, Education, and Opportunity among Chinese Americans*. Stanford, CA: Stanford University Press, 2004. 0804749841

- Lubetkin, M. John. *Jay Cooke's Gamble: The Northern Pacific Railroad, the Sioux, and the Panic of 1873*. Norman: University of Oklahoma Press, 2006. 0806137401

- Ma, Eva Armentrout. *Hometown Chinatown: A History of Oakland's Chinese Community*. New York: Garland Pub, 2000. 0815337604

- Marcus, Fred. *Survival in Shanghai: The Journals of Fred Marcus, 1939–49*. Berkeley, CA: Pacific View Press, 2008. 1881896293

- McLain, Charles J. (ed.). *Chinese Immigrants and American Law*. New York: Garland Pub, 1994. 0815318499

- McClain, Charles J. *In Search of Equality: The Chinese Struggle Against Discrimination in Nineteenth-century America*. Berkeley: University of California Press, 1994. 0520205146

- McCunn, Ruthanne. *Thousand Pieces of Gold: A Biographical Novel*. Boston: Beacon Press, 2004. 080708381X

- McCunn, Ruthanne. *Wooden Fish Songs*. Seattle: University of Washington Press, 2007. 0295987146

Links online at <TCNFCA.com>.

- Meagher, Arnold. *The Coolie Trade: The Traffic in Chinese Laborers to Latin America 1847–1874.* Philadelphia, PA: Xlibris Corporation, 2008. 1436309425

- Minnick, Sylvia Sun. *Samfow: The San Joaquin Chinese Legacy.* Fresno, CA: Panorama West Pub, 1988. 0944194095

- Minnick, Sylvia Sun. *The Chinese Community of Stockton.* Chicago, IL: Arcadia Pub, 2002. 0738520535

- Morse, Hosea. *The International Relations of the Chinese Empire. Volume 1. The Period of Conflict 1834–1860.* Boston: Elibron Classics, 2007. B004IIKABO

- Morse, Hosea. *The International Relations of the Chinese Empire. Volume 2. The Period of Submission. 1861–1893.* Boston: Elibron Classics, 2007. 1402193165

- Morse, Hosea. *The International Relations of the Chinese Empire. Volume 3. The Period of Subjection 1894–1911.* Boston: Elibron Classics, 2007. 1402182546

- Motomura, Hiroshi. *Americans in Waiting: The Lost Story of Immigration and Citizenship in the United States.* New York: Oxford University Press, 2007. 0195336089

- Mullen, Kevin. *Chinatown Squad: Policing the Dragon: From the Gold Rush to the 21st Century.* Novato, CA: Noir Publications, 2008. 0926664107

- Mungello, D. *The Great Encounter of China and the West, 1500–1800.* Lanham, MD: Rowman & Littlefield Publishers, 2009. 0742557987

- Murray, Marian. *Plant Wizard: The Life of Lue Gim Gong.* Atheneum, 1970. 0027677508

- Nathan, Andrew, and Ross, Robert S. *The Great Wall and the Empty Fortress: China's Search for Security.* New York: W. W. Norton, 1998. 0393317846

- Ngai, Mae. *The Lucky Ones: One Family and the Extraordinary Invention of Chinese America.* Boston MA: Houghton Mifflin Harcourt, 2010. B005MWLFPK

- Nguyen, Mimi Thi (ed.). *Alien Encounters: Popular Culture in Asian America.* Durham, NC: Duke University Press, 2007. 0822339226

- Nokes, R. Gregory. *Massacred for Gold: The Chinese in Hells Canyon.* Corvallis, OR: Oregon State University Press, 2009. 0870715704

- Nuys, Frank. *Americanizing the West: Race, Immigrants, and Citizenship, 1890–1930.* Lawrence, KS: University Press of Kansas, 2002. 0700612068

- Pascoe, Peggy. *What Comes Naturally: Miscegenation Law and the Making of Race in America.* Oxford New York: Oxford University Press, 2010. 0199772355

- Paterson, Thomas, and Clifford, J. Garry. *American Foreign Relations: A History.* Boston, MA: Wadsworth Cengage Learning, 2010. 0547225644

- Paulsen, George E. *The Gresham-Yang Treaty.* University of California Press, 1968. B0007GTSG4

- Peffer, George. *If They Don't Bring Their Women Here: Chinese Female Immigration Before Exclusion.* Urbana: University of Illinois Press, 1999. 0252067770

Links online at <TCNFCA.com>.

- Qin, Yucheng. *The Diplomacy of Nationalism: The Six Companies and China's Policy Toward Exclusion*. Honolulu: University of Hawaii Press, 2009. 0824832744

- Quan, Robert. *Lotus Among the Magnolias: The Mississippi Chinese*. Jackson: University Press of Mississippi, 1982. 1934110043

- Riggs, Frederick Warren. *Pressures on Congress: A Study of the Repeal of Chinese Exclusion*. Oxford University Press, 1950. B0000CHSN4

- Risse, Guenter. *Plague, Fear, and Politics in San Francisco's Chinatown*. Baltimore: The Johns Hopkins University Press, 2012. 1421405105

- Ristaino, Marcia. *Port of Last Resort: Diaspora Communities of Shanghai*. Stanford, Calif. London: Stanford University Press Eurospan, 2004. 0804750238

- Roberts, J.A.G. *China to Chinatown: Chinese Food in the West*. Reaktion Books, 2004. 1861891334

- Roediger, David (ed.). *The Best American History Essays 2008*. New York: Palgrave Macmillan, 2008. 0230605915

- Ross, James. *Escape to Shanghai: A Jewish Community in China*. New York Toronto: Free Press Maxwell Macmillan Canada Maxwell Macmillan International, 1994. 0029273757

- Saxton, Alexander. *The Indispensable Enemy: Labor and the Anti-Chinese Movement in California*. Berkeley: University of California Press, 1971. 0520029054

- Schmidt, Hans. *Maverick Marine: General Smedley D. Butler and the Contradictions of American Military History*. Lexington, KY: University Press of Kentucky, 1987. 0813109574

- Schulp, Leonard C. and Ryan, James G. *Historical Dictionary of the Gilded Age*. Armonk, NY: M.E. Sharpe, 2003. 0765603314

- Seagrave, Sterling. *Dragon Lady: The Life and Legend of the Last Empress of China*. New York: Vintage Books, 1993. 0679733698

- Seagrave, Sterling. *The Soong Dynasty*. New York: Harper & Row, 1985. 0060913185

- See, Lisa. *On Gold Mountain: The One-hundred-year Odyssey of My Chinese-American Family*. New York: Vintage Books, 1996. 0307950395

- Shah, Nayan. *Contagious Divides: Epidemics and Race in San Francisco's Chinatown*. Berkeley: University of California Press, 2001. 0520226291

- Shilpa, Dave, and Nishime, Leilani (eds.). *East Main Street: Asian American Popular Culture*. New York: New York University Press, 2005. 0814719635

- Siu, Paul C.P. *The Chinese Laundryman: A Study of Social Isolation*. New York: New York University Press, 1987. 0814778747

- Skrentny, John. *The Minority Rights Revolution*. Cambridge, MA: Belknap Press of Harvard University Press, 2002. 0674016181

- So, Yan-Kit. *Classic Food of China*. London: Macmillan, 1992. 0333569075

- Soong, May-ling (Madame Chiang Kai-shek). *This is Our China: Selections from the Writings of Madame Chiang Kai-shek*. New York: Harper & Brothers, 1940. B000V77WEE

Links online at <TCNFCA.com>.

- Spence, Jonathan. *The Chan's Great Continent: China in Western Minds.* New York: W.W. Norton & Co, 1999. 039331989X

- Stefoff, Rebecca. *Journey to Gold Mountain: The Chinese in 19th-century America.* New York: Chelsea House, 1994. 0791021777

- Sterckx, Roel. *Food, Sacrifice, and Sagehood in Early China.* New York: Cambridge University Press, 2011. 1107001714

- Sterckx, Roel. *Of Tripod and Palate: Food, Politics and Religion in Traditional China.* New York: Palgrave Macmillan, 2004. 1403963371

- Storch, Tanya (ed.). *Religion and Missionaries in the Pacific, 1500–1900.* Burlington, VT: Ashgate Publishing Company, 2006. 0754606678

- Storti, Craig. *Incident at Bitter Creek: The Story of the Rock Springs Chinese Massacre.* Ames: Iowa State University Press, 1991. 0813814030

- Takaki, Ronald. *Spacious Dreams: The First Wave of Asian Immigration.* New York: Chelsea House Publishers, 1993. 0791022765

- Takaki, Ronald. *Strangers from a Different Shore: A History of Asian Americans.* Boston: Little, Brown, 1998. 0316831301

- Tannahill, Reay. *Food in History.* New York: Three Rivers Press, 1989. 0517884046

- Tchen, John Kuo Wei. *New York before Chinatown: Orientalism and the Shaping of American Culture, 1776–1882.* Baltimore, MD: Johns Hopkins University Press, 2001. 0801867940

- To, Wing-kai. *Chinese in Boston, 1870–1965.* Charleston, SC: Arcadia Pub, 2008. 0738555290

- Tobias, Sigmund. *Strange Haven: A Jewish Childhood in Wartime Shanghai.* Urbana, IL: University of Illinois Press, 2009. 0252076249

- Tom, Brian. *Marysville's Chinatown.* Charleston, SC: Arcadia Pub, 2008. 0738559768

- Tom, Lawrence. *Sacramento's Chinatown.* Charleston, SC: Arcadia Pub, 2010. 073858066X

- Tsai, Shih-Shan Henry. *China and the Overseas Chinese in the United States, 1868–1911.* Fayetteville: University of Arkansas Press, 1983. 0938626191

- Tsai, Shih-Shan Henry. *The Chinese Experience in America.* Bloomington: Indiana University Press, 1986. 0253203872

- Tung, May, and Trepper, Terry S. *Chinese Americans and their Immigrant Parents: Conflict, Identity, and Values.* New York: Haworth Clinical Practice Press, 2000. 0789010550

- Tung, William L. *China and the Foreign Powers: The Impact of and Reaction to Unequal Treaties.* Dobbs Ferry, NY: Oceana, 1970. 0379004631

- Tung, William L. *The Chinese in America, 1820–1973; A Chronology and Fact Book.* Dobbs Ferry, NY: Oceana, 1974. 0379005107

- Twain, Mark. *A Tramp Abroad, Following the Equator, Other Travels.* New York: Library of America, 2010. 1598530666

Links online at <TCNFCA.com>.

- Twain, Mark. *The Innocents Abroad; Roughing it*. New York: Library of America, 1984. 0940450259

- Twain, Mark. *The Wit & Wisdom of Mark Twain*. New York: Perennial, 2005. 0060751045

- U.S. Senate. *Remission of Chinese Indemnity: Hearing Before the Committee on Foreign Relations, United States Senate, S.J. Res. 33, May 25, 1908*. 1113393254

- Waley, Arthur. *The Opium War through Chinese Eyes*. Stanford, CA: Stanford University Press, 1958. 0804706115

- Wang, Dong. *China's Unequal Treaties: Narrating National History*. Lanham, MD: Lexington Books, 2008. 073912806X

- Watanna, Onoto. *A Half Caste and Other Writings*. Urbana: University of Illinois Press, 2003. 0252070941

- Weatherford, Jack. *Genghis Khan and the Making of the Modern World*. New York: Crown, 2004.

- Weber, Judith Eichler. *Forbidden Friendship*. Silver Moon Press, 2004. 1893110427

- Wicker, Elmus. *Banking Panics of the Gilded Age*. Cambridge, UK New York: Cambridge University Press, 2000. 0521770238

- Wills, John E. *China and Maritime Europe, 1500–1800: Trade, Settlement, Diplomacy, and Missions*. Cambridge New York: Cambridge University Press, 2011. 0521179459

- Wong, K. Scott (ed.). *Claiming America: Constructing Chinese American Identities during the Exclusion Era*. Philadelphia: Temple University Press, 1998. 1566395763

- Wong, Kevin. *Americans First: Chinese Americans and the Second World War*. Cambridge, MA: Harvard University Press, 2005. 0674016718

- Wong, Wayne. *American Paper Son: A Chinese Immigrant in the Midwest*. Urbana: University of Illinois Press, 2006. 0252072634

- Wong, William. *Oakland's Chinatown*. Charleston, SC: Arcadia, 2004. 0738529257

- Wood, Douglas. *Franklin and Winston: A Christmas that Changed the World*. Cambridge, Mass: Candlewick Press, 2011. 0763633836

- Wood, Frances. *No Dogs and Not Many Chinese: Treaty Port Life in China, 1843–1943*. London: John Murray, 2000. 071956400X

- Wu, Cheng-Tsu (ed.). *Chink! A Documentary History of Anti-Chinese Prejudice in America*. New York: World Publishing Company, 1972. 0529044722

- Wu, Frank. *Yellow: Race in America: Beyond Black and White*. New York: BasicBooks, 2003. 046500640X

- Wunder, John R. *Chinese in Trouble. Criminal Law and Race on the Trans-Mississippi West Frontier*. Western Historical Quarterly, 1986. B0021ZDENW

- Yao, Steven. *Foreign Accents: Chinese American Verse from Exclusion to Postethnicity*. New York: Oxford University Press, 2010. 0199730334

Links online at <TCNFCA.com>.

- Ye, Weili. *Seeking Modernity in China's Name: Chinese Students in the United States, 1900–1927*. Stanford: Stanford University Press, 2001. 0804736960

- Yep, Laurence. *Dragon Road: Golden Mountain Chronicles: 1939*. New York: HarperCollins, 2008. B0042P59TG

- Yep, Laurence. *The Dragon's Child: A Story of Angel Island*. New York: HarperCollins, 2008. 0062018159

- Yep, Laurence. *Dragon's Gate*. New York: HarperTrophy, 1995. 0064404897

- Yep, Laurence. *The Traitor: Golden Mountain Chronicles, 1885*. New York: HarperCollins, 2003. 1439547602

- Yi, Henry Pu. *The Last Manchu: The Autobiography of Henry Pu Yi, Last Emperor of China*. New York: Skyhorse Pub, 2010. 1602397325

- Yun, Lisa. *The Coolie Speaks: Chinese Indentured Laborers and African Slaves in Cuba*. Philadelphia: Temple University Press, 2008. 1592135811

- Yung, Judy, and Chang, Gordon. *Chinese American Voices: From the Gold Rush to the Present*. Berkeley: University of California Press, 2006. 0520243102

- Yung, Judy. *San Francisco's Chinatown*. Charleston, SC: Arcadia Pub, 2006. 0738531308

- Yung, Judy. *Unbound Feet: A Social History of Chinese Women in San Francisco*. Berkeley: University of California Press, 1995. 0520088670

- Yung, Judy. *Unbound Voices: A Documentary History of Chinese Women in San Francisco*. Berkeley: University of California Press, 1999. 0520218604

- Yung, Wing. *My Life in China and America*. Hong Kong: Reprinted by China Economic Review Pub, 2007. 9889987457

- Zee, A. *Swallowing Clouds*. Seattle: University of Washington Press, 2002. 0295981911

- Zhao, Xiaojian. *Remaking Chinese America: Immigration, Family, and Community, 1940–1965*. New Brunswick, NJ: Rutgers University Press, 2002. 0813530113

- Zhao, Xiaojian. *The New Chinese America: Class, Economy, and Social Hierarchy*. New Brunswick, NJ: Rutgers University Press, 2010. 0813546923

- Zhou, Min. *Chinatown: The Socioeconomic Potential of an Urban Enclave*. Philadelphia: Temple University Press, 1992. 156639337X

- Zhou, Min. *Contemporary Chinese America: Immigration, Ethnicity, and Community Transformation*. Philadelphia: Temple University Press, 2009. 1592138586

- Zhu, Liping. *A Chinaman's Chance: The Chinese on the Rocky Mountain Mining Frontier*. Boulder: University Press of Colorado, 2000. 087081575X

- Zia, Helen. *Asian American Dreams: The Emergence of an American People*. New York: Farrar, Straus, and Giroux, 2001. 0374527369

Links online at <TCNFCA.com>.

Index

References are to chapter and section numbers.

A

Abolitionist movement, 2.26, 5.21–5.22

Abrogation of all treaties with China (Geary Act), 8.10, 8.21–8.22, 8.24

Absenteeism and voting in House and Senate, 2.14

Absolute exclusion proposals, 7.10–7.30, 8.10, 8.31

Ackerman, Kenneth, 2.23

Adams, Robert, 9.30

Africans. *See also* Race-mixing as negative for U.S.; Slavery

  Americanization of, 1.30, 2.10

  Chinese compared to, 1.30, 3.90, 4.40, 4.60, 5.20, 7.59, 9.30

  inferiority of, 3.80

  Oregon restrictions on negroes and mulattoes, 3.70

  Southern states seeing racial hypocrisy in Chinese vs. African treatment, 7.59

Ah Lung, In re (1883), 6.20

Akaka, Daniel, *epilogue*

Allen, A. Leonard, 11.40

Amendments (1884), Ch. 6

  overview, 6.0

  House debate on, 6.10

  House vote on, 6.10

  presidential (Arthur) signing, 6.20

  purpose to stop immigration from Hong Kong and Singapore, 6.10

  Senate debate on, 6.20

  Senate vote on, 6.20

American Federation of Labor (AFL), 9.23–9.24, 11.30, 11.52

American Legion, 11.30–11.40

American Party. *See* Know-Nothing Party

Ancestor worship, 2.24

Andrews, Charles O., 11.51–11.52

Angel Island (entry point for Asian immigrants), 9.17, 10.22

Angel Island (Lee & Yung), 9.17

Angell, James B., 3.10, 3.80

Angell Treaty (1880), *Appendix 5. See also* Senate debate on twenty-year exclusion bill (1882)

  Article I, 3.60

  Article II, 3.60

  China's withdrawal from Gresham–Yang and, 10.10

  Chinese labor distinctions, 3.30

  Geary Act (1892) and, 8.10

  legislation to implement, 3.20, 3.50–3.60

  negotiations and terms of, 3.80–3.90, 4.60

  purpose of, 3.0, 3.31

  Scott Act (1888) and, 7.51, 7.56

Anthony, Henry, 1.20

Anti-miscegenation laws, 9.30

Appeals of immigration officers' decisions

  Extension Act (1902) and, 9.10

  Permanent Law (1904) and, 10.20

Appropriations bill (1904), 10.20

Arcadia Conference (1941–1942), 11.33

Arizona and Chinese immigrants, 6.10

Arthur, Chester

  approval of ten-year exclusion law (1882), 5.70

  signing Amendments (1884), 6.20

  veto of twenty-year exclusion bill (1882), 4.0, 4.80, 5.20, 7.52, *Appendix 6*

Asiatic Barred Zone, 11.20–11.40, 11.52

Assassination of Garfield, 3.20

Asylum as purpose of immigration, 2.10, 4.40, 9.30

B

Barkley, Alben, 11.52

Bayard, Thomas F., 3.50, 7.30, 7.56

Bayard–Zhang Treaty (1888)

  overview, 7.0

  Bayard's role, 3.50

  China's reaction to, 7.41, 7.56–7.57, 7.70, 8.24

  House debate on, 7.40

  President Cleveland's response to Senate, 7.21

  Senate concurrence in House amendment to, 7.41

  Senate consent to ratify, 7.30

  Senate debate on, 7.10–7.20, 7.31

Bayne, Thomas, 4.50

Beck, James B., 2.23

Benevolent organizations, 2.10

Bennett, John B., 11.20–11.40

Bercuson, David, 11.33

Berry, Campbell, 4.40

Bertillion, Alphonse, 9.17

Biddle, Francis, 11.52

Biggert, Judy, *epilogue*

Birthright citizenship
Extension Act (1902) and, 9.19, 9.24, 9.30, 9.32, 9.41
Fourteenth Amendment and, 3.80, 9.10
Permanent Law (1904) and, 10.20

Black population. *See* Africans

Blaine, James G.
on Fifteen Passenger bill (1879), 2.23–2.24, 2.26–2.27, 4.60
on Naturalization Act (1870), 1.30
presidential election (1884), 7.52

Blair, Henry
on Geary Act (1892), 8.22
on Scott Act (1888), 7.56, 7.59

Booth, Newton, 2.22

Boxer Protocol (1901), 9.12

Boxer Rebellion (1900), 9.11–9.12, 9.22, 11.30

Boycotts by Chinese, 10.21

Bradley, James, 3.41, 9.22

Breckinridge, William, 8.10

Brents, Thomas, 6.10

Brick, Abraham, 9.31

British-Chinese relations, 2.12, 4.60, 6.10, 9.14, 11.32

British colonies with Chinese populations, immigration from, 8.20–8.21, 11.30–11.40, 11.52

British Columbia, crossings of Chinese into U.S. from, 6.10, 8.21, 8.24

Brown, Joseph E.
on Scott Act (1888), 7.55–7.56, 7.70
on twenty-year exclusion bill (1882), 3.60, 3.90

Brown, Scott, *epilogue*

Browne, Thomas M., 4.60, 6.10

Bruce, Blanche, 2.23

Buck, C. Douglass, 11.51

Buck, Pearl S., 11.30

Buckner, Aylett, 4.50

Bureau of Immigration, 9.17

Burlingame Treaty (1868), *Appendix 2*
abrogation, effect of, 2.10, 2.26, 2.30–2.40
advantages of, 2.26, 4.50
amendment of Angell Treaty (1880), 3.31
Article V, 2.10, 7.57
Article VI, 2.10
Grover attack on, 2.22
litigation based on rights granted to Chinese under, 7.11
missionaries and, 4.60
Morgan desire to renegotiate, 2.22
purpose of, 2.0, 2.40, 3.90
Republican Party and, 7.52
severabliity not possible, 2.40
summary of, 1.30, 2.12, 4.80

Burns, Robert, 2.10

Busbey, Fred E., 11.30

Butler, Matthew C.
on Geary Act (1892), 8.21
on Scott Act (1888), 7.52

Butterworth, Benjamin, 4.50, 4.70

C

Cairo summit meeting (November 1943), 11.30

California and Chinese immigrants
Amendments (1884) and, 6.10
anti-miscegenation law, 9.30
Chinese Exclusion Commission of the State of California, 9.41
Fifteen Passenger bill of 1879 and, 2.22–2.23
presidential election (1888), 7.80
repeal legislation (1943) and, 11.52

Scott Act (1888) and, 7.52
ten-year exclusion law (1882) and, 5.40
twenty-year exclusion bill (1882) and, 3.20, 3.50, 3.90, 4.20–4.30, 4.50–4.60

Calkins, William H., 4.10, 4.40–4.50

Call, Wilkinson
on Bayard–Zhang Treaty ratification (1888), 7.20
on Geary Act (1892), 8.24, 8.31
on Scott Act (1888), 7.20, 7.55–7.57
on ten-year exclusion law (1882), 5.50

Canada
Chinese immigration to, 8.42
crossings of Chinese into U.S. from, 6.10, 7.10–7.20, 8.24

Cannon, Joseph, 4.70

Cardin, Ben, *epilogue*

Carmack, Edward, 9.24

Carpenter, Matthew Hale, 1.30

Carper, Tom, *epilogue*

Casserly, Eugene, 1.20

Cassidy, George W., 4.30

Census. *See* Chinese population in U.S.

Central Pacific Railroad, 3.41

Certificates of identification, 8.30–8.32, 9.17, 9.30

Chae Chan Ping v. United States (1889), 8.10, 9.16

Chandler, William, 8.21–8.22, 8.24

Chang, Iris, 2.11, 11.22

Chew Heong v. United States (1884), 7.10, 9.16

Chiang Kaishek, 10.22, 11.0, 11.10, 11.30, 11.52

Chiang Kaishek, Madame (Soong Meiling), 10.22, 11.10, 11.30–11.31

"Chicken Oath," 2.25

References are to chapter and section numbers.

China. *See also* Qing Dynasty
changes in due to blocked immigration of dissidents, 5.50
diplomacy with U.S. *See* Diplomacy, China–U.S.
end of dynastic rule, 11.10
missionaries to, 4.60
objections to treatment of Chinese in U.S., 9.18
reaction to Bayard–Zhang Treaty, 7.41, 7.56–7.57, 7.70, 8.24
reaction to Extension Act (1902), 9.18
reaction to Permanent Law (1904), 10.21
republic founded, 11.10
restaurant culture in, 8.41
return to China by Chinese immigrants, 6.10
trade relations with U.S. *See* Trade relations between U.S. and China
treaty concessions (overview), 11.32
withdrawal from Gresham–Yang Treaty (1894), 10.0, 10.10
World War II and, 11.10–11.20

Chinatown, 2.10, 2.22, 7.59, 9.15

Chinese civilization and customs, impenetrability of
Amendments (1884) and, 6.10
Extension Act (1902) and, 9.16, 9.18, 9.20, 9.23, 9.30–9.32
Geary Act (1892) and, 8.21, 8.24
repeal legislation (1943) and, 11.30–11.40, 11.52
Scott Act (1888) and, 7.52, 7.55
twenty-year exclusion bill (1882) and, 3.20, 3.50–3.90, 4.30, 4.50–4.70

Chinese Communists, 11.10, 11.52

Chinese Exclusion Act of 1882. *See* Ten-year exclusion law (1882)

Chinese Exclusion Commission of the State of California, 9.41

Chinese Exclusion Convention (1901), 9.0

Chinese food and restaurants, 8.41

Chinese laborers
American desire to exploit, 5.20–5.30, 9.24
ban to include both skilled and unskilled, 3.40, 3.90, 4.90, 5.30, 5.50
definition of, 5.40–5.50, 9.14, 9.18, 9.21
Panama Canal Zone construction, 10.20
Permanent Law (1904) and, 10.20
reentry and right of return to U.S. *See* Reentry and right of return
seamen, 9.10, 9.24, 9.32, 9.41
ten-year exclusion. *See* Ten-year exclusion law (1882)
on transcontinental railway, 3.41, 8.24
twenty-year exclusion. *See* Twenty-year exclusion bill (1822)
unacceptable class and character of, 4.70

Chinese massacre of 1871, 7.59

Chinese Oath, 2.25

"Chinese person," defined
Geary Act (1892) and, 9.30
Permanent Law (1904) and, 10.20

Chinese population in U.S., 2.29, 3.30, 4.60, 6.10, 8.21, 9.16–9.18, 11.30

Chinese Six Companies. *See* Six Companies (Chinese Consolidated Benevolent Association)

Chu, Judy, *epilogue*

Chungking authorities, 11.30

Churchill, Winston, 11.30, 11.33

Chy Lung v. Freeman (1875), 3.50, 9.17

Citizens Committee to Repeal Chinese Exclusion, 11.30

Citizenship. *See also* Birthright citizenship
European immigrants. *See* European immigration, distinguished from Chinese immigration
Extension Act (1902) and, 9.10, 9.19, 9.24, 9.30–9.32
Fifteen Passenger bill (1879) and, 2.10, 2.22, 2.40
Permanent Law (1904) and, 10.20
removal of bar (1942 & 1943), 11.20
Scott Act (1888) and, 7.10, 7.55
ten-year exclusion law (1882) and, 5.40–5.50
twenty-year exclusion bill (1882) and, 3.30–3.50, 3.90, 4.30, 4.50

Civil unrest, ban on Chinese immigration to prevent, 3.40, 3.90, 4.70, 5.30

Clark, James Beauchamp "Champ," 9.30–9.32

Clash of civilizations. *See* Chinese civilization and customs, impenetrability of

Cleveland, Grover
Bayard-Zhang Treaty and, 7.41
Bayard–Zhang Treaty and, 7.0
on Fifteen Passenger bill (1879), 2.23
negotiations with Chinese emperor to end Chinese immigration, 7.21
presidential elections (1884 & 1888), 7.52, 7.80
Scott Act (1888) signed by, 7.62, 7.70

Cloture rule, 2.28

References are to chapter and section numbers.

Coe, Andrew, 8.41

Coffee, John Main, 11.30

Coffman, Mike, *epilogue*

Coke, Richard, 8.31

Communism. *See* Chinese Communists

Conference reports, procedure for, 8.31

Confucian traditions and family relationships, 2.24

Conkling, Roscoe
on Fifteen Passenger bill (1879), 2.23, 2.26
on Naturalization Act (1870), 1.20–1.30

Consistency with treaties, as issue for enacted laws, 10.10–10.20

Constitution, U.S. *See also* Fourteenth Amendment
Article I, section 7, 2.50
Article VI, 2.10
Caucasian race only race intended to be admitted to U.S., 3.50
on distinction between native-born persons and foreigners, 1.30
First Amendment, 9.24

Contract labor. *See* Coolie contract labor

Coolie contract labor
Fifteen Passenger bill (1879) and, 2.10, 2.26, 2.40
Geary Act (1892) and, 8.21
Naturalization Act (1870) and, 1.20–1.30
repeal legislation (1943) and, 11.40
Scott Act (1888) and, 7.54
ten-year exclusion law (1882) and, 5.20, 5.50
twenty-year exclusion bill (1882) and, 3.80, 4.10

Coons, Chris, *epilogue*

Corbett, Henry W., 1.20–1.30

Country quota system, 11.10, 11.21, 11.30–11.40, 11.52

Cox, Samuel, 7.62

Crocker, Charles, 3.41

Cullen, William, 4.70

Cullom, Shelby Moore
on Extension Act (1902), 9.14, 9.16, 9.18
on Permanent Law (1904), 10.20

Curtis, Carl, 11.30

Cutting, John T., 8.10

D

Davis, Cushman, 8.22–8.23

Davis, David, 4.90

Dawes, Henry L.
cited in 2011 congressional apology for exclusionary laws, *epilogue*
on Fifteen Passenger bill (1879), 2.26
on ten-year exclusion law (1882), 5.40
on twenty-year exclusion bill (1882), 3.70, 3.90

Dawes, Rufus, 4.70

Declaration of Independence, 1.20, 1.30, 2.22–2.23, 3.40, 4.30

De Gobineau, Count, 3.50

De Lima v. Bidwell (1901), 9.32

Democratic Party
1880 platform, 3.20–3.21, 4.20, 4.40, 4.70
1884 platform, 11.30
on admission of Chinese, 4.70, 6.10, 7.31, 7.53
Extension Act (1892) and, 9.32
opposition to Chinese immigration, 4.70, 5.30, 6.10
Scott Act (1888) and, 7.62

Democratic principles, 2.23, 3.30

Deportation proceedings, 8.23, 8.30–8.40, 9.17

Detaining arriving Chinese immigrants, 7.10, 9.10, 9.17, 10.22

Deuster, Peter, 4.40

Dickstein, Samuel, 11.20–11.30

Dillingham, William P., 9.18–9.19, 9.24

Diplomacy, China–U.S.
Extension Act (1902) and, 9.18
Geary Act (1892) and, 8.21, 8.23
Scott Act (1888) and, 7.53, 7.57
twenty-year exclusion bill (1882) and, 3.31, 4.40–4.60, 4.80
World War II and, 11.30

Diplomats
Geary Act (1892) on, 8.21, 8.24, 8.31
Scott Act (1888) on, 7.10
ten-year exclusion law (1882) on, 5.30

Dirksen, Everett M., 11.30

Disease-carriers, Chinese as. *See* Health threats posed by Chinese immigrants

Documentation required for Chinese immigrants, 3.60, 3.90, 4.90, 6.10, 9.17. *See also* Certificates of identification

Dolph, Joseph Norton
on Bayard–Zhang implementation bill (1888), 7.31
on Geary Act (1892), 8.20–8.21, 8.31

Dondero, George, 11.30

Douglas, William H., 9.32

Du Caurroy, Adople-Marie, 1.31

Dunn, James R., 9.17

E

Eaton, William, 6.10

Economic concerns as reason to deny Chinese immigration, 2.22, 3.20–3.30, 8.24. *See also* Labor protectionism

Edmunds, George
on Fifteen Passenger bill (1879), 2.26

on Naturalization Act (1870), 1.20

on ten-year exclusion law (1882), 5.50

on twenty-year exclusion bill (1882), 3.70–3.90

Educational purposes, entry for, 2.26. *See also* Students

Electoral College

Harrison election, 2.23, 7.52

Hayes election, 3.21

Elmer, William P., 11.30

European immigration, distinguished from Chinese immigration

Extension Act (1902) and, 9.18, 9.20

Fifteen Passenger bill (1879) and, 2.0, 2.10, 2.22–2.23

Geary Act (1892) and, 8.23

House debate on twenty-year exclusion bill (1882) and, 4.20, 4.40, 4.60–4.70

quota system and, 11.30

Senate debate on twenty-year exclusion bill (1882) and, 3.40, 3.60–3.70, 3.90

Europe-first strategy (World War II), 11.30, 11.33

Eustis, James B., 2.26

Evarts, William M., 7.57

Expatriation

Angell Treaty (1880) and, 3.30

Burlingame Treaty (1868) and, 2.22, 9.14

Geary Act (1892) and, 8.21, 8.23

Scott Act (1888) and, 7.55, 7.57

twenty-year exclusion bill (1882) and, 3.70, 4.60

Expressio unius est exclusio alterius, 9.21

Extension Act (1902), Ch. 9, *Appendix 9*

overview, 9.0

China's reaction to, 9.18

House debates on, 9.30–9.32

presidential (Roosevelt) signing, 9.41

resolving differences between Senate and House, 9.40–9.41

Senate debates on, 9.10–9.14, 9.18–9.21, 9.23–9.24, 9.40

Senate vote on, 9.24

shortcomings of, 10.10

Extraterritoriality, 11.30, 11.32

F

Fair, James, 3.70

Fairbanks, Charles, 9.11, 9.23–9.24

Farley, James T.

on ten-year exclusion law (1882), 5.20–5.40

on twenty-year exclusion bill (1882), 3.40–3.60, 3.80–3.90, 4.90

Federal Council of Churches of Christ in America, 11.30

Federal courts on issue of Chinese immigration, 7.10–7.11. *See also* Appeals of immigration officers' decisions

Feinstein, Dianne, *epilogue*

Felton, Charles, 8.21, 8.24

Fenby, Jonathan, 9.12

Fenton, Reuben, 1.20–1.30

Field, Stephen, 6.20, 8.10, 9.16

Fifteen Passenger bill (1879), *Appendix 4*

overview, 2.0

absenteeism and pairs in House and Senate votes, 2.14

Democrats vs. Republicans in voting for, 7.52

House attempt to override presidential veto, 2.50

House concurring in Senate amendments, 2.30

House debates on, 2.10

House vote on, 2.14, 2.30

presidential (Hayes) veto of, *Appendix 4*, 2.0, 2.40, 4.60–4.80, 5.20

Senate debates on, 2.20–2.22

Senate vote on, 2.26

Fifteen Passenger bill of 1879, Ch. 2, *Appendix 4*

overview, 2.0

absenteeism and pairs in House and Senate votes, 2.14

compared to twenty-year exclusion bill, 3.30

House attempt to override presidential veto, 2.50

House concurring in Senate amendments, 2.30

House debate on, 2.10

House vote on, 2.14, 2.30, 4.70

presidential (Hayes) veto of, 2.0, 2.40, 4.60–4.80, 5.20, *Appendix 4*

Senate debate on, 1.30, 2.20–2.22

Senate vote on, 2.26

Fifteenth Amendment, 1.0, 1.30

Fillmore, Millard, 3.32

First Amendment, 9.24

Fish, Hamilton, III, 11.30

Flower, Roswell G., 4.40

Fong Yue Ting v. United States (1893), 8.40, 9.30

Foraker, Joseph, 9.16, 9.21, 9.24

Force Act of 1870, 1.0

Forced labor contracts. *See* Coolie contract labor

Ford, Thomas F., 11.40

Fourteen Diamond Rings v. United States (1901), 9.19

Fourteenth Amendment, 3.80, 5.22, 7.11, 9.10, 9.30, 9.32

Fowler, Joseph, 1.30

Fraudulent entry of Chinese, 7.51, 7.56, 9.11, 9.30

Free Soil movement, 2.26

References are to chapter and section numbers.

Friedberg, Aaron L., 11.32

Frye, William P., 9.24

Fugitive Slave Laws, 4.60

G

Gallinger, Jacob H., 9.11, 9.18, 9.20

Garfield, James
abolition of slavery and, 5.21
assassination of, 3.20
Fifteen Passenger bill of 1879 and, 2.10, 3.20
Morey letter and, 4.20
presidential election (1880), 3.21
twenty-year exclusion bill (1882) and, 4.40

Garland, Augustus, 4.90

Gearhart, Bertrand "Bud," 11.30

Geary, Thomas J., 8.10, 8.32

Geary Act (1892), Ch. 8
overview, 8.0
bicameral agreement and conference report, 8.30
House debates on, 8.10, 8.32
politics and immigration enforcement, 9.17
Senate amendments offered, 8.24
Senate debates on, 8.20–8.24
Senate vote on, 8.24

Gelber, Harry G., 1.30, 9.16

Gentlemen's Agreement with Japan (1907), 11.52

George, James Z.
on Scott Act (1888), 7.52–7.54
on twenty-year exclusion bill (1882), 3.60

George, Melvin C.
on Amendments (1884), 6.10
on twenty-year exclusion bill (1882), 4.60

Gilbert, Abijah, 1.20

Gillett, Frederick H., 9.31

Glascock, John Raglan, 6.10

Gompers, Samuel, 9.10, 9.17, 9.24

Goodwill of U.S. as part of Angell Treaty negotiations, 3.80

Gorman, Arthur Pue, 7.56

Gossett, Ed Lee, 11.30

Grant, Ulysses S., 2.10

Gray, John Henry, 8.41

Green, Henry, 9.31

Gresham–Yang Treaty (1894), 9.0, 9.10–9.11, 9.16, 9.21, 9.32, 9.41, *Appendix 8*
China's withdrawal from, 10.0, 10.10

Grover, La Fayette
on Fifteen Passenger bill (1879), 2.22
on ten-year exclusion law (1882), 5.20
on twenty-year exclusion bill (1882), 3.40, 3.90

Guangdong Province, ties with benevolent organizations, 2.10

Guomindang Party (Chinese Nationalist Party), 11.10

H

Habeas corpus, 7.10, 7.51, 8.10, 8.30–8.31, 8.40

Hamlin, Hannibal
cited in 1943 debate on repeal, 11.30
on Fifteen Passenger bill (1879), 2.20, 2.23, 2.26
on Naturalization Act (1870), 1.30

Hammond, Nathaniel, 6.10

Hancock, Winfield Scott, 3.20–3.21

Harrison, Benjamin, presidential election (1888), 2.23, 7.52, 7.80

Harte, Bret, 2.10

Hatch, Orrin, *epilogue*

Hawaii, Chinese exclusion from, 9.0, 9.10, 9.16, 9.18, 9.20, 9.23

Hawley, Joseph R., 3.90

Hay, John, 9.21

Hayes, Rutherford B.
Chinese relations with, 2.23
commissioners appointed to negotiate Angell Treaty, 3.10, 3.80
Electoral College deciding presidential election of, 3.21, 7.52
veto of Fifteen Passenger bill, *Appendix 4*, 2.0, 2.40, 4.60–4.80, 5.20

Hazelton, George C., 4.70

Health threats posed by Chinese immigrants, 2.22, 4.10, 4.40

"The Heathen Chinee" (Harte), 2.10

Heitfeld, Henry, 9.23

Helborn, S.G., 3.70

Henderson, David, 4.70

Henley, Barclay, 6.10

Hepburn, William P., 4.70

Herwig, Holger, 11.33

Heyburn, Weldon B., 10.20

Hinshaw, John, 11.30

Hiscock, Frank, 8.23

History of the Diversity of the Races (De Gobineau), 3.50

Hitt, Robert Roberts
on Amendments (1884), 6.10
on Bayard–Zhang implementation bill (1888), 7.40
on Extension Act (1902), 9.30
on Geary Act (1892), 8.10

Hoar, George Frisbie
on Amendments (1884), 6.20
cited in 1943 debate on repeal, 11.30
cited in 2011 congressional apology for exclusionary laws, *epilogue*
on Extension Act (1902), 9.19, 9.24

References are to chapter and section numbers.

on Fifteen Passenger bill (1879), 2.23

on Scott Act (1888), 7.56

on ten-year exclusion law (1882), 5.20–5.30

on twenty-year exclusion bill (1882), 3.30–3.60, 3.80–3.90

Hoeven, John, *epilogue*

Holman, Rufus C., 11.51–11.52

Homeland Security, Department of, 9.17

Hong Kong, 11.30

Hoogenboom, Ari, 2.26, 2.40

Hooker, Charles E.
on Extension Act (1902), 9.31–9.32

on Geary Act (1892), 8.10

on twenty-year exclusion bill (1882), 4.50

House of Representatives
bill manager's role, 4.61

motion to recommit, 11.41

presiding over, 1.22

procedural questions and use of precedent, 4.91

House Committee of the Whole
Amendments (1884) consideration, 6.10

repeal (1943) consideration, 11.40

role of, 1.11

House Committee on Education and Labor
Fifteen Passenger bill (1879) and, 2.10

ten-year exclusion legislation (1882) and, 5.0, 5.10

House Committee on Foreign Affairs
on Bayard–Zhang implementation bill (1888), 7.40

on Extension Act (1902), 9.30

House Committee on Immigration and Naturalization, 11.20–11.40

House debate on Amendments of 1884
May 3, 1884, 6.10

House debate on Bayard–Zhang implementation bill (1888)
August 1888, 7.40

House debate on Extension Act (1902)
April 4, 1902, 9.30

April 5, 1902, 9.31

April 7, 1902, 9.32

House debate on Fifteen Passenger bill (1879)
January 28, 1879, 2.10

House debate on Geary Act (1892)
April 4, 1892, 8.10

May 4, 1892, 8.32

House debate on repeal legislation (1943)
October 11, 1943 (House Committee Report), 11.10

October 20, 1943, 11.30

October 21, 1943, 11.40

House debate on Scott Act (1888)
September 3, 1888, 7.51

September 20, 1888, 7.62

House debate on ten-year exclusion law (1882)
April 17, 1882, 5.10

May 3, 1882, 5.60

House debate on twenty-year exclusion bill (1882), 4.10–4.70
overview, 4.0

March 14, 1882, 4.10

March 15, 1882, 4.20

March 16, 1882, 4.30

March 18, 1882, 4.40

March 21, 1882, 4.50

March 22, 1882, 4.60

March 23, 1882, 4.70

House Immigration and Naturalization Committee, 11.30

Howe, Timothy, 1.20, 1.30

H.R. 282 (2011), *epilogue*

H.R. 1798. *See* Amendments (1884)

H.R. 1882. *See* Repeal (1943)

H.R. 2201. *See* Naturalization Act (1870)

H.R. 2423. *See* Fifteen Passenger bill (1879)

H.R. 3070. *See* Repeal (1943)

H.R. 5804. *See* Ten-year exclusion law (1882)

H.R. 6175. *See* Geary Act (1892)

H.R. 11336. *See* Scott Act (1888)

H.R. 13031. *See* Extension Act (1902)

H.R. 15054. *See* Appropriations bill (1904)

I

Immigration Act (1917), 11.20–11.30, 11.52

Immigration Act (1924), 11.20–11.30, 11.52

Immigration and Naturalization Service (INS), 9.17

Immorality and social decay
of Chinese, 2.10, 2.22, 3.20, 3.80, 4.20–4.30, 4.50–4.70, 5.50, 6.10, 9.16, 9.32, 11.40

immigrants coming to U.S. for immoral purposes, ban on, 2.13

Imperialists, Chinese as, 1.30

Imperialists, U.S. as, 9.22

Indemnification to China for injuries suffered by Chinese in U.S., 7.30, 7.70

Indiana's law prohibiting contracts with colored people, 4.60

Indian policy of U.S., 2.10

Ingalls, John J.
on Scott Act (1888), 7.54

on ten-year exclusion law (1882), 5.30

on twenty-year exclusion bill (1882), 3.50, 3.90

Interpreters for examination of Chinese immigrants, 9.17

References are to chapter and section numbers.

In transit, Chinese entry into U.S. for purpose of, 4.90, 7.30

I-yao Shen, 10.21, 11.21

J

Japan-China relations, 9.23, 11.10, 11.30

Japan-U.S. relations, 11.52

Japanese racist propaganda (World War II), 11.30

Jen, Gish, 8.41

Jenkins, Thomas A., 11.30–11.40

Jews, discrimination against, 2.10, 3.30

Johnson, Hiram, 11.52

Jones, John P.
    on Amendments (1884), 6.20
    on twenty-year exclusion bill (1882), 3.50, 3.90

Joyce, Charles, 4.60

Judd, Walter, 11.30–11.40

K

Kahn, Julius, 9.30, 9.32

Kasson, John, 4.60–4.70, 5.10

Kearney, Denis ("sandlot orator"), 2.10–2.11, 3.20, 9.15

Keifer, J. Warren, 5.10

Kennedy, Martin J., 11.30

Kilgore, Constantine, 7.62

Kinkead, John, 3.70

Kirk, Mark, *epilogue*

Knights of St. Crispin, 5.40

Know-Nothing Party, 1.20, 3.32

Kuomintang of China (KMT), 11.10

L

Labor organizations. *See* Unions

Labor protectionism. *See also* Chinese laborers; Coolie contract labor; Unions
    Amendments (1884) and, 6.10

Fifteen Passenger bill (1879) and, 2.0, 2.10, 2.22, 2.26
    repeal legislation (1943) and, 11.30, 11.52
    ten-year exclusion law (1882) and, 5.30, 5.50
    twenty-year exclusion bill (1882) and, 3.20, 3.50, 4.40–4.60

Lamb, John, 6.10

Lanius, Anna, 10.22

League of Nations and racial equality, 11.52

Lee, Erika, 9.17

Leibovitz, Liel, 9.12

Li, Laura Tyson, 11.31

Lincoln, Abraham, 3.41

Litigation in federal courts, 7.10–7.11. *See also* Appeals of immigration officers' decisions

Lodge, Henry Cabot, 9.11, 9.20, 9.23–9.24

Loughborough v. Blake (1820), 9.19

Loyalty oath and naturalization, 1.30

Luce, Henry R., 11.10

Lum, Walter U., 9.17

M

Magnuson, Warren, 11.20–11.40

Magnuson Act. *See* Repeal (1943)

Mallory, Stephen Russell, 9.19

Manchus, 9.16

Manderson, Charles, 8.24

Mansfield, Mike, 11.30

Mao Zedong, 11.52

Mason, Noah M., 11.30

Massachusetts and Chinese immigrants, 3.90, 5.40

Matthews, Stanley, 2.22–2.23

Maxey, Samuel B.
    on Fifteen Passenger bill (1879), 2.26

    on twenty-year exclusion bill (1882), 3.50, 4.90

Maybank, Burnet, 11.51

McClure, Addison, 4.50

McCoid, Moses, 4.70

McCormack, John W., 11.30

McCreary, James B., 8.40

McCreary Amendment (1893), 8.40

McCullough, David, 1.31

McDougal, John, 7.52

McKinley, William, 2.10, 4.70, 9.21–9.22, 9.32

McLane, Robert Milligan, 4.60

McLaurin, John L., 9.21

McMillin, Benton, 7.62

McPike, A.J., 3.70

Meacham, Jon, 11.33

Merchants
    Amendments (1884) on, 6.10
    Angell Treaty (1888) on, 3.60
    Bayard–Zhang Treaty on, 7.10, 7.30
    definition of, 7.40, 9.0, 9.10, 9.32
    Geary Act (1892) on, 8.24
    Scott Act (1888) on, 7.10

Mexico, Chinese immigration to, 8.42

Miller, Candice, 5.21

Miller, John F.
    on Amendments (1884), 6.20
    ten-year exclusion law (1882), 5.20
    twenty-year exclusion bill (1882), 3.10–3.20, 3.50, 3.70–3.90

Miller, Matthew, 9.12

Miller bill (S. 71). *See* Twenty-year exclusion bill (1822)

Mining
    Chinese forbidden from holding claims, 1.21, 1.33
    success of Chinese miners, 5.22

References are to chapter and section numbers.

Mining Law of 1866, 1.21

Missionaries to China, 4.60, 11.30

Mitchell, John H.
on Bayard–Zhang implementation bill (1888), 7.0
on Bayard–Zhang Treaty ratification (1888), 7.10
on Extension Act (1902), 9.10, 9.21, 9.24
on Fifteen Passenger bill (1879), 2.23
on Geary Act (1892), 8.24
on Scott Act (1888), 7.0, 7.10, 7.52, 7.56

Mixed-race persons with Chinese blood, 9.30, 9.32, 11.52

Mondell, Frank Wheeler, 9.32

Moore, William Robert, 4.40–4.50

Morey letter (1880), 4.20

Morgan, John Tyler
on Bayard–Zhang implementation bill (1888), 7.31
on Fifteen Passenger bill (1879), 2.22
on Geary Act (1892), 8.23, 8.31
on Scott Act (1888), 7.59
on ten-year exclusion law (1882), 5.20, 5.50
on twenty-year exclusion bill (1882), 4.90

Morrill, Justin, 2.26, 2.30

Morrill Land-Grant Colleges Act of 1862, 2.26

Morrison, Cameron, 11.30

Morrow, Judge (U.S. circuit court), 8.10

Morrow, William, 7.51, 7.62

Morton, Levi P., 8.31

Morton, Oliver
on Fifteen Passenger bill (1879), 2.10, 2.26
on Naturalization Act (1870), 1.20
on twenty-year exclusion bill (1882), 3.40

Morton Committee (1876), 2.10, 3.40, 4.30

Most favored nation status
for Chinese merchants coming to U.S., 6.10
for U.S. in trade with China, 2.40, 9.21

Motion to recommit (House of Representatives), 11.41

Murray, Patty, *epilogue*

N

Naphen, Henry, 9.30, 9.32

National origins quota system, 11.10, 11.21, 11.30–11.40, 11.52

Nativists, 5.22, 9.31

Naturalization Act (1870), Ch. 1, *Appendix 3*
overview, 1.0
of Africans, 1.30
Chinese not allowed to vote, 1.0
Committee of the Whole on Sumner amendment, 1.10
of first Chinese student to graduate from American university, 1.32
loyalty oath and, 1.30
Senate debate on Sumner amendment, 1.20–1.30
Senate vote on, 1.30
Williams amendment to Sumner's amendment, 1.30

Negroes. *See* Africans

Nevada and Chinese immigrants, 3.20, 3.50, 4.30, 4.50
Amendments (1884) and, 6.10
anti-miscegenation law, 9.30
presidential election (1888), 7.80

News Letter (San Francisco) on examination of Chinese immigrants, 9.11

New York City, Chinese population in, 7.10

NG Poon Chew, 9.17

1902 extension. *See* Extension Act (1902)

North Adams, Massachusetts, Chinese strikebreakers in, 5.40

O

Oath swearing by Chinese, 2.23, 2.25, 4.60

Open Door Policy (McKinley), 9.21–9.22

Opium War, 2.12, 9.14, 11.32

Oregon and Chinese immigrants, 3.40, 3.70, 5.30
Amendments (1884), 6.10
presidential election (1888), 7.80

Oregon Constitution and restrictions on Chinese, 1.33

Orth, Godlove S., 4.60

Otjen, Theobald, 9.31

P

Pacheco, Romualdo, 4.70

Pacific state senators, 1.30

Pagans, Chinese as, 1.30

Page, Horace
on Naturalization Act (1870), 2.10, 2.13
on ten-year exclusion law (1882), 5.10, 5.60
on twenty-year exclusion bill (1882), 4.10–4.50, 4.61, 4.70

Page Act of March 1875, 2.13

"Pairs" voting in House and Senate, 2.14, 2.28

Pakula, Hannah, 10.22, 11.31

Palmer, Henry W., 9.30

Panama Canal Zone construction, Chinese workers on, 10.20

Panic of 1873, 9.15

Paris Peace Conference (1919), 11.52

Partisanship and Chinese immigration, 1.30, 6.10, 7.0

Passports. *See* Documentation required for Chinese immigrants

Patterson, James, 1.20

References are to chapter and section numbers.

Patterson, Thomas
  on Extension Act (1902), 9.16, 9.24
  on Permanent Law (1904), 10.10
Payson, Lewis, 7.62
Pearl Harbor, 11.33
Pendleton, George, 5.50
Penrose, Boies, 9.10–9.11, 9.19, 9.23
Perez v. Sharp (1948), 9.30
Perkins, George C., 9.16, 9.32
Perkins, James B., 9.30
Permanent Law (1904), Ch. 10, Appendix 10
  overview, 10.0
  China's reaction to, 10.21
  Senate debates on, 10.10–10.20
Pfaelzer, Jean, 3.41
Phelan, James D., 9.0
Philippine Commission, 9.30, 9.32
Philippines
  Chinese exclusion from, 9.0, 9.10, 9.16, 9.18–9.20, 9.23, 9.30
  as U.S. territory, 9.19
Pin, Paul Yu, 11.30–11.40
Platt, Orville
  on Amendments (1884), 6.20
  on Extension Act (1902), 9.0, 9.11, 9.19, 9.21, 9.24, 9.40–9.41
  on Geary Act (1892), 8.24, 8.31
  on Scott Act (1888), 7.55
  on twenty-year exclusion bill (1882), 3.11, 3.80
Political impetus to Chinese exclusion, 7.52
Pomeroy, Samuel, 1.30
Powderly, Terence V., 9.17
Precedents, use of, 4.91
Presidential elections. See also Electoral College
  1880, 3.21
  1884, 7.52
  1888, 2.23, 7.52, 7.80
Presidential veto. See Veto, presidential
Presumption of guilt, 8.31, 8.40
Prison sentence for unlawful Chinese presence in U.S. (Geary Act), 8.10, 8.21–8.22
Pritchard, Jeter, 9.23
Prostitution
  ban (Page Act of March 1875), 2.13
  threat of, 2.22
Public health, Chinese as danger to, 2.22, 9.31
Public opinion
  anti-Chinese mass meetings and, 3.70
  change in attitude toward Chinese immigrants, 4.30
  Chinese Americans' reaction to repeal (1943), 11.50
  Congress's need to respond to, 4.50, 5.30, 7.52

Q

Qing Dynasty, 2.12, 9.11, 9.16, 9.18, 11.10
Quay, Matthew S., 9.24
Quota Act (1921), 11.21
Quota Act (1924), 11.21
Quota system (national origins), 11.10, 11.21, 11.30–11.40, 11.52

R

Race-mixing as negative for U.S.
  Amendments (1884) and, 6.10
  Bayard–Zhang implementation bill (1888) and, 7.40
  Extension Act (1902) and, 9.16, 9.31
  Naturalization Act (1870) and, 2.10, 2.22–2.23, 2.26
  Scott Act (1888) and, 7.40
  ten-year exclusion law (1882) and, 5.20

twenty-year exclusion bill (1882) and, 3.20–3.30, 3.50, 3.90, 4.50, 4.70
Racial legislation. See White supremacy
Racially derogatory language
  in House debates, 4.30–4.50, 6.10
  in Senate debates, 1.30, 3.20, 8.23
Radcliffe, George, 11.51
Radical Republicans, 1.20
Raids for illegal immigrants, 9.17
Railroads
  Chinese workers involved in building, 3.41, 8.24
  Panic of 1873 and, 9.15
Ramsey, Alexander, 1.30
Randall, Samuel, 2.10
Rayburn, Sam, 11.60
Real estate ownership, Chinese forbidden from holding, 1.33
Reed, Thomas, 4.70
Reentry and right of return
  Amendments (1884) and, 6.20
  Bayard–Zhang implementation bill (1888) and, 7.0, 7.30–7.40
  Extension Act (1902) and, 9.15
  Scott Act (1888) and, 7.0, 7.30–7.40, 7.52, 7.55, 7.70, 9.17
Registration of Chinese in U.S.
  Angell Treaty, 3.60, 3.80
  Geary Act (1892), 8.40
  1902 Extension Act and, 9.10
  in Philippines, 9.30
Reid, Harry, epilogue
Repeal (1943), Ch. 11, Appendix 11
  overview, 11.0
  House Committee Report, 11.20
  House debates on, 11.30–11.40

House vote on, 11.40

presidential (Roosevelt) signing, 11.60

Senate committee consideration, 11.50–11.51

Senate debates on, 11.52

Republican Party

1880 platform, 3.21, 4.20, 4.40, 4.60–4.70

on admission of Chinese, 1.30, 4.50, 5.30, 6.10, 7.31, 7.52–7.54, 9.23

Scott Act (1888) and, 7.62

Restaurant culture in China, 8.41

Return to China by Chinese immigrants, 6.10

Revels, Hiram, 1.20

Reynolds, Robert Rice, 11.52

Rice, William W.

on Amendments (1884), 6.10

on Naturalization Act (1870), 1.30

on ten-year exclusion law (1882), 5.10

on twenty-year exclusion bill (1882), 4.20, 4.70

Righteous and Harmonious Fists, 9.12

Robertson, Thomas, 1.30

Robinson, George, 4.70

Robsion, John Marshall, 11.30

Rock Springs massacre (1885), 8.21–8.22

Roosevelt, Franklin D., 11.0, 11.30, 11.33

Roosevelt, Theodore

Extension Act (1902) and, 9.0, 9.22, 9.32

Gentlemen's Agreement with Japan (1907) and, 11.52

Permanent Law (1904) and, 10.21

Rowe, William T., 9.12

Rubio, Marco, *epilogue*

Russo–Japanese War of 1905, 11.30

S

S. 71. *See* Twenty-year exclusion bill (1822)

S. 2960. *See* Extension Act (1902)

S. 3304. *See* Bayard–Zhang Treaty (1888)

S. 5344. *See* Permanent Law (1904)

Sabath, Adolph J., 11.30

Sanders, Wilbur Fiske, 8.23

Sandlot orators, 2.10–2.11, 3.20, 4.20–4.30, 9.15

Sandmeyer, Elmer C., 9.0

San Francisco

Chinatown protests over registration requirements (1892), 8.40

Chinatown riots (1873), 9.15

clearing immigration at port of, 7.51, 8.10

immigration officials, 9.17. *See also* Angel Island

repeal of exclusion laws (1943) and, 11.50

San Francisco Chronicle on Chinese immigration, 6.10

Sargent, Aaron, 2.21–2.23, 2.26, 2.30

Sargent, Frank P., 9.17

Saulsbury, Eli, 3.50

Schurz, Carl, 1.30

Scott, John, 1.30

Scott, William, 7.51, 7.58

Scott Act (1888), Ch. 7

overview, 7.0

House debates on, 7.51, 7.62

political parties and, 5.30

politics and immigration enforcement, 9.17

presidential (Cleveland) signing, 7.62, 7.70

Senate debates on, 7.10, 7.52–7.55

Senate motion to reconsider, 7.56–7.60

Senate vote on, 7.56

Senate vote on motion to reconsider, 7.61

Scranton, Joseph, 4.50

Seaman provision of 1902 Extension Act, 9.10, 9.24, 9.32, 9.41

Second War Powers Act (1942), 11.20

Self-preservation

Extension Act (1902) and, 9.30, 9.32

Fifteen Passenger bill (1879) and, 2.0, 2.10, 2.22–2.23, 2.27

repeal legislation (1943) and, 11.52

twenty-year exclusion bill (1882) and, 3.20–3.30, 4.60

Senate

cloture rule, 2.28

division vote, 3.90

Majority Leader, 2.21, 2.28

Minority Leader, 2.28

nineteenth-century vs. modern form of, 2.28

"pairs" voting, 2.28

president pro tempore, 1.22

presiding over, 1.22

procedural questions and use of precedent, 4.91

quorum calls, 2.28, 7.56

Rule 19, 4.90

unanimous consent agreements, 2.28

Senate Committee of the Whole

Amendments (1884) consideration, 6.20

Extension Act (1902) and, 9.13, 9.18, 9.40

Fifteen Passenger bill (1879) consideration, 2.21–2.24

H.R. 2201 consideration, 1.20

procedure, 1.12, 2.28

role of, 1.12

Sumner amendment and, 1.10

ten-year exclusion law (1882) consideration, 5.20

twenty-year exclusion bill (1882) consideration, 3.90

Senate Committee on Foreign Relations

Bayard–Zhang Treaty ratification (1888) and, 7.10–7.20

Geary Act (1892) and, 8.20–8.24

Scott Act (1888) and, 7.10, 7.52, 7.56

substitute amendment to bill S. 71 (twenty-year exclusion), 3.10–3.11, 3.50–3.90

ten-year exclusion law (1882) and, 4.90, 5.10–5.20, 5.50

Senate Committee on Immigration, 11.50–11.51

Senate Committee on the Judiciary, 1.10–1.30

Senate debate on Amendments (1884)

July 3, 1884, 6.20

Senate debate on Bayard–Zhang Treaty ratification (1888)

January 12, 1888, 7.10

March 1, 1888, 7.20

Senate debate on Extension Act (1902)

April 4, 1902, 9.10

April 5, 1902, 9.11

April 7, 1902, 9.13

April 8, 1902, 9.14

April 9, 1902, 9.18

April 10, 1902, 9.19

April 12, 1902, 9.20

April 14, 1902, 9.21

April 15, 1902, 9.23

April 16, 1902, 9.24

Senate debate on Fifteen Passenger bill (1879)

background, 2.20

February 12, 1879, 2.21

February 13, 1879, 2.22

February 14, 1879, 2.23

February 15, 1879, 2.26

Senate debate on Geary Act (1892)

April 13, 1892, 8.20

April 21, 1892, 8.21

April 23, 1892, 8.23

April 24, 1892, 8.24

Senate debate on naturalization bill (1870)

background, 1.10

July 2, 1870, 1.20

July 4, 1870, 1.30

Senate debate on Permanent Law (1904)

April 8, 1904, 10.10

April 22, 1904, 10.20

Senate debate on repeal legislation (1943)

November 16, 1943 (Senate Committee consideration), 11.51

November 26, 1943, 11.52

Senate Committee on Immigration receipt of bill, 11.50

Senate debate on Scott Act (1888)

January 12, 1888, 7.10

March 1, 1888, 7.20

September 3, 1888, 7.52

September 4, 1888, 7.53

September 5, 1888, 7.54

September 6, 1888, 7.55

September 7, 1888, 7.56

September 10, 1888, 7.57

September 11, 1888, 7.58

September 13, 1888, 7.59

September 14, 1888, 7.60

September 17, 1888, 7.61

Senate debate on ten-year exclusion law (1882)

April 25, 1882, 5.20

April 26, 1882, 5.30

April 27, 1882, 5.40

April 28, 1882, 5.50

Senate debate on twenty-year exclusion bill (1882), 1.10, 3.20–3.90

background, 3.10

February 28, 1882, 3.20

March 1, 1882, 3.30

March 2, 1882, 3.40

March 3, 1882, 3.50

March 6, 1882, 3.60

March 7, 1882, 3.70

March 8, 1882, 3.80

March 9, 1882, 3.90

April 5, 1882 (veto override), 4.90

Seward, William, 1.30, 3.20

Shanghai Commerce Association, 10.21

Sherman, John

on Bayard–Zhang Treaty ratification (1888), 7.20

on Fifteen Passenger bill (1879), 2.22

on Geary Act (1892), 8.21–8.22, 8.24, 8.31

on Naturalization Act (1870), 1.30

on Scott Act (1888), 7.20, 7.52, 7.55–7.57, 7.59

on twenty-year exclusion bill (1882), 3.90, 4.90

Sherwood, Robert, 11.33

Ships transporting Chinese immigrants, penalties on, 9.30, 9.32

Simmons, Furnifold M., 9.13

Sisson, Albert, 3.41

Six Companies (Chinese Consolidated Benevolent Association)

coercive nature of labor contracts of, 3.80, 4.60, 5.0

labor contracts arranged by, 2.10, 3.20, 4.40

litigation brought by, 7.11

power and scope of, 9.11

protesting to Congress about labor agency charges, 4.60

San Francisco Chinatown riots (1873) and, 9.15

Skilled labor. *See* Chinese laborers

Skinner, Charles R.

on Amendments (1884), 6.10

References are to chapter and section numbers.

on twenty-year exclusion bill (1882), 4.40

Slater, James H.
on ten-year exclusion law (1882), 5.30
on twenty-year exclusion bill (1882), 3.60

Slavery, 3.40–3.50, 3.90, 4.60. *See also* Abolitionist movement

Soennichsen, John, 9.15

Soong Ailing, 10.22

Soong Chingling, 10.22

Soong Meiling. *See* Chiang Kaishek, Madame

Speer, Emory, 4.40

Spooner, John, 9.16, 9.23

Sprague, William, 1.30

Squire, Watson, 8.24

Stanford, Leland
on Scott Act (1888), 7.53
on twenty-year exclusion bill (1882), 3.41

State courts dealing with Chinese immigration and naturalization, 3.40, 3.90, 4.30, 7.56

State regulation of immigration, 9.17. *See also specific states*

Stewart, William M.
on Bayard–Zhang implementation bill (1888), 7.31
on Bayard–Zhang Treaty ratification (1888), 7.10
on Extension Act (1902), 9.19, 9.24
on Geary Act (1892), 8.23, 8.24
on Naturalization Act (1870), 1.0, 1.20–1.21, 1.30
on Permanent Law (1904), 10.20
on Scott Act (1888), 7.52, 7.56, 7.58

Strobridge, James, 3.41

Students
Angell Treaty (1888) on, 3.60

Bayard–Zhang Treaty on, 7.30

Extension Act (1902) on, 9.0, 9.10–9.11, 9.18

Geary Act (1892) on, 8.24

ten-year exclusion law (1882) on, 5.30

Substitute amendment to a bill, 3.11

Sulzer, William, 9.32

Sumner, Charles
cited in 1943 debate on repeal, 11.30
cited in 2011 congressional apology for exclusionary laws, *epilogue*
on Fifteen Passenger bill (1879), 2.26
on Naturalization Act (1870), 1.0, 1.10–1.31

Sun Yat-sen, 10.22, 11.10

Swanson, Claude, 1.12

Swift, John Franklin, 3.10, 3.80, 5.0

T

Taft, William Howard, 9.30

Taylor, Bayard
on Extension Act (1902), 9.30
on Fifteen Passenger bill (1879), 2.10

Taylor, Ezra, 4.30

Teachers
Angell Treaty (1888) on, 3.60
Bayard–Zhang Treaty on, 7.30
Extension Act (1902) on, 9.0, 9.10–9.11, 9.18
ten-year exclusion law (1882) on, 5.30

Teller, Henry
on Geary Act (1892), 8.23
on Scott Act (1888), 7.52–7.56
on twenty-year exclusion bill (1882), 3.60–3.90

Ten-year exclusion law (1882), Ch. 5, *Appendix 7*

overview, 5.0

Democrats vs. Republicans in voting for, 7.52

enforcement failure of, 6.10

enrollment, 5.70

expiration of, 8.40

House concurrence in Senate amendments, 5.60

House debate on, 5.10

House vote on, 5.10

litigation over, 7.10, 7.11

presidential (Arthur) approval, 5.70

repeal proposed, 6.10

Senate debate on, 5.20–5.50

Senate vote on, 5.50

Texas and Chinese immigrants, 3.50

Textile trade, 3.60, 9.21, 9.23

Thayer, John, 1.20

Thomas, Elbert, 11.52

Thompson, Thomas, 7.40

Threat presented by Chinese immigration, 2.10, 2.22

Thurman, Allen
on Fifteen Passenger bill (1879), 2.23, 2.26
on Naturalization Act (1870), 1.30

Tilden, Samuel, 3.21

Timeline for American immigration laws, *Appendix 12*

Tong Duck Chung Company, 1.33

Tourists
Angell Treaty (1888) on, 3.60
Bayard–Zhang Treaty on, 7.30
Geary Act (1892) on, 8.24
ten-year exclusion law (1882) on, 5.30

Townsend, Martin, 2.10

Townshend, Richard W.
on ten-year exclusion law (1882), 5.30

Bayard–Zhang Treaty on, 7.30

Extension Act (1902) on, 9.0, 9.10–9.11, 9.18

Geary Act (1892) on, 8.24

ten-year exclusion law (1882) on, 5.30

References are to chapter and section numbers.

on twenty-year exclusion bill (1882), 4.70

Trade relations between U.S. and China. *See also* Most favored nation status

  Extension Act (1902) and, 9.10, 9.21, 9.23, 9.30

  extraterritoriality and, 11.32

  Geary Act (1892) and, 8.23

  Permanent Law (1904) and, 10.21

  twenty-year exclusion bill (1882) and, 3.60, 4.10, 4.30, 4.50

Transcontinental railway, 3.41, 8.24

Transient nature of Chines immigration, 2.27

Treasury Department procedures, 7.41, 9.11, 9.21, 9.24, 9.30

Treaty obligations, 2.10. *See also* Burlingame Treaty (1868)

  abrogation of, 2.20

Treaty of Nanking (1843), 2.12, 9.14

Treaty of Paris (1898), 9.19, 9.30

Treaty of Tientsin (1858), 2.40, 7.53, 9.14, 9.21, 9.23

Trescot, William Henry, 3.10, 3.80

Trumbull, Lyman

  on Fifteen Passenger bill (1879), 2.26

  on Naturalization Act (1870), 1.20–1.30

Tully, Pleasant B., 6.10

Turner, George, 9.18, 9.23–9.24, 9.41

Twenty-year exclusion bill (1822)

  Democrats vs. Republicans in voting for, 7.52

  House debate on, 4.10–4.70

  House vote on, 4.70

presidential (Arthur) veto of, *Appendix 6*, 4.0, 4.80, 5.20, 7.52

Senate debate on, 1.10, 3.20–3.90

Senate vote on, 3.90

Senate vote to override veto, 4.90

U

Unions

  opposition to Chinese immigration, 4.50, 5.22, 9.17, 9.23–9.24, 11.0, 11.30

  strikebreakers, Chinese shoemakers as, 5.40

V

Vallejo, California, resolution seeking protection from Chinese influx, 3.70

Vest, George M.

  on Scott Act (1888), 7.59

  on ten-year exclusion law (1882), 5.40

Veteran opposition to Chinese immigration, 11.30–11.40

Veterans of Foreign Wars, 11.40

Veto, presidential

  Fifteen Passenger bill (1879), vetoed by Hayes, 2.0, 2.40, 4.60–4.80, 5.20, *Appendix 4*

  House attempt to override veto of Fifteen Passenger bill (1879), 2.50

  twenty-year exclusion bill (1882), vetoed by Arthur, 4.0, 4.80, 5.20, 7.52, *Appendix 6*

Vice President as presiding officer of Senate, 1.22

A Visit to India, China and Japan in the year 1853 (Taylor), 9.30

Vorys, John Martin, 11.40

Votes on bills. *See specific piece of legislation*

Voting rights, denied to Chinese, 1.0, 1.30, 3.40, 4.50–4.60

W

Wallace, Henry, 11.60

Walsh, James, 11.30

War Brides Act (1945), 11.22

Warner, Willard, 1.20–1.30

Washburn, William D., 4.60

Washington Post on Scott Act (1888), 7.62

White, Compton I., 11.40

White, Harry, 2.30

White supremacy, 2.23, 3.40, 3.60–3.80, 11.52. *See also* Self-preservation

White witness requirement, 8.0, 8.24, 8.31

Williams, Charles G., 4.40, 4.50

Williams, George, 1.20–1.30

Willis, Albert Shelby

  on Amendments (1884), 6.10

  on Fifteen Passenger bill (1879), 2.10, 2.30

  on ten-year exclusion law (1882), 5.0, 5.10

  on twenty-year exclusion bill (1882), 4.30–4.40

Wilmeth, James L., 11.52

Wilson, Henry, 1.30

Wilson, James

  on Geary Act (1892), 8.21

  on Scott Act (1888), 7.56–7.57

Wilson, Woodrow, 11.52

Women immigrants and Page Act, 2.13

Wong Kim Ark; United States v. (1898), 9.19, 9.30

World War II, 11.10–11.20, 11.22, 11.33

Wright, James A., 11.30–11.40

Wu Tingfang, 9.18

Y

Yung, Judy, 9.17

Yung Wing, 1.32

Z

Zhonghua Huiguan. *See* Six Companies

References are to chapter and section numbers.

Acknowledgments

My law firm, Covington and Burling, has a long history of pro bono service. In 2010, we agreed to act as pro bono counsel for a consortium of Chinese-American organizations that wanted Congress to acknowledge and express regret for a long record of Chinese exclusion legislation passed in the late nineteenth and early twentieth centuries. At Covington, I was the lead partner responsible for this effort.

To secure redress, we had to convey accurately exactly what Congress had done. That history was far more extensive than we, or even our clients, initially understood. It involved passage of nine major legislative measures, seven of which became law, as well as action on several Sino-American treaties, and anti-Chinese provisions within other statutes.

Wonderful histories of the Chinese in America have tangentially mentioned Congress' role. But since no previous book has focused on congressional exclusion policy debates, this volume will add an important dimension to grasping the special hardships that Chinese immigrants bore in this country.

I am very grateful to Chug Roberts, president and publisher of TheCapitol.Net, for his openness to this idea and for bringing this book to life. Through publications and seminars, his company greatly enhances public understanding of Congress.

At Covington, Beth Bell has been my principal collaborator, both on our pro bono project and the book. She read thousands of pages of congressional materials in parallel with me. Beth is a superb lawyer on a path to a brilliant career. I greatly value her ideas, analysis, and editing. Erica Lai and Allegra Han, also with me at the law firm, have done much to serve our project and have helped to shape this book. I thank them all.

I also thank Carrie Ansell, a superb legislative librarian at Covington. Carrie brought to my attention all the relevant congressional debates and documentation. Without her indispensable skills, research would have been much more difficult, and I would have missed crucial information.

I am especially grateful to Dr. Sue Fawn Chung, Professor of Asian History at the University of Nevada, Las Vegas, for her essential insights on the historical context for this story.

My wife, Celeste, developed the title for this book. She read every page and offered numerous useful suggestions for how the text could be improved. Readers will benefit a lot from her involvement. The daughter of an immigrant, she has a substantial emotional attachment to this story. She also shares my love and respect for the Chinese people.

Martin B. Gold
Washington, DC Summer, 2012

About the Author

MARTIN B. GOLD is a partner in the law firm of Covington & Burling, LLP. Co-chair of Covington's Government Affairs Practice Group, he led the firm's pro-bono efforts to assist the 1882 Project, which sought resolutions from the Senate and House to express regret for passage of the Chinese exclusion laws. He was instrumental in the Senate and House passing expressions of regret for the Chinese exclusion laws: S. Res. 201 in October 2011, and H. Res. 683 in June 2012. In 2012, he was awarded the "Champion of Justice Award" by the Chinese American Citizens Alliance for his work on the project.

Mr. Gold is the author of *Senate Procedure and Practice* (2004, 2008), a widely consulted manual on Senate floor process. He lectures on that subject within the Senate itself and for TheCapitol.Net. He has also authored *The Grand Institution* (2011), a primer on the Senate that was prepared and translated for use in China.

Mr. Gold has been a guest lecturer in Beijing at Tsinghua University and at the Beijing Foreign Studies University. In addition, he has spoken at Moscow State University, the Moscow State Institute for International Relations, and consulted for the Federation Council of the Russian Federal Assembly, and the State Parliament of Ukraine. He has also spoken frequently on political and legislative matters before U.S. academic institutions and other domestic audiences, as well as foreign embassies.

In 2006, President George W. Bush appointed Mr. Gold to the United States Commission for the Preservation of America's Heritage Abroad. In that capacity, he was instrumental in American recognition of Dr. Ho Feng Shan, a Chinese diplomat who rescued Austrian Jews from the Holocaust.

Mr. Gold is a graduate of the Washington College of Law at The American University. At the Senate, he served on the staffs of Senator Mark O. Hatfield (R–OR), and Majority Leaders Howard H. Baker, Jr. (R–TN), and Bill Frist (R–TN). He was also a professional staff member of the Senate Select Committee on Intelligence and was Minority Staff Director and Counsel for the Senate Committee on Rules and Administration.

CPSIA information can be obtained at www.ICGtesting.com
Printed in the USA
LVOW03s2232280914

406298LV00007B/66/P